INTER/CULTURAL COMMUNICATION

To my spouse Michael Andrew Kurylo and our children Anastacia Victoria Kurylo 2.0 and Lincoln Andrew Obama Kurylo.

INTER/CULTURAL COMMUNICATION

Representation and Construction of Culture

Edited by

Anastacia Kurylo

Marymount Manhattan College

SAGE

Los Angeles | London | New Delhi
Singapore | Washington DC

Los Angeles | London | New Delhi
Singapore | Washington DC

FOR INFORMATION:

SAGE Publications, Inc.
2455 Teller Road
Thousand Oaks, California 91320
E-mail: order@sagepub.com

SAGE Publications Ltd.
1 Oliver's Yard
55 City Road
London EC1Y 1SP
United Kingdom

SAGE Publications India Pvt. Ltd.
B 1/I 1 Mohan Cooperative Industrial Area
Mathura Road, New Delhi 110 044
India

SAGE Publications Asia-Pacific Pte. Ltd.
3 Church Street
#10-04 Samsung Hub
Singapore 049483

Printed in the United States of America

*A catalog record of this book is available from the
Library of Congress.*

978-1-4129-8693-9

This book is printed on acid-free paper.

Acquisitions Editor: Matthew Byrnie
Editorial Assistant: Stephanie Palermini
Production Editor: Eric Garner
Copy Editor: Gretchen Treadwell
Typesetter: C&M Digitals (P) Ltd.
Proofreader: Laura Webb
Indexer: J. Naomi Linzer
Cover Designer: Gail Buschman
Marketing Manager: Liz Thornton
Permissions Editor: Karen Ehrmann

SFI Certified Sourcing
www.sfiprogram.org
SFI-00453

12 13 14 15 16 10 9 8 7 6 5 4 3 2 1

Brief Contents

Detailed Contents

Ronald L. Jackson II, University of Illinois at Urbana-Champaign
Cerise L. Glenn, The University of North Carolina at Greensboro
Kesha Morant Williams, Penn State Berks

Howard Giles, University of California, Santa Barbara
Jane Giles, Van Buren Consulting

PART III: NAVIGATING INTER/CULTURAL COMMUNICATION IN A COMPLEX WORLD

Chapter 10: Advocacy

Rachel Anderson Droogsma, Nebraska Wesleyan University

Chapter 11: Media and Culture: The "Reality" of Media Effects

Mark P. Orbe, Western Michigan University

Chapter 14: Interpretivist Approach to Culture

Chapter 15: Challenges and Opportunities in Inter/Cultural Communication

PART V: APPENDICES: STUDIES OF INTER/CULTURAL COMMUNICATION 349

Appendix A: Navajo Culture Explored Through Ethnography 351

Charles A. Braithwaite, University of Nebraska–Lincoln

Appendix B: Local Culture Explored Through Discourse Analysis 361

Kathleen C. Haspel, Fairleigh Dickinson University

Appendix C: Dagaaba Culture of Ghana Explored Through Rhetorical Analysis   369

Anthony Y. Naaeke, Marymount Manhattan College

Appendix D: Transnational Dominican Culture Through Phenomenological Analysis   379

Wilfredo Alvarez, Northeastern Illinois University
Mark P. Orbe, Western Michigan University
Ewa L. Urban, Western Michigan University
Nayibe A. Tavares, Western Michigan University

Appendix E: South African Culture Explored Through Content Analysis   389

Adrian Furnham, University College London

Preface

*I*nter/Cultural Communication is a text for the introductory intercultural communication course that was developed from my belief that students today need a fuller, more complete range of approaches to studying communication within and between cultures. In this book, I have worked with a group of intercultural communication scholars and researchers to present students with multiple approaches—*social scientific, interpretivist, critical,* and *dialogic*—that reflect current research, perspectives, and theories in the field. The hope is that students will gain an appreciation for the diversity of issues relevant to understanding cultural and intercultural communication and the different methodologies this understanding requires.

A DIVERSE APPROACH TO STUDYING INTERCULTURAL COMMUNICATION WITH AN INCLUSIVE VIEW OF CULTURE

In proposing and editing this textbook on inter/cultural communication, I was reminded of a question asked of me at the first National Communication Association convention I attended. As a first semester doctoral student joining my new scholarly community, I was introduced to another doctoral student who asked, "What methodology do you use in your research?" I responded in a way I thought appropriate, "I haven't decided yet." To my great surprise, the conversation ended there. This brief conversation made me feel uncomfortable, dismissed, and alienated.

Periodically, I would revisit this brief conversation as I pursued my doctorate and ask myself, "What methodology *should* I use?" In my quest for an answer, I worked with experimental design, thematic analysis, feminist criticism, and conversation analysis. I bounced from one faculty member to another in the search for *my* methodology. Luckily, I had the good fortune of taking a research methods class with Dan O'Conner at Rutgers University who made clear to his students the law of the instrument, also known as "Maslow's hammer." As Maslow (1969) proffered in *The Psychology of Science,* "It is tempting, if the only tool you have is a hammer, to treat everything as if it were a nail" (p. 15). Accordingly, I would aspire to have a variety of methodological tools in my researcher's tool belt so that I can see the topic of my research for what it is, rather than for what I need it to be in order to suit my methodology. Putting this into practice was not easy. Most faculty are fluent in a dominant methodology, and guiding students in a multimethod project not yet conceptualized fully is a difficult task for even the most experienced dissertation advisers. Moreover, learning multiple methodologies takes significantly more time than learning a single methodology especially for a student new to a field. Despite the challenges, I have come to view myself as a multimethod researcher.

As I worked on *Inter/Cultural Communication,* I was regularly reminded of that conversation about methods from my first academic convention. Essentially, I was being questioned about my cultural identity. I could not articulate it then, but, in retrospect, my initial discomfort with the question and my struggle with trying to claim a single methodology throughout my doctoral work was a result of my resistance to being labeled and categorized. Why did I have to choose one methodology? Similarly, people are too often categorized into singular identities. This occurs despite their ability to self-identify with multiple identities and despite the regularity with which people redefine their identities. As a result, and much like my experience seeking a singular methodology, people seek to find their "true" selves, attempt to get back to their roots, and even suffer from identity crises. Eventually, as I did with a methodology, people can begin to understand and become comfortable with the multiple identities with which they identify (Gergen, 1992).

The seemingly innocent question of methodology has allowed me to understand who I am, who I am in relation to others, and how others view me. I hope this textbook will guide students toward similar insight about their own identities. Toward this end, *Inter/Cultural Communication* resists relying solely on the social scientific approach that has dominated intercultural communication curriculum. This approach typically involves applying interpersonal communication topics to an intercultural context and is often expressed through the metaphor of "bridging" differences "across" cultures. *Inter/Cultural Communication* extends beyond this approach to provide a wider and deeper view of inter/cultural communication.

Specifically, the four approaches articulated by Deetz (1996) provide the basis for this text. These include the social scientific approach (i.e., normative) as well as the interpretivist, critical, and dialogic social constructionist approaches. These approaches and the increasing acceptability of multimethod research reflect current trends in the cultural and intercultural communication fields. The mission of this text is to weave these multiple approaches together in order to provide students with an appreciation for the diversity of issues relevant to understanding cultural and intercultural communication. Through this text students will become more aware of the complexity of their own and others' identities and feel more comfortable within those moments in which they find themselves and others labeled and categorized.

Inter/Cultural Communication introduces students to current topics in inter/cultural communication discussed by 44 contributors among whom are well-known and emerging scholars in the field. The case studies, narratives, examples, and images reflect perspectives and groups that provide a depth and breadth of coverage of varied cultural experiences. This book covers many of the same topics and theories discussed in traditional intercultural communication textbooks. However, *Inter/Cultural Communication* is unique from these other texts in the following ways.

- *Inclusive understanding of culture.* This text is founded on a broad definition of culture that is inclusive of gender, race, sexual orientation, ethnicity, class, geographic location, generational identity, and so forth. This broad definition is reinforced throughout the text within narratives, case studies, examples, and images.

- *Focus on learning about underrepresented cultural groups.* Students will encounter numerous in-depth and insightful opportunities to learn about cultural groups through narratives, case studies, and examples provided throughout the text including those that are commonly discussed as well as those often overlooked or taken-for-granted such as Native Americans, homeless, and librarians.
- *Integrated coverage of interpersonal topics.* Interpersonally oriented intercultural communication topics such as verbal and nonverbal communication, listening, and conflict have been integrated throughout the chapters, rather than compartmentalized in isolated chapters, to demonstrate their impact on a range of intercultural topics.
- *Emphasis on research.* The text offers a research component comprising chapters on each of the social scientific and interpretivist research approaches. Additionally, the seven case studies included in the appendices can be incorporated by an instructor along with the research methods text box in each that describes how the specific study was conducted. The case studies are valuable for gaining insight into specific cultural groups even if the instructor wishes not to emphasize research methods.
- *Current topics in inter/cultural communication discussed by well-known and emerging scholars in the field.* Chapters, case studies, narratives, examples, and images these contributors provide reflect a variety of perspectives and cultural groups. These enable instructors to update and to help students engage with their intercultural curriculum.

LEARNING GOALS

In order to accomplish its mission of making students more informed, effective, and ethical communicators in a variety of communities and cultures, *Inter/Cultural Communication* is built around ten learning goals for students.

1. To examine basic concepts, issues, and theories in and approaches to inter/cultural communication that provide a foundation from which students can navigate communication across literal and figurative cultural borders.

2. To explore how culture influences but does not predetermine the behaviors of its members.

3. To engage in discussion of the relationship between culture and communication and be aware of their participation in the collaborative co-construction of culture.

4. To gain insights about, knowledge of, and appreciation for the experiences, behaviors, and perspectives of their own and other cultural groups.

5. To increase their self-awareness and self-reflexivity about the ways in which cultural identities develop and are maintained, and the impact of culture on their lives and their communication practices as cultural beings.

6. To achieve greater intercultural communication competence in a complex social world.

7. To think critically about the dynamics of cultural and intercultural relationships.

8. To better appreciate the role media and technology play as cultural agents on local and global scales.

9. To be able to apply text concepts to everyday practical situations as well as current national and international events.

10. To understand ethical issues relevant to inter/cultural communication.

FEATURES

Inter/Cultural Communication introduces a number of pedagogical features to help enhance students' understanding and to encourage them to connect the skills and concepts they explore in the text to their real-world inter/cultural encounters.

1. Each chapter begins with a "Journey Through Chapter" section. This feature provides students a brief overview of the chapter and specifies whether the chapter focuses on social scientific or social construction and whether the chapter deals with representations or constructions. This feature also provides a statement of the souvenir or learning goal(s) for the chapter.

2. Reflection questions in captions and text boxes invite students to engage interactively with chapter material. These questions can be assigned as homework to make sure students have read the chapter, as questions to prompt journal entries, or as the basis of graded essay assignments.

3. Throughout the main chapters where relevant, students are encouraged to "Take a Side Trip" to read a case study in order to further explore the issue being discussed. In this way, students need not wait for an instructor to assign case studies but can read these as relevant to their interests and when they have the time to do so. This feature is also incorporated to reinforce that case studies are not singularly associated with specific chapters and, rather, can be incorporated throughout the semester as instructors and students find them relevant.

4. In each chapter, "Living Culture" narratives provide students first-hand insight into the experience of living as a member of a particular culture. Students are invited to consider questions about the narrative that transcend the author's experience. Narratives reflect the broad definition of culture the text takes and include discussion of issues related to the following: Pakistani identity, sexual orientation, HIV-positive culture, homelessness, punk rockers, race, socioeconomic class, and librarians, among others.

5. The main text of each chapter ends with the opportunity to "Continue Your Journey Online." This feature provides a single website that students can visit in order to

further grapple with the concepts in the chapter. Websites are selected because of their longevity and because of the vast amount of content they contain to allow students to explore a variety of content for an extended period of time, if desired.

6. Through the "Say What?" section that appears at the end of the chapter, students have the opportunity to eavesdrop and reflect on conversations in which cultural stereotypes are communicated. These are revealing about the way cultural groups are distinguished from one another in conversation. Questions are provided to aid with reflection on these sometimes disturbing, yet real-life, scenarios.

7. Review questions are included at the end of each chapter to aid students in reviewing the material. These questions add an element of critical thinking to the review process in addition to providing the opportunity to revisit chapter concepts.

8. Key terms are highlighted at the end of each chapter, along with definitions for each term in the Glossary.

9. Case studies discuss seven distinct cultures using seven distinct methodologies. These case studies provide unique and deep insight into various cultures while taking students on guided tours of the research process. Through these case studies, students can begin to question their own taken-for-granted understanding of cultures and envision new ways of gaining knowledge about cultural groups. Case studies reflect the broad definition of culture taken by the text and include discussion of issues related to the following: Japanese, Korean, South African, and transnational Dominican culture, as well as Dagaaba culture of Ghana, local culture, and Navajo culture.

ORGANIZATION OF THE TEXT

The following overview of the text gives a general idea of its content, its procession from chapter to chapter, and its overall logic. After its Introduction for Students, *Inter/Cultural Communication* is divided into five parts. The first part, Introduction to Inter/Cultural Communication, includes five chapters that discuss basic concepts relevant to inter/cultural communication. In Chapter 1, "Culture and Communication," I introduce foundational concepts relevant to inter/cultural communication, distinguish between cultural generalizations and individual behavior, explain why inter/cultural communication is important to study, and discuss the theoretical approaches that guide the rest of the text.

In Chapter 2, "Intercultural and Cross-Cultural Communication," Watson discusses cultural mores and the beginnings of cross-cultural communication research, two dominant traditions in cross-cultural research, nine specific cross-cultural dimensions, face-negotiation theory, and the willingness to communicate concept. In Chapter 3, "Intercultural Communication Competence," Arasaratnam introduces that concept, describes variables that influence it, presents four theoretical models of intercultural competence, and suggests ways that people can develop their competence to better prepare for and engage in intercultural communication.

In Chapter 4, "A Communication Theory of Culture," Carbaugh introduces four concepts of culture and presents, as an integration of these, a fifth concept of a communication theory of culture in which culture is viewed as a co-constructed product of communication processes. In Chapter 5, "Culture in Conversation," Robles provides a focused discussion on how culture appears in conversation. As part of this discussion, she explores speech communities, communication practices such as speech acts, person referencing, and conflict.

The second part of *Inter/Cultural Communication,* Distinguishing Self and Other, provides insight into identity and group membership. The section begins with Jackson, Glenn, and Morant's discussion in Chapter 6, "Self-Identity and Culture." This chapter presents concepts related to identity and culture, discusses the development of self-identity, and explores three theories of identity negotiation. Giles and Giles extend this discussion in Chapter 7, "Ingroups and Outgroups," by exploring how cultural group membership is enacted through ingroup and outgroup processes. Students will learn how language is used to identify and distinguish between ingroups and outgroups and explore how intergroup boundaries, group vitality, and communication accommodation theory describe important aspects of intergroup communication processes. In Chapter 8, "Privilege and Culture," Yep discusses how culture can constitute privilege for dominant groups in ways that normalize their identity and renders it invisible. In doing so, Yep discusses basic concepts relevant to privilege and culture including power, globalization, and hierarchies of cultures in order to understand how privilege, power, and culture intersect. Harris's discussion in Chapter 9, "Co-Cultural Group Membership," addresses relevant concepts for this topic including double consciousness, feminism, and other theories. The chapter provides two in-depth examples of co-cultural groups in academic settings and explores the implications of co-cultural group membership on intercultural communication.

The third part of *Inter/Cultural Communication,* Navigating Inter/Cultural Communication in a Complex World, addresses issues related to navigating a culturally complex world by emphasizing practical applications of inter/cultural communication to issues of advocacy and traditional and new media to enable students to become more aware of and take ownership over their role in inter/cultural communication processes. In Chapter 10, "Advocacy," Droogsma provides practical suggestions for how students may become advocates for their own and other groups through volunteering, activism, paper topic selection, and so forth. Her discussion also addresses the problems associated with advocacy and the issues related to who constitutes a legitimate advocate. In Chapter 11, "Media and Culture," Orbe helps the reader navigate through theories of media related to cultural representations and constructions, and applies these theories to reality television concluding with a discussion of media literacy. In Chapter 12, "Technology and Culture," Dumova discusses the ability of Web 2.0 technologies to generate shared intercultural spaces, foster global intercultural conversations, and reduce barriers to intercultural communication as well as promote educational opportunities and stimulate cultural exchange. Relevant societal, legal, and ethical issues are also addressed.

In the fourth part of *Inter/Cultural Communication,* Looking to the Future of Inter/Cultural Communication: Research and Practice, van Oudenhoven and Boromisza-Habashi present methodological approaches for the study of inter/cultural communication in a basic, direct, and relatable way. In Chapter 13, "Social Scientific Approach to Culture," van Oudenhoven presents a social scientific approach by discussing its research methods, ethics, and limitations. In Chapter 14, "Interpretivist Approach to Culture," Boromisza-Habashi presents an interpretivist approach based in the social constructionist perspective by discussing its research methods, ethics, and limitations. These chapters are supplemented by the case studies included as appendices which each focus on a particular culture and methodology. Instructors who do not wish to include a research component in their course can omit Chapters 13 and 14 from their course curriculum without affecting the flow of the text. In Chapter 15, "Challenges and Opportunities in Inter/Cultural Communication," I discuss some challenges and opportunities presented by inter/cultural communication and relevant concepts and theories associated with these. The chapter concludes with insights about the role students play in the future of inter/cultural communication.

The fifth section of *Inter/Cultural Communication* provides the appendices. Each presents one research report in an accessible case study format that discusses a specific culture explored through one research methodology. These provide deep and intriguing insight into a cultural group to which students might not otherwise be exposed. They supplement the optional research component of the text by providing representative research methodologies used within social scientific and interpretivist approaches. Case studies representing the following social scientific methodologies are provided: content analysis, survey research, and experimental design. Case studies representing the following interpretivist methodologies are provided: ethnography, discourse analysis, rhetoric, and phenomenological analysis. Some of these methods are commonly used in inter/cultural research. Others are less frequently used but nonetheless produce unique findings.

Inter/Cultural Communication provides insights that will enable students to engage with the diversity of people with whom they come into contact in their travels, communities, workplace, home, and online. Students will become more aware of their own cultural identities and be able to apply their newfound knowledge to their everyday interactions. They will begin to understand how their communication is a powerful tool through which to facilitate change—both in their own and others' lives. Most importantly, *Inter/Cultural Communication* will provide students with knowledge and skills enabling them to deal with yet unfamiliar cultures in yet unknown contexts with regard to yet unimaginable issues.

ACKNOWLEDGMENTS

No text can exist without the help from and collaboration with innumerable others. First and foremost, I appreciate the excellent quality of work produced by my 44 contributors to the text. Perhaps more importantly, I appreciate their endless patience with my input, specifications, and invasion of and indulgences with their contributions.

I would like to also thank former students who have helped as research assistants on this project, specifically Jack Bennett, Camela Weekes, and Meagan Ballenger who provided tremendous help with various important and not always so small tasks. Jack and Camela in particular have each worked with me for over 2 years on various projects and have always provided helpful sounding boards for my ideas. I would also like to thank Jeanne Zalesky at Pearson for her ecouragement and faith in this text.

I would like to thank Benjamin Broome from Arizona State University; Debbie Borisoff, Dan Hahn, and Radha Hegde from New York University; Brian Cogan and Janice Kelly from Molloy College; Bill Edwards from Columbus State University; Mark Frank from Buffalo

University; Mike Hostetler from St. John's University; Katie LeBesco, Corey Liberman, David Linton, Rebecca Mushtare, Anthony Naaeke, MJ Robinson, Alister Sanderson, Peter Schaeffer, and Laura Tropp from Marymount Manhattan College; Dan O'Conner, Jenny Mandelbaum, Harty Mokros, Marie Radford, and Lea Stewart from Rutgers University; and Jack Sargent from Kean University. Each deserves my debt of gratitude for serving as mentors, providing feedback on my ideas, and/or guiding me throughout the process of producing this text.

Additionally, I would like to thank my family and friends. I have received tremendous support, guidance, and inspiration from those closest to me: my friends Rie Akazawa, Pat Velez, and Terry Wilburg, and family members Chrisann Lucchetto, Lillian Kurylo, Dan Serro, and, of course, Fran Shea. I have been especially fortunate to have received seemingly boundless support from my husband Michael Kurylo.

It is my pleasure to work with Todd Armstrong, Elizabeth Borders, Matt Byrnie, Nathan Davidson, Eric Garner, Stephanie Palermini, and Gretchen Treadwell at SAGE on this project. Their guidance, honesty, support, and enthusiasm for the project made me even more dedicated to producing *Inter/Cultural Communication*. I would also like to extend thanks to everyone else I may have inadvertently forgotten. It goes without saying that I owe these folks many, many, many thanks.

I especially appreciate the feedback from my reviewers who have provided insights that I have adopted with enthusiasm. Their feedback challenged me and my vision for the text and, ultimately, has helped to improve the quality of the text and make my vision for it stronger.

Milan Andrejevich, Ivy Tech
   Community College
Margaret Chojnacki, Barry University
Brian Cogan, Molloy College
Kay L. Colley, Texas Wesleyan University
Brad Crownover, College of Mount Saint
   Vincent
Randy K. Dillon, Missouri State
   University
Bosah Ebo, Rider University
Bill Edwards, Columbus State University

Richard Fiordo, University
   of North Dakota
Anita Foeman, West Chester
   University of Pennsylvania
A. M. Mason, Pittsburg State University
Lisa Schreiber, Millersville University
Jianglong Wang, Western
   Washington University
Minmin Wang, Rider University
MJ Woeste, University of Cincinnati
Jin Xu, Winona State University

REFERENCES

Deetz, S. (1996). Describing differences in approach to organization science: Rethinking Burrell and Morgan and their legacy. *Organization Science, 7,* 191–207.

Gergen, K. (1992). *The saturated self.* New York: Basic Books.

Maslow, A. (1969). *The psychology of science: A reconnaissance.* New York: Harper & Row.

Note to Students

When discussing intercultural communication, people often use the metaphor of "bridging" differences across cultures. This occurs regardless of whether the cultures discussed are geographic, political, religious, ethnic, or so forth. Consider the following quotes.

> *Throughout my ministry, I have sought to build* bridges *between Jews and Christians. I will continue to strongly support all future efforts to advance understanding and mutual respect between our communities.*
>
> ~ Billy Graham, evangelist, March 2, 2002

> *We have a long way to go before we are able to hear the voices of everyone on earth, but I believe that providing voices and building* bridges *is essential for the World Peace we all wish for.*
>
> ~ Joichi Ito, activist and entrepreneur, December 25, 2004

Through the bridge metaphor, cultures are represented as land masses separated by water. The bridge represents communication. Communication, like a bridge, enables people to connect with members of other cultural groups. This metaphor is useful to begin a discussion of intercultural communication. Yet, there is more to intercultural communication than is described by this metaphor.

The bridge metaphor suggests that each culture is a discrete island so different from other islands that there is no connection between them. However, when people from different cultures communicate, similarities mark it as much as differences. Consider those times when you have communicated about your similarity with another person despite perceived cultural differences. For example, you find yourself sitting on a train next to someone much older than you. Because the train is crowded, you are forced to sit awkwardly close. Suddenly, you realize this person is reading the same book as you. You make a joke about the book and both have a good laugh. In this example, your conversation is marked by similarity not difference. The bridge metaphor does not help to explain this and, instead, discounts such similarities between different cultural groups.

The bridge metaphor also suggests that a person living on a cultural island is a monolith representing a single cultural identity. However, every person embodies a variety of cultural identities. Through cultural communication, people express each of these cultural identities at various times and in various ways. In the train example, you may be both a college student and an avid fan of that particular book genre. You might have just as easily made an age related joke, "I'm used to being crowded because I'm a college student and commute all the time." However, instead of invoking your age, you made your book fan identity salient by commenting about the book. The bridge metaphor does not help explain nor does it allow for you to have multiple identities.

If you reflect for a moment on your own inter/cultural communication you may agree that the metaphor is limited. It does not capture the complexity of inter/cultural communication experience. Intercultural communication is not a problem to be solved by building a metaphorical bridge. Moving beyond the bridge metaphor, *Inter/Cultural Communication: Representation and Construction of Culture* presents communication both within and between cultures so that you can gain greater understanding of the complexity of inter/cultural communication. *Inter/Cultural Communication* does not offer a new metaphor to help simplify inter/cultural communication. Instead, the following 10 learning goals are offered to guide your engagement with the ideas in this text.

1. To examine basic concepts, issues, and theories in and approaches to inter/cultural communication that provide a foundation from which you can navigate communication across literal and figurative cultural borders.

2. To explore how culture influences but does not predetermine the behaviors of its members.

3. To engage in discussion of the relationship between culture and communication and be aware of your participation in the collaborative co-construction of culture.

4. To gain insights about, knowledge of, and appreciation for the experiences, behaviors, and perspectives of your own and other cultural groups.

5. To increase your self-awareness and self-reflexivity about the ways in which cultural identities develop and are maintained, and the impact of culture on your life and your communication practices as a cultural being.

6. To achieve greater intercultural communication competence in a complex social world.

7. To think critically about the dynamics of cultural and intercultural relationships.

8. To better appreciate the role media and technology play as cultural agents on local and global scales.

9. To be able to apply text concepts to everyday practical situations as well as current national and international events.

10. To understand ethical issues relevant to inter/cultural communication.

To achieve these goals you will need to both reflect upon and move beyond your current knowledge of, understanding of, and experience with inter/cultural communication. This is not an easy task, especially if you are reading this text as part of the mandatory reading for a required class. Nonetheless, by setting aside your expectations, working through your concerns and confusion, being open to the perspectives of others regardless of their group membership, and exposing yourself to new experiences, I am hopeful that this text will help you accomplish these as well as your own personal and professional goals.

PART I

Introduction to Inter/Cultural Communication

Culture and Communication

Anastacia Kurylo

Marymount Manhattan College

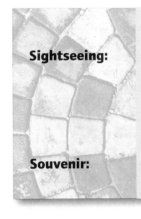

Journey Through Chapter 1

Sightseeing: On your journey, you will use the social constructionist and social scientific perspectives to visit basic concepts relevant to inter/cultural communication, distinguish between cultural generalizations and individual behavior, explain why inter/cultural communication is important to study, and discuss the theoretical approaches that guide the rest of the text. This chapter also introduces the views of culture as representation and construction.

Souvenir: After your journey, you will take away basic concepts, issues, and theories relevant to inter/cultural communication.

You probably don't realize it, but you have already begun to learn from this book. You have been introduced to new ideas just by reading its title: *Inter/Cultural Communication: Representation and Construction of Culture*. Each term in the title is meaningful. This section discusses key terms like those in the title, discusses why studying inter/cultural communication is important, and presents approaches used to study inter/cultural communication. Of the terms that the chapter discusses, the term *culture* is perhaps the most important even though it appears last in the title.

CULTURE

A culture is any group of people that share a way of life. The phrase "way of life" is one of the most recognizable and memorable phrases associated with culture (Kroeber & Kluckhohn, 1963). Way of life refers to the aspects of a culture that make up the life of its members including language, norms and values, and so forth. As a college student, the way of life you share with other college students may include a specific language such as the words *quad, ombudsman, registrar,* and *FAFSA,* as well as specific norms about where, when, and how to study. The shared aspects of a culture are infinite.

The term culture is often assumed to refer to nationality (Gudykunst & Mody, 2002). Additionally, you may think of culture as also referencing ethnicity, race, age, and gender because these are the most visibly salient categories you notice in other people when you see them for the first time (Stangor, 1995). However, culture refers to more than these groups. Cultural groups include those groups people are born into as well as groups that people voluntarily or involuntarily become a part of, such as those based on religion, phases of life (e.g., college), geographic location, sexual orientation, ability, socioeconomic class, and generational identity such as baby boomers or Generation Xers. Even this list of cultural groups only begins to expose the variety of cultures in the world. Edward Sapir (1932/1985), a celebrated scholar and early founder of intercultural communication, noted that there exists "infinitely variable groupings of human beings" (p. 519). Viewing culture broadly is important because it allows you to identify cultures that you might otherwise overlook.

Although you may view a person as representing a single culture, there are an infinite number of cultures with which any one person can identify. You are a certain gender, age, religion, reside in a specific geographic location, and so forth. You embody multiple cultural identities and are a composite of these. For example, your parents simultaneously have the identity of being parents to their children as well as of being children to their parents. This may sound complicated and even contradictory. However, people manage even their seemingly contradictory identities seamlessly.

Seamlessness is possible because only some identities are relevant in any given moment. Consider how your cultural identity as a child may be relevant to conversations with your parents but not matter in a college classroom. The reverse may also be the case. When you talk with your parents, your cultural identity as a college student is not always relevant. However, you can make any of your identities relevant at any moment by referencing the identity in your conversation. For example, you can discuss your grades with your parents over dinner and, as you answer a question in class, you can discuss your family life. Without always being aware of it, you actively and seamlessly manage your identities by making only certain identities salient in a given moment.

REFLECT 1.1: What cultures are part of your identity? Which were you born into, such as your race? Which did you choose, such as the organizations to which you belong? Which were chosen for you, such as your socioeconomic status? Of these, which do you identify with the most? Why?

COMMUNICATION

You manage your identities through your communication. At its most basic, communication can be defined as the use of symbolic code to send messages and create meaning. Another name for symbolic code is symbol. Symbols express meaning using language and behavior. Verbal communication involves the use of language to send and receive messages and create symbolic meaning. Nonverbal communication involves the use of behavior, other than verbal communication, to send and receive messages and create symbolic meaning. Symbols serve two purposes that are of interest for inter/cultural communication. First, symbols allow culture to be *represented* through verbal and nonverbal communication. Second, they allow culture to be created or *constructed* through verbal and nonverbal communication.

Symbols as Cultural Representation

People use symbols to represent meanings that are relevant to their experiences. Consider for a moment how you would explain love, freedom, or justice without using these symbols. It would take much longer, be more difficult, and likely produce more confusion than clarity to try to express these ideas without these symbols. Symbols provide a way to express cultural experience with others. A cultural representation involves the use of symbols to reflect various aspects of a shared group identity. In other words, culture can be expressed through symbols. This is the expressive function of communication. Consider the word *truthiness* coined on the U.S. American television program *The Colbert Report*. Colbert coined the word truthiness to provide a symbol for the idea of truth defined by what a person wants to be true, rather than what has been found to be true through evidence or logic. Because it represented this meaning in U.S. American culture well, truthiness became an entry in U.S. American dictionaries in 2006 and earned Word of the Year by Merriam Webster. Because culture can be represented symbolically, people are able to identify, understand, explain, and discuss aspects of their own culture and compare and contrast these to aspects of other cultures.

Symbols as Cultural Construction

In addition to serving as a representation of culture, symbols allow culture to be constructed. By communicating some symbols rather than any of the other potential symbols a person could communicate, people construct cultural identity. In this way, culture is not a preexisting entity represented in language, but rather a cultural construction created through the consistent and repetitive communication of symbols by people about a group identity. In other words, culture can be created through symbols. This is the creative function of communication. When eating certain food, engaging in certain mannerisms, using certain expressions and language, and by talking about a culture, people work together to create cultural meaning. By treating this meaning as real, people construct the culture itself as real. For example, by satirically coining the word truthiness in order to be humorous, Colbert helped to construct truthiness as a feature that exists in U.S. American culture. By laughing at Colbert's jokes about truthiness, his audience collaborates on treating this version of America as real. Through this construction process, America is created as a place in which truthiness is a common feature. Viewing culture as a construction exposes that culture is a product of communication practices. Culture cannot exist without people communicating it.

INTERCULTURAL AND CULTURAL COMMUNICATION

In your personal relationships, professional lives, and interactions with strangers you are regularly involved in intercultural and cultural communication. Intercultural communication is communication between and among those from different cultures. Even if you have never traveled outside of your town, no doubt you regularly interact with people from cultures other than your own. You may engage in intercultural communication in a variety of settings including your school, workplace, nearby neighborhoods, local events, online, and in your own family.

REFLECT 1.2: When was the last time you engaged in intercultural communication? What similarities and differences seemed to matter during this interaction?

In addition to engaging in intercultural communication, you engage in cultural communication, which focuses on the way in which communication enables people to create and negotiate their cultural identities within a cultural community. People often overlook cultural communication because it occurs more effortlessly than intercultural communication. As a result, cultural communication often seems invisible. You may not know where to find cultural communication even if you were to look for it. This is because you may take your own cultural identity for granted and not notice its importance in your daily conversation. For example, even in a recession when it is hard to pay bills and jobs are difficult to come by, your socioeconomic status or class may not stand out to you as something that is relevant to how you talk to other people because you may be surrounded by other people from the same class. Yet, the clothes you wear, what topics you talk about, your use of language, and numerous other aspects of your conversation all, nonetheless, communicate your group membership in that culture. You may not notice it because it seems to be standard practice to communicate in these ways within your cultural community. However, your cultural communication is as valuable to understand, study, and appreciate as your intercultural communication. Cultural communication and intercultural communication are relevant to all of your daily interactions with others.

The term inter/cultural communication in the title of this text draws attention to the point that each one of your conversations involves cultural as well as intercultural communication. All of your communication involves interacting with people who share some—but not all—of your cultural identities. Considering how complicated this could get, it is no wonder there are innumerable books and courses on these topics.

CULTURAL GENERALIZATIONS VERSUS INDIVIDUAL BEHAVIOR

You are no doubt familiar with countless symbols from your cultures. You can probably identify some important symbols from other cultures as well. For example, the Twin Towers are important and recognizable U.S. American symbols with which people from around the world are familiar. People use cultural symbols to identify members of a cultural group and to generalize about their way of life. You might infer that a person wearing a cross is Christian and extrapolate that the person has a strong belief in God and attends church regularly. Generalizations like these are statements about the characteristics and behaviors that describe a percentage of the members of a culture group. Generalizing about cultural groups is useful for many reasons. For example, without generalizations there could not be tourism books, like those published by Lonely Planet and Rick Steves, to guide travelers.

Generalizations can be verified through research. One way to do this would be to study a large representative sample of people from a particular culture's population to see if a trend exists in patterns of behavior. If a researcher found out that a majority of Christians attend religious service on Sunday, then it would provide the basis from which people could generalize beyond the sample used in the study to the general population of people from that culture. Knowing a generalization about a culture is helpful to understand where you may be similar to or differ from members. Generalizations also help you to be aware of how you might adapt to its behavior when interacting with someone from that culture. Generalizations about a culture affect how you think about and communicate with members of a culture.

When generalizing about a specific culture, people can erroneously view members of that culture as one-dimensional caricatures. In this way, generalizations can lead to stereotyping. Stereotyping occurs when people expect all cultural group members to have the same characteristics and engage in the same behaviors. This is problematic because not every member of a culture shares the exact same way of life as every other member of that culture all the time. Instead, there is considerable intracultural variety. This is because every person is a unique individual, even those from the same culture. Part of this uniqueness is that every person identifies with multiple cultures. Moreover, even two people who are members of the same set of cultures may behave entirely differently because of how these cultural identities intersect uniquely in each person. Unlike generalizations, stereotypes leave no room for individual differences.

Stereotypes are problematic because they can have undesirable consequences. These consequences occur when stereotypes provide an inaccurate or false basis for judgment and when they are "cognitive culprits in prejudice and discrimination" (Fiske & Taylor, 1984, p. 160; Fiske, 1998). Prejudice is a "hostile attitude" toward members of a cultural group because the person is a member of that group and is assumed to have qualities stereotypically associated with that group (Allport, 1954/1979, p. 7). Discrimination is the extension of prejudice into behavior in a way that causes different, negative, and consequential treatment of a member of the stereotyped group. Because stereotyping can provide an inaccurate basis for decision making and lead to prejudice and discrimination, avoiding stereotypes is wise.

Even generalizations, however, can be problematic because they can affect your ability to develop personal and professional relationships. Although a pattern may be observable when viewed across a large number of people, a specific single person may not enact it. If a behavioral pattern can be identified in 70 % of the population, you can generalize that this behavior is somewhat typical of that population. It does not mean, however, that a person from this culture engages in this behavior 70 % of the time. Behavior is binary. Any single member of a group either engages in the behavior or does not engage in the behavior. To expect otherwise is to assume that a person is above all else a member of a specific culture without the free will or agency to engage in behavior as an individual.

For example, the media reported much about the photograph in which U.S. Secretary of State Hillary Clinton covered her mouth with her hand while viewing the raid on Osama Bin Laden's compound in Pakistan and none of the men in the room did so. Her behavior was interpreted as a symbol of the shock of what she was witnessing and attributed to her gender because women are often generalized to be emotional. However, there are any number of reasons Clinton might have engaged in this behavior including, as she noted, that she may have been coughing at the time. Generalizations provide limited assistance when having a conversation with any one person. When you engage in cultural and intercultural communication, it is important to appreciate that each person is an individual above all else.

Photo 1.1   Does Hillary Clinton's reaction in this photo represent how all women would behave in this situation, or is it Hillary Clinton's individual way of behaving in this moment? Although people can behave in ways that match the characteristics attributed to their cultural group, these expectations do not always explain that behavior.

Copyright 2011 White House Photo by Pete Souza.

REASONS TO STUDY INTER/CULTURAL COMMUNICATION

Undergraduate students like yourself are already interculturally savvy. This is due in part to the accessibility of the media and Internet, which expose you to information from unfamiliar cultures. Television shows like *Passport to Europe* bring intercultural travel into your living room. In addition to the media, you may also have intercultural experience through your own travels abroad. Even if you have never left your town however, you may have had contact with those from other cultures at school, at work, or in other local opportunities to experience cultural diversity. Diversity refers to the presence of a variety of cultural groups.

Even if you have not had contact with much diversity, you may find that inevitably you will as you enter or continue in the workforce and travel domestically or abroad. For example, Figure 1.1 depicts how many people in the United States traveled internationally in 2010. In the future, if not previously, your international travel may be added to statistics like these. In some cases, your local area may increasingly become diverse around you as you grow older.

Pike County in Pennsylvania in the United States is an example of this. Its population has quadrupled since 1960 causing its demographic makeup to change so much that it has humorously been called "a distant suburb of New York City" (Squeri, 2002, p. 229). Educating yourself about intercultural communication will allow you to be better prepared for understanding your inevitable intercultural interactions.

Figure 1.1 International Travel Originating in the United States, January 2010.
How do world events shape your traveling habits? Economic downturns, natural disasters like earthquakes and tsunamis, and international and domestic terrorism may play a role often in subtle ways.

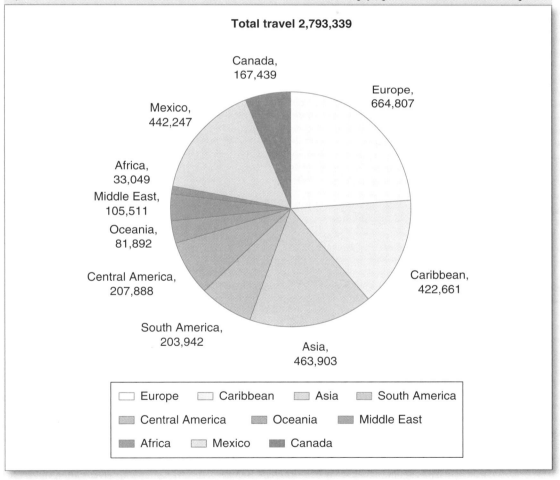

Source: Adapted from "U.S. Citizen Air Traffic to Overseas Regions, Canada & Mexico 2010" by Office of Travel and Tourism Industries. Available at http://tinet.ita.doc.gov/view/m-2010-0-001/index.html

A multicultural worldview is held by a person who is open-minded, worldly, and open to diversity. You may assume that those in large cities may have more opportunity for interaction with people from varied cultural groups and, therefore, would have a more multicultural worldview than those from rural areas. After all, large cities especially may have opportunities and resources that attract diverse populations. As a result, people living in a large city may more frequently come into contact with people from other cultures when conducting business, attending school, going to playgrounds, and so forth. Following this logic, those from rural populations may most benefit from studying inter/cultural communication.

However, this may not be the case. In big cities like San Francisco in the United States, the population is so dense that people do not need to have personal relationships with those from other cultures, though they may have professional relationships with each other. Although people from any number of cultural groups may work in and use integrated industries and public services, it may be the case that people are able to live isolated from other groups. Consider the ethnic enclaves in the three largest cities in North America as shown in Table 1.1. Regardless of whether you are from a rural or urban population and whether you work, live, go to school, or travel in a diverse place, you may find value in learning about intercultural communication.

Table 1.1   Ethnic Enclaves by City.

Is your community ethnically diverse? Even in the three largest U.S. cities, small culturally homogeneous communities exist.

Ethnic Group	Name(s) of Enclave
Chicago, IL	
African	Bronzeville
Chinese	Chinatown
Greek	Greektown
Indian	Little India
Irish	Beverly, Bridgeport, Canaryville, Mount Greenwood
Italian	Heart of Italy, Little Italy
Korean	Koreatown
Lithuanian	Lithuania Plaza
Mexican	Little Village, Pilsen
Middle Eastern and Central Asian	Assyrian District, Little Arabia
Polish	Garfield Ridge, Jackowo
Puerto Rican	Paseo Boricua
Swedish	Andersonville
Ukranian	Ukrainian Village
Vietnamese	Argyle Little Vietnam

Ethnic Group	Name(s) of Enclave
Los Angeles, CA	
African	Leimert Park, Watts
Armenian	Little Armenia
Chinese	Chinatown
Eastern European Jewish	Beverlywood, Fairfax District
Ethiopian	Little Ethiopia
Iranian	Little Persia
Japanese	Little Tokyo, Sawtelle
Korean	Koreatown
Mexican	Olvera Street
Filipino	Historic Filipinotown
Russian and Russian Jewish	West Hollywood
Thai	Thai Town
New York City, NY	
African	Harlem, Bedford Stuyvesant
West Indian	East Flatbush
Chinese	Chinatown
Dominican	Inwood
Dominican	Washington Heights
Eastern European Jewish	Borough Park, Crown Heights, Lower East Side
Filipino	Little Manila
German	Yorkville
Greek	Astoria
Indian	Little India
Irish	Woodlawn, Gerritsen Beach, Hell's Kitchen, Woodside
Italian	Arthur Avenue, Little Italy, Bensonhurst, Carroll Gardens, Cobble Hill, Little Italy of the Bronx
Korean	Koreatown
Latin American and Caribbean	Hamilton Heights, Jackson Heights, Loisaida
Polish	Greenpoint, Little Poland, Williamsburg
Puerto Rican	Spanish Harlem
Ukranian	Little Odessa, Little Ukraine

Source: Adapted from "List of named ethnic enclaves in North American cities" by Wikipedia. Available at http://en.wikipedia.org/wiki/List_of_named_ethnic_enclaves_in_North_American_cities.

Because of your background and amount of experience with diversity, you might think you already have a multicultural worldview and that you may gain no benefit from further education about intercultural communication. However, consider whether the people around you share this multicultural worldview. For example, do you have family or friends who talk louder when conversing with someone who looks elderly but does not necessarily have difficulty hearing, or who argue that people who do not speak the country's primary, though not necessarily official, language correctly are stupid? Even if you have a multicultural worldview, learning more about intercultural communication can help you communicate with others who do not.

REFLECT 1.3: Why do you want to learn about inter/cultural communication? What are the hardest and easiest things you will need to change in order to be a better inter/cultural practitioner?

INTERCULTURAL IMPERATIVES

In addition to the way in which your personal experiences may motivate you to learn more about inter/cultural communication, six intercultural imperatives articulated by Martin and Nakayama (2007) urge people toward greater awareness about intercultural communication. These imperatives represent societal level reasons for why people benefit from broader cultural awareness.

Demographic Imperative

The demographic imperative suggests that people are motivated to be culturally aware in response to changes in the makeup of a culture's population such as size, gender, age, and so forth. For example, some U.S. American schools have begun to offer Mandarin language education in response to the increased population in China and its political significance for the United States. The importance of the demographic makeup of a population and its relevance to a person's culture can motivate that person to have a greater cultural awareness.

Economic Imperative

The economic imperative suggests that people may be motivated to be more culturally aware in order to benefit from and be responsive to political, social, economic, and environmental events around the world that shape global economies. In 2010, a 3-month long oil spill by BP caused a significant impact on the fishing and tourism industries in the Gulf Coast of the United States. In turn, this has had an economic impact on restaurant owners, environmental groups, and financial institutions in the United States and worldwide, including lowering the value of BP's stock and making seafood from the Gulf Coast difficult to procure. When opportunities for economic success and failure transcend geographic borders, intercultural awareness can be an asset.

Ethical Imperative

The ethical imperative suggests that people may be motivated to have a multicultural worldview in order to be moral, just, and fair. In 2006, Google began to operate their search engine Google.cn which filters content consistent with the Chinese government's censorship policies enacted to protect Chinese citizens from what it views as potentially harmful information.

Photo 1.2 Have you heard of the Occupy Wall Street movement? Although often overlooked, your socioeconomic status is one of your cultural groups. The Occupy Wall Street movement was created in response to economic disparities in the United States. The movement and its slogan, "We are the 99%" helped draw attention to socioeconomic status as a culture.

Copyright 2011 Michael Kurylo.

Critics argued that the new site violated Google's well-known "don't be evil" mantra because it promoted censorship. Google responded that it was ethically more responsible to work with the Chinese government to provide some access to content than it would be to disavow censorship outright in a way that would cause the Chinese government to block Google access to China entirely. Grappling with ethical issues can motivate increased intercultural awareness in order to better understand a variety of perspectives.

Peace Imperative

The peace imperative suggests that people may be motivated to be more culturally aware in order to create or maintain stability interculturally. For example, a desire to facilitate greater stability in Iraq and, yet, withdraw U.S. American troops motivated military personal and elected officials, among others, to increase their understanding of Middle Eastern cultures in order to accomplish these goals. In order to accomplish peace initiatives like ending war, thwarting terrorism, and assuaging civil unrest, people are motivated to improve their inter-cultural understanding.

Self-Awareness Imperative

The self-awareness imperative suggests that people may be motivated to be more culturally aware in order to be self-reflexive and understand their thoughts and behaviors. Imagine having an unsettling disagreement with a friend who, unlike you, is in favor of mandatory military service. You reflect on the disagreement and commit to research additional information online. You find out that in some countries, citizens share participation in military service equitably, such as in Greece where the minimum required military service is 9 months. You realize that in a voluntary army, someone like yourself from a higher socioeconomic class would not need to serve in the military. Instead, people in a lower socioeconomic class like your friend would be disproportionately recruited and enlisted taking on the brunt of the risks associated with military service. Your increased self-awareness helps you understand the root of your differing opinions. A desire to be self-aware is a strong motivation to gain greater intercultural awareness.

Technological Imperative

The technological imperative suggests that people may be motivated to be more intercultur-ally aware in order to be connected to the global village. The global village refers to the idea that even though people may be far away from each other geographically, technology enables the world to feel like it occupies a much smaller space. As a result, technology motivates and enables people to be engaged interculturally. Consider the current text. Its contributors reside in different towns, cities, states, countries, continents, and hemispheres and most have never met each other in person. The availability of technology encourages this type of collaboration and motivates people to connect with others in ways that require increased intercultural awareness.

At this point, you may have concluded that inter/cultural communication is an important topic to study. Taking a class in intercultural communication and reading this text are a good start. Both are based on the work of inter/cultural communication scholars who study inter/cultural communication from various approaches. For example, some researchers are ori-ented heavily toward statistics and focus on how much (amount), how often (frequency), and for how long (duration) people do things. Other researchers are instead interested in the words people communicate, the situations in which they communicate these, and the mean-ings these words have for these situations. The approach a researcher takes provides a framework within which that researcher explores a topic and, ultimately, produces the content you learn in your coursework. Whether or not you conduct your own research on inter/cultural communication, it is important to understand the foundation of the content you are learning. The following section discusses the approaches researchers take to study inter/cultural communication.

APPROACHES TO THE STUDY OF INTERCULTURAL COMMUNICATION

If your roommate told you she lost something, but neglected to tell you what she lost, you would have a hard time finding it, short of a lot of luck. But once she tells you what she lost, her glasses for example, you have a better chance to find them even if you cannot remember exactly what they look like. If you are going to look for something, whether it is a pair of glasses or anything else, knowing what you want to look for will make your search more productive because that gives you an idea of how you might look for it. Glasses may be found on a desk, in a bathroom, or by a bed for example. A theoretical approach provides researchers with preexisting ideas about what is important to look for and how to do so. Specifically, four approaches provide the framework from which researchers have studied inter/cultural communication. These include (1) the social scientific approach as well as the (2) interpretivist, (3) critical, and (4) dialogic social constructionist approaches. All four of these approaches are important for the study of inter/cultural communication and are represented in this text. A fundamental distinction among these four approaches is between the social scientific approach and the social construction approach that guides the interpretivist, critical, and dialogic approaches.

Social Scientific Approach

Historically, a social scientific approach has been the most common approach used to study inter/cultural communication (e.g., Goldstein, 2008; Lustig & Koester, 2010; Neuliep, 2005). A social scientific approach stresses the way in which cultures are represented symbolically and helps to distinguish differences and similarities among cultures. Although this approach appreciates the importance of similarities, it emphasizes understanding cultural differences that may cause miscommunication. As a result, this approach is often referred to as a *differences approach*. Research from a differences approach attempts to explain past events and predict future events so that people can be equipped to foresee and adapt to problems that may occur in intercultural communication (e.g., Cooper, Calloway-Thomas, & Simonds, 2007; Dodd, 1998; Gudykunst, 2003; Klopf & McCroskey, 2007; Lustig & Koester, 2010; Milhouse, Asante, & Nwosu, 2001; Samovar, Porter, & McDaniel, 2007; Wiseman & Van Horn, 1995).

Imagine that you have prepared to travel abroad to the Dominican Republic. You have read about cultural differences between your culture and your host culture and are aware that, overall, the population in the host culture is much poorer than where you are from. When you arrive, you decide to immerse yourself in the local culture by shopping and taking tours while you enjoy the benefits of sightseeing and local low prices. Although you know that haggling is the norm in the culture, you pay full price for items even as others around you negotiate down by up to 50% because you understand that the sellers are probably poor and could use the money. As you tour nearby villages whose inhabitants welcome you with hospitality, you acknowledge the cultural differences by saying to other tourists and your guide that you "feel bad" for the local population and lament their poverty. You return from your travel tired from your excursions, with many memories, some great purchases, a sense of satisfaction that you have helped the local economy, and a new appreciation for the luxuries you take for granted like concrete floors and readily accessible tap water. Knowing about cultural differences equipped you to handle the problems that arose within your intercultural communication such as determining whether or not to haggle. Reading the guidebooks in advance of your trip allowed you to understand the host culture better and prepare you for what to expect in your travels.

Social Construction Approach

As reasonable as the previous scenario may have sounded to you, a social construction approach provides an alternate framework through which to view this scenario. A social construction approach stresses the way in which cultures are created through symbols. A social construction approach espouses the view that there is no reality of a culture outside of those who communicate about that culture. A culture exists by virtue of it being produced and reproduced in the moments of communication regardless of a person's awareness of this production process. Cultural similarities or differences are created through how people communicate about a culture. Within the social construction approach, inter/cultural communication has been studied using three specific theoretical approaches: (1) interpretivist, (2) critical, and (3) dialogic. An interpretivist approach guides researchers toward understanding how symbols are used in given contexts to create meaning by those who use them. A critical approach explores how power—such as power associated with wealth, whiteness, heterosexuality, or maleness—is constructed through the use of symbols and the impact of this power on people's lives. A dialogic approach focuses on conversation and the use of symbols in everyday talk to construct meaning. Not surprisingly, a social construction approach would explain your experience in the Dominican Republic in a different way than the social scientific approach did.

REFLECT 1.4: Which of the four approaches would you use if you were to study inter/cultural communication (social scientific, interpretivist, critical, or dialogic)? Why? Which would you be least likely to use? Why?

By discussing how you felt bad for the local population and commiserating about this with fellow tourists who agreed with you, you helped to produce the reality that these people were poor and that their way of life was unfortunate. At opportunities to immerse yourself in the cultural norm of haggling over a purchase price, you constructed pity by patronizingly paying twice the market rate. In doing so, you constructed your wealth and the poverty of the seller by indicating that you did not need to take part in the cultural norm because you could afford to pay more for the item. By contrasting their poverty with your culture's prosperity, you were able to bond with fellow tourists who collaborated with you to co-construct their cultures and your own as wealthy and prosperous. Through your communication, you reproduced the differences you had expected to find based on the guidebooks: a host culture in which its members were poor compared to your own wealthy culture. Not realizing your own role in constructing culture, you return from your travel tired, with memories, purchases, a sense of satisfaction, and a new appreciation for your own comparative wealth. A social construction approach provides the framework through which to understand that the culture you experienced is but one version of the host culture that you could have constructed through your communication.

LIVING CULTURE

The Social Construction of Race   *By Anita Foeman*

The first time I ran a set of DNA ancestry tests I asked a participant, "What result would be surprising for you?" A young blonde woman whom I selected for her candor responded, "I would be surprised if I had any Arab or African in my background. I just don't think anyone in my family would do *that* . . . I just don't know what I would do!" I wondered if she felt she might involuntarily break into a Negro spiritual if she found out she had African ancestry.

As an African American fully aware of the complex influences in my genetic past, the belief that one might and should be of pure ancestry was foreign to me. Now, having DNA tested more than 200 people, I am learning how rigid socially constructed racial identities can be and how profoundly the narratives that surround us influence them. In the process of interviewing and testing a diverse group of research participants, we engaged in a narrative process that began, on the spot, to reinvent each person's sense of self as a racial being.

In my DNA research, after we conduct a test, we receive a genetic profile in percentages of European, sub-Saharan African, East Asian, and Native American. These labs have different tests with different sensitivities. Responses from those who take the test tend to fall into one of two distinguishable categories: those who want diversity in their backgrounds and those who don't.

Among those who wanted diversity is one person who discovered Native American in her profile and responded, "You mean I'm not just white bread and mayonnaise!" Another said, "I feel like I have a little flava" and still another explained, "I have always been a diverse person and now I feel that my genes reflect that." One young man who identified as biracial with almost equal parts Asian and European plus a sliver of African and Native American felt confirmed as "a citizen of the world." Still another was pleased that she might "stick it in [her] racist parents' face." Several made comments like, "I can play basketball now," or "No wonder my son is so smart," or other statements most would never make in typical discussions about race. Those who wanted more diversity than they found were disappointed and responded in variations of, "That's it?!" One African American joked, "Wow, you mean I have to break it to my family that we're Black?" In each case, they felt that a diverse profile would enhance their narrative and support the identity they had built over time.

Among those who didn't want diversity in their backgrounds were people who felt uncomfortable with even the possibility of diverse ancestry.

(Continued)

LIVING CULTURE

(Continued)

One Chinese participant initially rejected taking part saying, "Oh no, I don't want to find out that I am anything but Chinese." When I responded saying that it isn't any big deal, stating, "I know that I have a diverse background," she blurted out, "But you know that you are all mixed up. I think I am pure." She apologized immediately and said, "You know what I mean." I have had people who self-identified as European, African American, Asian, and Latino each be upset by diverse findings. Underneath each objection was an identity concern. One woman who is strongly Black-identified became quite agitated when I asked her, "How could you not suspect [European ancestry] when you have green eyes?" she responded, "Well, we don't *talk* about [that]." And, indeed, many family narratives unfolded as if claims of purity in their ancestry made them pure.

Whites were most likely to be caught off guard by African ancestry. Several identified that they might have Native American ancestors, always substantiated by tales of a romanticized ancestor with beautiful long dark braids, but rarely African. When confronted with it in their DNA profile, they reacted, "Where did that come from?" Anti-miscegenation and one drop laws have apparently lead many Whites (though few African Americans) to believe a *pure White* narrative. In at least one instance after results came back with no Native American ancestry but measurable African ancestry, relatives revealed that this *Native American* ancestor was probably part black.

These experiences shed light on how we construct and maintain racial identities and how we respond to challenges to those identities. Given the popularity of DNA tests, new questions about how race will be viewed and discussed arise. Regardless of the answers, a new era in understanding racial identity is on the horizon. This new era will expose how identity is constructed as much out of conversation as any DNA profile.

Consider:

1. Why were some of the people in the study surprised and, in some cases, upset when they heard the results of their DNA profile testing?

2. What are the benefits and problems of DNA profile testing?

3. Does DNA profile testing provide evidence of racial differences or does it provide evidence of the social construction of race?

4. How might the experience of race shift in the future, if at all? Does structuration theory help to explain this? Why or why not?

WEAVING TWO DOMINANT APPROACHES

In research, a social scientific approach and a social construction approach are often treated as mutually exclusive (Deetz, 1994). Collier (2001) notes that these approaches have been "presented as polar opposites and dualistic extremes in past research" (p. 21). Nonetheless, some scholars have suggested that taking a combined approach is more useful. Baldwin and Hecht (1995) argue "against firm methodological and disciplinary boundaries" (p. 90). Essentially it is the cumulative knowledge produced by both of these approaches that provide the greatest benefit to students of inter/cultural communication. To navigate inter/cultural interactions, it is important to understand the differences and similarities between cultures and it is important to understand your role in creating these.

Structuration theory (Giddens, 1993) provides a way of weaving both approaches. Structuration theory articulates how representations and constructions intertwine to create reality. The first assertion of the theory is that people have agency to construct identities, relationships, and cultures as they like. In other words, people actively engage in social construction. Consider your hypothetical trip to the Dominican Republic. According to the United Nations Statistics Division, in 2007 48.5% of the country was below the national poverty line, something that would be reflected in most guidebooks. Despite these statistics, you have the ability to communicate about the culture in any number of ways. You might have told others you met on the trip that you thought the guidebooks were incorrect with their assertion about the poverty of the area and that you found members of the culture to demonstrate considerable financial wealth. As others hear your view of the culture, they may treat it as true by communicating with you in ways that support this version of reality. Although you have the agency to construct culture in any number of ways, the second assertion of structuration theory provides one reason why people might not buy into some constructions.

The second assertion notes that preexisting representations within a culture constrain social constructions. Giddens (1993) calls these representations *structures*; hence, structuration theory. These structures place a limit on how creative your constructions can be. For example, your construction of financial wealth in the Dominican Republic may not receive a lot of support from other people who share a representation of what financial wealth means that does not match what you experienced in that Dominican Republic. As a result, they may look at you strangely after hearing your remark on the wealth of Dominicans and ask, "what do you mean?" or "how can you think that?" Your ability to construct is limited by the necessity to do so within the representations that are common within a culture.

A third assertion of structuration theory is that because culture is both a representation and a construction, cultures can change over time. Giddens (1993) explains how people simultaneously reproduce culture within its current representations while they can actively work against those representations to produce that culture in a different way. For example, if you talk about the Dominican Republic as wealthy in spirit, pride, happiness, and so forth you may receive support for that construction because it works within an alternate but equally common representation of wealth. In this way, you may be able to construct the Dominican Republic in a way more reflective of your admiration for the culture. It should be noted that it is not only other people that can limit your ability to construct, but that you can also limit your own ability to construct. Consider that your construction of the Dominican Republic as predominantly poor in the original scenario was limited by the representations you learned from the guidebooks you read before you began your trip. During your trip, you may have sought examples that confirmed that view, and overlooked or disregarded evidence to the contrary. Hence the original information you received constrained your outlook such that you communicated in ways that treated this information as real.

This third assertion of structuration theory is powerful because it explains both how cultures change over time and why this change is often slow. However, civil unrest in Egypt, Libya, and Syria demonstrates that sometimes change can be surprisingly sudden. Recognizing your role in reproducing how a culture is represented and your ability to work toward constructing a different version of that culture with others is invaluable for your inter/cultural communication. This is because the consequences of this construction process impact your inter/cultural communication and relationships with others in ways you might never know. Imagine how the construction process in the Dominican Republic scenario might have played out in high stakes situations, such as if you are traveling as an exchange student, on a business trip, to visit family whom you have never met, or while applying for an international adoption.

FINAL THOUGHTS

Tracy (2002) argues, "[cultural] identities, then, are best thought of as stable features of persons that exist prior to any particular situation, *and* are dynamic and situated accomplishments, enacted through talk, changing from one occasion to the next" (p. 17). Tracy states further that "to understand everyday talk we need to keep both perspectives in mind" (p. 41). *Inter/cultural Communication* offers students a view of culture as both represented in and constructed through communication. This dual approach to inter/cultural communication will provide you with invaluable opportunities for practical understanding and personal reflection. By understanding both of these perspectives, appreciating when each is relevant to your own experiences, and understanding how they weave together, you will gain a broader and deeper understanding of inter/cultural communication.

CONTINUE YOUR JOURNEY ONLINE

Visit: http://911digitalarchive.org

The September 11 Digital Archive. Explore how cultural events provide the opportunity for inter/cultural communication. Search the site for references to cultural groups including Middle Eastern, lesbian, Latino, immigrant, American, and others. Use this primary source archive to broaden your understanding of the inter/cultural communication issues related to the terrorist attacks on September 11, 2001.

❝ SAY WHAT?

Say What? provides excerpts from overheard real-life conversations in which people have communicated stereotypes. As you read these conversations, reflect on the following questions.

- Have you been in conversations like this before?
- Is there any one of these conversations that stick out to you more than the others?
- What do you think of this conversation?
- How did the stereotype help or hinder the conversation?
- Was there another way the stereotyper could have communicated to convey the same point?
- How do you feel when you hear this conversation or the specific stereotype?
- Do any of these conversations bother you more than others? Why or why not?
- Do any concepts, issues, or theories discussed in the chapter help explain why?

- **Say What?** Expecting my male friend to respond to the story I had told him with sympathy, I was taken aback when he made the following comment. "Of course she crashed her car. She's a girl. I know at least three girls from my hometown who have crashed their cars at least once." To his comment, I responded with a look of disgust. "Of course? She's a girl?"

- **Say What?** I proceeded to tell her that Italian boys expect girls to wait on them hand and foot because their mothers always cater to them. This kind of catering leads to laziness. Italian boys think they are God's gift to women. They also think they're tough guys. Instead of concentrating on a solution to the problem, we just continued to bring up more bad qualities. The focus should have been on helping my coworker feel better.

- **Say What?** The other day my friend asked me to go out to eat to a restaurant. I told her that I would rather not spend the extra money. Her response to my decline was, "But your daddy's a doctor . . . you can afford anything," with an obnoxious tone in her voice. I immediately got defensive and said back, "Just because my parents have money does not mean that I can spend their money whenever I please. My parents teach me responsibility and I have to work for what I spend. I am sorry if your parents just hand it to you."

- **Say What?** "Asian women are bad drivers," my friend said to his girlfriend, with a sneer on his face. "Well, then," she said, "I guess you don't need a ride."

REVIEW QUESTIONS

1. How are symbols representations of culture? How are symbols constructions of culture? Provide at least one example for each.

2. Why is the term *inter/cultural communication* used in this chapter and the title of the text? Does its meaning warrant the use of a slash term or can the meaning be represented better with another symbol?

3. How is culture defined in the chapter? What is the simplest definition of culture discussed in the chapter? Based on the material discussed throughout the chapter, how might you define culture in more depth?

4. What is the difference between a stereotype and a generalization? Which contributes to prejudice and discrimination? How?

5. Based on the discussion at the start of the chapter, explain at least four reasons for studying intercultural communication.

6. What are the six intercultural imperatives discussed in the chapter? How might these intersect with each other?

7. Explain a social scientific approach. Provide one example of how you might study cultural variability in the amount, frequency, or duration of two cultures?

8. Think of an example of a specific situation that involved intercultural communication. Compare a social scientific approach and a social construction approach to culture applying each to the same example.

9. What is structuration theory? Why is it relevant to understanding culture?

10. Using the concepts from the chapter, explain the meaning of the first quote from Tracy (2002) in the final paragraph in the chapter.

KEY TERMS

communication 4

critical approach 16

cultural communication 6

cultural construction 5

cultural representation 5

culture 3

demographic
 imperative 12

dialogic approach 16

discrimination 7

diversity 8

economic imperative 12

ethical imperative 12

generalization 6

global village 14

inter/cultural
 communication 6

intercultural
 communication 5

intercultural imperative 12

interpretivist approach 16

multicultural worldview 10

nonverbal
 communication 4

peace imperative 13

REFERENCES

Allport, G. W. (1954/1979). *The nature of prejudice.* Cambridge, MA: Addison-Wesley.

Baldwin, J. R., & Hecht, M. L. (1995). The layered perspective on cultural (in)tolerance(s): The roots of a multidisciplinary approach to (in)tolerance. In R. L. Wiseman (Ed.), *Intercultural communication theory* (pp. 59–91). Thousand Oaks, CA: Sage.

Collier, M. J. (2001). *Constituting cultural difference through discourse.* Thousand Oaks, CA: Sage.

Cooper, P. J., Calloway-Thomas, C., & Simonds, C. J. (2007). *Intercultural communication: A text with readings.* Boston: Allyn & Bacon.

Deetz, S. (1994). The future of the discipline: The challenges, the research, and the social contribution. In S. Deetz (Ed.), *Communication yearbook, 17* (pp. 565–600). Thousand Oaks, CA: Sage.

Dodd, C. (1998). *Dynamics of intercultural communication* (5th ed.). New York: Harper & Row.

Fiske, S. T. (1998). Stereotyping, prejudice, and discrimination. In D. T. Gilbert, S. T. Fiske, & G. Lindzey, (Eds.), *The handbook of social psychology* (pp. 357–411). Boston: McGraw-Hill.

Fiske, S. T., & Taylor, S. E. (1984). *Social cognition.* New York: Random House.

Giddens, A. (1993). *The transformation of intimacy: Sexuality, love and eroticism in modern societies.* Cambridge, UK: Polity Press.

Goldstein, S. (2008). *Cross-cultural explorations: Activities in culture and psychology.* Boston: Allyn & Bacon.

Gudykunst, W. B. (2003). *Cross-cultural and intercultural communication.* Thousand Oaks, CA: Sage.

Gudykunst, W. B., & Mody, B. (Eds.). (2002). *Handbook of international and intercultural communication* (2nd ed.). Thousand Oaks, CA: Sage.

Klopf, D. W., & McCroskey, J. (2007). *Intercultural encounters.* Boston: Allyn & Bacon.

Kroeber, A. L., & Kluckhohn, C. (1963). *Culture: A critical review of concepts and definitions.* New York: Vintage Books.

Lustig, M. W., & Koester, J. (2010). *Intercultural competence: Interpersonal communication across cultures.* Boston: Allyn & Bacon.

Martin, J. N., & Nakayama, T. K. (2007). *Intercultural communication in contexts.* Boston: McGraw-Hill.

Milhouse, V. H., Asante, M., & Nwosu, P. O. (2001). *Transcultural realities: Interdisciplinary perspectives on cross-cultural relations.* Thousand Oaks, CA: Sage.

Neuliep, J. W. (2005). *Intercultural communication: A contextual approach.* Thousand Oaks, CA: Sage.

Samovar, L. A., Porter, R. E., & McDaniel, E. R. (2007). *Communication between cultures.* Belmont, CA: Wadsworth.

Sapir, E. (1932/1985). *Culture, language and personality.* D. G. Mandelbaum, (Ed.). Berkeley: University of California Press.

Squeri, L. (2002). *Better in the Poconos: The story of Pennsylvania's vacationland.* University Park: The Pennsylvania University Press.

Stangor, C. (1995). Content and application inaccuracy in social stereotyping. In Y. Lee, L. Jussim & C. McCauley (Eds.), *Stereotype accuracy: Toward appreciating group differences* (pp. 275–292). Washington, DC: American Psychological Association.

Tracy, K. (2002). *Everyday talk: Building and reflecting identities.* New York: Guilford Press.

Wiseman, R. L., & Van Horn, T. (1995). Theorizing in intercultural communication. In R. L. Wiseman (Ed.), *Intercultural communication theory* (pp. 2–6). Thousand Oaks, CA: Sage.

Intercultural and Cross-Cultural Communication

Bernadette M. Watson

The University of Queensland

Journey Through Chapter 2

Sightseeing: On your journey, you will visit intercultural and cross-cultural communication using a social scientific approach to learn about cultural mores, the beginnings of this research, and its two dominant traditions. You will learn how cultures are represented through nine specific dimensions, face-negotiation theory, and the willingness to communicate concept.

Souvenir: After your journey, you will take away an understanding of intercultural and cross-cultural communication that does not polarize cultures along the nine dimensions you will have learned.

This chapter provides a brief discussion of the beginnings of intercultural communication research and explores theories that seek to explain intercultural and cross-cultural communication behavior. Intercultural communication, introduced in Chapter 1, refers to the effects on communication behavior when different cultures interact together. Cross-cultural communication refers to how cultures vary in their communication behavior. It is not unusual for researchers to be interested in both these areas but the distinction is relevant for this chapter.

This chapter focuses on why it is that people from different cultures often understand and perceive the world differently from each other. For example, in many countries that have been influenced by the British and European cultures, it is traditional to see a bride wearing a white or cream-colored dress. Indeed, this is often how you are able to identify the bride. By contrast, traditional Indian brides wear red and green at their weddings. For Indians, white is strictly the color of mourning and is worn at funerals. It would be inappropriate for a Hindu bride to wear white because it would signify death.

Through reading this chapter, you will learn that a culture's beliefs and values shape how meaning is constructed for the people who live in that culture. You will see how it can be that people interpret the same behavior differently according to their cultural norms. At the end of this chapter, you will understand that cultures and communication are dynamic and changing. Thus, an important aim of this chapter is not to just describe differences between cultures, but to also extend the discussion to examine how different cultures respond to a similar situation in different ways.

CULTURAL MORES

Much miscommunication occurs because people are not aware of cultural differences. Importantly though, cultural mores, the components of a culture such as its norms, values, and customs, can be learned as you are learning them now. Individuals can conduct a great

Photo 2.1   What are some of the cultural mores of your cultural groups? Cultural artifacts like buildings embody cultural mores for future generations, if they last.

deal of research about a particular culture they intend to visit to ensure that cultural mistakes do not occur. Knowing and being familiar with a culture in which you live or to which you plan to travel is essential. If you do not fit within a culture, you may be viewed as not belonging or as an outsider. In order to understand how to fit in, it is important to remember that not all cultural practices are open and obvious; there are many cultural mores that are hidden. In fact, they can be so hidden that sometimes even the people who live in a culture may have never explicitly realized why certain kinds of behavior are not acceptable.

Every culture has both external, or more obvious, components, and internal components that can be easily overlooked. Examples of the external components of a culture are art, its use of color, its food, and religion to name just a few. The internal components of a culture are more subtle and tap into sometimes unspoken dimensions of a culture. Figure 2.1 uses the metaphor of an iceberg to describe some of the internal and external components of

Figure 2.1   The Culture Iceberg.

Are the aspects of your culture that you value the most on the visible portion of the cultural iceberg? Sometimes we take for granted what makes our culture unique without realizing that those from outside of our culture might not even know these exist.

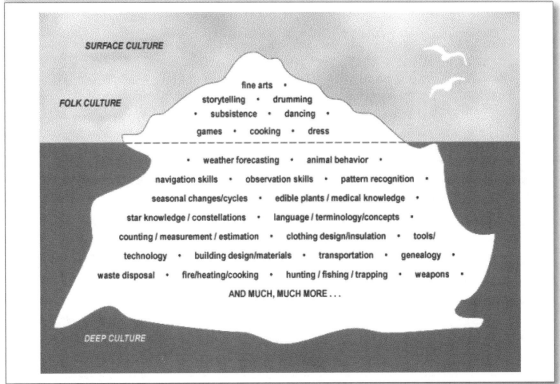

Source: Courtesy of American Foreign Service (AFS) Intercultural Programs, Inc. © 2010.

culture. Generally, people have low awareness of the internal components that exist in a culture. It is only in the study of psychology or communication that this is explicit knowledge.

How a person behaves during a funeral service is an example of how cultures can behave differently during similar situations. You may know that in regions such as the United Kingdom, Northern Europe, and North America funerals are often solemn affairs. Mourners communicate to the people around them their sadness and respect for the deceased by being quietly respectful, perhaps crying silently into a handkerchief, and wearing black or dark colors. These behaviors are examples of display rules. Display rules prescribe the type of emotional expression that has evolved over time to be considered appropriate in a given situation within a culture (Ekman & Friesen, 1969). In Middle Eastern countries, the display rules for a funeral can be different from those described previously. In these cultures, it is not expected that people will be reserved during a funeral. Rather, they are expected to vent their grief publicly and not to do so would be disrespectful. You have only to look at news coverage of funerals in the Middle East to see that people are openly showing their distress by shouting and wailing. In these cultures, it is appropriate to behave in this demonstrative manner.

Take a Side Trip:

If you would like to read more about related issues, visit Appendix F: Korean Culture Explored Through Survey Research.

Differences in display rules and other subtle cultural mores explain why intercultural communication competency training alone will not necessarily bring about effective mutually satisfying interactions. Table 2.1 provides further examples of how cultural mores vary across cultures. Being aware of these components of culture is important to enable successful interactions and relationships within that culture. Early intercultural and cross-cultural communication research was conducted for just this reason.

Table 2.1   Legal Ages Around the World.

In what way might cultural mores play a role here? Cultures vary in the ages they allow citizens to engage in certain behaviors and activities.

Country	Drinking	Smoking Cigarettes	Marriage Age Range	Military Service	Legal Working
Australia	18	18	16–18	17 (voluntary)	14.9
Brazil	18	None	16–18	17 (voluntary) 21 (conscript)	14
United States	21	18	16–21	18 (voluntary)	14
Nigeria	18	None	21	18 (voluntary)	No minimum
Russia	18	None	18	18 (conscript)	16
People's Republic of China	18	None	22 for males 20 for females	18 (conscript) No minimum (voluntary)	16

REFLECT 2.1: If you have been to a funeral, how did the people around you behave? What display rules might have been used? How do these display rules reflect your cultural mores?

BEGINNINGS OF THE STUDY OF INTERCULTURAL COMMUNICATION

Intercultural communication has been researched since the end of World War II (for a review see Leeds-Hurtwitz, 1990). The work of E. T. Hall was important in shaping this early research. In the 1950s, Hall worked with the American Foreign Service Institute (FSI). Hall's involvement with the FSI led to the establishment of a communication training program. The main aim of the program was to ensure diplomats working abroad knew the social mores and rules of their assigned country and so would neither cause offense by their behavior, nor mistakenly take offense at the behaviors they encountered. For example, raising your hand and bringing your thumb and forefinger together to make a circle in North America can mean "everything is fine." In Brazil, however, it has a very different connotation and literally means "screw you." In 1971, President Nixon used this gesture in Brazil and the crowd responded with anger. The skills training approach, used by the FSI program or by your intercultural communication class facilitated by the current text, continues to this day and is still an essential element for learning about intercultural communication.

TWO DOMINANT TRADITIONS IN INTERCULTURAL COMMUNICATION RESEARCH

As discussed in Chapter 1, research that focuses on differences between cultures often takes a social psychological approach. Social psychologists have played a large part in developing an understanding of intercultural communication. Their research can be said to fall into two major traditions: intercultural communication competence and intergroup communication. Both of these are discussed in depth in upcoming chapters. They are introduced here because they are foundational to understanding intercultural communication.

Intercultural Communication Competence

The first of these traditions, which represents the largest volume of work in this area, is known as intercultural communication competence (ICC). This approach began with the work of E. T. Hall at the FSI mentioned in the previous section. Those who follow this tradition make some critical assumptions. Specifically, they view intercultural communication as an interpersonal exchange between people who, because they come from different cultural backgrounds, have learned different social and communication rules. Newcomers to a culture must take the time to learn the language and social communication rules of that culture. As a result, the ICC approach focuses on people acquiring the necessary skills to be competent communicators within another culture.

Intergroup Communication

The second tradition in intercultural communication focuses on intergroup communication (IGC) (Giles & Watson, 2008). Those who work within this intergroup communication tradition make a different set of assumptions about the nature of intercultural communication than the ICC approach. The first of these assumptions is that the social and historical relations that exist between cultures influence how the two cultures communicate. To illustrate this perspective and why it is important, imagine two people meeting for the first time. One person comes from Israel and the other comes from Palestine. Even though they may both be able to converse in the same language, and know the correct communication behaviors of each culture, they may still not engage in mutually satisfactory communication. The reason for the communication failure may be that the two nations from which they come have a history of conflict. A history of poor relations between cultural group members can preclude effective communication.

REFLECT 2.2: Has the history of your cultural group ever played a role in how you thought about or behaved in certain situations? Provide an example and explain how.

A second assumption made by an intergroup communication tradition is the focus on group membership. Whereas researchers who take an ICC focus view communication as an interpersonal exchange, researchers in the second tradition view intercultural communication as an intergroup exchange. Rather than each person's individual identity as, say, James or Mary being significant, it is the social identity of each person (e.g., their membership in Israeli or Palestinian culture) that drives how the two interactants talk to each other. The communication between two people, who are representatives of two countries that are often hostile to each other, may be affected by the importance of their group membership.

A third assumption of an intergroup communication tradition is that it views the person's social identity (in this case, the country of origin of each speaker) as being a focal part of an interaction that can hamper effective communication. When a person views someone as belonging to a group which is not valued or is even actively disliked, it is likely that there will be little motivation for mutually effective communication. How a person behaves toward another is often governed by the beliefs held about a person's social identity. In the example of the interaction between the Israeli and the Palestinian, it could be that each has no desire to engage in competent and effective communication; instead, the group identity of each may have gotten in the way.

The IGC approach explains why knowledge learned from intercultural communication skills training may not equate to effective communication between people from different cultures, even though one side has read all the guidebooks about appropriate ways to behave. Individuals from one culture may not always be willing to acknowledge or show respect to the beliefs of another culture because they may not value that other culture. Indeed, in an extreme case, a person may deliberately flout the cultural rules in order to register disrespect. For example, a person visiting Japan may know that to wear outdoor shoes inside the home of a Japanese person would be considered rude behavior. From an ICC perspective, the way to achieve an effective interaction would be to remove one's shoes outside the home. From this perspective, no explanation for why a violation of this norm would occur apart from ignorance is offered. The IGC approach would say that if a person does not value or like the Japanese or a specific Japanese person, that person might deliberately keep the shoes on in order to display contempt. In other words, the person is motivated not to achieve effective positive communication.

Motivation is a key driver in our interactions with others and should not be underestimated (Giles, 1973). Consider your own motivations for taking this course and how these motivations affect your willingness to learn from this book. Thus, a key difference between the two intercultural communication traditions is motivation. The first tradition assumes (albeit implicitly) that people are motivated to communicate effectively with each other. The second tradition does not make this assumption and, instead, argues that effective communication depends not only on whether a person has the skills to interact with someone from a different culture, but also on a person's motivation to communicate with another. Unlike the ICC approach, researchers who focus on the importance of group identity highlight issues of conflict and discrimination between countries and cultures (Cargile & Giles, 1996). Such a focus recognizes that power and status differentials can lead to conflict. Neither approach is right or wrong; rather, they each focus on different aspects of intercultural communication.

In summary, both ICC and IGC approaches recognize diversity between cultures that can make effective communication difficult. Although the ICC approach takes as its starting point that mutually effective communication is the goal of interactants, IGC proponents argue that historical conflicts and tensions between cultures need to be acknowledged because it is possible that interactants from seemingly conflicting cultures may have no wish to achieve effective communication outcomes. Power and status are focal aspects of the IGC approach but are not important within ICC. It is just as important to explain why people might be motivated *not* to achieve effective intercultural communication as it is to understand when intercultural communication is successful. So far, you have learned about the beginnings of intercultural communication as a research area and two traditions from which researchers study intercultural communication. As you read through this chapter, you will learn how cultures across the world possess different values and beliefs, which in turn impact communication behavior. The next section covers some cultural differences that intercultural researchers have explored.

CROSS-CULTURAL DIFFERENCES

As you read about different countries and the people who inhabit those countries, you can imagine all of the diverse aspects of their lives. Houses may be differently constructed because of climatic differences; clothing may vary across countries, as may skin color and language. As this chapter has discussed, alongside these visible differences, there are other aspects of life that cannot be so easily observed. Hall's observations about the way people use physical space and about time explain two important aspects of culture that are often overlooked.

Physical Space

There is an unspoken rule that states we have a personal space around us into which strangers should not invade. Yet, you may never have thought about how your culture demands that you respect a person's space. Edward T. Hall invented the term proxemics to describe how people use space (Hall, 1966). Hall determined that the space around a person is comprised of intimate, personal, social, and public space. He observed that people from different cultures require different amounts of space in order to feel comfortable depending on the relationship that person has with the other person or people. For example, compared to Arabs, Australians need more personal space between themselves and their interactants. A stranger standing too close to an Australian will make the Australian feel uncomfortable and threatened.

Hall's research can be generalized to all Anglo-American cultures. If you are a member of an Anglo-American culture you may not consciously know why you feel affronted when a stranger seems to stand too close to you, but you know you feel anxious. If you live in Australia or the United States, try moving closer than 0.5 meters or 19 inches to someone you do not know and then try striking up a conversation. You will be assured of a reaction. Many Australians or U.S. Americans will not know why they get so upset when a stranger gets too close. This is because proxemics is an example of a hidden behavior. No one probably told you how close to stand when talking to a stranger compared to talking to a friend, but you know it from being in your culture and seeing how others behave.

Time

Hall (1959, 1984) also recognized that cultures view time in different ways. Hall found that some cultures (most noticeably northern Europe and the United States) have a monochronic concept of time. Hall (1984) also called this *M-time*. These cultures view time as following a linear trajectory and they allocate specific times to specific tasks. So if you have a 9:30 meeting for half an hour, you can expect the meeting to commence at 9:30 and finish at 10:00. By contrast, some cultures have a polychronic concept of time; also called *P-time* (Hall, 1984). Latin American, Asian, and Arab countries have this approach to time and are more likely to deal with many tasks at once. There is not one linear order for tasks. Hall noted that polychronic cultures tend to be countries where people are highly engaged with one another while monochromic are not.

Using the previous example, the meeting you have been asked to attend at 9:30 may not start on time and may continue for as long as it takes to get the business finished, even if this means the next person who has an appointment has to wait. In M-time cultures, such a disregard for time may be thought of as rude. However, P-time cultures argue that the person and relationships are more important and a person should not be constrained by the clock. In polychronic cultures, people are more important than the tasks and, as Hall (1966) comments, "the person with the most *push* gets served first" (p. 162) regardless of whether or not this person should be first. Note though that not all Europeans are monochronic; Hall describes how southern Europeans are more polychronic than their northern counterparts, which often leads to exasperation by the latter when tasks are not completed in a timely manner.

REFLECT 2.3: Given the amount of technology use by younger generations, do you think generational cultures can be said to be on different ends of the monochronic and polychronic continuum? If so, can you think of a specific example from your own life that demonstrates this? What miscommunication might result from this cross-cultural difference? How might a member of either group handle such miscommunication?

Hofstede's Five Cultural Dimensions

In the early 1980s, Geert Hofstede (1983) was interested in understanding and comparing how behaviors differ across cultures. He had access to results from a survey completed across 40 countries. He was particularly interested in the ways in which people from diverse cultures respond differently to the people around them. He categorized these varying responses into five cultural dimensions that differentiated people's behaviors across the countries surveyed. These dimensions are (1) individualism and collectivism, (2) masculinity and femininity, (3) uncertainty avoidance, (4) power distance, and (5) long- and short-term orientation. It is important to understand that the countries sampled provided broad ranging scores across a spectrum indicating a continuum rather than discrete high or low scores. Although these cultural classifications have been challenged (Fischer, Vauclair, Fontaine, & Schwartz, 2010; Merritt, 2000), they remain an important source for understanding cultural values as reflected across many countries. The dimensions are described briefly in the following sections.

Individualism and Collectivism

This value dimension represents the extent to which a culture accepts that each person can be independent and strive for personal needs over the needs of others. In an individualistic culture, self-reliance and individual achievement are positively valued. In a collectivist culture, the self is not as important as the social groups to which the person belongs, so self-credit is viewed as inappropriate. For example, in the workplace, people from a collectivist culture do not like to be singled out as individual achievers; rather they prefer that the entire group is recognized for the achievement. By contrast, a person from an individualist culture is pleased to be awarded recognition for contributions, even though the efforts of the entire group will be acknowledged. It is more important to a person in an individualist culture to not tarnish dignity and stature. This concern exists over and above any concern for a person's associates who may also be in the same situation. In collectivist cultures, the well-being and dignity of the group needs to be maintained before any thoughts about the self. A key difference here is the concern for self versus the concern for other.

Hofstede and Hofstede (2005) describe that in collectivist cultures a person is intrinsically linked to group membership. The well-being of the group brings about the well-being of the person. The two are not separate. Consider that with this understanding a married person might be viewed as being a member of a collectivist culture in which to be married presumes that each person in the married couple is concerned with the well-being of the other and that the two are necessarily connected because of their marriage license, shared address, potentially shared last name, and so forth. By contrast, in individualist cultures a person can be defined without any reference to social groups. Single people, as members of an individualistic culture, are concerned predominantly with their own well-being and are not necessarily tied to any other person in particular, though they may choose to be.

To understand how this difference translates in the work place, Hofstede and Hofstede (2005) listed what people from these two cultures chose as important work goals. Workers from an individualist culture rated having personal time to enjoy life outside of work, having freedom to choose how to best do their job, and having a challenge that leads to feeling a sense of achievement in their work as important. By contrast, workers from a collectivist culture rated as most important being able to obtain training at work, having a comfortable working environment, and being able to use their skills so that they could achieve at their work. In collectivist cultures, there is always a sense of togetherness that is less obvious in individualistic cultures.

Take a Side Trip:

If you would like to read more about related issues, visit Appendix G: Japanese Culture Explored Through Experimental Design.

Masculinity and Femininity

This value dimension represents the extent to which a culture is characterized by dominance. The use of the terms *masculinity* and *femininity* do not relate to the gender makeup of the population, but rather to the value placed on the attributes that have been traditionally assigned to each gender. From prehistoric times, men were often viewed as hunter-gatherers who used their strength to provide food for their families. Similarly, it is men who have often been viewed as the warriors. As a result of these behaviors, maleness has become associated with dominance. By contrast, from early times, females were depicted as the homemakers who cared for their children and cooked food. These behaviors have resulted in femaleness becoming associated with being nurturing. These male and female attributes are stereotypical representations and in reality people possess varying combinations of both male and female attributes. Nonetheless, according to Hofstede and Hofstede (2005), in a more masculine culture, it is important for the person to place emphasis on personal strength and external wealth as a means of dominance. By contrast, a more feminine culture focuses on nurturance in which relationships are important, there is equality between males and females, and people will not highlight accomplishments. For example, in feminine cultures such as the Netherlands and Scandinavian countries, the preferred method of resolving conflicts is through compromise and negotiation. By contrast, in cultures that have a strong masculine approach such as Mexico, it is more acceptable to resolve conflict by allowing people to stand up and fight to win (Hofstede & Hofstede, 2005, p. 143). Hofstede and Hofstede acknowledge this dimension is highly contentious.

Uncertainty Avoidance

The value dimension of uncertainty avoidance represents the extent to which a culture prefers order and structure and shuns ambiguity. Hofstede and Hofstede (2005) provide evidence of how people in high and low uncertainty avoidance cultures react to situations.

For example, they illustrate how low tolerance for uncertainty cultures, such as Japan, expect that teachers in schools reflect certainty and expertise which is unquestioned by students. In high tolerance for uncertainty cultures such as the United States, it is expected that a student will question their teacher and challenge concepts.

Power Distance

The dimension of power distance represents the extent to which a culture accepts inequality for people within the society and assents to centralized power and status differentials. In practical terms, power distance refers to the extent to which people are viewed as equal. Using education as an example again, you would find that in Australia it is normal for university students to call their lecturers by their first name. This is an example of low power distance. In countries such as Singapore, which has a much higher power differential, such familiarity would not be acceptable.

Long- or Short-Term Orientation

This value dimension was added after the first four value dimensions (Hofstede & Hofstede, 2005). Countries which demonstrate a short-term orientation tend to prefer fast results and focus on social and status obligations. In contrast, countries that have a long-term orientation tend to value patience and endurance that bring results over a long time, have low concern for status, and are willing to adjust to change. This concept can be summed up by considering the environmental disaster discussed in Chapter 1. Drilling for oil in the Gulf of Mexico provided the United States with a short-term solution to their desire for domestic sources of oil. However, this short-term orientation meant that the potential for long-term consequences on the environment, made salient during the 2010 oil spill, were overlooked.

Confucian Dynamism

It is important to remember that some aspects of a culture do not translate across cultures. Michael Bond and his colleagues (Chinese Culture Connection, 1987) found a dimension of culture that did not fit with any of Hofstede's dimensions. They called it Confucian dynamism and stated that it was a uniquely "oriental dimension" (p. 158) associated with the Asian work ethic. Confucian dynamism explains a cultural preference for employers or employees to be dependable, respectful, and desirous to ensure a harmonious relationship exists. It reflects the ideology of the philosopher Confucius who was born in China in 551 BC. His teachings address how to live life to embrace respect and harmony in all things. The Confucian dynamism dimension consists of eight items. Some of these items may be difficult for those from individualistic cultures to relate to. For example, one item is about "having a sense of shame." This item, although understood by Australians and U.S. Americans, does not easily relate to their work lives. Confucian Dynamism demonstrates that it is not always easy to understand what motivates other cultures. Someone who plans to commence work in Hong Kong would need to research not simply culturally acceptable behaviors such as bowing when you greet a colleague, but also to adapt to the more subtle cultural norms of that culture, which is hard to do.

High Context and Low Context Cultures

Another cultural dimension articulated by E. T. Hall is the extent to which a culture can be categorized as high or low context. Individuals from low context cultures provide a lot of detail in their conversations and they do not make assumptions about their speech partner's knowledge. Bernstein (1972) noted that such cultures are person focused in that each person is viewed as an individual with a unique context which cannot be known by others. Germany, the United States, and the United Kingdom are examples of cultures with a prevalence of low context language. In general, speakers there will provide a great deal of contextual information while they talk. In contrast, in high context cultures, speakers tend to use language and behavior that assumes much of what they know, you also know. Countries that use high context language include Japan and China. Bernstein stated that in such cultures there was a positional rather than a person focus. In a positional-focused culture people are viewed as being members of a collective and the context within which they reside is known. Thus, in these cultures, there are assumptions made about how much detail to provide and what is superfluous information.

Photo 2.2   Real or fake? In Japanese culture, restaurants often display plastic versions of their food to enable foreigners to know what to order because it is assumed they will not be able to read the menu. This type of accommodation allows foreigners to adapt more easily to a high context culture.

U.S. Americans and Australians usually use high context language only when they are communicating in intimate situations. For example, when family members talk together they often leave out unnecessary detail because they know much of the information is already known. Good friends operate in the same way and will leave out whole chunks of information because there is no need to relay information that both parties already possess. A stranger coming across two good friends speaking together may have difficulty following the conversation because so much is implicit in what is being said. Indeed, they may have nicknames for each other such as Stinky and Trouble, which to an outsider may seem insulting but are in fact names that have arisen from their long association and are in no way derogatory.

The dimension of high and low context language, like the other dimensions discussed, can explain how misunderstanding can occur when two people interact from different cultures. Note too that this may especially be the case when cultures appear to be similar. For example, Susan is an Australian girl holidaying in California in the United States. It may seem that there should not be too much difficulty in being understood. However, when she chats to Jess, a U.S. American she has just met, about how she managed to get good seats at a popular concert on a workday, difficulty emerges.

Susan: So I rang up my boss and I said I was really crook and that I couldn't come in to work. Then I went to the concert early and got good seats (laughs).

Jess: Sorry, you told your boss you were a crook?

Susan: No, I said I was crook (laughs).

Poor Jess does not have any idea what Susan is talking about. In Australian slang, to be crook means to be ill. So Susan was faking illness to go to the concert early. Jess will have to ask Susan what crook means if she is ever to understand the conversation.

E. T. Hall (1976) found that there was a strong association between high context and low context cultures and whether or not a person belonged to a collectivistic or individualistic culture. There are exceptions to this observation but as a general rule of thumb there is a strong relationship between level of language context and a culture. Hall noted that some cultures that are collectivistic often engage in high context language while individualistic countries had a preference for what he called low context language. Being a member of a collectivist or individualistic culture influences how people relate to and engage with others from that culture. This influences how much information you think is needed when talking to someone from outside of the culture.

REFLECT 2.4: Can you think of other cultural categories beyond those that are geographically determined where high context and low context cultures might apply? For example, how might high context and low context apply to Type A and Type B personality types?

It is clear then that understanding cultural differences is not easy. Some aspects can be taught and some are more subtle and hidden. In line with Hall's (1966) work on training diplomats for service overseas, there has been a great deal of focus on business negotiations and how they differ between cultures. For high context, collectivist cultures, it is important to get to know people well before you work with them. Hofstede and Hofstede (2005) recount how a Swedish company (high individualistic culture) despaired of finalizing business with a company from Saudi Arabia (collectivist culture) because so much time was taken up with the Saudis getting to know the Swedish company representative. Once a relationship between a person and the Saudi company had been established, it was important that this particular person remained in the contract negotiations. Establishing and maintaining good relationships is essential for business, with respect and trust being part of those relationships.

LIVING CULTURE

Interpreting Gestures   *Bill Edwards*

Columbus State University

Most of us delight in learning about gestures with different meanings from one culture to another. For example, the U.S. American gestures for okay (making a circle with thumb and first finger), victory (first two fingers spread to make the letter *V*), and approval (thumb up) are taken as insults in other cultures. So as a traveler, I read my travel guidebooks for tips about interpreting gestures, especially about those which might be offensive. Locals, I've found, also provide tremendous assistance when learning how to interpret cultural gestures.

On one of my first travels abroad, I had an opportunity to visit Guam for a month. Dr. Rhonda Kirkpatrick, then at the University of Guam, invited me to visit her intercultural communication class. The local students had several lessons they knew White U.S. American mainlanders, *haoles* (pronounced hau-le), enjoyed learning. One of the lessons they taught me was the way many indigenous people of the Mariana Islands, *Chamorros*, nonverbally greeted someone. The students told me to pay attention to their greeting gesture. I was dumbfounded when I noticed they were giggling. I obviously wasn't recognizing their greeting gesture. Finally, one student demonstrated the greeting and pointed to his forehead wiggling his brow up and down. I said, "Ah, now I see. I can do that," which resulted in some titters. I easily performed what I thought I had seen, only to be told I was doing it like a haole. What that meant was that I was wiggling my eyebrows as well as the brow muscles, whereas the islanders only use the brow muscles. I practiced for a few days trying to return the greeting, but I finally gave up. Two weeks later, after I had stopped trying, I said hello to one of the students and to my surprise he said, "You did it!" I still don't think I ever learned how to do it the way the locals did.

On an extended trip to Chennai, India, I began to notice an Indian gesture that was new to me. People would wag their heads shoulder-to-shoulder several times (similar in pace to a U.S. American head nod used to signal agreement). Because I noticed that Indians used nodding for agreement and

LIVING CULTURE

the headshake for disagreement, I came up with another meaning for the head-wagging gesture. It happened that I was with five international students one evening when one of the students demonstrated the same gesture and gave the same interpretation. Most of us agreed and we were impressed with ourselves for figuring out the correct interpretation of this gesture.

I decided I would share this discovery with my trusted Indian mentor, a person whom I had seen use the gesture many times. He firmly told me that we were incorrect and that it was a mannerism rather than a meaningful gesture. Of course, I didn't want to believe him so I asked another Indian, whom I also trusted to correct me, and she assured me that it was not a meaningful gesture like the shrug of the shoulder to say "I don't know."

What did I learn from these formal and informal lessons on interpreting gestures? When it comes to interpreting gestures, trust the locals to know what they mean.

Consider:

1. Why is nonverbal communication important for this author?

2. What benefit does learning about differences have for him as an intercultural traveler?

3. What techniques does the author use to better understand the cultures in which he is traveling?

4. Why might trusting locals be valuable for the intercultural traveler?

UNDERSTANDING DIFFERENCES AS CONTINUUMS

It is important to understand that difference does not mean that all members of a cultural group either engage in or do not engage in the behavior. Understanding that differences do not represent two opposite poles of behavior is important because otherwise you might assume extremes about a culture. This polarization could lead to stereotyping. One of the most commonly discussed of Hofstede's dimensions is the individualism and collectivism dimension discussed earlier. Stella Ting-Toomey (2008) noted that individualism-collectivism is an area of cultural difference that has far reaching effects. For this reason, this section uses the individualism-collectivism dimension in order to clarify the concept of dimensions. A culture is not either individualistic or collectivistic, for example, but can be placed along a continuum in which these are end points.

It is important to know that differences in cultures are in reality not so clear-cut as you might assume. The United States and Australia rank as the most individualistic countries in the world with scores of 91 and 90 respectively. By contrast, Guatemala ranks as the most collectivist culture with a score of 6. China, Singapore, and Thailand are three countries also known for being collectivist and they all have a score of 20 while their neighbor Japan scores 46. Much is made of differences between the West as individualistic and East as collectivistic. However, the fact that some South American countries are higher on the collectivist dimension than some Asian cultures provides a valuable piece of information. Much of what you read about culture is often simplistic and generalist. Although many cultures have the tendency to sit toward one end of the collectivistic to individualistic continuum, as you research more about any culture, you begin to see that no culture is purely collectivist or individualistic. Indeed, none of the dimensions discussed in this chapter are poles of behavior but instead are continuums along which behaviors may fall.

Additionally, where a culture may fall along any of the dimensions discussed in this chapter may change over time. Aspects of culture constantly alter, although some alter more slowly than others and give the impression of being static. For example, even religious beliefs that appear to be traditional and constant alter over time as people reinterpret beliefs to fit into their ever-changing world. So although Christian beliefs may seem fixed, there have been new rules allowing the introduction of female priests within only the last 15 years.

FACE NEGOTIATION THEORY

Good working relations are needed in all areas of life. It is important to be well regarded by others and have positive regard for your colleagues at work and those at home. Conflict can pose a threat to how you are regarded by others. Ting-Toomey introduced face negotiation theory (Oetzel & Ting-Toomey, 2003) to explain that often collectivist nations who also engage in high context language have a different focus when managing conflict than other cultures. Her findings reiterate how collectivists focus on group well-being over self, while individualists emphasize the self over and above the group. Specifically, she found that in individualistic nations, it was important for people to make sure they maintained a positive self-image even when they found themselves in embarrassing or conflict situations. In these situations, they would most likely try competition or collaboration conflict management styles. In contrast, rather than cause problems that would result in a loss of face, collectivists tended to use compromise, avoiding, and compliance conflict management styles.

Communicating a positive regard for self and others is known as managing face. Face is your positively valued social identity. Face-work refers to your management of your face. Identity management involves how you make yourself look good in the presence of others and how you make sure others are viewed positively as well. It also includes how you protect, regain, or save face when people use behavior to challenge your face through face-threats. Face-work is used so that a person recovers when they lose face in these ways. For example, in the United States it is assumed that a good teacher will encourage students to ask questions and stress that it is important to ask something even if to the students the question seems trivial. If a teacher is explaining a concept to a student and suspects that the student does not understand, the teacher could say something along the lines of, "This is a very difficult concept and takes time to absorb. Is there anything you would like to ask me before we move on?" In this way, the student who is having difficulty with the topic does not lose face by openly admitting a lack of understanding. Given the cultural differences you have been reading about in this chapter, it should not surprise you that how individualist cultures manage face differs from that of collectivist cultures. This next section looks at this in more detail.

Having self-respect and positive self-esteem is generally viewed as healthy. It is normal that you would want to be well thought of and liked by those whom you know. Generally, people do not like to look ignorant or stupid in front of others, especially those they want to impress. In fact, many people are guilty of pretending to understand something that is said to them when they do not. This kind of behavior ensures that a person does not appear ignorant in front of others. However, there are times when it is clear that you have made a mistake, failed at something, or let someone down. How do you manage your image in these situations? How do you behave when your credibility is thrown into question? These are some of the issues that Ting-Toomey (2008) has examined from an intercultural communication perspective.

Face in a collectivist culture is not simply about saving a person's reputation. The notion of face is far more complex. When U.S. American students were asked about self-face in terms of face saving, they answered that it was about the person looking good and maintaining a good name. By contrast, Japanese students were more concerned with ensuring the other person does not lose face (Oetzel & Ting-Toomey, 2003). This concern is referred to as other-face. In order to enhance your understanding of self-face and other-face, Table 2.2 provides a visual representation of face negotiation theory. Ensuring harmony is important for Japanese culture and disagreements happen behind the scenes (Irwin, 1996). For example, a Japanese businessman attending a board meeting in the United States where the majority of attendees are American would be horrified to see questions raised about every item on the agenda. Such disagreement would be unlikely to occur in Japan. Instead, the questions about the agenda would have been raised before the formal meeting, and at the board meeting, agenda items would proceed without interruptions. Although the Japanese may view the questions raised by attendees as signifying disharmony, the U.S. American may view it as healthy, robust discussion.

WILLINGNESS TO COMMUNICATE

Cross-cultural differences are so complex and subtle that they are often not possible to learn unless you immerse yourself in the culture. Such immersion requires an openness and respect for that culture. From an intercultural communication competence perspective,

Table 2.2 Visual Representation of Face Negotiation Theory.

Do the conflict styles that Face Negotiation Theory predicts reflect your cultural experience? Face Negotiation Theory is important for those conducting business interculturally.

Main Theoretical Concepts	Individualist	Collectivist
Face	Prioritizes self-face	Prioritizes other-face
Conflict style	Values competition	Values avoidance
	Values collaboration	Values accommodation
		Values compromise

this is always the case. However, an intergroup perspective suggests that historical differences between cultures, prejudice, and belief in cultural stereotypes can get in the way of effective communication such as between Hindus and Muslims in India or between Catholics and Protestants in Northern Ireland. Sometimes it can seem that there are often more reasons not to communicate effectively with another cultural group than to commence a mutually effective interaction. To understand other cultures and their values is to acknowledge that our own cultural values are not a gold standard; rather, every culture has merit. For some people, recognizing and respecting the relevance of other cultures does not come easily.

Research by MacIntyre, Babin, and Clément (1999) highlights the importance of a variety of both psychological and contextual variables that influence a person's desire to communicate with someone from another culture, which they named willingness to communicate (WTC). For example, what determines whether a person will try to learn a second language? These include, amongst other variables, a person's positive or negative attitudes towards another culture (Clément, Baker, & MacIntyre, 2003). The WTC approach is connected to the work of IGC in that if people feel antipathy towards another nation they may be less willing to study and speak the language of that other nation. This willingness to communicate dimension highlights how important it is to take into account the attitudes people have toward other cultures because it influences communication behavior.

FINAL THOUGHTS

A main goal of this chapter has been to identify some dimensions of cultural difference and to question how easy it is to understand another culture. This chapter has shown that cultural behaviors can be learned and that beliefs and rules can be actively understood. However, miscommunication can occur for at least two reasons. First, the person who is experiencing the new culture may not be well prepared and so makes mistakes. The ICC approach can explain what has gone wrong and people can be trained to better communicate in the new culture. Second, a person who is experiencing a new culture may not be motivated to follow the cultural rules. This person may be in a position to adapt but prefers not to do so. These issues are better understood through an IGC approach. By now, it should be clear that culture is multifaceted and even people living in their own culture do not always know why they respond the way they do in certain situations. How much more difficult must it be to fully know another culture if you cannot fully ever know your own?

CONTINUE YOUR JOURNEY ONLINE

Visit: www.geert-hofstede.com/hofstede_dimensions.php

Geert Hofstede's website. View and compare the specific scores for over 60 countries on his cultural dimensions. As you have fun exploring these, take some time to also think critically about their value and usefulness for understanding your own and other countries.

66 SAY WHAT?

Say What? provides excerpts from overheard real-life conversations in which people have communicated stereotypes. As you read these conversations, reflect on the following questions.

- Have you been in conversations like this before?
- Is there any one of these conversations that stick out to you more than the others?
- What do you think of this conversation?
- How did the stereotype help or hinder the conversation?
- Was there another way the stereotyper could have communicated to convey the same point?
- How do you feel when you hear this conversation or the specific stereotype?
- Do any of these conversations bother you more than others? Why or why not?
- Do any concepts, issues, or theories discussed in the chapter help explain why?

- **Say What?** I overheard a conversation between two coworkers. Mary claimed that she had told Bill the location of the package and asked him to please mail it, as it was a priority. Bill argued that he never heard her say anything about a package and in turn never mailed anything for her. With a roll of her eyes and a sigh, Mary turned to Bill and said "Augh, ya know, men never listen to anything women have to say." In response, Bill turned and walked out of the room and Mary waited patiently to pay at the register.

- **Say What?** "I couldn't stand him. I had him last semester. He was the worst." I of course asked Christina why she felt like this. She responded, "He didn't like me because I am Egyptian." Professor Cohen was not only Jewish but in fact a rabbi. She brought it to my attention that for thousands of years, Egyptians and Jewish people have a long history of bitter resentment and hatred toward the other. Cristina continued to ramble on about how being Jewish resulted in the two of them not seeing eye-to-eye. She accused him of giving her a lower grader than she deserved. I responded, "He seems interesting."

- **Say What?** My father is a builder, which means he manages the designing, building, and sales of homes. He brought up a situation when an Indian family came in to purchase a home. He said that he knew from the beginning that they would be trouble. He explained that all Indian people try to "screw you as much as they can because they don't like White people and they're always out to save money." My first reaction to his comment was a request for him to at least explain to me why he would believe such things of any Indian family that comes in to buy a home.

- **Say What?** She asked me how I perceive Russia as someone who lives in the United States. I told her that I view Russia as a really poor country where everyone gets paid the same amount of money whether they are doctors or garbage men. She laughed and said that I had the wrong idea. I was curious about how Russia really was so I asked her to explain it to me.

REVIEW QUESTIONS

1. Why is miscommunication a problem, especially for intercultural communication?

2. Based on the discussion at the start of the chapter, what were the early goals of the study of intercultural communication?

3. Compare and contrast the intercultural communication competence tradition with the inter-group communication tradition, as discussed in the chapter.

4. Why does the existence of internal and external components of a culture make communicating with those from different cultures complicated?

5. If a wedding begins at 6 pm in a culture that uses monochronic time, what time would people arrive? What if the culture used polychronic time? How might this difference cause conflict?

6. Based on the chapter, what are Hofstede's cultural dimensions? Does each dimension describe a continuum or a dichotomy of cultural behavior? Explain your answer.

7. According to the chapter, why is Confucian dynamism distinguished from other intercultural dimensions?

8. What might you do to find out how to behave appropriately in a high context culture, based on what you learned in the chapter?

9. Provide an example of a face-threat in a recent conversation you have had. How was it managed successfully for all those involved? What role did individualism, collectivism, or both play in the example you provided? As discussed in the chapter, can face negotiation theory explain what happened in this example?

10. After reading the chapter, would you conclude that it is easy or difficult to know another culture? Why?

KEY TERMS

collectivist culture   33

Confucian dynamism   35

cross-cultural communication   25

cultural mores   26

display rules   28

external component   27

face   40

face negotiation theory   40

face-threat   40

face-work   40

feminine culture   34

high context culture   36

identity management   40

individualistic culture   33

intercultural communication competence (ICC)   29

intergroup communication (IGC)   30

internal components   27

long-term orientation   35

lose face   40

low context culture   36

masculine culture   34

monochronic   32

other-face   41

polarization   39

polychronic   32

power distance   35

proxemics   32

save face   40

short-term orientation   35

uncertainty avoidance   34

willingness to communicate (WTC)   42

REFERENCES

Bernstein, B. (1972). Social class, language and socialization. In P. P. Giglioli (Ed.), *Language and social context* (pp. 157–178). London: Penguin.

Cargile, A. C., & Giles, H. (1996). Intercultural communication training review, critique, and a new theoretical framework. In B. Burleson (Ed.), *Communication Yearbook, 19* (pp. 385–423). Thousand Oaks, CA: Sage.

Chinese Culture Connection. (1987). Chinese values and the search for culture-free dimensions of culture. *Journal of Cross-Cultural Psychology, 18,* 143–164.

Clément, R., Baker, S. C., & MacIntyre, P. D. (2003). Willingness to communicate in a second language: The effects of context, norms, and vitality. *Journal of Language and Social Psychology, 22,* 190–209.

Ekman, P., & Friesen, W. (1969). The repertoire of nonverbal behavior: Categories, origins, usage, and coding. *Semiotica, 1,* 49–98.

Fischer, R., Vauclair, C. M., Fontaine, J. R. J., & Schwartz, S. H. (2010). Are individual-level and country-level value structures different? Testing Hofstede's legacy with the Schwartz value survey. *Journal of Cross-Cultural Psychology, 41,* 135–151.

Giles, H. (1973). Accent mobility: A model and some data. *Anthropological Linguistics, 15,* 87–105.

Giles, H., & Watson, B. (2008). Intercultural and intergroup communication. In W. Donsbach (Ed.), *International encyclopedia of communication* (Vol. VI, pp. 2337–2348). Oxford, UK: Blackwell.

Hall, E. T. (1959). *The silent language.* New York: Doubleday.

Hall, E. T. (1966). *The hidden dimension.* Garden City, NY: Doubleday.

Hall, E. T. (1976). *Beyond culture.* New York: Anchor Books/Doubleday.

Hall, E. T. (1984). *The dance of life: The other dimension of time.* New York: Anchor Press/Doubleday.

Hofstede, G. (1983). National cultures revisited. *Cross-Cultural Research, 18,* 285–305.

Hofstede, G., & Hofstede, G. J. (2005). *Cultures and organizations: Software of the mind* (2nd ed.). New York: McGraw-Hill.

Irwin, H. (1996). *Communicating with Asia.* St Leonards, NSW: Allen & Unwin.

Leeds-Hurtwitz, W. (1990). Notes in the history of intercultural communication: The foreign service institute and the mandate for intercultural training. *Quarterly Journal of Speech, 76,* 262–281.

MacIntyre, P. D., Babin, P. A., & Clement, R. (1999). Willingness to communicate: Antecedents and consequences. *Communication Quarterly, 47,* 215–229.

Merritt, A. (2000). Culture in the cockpit. Do Hofstede's dimensions replicate? *Journal of Cross-Cultural Psychology, 31,* 283–301.

Oetzel, J. G., & Ting-Toomey, S. (2003). Face concerns in interpersonal conflict: A cross-cultural empirical test of the face negotiation theory. *Communication Research, 30,* 599–624.

Ting-Toomey, S. (2008). Intercultural conflict styles and facework. In W. Donsbach (Ed.), *The international encyclopedia of communication.* Malden: MA: Blackwell.

Intercultural Communication Competence

Lily A. Arasaratnam

Alphacrucis College

Journey Through Chapter 3

Sightseeing: On your journey, you will visit with intercultural communication competence and its relevant variables taking a social scientific approach. You will be presented with four theories of intercultural communication competence that build upon the representations of culture discussed in Chapter 2, and explore ways to develop your own intercultural communication competence.

Souvenir: After your journey, you will be better equipped to be a competent intercultural communicator by integrating knowledge that you already have with related theories.

Intercultural communication is an everyday reality for many people who live in industrialized societies. Though competence in intercultural communication can be developed, like any other skill, research shows that some aspects of intercultural communication competence (ICC) are more inherent in a person's personality. Despite the proliferation of literature on handy tips to improve a person's communication competence, it is essential for a student of communication to gain a deeper understanding of the factors that contribute to what is perceived as competent communication, beyond the superficial checklists. This chapter addresses the concept of communication competence, particularly in intercultural settings, and discusses relevant variables and theories. The chapter concludes with suggestions for how you can further develop your intercultural communication competence.

Before diving into the specifics of intercultural communication competence, it is helpful to briefly examine the nature of intercultural communication itself. It is necessary to ask the question of what makes a communication exchange *intercultural*. Does it depend on the cultural identities of the individuals involved? What about people who do not identify with just one culture, such as someone who is born to parents from different cultures or someone born in one culture and raised in another? When do people engage in intercultural communication? Arasaratnam (2011) addresses these questions in the following way:

> In most industrialized nations it is not uncommon for a person to be born in one country, educated in another, and perhaps be employed in yet another. Depending on the extent to which the person assimilates each of those country's cultural norms, she or he may have a unique cultural identity that is hard to categorize. When does such an individual participate in intercultural communication (as opposed to interpersonal communication)? Perhaps the determining factor is when cultural differences between the relevant individuals affect the communication exchange in ways which would have been insignificant had those differences not existed. I see these particular communication interactions as occurring in *intercultural spaces*. These are not spaces in the physical sense of the word. They are instead symbolic markers of these particular types of communication exchanges. (p. 1)

Hence one way of viewing intercultural communication is as communication that unfolds in symbolic intercultural spaces. These are moments when a communication exchange has been affected by cultural differences. Now that the nature of intercultural communication has been examined briefly, it is also helpful to discuss what is meant by communication competence in general, before discussing the specifics of intercultural communication competence.

COMMUNICATION COMPETENCE

One of the commonly used definitions of communication competence is that competent communication is effective and appropriate (Spitzberg & Cupach, 1984). A communication exchange is effective when the speaker's goals are accomplished in that particular exchange. A communication exchange is appropriate when these goals are accomplished in a manner that is both expected and accepted in that given social context. For example, assume that Mike, an undergraduate student, wishes to request an extension for his assignment due date from his professor. The exchange might unfold like this:

Mike: Hello Dr. Patel. May I please have two extra days to complete my essay on cultural adaptation?

Dr. Patel: Oh? Why do you need the extra time?

Mike: My dad fell ill unexpectedly last week and I had to spend most of my time at the hospital, and so I didn't get to work on my essay during the evenings as I had hoped. But I have brought what I have done so far to show that I did begin work on it a few weeks ago and am not asking for the extension because I haven't started on it. Here, as you can see, I've finished the literature review and fleshed out the structure of the essay.

Dr. Patel: Yes, I see. Okay, Mike, as you have clearly been doing your work diligently, I'll grant you the 2-day extension. I hope your father gets well soon.

Mike: Thank you, Professor. Yes, my dad is much better now. Thank you for the extension—I appreciate it.

In this exchange, Mike's goal was to get an extension for his assignment and he was successful in accomplishing this goal. Anticipating what was necessary to accomplish his goal, Mike brought the necessary evidence to convince Dr. Patel that he was not asking for an extension due to lack of initiative on his part. Further, he accomplished his goal by behaving in a manner that is socially expected and accepted in an exchange between a professor and a student. He addressed the professor courteously, provided a reasonable explanation for his request, and conducted himself in a polite manner. In this exchange, Mike demonstrates competent communication.

Though the exchange between Mike and Dr. Patel is a simple example, it illustrates that prior knowledge of social expectations as well as the skills to meet these expectations are useful when it comes to communicating competently. In intercultural situations, however, this prior knowledge is not always available. There are several variables that contribute to competence in intercultural contexts.

COMPETENCE IN INTERCULTURAL COMMUNICATION

Needless to say, what is considered effective and appropriate varies from culture to culture based on the values and social expectations of the context. As introduced in Chapter 2, intercultural communication competence (ICC) is the use of effective and appropriate communication in a context where cultural variables significantly influence the outcome of the interaction. ICC can be characterized as encompassing four levels of competence (Bhawuk, 1998; Howell, 1982). These stages of competence will be illustrated through an example of dancing.

REFLECT 3.1: What is your level of intercultural competence?

Unconscious Incompetence

Unconscious incompetence indicates that the communicator is not only communicating without being effective or appropriate, but also is unaware of this. Consider Bill, who loves salsa dancing and assumes that he is an excellent dancer, but in reality is clumsy and uncoordinated. Though Bill might consider himself graceful, the onlookers shake their heads in bewilderment wondering how someone could be such a terrible dancer. Bill in this instance is unaware or unconscious of his incompetence. This is arguably the lowest level of intercultural communication competence.

Conscious Incompetence

Conscious incompetence indicates that the communicator is aware of not communicating as effectively as expected and not exhibiting the appropriate behaviors in an intercultural context, but does not know the particulars of what contributes to this incompetence. With the awareness of this incompetence, the person is in a better position to address the matter compared to if the person was at the unconscious incompetence level. Consider the example of Bill again. If Bill is aware that he is not a graceful dancer but is not sure how to correct his mistakes, that would represent the conscious incompetence stage.

Conscious Competence

A communicator who is at the conscious competence level deliberately adapts competent behavior and is alert to the nuances of the communication context. Assume Bill starts taking salsa lessons and begins to understand the basics of the dance. From an onlooker's perspective, Bill looks like a competent salsa dancer because he dances without making mistakes. However, still being fairly new to salsa dancing, Bill counts the steps carefully in his head and is conscious of his every movement while dancing.

Unconscious Competence

Unconscious competence indicates that the communicator is at ease and conversant in communicating with people of other cultures and, consequently, communicates competently without conscious effort. Intercultural communication competence comes naturally to this communicator. Going back to the example of Bill, after several months of dancing salsa, Bill will get to a stage where he is no longer counting the steps in his head. Instead, he lets the music flow through his body and, without Bill having to deliberately remember what his next step should be, his feet naturally move to the rhythm of the music with ease.

There is some debate among scholars as to whether unconscious competence is preferable to conscious competence. Some think that unconscious competence is the ideal state given the effortless way in which a communicator at this stage exhibits intercultural communication competence. Others disagree. Those who argue that conscious competence is preferable suggest that a communicator who is at the level of unconscious competence may not be alert to subtle variations in new contexts and, therefore, may not be learning and adapting continuously.

Photo 3.1   What did you bring home from your last trip? Because cultures are unique, tourists often bring home tangible cultural objects and new understandings of the visited culture as mementos. Tourists, as guests in another culture, benefit from increased intercultural communication competence whether haggling for souvenirs like these or taking part in a business meeting.

Copyright 2011 Anastacia Kurylo.

VARIABLES THAT INFLUENCE INTERCULTURAL COMMUNICATION COMPETENCE

Over the years, several variables have been identified that contribute to intercultural communication competence, such as your experience with education, training, living or traveling abroad, and so forth. This section highlights some of these key cognitive, affective, and behavioral variables that are associated with intercultural communication competence.

Cognitive Complexity

Cognitive complexity refers to your ability to form unique categories in your mind. The more the person has cognitive complexity, the more this individual is able to form categories that are distinct and rely less on generalization. For example, you can put an apple, a banana, and a pineapple in the general category of fruit. However, each of these types of fruit is unique. If you put each one of these fruit in a category of its own, then you have accomplished a categorization system that is differentiated and not generalized.

Consider another example. On the first day of class, a professor named Fran looks at a group of students and places them in the category of *my 8 am intercultural communication class*. But as the semester progresses, the professor begins to know the students and to form more complex categories that differentiate the class into groups such as *the interactive students* and *the quiet students*. Ideally, if she is able, she will eventually form a unique category for each of the students in the class. Hence from a general group of *my 8 am intercultural communication class* the professor differentiates the group into unique smaller categories of *Alison, Rita, Juan,* and so on.

Cognitive complexity influences intercultural communication competence because it enables individuals to rely less on generalizations or stereotypes, thus facilitating a more tailored approach to communicating with individuals and allowing for the flexibility to incorporate new information. Relating cognitive complexity to the anxiety/uncertainty management (AUM) model of intercultural communication competence, Gudykunst (1995) argues that the higher the level of cognitive complexity, the greater a person's ability to manage anxiety and uncertainty in intercultural interactions.

Ethnocentrism

One of the early definitions of ethnocentrism is by Sumner (1907/2002), who defines it as the, "name for this view of things in which one's own group is the center of everything, and all others are scaled and rated in reference to it" (p. 13). Since then researchers have used several variations of this definition to engage this concept of ethnocentrism. An ethnocentric individual views the world from the perspective of that person's own culture and evaluates other people and cultures using cultural values from their own culture as the ideal forms.

REFLECT 3.2: If you have trouble understanding someone's accent, what do you do? How might this way of handling it reflect ethnocentrism, if at all? In what other ways might a person handle this situation?

For example, an ethnocentric U.S. American might look at an Indian who uses fingers to eat rice and say, "That's so uncivilized!" because, according to the Western customs, "civilized" individuals eat with utensils. However, from the cultural perspective of the Indian, it is perfectly civilized practice to eat with fingers. Ethnocentric attitudes debilitate effective intercultural communication (Gudykunst & Kim, 2003) because an ethnocentric person does not view another culture as equal in value. Therefore, the ethnocentric person is likely to engage in behaviors that are the result of ignorance, intention to offend, or both. Ethnocentrism can be harmful to intercultural communication competence because it prevents a person from being open to the idea that other people may have equally valid ways of doing things that may be completely different from the way someone does things in one's own culture.

Empathy

Empathy is the ability to put yourself in someone else's proverbial shoes and experience the thoughts and emotions from that person's perspective. It is a key asset in intercultural communication. A person who has the ability to empathize is able to relate to someone from a different culture at a personal level even without extensive prior experience interacting with people from other cultures (Arasaratnam, 2006; Arasaratnam & Doerfel, 2005). In the Multicultural Personality Questionnaire, which evaluates the extent of someone's multicultural orientation, cultural empathy is one of the key components (Van der Zee, Zaal, & Piekstra, 2003; Van Oudenhoven & Van der Zee, 2002). If you are an empathetic person, for example, you will be able to identify with perhaps an international student in your class even if you yourself have never studied abroad. You might think, "How will I feel if I go to a new country and I don't know anybody?" You might imagine yourself in that student's situation, "How have I felt in similar situations?" and, in doing so, experience the thoughts and emotions the other person might be experiencing.

Interaction Involvement

Interaction involvement requires mindfulness and active listening. Mindfulness means being an engaged participant in the communication exchange, being tuned-in and involved. An active listener pays attention to what the other person is saying, without being preoccupied with formulating a response. An active listener also asks relevant follow-up questions and displays appropriate nonverbal cues to demonstrate listening intently to the other person. These cues may include nodding, maintaining eye contact if relevant, and showing facial expressions that are appropriate to the topic of the conversation. Active listeners are comfortable with silences and pauses in conversation, and allow the other person to complete their thought without hastily interjecting their own thoughts.

Motivation

Motivation to seek intercultural contact or partake in intercultural interaction plays a key role in facilitating intercultural communication. People may have a variety of reasons for being motivated to engage in intercultural communication. For example, recently it has been discovered that people who are drawn to novel and exciting experiences, also known as high sensation seekers, are often motivated to seek intercultural contact because of the element of novelty involved in interacting with someone of a different culture (Arasaratnam, 2005; Arasaratnam & Banerjee, 2007). Perhaps you may be motivated out of desire to understand other worldviews and expand your horizons. Another motivation may be to communicate with someone from a different culture because you want to get to know that person better. Whatever the reason, when someone is genuinely motivated to engage in intercultural communication, they are perceived favorably by the person with whom they are interacting because they come across as being engaged and interested in the other person (Arasaratnam & Doerfel, 2005).

Positive Global Attitude (Toward Other Cultures)

Just as ethnocentrism hinders intercultural communication, a global outlook or positive attitude toward people from other cultures facilitates intercultural interactions. A person with a positive global attitude about people from other cultures is predisposed to seeking intercultural contact and forming intercultural friendships. Further, if you have a positive attitude toward people of other cultures, then you are likely to interpret any ambiguous behavior on their part in a positive light. This is helpful in intercultural interactions because often people come across situations in which they do not quite understand why someone from a different culture is behaving in a certain way because of unfamiliar cultural practices. But if you generally have a positive attitude toward people from other cultures, you are prone to view such unexplainable behavior in a positive light.

MODELS OF INTERCULTURAL COMMUNICATION COMPETENCE

Over the years, there have been several attempts made to represent intercultural communication competence in terms of conceptual models. Models of intercultural communication competence help you understand how different variables interact to produce the end result of intercultural communication competence. For example, if you want to know how to make a good cake, it is necessary to find out the ingredients that go into making a cake and the proportions of each of these ingredients that are required. Similarly, when studying the end result that is intercultural communication competence, it is helpful to look at the "ingredients" or variables that contribute to that end result. Further, identifying these variables helps you to not only introspectively reflect on your own intercultural skills but also recognize ways in which you can help other people improve their skills. These models provide useful frameworks through which to understand intercultural communication competence.

Thought processes, emotions, and behavioral skills work together to enable people to be competent intercultural communicators. These three dimensions of cognition, affect, and behavior are generally relevant to ICC. The cognitive dimension refers to the mental abilities that pertain to communication competence. The affective dimension refers to emotional abilities. The behavioral dimension refers to the applied skills that people have through their ability to communicate. Intercultural communication competence is an intricate product of interaction between these three broad categories. (For a more comprehensive list of models of intercultural communication competence, see Spitzberg & Chagnon, 2009). Select models of intercultural communication competence are discussed in this section.

Anxiety/Uncertainty Management Model

The anxiety/uncertainty management (AUM) model (AUM) (Gudykunst, 1993; 1995; 2002; Gudykunst & Nishida, 2001; Stephan, Stephan, & Gudykunst, 1999) is a well-known model in intercultural communication competence literature. The premise of this model is set in the context of communication with strangers. Gudykunst (1993) characterizes a stranger as someone who is geographically near, such that you can engage in communication, but culturally distant in that the person comes from a culture that is distinctly different from yours. In this model, Gudykunst draws a causal relationship between management of uncertainty and anxiety and effective communication. Gudykunst argues that there is a measure of uncertainty involved in communication with a stranger due to a person's potential inability to predict or explain the stranger's behavior due to cultural differences. In other words, when you meet someone from a different culture you cannot necessarily assume that this individual will behave in the same way as someone from your own culture. This uncertainty of not knowing how a stranger will behave may cause a measure of anxiety. Therefore, anxiety and uncertainty management are basic causes that contribute to effective intercultural communication.

According to the anxiety/uncertainty management model, as shown in Figure 3.1, the extent to which a person is able to manage anxiety influences the level of effective communication. Gudykunst (1995) defines effective communication in the anxiety/uncertainty management model as communication in which there are minimal misunderstandings. It is necessary to note that the term *effective* in the context of the AUM model is not identical to how it is conceptualized when you say effective in reference to intercultural communication competence. In the latter, effective refers to a person's ability to accomplish goals. In AUM, effective refers to having minimal misunderstandings. The AUM model gives you a perspective on how certain elements contribute to effective and appropriate communication.

The AUM model identifies self-concept, motivation to interact with strangers, reaction to strangers, social categorization of strangers, situational processes, and connection with hosts as some of the superficial causes that contribute toward intercultural effectiveness. Each of these elements is discussed as follows.

- *Self-concept* refers to elements such as your identity, self-esteem, whether you are proud of yourself or ashamed of yourself, and so forth.
- *Motivation to interact with strangers* can be influenced by various factors such as your need to conform to what your friends are doing, your own sense of security in your cultural identity, and your need for being able to know what to expect in a particular interaction.
- Your *reaction to strangers* is often influenced by the extent to which you are comfortable with ambiguity, your ability to empathize with people who are different from you, and your ability to be flexible and adaptable.
- *Social categorization of strangers* refers to the way you process information when it comes to categorizing someone as similar or different to you.
- *Situational processes* refers to the variables involved in the particular interaction, such as whether it is a formal or informal interaction, whether there are prescribed socially appropriate ways of behaving in such an interaction, and so forth.
- Finally, *connection with strangers* refers to the extent to which you feel a sense of affiliation with people who are culturally different.
- By identifying these variables, the AUM model highlights the relevant factors that are involved in an intercultural communication exchange.

As the AUM model depicts, mindfulness acts as a mediating variable between anxiety/uncertainty management and communication effectiveness in intercultural contexts. Gudykunst (1993) explains that a mindful communicator is alert to subtle nuances in conversation and adjusts communication according to the situation. Mindfulness involves continually creating new categories in your mind to accommodate new information that you are receiving. Instead of operating on autopilot, or mindlessly, a mindful communicator uses communication behavior deliberately.

Figure 3.1   The Anxiety/Uncertainty Management Model

How do you manage your anxiety and uncertainty in intercultural encounters? The AUM model examines these in intercultural encounters.

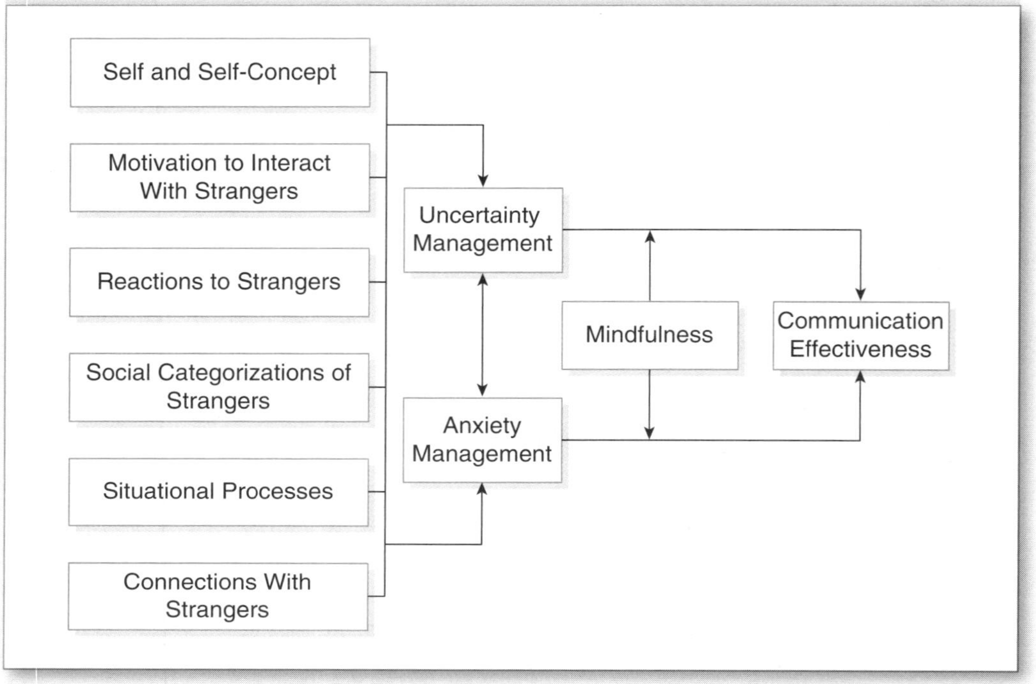

Source: Adapted based on the anxiety/uncertainty management model (Gudykunst, 1993; 1995; 2002; Gudykunst & Nishida, 2001; Stephan, Stephan, & Gudykunst, 1999).

Copyright 2011 Lily A. Arasaratnam.

For example, consider a situation whereby you are communicating with a friend from a different culture. Because you are familiar with your friend, you may be in a mind-set where you are not necessarily paying careful attention to subtle nonverbal cues or other cues that may be present in your conversation that might indicate there is a cultural factor involved in the conversation. Perhaps you asked your friend for a favor and your friend paused for a moment before agreeing to your request. If you were operating on autopilot, you may not have noticed the pause. But if you are a mindful communicator, you would pick up on the pause and consider whether there is some meaning, beyond your friend's verbal agreement, that you need to explore further.

The AUM model is not without its critics. For example, Yoshitake (2002) argues that characterizing effective communication as communication where there is minimal misunderstanding is a simplistic view of communication. Further, he notes that the AUM model is reflective of a Westernized view of communication processes. Hence, it is important to consider models that incorporate multiple cultural perspectives. The integrated model of intercultural communication competence is one such model.

LIVING CULTURE

A Punk. A Lifer.   *Brian Cogan*

Molloy College

I guess you could call me a lifer. That's the term lots of folks use to describe someone who is still in "the scene" after all these years. For most people, especially as they get older, music is secondary to lifestyle, but not for those of us, some well into our forties, that still proudly call ourselves *punks*. Music, to us, informs our lives and helps us find strength in being an outsider. We learn early on in school that most people are made uncomfortable by those that look and act different, especially punks.

But music is only one part of being a punk. Some people are familiar with the most popular radio-friendly punk bands, like the Ramones or the Clash, but for us, it goes much deeper. For those of us who still identify as punks and use the term *lifer* to identify ourselves and show that we are in for the long haul, punk is not simply listening to a specific kind of music (although that's part of it), but also being punk on a daily basis. The sad thing is, when most people think of punks, they think of fashion and body art, but that's just a small sample of what punks are like.

I guess the best way to describe who I am is as a punk, but it's not because I have a Mohawk haircut, live in a squat, or even have sleeve tattoos (I don't) but because being a punk leads me to try and live my life in a way that means consciously making a decision about the things I do on a daily basis. It means thinking about choices in food, drinks, clothing, and the way in which I engage with the world. A real punk will tell you, punk isn't about fashion, it's about DIY. The DIY (or do-it-yourself) ethic asks you to consider what your patterns of consumption are. Are you buying from people who make and sell their own art, music, literature, or crafts? Or are you buying from a large corporation that markets former boy-band members with spiky hair as commodified rebellion?

That's not to say I don't shop at mainstream stores, just that I limit myself in how much I buy at a regular grocery store as opposed to a food co-op or look for records at local independent record stores instead of buying online from a huge distributor that never really funnels the money back to the people who made it in the first place. Being a punk can be a bit of a job at times; there are almost always choices to be made (and don't even get me started on how straightedge vegan punks manage . . .) but I wouldn't trade my experiences in the scene for anything. Punk taught me at an early age that I can be an individual in a corporate world, and even three decades in, that's still how I want to live my life.

(Continued)

LIVING CULTURE

(Continued)

Consider:

1. What is a punk cultural identity?

2. How is the author a competent communicator within his culture according to his narrative?

3. The author suggests in his last sentence that he has to adapt his behavior to a "corporate world." What accommodative moves might he make to do so?

4. Would the author be able to maintain his punk identity in a corporate world? How do members of other cultures do so?

Integrated Model of Intercultural Communication Competence

In recent research, another model of intercultural communication competence has emerged. The integrated model of intercultural communication competence (IMICC) articulates that there are certain key variables that contribute to intercultural communication competence about which appears to be consensus amongst people of different cultures, despite cultural differences. The design of the IMICC was based on the in-depth responses of research participants who represented 15 cultural perspectives. Each participant was asked to describe a competent intercultural communicator. After these descriptions were collected, the researchers looked for commonalities in the participants' responses. The five variables that are identified in the IMICC are a result of this process (Arasaratnam, 2006; Arasaratnam, Banerjee, & Dembek, 2010; Arasaratnam & Doerfel, 2005). The IMICC recognizes five key variables that contribute to ICC as shown in Figure 3.2. The variables identified in this model were explained in more detail in the section on variables that influence intercultural communication competence. This model is one of the few models of intercultural communication competence that incorporates multiple cultural perspectives in its inception.

As the model shows, motivation and interaction involvement are two variables that have direct pathways to intercultural communication competence. Motivation in turn is influenced by positive global attitude and interaction involvement is influenced by empathy. Empathy also influences positive global attitude. Experience or training in intercultural communication influences a person's global attitude, which in turn influences that person's motivation to interact with people from other cultures, and this motivation then leads to more experience and possibly more training.

One of the questions that the integrated model of intercultural communication competence answers is the question of why some people who are widely educated and experienced international travelers still come across as incompetent intercultural communicators,

Figure 3.2   The Integrated Model of Intercultural Communication Competence

What can you do to be a more interculturally competent communicator? Several models of intercultural competence have been created. This model aims to be more inclusive than others proposed.

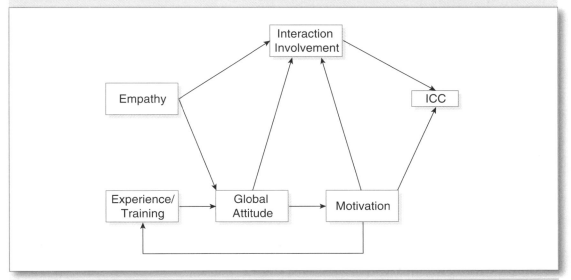

Source: Adapted based on the integrated model of intercultural communication competence (Arasaratnam, 2006; Arasaratnam, Banerjee, & Dembek, 2010; Arasaratnam & Doerfel, 2005).

Copyright 2011 Lily A. Arasaratnam.

while others from rural towns who may never have traveled abroad or interacted with someone from a different culture are able to exhibit competent intercultural communication behaviors. As the model depicts, even if someone is not well traveled or formally trained in intercultural communication, that person may still be perceived as a competent intercultural communicator if empathetic and a good listener—key variables identified in the IMICC. To understand the model better, consider this example. Assume you are communicating with Ted, who is from a different culture to yours. From Ted's perspective, the extent to which you come across as a competent communicator depends on certain variables. First, it depends on whether Ted thinks you are truly interested in him and interested in what he has to say. If you have a positive attitude toward people from other cultures and are motivated to inter-act with people from other cultures, this is likely to show in the way you interact with Ted in a friendly open way. Further, while Ted is speaking to you, he may observe whether you are paying attention and whether you ask appropriate follow-up questions. If you do, you exhibit that you are a good listener. An empathetic person is able to listen well because that person is able to consider the situation from the other person's perspective, think about the feelings that the other person might have regarding the situation, and react accordingly. Also, according to the model, if you have prior experience with intercultural communication through study, or travel, or friendships with people from other cultures, then you are likely to have a positive attitude toward people of other cultures and hence be motivated to communicate with them; this in turn is perceived favorably by the person from the other culture.

Identity Negotiation Model

Another theoretical approach used frequently in intercultural communication competence literature is the identity negotiation model (Ting-Toomey, 1993; 2005). The identity negotiation model focuses on how identities are managed in intercultural interactions. Ting-Toomey defines intercultural communication competence as "the effective identity negotiation process between two or more interactants in a novel communication episode" (Ting-Toomey, 1993, p. 73). Novelty, in turn, is characterized as a situation that contains "both unpredictability and challenge" (p. 73), and identity is defined as "the mosaic sense of self-identification that incorporates the interplay of human, cultural, social, and personal images as consciously or unconsciously experienced and enacted by the individual" (p. 74). Ting-Toomey argues that individuals who have a secure sense of identity in terms of how a person fits in their culture and what that means in relation to other cultures, along with healthy self-esteem, are equipped to deal with novel and unpredictable situations, which are often found in intercultural interactions.

As you can observe in Figure 3.3, the identity negotiation model identifies cognitive, affective, and behavioral resourcefulness as key variables leading to effective identity negotiation. Cognitive resourcefulness refers to both the knowledge a person has, as well as that person's ability to use that knowledge to deal with unfamiliar and new situations. This quality is quite similar to what is described as mindfulness in the AUM model. It also encompasses cognitive complexity, which was explained previously. Affective resourcefulness refers to a person's ability to relate to self and others in various intercultural situations. This encompasses empathy, as identified in the integrated model of intercultural communication competence. Behavioral resourcefulness refers to a person's ability to be flexible, and behave in a way that is appropriate to the situation.

For example, consider a diplomatic situation where an ambassador from Country A says something to the ambassador from Country B that is offensive according to the cultural values of Country B. Country B's ambassador has the choice of either taking offence, or exercising cognitive, affective, and behavioral resourcefulness. Cognitively, this could be done by recognizing that Country A's ambassador probably did not know this comment was offensive and therefore it should not be taken personally. Affectively, choosing not to act on the feelings of anger or hurt that may have arisen when the comment was said could achieve this. Behaviorally, this could be done by gently explaining to Ambassador A why such a comment could be perceived as an offence or, if appropriate, steering the conversation to a different topic. Hence, the identity negotiation model explains intercultural communication competence in a dynamic way that includes a person's thinking, feelings, and actions in an intercultural situation.

Take a Side Trip:

If you would like to read more about related issues, visit Appendix D: Transnational Dominican Culture Through Phenomenological Analysis.

Figure 3.3 The Identity Negotiation Model

What are some cognitive, behavioral, and emotional resources you have? How do these affect your intercultural competence?

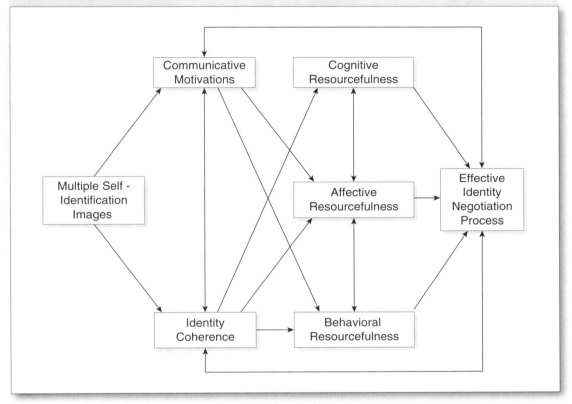

Source: Adapted based on the identity negotiation model (Ting-Toomey, 1993).

Copyright 2011 Lily A. Arasaratnam.

Pyramid Model of Intercultural Competence

Darla Deardorff (2006) proposes another model for consideration, namely the pyramid model of intercultural competence. This model shows the development of intercultural competence as a process from the personal level of attitudes to the interpersonal level of interacting with other people (Figure 3.4). Deardorff argues that mindfulness is a key variable in the process of building from attitudes and moving toward desired external outcomes. In other words, people need to be aware of what they are learning, as they progress up the pyramid. In reference to the pyramid model, Deardorff further explains that, "though individuals can enter these frameworks at any particular point, attitude is a fundamental starting point" (p. 255). For example, a person might have the ability to be adaptable and flexible depending on the context (at the desired internal outcome level of the

Figure 3.4   Pyramid Model of Intercultural Competence

What are some cognitive, behavioral, and emotional resources you have? How do these affect your intercultural competence?

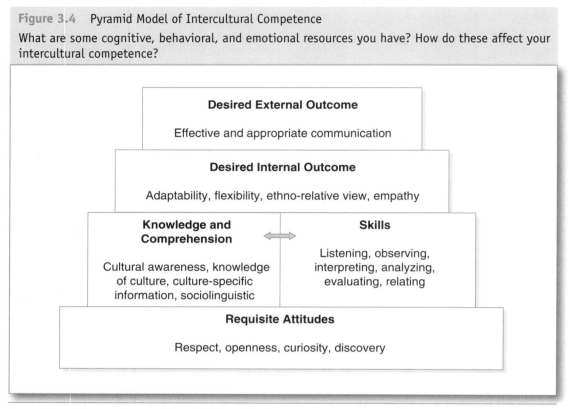

Source: Adapted based on the pyramid model of intercultural competence (Deardorff, 2006).

Copyright 2011 Lily A. Arasaratnam.

model), but not have culture-specific information about that context. But Deardorff implies that this is fine as long as the person has the attitudes conducive for intercultural competence, as identified in the requisite attitudes level of the model. Hence the model depicts various degrees of intercultural competence. Further, the pyramid model specifically accounts for language abilities, which are not specified in the other models discussed in this section.

It is interesting to note that there is a significant overlap in ideas in the models discussed in this section, highlighting the fact that research in intercultural communication competence repeatedly produces results that reiterate the cognitive, affective, and behavioral dimensions involved in intercultural communication competence.

REFLECT 3.3: Do any of these models contribute to your personal understanding of intercultural communication competence? Why or why not?

DEVELOPING INTERCULTURAL COMMUNICATION COMPETENCE

Some people are predisposed to be better at intercultural communication competence than others (Arasaratnam, 2005; Arasaratnam & Banerjee, 2007). Such people develop intercultural communication competence with greater ease and at greater levels compared to others. Naturally empathetic individuals are likely to be more tuned into the subtle cues of cultural variations and pick up on these more quickly. There is also some evidence to suggest that those who are naturally high sensation seekers are predisposed to intercultural contact-seeking behavior and hence likely to acquire more intercultural experiences. Predispositions aside, there are some deliberate measures people can take to improve their intercultural skills.

Exposure to and Engaging With Different Worldviews

Developing intercultural communication skills requires exposing oneself to new intercultural contexts and multiple worldviews. This can be accomplished through formal study of inter-cultural communication, traveling to cultures or communities that are significantly different from your own, interacting with people from other cultures, asking questions about another's culture, watching movies that unpack different cultural perspectives, and even studying world history to understand how historical events have shaped cultures and relationships between various groups. Exposure to worldviews that are different from your own helps you to expand your schematic frameworks and understand different ways of seeing a particular issue.

Practicing Role-Taking Behavior

Engaging in cognitive and emotional role-taking behavior is helpful in understanding multiple perspectives. For example, even though you may never have had the experience of being an international student, you could think about how you would feel if you were in a different country where you knew nobody, away from your family, in a strange culture where they speak a strange language. You could think about how you would feel if you had to read course material, listen to lectures, and write assignments in a different language and be graded on these. If you are able to deliberately engage in such role-taking exercises, you may be better equipped to empathize with, for example, international student classmates.

Practicing Active Listening

An active listener not only pays attention to what is being said and how it is being said, but also attends to what is being unsaid. Devito (2004) suggests that listening involves receiving, understanding, remembering (reconstructing the message in your mind), evaluating (placing a form of judgment or assessment on the message), and responding (giving some form of feedback). There is an added measure of complexity when cultural differences are involved in this process. Hence in intercultural interactions, active listening not only involves the aforementioned behaviors, but also requires the listener to consciously bear in mind that people interpret messages on the basis of their own understanding of cultural context. Therefore, there may be room for error and the other person's (cultural) perspective should be taken into consideration.

REFLECT 3.4: What techniques have you used in the past to become a competent intercultural communicator? Have these helped your intercultural communication? How? What might you do to improve in the future?

Seeking Regular Feedback

Just as you need feedback in your assignments to tell you how you are doing in your classes, you need feedback from friends, colleagues, and other sources such as books and media to inform you as to how you are progressing in your intercultural communication competence. Beamer (1992) argues that the competent intercultural communicator "will keep challenging his or her repository, in order to play a part in the matching of signs with the other communicator" (p. 288). Although you may have your own ideas about the extent of your competence, regularly evaluating your performance by soliciting feedback from other sources is an important and necessary part of developing intercultural communication competence. For example, if you have good friends from other cultures, you could ask them what they think about your intercultural communication skills and whether they could give you any suggestions for improvement. You could also ask friends from your own culture about your communication skills. Though at first it might be awkward to initiate a conversation like this, once you get past the awkwardness, you might find that your friends have valuable and honest feedback to share with you about how you can improve your communication skills. You might also find it is not awkward at all. Often people do not correct each other when they act in a slightly offensive way because they want to avoid a perceived potential conflict, do not want to hurt feelings, or are careful not to cause discomfort in a friendship. But if you voluntarily ask them to give feedback, they are likely to be more forthcoming about areas in which you can improve.

FINAL THOUGHTS

Despite the aforementioned steps that can be taken to improve your intercultural communication skills, it must be noted that intercultural communication competence is far more complex than a mere checklist. Generally speaking, a competent communicator is deliberately aware of the other person's cues and tries to discern that person's needs in the communication exchange so as to respond accordingly, just as Mike did at the start of the chapter. In intercultural interactions, this can be an even more challenging task due to the cultural differences involved in addition to personality differences and differences in communication styles.

As discussed in the discussion of intergroup communication theory in Chapter 2, even when people know what to do in a particular situation, they might simply not be able or willing to execute that behavior. For example, in a study involving international students in a graduate seminar in the United States, Arasaratnam (2003) notes that even though some of the international students knew the style of communication they needed to adopt in order to be appropriate in the classroom, they *chose* not to adopt it because this style of communication was in conflict with their own cultural ideals of "good" communication. In other words, there are instances when people may choose not to practice the behaviors that are considered effective and appropriate in a particular context even at the expense of coming across as incompetent, in order to remain consistent with their own beliefs. Further, Martin (1993) points out that understanding what people from other cultures view as "competent" intercultural communication is as important to understanding your own intercultural communication competence. But generally speaking, it is fair to say that as you learn good communication skills and expand your experience with intercultural interaction, you will begin to develop an understanding of how to navigate the subtle and pronounced cultural differences.

CONTINUE YOUR JOURNEY ONLINE

Visit: www.transitionsabroad.com

Transitions Abroad website. Explore the possibility of studying, working, traveling, or living abroad. Consider how intercultural communication competence might help in these endeavors.

---

66 SAY WHAT?

Say What? provides excerpts from overheard real-life conversations in which people have communicated stereotypes. As you read these conversations, reflect on the following questions.

- Have you been in conversations like this before?
- Is there any one of these conversations that stick out to you more than the others?
- What do you think of this conversation?
- How did the stereotype help or hinder the conversation?
- Was there another way the stereotyper could have communicated to convey the same point?
- How do you feel when you hear this conversation or the specific stereotype?
- Do any of these conversations bother you more than others? Why or why not?
- Do any concepts, issues, or theories discussed in the chapter help explain why?

- **Say What?** We all chitchatted and then one of my friends said, "I would never date a fat guy. I find them disgusting. They have no manners and eat like they have never seen food in their life. I also know that they can lose weight, but are too lazy to try. I was fat when I was young and I lost all my weight." The atmosphere became very uncomfortable at this time and no one knew what to say.

(Continued)

(Continued)

- **Say What?** We came across a new, prestigious store and began browsing. As I was about to show Mike a shirt that I found, his attention drew away from me. Two African American teenagers walking into the store held Mike's attention. I threw the shirt in his face. "What is wrong with you?" I asked. "Yeah, like they could afford anything in this store. And if they can, I bet you it's drug money," was his reply. At that second, I felt my face turn red, my blood pressure rise, and my heart start pounding. "Excuse me!" blurted out of my mouth loud enough for the entire store to hear.

- **Say What?** Chan asked me if I knew why women had smaller feet than men. I told him that I didn't know why. "So that they can get as close to the sink as possible," he responded mischievously. I said, "Hey!" because I thought that he was serious. Then I looked at his silly face, laughed and threw a pillow at him, which started a humongous pillow fight.

- **Say What?** A customer entered the bar, took one look at me, and began cursing to himself and his peers. Later he apologized for cursing me out and said that he was surprised that I had such a great choice and selection of hip-hop songs. It only seemed obvious that this statement referred to the fact that I was White. My question back to him was "What kind of music do I look like I carry?" The customer and his peers seemed hesitant to answer and kind of started laughing. However, they did say that they thought I would play more club, rock, and . . . more White music.

REVIEW QUESTIONS

1. What is communication competence? How does the chapter define effective and appropriate communication?

2. What are the four levels of intercultural communication competence? According to the chapter, which one is most desirable? Why?

3. Who are "strangers" according to the AUM model as discussed in the chapter?

4. Using the framework of the integrated model of intercultural communication competence discussed in the chapter, explain why someone who has no experience or training in intercultural communication may still be perceived as a competent intercultural communicator compared to someone who is a seasoned world traveler.

5. What are the five key variables that contribute to intercultural communication competence? Use the dialogue at the start of the chapter to explain why at least two of these are important for intercultural communication.

6. Based on the chapter discussion, identify two practical steps you can take to develop your intercultural communication competence.

7. What is cognitive complexity? According to the chapter, why is it relevant to intercultural communication?

8. Why does the chapter say ethnocentrism is harmful to intercultural communication?

9. Why is a positive attitude toward people from other cultures beneficial for intercultural communication, according to the chapter?

10. What advice does the chapter give on how to become an interculturally competent communicator?

KEY TERMS

affective dimension   54

affective resourcefulness   60

anxiety/uncertainty management (AUM) model   54

behavioral dimension   54

behavioral resourcefulness   60

cognitive complexity   51

cognitive dimension   54

cognitive resourcefulness   60

communication competence   48

conscious competence   50

conscious incompetence   49

effective communication   55

empathy   53

ethnocentrism   52

high sensation seekers   53

identity   60

identity negotiation model   60

integrated model of intercultural communication competence (IMICC)   58

interaction involvement   53

mindful communicator   55

mindfulness   55

novelty   60

pyramid model of intercultural competence   61

stranger   54

symbolic intercultural space   48

unconscious competence   50

unconscious incompetence   49

REFERENCES

Arasaratnam, L. A. (2003). Competing cultural voices: An ethnographic study of international students in American graduate education. Paper presented at the annual convention of the National Communication Association, Miami, FL.

Arasaratnam, L. A. (2005). Sensation seeking and international students' satisfaction of experiences in the United States. *Journal of Intercultural Communication Research, 34,* 184–194.

Arasaratnam, L. A. (2006). Further testing of a new model of intercultural communication competence. *Communication Research Reports, 23,* 93–99.

Arasaratnam, L. A. (2011). *Perception and communication in intercultural spaces.* Lanham, MD: University Press of America.

Arasaratnam, L. A., & Banerjee, S. C. (2007). Ethnocentrism and sensation seeking as variables that influence intercultural contact-seeking behavior: A path analysis. *Communication Research Reports, 24,* 303–310.

Arasaratnam, L. A., Banerjee, S. C., & Dembek, K. (2010). The integrated model of intercultural communication competence (IMICC): Model test. Unpublished paper presented in the annual convention of the International Communication Association, Singapore.

Arasaratnam, L. A., & Doerfel, M. L. (2005). Intercultural communication competence: Identifying key components from multicultural perspectives. *International Journal of Intercultural Relations, 29,* 137–163.

Beamer, L. (1992). Learning intercultural communication competence. *The Journal of Business Communication, 29,* 285–304.

Bhawuk, D. P. S. (1998). The role of culture theory in cross-cultural training: A multimethod study of culture-specific, culture-general, and culture theory-based assimilators. *Journal of Cross-Cultural Psychology, 29,* 630–656.

Deardorff, D. K. (2006). Identification and assessment of intercultural competence as a student outcome of internationalization. *Journal of Studies in International Education, 10,* 241–266.

Devito, J. A. (2004). *The interpersonal communication book.* Boston: Pearson Education.

Gudykunst, W. B. (1993). Toward a theory of effective interpersonal and intergroup communication: An anxiety/uncertainty management (AUM) perspective. In R. L. Wiseman & J. Koester (Eds.), *Intercultural communication competence* (pp. 33–71). Newbury Park, CA: Sage.

Gudykunst, W. B. (1995). Anxiety/uncertainty management (AUM) theory. In R. L. Wiseman (Ed.), *Intercultural communication theory* (pp. 8–58). Thousand Oaks, CA: Sage.

Gudykunst, W. B. (2002). Intercultural communication. In W. B. Gudykunst & B. Mody (Eds.), *Handbook of international and intercultural communication* (pp. 179–182). Thousand Oaks, CA: Sage.

Gudykunst, W. B., & Kim, Y. Y. (2003). *Communicating with strangers: An approach to intercultural communication.* New York: McGraw-Hill.

Gudykunst, W. B., & Nishida, T. (2001). Anxiety, uncertainty, and perceived effectiveness of communication across relationships and cultures. *International Journal of Intercultural Relations, 25,* 55–72.

Howell, W. S. (1982). *The empathic communicator* (pp. 29-33). Belmont, CA: Wadsworth.

Martin, J. N. (1993). Intercultural communication competence: A review. In R. L. Wiseman & J. Koester (Eds.), *Intercultural communication competence* (pp. 16–29). Newbury Park, CA: Sage.

Spitzberg, B. H., & Chagnon, G. (2009). Conceptualizing intercultural competence. In D. K. Deardorff (Ed.), *The SAGE handbook of intercultural competence* (pp. 2–52). Thousand Oaks, CA: Sage.

Spitzberg, B. H., & Cupach, W. R. (1984). *Interpersonal communication competence.* Beverly Hills, CA: Sage.

Stephan, W. G., Stephan, C. W., & Gudykunst, W. B. (1999). Anxiety in intergroup relations: A comparison of anxiety/uncertainty management theory and integrated threat theory. *International Journal of Intercultural Relations, 23,* 613–628.

Sumner, W. G. (1907/2002). *Folkways: A study of mores, manners, customs and morals.* Mineola, NY: Dover Publications.

Ting-Toomey, S. (1993). Communicative resourcefulness: An identity negotiation theory. In R. L. Wiseman & J. Koester (Eds.), *Intercultural communication competence* (pp. 72–111). Newbury Park, CA: Sage.

Ting-Toomey, S. (2005). Identity negotiation theory: crossing cultural boundaries. In W. B. Gudykunst (Ed.), *Theorizing about intercultural communication* (pp. 211–233). Thousand Oaks, CA: Sage.

Yoshitake, M. (2002). Anxiety/uncertainty management (AUM) theory: A critical examination of an intercultural communication theory. *Intercultural Communication Studies, 11,* 177–193.

Van der Zee, K. I., Zaal, J. N., & Piekstra, J. (2003). Validation of the multicultural personality questionnaire in the context of personnel selection. *European Journal of Personality, 17,* 77–100.

Van Oudenhoven, J. P., & Van der Zee, K. I. (2002). Predicting multicultural effectiveness of international students: The Multicultural Personality Questionnaire. *International Journal of Intercultural Relations, 26,* 679–694.

CHAPTER **4**

A Communication Theory of Culture

Donal Carbaugh
University of Massachusetts Amherst

Journey Through Chapter 4

Sightseeing: On your journey, you will visit with five concepts of culture and engage in an in-depth discussion of a communication theory of culture. This discussion demonstrates how culture can be viewed as a construction, rather than a representation by introducing a social constructionist approach applied to inter/cultural communication.

Souvenir: After your journey, you will take away an understanding of how culture is produced in moments of interaction and how this understanding is distinct from that which the other concepts of culture provide.

The "culture" concept has been adopted by many people, each intent on using it for some purposes rather than for others (Bauman, 1999). This can be a healthy sign of fertile intellectual soil as you seek to understand various circumstances and particular practices among peoples in the world today. Some of the issues addressed in earlier discussions of this concept have included the relationship between languages and cultures, the ways cultures penetrate societies, the role of cultural analyses in historical studies, a robust understanding of intercultural encounters, the integration of cultures, interpretations of visual media, dynamics in chat rooms or blogs, relations between nature-environment and peoples' places, as well as the practical activities of everyday living. There is much here to think about.

This chapter does three general things. First, following Bauman (1999), it discusses some prominent uses of the culture concept. Second, it introduces a communication theory of culture and uses that theory as a basis for reflecting upon earlier uses of the culture concept. Third, the chapter concludes by briefly summarizing some of the possibilities of this approach for the study of communication and culture. To begin, the following section discusses four ways people have used the concept of culture.

FOUR USES OF THE CULTURE CONCEPT

Generic Concept

People make sense of the cosmos, of beings and things in nature, through ways of speaking that are customary to them. People have "ways" of speaking about human beings and animals. In the process of speaking about these, people learn which are like and which are not like human beings in their appearance or in their activities. How is it, you might ask, that people are different from chimpanzees? Explanations typically involve how people have developed a sophisticated use of language, like these words on this page. Other points are made about refined use of tools like the use of computers. Still others refer to the finer arts of music, painting, and sculpture.

A way of entitling these lines of thought is to say, that humans have developed culture while other animals do not. In this sense, humans are said to be culture-bearers in a way animals have not. To be a culture-bearer is to learn in a specialized way, to act in particular ways, to believe particular things, and to feel certain ways about the world. Culture here

Photo 4.1   Do you remember when you were *not* aware of cultural expectations? Newborns come into the world without culture. Yet, even at this young age, gender and class identities are being constructed through a blue bath mat, indoor plumbing, and expensive toys.

Copyright 2010 Michael Kurylo.

means things like sophistication in language ability, artistic expression, musical abilities, as well as other qualities that highlight uniquely human accomplishments. When culture is used in this basic way to distinguish the human animal from other animals it takes the form of a generic concept that locates culture within the human species, as a species-wide ability and as a way of viewing humans above and unlike all other species.

Distinctive Concept

As people began traveling beyond their homelands, they noticed that human habits and customs differed. Among one group, people were greeted with a bow, in another by the clasp of the arm, or elsewhere by a kiss. These differences in habits and customs can be described by the idea of culture as a distinctive concept. Here, culture is used as a way to distinguish the habits of one human group from another human group. If a customary postdinner moment in some parts of East Asia includes burping from a guest as a compliment to the host, this can be understood to be distinctive to this group and unlike other groups. This idea of culture helps distinguish the range of customs and habits that are distinctive to one group. It highlights the uniqueness of that cultural group versus another and the exclusiveness of that group from others.

> ### Take a Side Trip:
>
> If you would like to read more about related issues, visit Appendix F: Korean Culture Explored Through Survey Research.

Exclusiveness used in reference to the distinctive concept of culture means that a cultural group may not welcome intrusion from outside groups. This may be obvious in homogenous cultures in which there is little variability in the cultural makeup of its group members. Some such cultures like Amish, Mormon, or Hasidic Jewish communities require those from outside their group to go through rigorous procedures to be accepted into the culture, if they are accepted at all. Heterogeneous cultures that are comprised of considerable group variability can be distinctive as well. New York, known as the melting pot, is also a notoriously distinctive culture as suggested by the song lyrics "I want to be a part of it, New York, New York." As the generic concept of culture distinguished humans from other species, the distinctive concept distinguishes the unique qualities of a particular human group that set it apart from other groups.

Evaluative Concept

The evaluative concept of culture suggests that within any human group there are values that tend to be championed as good and as higher than the others that are viewed as less good or lower in value (see Table 4.1). Teens might thoroughly enjoy popular music such as rap or rock music, wear their hair in a popular style, and, like other kids, get absorbed in a vibrant youth culture. Many of their parents, in contrast, might not value these to the same extent and may want to be sure to expose their children also to "the finer things in life." These might include attending theatrical performances or orchestral concerts, reading great works of

Table 4.1   Proverbs.

What proverbs do you remember hearing while you were growing up? Cultural group members communicate proverbs to reproduce cultural values for each generation.

Country of Origin and Use	Proverb	Cultural Value(s)	Meaning of Proverb
Cameroon	What an old man can see sitting, a young man cannot see standing.	A patriarchal and status-oriented hierarchy.	In contrast to the young, no matter how much effort they exert, elderly, particularly males, are wise because of their age and experience and their viewpoints should be valued and advice heeded.
Mexican	Better to die on your feet than live on your knees.	Machismo, a strong sense of honor, and a cultural history of revolution.	Honor is achieved through action, or at an extreme fighting, even if it has considerable costs rather than waiting or being subservient to others.
Scottish	Ne'er cast a clout till May be oot.	Realism, reserve, and independence.	Don't put winter clothes away until the flowers bloom; it warns to always be prepared.
U.S. American	Good fences make good neighbors.	Individualistic tendencies and privacy.	Good relationships are built upon knowing boundaries and distinctions between what is a possession of one person or of another.

Source: Adapted from "Cameroon," "Scotland," "United States of America," and "Mexico" Culturegrams by Culturegrams. Available at www.culturegrams.com/.

Copyright 2010 Anastacia Kurylo.

literature, as well as attending choral events, all in order to broaden their kids' exposure to the variety of things life offers. Implicit in these parental actions is helping children learn through diverse experiences so their judgments about what is better and lesser in their lives can be informed by a breadth of experiences. Judgments of this type tend to pervade any group, but what constitutes the so-called finer things may vary from one group to the next and can fall along lines of class, race, region, gender, or many other differences within groups.

Applied in this way, the idea of culture as an evaluative concept moves from the distinctive concept, which expresses that there are differences between groups, to a judgment of difference within a group in which some qualities are deemed better than others. As such, it is used to distinguish, for example, the high arts and letters within a group, from the lower and lesser forms. To be cultured, in this sense, is to claim access and appreciation to the best that society has to offer. To lack culture, in this evaluative sense, is to be ignorant, vulgar, or unappreciative of the "finer" arts and aspects of life.

To further illustrate culture as an evaluative concept, consider the case of a doctoral student who, several years ago, proposed a study to his dissertation committee. The study focused upon culture in a U.S. American prime-time television talk show hosted by Phil Donahue. A committee member replied to this proposal with a comment of exasperation:

"Doctoral research typically focuses on important figures like Max Weber, Sigmund Freud, Hans Georg Gadamer, or John Dewey and you're going to study a talk-show host, Phil Donahue?!" The remark presumes a properly cultured person—evidently unlike this doctoral student—knows what is proper for academic study and appreciation. In turn, those less cultured types do not have their proper senses. The society is then stratified between those adhering to the higher and those adhering to the lower values. Within the evaluative concept of culture, high culture is associated with the upper class and the value placed on the fine arts and education and low culture is associated with the lower class, those who are less well educated, and popular culture.

Cognitive Concept

Culture can be understood as a mental or cognitive concept. This usage identifies culture as a kind of collective lens used to perceive the world, a filtered way of sensing, believing, and feeling. Claims within this cognitive concept identify culture within the internal workings of the mind, the templates for thought, routine dispositions, and specific characteristics. Note that culture in the cognitive sense is located inside the person, as a part of the mental makeup a person uses when being-in-the-world. The idea of being-in-the-world draws attention to the particularities of a person's senses about things, beliefs about people or classes of people, and emotions.

An example of culture as a cognitive concept can be seen in an instance when a highly educated government official visited a farmer in India who had been working his land successfully for generations. The official was a specialist in "soil productivity" and the farmer, upon meeting the official, addressed him as "sir" and "your grace." The government official recommended that the farmer use organic fertilizer. The farmer had tried organic fertilizer previously with good yield. Nonetheless,

Photo 4.2 What is the view from your window? How does this filter your perception, identity, and behavior? What we see each day impacts who we are and how we view the world around us, often in unknown ways.

Copyright 2010 Bill Edwards and Anastacia Kurylo.

as the farmer and others in his community had done repeatedly in conversations with those in higher status, the farmer replied to the official by referring to himself as an "illiterate" and "ignorant fellow." How might you account for this deprecating stance of the farmer? One account is that the collective mind of people in this community not only expect but act upon rigid differences in power. The official is deemed higher in status and the farmer lower, with the higher status person regarded by all, including this farmer, as the knowledgeable person deserving of deference. Presumably, the lens the farmer uses to interact with the official illustrates how culture is used as a filter. His lens guides him to show respect to anyone above a person's own status—even if the person's statements in that moment may not warrant such respect.

REFLECT 4.1: Which concept of culture do you use the most? Why?

A COMMUNICATION THEORY OF CULTURE

The previous conceptions and uses of the culture concept are valuable. There are times when it is useful to distinguish human qualities from the nonhuman, to distinguish one group's features from another's, to understand what is valued more and less, and to think of habits of the collective mind. The current chapter does not seek to dismiss the kinds of claims each of these uses of the culture concept brings with it. Rather, this chapter wants to embrace each by proposing a way of relocating these ideas about culture from the species, groups, classes, and minds into the domain of communication practice. Communication practice is a fifth understanding of culture. Communication practice refers to expressive action performed in specific contexts; that is, how people actually do communication in their specific social scenes. This section addresses this fifth understanding of culture from a communication theory of culture perspective. A communication theory of culture views culture as a social construction produced through communication practices within cultural discourse. Cultural discourse is the "historically transmitted expressive system of communication practices, of acts, events, and styles, which are composed of specific symbols, symbolic forms, norms, and their meanings" (Carbaugh, 2007, p.169).

Rather than locating culture inside a person, groups of people, or within human minds, the remainder of this chapter theorizes culture as an ever-present dimension of communication practices. According to Carbaugh (1996), from a social construction approach any particular identity can be viewed as

a set of communicative practices that is more noticeable or salient in some social scenes than in others. Just as an individual is more adept at some identities (e.g., being a teacher, or an Argentinean) than others (e.g., being a business executive, or a Russian), so too are social scenes designed for some identities more than others. This is a way of . . . moving the site of identity from the individual into actual scenes of communicative action. (p. 25)

In this way, culture is produced in the interactional moment that meaning is given, rather than by virtue of it being reflected in the behavior of a large number of people.

This concept of culture is informed by various field-based studies that have used this approach and resonate with the idea that culture is socially constructed (see Galanes & Leeds-Hurwitz, 2009). For example, some of these studies have carefully examined cultural discourses of gender in Finland (Berry, 1997), hate speech including folk models of the proper person in Hungary (Boromisza-Habashi, 2007), intercultural interactions among U.S. Americans, Finns, Russians, English, and Native Americans (Carbaugh, 2005), meanings of dialogue in several different languages (Carbaugh, Boromisza-Habashi, & Ge, 2006), indigenous and nonindigenous models of rhetoric and consciousness (Carbaugh & Wolf, 1999), cultural notions for expressing interpersonal life in Colombia (Fitch, 1997), Israeli history through its prominent expressive genres (Katriel, 2005), cultural discourses about water (Morgan, 2003, 2007), Finnish cultural speech and language (Poutiainen, 2005), nonverbal ways of communicating with nature (Scollo, 2005), local forms of political praxis in the United States (Townsend, 2006), an optimal form for Finnish public discourse (Wilkins, 2005), and Arab narratives of identity in the United States (Witteborn, 2007). This is not a comprehensive listing but it is a suggestive one that illustrates how the approach has been widely and productively used.

Imagine you are a speaker in a courtroom and you want to persuade a jury and a judge not to develop the area on a mountainside because you view it as an important site of nature. This was the task in a courtroom in Arizona. Some who participated stated an argument about the costs of such development and the resulting destruction to the mountain. For these participants, the practice of arguing in a verbal form was familiar and seemed appropriate to them as a way of stating their case in court. However, for some Native American participants, the best way they knew to honor a natural site such as this mountain—which in this case was a sacred location—was in the use of silence. For these people, silence was appropriately respectful as a way of standing in support of the site because the silence acknowledged from their view that it is presumptuous to put the creator's sacred site into words. In this way, silence was a communication practice designed to express reverence for a spiritual place in the hope of stopping its development. Each communication practice, arguing in words and standing in silence, was used in a courtroom context, yet each used different traditions of expression to express their meaning.

REFLECT 4.2: How do you produce your cultural identity through your verbal and nonverbal behavior? Are you aware of it when you are doing it?

FOUR PROPOSITIONS OF A COMMUNICATION THEORY OF CULTURE

Four central propositions help further explain the value in viewing culture from a communication theory of culture perspective. The first proposition is that communication practice involves a complex system of symbols, symbolic forms, and their meanings.

A Complex System of Symbols, Symbolic Forms, and Their Meanings

As people communicate and engage in the ongoing flow of their everyday social life, they do so through communication practices. As with Native American and non-Native people in the preceding example, these practices not only reveal but create their view of the world. A cultural analyst can gain access to that world by noticing key symbols that are being used, prominent symbolic forms that are being practiced, such as arguing verbally and being silent, and by interpreting the meaningfulness of those symbols and symbolic forms to those who use them. Both symbols and symbolic forms are rich with local meanings, deep in feeling, and broadly accessible to people. As discussed in Chapter 1, symbols are key words, expressions, images, circumstances, actions, or phrases used to conceive of and evaluate parts of a culture that participants deem richly significant and important. For example, the Hebrew symbol, *dugri* or talking "straight" with someone has a local, deep, and broad role in shaping Israeli communication and culture. Similarly, in China the symbol of *Xue Lei Feng,* which refers to "learning from Lei Feng," plays a rich role in an evolving Chinese culture. Each illustrates how communication practices can involve potent and prominent symbols that are understood deeply by cultural members.

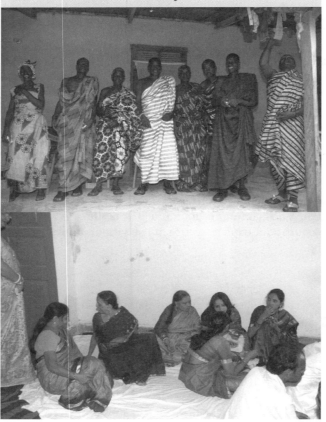

Photo 4.3 How is your current appearance a carrier of meaning for your culture? Physical appearance in a culture constructs cultural identity.

Although similar to symbols, symbolic forms are larger units, communication acts within larger sequences of actions. Analysts have explored symbolic forms as ritual, myth, and social drama (Philipsen, 1992) and as key terms and tropes (Carbaugh, 1996). Additionally, native terms can also be used to draw attention to participants' symbolic forms such as *soul talks* in Russia, *tea meetings* in Japan, *services* among Quakers, or *griping sessions* in Israel or Bulgaria. Each of these terms, and innumerable others, help the analyst identify ways in which communication practice is made meaningful and shapes cultural lives. A second proposition central to understanding a communication theory of culture is that communication practices, like those just discussed, are meaningful to participants in a culture.

Meaningful Practices to Participants

Communication practices involve systems of shared, common, and public meanings. Cultural analysts seek to discover and interpret these systems. Elsewhere, the interpretive aspects of cultural discourse theory, which explores these systems, have been discussed in some detail (Carbaugh, 2005, 2007). This section provides a few observations on this topic.

Communication practices generally, as well as cultural symbols and symbolic forms specifically, are potent carriers of meaning. They can carry great depth of insight and feeling concerning a person's ways of doing things. These meanings are often taken-for-granted knowledge in a person's community. That is to say, communication practice is something that typically you do not have to think about; it is just assumed. Practices, symbols, forms, and norms all carry deep meanings for cultural group members. Yet, these may only be made explicit when a cultural analyst articulates them in the form of cultural premises. For example, you might never think that people could be anything other than individuals. Yet, if you were among the Gurung people in Nepal, you might never think people could be anything other than particles of subatomic energy. Taken-for-granted knowledge like this typically takes the form of premises pertaining to (1) beliefs about what exists and (2) beliefs about what is better or worse.

REFLECT 4.3: Can you think of an example of when you have been forced to become aware of taken-for-granted knowledge about your culture? What did you realize about your culture? How did it make you feel?

As you go about your everyday routine, you express yourself culturally. As you greet others, listen to lectures, or attend a movie, you are, perhaps unwittingly, also acting as an agent in producing culture. In this way, and with the help of others, you construct what you think of as your shared lives and in doing so live in ways that are true to your perception of your community and your social scenes. A community is an organization of diverse people and practices. A social scene is a place people can identify and recognize as significant in their lives such as a church service, a sporting event, a family dinner, or a courtroom. Typically, you do not have to think about your use of culture. But sometimes you do, as when your communication practices reach a boundary. For example, in the courtroom routine mentioned earlier, one group's aggressive behavior might disadvantage others who are standing silent by not allowing their traditional communication practice to be expressed fully as the vocal group minimizes the potential impact of the silent group. Culture, then, is both active in the process of communication and is a product of that communication.

This idea that cultural practices are meaningful to participants in a culture can be summarized in three basic points. First, culture is housed in communication practices. Communication is the place where culture is active, applied, challenged, and changed. As you go about your communicative routines, you are producing your culture.

Second, as you communicate, you are actively producing a particular set of practices, unique to your cultural scenes and community. These particular practices mark you as a member of a specific group and not others with a badge of shared identity that is unlike that shared by others elsewhere. Gerry Philipsen (1989) has written about this as a process of membering. As you use your culture, you identify yourself in membership with some people and not with others. Table 4.2 shows how language can be used for membering. The process whereby you associate yourself with some groups of people and not others is discussed in more depth in Chapter 7.

Third, diversity and plurality is important in the world today. As in the courtroom, social scenes and communities can have active in them multiple practices through many cultural traditions. An understanding of and the ability to act productively within this variety of communication practices is valuable because they are markers of a person's identity. Moreover, multiple cultural identities and diversity in communication practices are active in social scenes and communities.

Prior studies have created a way of interpreting the meaningfulness of communication practices for participants. In short, these studies provide a way of investigating deeply the extent to which people produce culture as they communicate. This depth can be mined by exploring five potential hubs of meaning: (1) being, (2) relating, (3) acting, (4) feeling, and (5) dwelling, with the others radiating (as radiants) from each hub. To explore these an analyst would focus on a specific communication practice of interest, such as a greeting, and ask about it with the following questions:

1. About being: What is presumed about the person (roles, institutions) for this practice to be done in this way?

2. About relating: What is presumed about social relationships (roles, institutions) for this practice to be done in this way?

3. About acting: What is presumed as a model for social action for this practice to be done in this way?

4. About feeling: What emotion is presumed, expressed, or countered for this action to be done in this way?

5. About dwelling: What is presumed about this place, or person's relations to nature, for this action to be done in this way?

This way of interpreting meanings has been shown to be particularly useful in constructing cultural interpretations of activities such as greetings, work meetings, arguing, listening to others, political speeches, and much more. Generally there are two points of interpretation that help to explicate the communication practices participants perform and understand (Carbaugh, 1995, 2005; Philipsen, 1992). First, you would interpret the meaningfulness of a communication practice by formulating premises of belief and value related to each of the five hubs. Second, you would interpret the radiants of meanings that are active in that practice. This approach is particularly valuable because it provides a means through which to expose otherwise taken-for-granted cultural knowledge and construction.

An Expressive System of Culture

A third central proposition of a communication theory of culture is that culture is an expressive system. Culture can be understood as the practices of people in place, as something people do with each other, as a system of practices, as a way of organizing themselves

Table 4.2 Hamlet.

Have you read these words before? Cultures develop in response to shared events, interests, language, and so forth. Using the Klingon language would enable you to be identified as a member of a specific community based on a media phenomenon generated by the television program *Star Trek* cultural, known as Trekkies.

To Be, Or Not To Be Soliloquy	To Be, Or Not To Be Soliloquy (Klingon Version)
Hamlet: Prince of Denmark	The Klingon Hamlet: The Tragedy of Khamlet, Son of
Act 3 Scene 1	the Emperor of Qo'nos
by William Shakespeare	Act 3 Scene 1

Hamlet: To be, or not to be: - that is the question: -
Whether 'tis nobler in the mind to suffer
The slings and arrows of outrageous fortune,
Or to take arms against a sea of troubles,
And by opposing end them? - To die: - to sleep; -
No more; and by a sleep to say we end
The heart-ache and the thousand natural shocks
That flesh is heir to, - 'tis a consummation
Devoutly to be wish'd. To die, - to sleep; -
To sleep! perchance to dream: - ay, there's the rub;
For in that sleep of death what dreams may come,
When we have shuffled off this mortal coil,
Must give us pause: there's the respect
That makes calamity of so long life;
For who would bear the whips and scorns of time,
The oppressor's wrong, the proud man's contumely,
The pangs of despis'd love, the law's delay,
The insolence of office and the spurns
That patient merit of the unworthy takes,
When he himself might his quietus make
With a bare bodkin? who would fardels bear,
To grunt and sweat under a weary life,
But that the dread of something after death, -
The undiscover'd country, from whose bourn
No traveller returns, - puzzles the will,
And makes us rather bear those ills we have
Than fly to others that we know not of?
Thus conscience does make cowards of us all;
And thus the native hue of resolution
Is sicklied o'er with the pale cast of thought;
And enterprises of great pith and moment.
With this regard, their currents turn awry,
And lose the name of action.- Soft you now!
The fair Ophelia! Nymph, in thy orisons
Be all my sins remember'd.

Hamlet: taH pagh taHbe'. DaH mu'tlheghvam vIqelnIS.
quv'a', yabDaq San vaQ cha, pu'je SIQDI'?
pagh, Seng bIQ'a'Hey SuvmeH nuHmey SuqDI',
'ej, Suvmo', rInmoHDI'? Hegh. Qong-Qong neH-
'ej QongDI', tIq 'oy', wa'SanID Daw"e' je
cho'nISbogh porghDaj rInmoHlaH net Har.
yIn mevbogh mIwvam'e' wIruchqangbej.
Hegh. Qong. QongDI' ehaq naj. toH, waQlaw' ghu'vam!
HeghDaq maQongtaHvIS, tugh vay' wInajlaH,
volchaHmajvo' jubbe'wI' bep wIwoDDI';
'e' wIqelDI', maHeDnIS. Qugh DISIQnIS,
SIQmoHmo' qechvam. Qugh yIn nI'moH 'oH.
reH vaq 'ej qIpqu' bov; mayHa'taH HI';
Dochchu' HemwI'; ruv mImlu'; tIchrup patlh;
'oy'moH muSHa'ghach 'Il vuvHa'lu'bogh;
quvwI'pu' tuv quvHa'moH quvHa'wI'pu';
qatlh Hochvam lajqang vay'? wa' taj neH l0'DI',
Qu'Daj Qatlh qIllaH ghaH! tep qengqang 'Iv?
Doy'moHmo' yInDaj, bepmeH bechqang 'Iv,
mISbe'chugh neHtaHghach, ghaH ghIjmo' DuHvam:
Hegh tlha' vay': Hegh tlha' qo"e' tu'bogh pagh.
not chegh lengwI'ma', qo'vetlh veHmey 'elDI'.
vaj Seng DIghajbogh, lajtaHmeH qaq law';
latlh DISovbe'bogh, ghoSchoHmeH qaq puS.
vaj nuch DIDa 'e' raDlaw' ghobmaj, qelDI'.
'ej, plvmo', wovqu'taHvIS wuqbogh qab,
'oH ropmoH rIntaH Sotbogh qech ghom Hurgh.
'ej Qu'mey potlh DItulbogh qll je qechvam.
vIDHa'choH nab. baQa'! 'ovelya 'IH!
toH be', qa"a'pu'vaD bItlhobtaHvIS,
jIyempu' 'e' yIQIjehoH je.

From the Klingon Hamlet—a translation of the tragic Shakespearian play. Adapted from William Shakespeare's Hamlet/ Available at http://shakespeare.mit.edu/hamlet/full.html. Public Domain. Adapted from Shoulson, M. (Ed.). (2000). *The Klingon Hamlet: The tragedy of Khamlet, son of the Emperor of Qo'nos.* (N. Nicholas & A. Strader, Trans.). New York: Pocket Books. Copyright 2000 by Pocket Books.

together, and as a way of accounting for that organization. The organization that can be called culture is a practical art, a system for acting that is commonly accessible, mutually intelligible, and deeply felt (Carbaugh 2005). More specifically, the cultural expressive system is the life-blood of culture composed of three types of communication practices that are prominently active in social scenes: (1) specific acts, (2) events, and (3) styles of social interaction.

This expressive system is characterized by its part-whole nature (see Geertz, 1983, pp. 69–70). In other words, you can understand a part, such as greeting by handshaking and body bumping, only by understanding the larger scene in which it is produced. For example, in Israel, a person will hear acts of "talking straight"' or *dugri* speaking especially among Sabra Jews (Katriel, 2005). These acts do not stand alone but are parts of larger social sequences such as social dramas of living, ritualized forms of action, and an ethos of *gibush* or collective action that is championed and at times cherished. Dugri is also a style of speaking that can be marked as confrontational, plain and direct, and runs counter to other styles, such as *musayara* among Israeli Arabs.

Take a Side Trip:

If you would like to read more about related issues, visit Appendix A: Navajo Culture Explored Through Ethnography.

The concept of expressive system is used here to make three points. First, culture exists in communication practices of people in places. Second, any one communication practice—a communication act, event, or style—is part of a system of expressive practices. Third, as a result, this system of communication practices is the site of culture because it is through these communication practices that culture is created and expressed and, therefore, is cultivated.

An Expressive System That Is Historically Transmitted

An expressive system has precedents and these can be understood through its history or histories. For example, the *dugri* style of talking straight is designed to counter a past of being silenced, of being not heard from, of being indeed subjects of extermination. Against these forces, it is said, a person's will must be heard, must be heard forcefully, and must speak the truth in a straight manner, even as, or especially as an act of confrontation. Knowing the historical roots of this cultural practice helps enrich a person's sense of the practice and all that it brings with it.

In China, there is a well-known figure, Lei Feng. Lei Feng was a soldier who gave his life in service to others. After his accidental death in August 1962, Mao Zedong, the then Chinese leader, called on the whole country to learn from him and a national holiday of March 5th was established to celebrate the life of Lei Feng and the ethic of altruism he represented. Although this ethic was robust during the Mao era, as time has passed the symbol of Lei Feng has changed. No longer is the ethic of service to others assumed in an unquestioned way. In China today, especially among members of the younger generation, this symbol and meaning of altruism is questioned, with responses to it asking, what do I get in return? Morphed from its original meaning, the symbol now sounds a cautionary note in response to its past meaning: Don't be a fool by denying your self-interest.

The example from China helps make the point that communication practices ignite tension between a creative impulse and common practice. These tensional forces, which were discussed in Chapter 1 as the hallmark of structuration theory (Giddens, 1993), at once evoke history and create meaning anew (Carbaugh, 1994). Analyzing practices along this dimension helps develop insights about what is being evoked from the past and what is being created in the present. This creative evocativeness provides a tool for understanding culture as an expressive system that is historically transmitted, but also one that can creatively employ or react to that history.

LIVING CULTURE

Latin Dancing?   *By Anonymous*

There are many things in life that a person expects or is aware that they may encounter. Unfortunately stereotypes have become one of those things. We live in a day and age where categorization is a natural response and where we place people in the groups that we believe they should belong. We often generalize people into categories and make assumptions about the kinds of people that belong in a particular group. Naively, I assumed that because I am a member of what is generally the majority, I did not think that stereotypes would ever be a part of my life. However, I came to find out that not only would they be a part of my life, but it would be because I am a member of the majority that stereotypes are so prevalent.

As a competitive ballroom and Latin dancer, I often teach group classes in exchange for lessons or just as favors to people who are interested in learning. Upon request of a friend (Rob), I had agreed to teach his roommate (Bob) to do some mambo and cha-cha. Before meeting, the only information that Bob knew of me was that I was a competitive dancer who knew how to teach the steps; he was told nothing of my appearance. Although he knew nothing about me, I soon came to find out that he had his own preconceived ideas of how I would look.

We met early in the morning at a studio in which I often practiced. He came in the door and I greeted him, "You must be Bob, nice to meet you." He looked almost stunned. He said nothing at first, and then asked, "Yes, hi and umm where could I find Jane?" as he looked past me to the empty wooden floor. "That's me." I responded. He looked perplexed as he asked, "So you're going to teach me Latin dancing?" with an almost sarcastic tone. I responded, "Yep, that's me" trying to avoid the awkwardness. I persisted, "You can change your shoes over there and I'll be right with you." I knew that this might happen. It had happened before, and it was happening again.

(Continued)

LIVING CULTURE

(Continued)

As I walked away, he followed and continued, "I'm sorry, but with all due respect, what could you teach me about Latin dancing?" He was about 5'9", dark skinned, of Puerto Rican desent looking at a fair-skinned, red-haired girl. Feeling offended, I asked him why he thought I could not teach him. He simply responded, "Well look at you ... you look more Irish than anything!" This was the problem. I did not fit the mold he perceived for a Latin dancer. He expected someone much more like him, someone from his heritage. He wanted to identify himself with me, and with the way I looked he couldn't. I proceeded to explain that I have had many years of training as a dancer, and that one's ethnic background has nothing to do with their ability. However, my explanations did little in the way of persuading him in his beliefs. He said that I could not possibly be able to move like the *other* girls did. It was as if we had hit a roadblock; he did not want me teaching him because "the rhythm was not in my blood." However, I was determined to prove my point. So, we struck a deal; he would wait for my dance partner to come and I would show him that I could dance.

Sure enough, my partner arrived and we danced for Bob. Bob sat in the chair looking on in astonishment. I had become a different person on the floor; I came to life and put in every last ounce of myself so that I could prove that the shade of my skin or my ethnic background has nothing to do with my ability. When we finished, he came over, shook my hand and said, "I stand corrected."

Consider:

1. What is it that the author says she knew might happen? How does she feel about this? Why?

2. What concepts of culture are being referenced in this Living Culture narrative?

3. How is dancing used as a cultural symbol in the narrative? Does the meaning of this symbol change at the end of the narrative? If so, how?

4. How is this conversation an example of a cultural moment?

CULTURAL MOMENTS

Culture is socially constructed through communication practices enacted in cultural moments. Cultural moments are instances in time in which culture is communicated in language and behavior in ways that reveal culture as a social construct despite its usual taken-for-granted nature. This section provides three examples of cultural moments that have been studied through a communication theory of culture perspective in which the communication of culture, usually taken-for-granted, can be identified.

Carbaugh (2005) provides a transcript from a *60 Minutes* segment in which Morley Safer interviews Finnish author and radio personality Jan Knutas. In the interview, Knutas talks about the discomfort he experiences when pressured by U.S. American social norms of small talk. Carbaugh points out that although Americans may at times feel annoyed when engaging in small talk, Knutas uses the term "horrifying" (p. 48) and invocations of "oh god" (p. 49) to describe his experience with American small talk. Through his communication, Knutas constructs small talk as something distinctly American and taken-for-granted in America as normal, but as a horrifying experience to him as a Finnish man. The example demonstrates the social construction of his cultural identity as a Finnish person with a preference for Finnish norms who will accommodate an U.S. American cultural norm albeit reluctantly. In addition to constructing cultural identity as shown in this example, cultural moments can also invoke cultural identity for practical reasons as shown in the following two examples.

Mokros (2003) used videotaped data from an ethnographic research site to gain insight into "how otherness is employed to resolve practical problems of identity within interaction" (p. 255). He provides an example of a cultural moment in which the communication of identity in the form of a stereotype is used as a tool to accomplish practical goals within a conversation. In this cultural moment, a vendor gets into a physical fight with a customer. After the conflict, the vendor communicates the stereotype that the customer was being stingy or cheap because he is Jewish. In doing so he provides a justification for his behavior, which he viewed as warranted because to him the customer was being too selective in picking out a product. By communicating the stereotype, he constructs the cultural identity of the customer in a way that made the customer look as if he was in the wrong. The stereotype allowed the blame to be shifted to the customer so that the vendor's behavior in the conflict might be justified. This example demonstrates a cultural moment in which culture is invoked and used as a tool to accomplish practical interactional goals.

Hopper (2003) looked at transcripts of interpersonally communicated stereotypes to understand how gendered identity is constructed in communication processes. His examples involve cultural moments in which gender stereotypes are communicated in ways that construct differences between men and women where none may exist. For example, Hopper discussed a heterosexual romantic couple who assign "household chores" according to gender stereotypes (p. 109). Cultural moments in which gender identity is invoked can reinforce gender differences as meaningful symbolic distinctions. In addition and similar to the previous example, cultural moments like these provide practical benefits for those in the interaction. Hopper explains how invoking gender differences in conversation can be used to soften a critique to a romantic partner. Hopper notes that perhaps "it is easier to critique . . . if the critique fits your stereotypes about the way men are" (p. 117).

REFLECT 4.4: When have you recently had a cultural moment? What did you learn in this moment about your culture or someone else's?

FINAL THOUGHTS

Through the topics and examples discussed in this chapter, you can begin to appreciate the varied conceptualizations of the idea of culture, understand better a focus on culture as a communication practice, and appreciate the variety of ways in which culture is actively produced in communication practices. This fifth understanding of the concept of culture as a communication practice can be said to incorporate the four other ways, discussed at the start of the chapter, in which the concept of culture can be viewed in a generic way, in a distinctive way, in an evaluative way, and in a cognitive way. All of these concepts of culture can be explored in an integrative way within a communication theory of culture. In other words, the fifth view resituates those earlier concepts of culture from species, groups, classes, and lenses into communication practices. Through your communication of culture in symbols and symbolic forms you express yourself as uniquely human (the generic concept), identify distinct features of groups to distinguish groups from each other (the distinctive concept), make judgments about how one group's ways are typically better than others' (the evaluative concept), and normalize human action within groups in such a way as to create lenses or expectations for behavior (the cognitive concept).

Unlike the four concepts of culture as originally articulated, the fifth concept of culture, incorporating these four, positions you to explore the relationship between languages and cultures, the ways cultures infuse societies, the role of cultural analyses in historical studies, a robust understanding of inter/cultural encounters and hybrid cultures, interpretations of visual media, relations between nature-environment and peoples' places, as well as the practical activities of everyday living. Living and studying with a communication view of culture, there is much good work to do.

CONTINUE YOUR JOURNEY ONLINE

Visit: http://whc.unesco.org/en/list

UNESCO World Heritage List. Take a tour of countries you may otherwise never get a chance to visit in person. Explore the representations of culture in the images and text on the site. Consider the value of this site for preserving, protecting, and constructing "world cultural and natural heritage."

Notes

The author is indebted to Xinmei Ge and her current dissertation studies for analyses of these Chinese discursive phenomena. Her studies are being completed at the University of Massachusetts under the author's direction.

Parts of this chapter were delivered as a keynote lecture prepared for the international conference on Hybrids, Differences, Visions: The Study of Culture II. University of Modena, Italy, October 19–20, 2007.

Parts of this chapter appear in Donal Carbaugh. Resituating cultural studies in communication: Cultural discourse theory. In Claudio Baraldi, Andrea Borsari, Augusto Carli (Eds.), *Culture and the human sciences.* Aurora, CO: The John Davies Group (in press).

The author thanks Anastacia Kurylo for assistance in adapting the chapter for this volume.

❝ SAY WHAT?

Say What? provides excerpts from overheard real-life conversations in which people have communicated stereotypes. As you read these conversations, reflect on the following questions.

- Have you been in conversations like this before?
- Is there any one of these conversations that stick out to you more than the others?
- What do you think of this conversation?
- How did the stereotype help or hinder the conversation?
- Was there another way the stereotyper could have communicated to convey the same point?
- How do you feel when you hear this conversation or the specific stereotype?
- Do any of these conversations bother you more than others? Why or why not?
- Do any concepts, issues, or theories discussed in the chapter help explain why?

- **Say What?** We met up with some other friends and all we did was boast about how good our basketball team was. Mike asked us what was the big deal about winning 10 games in a row because the teams probably sucked. John retaliated by saying that we even beat a team full of African Americans, Mike then stated, "Just cause they're Black doesn't mean they're good." John, after a brief moment of silence, tried to cover up by saying that the opposing team was pretty good, but I was there and I know that Mike was right. The team with the African Americans wasn't all that great.

- **Say What?** On a very physical play a player took the ball in toward the basket and was fouled, the team captain insisted that I was "giving all the calls to the White team." I gave the team captain a technical foul because of the nature of his comment. This incited him further and he had to be taken aside by his teammates to be calmed down. He spat out some further biased comments, but I opted not to throw him out of the game. I did not want him to be able to use "the racist referee" as his excuse for losing the game.

- **Say What?** I was training a new girl at work. Now this girl is a tiny girl so I said to her, "This tray is very heavy; I'll show you an easy way to carry it since you're a little girl. It will be easier to rest in on your shoulder instead of holding it up in the air." This did not go over well with this new girl. She got very offended and grabbed the heavy tray, held it high in the air and said with an attitude, "Even little girls can handle big jobs!"

- **Say What?** I had asked her about possibly going out after work one of these days to grab a bite to eat. She agreed, but she wanted to wait until she got next week's paycheck so that she would have some money. I told her she doesn't need to have money. She responded by asking why. I went on to tell her that I would have to pay because that's just how things are. She quickly became annoyed and told me that I was an idiot for thinking that way. In reality, she did make a lot more money then me and I really didn't have a lot of money to spend. She knew that too.

REVIEW QUESTIONS

1. What are the first four concepts of culture discussed in the chapter? Define each.

2. What is distinct about the fifth concept of culture from the four previously discussed in this chapter?

3. How does the fifth concept of culture incorporate the previous four concepts of culture discussed? Be specific. Provide examples as appropriate.

4. What is a communication theory of culture, according to the chapter? How does this approach relate to social construction?

5. When do we socially construct our cultural identity, according to the chapter? When don't we?

6. How do people use symbols to construct culture? Based on the chapter discussion, why do you think this process requires collaboration by others?

7. What does the chapter mean when it says that symbols are part of an expressive system?

8. If culture is situated in practices of people in place, what role does our preexisting knowledge about cultures play in this social construction? Incorporate the five hubs of meaning into your answer.

9. How is culture constructed in the three examples of cultural moments provided in the chapter?

10. When you think of culture being constructed through communication, which cultures do you think of as being constructed? Why? If culture is constructed in communication, what limit, if any, is placed on the amount or variety of cultures than can be constructed?

KEY TERMS

being-in-the-world   73

cognitive concept of culture   73

communication practice   74

Communication theory of culture   74

community   77

cultural discourse   74

cultural expressive system   80

cultural moment   82

culture-bearer   70

distinctive concept of culture   71

evaluative concept of culture   71

exclusiveness   71

generic concept of culture   71

heterogeneous culture   71

high culture   73

homogenous culture   71

lens   73

low culture   73

membering   78

part-whole nature of an expressive system   80

practices of people in place   78

social scene   77

symbolic forms   76

taken-for-granted knowledge   77

tensional force   81

REFERENCES

Bauman, Z. (1999). *Culture as praxis.* Thousand Oaks, CA: Sage.

Berry, M. (1997). Speaking culturally about personhood, motherhood and career. In I. Aaltio-Marjosola & G. Sevon (Eds.), *Gendering organization topics. Hallinnon tutkimus (Administrative Studies), 4,* 304–325.

Boromisza-Habashi, D. (2007). Freedom of expression, hate speech, and models of personhood in Hungarian political discourse. *Communication Law Review, 7,* 54–74.

Carbaugh, D. (1994). Cultural communication and intercultural encounters: Personhood, strategic action, and emotions, *Teoria Sociologica, 3,* 17–45.

Carbaugh, D. (1995). The ethnographic theory of Philipsen and Associates. In D. Cushman & B. Kovacic (Eds.), *Watershed theories of human communication* (pp. 269–297). Albany: State University of New York Press.

Carbaugh, D. (1996). *Situating selves: The communication of social identities in American scenes.* Albany: State University of New York Press.

Carbaugh, D. (2005). *Cultures in conversation.* New York: Lawrence Erlbaum.

Carbaugh, D. (2007). Cultural discourse analysis: Communication practices and intercultural encounters. *Journal of Intercultural Communication Research, 36,* 167–182.

Carbaugh, D., Boromisz-Habashi, D., & Ge, X. (2006). Dialogue in cross-cultural perspective. In N. Aalto & E. Reuter (Eds.), *Aspects of intercultural dialogue* (pp. 27–46), Koln, Germany: SAXA Verlag.

Carbaugh, D., & Wolf, K. (1999). Situating rhetoric in cultural discourses. *International and Intercultural Communication Annual, 22,* 19–30.

Fitch, K. (1997). *Speaking Relationally.* New York: Guilford Press.

Galanes, G. J., & Leeds-Hurwitz, W. (Eds.). (2009). *Socially constructing communication.* Cresskill, NJ: Hampton Press.

Geertz, C. (1983). *Local knowledge: Further essays in interpretive anthropology.* New York: Basic Books.

Giddens, A. (1993). *The transformation of intimacy: Sexuality, love and eroticism in modern societies.* Cambridge, UK: Polity Press.

Hopper, R. (2003). *Gendering talk.* East Lansing: Michigan State University Press.

Katriel, T. (2005). *Dialogic moments: From soul talks to talk radio in Israeli culture.* Detroit, MI: Wayne State University Press.

Mokros, H. (2003). *Identity matters: Communication-based explorations and explanations.* Cresskill, NJ: Hampton Press.

Morgan, E. (2003). Discourses of water: A framework for the study of environmental communication. *Applied Environmental Education and Communication, 2,* 153–159.

Morgan, E. (2007). Regional communication and sense of place surrounding the Waste Isolation Pilot Plant. In B. Taylor & W. Kinsella (Eds.). *Nuclear legacies: Communication, controversy, and the U.S. nuclear weapons complex* (pp. 109–132). Lanham, MD: Lexington Books.

Philipsen, G. (1989). Speech and the communal function in four cultures. *International and Intercultural Communication Annual, 13,* 79–92.

Philipsen, G. (1992). *Speaking culturally: Explorations in social communication.* Albany: State University of New York Press.

Poutiainen, S. (2005). Kulttuurista puhetta deittaamisesta. *Puhe ja Kieli, 25*(3), 123–136.

Scollo, M. (2005). Nonverbal ways of communicating with nature: A cross-case study. In S.L. Senecah (Ed.), *The environmental communication yearbook, Vol. 1* (pp. 227–249). Mahwah, NJ: Lawrence Erlbaum.

Townsend, R. M. (2006). Local communication studies. *Quarterly Journal of Speech, 92,* 202–222.

Wilkins, R. (2005). The optimal form: Inadequacies and excessiveness within the *asiallinen* [matter of fact] nonverbal style in public and civic settings in Finland. *Journal of Communication, 55,* 383–401.

Witteborn, S. (2007). The expression of Palestinian identity in narratives about personal experiences, *Research on Language and Social Interaction, 40,* 145–170.

Culture in Conversation

Jessica S. Robles
University of New Hampshire

Journey Through Chapter 5

Sightseeing: On your journey, you will use the social constructionist approach from a dialogic perspective to explore how culture is a construction produced through conversation in speech communities and in communication practices, such as speech acts, person referencing, and conflict.

Souvenir: After your journey, you will take away an ability to analyze how culture is communicated in conversation and understand its role in conflict.

You go to a coffee shop in a city where you have never been. You order your drink, give the cashier some money, and collect your change. You wait for your drink to be made, then take your drink and leave. As a description of getting coffee, this may seem like too much information. If you mention it at all to someone, you would probably just say, "I got coffee" or even just hold up your to-go cup. The incident is unremarkable because it went as you would expect and a lot of description would seem unnecessary.

On the other hand, an interaction in a coffee shop may feature noticeable communication differences between each person in the situation. You might use a different word for the drink you are ordering than the cashier does. You might pronounce certain words differently. Or maybe you follow different social rules for how to order drinks in a coffee shop. If such differences are unexpected, you might be more likely to remember them and share them with others. These characteristics of the interaction could indicate a cultural or intercultural situation. This is because features of talk—word choices, pronunciation, phrasing—often refer to culturally marked ways of speaking. The following section discusses some basic concepts related to cultural ways of speaking and is followed by sections on speech communities, cultural communication practices, and conflict.

INTRODUCTION TO CULTURAL WAYS OF SPEAKING

Ways of speaking are viewed as culturally marked because of the concept of indexicality. Indexicality means that one thing (e.g., communication) refers to or is associated with another thing (e.g., cultural background) (Ochs, 1990). A list of people and ideas in an index at the back of a book provides page numbers where you can look up larger explanations of the listed items. In a similar way, what people say and how people say things refer to general cultural patterns that are not explicitly referenced in a conversation. However, indexicality triggers awareness of a cultural context. Fluency in the abbreviations used in text messages and online communication indexes membership in a technologically savvy community. As another example, if you are dining in France, asking for the check long after finishing dinner is considered the norm. If a table asks for the check as soon as they are finished eating it will index a cultural background to make sense of the strange behavior. For example, the waiter might conclude the diners are U.S. Americans, who do not tend to linger after a meal. Indexicality references ways that culture seems to influence how people talk and can help people make sense of an unexpected or awkward interaction.

Knowing what people say and how they say it is useful for understanding how culture is indexed in an interaction. Consider a transcribed version of the coffee shop example in which you can see what each communicator actually said. A transcript is a verbatim typed-out version of exactly what each person said (Roberts, 2008). A transcript from an audio recording of a real coffee-shop encounter is as follows:

Customer: I'll have a latte.

Cashier: What?

Customer: Latte?

Cashier: Cafe au lait?

Customer: Latte.

Cashier: Oh, a latte.

In this instance, you have a conversation that does not seem to have proceeded as planned. This example is likely to bring up *why* questions: why, for example, did the customer have to give his order three times? As a result, it is an experience that might be noticed and even described later to others. When something is accountable, it demands an explanation (Buttny, 1993). In the coffee shop example, you may wonder why the cashier did not understand the order. The situation's strangeness demands a reason for the "problem." A cultural reason might include the dialect or way the words were pronounced. Other examples include showing up late for class. This event is accountable because you need to give a reason why; you have to explain yourself. Likewise, declining an invitation to dinner is also accountable. Why some situation happened or some action occurred is potentially attributable to any number of reasons.

In everyday life, people generally do not ask why when things go as expected. Instead, people ask why when something surprises or goes awry. During such instances, your assumptions about how "normal" interaction should occur—for example, that the cashier should appropriately hear, understand, and respond to your order—are revealed. Such assumptions are taken-for-granted in that they are assumed to be true, expected, and ordinary. You are unlikely to think about or question what is taken-for-granted unless something goes wrong. You probably take it for granted that if you text your friend a question, she will respond fairly promptly. If she does not, you may make note of it and try to make sense out of it. In the interaction and stories told about it thereafter communicators construct the meanings of and reasons for violations of taken-for-granted practices also known as breaches. Because cultural groups may share ways of communicating, "coming from different cultures" is sometimes offered as a reason for communication breaches, misunderstandings, and conflicts.

> **REFLECT 5.1:** Have you ever invoked generational identity as an explanation of someone's behavior? How? What other cultural groups have you invoked in order to explain a breach, misunderstanding, or conflict?

SPEECH COMMUNITIES

As mentioned in Chapter 4, one way of dividing up cultural communities is by ways of speaking. A speech community defines a group not strictly by ethnicity, region, religion, or other cultural markers, but by speech codes. Speech codes are patterned ways of speaking which are shared and intelligible among community members (Carbaugh, 1996; Fitch, 1994). The same speech codes do not exist everywhere because they are specific to and useful for a specific cultural context. For example, anyone who works in a restaurant—where people are hustling and bustling with trays of food—will understand why you need to give a verbal warning if you are behind someone. Why? Because if the person in front of you turns around suddenly without knowing you are there, the food could go flying! On the other hand, it would be strange to shout "behind you!" as you walk behind a coworker in a clothing store or legal office.

An important aspect of speech codes is interpersonal ideologies, which are the norms for speaking to different people, including how and under what circumstances particular codes should be employed (Fitch, 1998). Interpersonal ideologies are the logic or "reasoning" behind speech codes. They are the community's answer for why the speech code exists. Interpersonal ideologies are rules for interaction. An interpersonal ideology such as "respect your elders" may cross many cultural boundaries. But the speech code for "respect your elders" may be as varied as being polite and paying attention in the United States to following elders' romantic advice in Korea. Table 5.1 outlines examples of different codes for respecting elders in the United States and Korea (Sung, 2004).

Communities can also have different interpersonal ideologies and different codes to go along with them. In Internet blog posts by Christians and Muslims, members use U.S. religious Internet speech communities' conventional ways of speaking to perform the appropriate code which represents the values in their respective communities. Christianblog.com and TalkIslam.info are comparable blogs because both are active and occur in the same format. Each website features lists of posts by bloggers who self-generate topics, unlike other

Table 5.1   Interpersonal Ideology.

What codes are communicated in your culture to express respect for elders? In the United States and Korea, the codes are distinct. A culture might incorporate a variety of codes into their way of communicating in order to express respect to elders.

Common Codes in the U.S.	Common Codes in Korea
Display affection such as hugging.	Bow when greeting.
Ask how they are doing.	Give them material gifts.
Listen to their words.	Call them by an appropriate title of honor.

Copyright 2011 Jessica S. Robles.

websites which feature blogs in response to articles or videos or are primarily for social networking. Neither of these blog sites represents the Christian or Muslim communities broadly—rather, they are their own speech communities within the larger ones.

In the blogs on TalkIslam.info, participants often reference current events and discuss various views on Islam. They identify particular people and groups who display hostility toward Islam and frequently reference "ignorance" as a problem with other groups' opinions about Islam. The blogs cover a vast range of topics but in identifying community issues, the ignorance of outsiders is a common theme in the following quotes from TalkIslam.info:

- "European Christians allying with secularists against Islam are basically dupes. The secularists want to destroy us all. If anything, they are the common enemy against our shared values."
- "Forgive the hyperbole, but I think that to many religiously illiterate Christians today the traditions you're talking about are almost as alien and 'external' as Ramadan. Many American Christians can't even give a coherent explanation for the differences between a Catholic and a Protestant, so I'm not optimistic they can grasp pre-Reformation religious practice."
- "A lot does go to bad stereotypes by rather ignorant and aggitated [sic] folks."

In the blogs on Christianblog.com, participants focus on spiritual and philosophical discussions that are more personal or related to everyday life. They regularly draw on the ideas of belief in Christ and sinfulness as important questions for the community. The blogs are varied but when discussing problems with the Christian community, the weak Christianity of so-called Christians is a common theme:

- "An unsaved man can choose to do right and still do wrong in the eyes of God. The intent was right. The action was wrong because Christ was still rejected and there was no righteousness from God within the heart of man."
- "Are the churches of our day lukewarm? Wanting to fill seats, they worry about offending with the word of the Lord. They concern themselves with numbers, not about truth."
- "It is time we focus on Jesus Christ. Jesus Christ is the WAY, the TRUTH, and the LIFE. Without Jesus Christ, we have none of these. It is that simple."

Whereas the TalkIslam.info blog identifies community problems as coming from the outside—from "Islamophones," "secularists" and religious groups within outside Islam in general—the Christianblog.com blog identifies community problems as coming from the inside—from "lukewarm" Christians and well-intentioned people who reject Christ. Table 5.2 shows what speech codes are present in the blog posts and the interpersonal ideologies to which the speech codes are tied.

Table 5.2 Speech Codes and Interpersonal Ideologies.

How are your communication practices tied to your beliefs? In religious communities, certain ways of talking and arguing about beliefs are ways of showing faith, knowledge, and other markers of spiritual membership.

Website	Common Speech Codes	Ideological Logic
TalkIslam.info	References to Islamic practices: Ramadan, etc.	References to Islamic practices display familiarity and active participation in Islam. Posts discuss the value of such practices, particularly discipline and sacrifice as community norms. Distinctions are made between similar practices (i.e., fasting = lent) in other religions. The meaning of the "same" practice is unique to the community.
	References to Islamophobia, hate, or persecution: know nothing about Islam, vilify Islam, etc.	The fear and hate of Islam is based on ignorance. This is presented as the ultimate threat to Islam. Even among blog posters, the claim that the other does not know enough about Islam is a common challenge in arguments.
	Displays of knowledge regarding subtleties of Islam: Islam is, etc.	Displaying formulations of important Islamic values and nuances of Islamic laws outside the United States again demonstrates the problem of attacks on Islam being based in stereotypes and ignorance.
Christianblog. com	Dedication to Christ as a condition of community inclusion: only Christ can save you, etc.	Good deeds are not enough; one is a sinner if one has not "fully" accepted Christ. Someone can participate minimally in Christian practice (go to church, pray) and still be a sinner.
	Formulaic references to Christ: Christ is life, Jesus Christ is the way, Christ is love, etc.	References to Jesus Christ display that the blogger is in the category of "saved" and therefore has authority to comment on the sin of others. Conventional expressions are peppered throughout posts to emphasize the focus on Christ.
	Scripture quotations: Joshua 24.15, Romans 10, etc.	Almost every post includes quotations from Scripture. Displaying intimate knowledge of exact Biblical quotations and producing them in appropriate arguments emphasizes the closeness to God as being aligned with deep familiarity of God's words (through Christ).

Speech communities, as with any cultural category, are not homogenous. From a cultural perspective which focuses on conversation, culture is not something that people carry around, live in, or "are" in some obvious sense; rather, culture is a symbolic and material category for patterned ways of communicating (Fitch, 1998). People do not have culture, but instead display, perform, and participate in culture. Cultural participation refers to the extent to which people use particular speech codes and other communicative modes in order to display membership in socially recognizable communities. If you study abroad in Japan, you may notice some people are more traditional than others. Not everyone in Japan will bow deeply forward from the waist. Often, particularly among younger people of similar social status, a quick nod of the head and slight angling of the upper body will do (Tohyama, 1991). People choose which aspects of cultural life to take on as their own. You might participate minimally in your regional community, but actively in a religious community.

REFLECT 5.2: When was the last time you communicated your culture to someone else? How did you do this? In what way did people respond? Why do you think they responded this way?

The enactment of cultural participation in conversation is inherently dialogic (Bakhtin, 1981). This means that cultural enactments interact with, can be compared to, and exist in dialogue with other cultural enactments. A cultural enactment describes a situation where people do a cultural communication practice, such as speaking a certain language. If you speak Spanish, you speak a language that has multiple varieties all over the world. Spanish spoken in Mexico is a bit different from Spanish spoken in Spain, but Mexican Spanish is dialogic with Spain's Spanish because they can contrast with and relate to each another. In the following example of a family living in Finland, two languages are used in dialogic contrast. The choice of what language to speak and when to speak index culture.

1	Albert:	Jan had to wait til nine to start so I was just talking to Mom before
2		she had—but um Ivan has a card ((kisses Tina)) for Ivan waiting for
3		him on the computer ((sets Tina down))
4	Mina:	Will you take this to JR? ((to Tina))
5		(18 seconds deleted)
6	Tina:	((speaking in Finnish))
7	Mina:	((speaking in Finnish))
8		(2.0)
9	Tina:	speaking in Finnish =
10	Mina:	= speaking in Finnish
11	Albert:	You wanna see the email Ivan?

Transcript Notation. Researchers often use transcripts to study conversation. Symbols represent the meaning of nonverbal communication within the conversation, such as the following, adapted from Jefferson's system (Atkinson & Heritage, 1984). This system is used throughout the rest of the chapter.

=	indicates that one event followed the other with no silence
(( ))	surrounds notes on details of the interaction
__	emphasis
:	stretched or elongated sound
( )	encloses items that are in doubt
[	marks the onset and termination of simultaneous activities
°	encloses words that are quieter than surrounding talk
-	represents a short un-timed pause of less than a second
(Numbers)	denotes elapsed silence in tenths of seconds
Capitalization	indicates louder volume than surrounding talk

In this transcript, Mina is a native Finnish speaker who speaks fluent English, while Albert is a native U.S. English speaker who speaks some Finnish, and their children are bilingual in both languages. Albert has been working in the other room, but came to deliver a message about Ivan's birthday while the rest of the family eat dessert (Lines 1–3). After Tina returns from taking candy to the researcher, she initiates a conversation with her mother in Finnish (Line 6). She and her mother are both fluent English speakers, so Tina participates culturally by the action of choosing a language that indexes Finnish rather than U.S. American.

It is interesting also that rather than carrying on a side conversation in English with Ivan—which he could easily do because Tina and Mina appear to be speaking to each other exclusively—Albert instead waits for the conversation in Finnish to end before speaking in English to Ivan (Line 11). The performance of English and Finnish in the same familial context puts the two languages in contrast with each another. In this interaction, the languages of English and Finnish interact dialogically. As a result, analyzing one without the other would be incomplete.

In addition to being analyzed in an inter/cultural communication textbook, cultural enactments can also be noticed and commented on by people in the interaction in which they occur. This indicates that people are aware of and can draw upon the idea of culture to make sense of what is going on (Schegloff, 2007). In orienting to culture, conversational participants would explicitly label their own or others' practices as cultural. For instance, a person is orienting to culture if saying, "That's the American way." If you travel outside of where you grew up, the contrast between what is normal for you and the people around you will probably result in you talking about cultural differences explicitly. You might say things like "that's just how they do it in South Africa," or "I don't know how to talk to people in Cambodia." People can even use the term *culture,* rather than referencing a specific speech community explicitly, in order to orient to culture as in this example of an interview between U.S. American and Thai exchange students:

I: Was it hard to adjust to coming here?

R: Yes, at first I had some cultural problems ((laughs)).

There are a number of communication practices which demonstrate cultural variability and which discourse analysts study. Cultural communication practices are methods by which people in a conversation index and participate in cultural interaction. The next section introduces several potentially cultural communication practices.

CULTURAL COMMUNICATION PRACTICES

Accent

People use many cultural communication practices to index their participation in particular speech communities. This section discusses some ways in which talk can index culture and indicate a cultural moment in everyday life. Perhaps one of the most apparent communication practices which conversational participants notice is how talk sounds. An accent is a way of pronouncing words that is indicative of a specific speech community. Ways of pronouncing that are not consistent with how others in the speech community talk index a cultural difference. Consider another version of the transcript from the beginning of the chapter:

1   Customer: I'll have a la-tay.

2   Cashier: What?

3   Customer: La-tay?

4   Cashier: Cafay oh lait?

5   Customer: La-tay.

6   Cashier: Oh, a lah-tay.

In this version of the transcript, you can see that each speaker pronounces the trouble word, *latte,* differently. The customer is pronouncing it with a short *a*, as in the word *cat* in Lines 1, 3, and 5. The cashier does not identify the term because the cashier, as seen at the end in Line 6, pronounces latte as in the word *car.* Notice also that this struggle between the word the customer produces and the sound the cashier expects to hear causes the cashier to supply a candidate for the customer's order which is something in between—a café au lait, pronouncing *lait* with a long *a*, like the word *late.*

You can imagine that once the participants identify the pronunciation difference, they might remark on it to one another. The customer might have said, "Sorry, I've never heard it said that way" or the cashier might have said, "Where is your accent from?" or even "Where are you from?" The cashier might have at that point displayed an orientation to culture by associating the accent with a region or country, which is how most people in everyday life understand culture as in such descriptions as a *southern accent* or a *Russian accent*.

Language Selection

Language selection is an even more marked indicator of culture than accent particularly when the language differs from how others speak in the community. Language selection refers to what language a person chooses to speak at a particular moment (Tracy, 2002). Though two people may hear each other as having different accents, that both people in the conversation are speaking the U.S. English language would still include them in a larger cultural category. If a group of people are speaking Farsi in an area of mostly British English speakers, or if someone asks for directions in Korean in an area where Japanese is the dominant language, then a particular cultural identity will be indexed through this language selection. Additionally, bilingualism, multilingualism, and code switching index participation in several cultural communities (Bailey, 2000b). Code switching occurs when a person goes back and forth between languages in a single conversation as indicated in the earlier example of the Finnish-American family.

Conversational Style

In contrast to accent and language selection, a more subtle aspect of language and dialect is conversational style. Conversational style refers to aspects of directness and intonation in speech, which are ways of producing particular speech codes (Tannen, 1981). One notable stylistic difference that is visible in different speech communities involves the way in which questions are asked. Some questions may have a very direct format, such as "Do you want a biscuit?" while others are more indirect, for instance, "Would you perhaps like a biscuit?" The latter is perceived as being more polite than the former in some cultural contexts, although in others it might be viewed as too wordy. More indirect conversational style is often associated with "women's language" or a more "feminine" style (Lakoff, 1973). Intonational style refers to where tone rises and falls. In U.S. English, questions usually end with a rising tone; in British English, for many kinds of questions, the tone rises in the middle of the utterance and falls slightly at the end (Gumperz & Cook-Gumperz, 1982).

Speech Acts

Another aspect of style involves what social action individuals are trying to achieve with their talk. For example, a *question* can be completing a certain action, which is not just about seeking information. Speech acts name utterances, like those grammatically known as questions, by their social function: When someone says something, they are also doing something or making something happen (Searle, 1969). For example, in the previous paragraph, the question about the biscuit is really an offer. An offer is not just any kind of action, but an attempt to give something to another person. Asking a question is just one way of "doing" an offer. You could also "do" the offer nonverbally just by holding a tray of biscuits toward the other person. Not all questions are offers, obviously. Questions can seek information, challenge someone's opinions, or ask permission to do something. In the next example, Matt speaks to his girlfriend in the format of a question.

Matt: Do you think it's courteous to call somebody and check in on them every five minutes? I mean, don't take it the wrong way.

Matt's utterance begins with "do you think" and ends with rising intonation, indicating a question. The "do you think" at the beginning of a sentence is often a formulaic way of asking for someone's opinion rather than asking for, say, information. It could also potentially be used as a politeness marker before a request as in, "Do you think I could get one of those envelopes?" However, the function of Matt's entire utterance does not seem to be asking for an opinion, but rather challenging the other person to provide an account for the action of "calling somebody and checking in on them every 5 minutes." The fact that Matt follows up the "question" with a disclaimer ("don't take it the wrong way") shows that Matt is aware of the challenging or even face-threatening nature of his so-called question. Speech acts can be enacted across cultural groups in similar ways, such as similarities between British English and U.S. American English. Some examples of speech acts include (Searle, 1969):

- *Commissives* commit a person to a future action such as a threat or a promise.
- *Declarations* create the social reality they state such as a marriage or sentencing someone to prison.
- *Expressives* display attitudes and emotions such as thanking someone.
- *Directives* get someone to do something such as ordering or commanding.

The same speech acts can also be expressed in a different way depending on culture. For instance, in Columbia it is common to do the speech act of directing—getting someone to do something—in a direct way: "Get me a coffee" rather than "would you mind getting me a coffee?" (Fitch & Sanders, 1994). In a similar example to the one described in the previous paragraph, a Dutch speaker also demands an account for questionable behavior, but much more directly:

D: goed je gezegd, ja. maar we willen weten waarom het gebeurt iedere keer

Well you said so, yeah. But we want to know why it happens every time.

Culture-specific speech acts describe social actions (i.e., speech acts) that are particular to a speech community. For example, in Australia *chyacking* refers to playful insults ritually exchanged among friends (Wierzbicka, 1991). In Israel, *kiturim* is a ritual form of griping which is distinct from the concept of griping common to many speech communities because it can only be about publically significant problems (Katriel, 1990). Not all publically significant gripes count as kiturim, either. Table 5.3 notes the rules for when a speech act counts as kiturim.

Table 5.3   Rules for *Kiturim*.

Do you think kiturim should count as a speech act? Why or why not? Can you think of any cultural specific speech acts for the cultural group to which you belong?

Participants of Kiturim	Kiturim usually occurs face-to-face with intimates and provides a sense of solidarity. (Kiturim with less intimate people will be more topically general.)
Control of Situation	Kiturim is about events people individually cannot control.
Relationship to Problem	Kiturim cannot be too personal or directed toward someone who can solve the problem (see about)—this would transform it into "complaining."
Attitudes Toward Kiturim	Kiturim is seen as negative, as something that occurs because talking is all that can be done about the problem.
Solutions for Kiturim	Because talking is all that can be done, the alternative to kiturim is to change one's outlook (because the situation can't be changed).

A more extended speech act practice with cultural variability is how people "do" narrative or tell stories. The organization of stories and what makes them worth telling can differ (Labov, 1997), as can the sorts of stories deemed appropriate for telling. Narratives present culturally appropriate versions of the self. In the United States, telling stories about your job or your personal achievements is valued in ways that are not elsewhere (Linde, 1993) because of the importance of individualism and competition for U.S. Americans. In contrast, in Columbia, a *palanca* narrative (meaning "lever") is a story that demonstrates how a person has helped another advance professionally. The cooperation involved in the story implicates the value of community for Columbians (Fitch, 1998). Stories may have particular practices within them that are culturally specific functions too. In Estonian stories, the word *see,* similar in meaning to the English *this,* functions as a filler which can also request collaboration from the listener, as in the following example in which the listener supplies the sought-after word (Keevallik, 2010):

M: a koige tahtsam on see

   but most important is this

L: ajalugu

   history

M: e jah

   yeah

Another important aspect of conversation with cultural implications is how interaction unfolds. In many dialects of U.S. English, people engage in turn-taking in which they go back-and-forth quickly in conversation, literally take turns talking. U.S. English-style turn-taking overwhelmingly includes quick speaker changes and little overlapping speech (Sacks, Schegloff & Jefferson, 1974). A typical example of minimal overlap is reproduced as follows:

1 Claire: [Uh]

2 Chloe: [Well] Then it was her fault [Claire].

3 Claire: [Yeah] She said no one trump.

In other speech communities within and outside of the United States, however, longer pauses may occur between speakers with more or less than the expected overlap (Philips, 1990). In a study comparing U.S. English speakers and Spanish speakers, Berry (1994) offered many examples in Spanish such as the following, which looks quite different from the previous example with Claire and Chloe:

1 Marisa: si of un reportaje de horas end la televi[sion].

2 Paula: [si] pero

3 Marisa: y han y han encontrado agendas con direcciones [de los].

4 Paula: [pero Ma]risa

5 Marisa: [de los]

6 Paula: [eso]

7 Marisa: pisos

8 Paula: sabes como funciona ETA? [funciona a]si

9 Marisa: [(muffled)]

10 Emi: [uando unos bajos otros suben y]

10 Paula: [(muffled) en piramide. Exacto. [O sea]

11 Marisa: [yeah]

12 Paula: [cogen a los tres]

11 Emi: [(muffled) o sea]

12 Paula: gordos e inmediata-.

Although there are cultural differences in conversation, most of the basic interactional principles in human communication appear to be cross-cultural. Almost all speech, in any context, displays progressivity. **Progressivity** is a progression or advancement toward completing certain conversational actions. If Person A invites Person B to a party, Person B will be obliged to accept or decline the invitation—regardless of Person B's answer, how long B takes to provide it, or in what format the speech act is produced. In an example of intercultural front desk encounters at a university-sponsored English language program, Kidwell (2000) demonstrates how the progressivity inherent in interaction—the way in which what people say sets up what should come next to advance the action—moves the conversation forward so that the students can complete their business:

Example 1   S: aHhaaii.

R: Hi.

S: I want to talk to you I need

Example 2   R: Hhaai.

S: Uh can I:: (.) copy this here

Example 3   R: Hi.

S: Hi. I have a question.

In each of these examples, a greeting is followed by an opening of interactional business by including a speech act which quickly identifies that the student has something which the receptionist can potentially help including, respectively, a request for documents, a request to make copies, and a question about a class change. Although the interactions are intercultural, the institutional setting and the progressivity of interaction provide a common ground so that what you see is a similarity rather than difference.

Linguistic choices are a quickly identifiable cultural indexical. Linguistic choices refer to differences in words people use. Different words can mean the same thing, such as *sidewalk* in U.S. English and *pavement* in British English. The same words or phrases can also mean different things, such as *knocked up* which means "knocked at the door" or "went to visit" in British English and "got pregnant" in U.S. English. The words people use and the way they are pronounced can indicate someone's speech community such as the various words for a flavored fizzy beverage (*soda, soda pop, pop, cola*). Apparently, even U.S. English Twitter posts show regional variation. Californians write *koo* or *coo* for "cool." New Yorkers write *suttin* for "something." Southerners write *y'all* for "all of you" (Yates, 2011).

Person Referencing

Person referencing refers to different terms for referencing and addressing people, including forms of address, honorifics, and membership categorization devices. Forms of address, or ways of calling and referring to people, can also be culturally distinct. The difference between *mom* and *mum* in U.S. and British English is not a difference of accent. Instead, they are two different words that refer to the same relationship. Honorifics are another way of calling people. Honorifics are titles or other terms which reference status. For example, you might say Dave or Professor Brown in English or use an informal *tú* or a formal *usted* for *you* in Spanish. Forms of address such as nicknames, too, can be culturally specific, such as calling someone *sweetie* in U.S. English, *mi amor* (my love) in Columbian Spanish, *love* or *ducks* in British English, or *zolotce* (treasure) in Russian.

People's actual names also have cultural implications (Carbaugh, 1996). Names common in one speech community may be less common or nonexistent in another. As such and not surprisingly, names index culture. Someone called Jane is more likely to speak English than Portuguese, and versions of Jane such as *Jana* and *Juana* will often be expected to be attributable to Russian and Spanish speakers, respectively. The way in which names index culture is so strong, in fact, that people who intend to live outside their home speech community will often change their name to one more common in their new community. In many East Asian communities where English is taught as a second language, teachers provide students with "English" names, so that someone named Xie (pronounced Zee) might also be called Steve (Hsu, 2009). In the past in the United States, people often "Americanized" their last names, shortening them (Bobanova to Boban) or altering them more dramatically (Cyman to Seaman, Przystawski to Preston, etc.). The famous martial artist and actor Jet Li was born Li Lianjie.

How people select names when they marry can also index culture. In some communities it is traditional for a wife to take the husband's last name, whereas in others the last names are combined (Carbaugh, 1996). Though the former is still dominant in U.S. American culture, other options are becoming viable. Furthermore, the assumption behind who-takes-whose-name is likely to become less obvious over time as same-sex marriages becomes more commonplace including legalization in New York and Washington in recent years.

REFLECT 5.3: Given that person referencing indexes culture, how might it be used to insult or offend someone? How would you handle a situation in which someone uses a person reference that makes you feel uncomfortable?

Membership Categorization Devices

Another cultural communication practice strongly linked to person referencing is the membership categorization device. Membership categorization devices are ways of referencing people that put them into assumed categories (Sacks, 1992). For example, referring to someone as so-and-so's brother categorizes that person on the basis of family relationships. Membership categorization can also label people by assumed cultural categories. Race, ethnicity, and nationality are common colloquial and legal categories based on purported features such as skin color, customs, language, birthplace, and citizenship. Regions and nations are common ways of culturally categorizing members of speech communities.

Membership categorization devices indicate what sort of differences people have decided should matter and, as such, membership categorization devices are social constructions. Eye color is not a common basis of categorizing people into groups, while hair color is slightly more salient. For example, there is a proliferation of stereotypes in U.S. American culture about blondes but not people with hazel eyes. Skin color, accent, and language are differences that have come to "stand out" to people, though these too are variable. In a diverse city like San Francisco, encountering someone with an accent may not, by itself be as remarkable as it would be elsewhere.

Not all culturally marked differences are explicitly attributed as reasons for an interactional event. Some distinctions are marked in language without any explanation, possibly without any awareness on the part of the speaker. Markedness is another, more implicit way of doing membership categorization. Markedness refers to ways in which people add to what they are saying in order to demonstrate that something is atypical. Referring to a male nurse, for example, adds the word *male* to *nurse* and displays the assumption that men are not usually nurses. This "marks" the nurse off as being unusual without the speaker ever having to say anything like "and you don't often see male nurses!" Simply by marking nurse with male, the speaker categorizes certain occupations based on gender expectations within the culture. The category of nurse in this case assumes that the membership will consist of females.

Mentioning any cultural category does some form of marking work and indicates implicitly what is taken-for-granted in the speaker's expectations about people, actions, and identities. For example, telling a story about a student's achievements and adding that she was blind indicates a cultural expectation about what categories of student are expected to excel. You would be unlikely to refer to someone's daughter as Chinese if you considered the daughter's parents Chinese. Similarly, saying *adopted daughter* indicates that most people in a *daughter* category are assumed to be biologically related (Suter, 2008).

Membership categorization indicates a stance toward the cultural category being referenced. A stance displays what is assumed to be a speaker's opinion, belief, or attitude (Ochs, 1993). "Unusualness" is just one stance which can demonstrate taken-for-granted assumptions. Speakers can also indicate interpersonal ideologies, social norms, and moralities. Naming a person's cultural category in a story about a disreputable act can explicitly provide a cultural category as a reason for the act, as well as link that category of person with the "bad" category of act. In this example, a reference to the category *Mexican* comes across as negative.

1   Christa: We could sell them at a yard sale (1.8) at the flea market you know Mexicans

2   Love that ki oh.

3   (3.0)

4   Valerie: No comment.

In this instance, Valerie and Christa have been discussing making paper maché globes in elementary school, and Christa jokingly suggests they could make paper maché globes before launching into her suggestion that they make the globes, and then attempt to sell them. By marking out Mexicans as being the sort of people who would buy a paper maché globe at a flea market, Christa implies a negative stereotype of Mexicans as either cheap or not being fashionable because flea markets are places where people can purchase cheaply out of date items. Valerie's reaction of "no comment" implies that Christa's comment is negative and worthy of some disapproval, perhaps because Valerie's boyfriend is from Mexico.

Take a Side Trip:

If you would like to read more about related issues, visit Appendix B: Local Culture Explored Through Discourse Analysis.

LIVING CULTURE

Let's Have the Men Clean Up

The following is a transcript of a Thanksgiving dinner. At any time there are two or three women in the dining room in which the video camera is placed. In an adjoining room, out of view of the camera, several men and one woman are watching football.

1		(3.0)
2	Laura:	ALRIGHT ((Laura's left hand motions to get Brenda's attention
3		simultaneously turning her head toward Brenda then Caren))
4		(1.0)
5	Laura:	°Let's see what the men's reaction will be°
6	Laura:	((Looks forward to living room)) Okay let's let- let's
7		have ((Leans forward)) the men clean up
8	Laura:	[((Leans back))
9		[(1.3) [
10	Brenda:	[((Looks up briefly towards living room, then to
11		Laura, then leaves the room with two handfuls of crumpled
12		napkins and other garbage from the table))
13	Laura:	It's the Y chromosome they don't hear it ((Shakes head))=
14	Laura:	((Leans forward)) =Who wants cheesecake?=
15	Laura:	=See ((leans back, looks at Caren, and gestures with right hand
16		palm up to Caren as if to say "I told you so"))
17	Caren:	((laughs))
18	Tom:	Right here you didn't ( )
19	Laura:	[((Laughs))
20	Caren	[((Laughs))
21	Laura:	It is the Y chromosome ((Nods head))=
22	Laura:	= ((Turns head to camera behind her)) I hope this test is
23		recorded=
24	Laura:	[((Turns head forward))
25	Caren:	[((Puts her feet on the chair in front of her))
26	Laura:	[(0.7)

LIVING CULTURE

27	Laura:	So <u>years</u> from now in a <u>biology class</u> they will <u>see</u>:
28		the difference
29		between the y chromosomes=
30	Laura:	= ((Leans forward)) Who wants to clean u:p. ((Leans
31		back))
32	Laura:	((Shakes head and makes palm up gesture similar to lines
33		15-16))
34	Brenda:	((Returns to dining room and continues cleaning table))
35		(2.5)
36	( ):	Laura˙ ask ( ) [not helping
37	(Caren):	Honey? [°Could you help me.°
38	Laura:	((Leans forward)) Alright the men are cleaning up
39	Laura:	[((Looks at Caren and makes palm-up gesture similar to
40		previous))
41	Brenda:	[((Looks up quickly toward living room))
42	(Fran):	(They) can't hear the games [too loud.
43	Laura:	[( ) Gets a beatin
44	Brenda:	((Quickly lifts head to look at living room))
45		(2.5)
46	Laura:	((Leans forward)) WHO WANTS CHEESECAKE?
47	Brenda:	((Quickly lifts head to look at living room))
48		(1.0)
49	Brenda:	[((Laughs as she walks out of the room with crumpled
50		napkins))
51	Laura:	[((Laughs, looks at Caren and makes same gesture from
52		15-16))
53	Caren:	[((Laughs, looks at Laura, lifts left hand palm down to Laura))
54	(Tom):	I do right here I say it every time you guys say it.
55	(Laura):	(theory)
56	Laura:	((Laura gets up)) All I know is the same theory is th- through
57		the Stone Age °is the same°

(Continued)

LIVING CULTURE

(Continued)

58		(0.7)
59	Caren:	OKAY you guys ((Claps her hands)) help clean up please
60		(2.0) ((Caren rocks the chair in front of her with her feet))
61	Laura:	((Looks to living room, then Caren))
62	Laura:	Kay ((gestures with both hands palms up and elbows bent then
63		starts cleaning))
64		(2.0)
65	Laura:	((Turns to living room)) ANYBODY WANT SOME ANDES
66		MINT
67	(Tom):	No thanks.
68	Laura:	((Looks at Caren, smiles and shakes head, and gestures
69		with both
70		hands palms up and elbows bent))
71	Caren:	((Laughs))
72		(4.0)
73	Caren:	((Gets up and clears her plate and Laura's from the table))

Consider:

1. What are the people in this interaction doing? What are some cultural ways of speaking used in this conversation?

2. What membership categorization device(s) is invoked in the conversation? How?

3. How is Laura, with the collaboration of others in the interaction, constructing gender norms through communication? For example, consider Laura's use of the phrase "the men" rather than "those watching football," which would also include the woman in that room.

4. Based on evidence from the transcript, who is cleaning? How does this compare to the gender assignment discussed in the conversation? Why is this comparison interesting?

CULTURE AND CONFLICT

Inter/cultural conflict is often invoked in conversation as a problem of communication error or misunderstanding. Even research studies of intercultural conflict across the communication field have tended to analyze conflict as the result of misunderstanding due to cultural difference (Jacquemet, 1999). This section focuses on intercultural conflict, though much of what is said about conflict between speech communities may be said of conflict within them. After all, assuming sharedness and homogeneity within speech communities is problematic because studies also note conflicts and controversies among people who are seemingly of the same cultural background (Boromisza-Habashi, 2010).

The origins of discourse analytic cultural research from such areas as ethnography of speaking and interactional sociolinguistics were deeply concerned with intercultural misunderstandings. Negative attributions made by speakers of cultural others were attributed to misidentifications of the meanings associated with different ways of speaking. For example, features of speech such as style and intonation were blamed for conflicts between British English and West Indian communities in England. The intonation pattern in the accent of West Indian English was perceived as rude from the perspective of the British English speakers, who expected a different intonation pattern, which for them sounded more polite. Similarly, when West Indian and British English research participants were asked to judge examples of one another's speech, each had a negative interpretation of the speakers' identities (Gumperz & Cook-Gumperz, 1982). Although West Indian evaluators had a positive interpretation of West Indian speakers as saying what they mean, they viewed British English speakers as being indirect and condescending. British English evaluators expressed a similar negative bias toward West Indian speakers referring to their behavior as somewhat rude, although they viewed the behavior of fellow British English speakers as calm and accurate.

Explanations of intercultural conflict as miscommunication assume that if speakers knew the different meanings of the speech codes in different speech communities, fewer conflicts would occur. This has long been an assumption of many perspectives on gender difference as well, presuming that if men and women learned what the ways of speaking mean for each other, and not just from their own perspectives, they would get along better (see Tannen, 1982). These perspectives, although not necessarily inaccurate all the time, have been challenged by critical scholars. Another explanation for gender conflict, for instance, is that men and women's assumptions about each other's roles and abilities lead them to interpret one another's communication negatively. Thus, rather than conflict arising out of misunderstanding, conflict arises out of a struggle over a person's place in society. In the example of a husband at the dinner table asking his wife "do you have any ketchup, Vera?" Cameron (1998) explains that the husband's utterance is an indirect way of asking Vera to get the ketchup and that Vera understands and complies with this "request" because, traditionally, women are assumed to know more about the ins-and-outs of the kitchen than men. If Vera were to ask her husband for ketchup in the same way, he would not necessarily hear the question, which sounds information seeking, as a request. In the potential ensuing conflict, Vera might be blamed for not having been direct enough in asking for the ketchup when in actuality it is not her indirectness that was the problem, but her gender role.

REFLECT 5.4: Do you agree that fewer conflicts would occur if speakers knew the different meanings of the speech codes in different speech communities? Why or why not?

Although intercultural conflict can occur due to misunderstanding, intercultural conflict also occurs because conversational participants choose to interpret one another negatively as a way of negotiating social status and enacting group boundaries. When interactions do not go as expected, there are multiple ways of deciding reasons for why this occurred. By attributing conflict to culture, participants construct cultural difference as problematic.

Bailey (2000a) provides an example of intercultural conflict in the context of immigrant Korean retailers and African American customers in Los Angeles. Amidst the backdrop of local concerns about these two groups in light of riots and shootings, Bailey analyzes how everyday interactions in convenience stores construct and reenact conflict by performing cultural difference. He first looks at the potential differences in Korean and African American communication behaviors. He articulates that Koreans value quietness and restraint and view service encounters as simple transactions, while African Americans value enthusiasm and friendliness and view service encounters as social occasions. He then interviews members of each group and finds that each person describes the others' communications as lacking in respect.

Rather than stopping there and attributing the conflict to misunderstanding, Bailey (2000a) analyzes video of actual interactions between the groups and finds that their communication exhibits divergence. Consistently, neither the Korean cashier nor the African American customer adjusts their communication style to accommodate the other's:

1	Cashier:	Two fifty ((rings up purchase and bags beer)) ((4.5))
2	Customer:	I just moved in the area. I talked to you the other day. You
3		[remember me]?
4	Cashier:	[Oh yesterday] last night.
5	Customer:	Yeah.
6	Cashier:	[(O:h yeah.)] ((Cashier smiles and nods.))
7	Customer:	[Goddamn, shit.] [Then you don't.]
8	Owner:	[New neighbor, huh?]
		((Customer turns halfway to the side toward the owner.))
9	Customer:	Then you don't know me.
10	Cashier:	[(I know you.)] ((gets change at register.))
11	Customer:	[I want you to know] me so when I walk in here you'll know me. I smoke
12		Winstons. Your son knows me.

As shown in this example, the African American's communication becomes more interpersonal and assertive, while the Korean's communication remains business focused. The Korean cashier gives no recognition of the African American customer, who pursues recognition (Line 2) and displays anger (Line 7) when the cashier's recognition is minimally given and perhaps not provided to the customer's expectation. The fact that the customer continues to accuse the cashier of not knowing him despite the cashier saying he does know the customer indicates that saying so is not enough. In this example, the conflict is not merely a misunderstanding. Bailey (2000a) points out that these groups have been interacting long enough to know each other's speech codes. Instead, this example demonstrates an emphasis on cultural differences and a persistence in judging those differences negatively.

Conflict markers are the communication practices employed during conflict and when talking about conflict that indicate serious interactional troubles. Conflict markers can include metadiscursive terms (e.g., descriptions such as *fight, quarrel, argument*), expletives and slurs, speech acts (e.g., threats), aggressive emotional displays (e.g., puffing up, physically indicating violence, going red in the face, shouting), and divergence (e.g., communicating in increasingly differentiated ways). In inter/cultural interactions, conflict markers may be culturally marked as well, involving explicit orientations to culture (e.g., using racial slurs) or implicit cultural communication practices (e.g., raising one's voice).

In the coffee shop example, for instance, there appears to be little or no evidence of a conflict. In fact, the possibility of a simple misunderstanding seems a reasonable explanation. The conversation could be indicative of a conflict with the inclusion of conflict markers in the transcript.

1	Customer:	I'll have a la-tay.
2	Cashier:	What?
3	Customer:	La-tay?
4		(1.5)
5	Cashier:	Cafay oh lait?
6	Customer:	LA-TAY
7	Cashier:	Oh, a lah-tay ((looking down)).

In this version of the transcript, you can see there is a long pause in Line 4. Though not necessarily indicative of conflict, long pauses in conversation can indicate minor troubles because, as was mentioned in an earlier section, most speaker exchanges in English-speaking contexts are rapid. The shout (Line 6) could be a conflict marker and the withdrawal of gaze (Line 7) could be intended as dismissive. Alone, however, these features are not enough to label this as *intercultural* conflict.

There is, however, a suggestive divergence present. The difference between *la-tay* and *lah-tay* seems easily surmountable because it is a small pronunciation difference. Yet, you'll notice that the cashier does not supply many guesses to what the customer is saying. Additionally, the customer makes no attempt to explain, pronounce differently, or otherwise assist the cashier with understanding the order. Instead, the customer merely repeats the word. It is also notable that after the interaction, nothing more is said. Neither person comments on the interaction and the transaction is not accompanied by the usual *thank you* or *you're welcome* phrases that are common to U.S. service encounters.

Although people are quick, at times, to assume that cultural differences are at the root of a conflict, as you can see there is still little evidence in this conversation to make such a claim. However, repeated enactment of this type of conflict would provide more substantive evidence for this type of claim. Imagine that the cashier is U.S. born of Indian parents and speaks

U.S. English; the customer is a White British English speaker. The coffee shop is in the United States and this sort of interaction regularly occurs between Indian American cashiers and British English customers. What if, in interviews with various cashiers and customers, each discussed the other as disrespectful? Then it would be a parallel to the case of Korean immigrant retailers and African American customers analyzed by Bailey (2000a). If that were the case, then this small conversation would quite likely demonstrate intercultural conflict. Despite this hypothetical possibility, this instance is the only one that exists.

Intercultural awareness is an important step in living in a diverse society, but it is not the only salve for the destructive potential of intercultural conflict. If awareness and education were all that were required, culturally diverse regions would be more harmonious. Instead, it often seems, the more different speech communities in contact with one another, the more marked the conflict. Communication is always a delicate interactional dance with another person. Because there are multiple goals in discourse, conversational choices are fraught with potential missteps. Interactional dilemmas refer to conversational choices, which, by serving one aim, directly compete with an equally desirable ideal (Tracy & Ashcraft, 2001). In intercultural communication, interactional dilemmas are especially apparent. Being culturally sensitive may solve some of the problems of ignorance, but assuming cultural differences can be equally problematic.

FINAL THOUGHTS

Conversation is the most common way of communicating culture. In the countless interactions you have in a day—stopping for coffee, texting your friend, e-mailing a professor, arguing with your roommate about the dishes—you communicate your participation in cultural communities. Just the sound of your voice and the way you say a single word can tell people a lot about your speech community. When you interact with your own speech communities, you tend not to notice the cultural elements of what you are doing. In contrast, speech community differences seem to stand out in intercultural interaction.

Intercultural communication and its challenges are common. And yet, they remain some of the most difficult interactions you might have. Being able to "hear" through a different accent or understand an unusual word choice is a skill requiring some exposure and training. Communication skills training alone cannot prepare communicators for all of the difficulties they might face from moment to moment when communicating interculturally. People must be willing to confront and examine their own taken-for-granted assumptions about what is normal even in the most basic of situations.

CONTINUE YOUR JOURNEY ONLINE

Visit: http://nixon.archives.gov/forresearchers/find/tapes/watergate/trial/transcripts.php

Watergate Trial Conversations at the Nixon Presidential Library and Museum website. Learn about U.S. American history and international affairs through these transcripts and audio files. Apply the concepts from the chapter to these primary sources of inter/cultural communication.

SAY WHAT?

Say What? provides excerpts from overheard real-life conversations in which people have communicated stereotypes. As you read these conversations, reflect on the following questions.

- Have you been in conversations like this before?
- Is there any one of these conversations that stick out to you more than the others?
- What do you think of this conversation?
- How did the stereotype help or hinder the conversation?
- Was there another way the stereotyper could have communicated to convey the same point?
- How do you feel when you hear this conversation or the specific stereotype?
- Do any of these conversations bother you more than others? Why or why not?
- Do any concepts, issues, or theories discussed in the chapter help explain why?

- **Say What?** When Tom told me his major was engineering, I responded by saying, "So you spend a lot of time doing work?" He told me that he has a lot of studying to do every night, and I asked if he had a lot of time to go out on weekends. He responded by saying that he always found time to have fun even though he had a full workload. Through this brief interaction, I expressed my preconceived notions about engineers and Tom responded in such a way that told me he knew that I was under the impression of a stereotype and that he had encountered this before.

- **Say What?** At Christmas dinner, a family member, continuing an otherwise innocuous conversation topic, said, "Yeah, well those immigrants don't even know how to speak English." My girlfriend's grandmother, who after 30 years of living in America still spoke broken English, agreed. I noted the irony but chose not to comment.

- **Say What?** The other day in one of my classes, I was having a conversation with my friend Joanne. She began to tell me how she thought I was a "snotty sorority girl" and perceived me as a bitch when we first met. I was very taken back by this and got noticeably offended. I could tell Joanne felt bad when she saw my reaction because she immediately tried to redeem herself. She went on saying that her opinion completely changed once she had met me and realized that she was putting me into a category of the typical sorority girl.

- **Say What?** At lunch one day, our lunch group was talking about some music award show. At one point, one of my colleagues was trying to pinpoint the name of a rapper. My supervisor turns to us and says, "Lisa must know who he is; she's all into that ghetto stuff." Prior to that, my supervisor never once asked what kind of music I listened to. He assumed because I'm Puerto Rican that I know everything about the urban/hip-hop world. I stayed quiet for a second, then started laughing and said, "What makes you think I know everything about hip-hop?" To this he responded hesitantly, "I don't know, just thought you would." I then told them I didn't know the answer and we all went on with our lunch.

REVIEW QUESTIONS

1. When was the last time you felt you had to give an explanation for something? Using the chapter content, explain why you were accountable in the situation? Did you feel the other person accepted your reasons?

2. What speech codes exist in your community? Who uses them and in what situations? According to the chapter, why might an outsider have trouble interpreting these?

3. What examples does the chapter provide of conversational style? What aspects of your conversational style indicate your cultural membership?

4. What situations do you think you would be more direct in? What about less direct? How does style of speaking relate to chapter concepts?

5. What are speech acts according to the chapter? What speech acts are present in your community?

6. If you think of a recent story you've heard from a friend or family member, what do you remember about it? What community values could it have been portraying? How do stories communicate culture according to the chapter?

7. Have you ever been in situations when you had a hard time getting a turn to talk? How, if at all, does the chapter help to explain why this happened? If you were in a conversation where others were having that difficulty, how could you get them participating without making it obvious?

8. How would you react if someone called you (or referred to you by) an unexpected name or term? Why do you think you would have that reaction? What are some of the dangers of membership categorization? Incorporate chapter concepts in your answer.

9. Have you ever had a conversation that felt "derailed" or awkward? Has it ever occurred in an intercultural encounter? Why did you think the conversation went that way at the time? Can you think of other potential explanations now that you have read this chapter?

10. Have you ever been in, witnessed, or heard a story about an intercultural conflict? What happened? What concepts from the chapter played a role, if at all?

KEY TERMS

accent   96

accountable   90

breach   91

code switching   97

conflict marker   109

conversational style   97

cultural enactment   94

cultural participation   94

cultural perspective   94

culture-specific speech
    act   98

dialogic   94

form of address   101

honorific   101

indexicality   90

interactional
    dilemma   110

interpersonal ideology   91

language selection   97

markedness   103

membership categorization
    device   102

narrative   99

orienting to
    culture   95

person referencing   101

progressivity   100

speech act   97

speech code   91

speech community   91

stance   103

transcript   90

turn-taking   99

REFERENCES

Atkinson, J. M., & Heritage, J. (Eds). (1984). *Structures of social action: Studies in conversation analysis.* Cambridge, UK: Cambridge University Press.

Bailey, B. (2000a). Communicative behavior and conflict between African-American customers and immigrant Korean retailers in Los Angeles. *Discourse and Society, 11,* 86–108.

Bailey, B. (2000b). Dominican American ethnic/racial identities and United States social categories. *International Migration Review, 35,* 677–708.

Bakhtin, M. M. (1981). *The dialogic imagination.* Austin: University of Texas Press.

Berry, A. (1994). Spanish and American turn-taking styles: A comparative study. *Pragmatics and Language Learning, 5,* 180–190.

Boromisza-Habashi, D. (2010) How are political concepts "essentially" contested? *Language & Communication, 30,* 276–284.

Buttny, R. (1993). *Social accountability in communication.* London: Sage.

Cameron, D. (1998). 'Is there any ketchup, Vera?' Gender, power and pragmatics. *Discourse & Society, 9,* 437–455.

Carbaugh, D. (1996). *Situating selves: The communication of social identities in American scenes.* Albany: State University of New York Press.

Carbaugh, D., Berry, M., & Nurmikari-Berry, M. (2006). Coding personhood through cultural terms and practices: Silence and quietude as a Finnish "natural way of being."*Journal of Language and Social Psychology, 25,* 1–18.

Craig, R. T. (2006). Communication as a practice. In G. J. Shepherd, J. St. John, & T. Striphas (Eds.), *Communication as . . . : Perspectives on theory* (pp. 38–47). Thousand Oaks, CA: Sage.

Fitch, K. (1994). Culture, ideology, and interpersonal communication research. In S. Deetz (Ed.), *Communication Yearbook* 17 (pp.104–135). Beverly Hills, CA: Sage.

Fitch, K. (1998). *Speaking relationally: Culture, communication and interpersonal connection.* New York: Guilford Press.

Fitch, K., & Sanders, R. (1994). Culture, communication, and preferences for directness inexpression of directives. *Communication Theory, 4,* 219–245.

Gumperz, J. J., & Cook-Gumperz, J. (1982). Interethnic communication in committee negotiations. In J. J. Gumperz (Ed.), *Language and social identity* (pp. 145–162). Cambridge, UK: Cambridge University Press.

Hsu, H. (2009, April 27). My name's Du Xiao Hua, but call me Steve: What's up with Chinese people having English names? *Slate.* Retrieved from http://www.slate.com/id/2217001

Jacquemet, M. (1999). Conflict. *Journal of Linguistic Anthropology, 9,* 42–45.

Katriel, T. (1990). 'Griping' as a verbal ritual in some Israeli discourse. In D. Carbaugh (Ed.), *Cultural communication and intercultural contact* (pp. 99–114). Hillsdale, NJ: Lawrence Erlbaum.

Kidwell, M. (2000). Common ground in cross-cultural communication: Sequential and institutional contexts in front desk service encounters. *Issues in Applied Linguistics, 11,* 17–37.

Keevallik, L. (2010). The interactional profile of a placeholder: The Estonian demonstrative *see.* In N. Amirdze, B. H. Davis, & M. Maclagan (Eds.), *Fillers, pauses and placeholders* (pp. 139–172). Amsterdam: John Benjamins Publishing Company.

Labov, W. (1997). Some further steps in narrative analysis. *Journal of Narrative and Life History, 7,* 395–415.

Lakoff, R. (1973). Language and woman's place. *Language in Society, 2,* 45–80.

Linde, C. (1993). *Life stories: The creation of coherence.* New York: Oxford University Press.

Ochs, E. (1990). Indexicality and socialization. In J. W. Stigler, R. A. Shweder, & G. Herdt (Eds.), *Cultural psychology: Essays on comparative human development* (pp. 287–308). Cambridge, UK: Cambridge University Press.

Ochs, E. (1993). Constructing social identity: A language socialization perspective. *Research on Language and Social Interaction, 26,* 287–306.

Philips, S. U. (1990). Some sources of cultural variability in the regulation of talk. In D. Carbaugh (Ed.), *Cultural communication and intercultural contact* (pp. 329–344). Mahwah, NJ: Lawrence Erlbaum.

Roberts, F. (2008). Transcribing and transcription. In W. Donsbach (Ed.), *International encyclopedia of communication* (Vol. XI, pp. 5161–5165). Oxford, UK & Malden, MA: Wiley-Blackwell.

Sacks, H. (1992). *Lectures on conversation* (2 Vols., G. Jefferson, Ed.). Cambridge, MA: Blackwell.

Sacks, H., Schegloff, E. A., & Jefferson, G. (1974). A simplest systematic for the organization of turn taking for conversation. *Language, 50,* 696–735.

Schegloff, E. A. (2007). *Sequence organization in interaction: A primer in conversation analysis.* Cambridge, UK: Cambridge University Press.

Searle, J. (1969). *Speech acts.* Cambridge, UK: Cambridge University Press.

Sung, J. (2004). Elder respect among young adults: A cross-cultural study of Americans and Koreans. *Journal of Aging Studies, 2,* 215–230.

Suter, E. A. (2008). Discursive negotiation of family identity: A study of U.S. families with adopted children from China. *Journal of Family Communication, 8,* 126–147.

Tannen, D. (1981). Indirectness in discourse: Ethnicity in conversational style. *Discourse Processes, 4,* 221–228.

Tannen, D. (1982). Ethnic style in male-female conversation. In J. J. Gumperz (Ed.), *Language and social identity* (pp. 217–231). Cambridge, UK: Cambridge University Press.

Tohyama, Y. (1991). Aspects of Japanese nonverbal behavior in relation to traditional culture. In Y. Ikegami (Ed.), *The empire of signs: Semiotic essays on Japanese culture* (pp. 181–218). Amsterdam: John Benjamins Publishing Company.

Tracy, K. (2002). *Everyday talk: Building and reflecting identities.* New York: Guilford.

Tracy, K., & Ashcraft, S. (2001). Crafting policies about controversial values: How wording disputes manage a group dilemma. *Journal of Applied Communication Research, 29,* 297–316.

Wierzbicka, A. (1991). *Cross-cultural pragmatics: The semantics of human interaction.* Berlin: Mouton de Gruyter.

Yates, J. C. (2011, January 11). Twitter full of regional "accents," study finds. *Huffington Post.* Retrieved from http://www.huffingtonpost.com/2011/01/11/twitter-full-of-regional-_n_807284.html

PART II
Distinguishing Self and Other

Self-Identity and Culture

Ronald L. Jackson II
University of Illinois at Urbana-Champaign

Cerise L. Glenn
The University of North Carolina at Greensboro

Kesha Morant Williams
Penn State Berks

Journey Through Chapter 6

Sightseeing: On your journey, you will visit concepts related to identity and culture, learn about the development of self-identity, and explore three theories of identity negotiation. Here you will find a unique integration of social scientific and social construction approaches that, respectively, view culture as a representation that impacts self-identity as well as a construction that creates self-identity.

Souvenir: After your journey, you will better understand how identity is negotiated through communication with others within a cultural context.

Understanding self-identity is important to inter/cultural communication because as you learn who you are, you learn how to communicate effectively with others. People often assume their cultural identities are "normal" and universal because they are largely developed and defined in group settings with people of similar cultural norms and values. People begin to "see" culture when they begin to interact with others who do not share their same beliefs and behaviors. These alternate cultural identities can often be regarded as different in ways that seem "abnormal" because they are not the same behaviors you learned. Understanding how you learn to define and communicate your sense of self is critical to promoting understanding of your own and other cultural identities. In order to better understand how self-identity is relevant to inter/cultural communication, this chapter introduces the concept of identity and related terms, discusses how identity is developed, and explores three theories that describe ways in which identity is negotiated with others.

IDENTITY

Identity, introduced in Chapter 3, is a broad-based term people use to characterize their sense of self. Examining self-identity, how you develop and communicate your sense of who you are to others, helps you answer the "Who am I?" question many people struggle to understand especially as they grow and mature from a child to adult. Inter/cultural communication scholars study how people construct and communicate their sense of self to others by incorporating the *how* and *why* questions into inquiries of identity. Further, you can understand these processes as manifestations of culture in that they are sets of beliefs and behaviors of particular groups. Although culture has traditionally been defined by characteristics such as race, ethnicity, and nationality, inter/cultural communication scholars also address other aspects of cultural identity, such as gender and religion.

As you learn more about cultural identities, you learn that some aspects of who you are remain more salient than others, some seem more universal, and others seem different or even strange at times. So then how does culture impact and shape your sense of self? How do you learn what is expected and normal? How do you negotiate those aspects of your self that deviate from these norms? Understanding these questions often causes people to interrogate how they understand their own cultures, how they behave and communicate their identities, how cultural contexts impact their personal belief systems, how this affects their relationships, and various other issues that arise as they learn who they are and how to interact with others in their daily lives.

REFLECT 6.1: Have you ever traced your behavior to your cultural identity? What motivated you to do this? What did you find out? How did this impact your understanding of who you are?

The Role of Place and Space

In a philosophical sense, a person can explore identity by thinking of physical, metaphysical, mental, and discursive spaces and places. Places are physical, concrete, and tangible locations. These can be contrasted with spaces, which are metaphorical, elusive, intangible, or analogous psychological locations that frame a person's understanding of preferences surrounding closeness and distance. Both spaces and places in which people live help to define

Photo 6.1 What does your place of worship look like, if you have one? Belief systems are integral to self-identity.

Copyright 2010 Bill Edwards and Michael Kurylo.

who they are. Places are physically bound and may vary from the local barbershop to city hall to the classroom, the cinema, and beyond. Most people cultivate their understanding of place at an early age within their homes. Perhaps your home is the first place you ever remember knowing. As you grew, places such as school or a place of religious worship gained importance in your life. The significance of place for identity is often connected to the memories or cultural understandings that are attached to the place rather than the place itself.

While places are physical locations, spaces are psychological locations that frame understanding of preferences surrounding closeness and distance. Norms for space are developed through understanding of cultural knowledge. Although there are general accepted norms within specific cultures, there is variation of norms between cultures, families, and people. For example, people from contact cultures, such as South America or the Middle East, tend to need less personal space and touch during interaction; whereas, people from noncontact cultures, such as Great Britain and Japan, maintain more space and touch less frequently during interaction (Anderson, Hecht, Hoobler, & Smallwood, 2002). Regardless of their properties, spaces have a tremendous influence on how people think about their identity psychologically and socially. If you think about yourself, for example, as a citizen of your country, it is easy to see how both spaces and places impact identities.

People tend to only really think about their identities when they are in crisis or when they are displaced or moved from where people believe they belong. For a teenager or emerging adult, one crisis might involve the first day of high school. For an adult, a crisis might happen after the death of an aging loved one when a person's mortality and age are suddenly questioned all at once. Moreover, a person visiting or living in a different cultural context for the first time may feel out of place and experience culture shock. Culture shock is the discomfort you might feel because of unfamiliarity with environmental cues. These are all examples of identities in crisis and have been studied by psychologists, sociologists, and communication scholars as a means of trying to grapple with questions of self-identity. These questions are often ones that suggest that identities can be harmed, so they must be protected.

The Role of the Other

Perhaps the most fundamental lesson in all of this is that none of these things take place in a vacuum. They are all facilitated through communication with others. Anticolonialism scholar Frantz Fanon (1967) wrote in his famous treatise *Black Skin White Masks,* "To speak is to exist for the other" (p. 17). That means that the socially constructed discourse you use to communicate is bound by an I-Other dialectic explaining that how you view yourself is heavily influenced by how you view others and how they view you. These are intertwined in the core elements of self-identity: self, self-esteem, and self-consciousness.

When someone is treated as the *I* in an I-Other dialectic the individual is permitted agency or allowed the authority to define, name, or affect his or her identity within any given communication encounter. When someone is treated as *other*, the individual is being acted upon and controls little to nothing in the communication encounter. An example of this is the debacle involving Henry Louis Gates's arrest at his home. His neighbor mistakenly identified him as a burglar attempting to break into his own home and called the police. Gates attributed his mistreatment to racism on the part of the arresting officers who refused to let him immediately identify himself as the homeowner. In this case he felt *othered*. That is, he felt he was not permitted to define himself as an interactant with equal footing or equal authority to express himself. Instead, the officers seized legitimate authority over him. Hence, Gates was treated as *other* while the officer was the *I* in that I-Other dialectic. This example demonstrates what happens at a microlevel, but as you might imagine this becomes much more complex when dealing with national sovereignties or other collectives as identified via race, religion, gender, or class such as in the sociopolitical aftermath of Hurricane Katrina.

The self has historically been understood as a stable, core set of identities within a person that comprise that person's system for thinking and behaving. The self is inextricably linked to the mind, and yet it is not a contained unit unaffected by the social world (Coover & Murphy, 2000). The stability of the self is in some ways individuated, but in other ways influenced by society. Cognitive theorists have suggested that the mind develops its own feedback loops that automate activity based on parts of a person's identity that are most salient. When that loop is overloaded, overstressed, or interrupted, a person experiences an identity crisis and, at the extreme, perhaps a mental breakdown. So, the mind seeks to maintain congruence with social norms so that it does not experience such a crisis.

Social actors are constantly responding to the world around them. This is the foundation for self-esteem. Self-esteem refers to how people value themselves. Social and environmental cues facilitate self-appraisals. In order to feel good about your self, identity negotiations become standard as people try to reconcile the salience of their identities with the significance of those identities in the social context. To have a healthy self-esteem a person must also have a high sense of self-worth. The two go hand in hand and enable personal growth.

Another factor in personal growth is self-consciousness, which is defined as a general awareness of one's self in society. Self-consciousness also traverses dimensions of culture such as worldview, beliefs, ideals, and knowledge. Out of self-consciousness emerges a concern for categorization, labeling, typecasting, and prejudices. As mentioned earlier, people often understand their self-identities through cultural norms and beliefs. When people become aware of who they are in larger societal contexts, they organize their social identities to make connections with people and separate themselves from others. For instance, a Christian may categorize her sense of self with other Christians by using this label to refer to her system of religious beliefs. When others use this same label, it creates a sense of connection and belonging. A person with a high level of self-consciousness will be acutely aware of how others feel, and if the person has a high self-esteem will develop adaptive and protective mechanisms in defense of being psychologically harmed by the effects of categorization. A person with low self-consciousness may have an equal concern for protecting the self, but will likely be unable to do so due to being unaware of how the self is understood within any given context.

Developing a high self-consciousness is more easily done if a person perceives the capacity or ability to alter the circumstances. This is known as self-efficacy. People with higher self-efficacy believe they have the ability to perform well and master certain tasks. Those with lower self-efficacy may not think they can perform as well or avoid certain tasks. Consider academic performance, for example. Students with higher self-efficacy will believe they can do well in class and aim to earn an A or a B. Those with lower self-efficacy may view the A or B as unattainable and will aim for a C instead.

Self, self-esteem, and self-consciousness are three terms that are useful for understanding the nature and function of self-identity. Anthropologist Martin Sokefield (1999) maintains that the concepts of self and identity have shifted significantly since the 1960s. He argues that the old way of describing identity was as "a disposition of basic personality features acquired mostly during childhood and, once integrated, more or less fixed. This identity made a human being a person and acting individual. Inconsistency of personality . . . was regarded as disturbance or even psychic illness" (p. 417). With that prior definition, anyone with an identity conflict was essentially characterized as psychologically ill. However, the definition of identity has since expanded and so has identity research in general.

Inter/cultural communication scholars have paid special attention to how self-identity is constructed through creating shared meanings with others. For example, people learn

Photo 6.2 Is there a photograph like this in your family album? Identity is shaped in part by cultural similarities with parents and grandparents. However, because of generational identities you are also from different cultures than your parents and grandparents in many ways too.

Copyright 2010 Anastacia Kurylo.

at an early age to distinguish themselves from others. Your sense of self, however, is not constructed in isolation. It is heavily dependent on your interactions with others around you. This starts with basic practices, such as developing language skills and the practice of naming objects and ideas. For instance, one of the ways you begin to learn who you are is with the names your parents give you. You hear your parents, as well as other close relatives and family friends, address you by your names and over time you learn to identify your sense of self with that name and use it to identify yourself as a distinct individual when you interact with others. In addition to exploring the social construction of self, communication scholars have examined the complexities of developing cultural identities and how there are numerous aspects of self-identity that must be understood as dynamic negotiated communicative processes. Aspects of each of these important elements of identity are elucidated in this chapter through the discussions of theoretical advancements addressing the development, management, and negotiation of social identities.

THE DEVELOPMENT OF SELF-IDENTITY

In order to understand how you develop your self-identity, you must first understand how you arrive at your sense of reality and learn about who you are through communicative processes. The work of George Herbert Mead became known as symbolic interactionism. He based his ideas upon the notion that people socially construct reality.

Mead's Theory of Symbolic Interactionism

Symbolic interactionism is derived from the field of social psychology and explicates how people make sense of the world in their everyday interactions. This theory explains how people learn cultural norms and values, as well as create their sense of self, through these interactions. Theoretical tenets of symbolic interactionism assert that people do not construct their understanding of themselves and the world in isolation; rather they understand themselves and others through intersubjective interaction (Mead, 1934; Singleman, 1972) that produces shared meaning. Knowledge varies from person to person because individuals do not necessarily share the same experiences or the same meanings for these experiences. Reality, therefore, is dependent on interactions with others and is co-created through those interactions. For example, if you wanted to move out of state and change your name, you might be able to do so as long as you were able to be consistent with referring to yourself as that name with others you meet. If, however, you wanted to remain in your current environment and change your name, it would be more difficult because there is already a shared meaning that would need the participation of others in order to be changed.

In order to function as individuals and, yet, live in cohesive societies, people must create a shared system of understanding through the use of symbols. Language functions as a system of symbols with shared meaning. The English term *housecat,* for example, represents a small, furry, four-legged, domesticated animal that purrs. People who speak English learn that the term housecat is a symbolic representation of this particular thing. People who use other linguistic systems will use a different symbol to refer to that same thing, such as *gato* in Spanish. People learn and use language to create shared systems of meaning. Through interacting with others who speak that same language, whether the official language of the country or not, as shown in Figure 6.1, people learn what symbols represent particular things. Thus, people learn how to understand and communicate their ideas to others through the process of symbolic interactionism during which people agree that certain words represent particular objects and ideas.

People communicate with each other effectively through these shared meanings and understandings of particular symbols. Through the use of symbols and direct interaction, people

> ### Take a Side Trip:
>
> If you would like to read more about related issues, visit Appendix C: Dagaaba Culture of Ghana Explored Through Rhetorical Analysis.

also learn who they are due to the way the others respond to them (Mead, 1934). Mead labels a person's sense of individual identity as *the self*. He explains, "The self is something which has a development; it is not initially there, at birth, but arises in the process of social experience and activity that is, develops in the given individual as a result of his relations to that process as a whole and to other individuals within that process" (Mead, p.135).

Mead believes that the self possesses a high level of consciousness, which gives people the ability to self-reflect as they interact with others. Similar to Charles Cooley's notion

Figure 6.1 Countries With Official Languages.

Does anything in this pie chart surprise you? A nation's use of an official language or languages sends a message about its cultural identity and how it views cultural diversity.

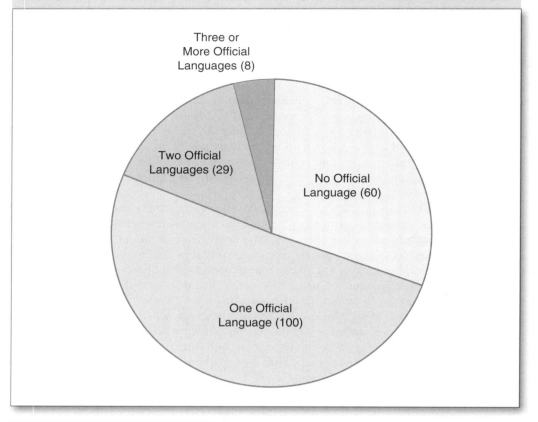

Source: Adapted from "Languages by Country" by InfoPlease. Available at www.infoplease.com/ipa/A0855611.html. Copyright 2010 Anastacia Kurylo.

of looking glass self, which asserts that people learn who they are by the image that is projected unto them by others, Mead (1934) asserts that people construct their self-identity based upon the perceptions of others. Each person has the ability to reflect upon self from a figurative distance in order to view self as an object. This ability to create distance allows people to internalize the perspective of others based on interaction, primarily in the form of language and dialogue, in an organized social environment (Mead, 1934). As this process occurs, people develop an idea of who they are by looking at themselves through the lens of how they think others perceive them. Mead terms this process the generalized other.

The Wedding Night

by Ida Craddock (1857–1902)

Yet there is a more solemn moment to follow. It comes when the last kisses of mother and girl-friends have been given, and the last grain of rice has been thrown upon the newly wedded pair, and the last hack driver and hotel or railway porter have been gotten rid of, and the key is turned in the bedroom door and the blinds drawn, and the young girl, who has never been alone in a locked room with a man in all her life, suddenly finds herself, as though in a dream, delivered over by her own innocent and pure affection into the power of a man, to be used at his will and pleasure. She, who has never bared more than her throat and shoulders and arms to the world, now finds that her whole body, especially those parts which she has all her life been taught it was immodest to fail to keep covered, are no longer to be her own private property; she must share their privacy with this man.

Fortunate indeed is the bride whose lover at such a moment is a gentleman in every fibre of his being.

For there is a wrong way and there is a right way to pass the wedding night.

In the majority of cases, no genital union at all should be attempted, or even suggested, upon that night. To the average young girl, virtuously brought up, the experience of sharing her bedroom with a man is sufficient of a shock to her previous maidenly habits, without adding to her nervousness by insisting upon the close intimacies of genital contact. And, incredible as it may sound to the average man, she is usually altogether without the sexual experience which every boy acquires in his dream-life. The average, typical girl does not have erotic dreams. In many cases, too, through the prudishness of parents—a prudishness which is positively criminal—she is not even told beforehand that genital union will be required of her. I once talked with a young married woman, the daughter of a physician, well educated, and moving in cultured society, who had been allowed to marry at the age of 20, in entire ignorance of this. She remarked to me: "I think the relation of husband and wife is something horrid. I knew, of course, before I married, that married people had children; but I supposed that God sent them babies, and that that was all there was about it. I was never told about the physical relation." Her husband was so lacking in self-control as to make her pregnant on her wedding night.

Consider:

Can you imagine experiencing this on your wedding night, if you get married? Even something as personal as our expectations of what will happen on our wedding night is culturally produced. If this seems outlandish, consider your reaction to this excerpt from *The Wedding Night*. Although this might seem old fashioned to you, her book was controversial in its time. Ida Craddock was arrested and sentenced to jail time for being so blunt.

Enculturation and Acculturation

Communication scholars often refer to the process of developing individual identities as enculturation. Enculturation refers to the manner in which people first learn who they are through their interactions with people in their native cultural groups, such as family members, friends, and others in their communities. During this time, people learn about cultural values and norms and begin to develop their sense of identity and their conceptions of the world around them. As they age and expand their social networks (e.g., through attending school), people expand their conceptions of the worlds they inhabit. People continually adjust their sense of self through these interactions, with some aspects of their sense of self being reinforced and others being challenged. The process of learning and adapting to others who are not in a shared cultural group is referred to as acculturation. For example, oftentimes when studying abroad students adopt a second culture by embracing and having continuous first-hand contact with the people and environment where they are immersed. Through acculturation the students become a part of, rather than observers of, their new environment.

The process of enculturation is crucial to the development of self. It allows people to understand who they are as they interact with members of their native cultural groups by helping them each form a unique sense of identity while they also learn to understand what members of these groups expect from them. Mead (1934) theorizes that the self, therefore, consists of two parts: the *me* and the *I*. The me comprises the part of the self that instructs a person how to interact with others in daily encounters. Therefore, the *me* is dependent on the environment. The *I*, on the other hand, remains the same at all times in that it is not manipulated or shifted by outside influences. The *I* comprises the other part of the self that is not regulated by the *me*, which causes it to be more spontaneous in nature. Unlike the *me*, the *I* is not influenced by the perception of others which makes it more rebellious. The self, therefore, consists of negotiations between *I* and the *me*.

People learn to adjust their notions of self based on the new social roles they take on as they grow older and interact with new people. Mead (1934) asserts that a person's relationship with certain groups determines which part of that person's self will be used in specific dialogic encounters. Mead explains, "We carry on a whole series of different relationships to different people. We are one thing to one man and another thing to another . . . We divide ourselves up in all sorts of different selves with reference to our acquaintances" (p. 142). These new situations cause people to adjust and redefine themselves (Blumer, 1969). The ability to create shared systems of meaning and internalize the perceptions of others allows organized social interactions to occur (Mead, 1934). Based on Mead's arguments, people perceive their self-identity differently depending upon the nature of dialogue and interaction they have with various groups. This process becomes more complicated as people interact with more and more people in their daily lives. Self-identity, therefore, is never cemented, but constantly changes or is challenged as people expose themselves to more people and shape ideas about their sense of self.

REFLECT 6.2: What aspects of your self-identity change as you interact with others in different settings? Why?

Sources of Identity

Your cultural identity is a reflection of how your social and cultural groups influence your thoughts and behaviors. Cultural identities are made up of connections with and acceptance into a group that has shared symbols, meanings and, norms for conduct. Cultural identities encompass all types of identities (e.g., gender identity, sexual identity, age identity, and race and ethnicity identities) associated with social and cultural groups. The social scientific perspective, introduced in Chapter 1, posits that all people have an individualized identity (independence and self-reliance), a familial identity (interdependence with others) and a spiritual identity (connectedness to others and power outside of one's self) (Martin & Nakayama, 2010). Roland (1988) asserts that these three identities are present in each person. However, how these three identities develop and emerge is dependent on culture. For example, in many Eastern countries familial and spiritual identity are more significant than individualized identity, while in many Western countries individualized identities surpass familial and spiritual identity.

Because identity is cultural, it is not only a part of ourselves, but is also a part of a societal social hierarchy. For example, in the United States, heterosexual identity and Christian religious identity are majority identities because they are representative of dominant groups in society. Dominant groups are composed of people in society with greater power, privileges, and social status. Homosexuality identity and Islamic religious identities are minority identities (Peek, 2005; Rodriguez & Ouellette, 2000) because they represent those without power, privilege, or social status and are, therefore, not representative of dominant groups in society.

The importance of an identity changes depending on the situation and the value placed on that identity in the numerous social roles people play in their daily lives. Although a person may be an employee, student, parent, child, athlete, a Japanese person, a librarian, a talk-show caller, and a volunteer, the value of each role is dependent on the situational context. If you are at work, it may not matter much that you are also someone's child; however, when interacting with your parents, it is your role as an employee that becomes less significant (Castells, 2009).

The role that someone ascribes to you versus the role that you give to yourself is not always the same. Cultural identities are endorsed, discussed, disputed, or reinforced through avowal and ascription. Avowal is the process by which individuals portray themselves, whereas ascription is the process by which others attribute identities to them (Martin & Nakayama, 2010). For example, you may view yourself as a mature young adult who is successfully progressing through college, while your parents may view you as their inexperienced child who is in need of guidance. While you avow your identity as mature and independent, your parents ascribe you an inexperienced and dependent identity. Over time, people acquire new roles and eliminate existing roles through communication with other people.

THEORIES OF IDENTITY NEGOTIATION

With so many sources of identity, the question then becomes how do people manage these multiple sets of 'me' and the layers of their identity? How do people negotiate their identities when others ascribe conflicted roles to them? Three models of identity management recognize the significance of communication, power, and social construction of identities: cultural contracts theory, identity management theory, and the communication theory of identity.

Cultural Contracts Theory

Cultural contracts theory (CCT), developed by Ronald Jackson (2003), is one model used to explain how avowals and ascriptions can result in various conditions under which identity conflicts must be managed. Contracts are sets of expectations. Interestingly, Jackson developed this theory while purchasing his first home. He discovered a home contract is a lot like the figurative contracts people sign every day in interaction with others. There is a set of clear expectations (e.g., courtesy behaviors, norms of reciprocity) and then there is the small print (e.g., hidden rules, presumptions, anticipations) that may contribute not only to communication failure but also to how one defines one's self in any given encounter.

The CCT maintains that as people negotiate identities they are also agreeing to figuratively "sign" one or more contracts. For example, imagine an interracial couple from two different religious backgrounds. One may pray before a meal and one may not. One may want to celebrate certain rites of passage for their children and another may not. Due to these differences in belief, this couple will need to coordinate meanings and they will need to figure out how to respect each other's identities. The CCT basically suggests that people tend to negotiate their identities within and outside of the groups to which they belong. This identity negotiation, for example, can manifest itself in terms of basic code switching behavior, such as when a teenager talks one way to his parents or teachers, but changes his tone and vocabulary when talking to friends, oftentimes incorporating the use of slang or colloquial expressions in the latter.

The theory outlines three different contract types: (1) ready-to-sign, (2) quasi-completed, and (3) co-created contracts. The ready-to-sign contract is essentially one that suggests assimilation. It is as though another person has a contract in her pocket and when she encounters different values, norms, or beliefs, the expectation is that this conflict is best resolved by the other party "signing" or agreeing to the ready to sign contract. This contract is potentially the most problematic unless both parties agree to a homogenous way of doing things.

REFLECT 6.3: Which type of contract seems most appropriate for you and which most unusual? How might the characteristics of your culture, for example, the cultural dimensions discussed in Chapter 2, explain this?

The quasi-completed contract is most well aligned with what is known as accommodation. This implies a temporary adjustment of behavior. It may also mean that a part of a person's identity is accepted while another is rejected or not appreciated. This happens all the time in the workplace. For example, it is possible that a person's race or gender is appreciated at times, but when there appears to be an over-identification with one's culture, problems may arise. One example of this is when a Catholic middle school kid in New York City decided to come to school one day with "locks," or dreadlocks. The principal and teachers were astonished and demanded that the child go home and change this hairstyle by the next day or else he would be expelled. The school administrator argued that this hairstyle was not in keeping with the school dress and appearance code. The parents argued that this was a clear rejection of the child's culture. Unfortunately, because the school ultimately decided to stand by its policy, the parents disenrolled the child. This is a prime example of a quasi-completed contract, which basically says, "I accept you up until a point."

The final contract is the co-created contract. This one seems perfect on the surface. It allows for a peaceful, harmonious acceptance and appreciation for all identities. This is because when all parties co-create their set of expectations, it facilitates a more valuable relationship. Of course, all contracts have small print. So, it is important that even these fine details are revealed in this co-creative process.

The CCT helps to explain what happens when people have misalignments with others in terms of their beliefs, values, or norms. There are also other models of identity management relevant to inter/cultural communication, such as the identity management theory and communication theory of identity.

Identity Management Theory

Identity management theory (IMT) asserts that in addition to cultural identities, relational identities are your most significant identities. Relational identities — in which the *we,* not *I* or *you,* is emphasized—are privately shared systems of understanding between those involved in the relationship. Therefore, relational identity "arises out of communication and becomes an increasingly central influence on individual partners' ways of knowing, being and acting in relation to each other and the outside world" (Wood, 1982, p. 75). Identity management theory contends that people must be able to manage and negotiate these identities competently. Those who do not understand the relational or cultural identities are, in this context, unable to communicate competently (Cupach & Imahori, 1993).

Identity management theory also addresses the issue of face. As discussed in Chapter 2, face is your positively valued social identity. The term *face* is associated with a person's prestige, honor, or reputation. The identity management of face is face-work, which is how people protect or regain a face that has been lost or damaged (Imahori & Cupach, 2005) due to face-threats or face-attacks. For example, explore two friends in conflict. Evelyn secretly knows she is wrong; however, the negative response she received from Samuel and the embarrassment she felt after admitting errors in past conflict with Samuel has left her leery to accept the blame. In this example, the negative response and the past responses Evelyn received from Samuel are an example of attacking-face. Evelyn refusing to admit she is wrong is an example of saving-face because she is trying to protect her face from being looked at negatively. Evelyn may be more likely to admit her errors if Samuel used a giving-face approach, the support of another person's identity. In this example, face-giving would be Samuel making a purposeful effort to support Evelyn through positive language and action. Giving-face is often used to counter attacking-face.

REFLECT 6.4: Has anyone tried to impose an identity on you that you were not comfortable with? How did you communicate in a way that attempted to negotiate a different identity? Were you successful?

The practical application of identity management theory is found in examples such as the vernacular use of language and collective harmony. These are discussed in the following two paragraphs. In both cases, the messages have communal and cultural significance that is understood by those that ascribe to a specific cultural identity. In addition, group members must understand shared symbols and means as well as the norms for behavior. People who are not a part of this culture may misunderstand what is being communicated.

Vernacular language is usually described as a native or indigenous language that is not of a standardized variety. The vernacular is a language of comfort—a language used to express solidarity between people of the same ethnic or cultural heritage. The vernacular is the plain variety of language used within comfortable environments. The vernacular is based on a set of rules that a person is only familiarized with through everyday life experience (Hecht, Jackson, & Ribeau, 2003; Holmes, 2002; Smitherman, 2000; Winford, 2003). Winford (2003) explains, "You aren't sat down and taught the 'rules' of vernacular speech. It is through exposure and experimentation, that one learns the conventional and systematic ways of pronouncing, modifying, and combining words that are characteristic of their community's language variety (or varieties)" (p. 93).

Collective harmony is demonstrated when the needs of the group are more significant than the needs of the individual. This is expressed through verbal communication, such as call and response, humor and banter, vernacular use of language, and a desire to share in the struggles and successes of community members. The desire to share of self and material possessions is inherent in collectivist cultural identities. A sense of interconnectedness, inter-relatedness, sharing, and interdependence are central unifying concepts of these identities (Asante, 2003; Hecht, Collier, & Ribeau, 1993; Hecht, Jackson, & Ribeau, 2003).

The following excerpt from an urban radio program provides an example and explication of African American Vernacular English (AAVE) and collective harmony's connection to identity. A radio host asks a guest about complacency and issues affecting the African American community.

Well see I mean first of all that's ludicrous but see something got to get stirred up or the stuff in the pot gonna keep stankin' (laughs) the same way it's been stankin.' See people kill me when you they get scared to stir up stuff. If you don't stir it up it stays the same. It gets stuck on the bottom.

This example of AAVE highlights that vernacular language is comprised of much more than pronunciation and word choice, but also includes elements like metaphor and style. In addition, it supports the need for collective harmony and understanding amongst the group.

In relationship to collective harmony, the speaker suggests that in order for the Black community to move forward, the needs of the group must be more significant than the needs of the individual. Stirring the pot of greens (referenced in the full source) is a metaphor for engaging and motivating the Black community. The speaker's stirring of the pot example was referencing a recent court case in which many people believed defendants were treated unfairly. When the speaker asks listeners to "stir the pot," he is asking them to respond even if the issue does not directly affect them. The speaker uses the oral tradition in an interactive and narrative form by couching a significant message within a creative analogy. Those without this cultural history (e.g., interlocutor) may walk away believing the speaker literally means people should stir the greens so that they will not get burned and begin to smell badly. In the excerpt, harmony is expressed through this vernacular use of language and a desire to share in the struggles of community members.

The identity management theory contends that to communicate competently, relational and cultural identities must be understood. This idea is supported through this example. IMT scholars also assert that an interlocutor (e.g., a person outside of the cultural group) may attempt to enter the group but must learn how to communicate competently within this intercultural situation (Imahori & Cupach, 2005). Identity management theory asserts that there are three phases people must encounter within intercultural interpersonal relationships. The intercultural dyad must first stumble or be willing to make mistakes as they search for similarities within their identities. Next, the pair must develop their own contextual relational identities; and finally they must use their new relational identities to negotiate their distinctive cultural identities.

LIVING CULTURE

The Dilemma of Nationalism in Pakistan *Satarupa Dasgupta*

Princeton, New Jersey, United States

Construction of identity is always a complex task in this age of globalization. Imagine being torn between two identities—a global one and a national one, and both being equally important to you. Such a dilemma of identity construction is rocking the Islamic world. Being Indian and South Asian, I was curious how such identity construction manifests itself in our neighboring Islamic state, Pakistan. In Pakistan, the global identity centers around the *ummah*, which is an imagined collective body of faithful Muslim. The *ummah* is a transnational community of Islam that is not confined by geographical boundaries (Al-Ahsan, 2002). The *ummah* directly challenges the idea of national, ethnic, and cultural allegiances (Castells, 2004). The resulting identity negotiation between global and national forms can be seen in letters to the editor published between 2002 and 2008 of *Dawn,* the oldest and the most widely circulated English newspaper in Pakistan. I undertook a key word search and content analysis of relevant letters focusing on the idea of the *ummah* to explore how identity is negotiated.

Some of the letters point out the importance of the *ummah* over a national identity. Others note that a global Muslim identity is less important than nationalistic, ethnic, and cultural leanings.

(Continued)

LIVING CULTURE

(Continued)

Voices in Favor of the Ummah

I found that the description of the *ummah* in these letters often highlights the *Quranic* idea of a borderless state inhabited by pious Muslims and governed by Islamic law. "'*Ummah*' thus carries universal relevance . . . no Muslim has precedence over the other either on the basis of color, caste or social status" (Aleem, 2005, para. 11). In this way, Muslim identity supersedes all other potentially competing identities. Some letters highlight the relative importance of an Islamic community over nationalism. "The bottomline that determines a Muslim's attitude and behavior is his or her strength of faith in God. If it is as strong as it should be or used to be in the past, then Islam provides a far better bonding than culture or other factors ever can" (Aleem, 2005, para. 11). Thus, the conflicting relationship between nationhood and religion is noted. In many letters that spoke about the ummah, global Islamic fraternity displaces national identity.

Voices Speaking for the Nation

Some letter-writers do not think that the *ummah* is more important than national or ethnic identities. These note that the collective Islamic identity of the *ummah* is broken by linguistic, cultural, social, and national divisions. "In Pakistan, most Muslims (85% and more) are neither from one ethnic stock nor do they speak one language . . . religion also cannot cement one Muslim with the other, because in between is culture, which is a stronger adhesive than religion" (Yunus, 2005, para. 11). I found that these letter-writers tend to connect nationalism with modernity and multiculturalism in a global society. As one writer notes, "Today socially, ethnically and temperately there is a wide difference between a North African Muslim and a West African or a Mid-Eastern or an Afghan or an Indian Muslim"; consequently the solidarity promised by a global Islamic confraternity can be viewed as "elusive" at best (Haider, 2003, para. 24). With these letters I did not notice any effort to differentiate between the sacred and the secular or an attempt to explore the relationship between the *ummah* and nationalism in conflicting terms. Rather, according to these letter-writers, it is nationalism along with ethnic, linguistic, and cultural allegiances that help to shape identity negotiation in the Islamic *ummah*.

Islamic Identity Versus National Identity

It seems that the pursuit of identity creation through the discourses of religion and nationalism is part of a complex process that results in opposing

LIVING CULTURE

viewpoints in the Pakistani populace. The following remark of Malik (1999) offers a relevant observation:

> In the more recent years, Islamic elites, seeing more prospects for globalization of the Islamic community, have discovered a new vigor in their ideal for *ummah* but have concurrently resigned themselves to the reality of nation-states. However, there is no denying the fact that the state in the contemporary Muslim world has been transformed into an ideological battleground for various polarized groups. (p. 6)

References

Al-Ahsan, A. (1992). *Ummah or nation? Identity crisis in contemporary Muslim society.* Leicester, UK: The Islamic Foundation.

Aleem, A. (2005, August 17). Defining the ummah. *Dawn (letters to the editor).* Retrieved from http://www.dawn.com/2005/08/17/letted.htm

Castells, M. (2004). *The power of identity* (3rd ed.). Malden, MA: Blackwell.

Haider, M. (2003, Jan. 28). *Iraq crisis and Pakistan. Dawn (letters to the editor).* Retrieved from http://www.dawn.com/2003/01/28/letted.htm

Malik, I. H. (1999). *Islam, nationalism and the West.* Oxford, UK: St. Anthony's College.

Yunus, K. K. (2005, August 6). Defining ummah. *Dawn (letters to the editor).* Retrieved from http://www.dawn.com/2005/08/06/letted.htm#2

Consider:

1. What is the identity conflict discussed here?

2. How does history play a role in this identity conflict?

3. Why is spiritual belief such an important part of self-identity?

4. What feeling does this narrative evoke from you? Why? What does that response have to do with your own self-identity?

The Communication Theory of Identity

So far you have learned how you shape your self-identities through relating to others. The communication theory of identity (CTI) specifically examines how *communication* shapes and reflects identity. Instead of focusing on cognition, CTI foregrounds the communicative nature of self-identity and the social identities people enact when they interact with others. The communication theory of identity asserts that identity is a dynamic phenomenon; however, it cannot be separated from communication. Communication impacts the formation, maintenance, and modification of identity. It also serves as a process for externalizing identity (Hecht, 1993; Hecht, Jackson, & Ribeau, 2003). Through social interactions with others, people develop multiple and shifting identities. According to Hecht, Jackson, and Ribeau (2003), CTI contains nine basic assumptions as follows:

1. Identities have individual, enacted, relational, and communal properties.
2. Identities are both enduring and changing.
3. Identities are negotiable.
4. Identities are affective, cognitive, behavioral, and spiritual.
5. Identities have both content and relationship levels of interpretation.
6. Identities involve both subjective and ascribed meanings.
7. Identities are codes that are expressed in conversations and define membership in communities.
8. Identities have semantic properties that are expressed in core symbols, meanings, and labels.
9. Identities prescribe modes of appropriate and effective communication. (p. 235)

As the first assumption states, interconnected layers comprise identity: (1) individual, (2) enacted, (3) relational, and (4) communal. The individual layer refers to the intrapersonal identity a person possesses, consisting of self-concept and self-image. The earlier discussion of self-esteem and self-efficacy explains other aspects of intrapersonal identity. The self, in turn, becomes enacted and expressed through communication exchanges with others. The enacted layer consists of the ways in which you decide both consciously and unconsciously, to project your identities to others when you interact with them. You enact your identity in ways that project the image of your sense of self (either as you really are or in ways that you hope others perceive you to be) when you communicate. Social roles also shape identity. In the relational layer, identity is produced and negotiated throughout communication in relationships (Hecht, 1993). For example, a person's identity as a mother or father is shaped through communication with a spouse or children. Members of a group share a sense of identity in the communal layer; therefore, identities emerge out of networks and groups.

Each layer of identity reflects a locus for your identity, which at times reinforces and at other times contradicts one or more layers. In this way, the majority of the assumptions (1, 2, 4, 5, 6, 7, and 9) of CTI describe dialectical tensions. Goodall and Goodall (2002) describe dialectics as the "interaction of two opposing arguments or forces" (p. 181). Assumptions 2 through 6 explain how efforts to reconcile or negotiate these tensions with regard to identities, often referred to as identity negotiation, result in issues such as stress and fragmentation. Fragmentation occurs when aspects of your social identities do not feel integrated with others, contributing to feelings of distance and alienation. Identity negotiation becomes a complicated and dynamic process due to "the competing forces in society that push and pull individuals toward a variety of identities" (Hecht, Jackson, & Ribeau, 2003, p. 66). Jung and Hecht (2004) describe how at times these identities can cohere, resulting in interpenetration; yet at other times they can contradict, which causes identity gaps that people are forced to reconcile or they experience fragmented identities.

Assumptions 7 and 8 reflect aspects of symbolic interactionism that explain how people use symbols and language to create shared systems of meaning. CTI elaborates by explaining how these processes are inherently communicative. Therefore, identity does not merely reside in the language codes people create; it becomes enacted as it is expressed through communicative exchanges, such as conversations, with others. The last assumption describes how efforts to shape identity result in normative and effective ways to communicate to others. People learn appropriate ways to refer to aspects of their social identities to gain a desired response. For example, parents talking to their teenager may use the term *young adult* instead of *child* to reflect that teenager's transition to adulthood, which comes with more mature behavior and responsibilities. As you can tell, the multiple sets of *me* and the layers of identity can foster confusion and difficulty maintaining your sense of self-identity. Simultaneously, these allow your sense of self to continue to grow and develop. The communication theory of identity provides a useful frame for understanding the complexities of self-identity in various cultural contexts discussed in this chapter.

FINAL THOUGHTS

Although the concept of identity may seem to be something that is developed individually, research supports that a person's multiple identities are shaped and influenced by society in general as well as by those with whom that person interacts. Nakayama (2000) poses an important question about identity when he asks, "Who am I perceived to be when I communicate with others?" (p. 14). This quote emphasizes that although people may avow a certain identity, those that surround them may ascribe a very different identity. It also challenges people to address whose interpretation of identity "wins." For example, as mentioned in Chapter 1, when you talk to your parents you are in your daughter or son identity. In this context, the daughter or son identity wins over your student or teacher identities. This however is a relatively simplistic example. How do you address issues of self-identity in more complicated situations? In *Why Am I Who I Am?* Ferdman (2000) explores a series of questions on this issue.

> How do I make sense of and give coherence to the paths my life has taken? What cultural and historical interpretations do I give these paths, so as to see myself as a social and cultural being connected to (or in some cases disconnected from) human collectives defined in terms of ethnicity, nationality, gender, race, profession, and other such dimensions of social identity? These are especially important and engaging questions in a world in which more and more of us confound and defy systems of social classification and are constantly crossing and often blurring cultural boundaries. (p. 19)

Ferdman's (2000) passage supports the assertion that your self-identity does not fit neatly into a box. It also alludes to your responsibility to consider the multiplicity of a person's identity during communication interactions. If you presume that effective communication occurs when the message sent is the message received, how do you rectify the influence of assumptions about physical appearance, religious affiliation, culturally identifying names, and other identifying features that influence your communication? To rectify these assumptions, people embrace and effectively employ the tenets of intercultural communication competence discussed in Chapter 3. First, you must acknowledge that your histories shape the way you send and receive messages as well as your assumptions about those affiliated with particular groups. Second, you must understand that your societal, cultural, and individual histories not only address the question of "Who am I?" but also the how and why of self-identity formation.

Each identity has a shared system of meaning only understood by those that are a part of the identity. However, people must also recognize the importance of the individual-cultural dynamic through which they can acknowledge that not everyone in a particular cultural identity is the same. It allows people to recognize connections between a person and his or her cultural identity, but it also leaves room to embrace the person as an individual. The individual-cultural dynamic encourages people to embrace both a person's individual and individual cultural identities.

CONTINUE YOUR JOURNEY ONLINE

Visit: www.census.gov/people/

The U.S. Census Bureau website. Find out statistics about the cultural groups that comprise your identity. Learn about yourself by exploring how your identity is represented in U.S. American culture.

66 SAY WHAT?

Say What? provides excerpts from overheard real-life conversations in which people have communicated stereotypes. As you read these conversations, reflect on the following questions.

- Have you been in conversations like this before?
- Is there any one of these conversations that stick out to you more than the others?
- What do you think of this conversation?
- How did the stereotype help or hinder the conversation?
- Was there another way the stereotyper could have communicated to convey the same point?
- How do you feel when you hear this conversation or the specific stereotype?
- Do any of these conversations bother you more than others? Why or why not?
- Do any concepts, issues, or theories discussed in the chapter help explain why?

- **Say What?** I asked him if he considered himself a feminist. He looked at me with a disgusted look and said, "No, do I look like a lesbian to you?" I smiled and sort of laughed. Then I said to him that feminists weren't lesbians, and in fact both men and women do consider themselves feminists. I told him that there was no reason to be afraid of the word *feminist*. If he believed in women's rights, he should be proud to be a feminist; many ladies around campus would even like him more for it.

- **Say What?** A few of the servers were hanging around the waiter's station where there is a view of the dining room. My coworker watched the hostess sit a table of Black people in his station and he was noticeably annoyed. He said, "Great a table of Blacks." There were three other people around and they laughed, and said, "Aw man that stinks." After serving the table though, Mike found he was tipped 15%.

- **Say What?** My coworkers and I were sitting down and discussing what we should get for our boyfriends and girlfriends for the upcoming holiday. My friend Jane suggested that a cute idea would be to buy our boyfriends a dozen roses and heart shaped candy—the opposite of the cliché. All the guys started laughing, saying that the gift idea was dumb and no real man wants to get flowers on Valentine's Day; it was the women who get the flowers. The conversation further progressed with the men saying women are dainty and men are macho; therefore flowers are a girlie gift.

- **Say What?** "You know, with the blonde hair, the big eyes and the big smile, you seem like an airhead but when somebody talks to you its obvious that you're actually a pretty smart girl." When he made his comment, I became a little offended and surprised. I replied "Oh" and proceeded to explain that that was not the first time that people had used that stereotype against me.

REVIEW QUESTIONS

1. What examples can you think of that distinguish the concepts of space and place based on how these are used in the chapter?

2. According to the chapter, when do people most think about their identities?

3. Discuss an example from a movie or television show that can be used to explain the I-Other dialectic discussed in the chapter.

4. Explain the following terms introduced in the chapter: self, self-esteem, self-consciousness, self-efficacy, identity, and self-identity. How do they relate to each other?

5. This chapter explores self-consciousness and identity management. How are these related?

6. What is symbolic interactionism as discussed in the chapter? What does it have to do with symbols and self?

7. What is the difference between enculturation and acculturation? How do these terms relate to the concepts of vernacular language and collective harmony discussed later in the chapter?

8. What is meant by the statement, "To speak is to exist for the other"? How would the chapter explain that this is relevant to self-identity?

9. What is identity management theory? It includes some of the same terms from the discussion in Chapter 2 on face negotiation theory. How are the two theories similar or different?

10. How is identity development facilitated through communication with others? Defend your answer based on the communication theory of identity.

KEY TERMS

acculturation   126

ascription   127

avowal   127

co-created contract   129

collective harmony   130

communal layer   134

communication theory
   of identity (CTI)   133

contact culture   119

cultural contracts theory
   (CCT)   128

cultural identity   127

culture shock   120

dialectical tension   134

dominant group   127

enacted layer   134

enculturation   126

fragmentation   134

generalized other   124

giving-face   129

identity gap   134

identity management
   theory (IMT)   129

identity negotiation   134

individual layer   134

interpenetration   134

I-Other dialectic   120

looking glass self   124

majority identity   127

minority identity   127

noncontact culture   119

quasi-completed
   contract   128

ready-to-sign
   contract   128

relational identities   129

relational layer   134

self   120

self-consciousness   121

self-efficacy   121

self-esteem   121

self-identity   118

symbolic
   interactionism   123

vernacular language   130

REFERENCES

Andersen, P. A., Hecht, M. L., Hoobler, G.D., & Smallwood, M. (2002). Nonverbal communication across cultures. In W. B. Gudykunst & B. Mody (Eds.), *Cross-Cultural and intercultural communication* (pp. 73–90). Thousand Oaks, CA: Sage.

Asante, M. (2003). *Afrocentricity: The theory of social practice (revised and expanded)*. Chicago: African American Images.

Blumer, H. (1969). *Symbolic interactionism: Perspective and method*. Englewood Cliffs, NJ: Prentice Hall.

Castells, M. (2009). *The power of identity.* Cambridge, MA: Blackwell.

Coover, G., & Murphy, S. (2000). The communicated self: Exploring the interaction between self and social context. *Health Communication Research, 26,* 125–147.

Cupach, W. R., & Imahori, T. T. (1993). Identity management theory: Communication competence in intercultural episodes and relationships. In R. Wiseman & J. Koester (Eds.), *Intercultural communication competence* (pp. 112–131). Newbury Park, CA: Sage.

Fanon, F. (1967). *Black skin white masks.* New York: Grove.

Ferdman, B. M. (2000). Why am I who I am: Constructing the cultural self in multicultural perspective. *Human Development, 43,* 19–23.

Goodall, H. L., Jr., & Goodall, S. (2002). *Communicating in professional contexts: Skills, ethics, and technologies.* Belmont, CA: Wadsworth/Thomson Learning.

Hecht, M. L. (1993). A research odyssey: Towards the development of a communication theory of identity. *Communication Monographs, 60,* 76–82.

Hecht, M. L., Collier, M. J., & Ribeau, S. A. (1993). *African American communication: Ethnic identity and cultural interpretation.* Newbury Park, California: Sage.

Hecht, M. L., Jackson, R. L., & Ribeau, S. A. (2003). *African American communication: Exploring identity and culture* (2nd ed.). Mahwah, NJ: Lawrence Erlbaum.

Holmes, J. (2002). *An introduction to sociolinguistics.* New York: Longman.

Imahori, T. T., & Cupach, W. R. (2005). Identity management theory: Facework in intercultural relationships. In W. B. Gudykunst (Ed.), *Theorizing about intercultural communication* (pp. 195–210). Thousand Oaks, CA: Sage.

Jackson, R. L. (2003). Cultural contracts theory: Toward an identity negotiation paradigm. In P. Sullivan & D. Goldzwig (Eds.), *New Approaches to Rhetoric.* (pp. 89–107). Thousand Oaks, CA: Sage.

Jung, E., & Hecht, M. L. (2004). Elaborating the communication theory of identity: Identity gaps and communication outcomes. *Communication Quarterly, 52,* 265–283.

Martin, J. N., & Nakayama, T. K. (2010). *Intercultural communication in contexts* (5th ed.). Boston: McGraw Hill.

Mead, G. H. (1934). *Mind, self, and society.* Chicago: The University of Chicago Press.

Nakayama, T. K. (2000). Dis/orienting identities: Asian Americans, history, and intercultural communication. In A. González, M. Houston & V. Chen (Eds.), *Our voices: Essays in ethnicity, culture, and communication* (pp. 13–18). Los Angeles: Roxbury.

Peek, L. (2005). Becoming Muslim: The development of religious identity. *Sociology of Religion, 66,* 215–242.

Rodriguez, E. M., & Ouellette, S. C. (2000). Gay and lesbian Christians: Homosexual and religious identity integration in the members and participants of a gay-positive church. *Journal for the Scientific Study of Religion, 39,* 333–347.

Roland, A. (1988). *In search of self in India and Japan: Toward a cross-cultural psychology.* Princeton, NJ: Princeton University Press.

Singleman, P. (1972). Exchange as symbolic interaction: Convergences between two theoretical perspectives. *American Sociological Review, 37,* 414–424.

Smitherman, G. (2000). *Talking that talk.* New York: Routledge.

Sokefield, M. (1999). Debating self, identity, and culture in anthropology. *Current Anthropology, 40,* 417–431.

Winford, D. (2003). Ideologies of language and socially realistic linguistics. In S. M. G. Smitherman, A. F. Ball, & A. K. Spears (Eds.), *Black linguistics: Language, society and politics in Africa and the Americas* (pp. 21–39). New York: Routledge.

Wood, J. (1982). Communication and relational culture: Bases for the study of human relationships. *Communication Quarterly, 30*(2), 75–84.

CHAPTER 7

Ingroups and Outgroups

Howard Giles

University of California, Santa Barbara

Jane Giles

Van Buren Consulting

Journey Through Chapter 7

Sightseeing: On your journey, you will visit ingroups and outgroups and learn about intergroup boundaries that construct differences between cultural groups. Taking a social construction perspective, you will explore how language is used to identify and distinguish between ingroups and outgroups, and explore how group vitality and communication accommodation theory describe important aspects of intergroup communication processes.

Souvenir: After your journey, you will take away an understanding of intergroup communication processes and the role of language in group identity.

This chapter introduces some key elements from an intergroup communication perspective (see Giles & Watson, 2008), one of many different ways of exploring intercultural relations. This approach studies the effects of talking to someone from another culture based *solely* on that individual's membership in that group, rather than talking to the person based on individuating information, that is, unique characteristics, such as personality or temperament. The former would be considered a highly intergroup interaction, whereas the latter would be much more inter-individual in nature (Tajfel & Turner, 1986). Intercultural encounters can be either of these extremes—and, sometimes, with the same person on different occasions. For example, conversing with a newly fostered sister from China as though she was just one longstanding member of the family on one day yet on the next (perhaps because she seems overly demanding) treating her as a complete outsider.

Actually, it is difficult to locate interactions that are not intergroup, at least to some degree (see Giles, Reid, & Harwood, 2010; Harwood & Giles, 2005). Take, for instance, the following snippet from a conversation between John and Frangelica who are of Irish and Sicilian heritage respectively:

> You are so, so special and unique, with the most bubbly personality! The fact that we're from so very different backgrounds does not affect my feelings toward you one bit. It's *you* who I love—this has nothing, nothing to do with where you came from . . .

Although John's sentiments are highly personal, idiosyncratic, and hence very inter-individual in character, all this is expressly contrasted with Frangelica's different ethnic heritage and, therefore, her social identity is also salient in this conversation. Concepts introduced subsequently, such as ingroups and outgroups, intergroup boundaries, and group vitalities, are important to the study of intergroup communication and can assist when analyzing interactions with those from another culture (be it national, organizational, generational, etc.). To inform about these topics, the chapter provides a discussion of ingroups and outgroups and the role language plays in group identification. In order to explain how distinctions between ingroups and outgroups are communicated, intergroup boundaries are explored followed by a section on labeling. Next, group vitality, an important aspect of group identity, is discussed. Finally, the chapter explores communication accommodation theory and its role in intergroup processes.

REFLECT 7.1: Are you currently living in a community comprised of mostly members of your own cultural group? What benefits can be gained from living in such a community?

INGROUPS AND OUTGROUPS

An ingroup is a social category or group with which you identify strongly. An outgroup, conversely, is a social category or group with which you do not identify. An important characteristic of the in-outgroup dichotomy is that groups mark their identities communicatively by the distinctive language and speech styles they create and use, the dress codes they adopt, and the festivals and pageants that highlight their unique traditions and rituals, and so forth. In this way, language and communicative features are important devices for creating an *us* and *them* (see Gaudet & Clément, 2008) as indicated in the following examples of in- and outgroup labels:

- Christian versus Heathen
- Muslim versus Infidel

- Zhong Guo Ren versus Wai Guo Ren (Chinese versus non-Chinese)
- Nihonjin versus Gaijin (Japanese versus "out people")
- Jew versus Goyim

A broader example is from a videotape allegedly from former Al-Qaeda militant leader Osama bin Laden that proclaimed: "The world has been divided into two camps. One under the banner of the cross and another under the banner of Islam."

People have many cultural identities that they can call upon. These might include being a student, a surfer, a sporty guy, and so on. Clearly, people can have multiple identities. A person can simultaneously be a Korean who values their ethnic heritage, but is also proud to have become an American citizen. Both components of this dual identity are salient, and each one is triggered on different occasions as being more central to who that person is at that moment. Korean Americans who visit Korea are often surprised—even

Photo 7.1 Do you see difference or similarity? Preference for people who think, look, and act like you is common. This perceived similarity both enhances friendships and limits opportunities to make friends. In this photo, group membership is not produced by visual race or ethnicity. Instead group membership is produced by the shared activities these children engage in and enjoy together.

when visiting to retrieve some of their lost cultural heritage—to discover that locals see and hear them only as American. Hence, what constitutes the major components of a social identity can vary radically between different outgroups; sometimes the language spoken is key to being an authentic member of a group, but for others it could be birthright. Knowing what are the essential ingredients of an outgroup's identity can be important diagnostic information, as by this means you know best how to accommodate to them. So when in the West Bank or the Gaza Strip, it has been argued that feeling subjugated and having continually endured conflict are emotional dimensions of a Palestinian identity (see Ellis, 2006).

REFLECT 7.2: List the groups of which you are a member, and rank order them in terms of (1) their positive value to you, and (2) the salience these social identities may assume in day-to-day conversations.

Social identity theory proposes that when an ingroup identity is made or becomes salient, people often wish to emphasize characteristics of their group that they hold dear (Tajfel & Turner, 1986). Communicative symbols are often evoked in this regard and, depending on the intercultural setting involved, can include emphasizing organizational jargon, feminist sentiments, adolescent colloquial phrases, or ethnic accents (Giles & Johnson, 2009). The theory suggests that by expressing its distinctive characteristics, people can thereby assume unqualified pride in their membership in this group. Moreover, the theory suggests that by such expressed public identification with the group, this translates into a greater sense of personal worth. An example would be a Jamaican switching into the local creole when talking to an American tourist on the island, despite the Jamaican's ability to speak standard English. In this way, ingroup members can play off of outgroup members to further bolster their valued ingroup identity as well as their own self-esteem.

LANGUAGE AND INGROUP IDENTIFICATION

Language can be a critical determinant of whether someone views another as an authentic ingroup member or an outgroup imposter. Indeed, even one sound can cause detection as with the notion of linguistic shibboleths, which are words or terms that when communicated can identify someone as being a member of a distinctive group. In the Bible (Judges 15, 5–6), an account is provided of the Gileadites who captured large numbers of Ephraimites. If a person answered negatively to the question, "Are you an Ephraimite?" they would then be required to pronounce *Shibboleth*. If the captured said, *Sibboleth* because they could not articulate the appropriate *sh* sound, then their outgroup status was revealed and they were duly killed (along with, purportedly, 42,000 other Ephraimites).

< Kiedy ranne wstaja zorze

Kiedy ranne wstaja zorze,

Tobie ziemia, Tobie morze,

Tobie spiewa zywiol wszelki:

badz pochwalon Boze wielki!

Tobie spiewa zywiol wszelki:

badz pochwalon Boze wielki!

A czlowiek, który bez miary

obsypany Twymi dary,

cos go stworzyl i ocalil,

a czemuzby Cie nie chwalil?

Cos go stworzyl i ocalil,

a czemuzby Cie nie chwalil?

Ledwie oczy przetrzec zdolam,

wnet do mego Pana wolam,

do mego Boga na niebie,

i szukam Go kolo siebie.

Do mego Boga na niebie,

i szukam Go kolo siebie.

Wielu snem smierci upadli,

co sie wczoraj spac pokladli,

my sie jeszcze obudzili,

bysmy Cie, Boze chwalili.

My sie jeszcze obudzili,

bysmy Cie, Boze chwalili.

* * *

Do you understand what this says? Language, whether in interpersonal communication, in a business context, or in the media, is one way in which people communicate their ingroup status. If you understand that this is a Polish lullaby titled "When the Morning Dawns Break," then you are an ingroup member with others who share this language.

In general, there is a positive correlation between your identification with a particular ingroup and your expressed use of that group's distinctive communication style. However, in some settings, these ingroup patterns can be predicted more by the groups in which a person does not wish to be identified than ones in which they do. For example, Catalonian speakers' decision to use the language Catalan with a Castillian speaker in Barcelona rather than Castillian Spanish is predicted more by the Catalonians' rejection of a Spanish identity than it is by the strength of their Catalonian identity (Giles & Viladot, 1994). In like fashion, if writing to a Catalan colleague in Barcelona, it might be prudent not to address the envelope being mailed to Spain. Likewise, many Britons will not appreciate or respond well to receiving mail addressed to them in Europe as they do not view themselves as part of that continent; rather they would prefer the address to be Britain or UK.

The use of an ingroup language or speech style can be a critical feature of what it means to be a member of many groups. Moreover, the importance of language as a component of a person's social identity can change over the lifespan. For instance, not bringing up your child to speak Cantonese if, say, you have emigrated from Hong Kong to Vancouver may not be that relevant to a Chinese-Canadian teenager whose core identity at that time is an adolescent peer identity anyway. However, later in life, it is fairly common for Chinese emigrés not to

Take a Side Trip:

If you would like to read more about related issues, visit Appendix D: Transnational Dominican Culture Through Phenomenological Analysis.

feel entirely and fully Chinese, to feel resentful of their parents for not passing on this linguistic gift to them, and to begin avidly taking Chinese language classes.

Knowing the statuses of different languages in a culture being visited can be informative because many nations have more than one official language, as is the case with Switzerland which has four. In addition, knowing that there are different forms of the same language as in Arabic and German can be informative for making appropriate language choices. The "lower" form of the language is typically for use in informal contexts in the home and the neighborhood, whereas as the "higher" form is used in formal institutional contexts, such as in church services and in professional situations (e.g., addressing an instructor with two doctorate degrees as Herr Professor Dr. Dr.).

INTERGROUP BOUNDARIES

Because of their role in intergroup communication, it is important to recognize intergroup boundaries. These are symbolically equivalent to geographical borders, yet are reflected in more psychological and communicative dimensions. For example, you communicate intergroup boundaries when you contend that you have different ways of looking at the world, spiritual rituals and moral standards, and so forth. Intergroup boundaries can be found in food and drink, and even in the use of utensils. Brits are often regarded as impolite by some Americans for their use of eating utensils, by retaining the knife in their hand rather than setting it down. Americans are regarded by some Brits as "shovelers" for their ubiquitous use of the fork while eating because it is impolite to turn a fork over when eating with one in Britain. To get the right eating practices involves cultural knowledge (see Cleveland, Laroche, Pons, & Kastoun, 2009). Asking for chopsticks in Thailand can be seen as curiously ignorant when most ethnic Thais actually do not use these, but a fork! Given the vehement reactions using outside practices can evoke, a "bilingual eater" would accommodate local practices.

Language and physiognomy can be vivid intergroup boundaries felt as impervious to the extent that they limit the ability of a person to become a genuine member of the group in the eyes and ears of its members. Although permeability of intergroup boundaries such as being bicultural and a nativelike speaker of another group's language is possible (Kim, 2001), some groups contend that their characteristics are so unique as to be quite inaccessible (and impermeable) to outgroups. For instance, people in Japan, at least in the recent past, have felt Westerners cannot readily learn their language and, thereby, their cultural identity is rigorously held to be impermeable. In this vein, Americans who are fluent Japanese speakers sometimes find that Japanese locals will not respond or accommodate back to them in Japanese but, rather (and if they are bilingual), will continue in English for however long the

American persists in speaking Japanese. In other words, an outsider's seemingly over-accommodative and invasive use of Japanese is difficult to tolerate when locals intransigently adhere to cultural boundaries.

LABELING

Labels can be used to delineate boundaries. For example, knowing that many Hong Kongers will generically label all German, Swede, or Irish persons *Westerners* is valuable information to have in terms of how you may be viewed there. In parallel, Britons may label an American as a *Canadian,* or an American may ascribe Australianess to a New Zealander, and be surprised by the disgust their miscategorization evoked! Appreciating social sensitivities such as these is important when receiving and giving cultural labels and understanding the affect that these can evoke. When asked, in a study, to consider how Belgian and Dutch students felt one week after the 9/11 attacks in the United States, those who were told the experiment was about Arab and Western reactions expressed more fear about future terrorist attacks than those who were informed that the investigators were examining American and European reactions (Dumont, Yzerbyt, Wigboldus, & Gordij, 2003) because of the labels with which they associated themselves.

After 9/11, many Sikhs from India (who are renowned for their turbans and beards) are often falsely attributed as Muslims. As a consequence and because of anti-Muslim racism, they have been subject to vicious ethnic slurs and some even have had their property fire-bombed. The act of being falsely foisted with an outgroup label is known as categorization threat for the recipient. The term *threat* is intended to reflect the potential dire consequences of the label. Another example of this is when someone's citizenship status is called into question. It has been estimated that one-third of Asian-Americans who were born in the United States are frequently asked: "Where do you *really* come from?" (Cheryan & Monin, 2005). This is called identity denial because those asking the question deny those being questioned their own identity as American. The defensive reaction to this type of identity denial is often characterized by communicating allegiance to American values (e.g., feeling moved when the national anthem is played) and espousing American practices (e.g., playing basketball and baseball).

Knowing how outgroups use ethnic slurs or ethnophaulisms and what their social meanings might be is critical information on how a society views groups and their relative positions within the intergroup status hierarchy. This term denotes the fact that most groups in contact have more or less status (and power), and that there is often a multicultural consensus about the rank ordering of social groups in a particular society. Hence, there can be a relationship between a group's position in the intergroup status hierarchy and the more frequently offensive slurs aimed at this group. These ethnophaulisms are multidimensional in terms of their complexities and valence. In terms of the latter, ethnic slurs vary along a dimension of negativity. *Taffy* is a somewhat innocuous term for a Welsh-American (and simply refers to the River Taff that flows through the capital city of Wales). Other slurs are, of course, way more pernicious—and certainly so evident that they do not need to be highlighted here. Studies by Mullen and his associates (e.g., Mullen & Smyth, 2004) have shown that the less complex and more negative the slur assigned to an ethnic group, the members of that group are less likely to marry into the mainstream dominant group, more likely to hold low-paid occupations, appear less attractively in children's literature, and are even more likely to commit suicide. In other words, the simpler and worse an outgroup is viewed, the more negative consequences there are for those having that group membership. Researchers have also shown that the origins of labels people adopt for their ingroup, called ethnonyms, can be symbolically important (Mullen, Calogero, & Leader, 2007). Indeed, it has been shown that the more complex or the more diverse an ingroup reflects ethnonyms, the less intergroup hostility they experience.

REFLECT 7.3: Think about the ethnic groups in your city or province. What labels, if any, do you hear or see associated with these groups?

Direct slurs can sometimes be viewed as less harmful than more subtle, indirect expressions of disdain. In one study, Leets and Giles (1997) had people read a vignette that depicted a Euro-American publicly proclaiming at a bus stop about not wishing to board a bus driven by an Asian-American when it arrived. In one condition, a repeated sequence of ethnophaulisms (too offensive to specify here) were expressed that were in contrast to the other condition where the sentiment was expressed in a more indirect way, namely: "I don't feel comfortable taking your bus. I'll wait for the next one and see if I feel safer with that one." Anglo-American readers of the vignette reported that the direct slurs were far more harmful to the target than the indirect; however, the Asian-American readers (avowedly accustomed to frequent ethnic slurs) reported that it was the *indirect* message that was the most harmful. Arguably, indirect confrontations are quite difficult to manage communicatively, leading to uncertainty about how to respond effectively and, therefore, are associated with heightened anxiety.

Linguistic subtleties can be viewed in another way by listening to the language people use to describe or report on the actions of ingroups and outgroups—and this pertains to the so-called linguistic intergroup bias (see Sutton & Douglas, 2008). This effect manifests when people describe differently those that do honorable acts depending on their group memberships. If your ingroup is behaving in a socially positive manner, then the act is described in terms of global traits. For example, giving to a charity is talked about solely in terms of the *generosity* of the donor. However, if an outgroup member committed this very same act, they may be described only in *specific* behavioral terms—as giving so much money to a particular charity. This allows perceptions of ingroup members overall to be favorable, although for outgroup members it doesn't generalize beyond the single act. When doing despicable acts, people talk about ingroup and outgroup actions in the correspondingly converse ways. This, then, allows outgroup members overall to be viewed negatively for engaging in even a single negative act, although the same act for an ingroup member is less likely to affect the overall impression someone has of them. In these ways, intergroup actions are linguistically sustained as stereotypically positive for the ingroup and reaffirmed as far less so for the outgroup.

**LIVING
CULTURE**

Crip Mate   *David Linton*

Marymount Manhattan College

"Was she always . . . ?" "When did she . . . ?" "Did you know her before . . . ?" People want to know if I fell in love with and married my wife before or after she had the accident that severed her spinal cord and required her to use a wheelchair.

People who use wheelchairs come to expect rude inquiries, "What happened to you?" Different response strategies emerge. Feigned innocence: "What do you mean?" Belligerence: "It's none of your damn business." Heroic dramatization: "I was dropped behind enemy lines and my chute didn't open." Ju-Jitsu: "I'm fine, thanks. What happened to you?"

After more than 25 years of thinking about how to answer those intrusive questions, I'm still not sure how to respond. If I answer that we were married before she became disabled, then the pity look would appear. "Oh, you poor man," you could almost hear them thinking, "what a burden to have thrust upon you." Next they'd want to know how long I had been married before "it" happened, whether I had been able to have a family, how I had borne up under the extra responsibilities that must come to a person wed to one with a disability.

When people learn that Simi became disabled years before we met, a different set of fantasies plays out to figure out why an AB (one of the disability community's slang for able bodied folks like me) would enter a relationship with someone with a disability. The first is that we have some sort of martyr complex, a need to sacrifice ourselves for the good of another. At times this makes us seem noble, generous, self-sacrificing. The other theory is that we are secret fetishists, that we get kinky pleasure out of physical intimacy with bodies that have undergone scarring trauma. Of course, there are those who understand that love is not necessarily bound by conventions. Falling in love with someone is a full body and soul experience.

I won't deny that in addition to her beauty and sexy ways I was intrigued by Simi's disability and the way it shaped how she experienced the world. At the age of 23 Simi was injured in an automobile accident. Both her husband and her best friend were killed so her scars were both internal and external. By the time we met in graduate school, she'd been through rehab, had her own apartment, her own life, and had created a new advocacy organization called the Coalition for Sexuality and Disability. She had already cut out a place for herself in the world of disability culture. I was fascinated by the whole package.

(Continued)

LIVING CULTURE

(Continued)

After a few conversations during class breaks I asked her to have dinner with me. We set a time and she mentioned, "I'll be wearing a red carnation so you'll be able to find me." It wasn't until that night when she *wasn't* wearing a carnation that I realized that she was toying with my feigned indifference to her disability. There was something about her wry humor that let me know I was dealing with someone who would shake up my assumptions and open me to new ways of looking at the world. The wheelchair does not diminish the fact that she was and is a beautiful, interesting woman. And the life she has led and the insights she has gained and shared with me because of the wheelchair make her all the more intriguing. Simply put, she inhabits an exotic world.

As a disability activist, writer, and filmmaker, Simi is deeply involved in that world and, as her mate, I am allowed entry. Members of the disability community are comfortable calling each other *crips* as a term of bonding and affection but of course I am not entitled to the term. But they do have a word for people like me, a label that bestows on us status and distinction: *crip mate.*

Consider:

1. The essay begins with a set of questions. Does the author ever provide the reader with answers to these? If so, what do you think the answers are?

2. What ingroups and outgroups are identified in this essay?

3. What are the characteristics of the ingroups and outgroups in this essay?

4. What do you think about labels that are considered proprietary to certain groups like crips?

GROUP VITALITY

The concept of group vitality has received a lot of attention in the multicultural literature. It refers to how much a group has social advantages in terms of pride in its history, sheer numbers of its members, and the visibility of its culture and communicative codes in the important layers of society. It is made up of three separate, but interrelated, dimensions of status, demographics, and institutional support that are each discussed in the next few sections. One of the means of deciding whether your ingroup has a positive identity or not is to compare the group's characteristics along these vitality dimensions with that of the outgroup. For instance, how does your group fare in terms of its language's use in the media, educational curricula, and in local commerce vis-à-vis that of the outgroup? The vitality of an ingroup, as well as an outgroup, can, arguably, be measured objectively. You can count the number of demonstrators seen to protest the new illegal immigrant policies adopted in Arizona to inform you about the group vitality of immigrants. However, data collection is not immune from biases. How do you decide how many people are actually participating in a march, and for how long? This is an unenviable analytical task.

Just as important as *objective* vitality are its perceptual dimensions, namely subjective group vitality (Giles, Bourhis, & Taylor, 2009), that is, how people view their own and others group vitalities. It has been argued that we are aware of the vitalities of all the social groups to which we belong by mere (yet continual) perusals of media depictions and reports of relevant intergroup scenes. Further, ethnolinguistic identity theory contends that the higher your ingroup vitality, the more members are willing to invest in their ingroup emotionally,

Photo 7.2 What value does celebration have to you? Celebrations and rituals such as those that occur for holidays, weddings, funerals, and parades have value for culture. For example, celebrations provide the opportunity for members of a community to show their cultural solidarity and pride. This may be especially important for groups with a low group vitality.

psychologically, and with respect to collective action to foster their own group's interests (Giles & Johnson, 2009). Put another way, there appears little merit in, or gain from, possessing a vitality that has a consensually low subjective vitality in terms of its status, demographic health, and institutional support. Ingroups and their cultures, including their languages and literatures, will survive and flourish (e.g., Catalan, Navajo, Irish Gaelic, and Luxembourgish), continue to be creative and innovative, and expand and be socially influential, if they have high perceived ingroup vitality. In general, high vitality groups are usually dominant groups, those in the upper echelons of any intergroup status hierarchy, whereas low vitality groups are marginalized groups, those relegated toward the bottom end of this continuum.

It is important to note that for dominant groups to maintain their social privileges and advantages, they might need to control public information that perpetuates low subjective vitality among subordinate groups. Members of low vitality groups, for their part, may be disposed to assimilate into other more prestigious collectivities to gain enhanced personal worth and dignity. Consequently, their communication codes might fade away into oblivion in a manner referred to as language suicide.

> **REFLECT 7.4:** How are ethnic minorities in your hometown represented in radio and on television? If you think there are differences between how groups are represented, why do you think this might be?

Status

One important subdimension of group vitality has been labeled status. This refers to the influence and power a group has economically, historically, socially, and linguistically. For example, regarding the latter, Greek may not have high status as an international language; yet, in Melbourne (purportedly the second largest "Greek city"), it has accrued considerable local currency. Groups with high vitality will usually have a history of which they are proud and this can be reflected in school texts, TV serials, monuments, painted street wall murals, and so forth. However, sometimes flawed historical events, such as military defeats, can be mobilizing even hundreds of years later (e.g., the Battle of Bannockburn for the Scots) as the ingroup ponders its cultural survival in the face of colonializing influences and aggression. Communicating history is a potent intergroup force. This can be illustrated not only in Japan's prior refusals to apologize for their militaristic actions in World War II, but in its reinforcing historical biases in these regards in educational texts for Japanese school children (Edwards, 2005).

Other subdimensions of this status vitality factor include economic and linguistic statuses whereby certain groups seem to excel in business and commerce, and their language and dialect is still an important mode of communication. In the latter regard, note the impressive

Take a Side Trip:

If you would like to read more about related issues, visit Appendix C: Dagaaba Culture of Ghana Explored Through Rhetorical Analysis.

resurrection and revitalizing of ethnic languages in the wake of both the dissolution of the former Soviet Union and Yugoslavia. Interestingly, as globalization takes hold of market economies, languages—as precious resources of ingroup vitality—can take on unprecedented social capital with a group's desires for cultural distinctiveness and authenticity. For example, many ethnic minorities and smaller cultures have feared being homogenized by the establishment of the European Union. This concern can then lead to cultural and linguistic revitalization (as with the increased use of, and support for, the Breton, Basque, and Frisian languages) in ways that could never have been predicted decades earlier.

Demographics

Demographics (that is, the population and location features of groups) are, too, a key dimension of group vitality. Hence, attempted massacres, genocide, and ethnic cleansing perpetrated against certain groups can be seen as concrete means of delimiting the violated group's perceived strength. Interestingly, such acts of atrocity are still committed all around the world (e.g., Nigeria and Indonesia) and in the cultural heartlands of outgroups, such as Christians slaying Muslims in their mosques and defiling their sacred places and the latter, in turn, desecrating churches, altars, and crosses. Demographic vitality can be manifest in a range of different means. For example, ingroup sanctions against those engaged in ethnic mixed marriages can be interpreted as one way of maintaining ingroup vitality, particularly when it is the female of a subordinate group that marries into a dominant group family. In this case, it is often the language and culture of the woman that is lost and not passed onto future generations because of her ingroup's low group vitality.

When immigrants enter and settle in a country or region of which they are not native, the spread of their languages within it (e.g., Spanish into the western states of the United States and East European languages and Turkish into Western Europe) may be considered, by some longstanding residents, as a diminution of their own host group's language. Mainstream backlashes often result as a way of ameliorating the threat. Oftentimes immigrating groups and refugees (such as the Hmong in the United States) are strategically dispersed across a nation's territory by the host government agencies so as not to have them concentrated in demographically strong enclaves. Acting in this way can diminish the dispersed group's cultural solidarity and, thereby, stymie their potential to possess economic and political muscle.

Emigration is the movement, voluntary or forced, of one group to another geographical and culturation space. Emigration, especially of a group's educated youth, can decrease ingroup vitality. Much attention has been given to so-called White flight in certain areas of the United States where Euro-Americans parents withdraw their children from schools where African American and Hispanic children are seen as becoming more dominant, and therefore vitality threatening. San Francisco has recently seen the emergence of "Black flight" whereby African Americans have moved out of the city to other areas. As a result, Asian-Americans have moved into these neighborhoods, causing resentment, conflict, and crime among some of those remaining.

Institutional Support

Institutional support is the last important dimension of a group's vitality and refers to the extent to which a group and its culture are reflected in the main structures of society, such as in the media, politics, the law, and so forth. The use of the ingroup language in ethnic newspapers, newsletters, magazines and Internet sites, as well as the ability to see it in the national and international news on the TV, are potent forms of high vitality. Indeed, in one study, institutional support was perceived as the most important of the three vitality factors (Giles, Rosenthal, & Young, 1985). Knowledge of, as well as talk about (see Harwood, Giles, & Bourhis, 1994), a group's presence in the educational curriculum, its continued use in religious settings, and even the growth of its own unique places of worship can make profound statements about its cultural capital. In Britain for instance, it has been estimated that there are no less than 1,600 mosques there for worship. Moreover, attention given to the building of mosques and their minarets (symbolically represented as guided missiles in the Swiss media) brought about a wave of indignation amongst non-Muslims in Switzerland. Likewise, the construction of Israeli settlements in Arab communities, be it considered legitimate from the Jewish side or not, is a threat to Palestinian vitality as well as the permeability of the group's cultural boundaries.

The linguistic landscape is a powerful means of establishing and legitimizing a sense of ingroup pride and vitality. The visual and sensory energies of neighborhoods like Little Italies and Chinatowns in the United States, as discussed in Chapter 1, are replete with ethnically distinctive odors, and with signage widely proclaiming that the ethnic tongue (at least in terms of road and shop signs) is very much alive and well. Moreover, the groups' festivals, music and song, sculptures and fine art, as well as many other cultural artifacts in the home are markers of ingroup solidarity and valued distinctiveness.

Certainly, relative group vitalities are not a static phenomenon, and a person's appraisal of them should not be considered etched in stone. Groups continually vie for an increasing share of overall vitality as this, in part, contributes to their survival in the local intergroup, as well as sometimes the global, scene. In other words, just because a traveler formulated a vitality profile for a cultural destination a few years earlier does not mean that the profile would be the same now. Because of all sorts of intergroup and international forces, vitality profiles are not static—they are quite malleable.

COMMUNICATION ACCOMMODATION THEORY

Communication accommodation theory is a framework that explores the reasons for, and consequences arising from, speakers converging toward and diverging away from each other (see Gallois, 2008; Giles & Ogay, 2006). Typically, recipients generally receive convergent moves favorably. This accommodation conveys respect and effort that, in turn, renders appreciative responses, such as liking and altruism. For recipients, the effects of intergroup accommodation can also generalize to broader and more positive feelings about the entire culture and group to which the converger belongs. Naturally, the consequences of this are interactional satisfaction that can yield a range of other social payoffs, such as a general pleasure at being in the culture and with its people, a desire to revisit at a later time, the fostering of business deals in the future, and so forth.

It must be borne in mind that any cultural group is often made up of quite heterogeneous subgroups and members who will hold widely differing values, beliefs, and various ways of expressing their identities. In other words, meeting up with people from another culture does not mean you will engage a monolith. Even when you accommodate, you will want to be sensitive to the inevitable variability of people even within a single cultural group (see Gallois & Callan, 1997).

Convergence

Accommodating to an outgroup language—even in terms of simple hellos, expressing thanks, and ordering, say, drinks can demonstrate convergence in which you are tying to join with outgroup members. Accommodative moves like these are behavioral attempts to accommodate that may be welcomed and can engender genuine cooperative responses in many cultures. That said, such affiliative approaches would have to be viewed as accommodative as sometimes people hear what they wish to. Work on the retroactive speech halo effect (Ball et al., 1982) is relevant here, and is built upon the notion that fast speech rates and standard accents are construed as positive attributes of speakers across many cultures. Hence the effect is manifest in that if a person believes a speaker is of high status, they would be heard to *sound* more standard accented and faster in speech rate than if no status information was available about them or, especially, if they were known to be of low status. In this way and as shown in Figure 7.1, accommodative moves, such as a Japanese-fluent American speaking Japanese to a Japanese person, are susceptible to biases and may be not always be received in the way they were intended.

Figure 7.1 Intergroup Model of Accommodative Processes.

Does this model explain your intercultural encounters? The complexity of intercultural communication is often hard to grasp. This model provides an explanation of how these interactions might work.

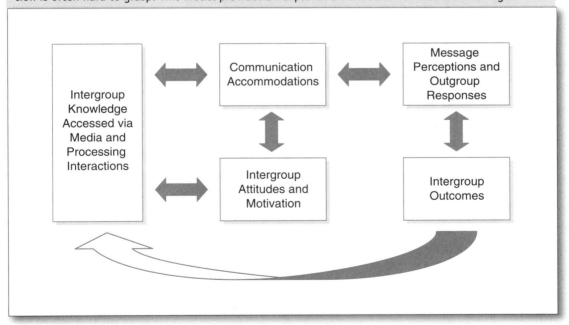

Source: Adapted based on communication accommodation theory (Gallois, 2008; Giles & Ogay, 2006).

Copyright 2011 by Howard Giles and Jane Giles.

Interestingly, this caution is contrary to the accommodative advice suggested earlier and, hence, important to appreciate and anticipate; otherwise, it can lead to resentment and a dissatisfactory intergroup climate. In light of this caution, locals could construct a Japanese-fluent American switching back into English as the appropriate accommodative move. Hence, accommodations are not simply the province of sociolinguistic acts alone but also other variables involved.

The keen observer of an intergroup scene should find it informative to determine which and how many ethnic minority groups are located in a targeted cultural milieu and to explore their interrelationships within the culture; Italy, for instance, has at least 13 ethnolinguistic communities. Knowing, for instance, that America is a male-dominant culture that often treats women as a special class to be protected would allow every chivalrous act, like a man holding the door open for a woman, to make more sense. In tandem, observing norms within cultural behavior such as the kinds of jobs women are seen to be in, the roles they play in shopping, taking care of children, older people, and pets, their style of dress, and whether, as is the case in Kuwait, they have to buy hamburgers in a different location than men can be diagnostic of their social position.

Divergence

In intergroup interaction, social stereotypes about ingroups and outgroups can be triggered that could alter the ways messages are exchanged between intergroup members in such a way as to create divergence or a distance between ingroups and outgroups. Knowledge of stereotypes of various groups (and their subtypes), the kinds of emotions they stir up, and their attributed origins can also be as important information about the groups as the kinds of ethnophaulisms that exist about them. This can be especially important in terms of the outgroup or host culture's images of particular groups of foreigners and the reasons triggered to account for them. Particularly, knowing how you might be perceived by others, and why, can be enormously helpful in adapting to a culture and its members (see Reid & Anderson, 2010). This is a difficult situation to deal with and especially so, for example, when stereotypes of U.S. Americans (such as their being aggressive, arrogant, superior, imperialist, loud, and so forth) are written large on the linguistic landscape—as in graffiti on walls in large letters saying "Yanks Go Home!" What is even more frightening is the infrahumanization effect whereby people have a tendency to attribute and express human qualities to members of their ingroup, but less human and more animalistic properties to outgroups, such as *knuckleheads* or *gooks* (see Vaes & Paladino, 2010).

Although research on group vitality has been devoted mostly to interethnic group settings, it is important to underscore that other forms of cultural groupings—including the generations, organized street gangs, hearing impaired (and deaf culture), police, and so forth—all lend themselves to cogent analysis in these terms. Given power disparities and vitality disparities, intergroup accommodation is, more often than not, unidirectional to the extent that subordinate groups communicatively align themselves more with dominant groups than vice versa. This might be a problem for society because it hampers its ability to evolve or be empowered to embrace the cultural capital of another community that has its own enriching resources.

All this could lead to accommodative dilemmas, which occur when people have to communicatively manage others' miscategorizations of, or overt or covert abuse toward, their group in their conversations. For example, a U.S. American student studying abroad is questioned by the patriarch of her host family about whether she fits the stereotypes he holds of U.S. Americans. The student faces an accommodative dilemma because she has to manage how she responds to his questions in order to be accommodative while navigating his mischaracterization of U.S. American culture. Such situations are particularly challenging if people wish to amend an outgroup's feelings about, and images of, their ingroup. One intercultural sphere, namely intergenerational communication, has expended some modest effort in this direction by looking at the ways older people can deflect or manage situations (e.g., by being assertive or humorous) in which they have been patronized because of their age (Ryan, Kennaley, Pratt, & Shumovich, 2000).

The thrust of this chapter is that it is important, in all these respects, to understand how other groups (as well as meaningful subgroups within them) might perceive you and your cultural group, that is, how people label, stereotype, describe, and react to you. Group members need to inquire into the social origins of perceptions of their group, however illegitimate and disturbing these cognitions and emotions feel. In this sense, people need to appreciate that if another group member diverges away from them in speech style or nonverbally, and also denigrates them overtly or covertly, that they should not necessarily take this personally but, rather, take it as a more generic reaction to group membership in a perceived social category. In this way, personal respect and esteem can typically only be improved to the extent that the outgroup culture revises the image of the ingroup as a whole more positively, or views each person in the ingroup as unique individuals to be valued positively due to salient individuating information. Moreover, it is important to underscore *perceived* in the foregoing advisedly as sometimes people are categorized into cultural groupings erroneously by others based on inferences about the perceived character of their communicative styles; for example, being attributed by a U.S. American as English when you are Irish.

Intergroup Model of Accommodative Processes

The model depicted in Figure 7.1 is a summarized way of schematizing the argument developed in this chapter. Starting with the top left box, a person needs to garner knowledge about the outgroup(s) being visited, and relate this to ingroup ways of interacting. Such knowledge can be gained by direct face-to-face interactions, vicarious observations of, and even imagined contact with outgroup members (see Turner, 2010). Intergroup contact can come by way of conversations with, and observations of, the host culture through its media, literature, and knowledge of its history (Harwood, 2010). Interestingly, few intercultural communication programs are devised to provide potential vacationers (and business people) with recorded histories of the groups involved, let alone from both cultures' perspectives (Cargile & Giles, 1996).

Enriched by this intergroup knowledge, more positive attitudes toward the outgroup and increased motivations to be communicatively involved with them can be engendered (as well as perhaps new insights evoked about a person's ingroup, too). These intergroup attitudes and motivations (middle lower box in Figure 7.1) then allow a person to be better placed to make appropriate communicative accommodations to the outgroup and manage accommodative dilemmas, be it in terms of key words, phrases, or accepted dress styles for particular contexts, and so forth. In the ideal world, the outgroup will recognize these accommodations, and should reciprocal accommodations follow (see top right box), then positive intergroup outcomes (e.g., intercultural communication satisfaction) will ensue (see right lower box). The arrows in Figure 7.1 are bilateral to indicate feedback cycles as in the case of intercultural satisfaction promoting future, and perhaps more extensive, accommodations as well as satisfaction encouraging the pursuit of further intergroup knowledge.

FINAL THOUGHTS

A skeptic reading this chapter might conclude that intercultural encounters are a minefield that should be avoided at all costs! The intent, of course, has not been to spawn such fears, but rather, that you remain mindful of, and become more sophisticated about, complex intergroup dynamics as tourists, businesspeople and the like. This can help to navigate misattributions, miscommunication, and even conflicts and increase the benefits gained from intercultural interaction. Some cultures encountered greet people with open arms if their images of that group have been historically and politically positive, as well as economically and militarily supportive. Possibly and intuitively, it is these very cultures that people choose to embrace as they plan trips abroad in order to minimize the demands of the intergroup work referred to previously and enhance the intercultural satisfaction they so wish to enjoy. Even then, people need to be open and welcoming to those who inevitably and frequently enter (and, in some people's minds, invade) their own cultural space as refugees, visitors, and migrants. Hopefully, the model scheme in Figure 7.1 will be a useful heuristic for managing the plethora of intergroup and intercultural episodes that readers will inevitably encounter over their life spans.

CONTINUE YOUR JOURNEY ONLINE

Visit: www.babyboomers.com/

The National Association of Baby Boomers website. Learn about how this generation views its cultural identity. Explore issues that are important for this generation. How does this group construct itself through the website as distinct from other groups?

Note

We wish to extend sincere appreciation to the editor of this volume for her encouragement throughout the process and her wonderfully cogent and extensive comments on earlier drafts.

66 SAY WHAT?

Say What? provides excerpts from overheard real-life conversations in which people have communicated stereotypes. As you read these conversations, reflect on the following questions.

- Have you been in conversations like this before?
- Is there any one of these conversations that stick out to you more than the others? Why or why not?
- What do you think of this conversation?
- How did the stereotype help or hinder the conversation?
- Was there another way the stereotyper could have communicated to convey the same point?
- How do you feel when you hear this conversation or the specific stereotype?
- Do any concepts, issues, or theories discussed in the chapter help explain why?

- **Say What?** Jen walked right past the two of us mumbling something about how she can not stand how the house is always looking sloppy. She noticed a pot with rice stuck to it soaking in water and said, "See like this gook pot soaking in the sink; I am sick of this." Melissa and I just looked at each other and then laughed out loud and so did Jen. I informed Jen that it was me who was responsible for the pot of rice soaking in the sink and not our Chinese roommate.

- **Say What?** Shelly and I were discussing one of the girls that had come out to rush sorority, "Marie," who had been extremely shy, kind of hard to talk to, and lived in the honors dorm. She was very nice and seemed to be a little nervous. Shelly then implied that maybe we would not want her in sorority because she is probably a boring person and probably isn't too much fun to be around. I was kind of surprised that she was so blunt about it. Then after a couple of seconds I disagreed with her. I told her that not all shy, smart people were necessarily boring.

- **Say What?** This past Saturday my friend and I were at the bank standing in line. She just needed change. The line was really outrageous and she didn't want to wait. So she said, "I guess I have to wait in this line. I would ask someone in line for change but they don't look like they have any money." I said to her, "Wow isn't that a stereotype." The people in the line were all Mexican except us. I thought it was really ironic that she would assume that these people had no money yet they were standing in the bank.

- **Say What?** An African American individual started to walk in front of us. He was coming toward us and we could see that his dress was not very collegelike; he seemed to be in his mid-20s and did not seem to go to college. My friend was holding my left hand as the individual passed that side. As he moved closer, she proceeded to walk to the other side of me and squeeze tightly my left hand. The response that the individual took was to move into the street.

REVIEW QUESTIONS

1. What is the difference between intergroup and inter-individual interaction, as defined in the chapter? Why does this distinction matter for intercultural communication?

2. Do ingroups shift depending on which is salient at a given time or are they fixed regardless of context? Explain your answer by using and extending examples from the chapter.

3. How do people use labels to differentiate between ingroups and outgroups?

4. In your own words, explain social identity theory using one of the examples discussed in the chapter.

5. Why might categorization threat and identity denial discussed in the chapter relate to the concept of face discussed earlier in the text

6. Choose an example from an earlier chapter in the text. Explain how the concept of intergroup boundaries defined in this chapter applies.

7. When are the subdimensions of group vitality been particularly relevant? Provide an example and explain based on the discussion in the chapter.

8. Where does media fit in the model of accommodative processes provided in the chapter? Why is this an appropriate place for it in a model about accommodation?

9. Based on the discussion throughout the chapter, create a list of the characteristics we tend to assign to ingroup members and what characteristics we tend to assign to outgroups, regardless of which particular culture either represents.

10. The chapter discusses intergroup interaction in neither a positive or negative way, though some of the examples demonstrate both. Why is this neutral stance taken?

KEY TERMS

accommodative dilemma   157

accommodative move   155

categorization threat   147

communication accommodation theory   154

demographic   153

ethnolinguistic identity theory   151

ethnonym   148

ethnophaulism   147

group vitality   150

identity denial   147

individuating information   141

infrahumanization effect   156

ingroup   142

institutional support   153

intergroup boundary   146

intergroup communication perspective   141

intergroup contact   157

intergroup interaction   141

intergroup status hierarchy   147

inter-individual interaction   141

language suicide   152

linguistic intergroup bias   148

REFERENCES

Ball, P., Byrne, J., Giles, H., Berechree, P., Griffiths, J., McDonald, H., & McKendrick, I. (1982). The retroactive speech stereotype effect: Some Australian data and constraints. *Language and Communication, 2,* 277–284.

Cargile, A. C., & Giles, H. (1996). Intercultural communication training review, critique, and a new theoretical framework. In B. Burleson (Ed.), *Communication Yearbook 19* (pp. 385–423). Thousand Oaks, CA: Sage.

Cheryan, S., & Monin, B. (2005). Where are you *really* from? Asian Americans and identity denial. *Journal of Personality and Social Psychology, 89,* 717–730.

Cleveland, M., Laroche, M., Pons, F., & Kastoun, R. (2009). Acculturation and consumption: Textures of cultural adaptation. *International Journal of Intercultural Relations, 33,* 196–212.

Dumont, M., Yzerbyt, V., Wigboldus, D., & Gordijn, E. (2003). Social categorization and fear reactions to the September 11th Terrorist Attacks. *Personality and Social Psychology Bulletin, 29,* 1509–1520.

Edwards, J. (2005). Community-focused apologia in international affairs: Japanese Prime Minister Tomiichi Murayama's apology. *The Howard Journal of Communications,* 16, 317–336

Ellis, D. (2006). *Transforming conflict: Communication and ethnopolitical conflict.* New York: Rowman & Littlefield.

Gallois, C. (2008). Intergroup accommodative processes. In W. Donsbach (Ed.), *International encyclopedia of communication* (Vol. VI, pp. 2368–2372). Oxford, UK: Blackwell.

Gallois, C., & Callan, V. C. (1997). *Communication and culture: A guide for practice.* Chichester, UK: Wiley.

Gaudet, S., & Clément, R. (2008). Forging an identity as a linguistic minority: Intra and intergroup aspects of language, communication and identity in Western Canada. *International Journal of Intercultural Relations, 33,* 213–227.

Giles, H., Bourhis, R. Y., & Taylor, D. M. (2009). Towards a theory of language in ethnic group relations. In N. Coupand & A. Jaworksi (Eds.). *Subjective and ideological processes in sociolinguistics* (pp. 97–132). London: Routledge.

Giles, H., & Johnson, P. (2009). The role of language in ethnic group relations. In N. Coupland & A. Jaworski (Eds.) *Subjective and ideological processes in sociolinguistics* (pp. 144–187). London: Routledge.

Giles, H., & Ogay, T. (2006). Communication accommodation theory. In B. Whaley & W. Samter (Eds.), *Explaining communication: Contemporary theories and exemplars* (pp. 293–310). Mahwah, NJ: Lawrence Erlbaum.

Giles, H., Rosenthal, D., & Young, L. (1985). Perceived ethnolinguistic vitality: The Anglo- and Greek-Australian setting. *Journal of Multilingual and Multicultural Development, 6,* 253–269.

Giles, H., & Viladot, A. (1994). Ethnolinguistic identity in Catalonia. *Multilingua, 13,* 301–312.

Giles, H., & Watson, B. (2008). Intercultural and intergroup communication. In W. Donsbach (Ed.), *International encyclopedia of communication* (Vol. VI, pp. 2337–2348). Oxford, UK: Blackwell.

Giles, H., Reid, S. A., & Harwood, J. (Eds.). (2010). *The dynamics of intergroup communication.* New York: Peter Lang.

Harwood, J. (2010). The contact space: A novel framework for intergroup contact research. *Journal of Language and Social Psychology, 29,* 147–177.

Harwood, J., & Giles, H. (Eds.). (2005). *Intergroup communication: Multiple perspectives.* New York: Peter Lang.

Harwood, J., Giles, H., & Bourhis, R. Y. (1994). The genesis of vitality theory: Historical patterns and discoursal dimensions. *International Journal of the Sociology of Language, 108,* 168–206.

Kim, Y. Y. (2001). *Becoming intercultural: An integrative theory of cross-cultural adaptation.* Thousand Oaks, CA: Sage.

Leets, L., & Giles, H. (1997). Words as weapons—when do they wound? Investigations of harmful speech. *Human Communication Research, 24,* 260–301.

Mullen, B., & Smyth, J. M. (2004). Immigrant suicide rates as a function of ethnophaulisms: Hate speech predicts death. *Psychosomatic Medicine, 66,* 343–348.

Mullen, B., Calogero, R. M., & Leader, T. I. (2007). A social psychological study of ethnonyms: Cognitive representations of the ingroup and intergroup hostility. *Journal of Personality and Social Psychology, 92,* 612–630.

Reid, S. A., & Anderson, G. (2010). In H. Giles, S. A. Reid, & J. Harwood (Eds.), *The dynamics of intergroup communication* (pp. 91–104). New York: Peter Lang.

Ryan, E. B., Kennaley, D. E., Pratt, M. W., & Shumovich, M. A. (2000). Patronizing speech and assertive responses in the nursing home: Evaluative perceptions by staff, residents, and community seniors. *Psychology and Aging, 15,* 272–285.

Sutton, R. M., & Douglas, K. M. (Eds.). (2008). Celebrating two decades of linguistic bias research. *Journal of Language and Social Psychology, 27,* 105–109.

Tajfel, H., & Turner, J. C. (1986). An integrative theory of intergroup conflict. In S. Worchel & W. G. Austin (Eds.), *Psychology of intergroup relations* (pp. 2–24). Chicago: Nelson-Hall.

Turner, R. (2010). Imagining harmonious intergroup relations. *The Psychologist, 23,* 298–301.

Vaes, J., & Paladino, M. P. (2010). The uniquely human content of stereotypes. *Group Processes and Intergroup Relations, 23,* 23–39.

Privilege and Culture

Gust A. Yep

San Francisco State University

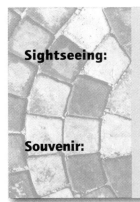

Journey Through Chapter 8

Sightseeing: On your journey, you will use the social constructionist approach from a critical perspective to visit basic concepts relevant to privilege and culture—including power, globalization, and hierarchies of cultures—in order to understand how privilege, power, and culture are constructions that intersect.

Souvenir: After your journey, you will take away an in-depth understanding of privilege and be able to articulate your status with regard to privilege within your own culture.

In the United States, a lot of people have Internet access, particularly if you are on a college campus. What does *access* mean? Does access mean easy availability—that is, you can get online anywhere and anytime you wish to do so? Does access mean affordability—that is, you can get online either for free or at a relatively low cost to you? Does access mean convenience—that is, you can get online easily and quickly? For many U.S. Americans, the Internet is accessible because it is often available, affordable, and convenient. This might give the impression that most people in the world have access to the Internet. Sadly, this is not true. In fact, for a lot of people in the world, the Internet is unavailable, too slow, or too costly to use. For others, it is the lack of sites in their own native languages, or a combination of all these factors.

In many ways, this modern technology that you probably take for granted has created two different groups of people—those who have access to it and those who do not. This group differentiation is connected to economic, political, and technological power. For example, huge economic and technological disparities exist between the United States and African nations, which are directly connected to differences in Internet access between people in the

United States and people in Africa. Based on these disparities, you can say that U.S. Americans, even in the current climate of higher levels of unemployment and loss of homes due to foreclosures and other economic challenges, are privileged when compared to other people in the world.

You may have never thought about ideas of power and privilege in relationship to culture before. It may have never occurred to you to do so. This may be because these concepts seem abstract and you might feel that they do not relate to you directly. These ideas might be uncomfortable to consider or you might feel that you do not know how to talk about them. These feelings and reactions are fairly common. Embrace them and pay attention to how they change as you engage with ideas about power and privilege in the chapter. The first section of this chapter discusses globalization, followed by sections discussing power, hierarchies of culture, and privilege. The chapter concludes by providing additional topics that will help you to understand the intersections between privilege, power, and culture.

GLOBALIZATION

Have you ever looked around your house to see where your belongings—personal electronics, school supplies, household products, clothes and accessories, and personal grooming products— were made? If you do, you are likely going to discover that these things, which you might use every day, are made by people from other cultures in other regions of the world. Have you ever wondered what communication with them would be like? If you have called customer service or technical assistance numbers, you might have already had some experience with this type of communication. For example, if you are having a problem with your computer, the representative at the other end of the technical assistance line might be in another state, or more likely, in another country. Although the name of the representative might be a Western one, you might detect an accent or a somewhat different speech pattern. Next time, ask where the person is located and you may be surprised to hear, "I am Johnny and I am at the call center in Bangalore, India."

The world has become increasingly global. Globalization is the process whereby people's lives and local communities are increasingly influenced by economic, technological, and cultural forces that operate worldwide. For example, many products, which you use every day, are produced by large international corporations and conglomerates (Lynn, 2010). They are designed in a country or perhaps by a transnational team that includes members from several cultures, the parts and components are manufactured in other regions of the world and assembled in factories located in various countries, and finally, the finished products are distributed and sold in the world market oftentimes not in the countries in which they were made. Globalization produces a global mass culture. You can readily see this when you travel. You can find a Big Mac, a can of Coke, a Banana Republic T-shirt, or an Apple computer in a lot of communities around the world. This global mass culture is fairly homogeneous—a Big Mac or can of Coke might be packaged in different languages or adapted to local markets but they will have a predictable taste whether you get them in Barcelona (Spain), Beijing (China), Johannesburg (South Africa), Rio de Janeiro (Brazil), or Sydney (Australia). However, a Big Mac and a Coke are treated as inexpensive fast food in the United States and more expensive

U.S. American food in Central America. Taking your date to a McDonald's will probably be viewed as cheap and tacky in the United States but expensive and unique in Central America. In other words, these global mass cultural products have different monetary and social values in different cultures.

REFLECT 8.1: How has globalization affected you? Think about your personal and professional lives. How has globalization affected other people you know?

People are living in a global village. This term, coined by media scholar Marshall McLuhan (1967), has been used to refer to a world in which various communication technologies bring people together from different regions of the globe. With the Internet, you can readily communicate with people in remote parts of the world, many of whom you will probably never meet in person. As indicated earlier, not everyone you communicate with has the same resources. In the United States, most people have access to televisions and computers. This is not true in other regions of the world. The differences in availability and access create feelings and perceptions of U.S. American privilege and highlight disparities in economic, military, and political power between cultures.

As a member of this global village, your ability to communicate with people from your own culture as well as other cultures is critical. Understanding how power and privilege operate in communication within and between cultures, the topic of this chapter, can help you become a more sensitive communicator. The chapter is divided into five sections. The first focuses on power and its related concepts in the context of inter/cultural communication. The next two sections use the concept of hierarchy to discuss relationships between cultures (hierarchies of culture) and social relations and interactions within a culture (cultural hierarchies). The fourth section examines privilege and power in inter/cultural communication. The chapter ends with a summary of the main ideas presented here.

POWER

What comes to mind when people talk about power? You might have images of a powerful figure such as the president of the United States or an international billionaire. Government and law, including officials who write legislation, such as politicians and lawmakers, and individuals who enforce them, such as police officers and court judges, might also come up. You might think about "power of the people," that is, how everyday people can collectively change the world through organizing around specific issues, such as campaigns to legalize marijuana. Is power always top-down, that is, coming from the more powerful to restrict and restrain the less powerful as in how a CEO can dramatically affect the lives of employees in an organization? Can power flow from the bottom-up, such as in community organizing to change some aspect of society? Is power always repressive, that is, to restrict or restrain people through the control of resources such as money, knowledge, and various social institutions? Is power inherent in certain people and institutions? As you can see, the concept of power is quite complex. This section explores some of these complexities.

Conceptualizing Power

Power is the ability to control circumstances (like access to financial, social, and cultural resources) and to get things done (like fulfilling personal goals and dreams and helping others achieve theirs). According to renowned French philosopher Michel Foucault (1978/1990), power is a network of relations that circulates through all social relationships—including intercultural interactions and cross-cultural encounters—and all levels of society. To put it differently, all individual and social relationships operate within relations of power. If you think about your experiences in the service industry—restaurants, for example—you can see how power operates. If you are a server, you are probably aware that having a good relationship with your customers (friendly attitude and efficient service) might increase your tips and perhaps even get a complimentary face-to-face comment or a nice online review for your establishment. If you are a customer, you might be aware that having a good relationship with your server (friendly attitude and polite requests) will make your dining experience more pleasant and enjoyable. You might have also heard stories about what some servers do to your food if they are angry with you. In other words, your relationship—from either perspective—is deeply influenced by relations of power (to tip, to complain, to increase enjoyment of your experience). This network of relations, Foucault adds, is not simply constraining and limiting (power over), as in the restaurant customers having all the power over the servers, but also productive and enabling (power to), as both customers and servers have different degrees and levels of power that enable their relationship. In sum, power is complex, dynamic, and omnipresent in all relationships, including those within a cultural context and between members of different cultures.

REFLECT 8.2: Michel Foucault said, "Power is everywhere." What did this French philosopher mean by his famous statement? Do you agree? Disagree? Why?

Levels of Power

There are two interrelated levels of power operating simultaneously in any given situation. The first level of power is macroscopic, which is the way power is set up in a given culture or society at a particular time in history. This level is about the circulation of power on a larger social scale and it includes government and politics, social policy and the law, religious institutions, educational systems, health care institutions, family and kinship systems, mass media, and other social institutions. This level of power is generally created by a few people—the more powerful, such as political and religious leaders—and affects the lives of virtually everyone in society. The second level of power is microscopic, which occurs in individual and social transactions—in conversations with others, interpersonal relationships, or inter/cultural encounters. These can be face-to-face (having a conversation with someone from a shared culture at the school cafeteria) or mediated (having a chat room exchange with someone from another culture in a different region of the world). Together, these two levels operate simultaneously, and often invisibly, in people's lives, in their relationships with particular others and with the larger social group.

Both macroscopic and microscopic levels of power are present in relationships between different groups in a culture. There are two dimensions of group-related power. The primary dimension refers to more permanent traits and the value society assigns to them. Some such attributes are race, ethnicity, culture, gender, sexual orientation, age, and ability. People will have more or less power in a culture depending on the intersections of these attributes. For example, according to feminist writer Audre Lorde (1984) and gender activist Kate Bornstein (1998), a young, heterosexual Latina who is a recent U.S. immigrant is likely going to have considerably less power than a gay European American who is a U.S. citizen in his 20s. He, in turn, is likely to have less power than his heterosexual counterpart, who is also a U.S. citizen, in his 50s. The secondary dimension of group-related power refers to more changeable attributes, such as socioeconomic status, educational background, marital status, and geographical location, that a particular society assigns different degrees of value to the person displaying them. For example, in the United States as well as in many other cultures, individuals who are wealthy, married, and coming from urban centers usually have more status and power than people who are poor or less wealthy, perhaps single, and residing in rural areas.

Ideology

Power influences the way people think and act. Ideology, a concept popularized by French thinker Louis Althusser (1971), refers to the collective beliefs, attitudes, perceptions, and values that are known to members of a culture and that guide their actions. For example, consumerism is a dominant ideology in numerous cultures. Shopping, the acquisition of objects and use of services, and the accumulation of material goods are activities that you probably engage in on a daily basis. Consumerism is omnipresent in U.S. culture, as communication scholar Marita Sturken (2007) observes that in times of national crisis and mourning, such as 9/11 and the Oklahoma City bombing, many U.S. Americans are driven to consume comfort objects such as World Trade Center snow globes, FDNY teddy bears and T-shirts, and Oklahoma City Memorial branded water. Although not everyone in U.S. culture endorses an ideology of consumerism, everyone is exposed to it on an ongoing basis. Consumerism is connected to capitalism, which is simultaneously an economic system, a cultural ideology, and a political system that govern that nation. Cultural ideology generally comes from the more powerful members of a culture—for example, owners of large corporations—who stand to profit from these ideas and practices.

Hegemony

According to philosopher Rosemary Hennessy (1995), hegemony "is the process whereby the interests of a ruling group [i.e., those with power] come to dominate by establishing the common sense, that is, those values, beliefs, and knowledges that go without saying" (pp. 145–146). In other words, hegemony refers to a temporary closure of meaning—that is, ideas become fixed—to support the interests and beliefs of the powerful by making their ideas unquestionable and commonsensical. This is accomplished not by overt violence or coercion but by the winning of consent, that is, the process of creating and maintaining acceptance and agreement to these ideas. Through this process, historically powerful groups—for example, the cultural elite and large businesses—exercise social authority, control, and leadership over the general population. For example, most people in Western cultures believe in the idea of marrying for love to the degree that marrying for other reasons, such as money and status, seem immediately suspect and even wrong. However, historian Stephanie Coontz (2005) points out that marriage has more to do with inheritance rights than love in most complex civilizations. In other words, wealthy individuals, through marriage, can keep the wealth in their families and pass it on to successive generations. She points out that "in some cultures and times, true love was actually thought to be incompatible with marriage . . . [while] other societies considered it good if love developed after marriage" (p. 16). Although marrying for love is a recent cultural invention, it is also a powerful one. Virtually everyone in the world has been exposed to it and, of those who have, most accept it without question. To the extent that you believe that marriage should be about love above all else, hegemony is working to naturalize certain meanings such as the way marriage is or should be. This is accomplished by making these seem natural and beyond question and foreclosing other possible meanings such as marriage for regulating property, sex, and child rearing. In this way, marriage is guided by the hegemony, but perceived as only motivated by love.

Otherness

When hegemonic ideas and social practices become taken-for-granted standards of a culture, they create a hierarchy of differences that vary in terms of the value they have for that culture. For example, returning to the idea of marriage, those individuals who marry because "they are in love" would be viewed as the standard for romantic relationships in most contemporary cultures. Those who marry because of economic necessity (e.g., money) and social aspirations (e.g., status) would be judged as having a lesser relationship—that is, one with less value—in those cultures. Those who are in arranged marriages might find themselves judged even more harshly, as *outdated, antiquated,* and even *primitive.* In other words, the individuals who did not marry for love may be *othered* in their culture.

Otherness refers to specific locations in a particular social group where individuals are deemed to have deviated from the cultural standard or center. The *other,* discussed in Chapter 6, and the center are intricately related to each other. For example, to say that arranged marriages are backward and primitive affirms, either implicitly or explicitly, that marriage for love is normal and contemporary. In this sense, the cultural standard cannot exist without its *others* as a contrast. Indeed, for the standard to maintain its normality and desirability in a culture, it needs its deviant and inferior others. For example, a person cannot say that marriage for love is normal in a culture except by comparing it to other forms of marriage that are deemed abnormal or, at least, less normal. The topic of ingroups and outgroups were discussed extensively in Chapter 7 and relates here. The cultural standard is connected to ingroups while otherness is associated with outgroups.

HIERARCHIES OF CULTURES

How do you think about various cultures around the world? You might consider them in terms of similarities—what they have in common—and differences—how they are unique and distinct from each other. When you think about differences, you might also be evaluating them in terms of specific values. For example, when you travel across various cultural communities you might talk about a culture, for example, as having better food, better public transportation system, less friendly people, and more primitive customs when compared to other groups. In this case, the values that you are using to assess these cultural differences would be the taste of their food, the efficiency of their transportation system, the friendliness of the people, and the nature of their customs. In the process of evaluating cultures, people are establishing and maintaining hierarchies. This section explores hierarchies of culture.

First-World and Third-World

What comes to mind when you hear *first-world*? Perhaps images of economic prosperity, advanced technologies, abundance of material goods, strong educational system, solid infrastructure, and stable democracy are conjured up. What about a *third-world* nation and culture? Images of poverty, lack of technology, abundance of raw materials, impoverished educational system, underdeveloped infrastructure, and unstable government might come to mind. As you can see, first-world and third-world nations and cultures are related to each other, with the former occupying the positive and the latter the negative end of a continuum of values related to economic, technological and educational development, or political stability. To put it differently, the concept of a developed and powerful first-world cannot exist without its relational other, the idea of an underdeveloped and poor third-world.

First-world was a term originally used to designate the dominant economic powers of the West, such as the United States, characterized by a capitalist system of production. Second-world was employed to refer to other economic powers, such as the

Photo 8.1 What rights and responsibilities do we have to other cultures? The ways we behave during times of war have consequences for people's lives. These pictures represent just a few of the atrocities we commit against others: atomic bombs, concentration camps, slavery, and genocide.

Copyright 2010 Bill Edwards.

Soviet Union and its satellites, featuring a socialist system of production. Originally used by politician and economist Alfred Sauvy (1952) to designate the nations that were aligned with neither the United States nor the Soviet Union, the concept of the third-world describes cultures constituted by the experience of being ruled or controlled by others. Such cultures are saturated with images of poverty, disease, and war. More recently, fourth-world was introduced to designate cultural groups of indigenous people who suffer even more economic marginalization and social oppression than groups ruled or controlled by foreign powers (Brotherston, 1992).

The classification of nations and cultures listed previously produces a distinct hierarchy that maintains the otherness of third- and fourth-world peoples. Criticizing this hierarchy, literary theorist and political commentator Aijaz Ahmad (2006) points out, "ideologically, this classification divides the world between those who make history [first- and second-worlds] and those who are mere objects of it [third- and fourth-worlds]" (p. 85). In spite of these criticisms, these cultural hierarchies continue to persist in the popular imagination.

Imperialism and Its Different Forms

When more powerful nations and cultures rule or control less powerful ones, you have colonialism and imperialism. They are distinct from each other. Colonialism, according to cultural critic Edward Said (1993), refers to the "implanting of settlements on distant territory" (p. 9). For example, many Latin American cultures—Argentina, Colombia, Ecuador, Mexico, Peru, Venezuela, among others—were colonized by Spain prior to the 20th century. As Spain exploited the local populations, depleted their natural resources, created new forms of government, and introduced Catholicism, local cultures and ways of living, indigenous languages and social institutions were dramatically, and sometimes violently, modified or destroyed.

Imperialism, on the other hand, refers to "the practice, theory, and the attitudes of a dominating metropolitan center ruling a distant territory" (Said, 1993, p. 9). Although direct colonialism has largely ended in the 21st century, imperialism continues in several forms. Wealthy nations, such as the United States and England, exercise their powerful influence on cultures around the globe through the dissemination of attitudes, ideas, practices, and products.

Cultural imperialism is pervasive today. It refers to the process of domination through the proliferation and global spread of cultural products. If you travel, you can readily see U.S. American brands—in foods and beverages, pharmaceutical products, clothing labels, and computer equipment, for example—in many cultures in the world. However, you are much less likely going to encounter these same types of products from other cultures in the United States. This asymmetrical proliferation of cultural products makes the U.S. culture dominant in a global world. With the rapid expansion of communication technologies, media imperialism, or the domination or control through media products, has become ubiquitous. U.S. media products, ranging from Hollywood films and television shows to music and the news are virtually everywhere in the world. They not only provide a U.S. perspective of reality that dominates the media world, but also displace local media products at the expense of local cultural viewpoints. Local communities and governments react negatively to this asymmetrical proliferation and expansion that tends to be largely unidirectional, originating from the first-world and spreading to cultures around the globe. Products from the third-world have limited distribution and markets in the first-world—take for example, how motion pictures from all over the world, including the third-world, get grouped into a singular category of *foreign films* in the United States.

Travel and Identity Tourism

Travel is the process of moving across various cultural contexts for relatively short periods of time. One of the reasons for travel is for leisure and recreation. Through travel, people learn more about themselves—their likes and dislikes, values and perceptions, and behavioral patterns— and other groups—their attitudes, beliefs, values, customs, and rituals. With the expansion of communication technologies, people can also travel virtually. Individuals can experience other worlds through these technologies without leaving the comforts of their own home. This ability has created opportunities for identity tourism, which refers to the process whereby individuals take on the identities of other cultures, races, ethnicities, genders, social classes, sexualities, and (dis)abilities for recreational purposes. For example, you can take on the identity of another cultural group when you are in an Internet chat room to experience communication from a different perspective. Although the process might be fun and insightful about the world of others, it also raises some serious ethical concerns including deception and manipulation of others.

Intercultural Transitions and Cultural Migrations

Intercultural transition refers to the process of moving between cultural contexts ranging from relatively short periods of time to long durations and permanent resettlement. Closely related to the concept of intercultural transition, cultural migration refers to the flow of people, social networks, and cultural values from one cultural context, such as a nation-state, to another. Individuals and groups migrate between different cultural boundaries for mostly economic and political reasons. Communication scholar Majid Tehranian (2004) notes that cultural migrations

Photo 8.2   What landmarks have you gone out of your way to visit? Millions of people travel around the world each year to visit the sites of other cultures. Tourism is a tremendous money-making industry. Souvenirs, media, and advertising all reproduce the iconic images of a cultural landscape in order to make money. Economic factors are strong motivators to continue political, economic, and social trends and policies within a culture.

Copyright 2010 Bill Edwards and Michael Kurylo.

Photo 8.3 How would you feel if you moved from your place of birth to another country in which you were a marginalized group? In this picture, poetry from Shizue Iwatsuki, a refugee living in a U.S. internment camp during World War II, is inscribed on granite boulders in the Japanese American Historical Plaza in Portland.

War and change,
My native land
Once so hard to leave,
Is behind me now
forever.

Copyright 2010 Michael Kurylo.

are currently at an all-time high, flowing from developing nations about equally to other developing countries and more industrialized ones, with a growing number of women among them. Such migrations are increasingly politicized, including greater mainstream media attention that can intensify anti-immigrant sentiments. They are also increasingly commodified with the rise of agencies that provide services to relocate individuals and groups from one cultural context to another.

Intercultural transition and cultural migration occur in different forms. Travel, as discussed in the previous section, is a form of voluntary intercultural transition characterized by its relatively short duration and the expectation to return to the original cultural context. Another form of voluntary intercultural transition is immigration. Immigration is the process of moving from one nation-state to another to settle more or less permanently. Not all intercultural transitions are voluntary. Some individuals or groups are forced to move to other cultural contexts for a variety of reasons—political, economic, social, and environmental. These people are refugees, some of which move away for relatively short durations. An example of refugees in the United States would be the internment of Japanese Americans during World War II, which occurred after Japan bombed Pearl Harbor. The U.S. government responded by confiscating the properties and material possessions of U.S. citizens of Japanese descent, who had nothing to do with the bombing, and quarantining these citizens by putting them in internment camps. Other refugees move away for a long time or even settle in a new cultural context. For example, after the U.S. occupation of Iraq in 2003, many Iraqis left their home country to start a new life and settling in cities of neighboring nations like Beirut.

REFLECT 8.3: Explore your family tree. Where does your family come from? What were their reasons for migration? What obstacles did they encounter?

PRIVILEGE

How do you think about various cultures inside the United States? Once again, you might think about them in terms of similarities—what they have in common with your own cultural background—or differences—how they are distinct from your own. As stated earlier, differences are not simply about how distinct two cultural groups are from one another. They generally include evaluation of distinctiveness in terms of a value system. For example, English professor Lindon Barrett (1999) maintains that race is associated with value as he unpacks U.S. cultural binarisms such as *alliterate, singing,* and *street* for blackness and *literate, signing,* and *academy* for whiteness to reveal the higher cultural value placed on whiteness. This section examines privilege and oppression in cultural hierarchies.

The Nature of Privilege and Oppression

Privilege and oppression are emotionally loaded words in the United States. Sociologist Allan Johnson (2001) urges people "to reclaim [them] so that we can use [them] to name and illuminate the truth" (p. 23). In other words, there is a need to have a deeper understanding of these terms if you want to become a more sensitive communicator. Privilege and oppression are actually two sides of the same coin. Whereas privilege creates open doors of opportunity, oppression slams them shut. Privilege is a frequently invisible and normalized process whereby a person is granted more value, and given better treatment, solely based on this person's membership in a group. For example, if a Muslim woman and her husband go to a health care provider in Singapore to discuss her recurrent headaches and he receives more attention from the practitioner than his wife through increased eye contact, care, and thoughtfulness, he is benefiting from gender privilege. It is important to note that privilege has nothing to do with anything a person has done or failed to do. Most people in a culture simply give some individuals more power based on perceived group membership (e.g., racial, class, gender, sexuality, nationality). In this sense, you might be involved in maintaining and perpetuating certain patterns of privilege in your culture and not be aware of doing so.

There are two types of privilege—unearned advantage and conferred dominance (McIntosh, 2009). Unearned advantage refers to entitlements that everyone should have, such as feeling that your life is valuable or experiencing safety in public spaces, but these are restricted to certain groups in a culture. When this occurs, it becomes an unearned advantage for the individual or group who receives such entitlements. For example, a heterosexual person can get married anywhere while a gay or lesbian person cannot do so in most states in this country or nations in the world. This is heterosexual privilege. Conferred dominance refers to the process of most people in a culture, consciously or unconsciously, giving one group power over another. In U.S. and Latin American cultures, for example, people routinely ask intensely invasive and inappropriate questions about the sexual lives of gay and lesbian individuals when such inquiries are deemed rude and impolite if directed at their heterosexual counterparts. In this instance, conferred dominance is granted to heterosexuals who may be less likely to be asked such questions, more likely to ask them without objection, and more likely to receive answers to them from those who may feel obligated to answer because of this dominance.

The flip side of privilege is oppression. Oppression refers to social forces that limit, restrict, block, and foreclose an individual's, or a group's, pursuit of a good life. For example, gay and lesbian people in the United States as well as in numerous cultures around the world represent an oppressed group not only because they do not have the same rights and privileges that heterosexuals take for granted but they also fear persecution, socially and materially, from members of their own culture. Finally, it is worth noting that belonging to a privileged category that has an oppressive relationship with another is quite different than an oppressive person who behaves in oppressive ways. For example, men (as a social category) oppressing women (as a social category) is a social fact in heteropatriarchal cultures. But this does not inform about how a particular man might think, feel, or behave toward a particular woman in the same culture. In other words, in a heteropatriarchy, men as a social group are oppressors while individual men may or may not act in oppressive ways toward women.

Degrees of Cultural Privilege

In any given culture, identities are given certain privileges based on their location on race, social class, gender, sexuality, ability, and national hierarchies at a particular moment in history. All of them are cultural inventions and social constructions whose meanings depend on history and geography. Although Jewish-, Italian-, and Polish-Americans are automatically categorized as white in the United States today, for example, historian David Roediger (2005) observes that they were not considered white until the 1920s and 30s; before then, they were caught in a "complicated racial inbetweenness" (p. 50). Similarly, classifications of people based on sexual identity—homosexual, heterosexual—in the contemporary West did not exist until the 19th century. Although people engaged in erotic same- and different-sex activities throughout history, their behaviors did not constitute a type of person or identity until fairly recently (Foucault, 1978/1990). These variations in meanings and the cultural importance attached to them suggest that race, social class, gender, sexuality, ability, and nationality are not transhistorical, inherent, and essential categories. They are social constructions influenced by historical and geopolitical factors intricately connected to power, privilege, and oppression and maintained through formal and informal communication practices.

> ## Take a Side Trip:
>
> If you would like to read more about related issues, visit Appendix E: South African Culture Explored Through Content Analysis.

Cultural privilege is not based on a singular identity but rather on a particular configuration of all of these identities altogether. This configuration of identities is called intersectionality, which refers to how race, social class, gender, sexuality, ability, and nationality are simultaneously operating to produce a specific type of person. Everyone in a culture has an intersectional identity; intersectionality is not simply about cultural members that have less power and privilege. Some intersections might appear to be more visible than others in a culture. For example, the identity of a poor, transgender, lesbian-identified woman from Ethiopia living in the United States might be more visible than the identity of a middle-class, European American, heterosexual man who is a U.S. citizen. The former might stand out because she is viewed as a member of the outgroup while the latter might blend in because he is perceived as a member of the ingroup. In actuality, both identities are intersectional with the former having less cultural privilege than the latter.

There are two types of intersectionality. The first is a roster-like approach that simply lists all of the aspects of a person's identity and considers these superficial characteristics of a person. The second is thick intersectionality which focuses on the complexities of a person's life and identity associated with race, class, gender, sexuality, ability, and national locations by understanding the individual's history and personhood "in concrete time and space, and the interplay between individual subjectivity, personal agency, systemic arrangements, and structural forces" (Yep, 2010, p. 173). In short, thick intersectionality pays attention to the lived experiences and the biography of the person. To understand your own identity using thick intersectionality, you might explore how you make sense of the different aspects of your identity by looking at how you have lived your life and the decisions you have made, your experiences with privilege and oppression, your responses to cultural expectations, and your interactions with social institutions at particular moments in your life.

Take a Side Trip:

If you would like to read more about related issues, visit Appendix G: Japanese Culture Explored Through Experimental Design.

The concept of intersectionality invites you to think about the complexities of identities in a culture within a specific historical period and geographical location (Carroll, 2011). It helps you to avoid simplistic—and often inaccurate and misleading—conceptions of yourself and others. You are not simply your race alone or your social class or gender and so forth. You are a complex and unique mixture of all of your identities. Even when you have the exact same race, class, gender, sexuality, ability, and national identities as someone else, the two of you are likely going to be different, largely depending on when or where you grew up. Although this might appear to be rather obvious when it comes to thinking about the complexities of your own identities, you might have been tempted to simplify the identities of others. For example, in an informal conversation, you may have focused solely on the other person's gender, treated others simply on the basis of their race, or focused mostly on someone's culture because it is different from your own.

Although it is beyond the scope of this chapter to examine the intricacies of cultural privilege and oppression related to all of the preceding identities, it is important to think about them intersectionally. You might also consider taking a communication course on gender or sexuality, a sociology class on social stratification, and a history course of different ethnic groups in a particular nation-state. They will give you a broader perspective on issues of cultural privilege and oppression. As you go through the next section, which seemingly focuses on race and whiteness, consider the discussion in intersectional terms.

LIVING CULTURE

New Jersey   *Anonymous*

I went to the doctor's office to get treated for a cold. After some time in the waiting room, I saw the doctor. His first question to me was "So, what brought you to this country?" Although this inquiry appeared innocent enough, this question hurt me because it was a stereotype. To me, not only did it state that I was a foreigner, but it also meant that I was not "American." I knew the doctor did not mean to hurt my feelings because he only was trying to make conversation. Like many people, the doctor misjudged my name because it was not like other "American" names like John, Mike, or Jack. Nonetheless, the stereotype had a detrimental effect on me, offending me to the point that I immediately answered "New Jersey," remaining mostly silent throughout the entire examination. The doctor apologized for his mistake, but it was too late. The visit was surrounded by a cold, silent atmosphere. Thus my doctor's visit was a prime example of the harmful consequences of a stereotype.

In my mind, the doctor was trying to use the stereotype in a beneficial way by opening communication and breaking the ice. By having some form of conversation, the silence and awkwardness of meeting someone new is lifted. Especially when talking with a medical professional, being open and comfortable is extremely important to describing the ailments affecting a person. However, the intent of the doctor's stereotype backfired because it was a wrong judgment based on weak evidence (my name). Instead of being more open with the doctor, I held information back. Thus, in a sense, the stereotype did not really have a beneficial aspect to me.

This stereotype, which labeled me as a foreigner, offended me, although I knew the doctor did not mean to hurt me. Sarcastically responding "New Jersey" to his question, I proceeded to tell the doctor of my aliments, even though the stereotype placed a barrier between me and the doctor. I no longer felt comfortable, mentally or physically. Although I was angry at first, I also felt depressed because I knew the doctor did not mean to offend me. Like many people before him, the doctor made a mistake in judging my name because it sounded foreign. Although my name has foreign origins, what common "American" name doesn't? Many names like Mike or John have origins in Germanic or Celtic languages and cultures, both of which *are foreign.* It would thus seem to be a mistake to judge people by their names alone. Yet, this mistake is prevalent in my life in the form of this foreign, un-American stereotype.

Although my response did produce an apology from the doctor, it led to a cold social atmosphere that was surrounded by silence. Still recuperating

LIVING CULTURE

from the effects of the stereotype, I made no attempt for small talk, and the doctor followed suit. Except for the actual examination, in which the doctor checked my ears, throat, and heartbeat, the rest of the proceedings consisted of silence. Seemingly the doctor noticed the effect of his question, and remained quiet to lessen any more damage. This relationship was far from what I came to expect from a doctor-patient relationship, where communication was open and both patient as well as doctor enjoyed each other's company. In the end, the silence was broken when the doctor told me about my prescription and I left with a low, unenthusiastic "thank you."

For a person who views himself as an "American," in spite of a foreign sounding name, stereotypes can challenge self-concepts and create conflicts between these images of self. It is no wonder that I sometimes feel like I am an alien to the world.

Consider:

1. How is privilege operating in this narrative?

2. Did the author find the apology sufficient? Why or why not?

3. What were the consequences of this cultural moment?

4. Why does being considered foreign matter to the author?

Whiteness

Whiteness is a complex, elusive, and slippery concept (Yep, 2007). There are six different ways to understand whiteness. They are: (1) whiteness as invisible and unmarked, (2) whiteness as an "empty" category, (3) whiteness as structural privilege, (4) whiteness as violence and terror, (5) whiteness as institutionalization of European colonialism, and (6) critical whiteness studies as an antiracist practice (Rasmussen, Klinenberg, Nexica, & Wray, 2001). Although they might overlap or even contradict each other, these conceptualizations can give you a deeper understanding of the elusiveness and complexities of whiteness. In addition, consider how whiteness is shaped and influenced by social class, gender, sexuality, ability, and nation. When someone talks about "white trash," what intersectionalities are conjured up?

If you are European American, have you thought about the meaning of being White? If you have not, you are certainly not alone. This is because whiteness is invisible and unmarked. For example, when people talk about Timothy McVeigh, the Oklahoma City bomber, they may not think about his whiteness. In contrast, when people talk about the 9/11 terrorists, their ethnic and religious identities immediately come up. Although whiteness is a major force in the social world, it conceals its power through its invisibility. *White,* by itself, may not have much meaning unless you compare it to other social groups such as *Black*. In this sense, it is an empty category that is solely defined by absence and appropriation (e.g., whiteness as an absence of color). As such, whiteness is a relational category that is, in the words of theologian Cornel West (1990), "parasitic on 'blackness' (and other racialized groups)" (p. 29). More simply stated, whiteness acquires meaning through its relationship to other groups.

You have probably heard that being White gives people many advantages in U.S. culture. Such advantages are part of the social structure. For example, until recently, the most powerful persons in the United States and arguably in the world—the presidents of the United States—have been White men. As structural privilege, whiteness is associated with unearned advantages, opportunities, and access to the social system. This view focuses on how social institutions such as education, health care, polity, the legal system, and the media, to name only a few, consistently favor Whites. Whiteness can also be viewed as an institutionalization of European colonialism. This perspective maintains that whiteness is a reproduction of colonial, neocolonial, and imperialist discourses of the West. Whiteness, in this view, is central to the creation and maintenance of racial hierarchies and the subjugation and exploitation of racialized others.

If you are a person of color, you might be aware, consciously or unconsciously, of the power of whiteness. For example, if you are an African American male walking in the city at night, you are likely going to be aware that the police might view you as a criminal to watch for rather than a citizen to protect. In this sense, whiteness can be viewed as violence and terror—the process through which it symbolically, psychologically, and materially harms individuals who are not White. Such harms can be manifested in many forms including symbolic erasure, fear and terror, and physical violence toward people of color. For example, in India as well as many other cultures, to be a beautiful woman is to have lighter skin and European features. To promote this standard of beauty, there is a huge cosmetic industry selling skin-whitening products promising to transform racialized others into "beautiful women."

As an antiracist practice, critical whiteness work examines how White identity is socially and historically constructed. Understanding this construction and its relationship to power and privilege offers the potential to destabilize and dismantle current systems of racial stratification. For example, social groups, including Whites, can envision other ways of defining beauty in a culture if they understand how whiteness operates intersectionally to produce cultural standards of beauty for both women and men.

How do these different ways to look at whiteness help you understand yourself and those around you? If you are European American—that is, White—you might not think about whiteness too much, if at all. You might be a student who is struggling financially to attend school and working hard to balance your academic, work, and personal lives. In fact, in your daily struggles, you may not feel privileged at all. This is because privilege has more to do with a social category than who you are as a person. That society gives you advantages—that is, privilege—because you belong to the social category of White people but you do not personally feel privileged is called the "paradox of privilege" (Johnson, 2001, p. 34). If you are a person of color, you are probably much more aware of whiteness in your daily life. You might see how you and other people of color get treated differently or have fewer opportunities than European Americans. You are, in these moments, experiencing how privilege and oppression are two sides of the same coin.

UNDERSTANDING PRIVILEGE, POWER, AND CULTURE

What comes to mind when you think about privilege, power, and culture? You might think about the power the United States has in the world. Do you come up with images of a mighty military, wealth and abundance, and political and economic authority? Do you have images of social alienation, political discord, and environmental crisis? You might think about how people from other cultures react to U.S. Americans. Do images of envy for the "American way of life" turn up? Do you have images of the privileged and entitled U.S. American overseas? This section examines how privilege, power, and culture operate in intercultural communication and discusses the importance of history.

Power and Intercultural Encounters

As discussed earlier in this chapter, power is an integral component of all social relationships, including intercultural ones. Indeed power cannot be detached from intercultural encounters. However, many people do not think about power in intercultural transactions. Some even believe that these interactions occur on a level playing field. Who benefits from this belief? What are its consequences? One potential outcome of this belief is blaming the disadvantaged person

Photo 8.4 Can you see change taking place in your culture? We produce, maintain, and change history through public displays in our communities. This picture of a pedestal with its statue of Lenin replaced by a cross represents Russia establishing itself as a democracy and the transition from one dominant group to another.

Copyright 2010 Anastacia Kurylo.

rather than examining the larger social system. This process of blaming uses the following logic: "Since everyone has the same power and opportunities and you failed, it must be your fault." As you have read in the previous section, not everyone has the same power and opportunities; thus, it is critical to recognize how power is present and at work in intercultural encounters.

Understanding History

History has implications for understanding intercultural communication. First, it might help you become a more sensitive communicator by making you more aware of how stories— histories—influence the way people relate to each other as individuals and groups. Second, it can make you more conscious of how power operates in stories people tell to make sense of themselves and others. Finally, it can expand your worldview by recognizing and understanding multiple perspectives on intercultural events in a globalized world. History refers to stories people tell themselves to make sense of who they are. There are three critical features to this definition.

First, history and power are intricately connected. What was told? Who told it? What was the purpose of the telling? What was the impact of the telling? These are questions related to power. When a story gains dominance in a culture, it becomes official and hegemonic. This, too, is directly connected to power. As feminist writer Gloria Anzaldúa (2000) points out, "History is fiction because it's made up, usually made up by the people who rule" (p. 242).

Second, history is alive and always present in intercultural encounters. As stories told—in a culture, nation, region, community, or family—they influence how people think, feel, and act. In this sense, history is very much alive in people's lives. For example, if you date someone from Russia and hear stories about that culture and its people, these stories are going to influence how you relate to other Russians you meet. Your interactions with your Russian date will become stories as well and they will affect the future of your relationship.

Finally, history is not singular—there is not simply one history—but plural—there are many stories people tell. Indeed individuals and cultural groups have histories, not history. You might want to try this. Choose a war that various cultural groups were engaged in—say, World War II—and read about what the French, Germans, Italians, Japanese, Russians, and U.S. Americans say about it in their history books. If you have family members who were involved in the war, ask them to tell you their version. Chances are that you are going to be reading and listening to very different stories about World War II. Do the winners tell the same stories as the losers of the war? Why? The stories you hear from the people and the version you read in a textbook are also likely going to be different. What you read in a textbook is considered more legitimate, more "official"; this is the hegemonic version of history. A textbook might emphasize victory over defeat, celebrate the heroism of certain intersectional identities—for example, White, heterosexual, able-bodied men—and downplay or erase the contributions of other intersectional identities—for example, women, gays and lesbians, transgendered people, and disabled individuals—to create and maintain a sense of collective pride and to produce a positive narrative about the culture and its dominant members. Even though the official account has more credibility in a culture, it is important to be aware that other stories circulate in the culture as well and the official version is not necessarily "true."

FINAL THOUGHTS

This chapter examined how power and privilege operate in encounters within and between cultures. It brought up emotionally loaded terms so that they can be unpacked and understood in intercultural communication. Power and privilege function in a dialectic of visibility-invisibility in most cultural contexts. On the one hand, they tend to be visible to those individuals and groups who suffer from the power and privilege dynamics of their culture. On the other hand, they tend to be invisible to those individuals and groups who benefit from such dynamics. Next time you have an encounter with someone from another culture, whether face-to-face or mediated by some technology, think about the different ways in which power and privilege influence your communication both positively and negatively.

CONTINUE YOUR JOURNEY ONLINE

Visit: www.digitalhistory.uh.edu/historyonline/ethnic_am.cfm

Digital History website. Explore the site to increase your understanding of immigration. Explore why history is important to understanding privilege. As you read, consider your own ethnic roots and what role immigration played in your family's history.

❝❝ SAY WHAT?

Say What? provides excerpts from overheard real-life conversations in which people have communicated stereotypes. As you read these conversations, reflect on the following questions.

- Have you been in conversations like this before?
- Is there any one of these conversations that stick out to you more than the others?
- What do you think of this conversation?
- How did the stereotype help or hinder the conversation?
- Was there another way the stereotyper could have communicated to convey the same point?
- How do you feel when you hear this conversation or the specific stereotype?
- Do any of these conversations bother you more than others? Why or why not?
- Do any concepts, issues, or theories discussed in the chapter help explain why?

(Continued)

Note

I thank Anastacia Kurylo, the editor of this volume, for her feedback and suggestions for additional examples included in the chapter.

(Continued)

- **Say What?** I asked her, "How about Boston Market? I really like their mashed potatoes." She glared down at her feet and sighed with disapproval. "Yuck!" she exclaimed. "You're out of your mind. I tried to go into that place last week with my sister, but I couldn't. There were only Black people working in there. I bet they steal tons of cash from the register and I'm not going to give them any more drug money." Inside, I freaked out. I couldn't believe what I was hearing, and had no idea what to say in response.

- **Say What?** Recently I was having a conversation with one of my father's colleagues . . . and he cracked a joke about my dad being cheap. I laughed and answered back by saying "I know." He took a pause and answered back "for being so cheap, that's a pretty nice BMW in the driveway!" This is a stereotype that I get all of the time. Just because my father has money, people think he spoils me rotten. The flip side, however, is the truth. I work very hard for the things I have accumulated. This is a large stereotype that really irritates me.

- **Say What?** They looked at John and said, "We asked for the president." John looked at them as if they were crazy and said, "She's the president." They looked back at me and I nodded my head and said, " Yes, I'm the president. What happened? Is there a problem?" Then they said, "Isn't the president male?" I said, "No, the vice president is male." Then they told me that that is who they were looking for. I insisted to them that I could help them with whatever they needed since Mark (the V.P.) was not around. They told me it was okay and I just shook my head and walked off.

- **Say What?** An extremely nice, black Mercedes cut us both off— one of those cars that many people dream of owning. My friend says, "Did you see that person driving that car?" I said no. Then she said, "Well, she was really ugly. Don't you think if you own such a beautiful car that you should be just as beautiful?" I couldn't believe she said that. I had no idea how to respond to this. At first I paused and took it all in. Then I rebutted with, "How can you say something like that?"

REVIEW QUESTIONS

1. In the start of the chapter, what does access have to do with privilege? In what other ways is the idea of access explicitly or implicitly referenced in the rest of the chapter?

2. How are globalization, colonialism, and imperialism different? Can you identify any points of overlap in the chapter among these terms?

3. What are the two dimensions of group-related power discussed in the chapter? Why are these important?

4. Why are consent and hegemony related to each other, according to the chapter discussion?

5. According to the chapter, why does a first-world require a third-world in order to exist? How do second- and fourth-worlds fit?

6. What does travel have to do with privilege? What types of travel does the chapter introduce?

7. How do the two types of privilege discussed in the chapter work to benefit some and not others? Use these concepts to explain whiteness in your own words.

8. Define intersectionality from the discussion in the chapter.

9. What is the paradox of privilege? Have you experienced this? If so, how? If not, why not?

10. Why does the chapter discuss history? Why would this be a recurrent theme in several of the chapters in an intercultural communication textbook?

KEY TERMS

colonialism   170

conferred dominance   173

consent   168

cultural imperialism   170

cultural migration   171

first-world   169

fourth-world   170

global village   165

globalization   164

group-related power   167

hegemony   167

history   180

identity tourism   171

ideology   167

immigration   172

imperialism   170

intercultural transition   171

intersectionality   174

macroscopic power   166

media imperialism   170

microscopic power   166

oppression   174

otherness   168

paradox of privilege   178

power   166

privilege   173

repressive   165

roster-like approach   175

second-world   169

structural privilege   178

thick intersectionality   175

third-world   170

unearned advantage   173

whiteness   177

REFERENCES

Ahmad, A. (2006). Jameson's rhetoric of otherness and the national allegory. In B. Ashcroft, G. Griffiths & H. Tiffin (Eds.), *The post-colonial studies reader* (2nd ed., pp. 84–88). London: Routledge.

Althusser, L. (1971). *Lenin and philosophy and other essays* (G. Brewster, Trans.). New York: Oxford University Press.

Anzaldúa, G. E. (2000). *Interviews/entrevistas* (A. Keating, Ed.). New York: Routledge.

Barrett, L. (1999). *Blackness and value: Seeing double.* Cambridge, UK: Cambridge University Press.

Bornstein, K. (1998). *My gender workbook: How to become a real man, a real woman, the real you, or something else entirely.* New York: Routledge.

Brotherston, G. (1992). *Book of the fourth world: Reading the Native Americans through their literature.* Cambridge, UK: Cambridge University Press.

Carroll, H. (2011). *Affirmative reaction: New formations of white masculinity.* Durham, NC: Duke University Press.

Coontz, S. (2005). *Marriage, a history: From obedience to intimacy or how love conquered marriage.* New York: Viking.

Foucault, M. (1978/1990). *The history of sexuality, Volume 1: An introduction.* (R. Hurley, Trans.) New York: Vintage Books.

Hennessy, R. (1995). Subjects, knowledges, . . . and all the rest: Speaking for what. In J. Roof & R. Wiegman (Eds.), *Who can speak? Authority and critical identity* (pp. 137–150). Urbana: University of Illinois Press.

Johnson, A. G. (2001). *Privilege, power, and difference.* Mountain View, CA: Mayfield.

Lorde, A. (1984). *Sister outsider: Essays and speeches.* Freedom, CA: The Crossing Press.

Lynn, B. C. (2010). *Cornered: The new monopoly capitalism and the economics of destruction.* Hoboken, NJ: John Wiley & Sons.

McIntosh, P. (2009). White privilege: Unpacking the invisible knapsack. In E. Disch (Ed.), *Reconstructing gender: A multicultural anthology* (5th ed., pp. 78–83). Boston: McGraw-Hill.

McLuhan, M. (1967). *The medium is the message.* New York: Bantam.

Rasmussen, B. B., Klinenberg, E., Nexica, I. J., & Wray, M. (2001). Introduction. In B. B. Rasmussen, E. Klinenberg, I. J. Nexica & M. Wray (Eds.), *The making and unmaking of whiteness* (pp. 1–24). Durham, NC: Duke University Press.

Roediger, D. R. (2005). *Working toward whiteness: How America's immigrants became white.* New York: Basic Books.

Said, E. (1993). *Culture and imperialism.* New York: Alfred A. Knopf.

Sauvy, A. (1952). *General theory of population* (C. Campos, Trans.). London: Methuen.

Sturken, M. (2007). *Tourists of history: Memory, kitsch, and consumerism from Oklahoma City to Ground Zero.* Durham, NC: Duke University Press.

Tehranian, M. (2004). Cultural security and global governance: International migration and negotiations of identity. In J. Friedman & S. Randeria (Eds.), *Worlds on the move: Globalization, migration and cultural security* (pp. 3–22). New York: I. B. Tauris.

West, C. (1990). The new cultural politics of difference. In R. Ferguson, M. Gever, T. T. Minh-ha, & C. West (Eds.), *Out there: Marginalization and contemporary cultures* (pp. 19–36). Cambridge, MA: MIT Press.

Yep, G. A. (2007). Pedagogy of the opaque: The subject of whiteness in communication and diversity courses. In L. M. Cooks & J. S. Simpson (Eds.), *Whiteness, pedagogy, performance: Dis/placing race* (pp. 87–110). Lanham, MD: Lexington Books.

Yep, G. A. (2010). Toward the de-subjugation of racially marked knowledges in communication. *Southern Communication Journal, 75,* 171–175.

CHAPTER **9**

Co-Cultural Group Membership

Tina M. Harris
University of Georgia

Journey Through Chapter 9

Sightseeing: On your journey, you will use the social constructionist perspective and take a critical approach to understand co-cultural group membership. To do so, you will learn about the concept of double consciousness and three theories that demonstrate how co-cultural group membership is constructed. The chapter will also discuss two examples of co-cultural groups in academic settings and explore the implications of co-cultural group membership on intercultural communication.

Souvenir: After your journey, you will take away a greater awareness of the experiences of co-cultural group members and in the process learn a variety of concepts and theories that help articulate these experiences.

$\mathbf{E}$ach person has characteristics and qualities that make that person unique. These include but are not limited to racial, ethnic, gender, physical capabilities, religious orientations, or sexual identities. What is most interesting about the self is that how people define and understand themselves is directly related to their group membership, which ultimately creates their standpoint. For example, a person who is female, of Latin American descent, from a middle-class family, a professor, and of a certain age group simultaneously belongs to several groups and connects to each one in a unique way. Her interactions with other cultural group members and society-at-large help her understand who she is, which is a co-created process. Your identities are directly impacted and shaped by your interpersonal networks (Orbe & Harris, 2008), which include those people whose opinions and perceptions are valued and trusted. These orientational others include family members, friends, and others. In contrast, and as discussed in Chapter 6, generalized others are those to whom you have no emotional or social connection and, so, do not play as large of a role in how you understand your self. As such, interactions and relationships with most people throughout the course of a person's life help that person to understand who he or she is as a person.

The goal of this chapter is to provide a space for advancing knowledge on the topic of marginalization, otherness, or co-cultural group membership (Johnsrud & Sadao, 1998; Sadao, 2003). To better understand co-cultural identities, this chapter teases out notions of otherness and co-cultural group membership in an effort to demonstrate how complex and imperative it is to understand how your identities are socially constructed, specifically those in the margins. It will also demonstrate how certain attributes that are static (unchanging) or fluid (changing) can create either permanent or temporary membership in a co-cultural group and effect communication with others. For example, Simon's identity as a gay male is fixed, but his transition from one socioeconomic status (SES) to another is more fluid.

Figure 9.1   State Policies on Same-Sex Marriage Rights in the United States.

Where do you stand on equal rights? Formal and systematic acceptance of co-cultural groups—such as those who are lesbian, gay, bisexual, and transgendered—within a dominant group varies from complete acceptance to complete rejection.

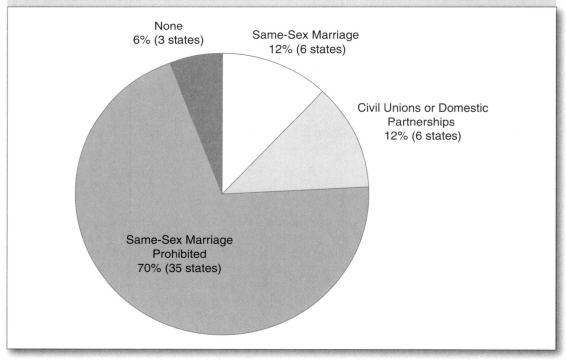

Source: Adapted from "State Policies on Same-Sex Marriage" by Stateline.org. Available at http://www.stateline.org/live/details/story?contentId=347390. Copyright 2010 by Anastacia Kurylo.

Note: States are identified once only by their most LGBT-friendly policies.

In either case, people like Steve have experiences that help them to understand inequalities (for example, depicted in Figure 9.1) resulting from systemic oppression. Research exploring these experiences will demonstrate how the process of othering via privilege is both a blessing and a curse in the construction of social identities, specifically co-cultural group membership.

CO-CULTURAL GROUP MEMBERSHIP

Research on identity has largely been focused on individuals or groups that do not fall into the mainstream. These people are oftentimes described as marginalized, or forced to the fringes of society where they are essentially ignored and deemed a part of the underclass. They are also considered the *other*, which is a term used in direct opposition to the mainstream. Thus, if you are not mainstream or do not conform to what society deems normal, then you are other or othered. Othered refers to being treated differently because of race, gender, sexual orientation, physical abilities, or religious identity. In contrast, members of the mainstream or dominant group are in the center and are rarely, if ever, forced into the position of thinking about their standpoint or identity.

REFLECT 9.1: Have you ever felt othered in a situation? Did it have something to do with your group membership? If so, how?

As discussed in the previous chapter, this position in U.S. American culture is commonly referred to as whiteness or White privilege and can be understood through the works of scholar and race relations expert Peggy McIntosh (1988), among others. Having White privilege means a person has a life of opportunities and benefits bestowed upon them because of their light or white skin color (see Tim Wise, 2008). Wise argues that this inherent power status unfortunately renders non-Whites powerless, underbenefitted, and *under*privileged, thereby perpetuating systemic oppression in ways oftentimes deemed unfathomable or ignored by said benefactors.

Over the past few decades, race and gender scholars such as bell hooks (1990), Patricia Hill Collins (1989a; 1989b; 1990; 1996a; 1996b), Marsha Houston (1994), and Beverly Tatum (2003), have offered clear evidence that the voices of these groups need to be heard. Because societal oppression still exists, it is imperative that researchers continue to conduct studies on issues of marginalization. Doing so will undoubtedly contribute to increased cultural sensitivity and understanding of the real ways in which privilege impacts your intercultural interactions.

Similar to marginalization, co-cultural group membership refers to a person's belonging to a nondominant group (see Orbe, 1998). Thus, if a person is not a part of the powerful, privileged group, then this individual is most likely part of a co-cultural group. In the United States, those who hold power are typically White, heterosexual, middle-to-upper class Christian males. Anyone who does not possess all of those qualities is most likely marginalized. Co-cultural group members include people of color, women, gays, lesbians, bisexuals, people with disabilities and those from a lower socioeconomic status.

An example of this is Steve, who is a low socioeconomic status heterosexual White male who is a first generation college student. Although he is a heterosexual White male, Steve is of a low-income bracket and does not have the same educational background as those in positions of power; therefore, his life experiences are markedly different from those in the dominant group. Steve does not represent traditional understandings of co-cultural group membership, which initially included people with physical traits, such as race and gender, who were subjected to systemic oppression. Oppression has evolved to include economic status, sexual orientation, and educational background, all of which adversely affect a person's day-to-day encounters. Hard work could possibly move him into a different economic group, but Steve's identity has been shaped by his status, which makes him different from the peers he might potentially have in this new economic class. Those "future peers" may have been born into an upper-class family and, therefore, do not have the same experiences or history as Steve. In this scenario, Steve symbolizes a way of thinking about difference that represents how there can be separation between groups despite individual or group efforts to move beyond these barriers.

REFLECT 9.2: If you are a member of a co-cultural group, how does it feel to be labeled as such? If you are not a member, how does that feel?

According to Orbe (1998), co-cultures are groups who are marginalized by "predominant societal structures" (p. 2), yet continue to make valuable contributions to society and their respective communities. In response to their oppressive state, co-cultural group members (CCGMs) are very likely to identify more strongly with their community than mainstream society. Think about CCGMs attending a predominately White institution (PWI) in the United States. Because they are not in the majority, they likely have experiences with isolation or being treated differently because of their race or ethnicity, and in an effort to cope, they may socialize more with other students who are like them. In terms of interracial interactions when they interact with members of the dominant group, however, co-cultural group members may do so in a way that affirms their racial, ethnic, or cultural identity. For example, John is a African American male with disabilities in an undergraduate research methods class. Although he is in the minority and his peers and professor do not make him feel very welcome, John does not let this bother him. In fact, he is empowered to speak up more in class and to share his opinions about his physical limitations as well as his race, which, he points out to his classmates and professor, are not being considered in research design. Instead of withdrawing and being discouraged, John feels even more empowered to succeed and excel in a somewhat oppressive environment.

Co-cultures have always coexisted simultaneously with other co-cultures, and over time, this state of coexistence was imbalanced or threatened because, in the United States for example, "one culture (that of European-American heterosexual middle- or upper-class males) has acquired a dominant group status in the major societal institutions (i.e., political, corporate, religious, and legal institutions) across the land" (Orbe, 1998, p. 2). As a byproduct of being a group occupying the position of power, dominant co-cultural groups relegate other co-cultural groups (CCGs) to the margins, thus rendering themselves powerful and the marginalized powerless within the predominant societal structures. Although they do not share in that power, co-cultural group members do not function less effectively. Co-cultural group members are able to succeed in the workplace, for example, or in other settings despite their lack of access to resources and opportunities typically afforded to dominant group members (for example, see Table 9.1 on page 192).

In response to their oppressive and marginalized state, co-cultural group members employ communication behaviors and strategies that aid them in maintaining balance between these two opposing worlds. Orbe (1998) identifies 25 strategies from which co-cultural group members can choose as they interact with dominant group members. In doing so, Orbe's goal is to understand the communication "between dominant group and co-cultural group members [as it is experienced] from the perspective of co-cultural group members" (p. 2). When co-cultural group members interact with dominant group members, they choose the communication strategy they believe is best.

An offensive or inappropriate behavior from a dominant group member might prompt a co-cultural group member to create psychological distance with that person. The strategy of

Photo 9.1 Is this image used for safety, entertainment, or marginalization? Cultural artifacts, like signs, are symbols that can capture lived experience. Mexicans running across the highway at the border to San Diego face considerable potential for harm. This sign cautions drivers to be careful. The sign is also emblazoned on T-shirts in San Diego as a symbol of this terrifying experience captured as a souvenir for tourists.

Photo 9.2   How do you feel when someone calls you by an epithet? Stereotypes are communicated in a variety of equally offensive and consequential ways. The stick figure in this graffiti represents a Muslim man wearing a turban, which "hides" a bomb. This offensive image portrays the stereotype of Muslims as terrorists.

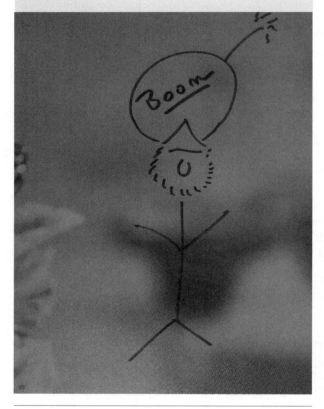

Copyright 2010 by Anastacia Kurylo.

maintaining interpersonal barriers may involve using nonverbals (e.g., space, eye contact, physical distance) or topical avoidance (e.g., topical shifts) to minimize or reduce communication with the offending group member. Orbe (1998) refers to *dispelling stereotypes* as another co-cultural communication practice. For example, Sofia is a Mexican woman who is close friends with Sheila, who is White. They are hanging out in Sofia's apartment having a good time when Sheila tells yet another offensive joke about Mexicans and explains that the stereotype does not apply to Sofia. Rather than ignore it, as usual, Sofia confronts her and tells her the comment is hurtful, insulting, and an unfair generalization about *all* Mexicans. She explains the stereotype is applicable to all people regardless of their race or ethnicity. Examples such as these demonstrate the "communication strategies that different 'non-dominant' group members use when interacting with members of dominant society" (p. 2). When co-cultural group members interact with dominant group members, they are oftentimes reminded of their marginalized status and respond from that perspective. Unfortunately, co-cultural group members are placed in the difficult position of having to navigate between two worlds. In this way, they are forced to grapple with oppressive forces that are longstanding and virtually impossible to dismantle.

DOUBLE CONSCIOUSNESS AND RACE

Double Consciousness

The genesis of the notion or reality of the other can be partially attributed to African American civil rights activist, scholar, and Harvard educated W. E. B. Du Bois who revolutionized and agitated social conceptions of blackness. Du Bois (1903/1989) introduced his concept of double consciousness in response to the U.S. Supreme Court's decision to uphold and preserve systemic racial segregation through Plessy v. Ferguson and the Jim Crow laws. He and other social scientists explained double consciousness as a marginalized person living simultaneously in two worlds: a Black world and a White world. He was able to articulate for African Americans their internal tensions and struggles resulting from living simultaneously in the two different worlds with vastly juxtaposed landscapes. Such a way of life forces one to live in a world where the individual is expected to adhere to dominant culture norms and rules but is limited in doing so because of otherness. As such, co-cultural group members must create strategies that will enable them to survive living this type of life. This tension is a reminder of their severely limited opportunities for social mobility and treatment as inferior beings; Du Bois's label of double consciousness captures the essence of this dichotomy. He addresses this imbalance in the following quote:

> It is a peculiar sensation, this double consciousness, this sense of always looking at one's self through the eyes of others. . . . One ever feels his twoness,—an American, a Negro; two souls, two thoughts, two unreconciled strivings; two warring ideals in one dark body. . . . The history of the American Negro is the history of this strife,— this longing . . . to merge his double self into a better and truer self. In this merging he wishes neither of the older selves to be lost. He would not Africanize America, for America has too much to teach the world and Africa. He would not bleach his Negro soul in a flood of white Americanism, for he knows that Negro blood has a message for the world. (p. 3)

This othering or racializing is a result of the racial hierarchy in society where darker skin (i.e., Black) is valued much less than is lighter skin (i.e., White). This process subsequently created an ideology about racial difference that continues to perpetuate qualitatively different life experiences that still exist today (Lumby & Coleman, 2010; Lyubansky & Eidelson, 2005).

Moving From Racial to Cultural Memories

Your social environments have a direct role in shaping not only your racial identities but your cultural identities as well. Through experiences within these social environments you learn who you are and are not. This creates what Dillard (2008) describes as racial/cultural memories, or "memories that change our ways of being (ontology) and knowing (epistemology) in what we call the present" (p. 90–91). For example, the childhood memory a co-cultural group member has of being excluded from social events or treated differently than her peers in school is a part of the process of becoming and knowing who she is as an individual. Although these experiences for co-cultural group members may be viewed as no different than those for any other child, there is a greater likelihood that those instances of isolation or alienation are due to their otherness and play a central role in their understanding of who they are in a power-centric society.

   Dillard (2008) explains re-membering as when a person recalls these events or "a particular event, feeling, or action from one's past experiences" (p. 90) and attempts to process these in light of one's present. This form of self-reflection aids in the sense-making process regarding an individual's marginal status. Similarly, Walker (1988) believes that the "concrete ways that racial/cultural memories influence the transformation of consciousness" (see Dillard, 2008, p. 90) are essential to knowing who you are. Memories of those life experiences allow you to

Table 9.1 Select Religious Observance Dates by Religion.

Which religious observances do you honor or celebrate? Different people, different families, different communities, and different cultures can choose to observe any variety of religious holidays. The dominant cultural group, however, decides which deserve a day off from work or school.

Observance	Date
Armenian Apostolic	
Christmas	January 6*
Baha'i	
Martyrdom of the Bab	July 9
Birthday of the Bab	October 20
Naw Ruz (New Year)	March 21
Ridván	April 21–May 2
Ninth Day of Ridván	April 29
Twelfth Day of Ridván	May 2
Declaration of the Bab	May 23
Ascension of Baha'u'llah	May 29
Buddhist	
Bodhi Day	December 8*
Paranirvana (Nirvana) Day	February 15*
Buddha's Birth	April 8*
Visakha Day	in April or May
Christian	
Feast of the Assumption	August 15
Reformation Day	October 31
All Saint's Day	November 1
All Soul's Day (Day of the Dead)	November 2*
Advent (Beginning of)	November 27 to December 3
Feast of the Immaculate Conception	December 8
Christmas Eve	December 24
Christmas	December 25
Epiphany	January 6
Shrove Tuesday	February 3 to March 9
Ash Wednesday	February 4 to March 10
The Feast of the Annunciation	March 25

Observance	Date
Palm Sunday	March 15 to April 18
Good Friday	March 20 to April 23
Easter	March 22 to April 25
Ascension Day	in May or June
Pentecost	May 10 to June 13
Coptic	
Christmas	January 7
Easter (Pascha)	April 4 to May 8
Ascension Day	May 14 to June 17
Pentecost	May 24 to June 27
Eastern Orthodox	
Christmas	January 7
Clean Monday	February 15 to March 21
Palm Sunday	March 28 to May 1
Holy Friday	April 2 to May 6
Easter (Pascha)	April 4 to May 8
Ascension Day	May 14 to June 17
Pentecost	May 24 to June 27
Hindu	
Janmashtami	in August or September
Navaratri / Dassehra	in September or October
Diwali (Festival of Lights)	October 13 to November 14
Maha Shivaratri (Shiva's Nights)	in February or March
Holi	in March
Ramanavami	in March or April
Islamic	
Ramadan	in August or July (2009–13)
Laylat al-Qadr (Night of Power)	in September or August (2009–13)
Eid al Fitr (Breaking of the Fast)	in September or August (2009–13)
Eid al-Adha (Feast of the Sacrifice)	in November or October (2009–13)
Muharram (New Year)	in December or November (2009–13)
Ashura	in December or November (2009–13)
Maulid an-Nabi	in January, February, or March (2010–14)

(Continued)

Table 9.1 (Continued)

Observance	Date
Jain	
Paryusana Parva	in August or September
Diwali Night (Lord Mahavir's Nirvana)	in October or November
Mahavir Jayanti	in March or April
Jewish	
Tisha B'av	in July or August
Rosh Hashanah (New Year)	in September or October
Yom Kippur (Day of Atonement)	in September or October
Sukkoth (Feast of Tabernacles)	in September or October
Shemini Atzeret	in September or October
Simchat Torah	in September or October
Hanukkah (Festival of Lights)	in Late November or December
Purim (Feast of Lots)	in February or March
Passover (Pesach)	in March or April
Yom Hashoah (Holocaust Memorial Day)	in April or May
Shavuoth (Festival of Weeks)	in May or June
Native American	
The dates of Native American observations and celebrations are seasonal events that vary by community and needs of those within the community.	
Sikh	
Diwali (Bandi Chhor Divas)	in October or November
Guru Nanak Dev Gurpurab (Bikrami Calendar)	in November
Guru Gobind Singh Gurpurab (Nanakshahi Calendar)	January 5
Vaisakhi	April 13 or 14
Zoroastrian	
Birthday of Prophet Zarathusthra (Zoroaster)	March 26*

Source: Adapted from "Equal Opportunity and Affirmative Action: Religious Observance Dates by Religion" by University of Minnesota. Available at www.eoaffact.umn.edu/resources/calendar/religion_dates.html. Copyright 2010 Anastacia Kurylo.

* Indicates that the typical date noted here may vary occasionally.

understand your place in the world and your respective community. Memories are also able to make connections between your racial/ethnic identity and the negative and positive experience(s) that impacted that understanding.

Hopson and Orbe (2007) refer to this recall process as critical memory. Critical memory is the process of remembering an important event related to one's standpoint. Hopson and

Orbe found critical memory to be salient for African American men. In their research, gender, in addition to race, shaped the overall identity of the study participants. Conversations with these men revealed that playing the game, or learning how to navigate through organizational structures, is frequently a difficult and taxing experience. Because of their co-cultural group membership, they are burdened with the expectation of succeeding and surviving in an oppressive organizational structure, which "hinges on the successful negotiation of several dialectical tensions" (Hopson & Orbe, 2007, p. 83). As discussed in Chapter 6, dialectical tensions are contradictions between opposing forces, such as autonomy versus connectedness, that ultimately ask that a person either choose or find balance between those tensions. This is difficult to accomplish considering that certain aspects of identity (i.e., race, sex, sexual orientation, disability) cannot be changed. As a result, co-cultural group members cannot fully assimilate or acculturate into the dominant group, thus leaving them with the task of spending a lifetime managing these experiences and their identity development process.

Other co-cultural groups experience expectations to assimilate. For example, Cohen and Avanzino (2010) found that people coping with disabilities are also a co-culture because they are marginalized and, as a result, use the same types of communication strategies when interacting with others as do other co-cultural group members. Participants in their study had real-world experiences with mainstream organizations (e.g., the workplace) and how these organizations deal with people who are different from them in terms of ability. Disabilities included blindness, cerebral palsy, muscular dystrophy, multiple sclerosis, congenital disability, and being wheelchair bound. People also varied in the extent to which their physical limitations impacted their work performance, if at all. Communication in the workplace tended to be both positive and negative.

People with disabilities reported pressure to adapt to the dominant culture (e.g., assimilate), which involved using communication behaviors that deflected attention away from their physical condition. This involved the purposeful use of language that avoided mentioning or drawing attention to their otherness. One participant explained that despite her efforts to encourage administration to adapt her workload to meet her physical needs, they chose to ignore her multiple requests, which resulted in her "'giv[ing] up' asking for accommodations" (Cohen & Avanzino, 2010, p. 286).

THEORIES OF CO-CULTURAL MEMBERSHIP

The general assumption undergirding the idea of co-cultural groups is that systemic oppression through homogeneity is pervasive and continues to affect a significant portion of any given population. There are various frameworks (i.e., theories) that attempt to enlighten the masses about the consequences of preserving hierarchies that continue to place less value on those who are not White, heterosexual, middle-to-upper class Christian males. They illustrate the ways in which various co-cultural group members of similar social status face equally oppressive struggles and barriers. Theories such as standpoint theory (Hartsock, 1983), muted group theory (Kramarae, 1981), and co-cultural group theory (Orbe, 1996) are examples of how such frameworks help people in a society to understand the far-reaching effect that their racial, gender, and physical differences have on the texture of lived experiences. As will be discussed, these differences are oftentimes framed as a negative human quality. However, it can be argued that all differences, regardless of social location, should be celebrated, not tolerated.

Standpoint Theory

Established by feminist sociology scholars (see Hartsock, 1983), standpoint theory acknowledges that people have certain standpoints that create a vantage point from which they view the world. Gender, race, class, and other lived experiences play a critical role in that process. Each person has varied experiences and as a result each person's standpoint will most likely be different. Identities, however, can be and are shared, thereby allowing people to relate to the experiences and realities of others. This "field of experience" (Orbe, 1998, p. 10) feeds into concrete or solid experiences that subsequently create your standpoint. For example, Stan and Ginger are married and decide to spend their date night at the movie theater. The psychological thriller has the action that Stan likes and the romantic relationship Ginger likes. Although watching the same movie, they have different reactions to a particularly violent scene involving a female character. In addition to their genders creating different perspectives, Ginger's childhood abuse caused her to have a visceral and highly emotional response to the scene. Although they discussed the film afterwards, Stan could not fully understand how Ginger thought the fictional account on screen related directly to her. So, not only is their gender standpoint contributing to this difference, but so are their personal histories.

Although not a complete list, examples of standpoint theory are feminist thought, Black feminist thought, Chicana feminist thought, and multiracial feminism. Each theory speaks to the multiple layers of marginalization that exist in society and continue to force women into spaces of variable marginality. Gender oppression is germane to each school of thought and has been at the base of these social movements directly informing the theories about gendered experiences within a patriarchal society. As a form of consciousness and social theory, feminism (Kramarae, 1981) is an active approach to addressing the oppression women experience in a patriarchal society. Initial efforts of the first wave of feminism addressed this disparity and aimed to level the playing field. Berger and Bettez (2007) explain that the first wave of feminism denotes the period when White abolitionist women and free Black women organized for the right to vote and won passage of the 19th Amendment. The second wave is identified as 1970s feminism, which challenged women's exclusion from the public sphere of employment and politics. The third wave is ongoing and "marks the ways in which young women manage some of the social and political freedoms gained from the previous generations."

Feminist Thought

Although intended to address the rights of all women (Kramarae, 1981), the feminist movement largely addressed the concerns and issues of White women who had the means and resources with which to advance their agenda. Their whiteness gave these early feminists privileges that other women did not have, yet they experienced societal oppression by men because they were perceived to be and treated as if they were weaker, less intelligent, and unparallel to men. The feminist movement was a political and social movement that brought to the foreground issues of marginalization and brought women liberation, to some extent, from an oppressive patriarchal society. Although it was successful in promoting social consciousness on these issues, it did not "recognize the centrality of the feminism of women of color in the Second Wave" of feminism (Thompson, 2002, p. 337). Thus, the other feminist frameworks with specific racial lenses and standpoints were introduced.

REFLECT 9.3: Would you describe yourself as a feminist? Why or why not? Does your answer reinforce the dominant culture or marginalization?

Black Feminist Thought

Patricia Hill Collins (1989a) introduced Black feminist thought, which serves as a tool of empowerment for oppressed women forced to live a life of double consciousness (Andrews, 2003): a gendered *and* racialized reality. Although their experiences with gender oppression were somewhat being addressed by the feminist movement, African American women had a reality where their experiences in a White patriarchal society were qualitatively different. They were experiencing double forms of oppression that their White counterparts did not have to face because they were also experiencing marginalization by the Black men in their community who did not support gender equality. As such, Black feminist thought was introduced to serve as a form of theoretical framework and social activism on behalf of African American women ignored by the feminist movement.

Chicana Feminist Thought

Similar to Black feminist thought, Chicana feminist thought (Garcia, 1997) speaks to the unique needs and experiences of Latin women including those who are of Mexican, Chicana, and of Hispanic descent. Theorists recognized the patriarchal system of machismo in particular as an oppressive force for these women. They, too, were forced to adopt a double consciousness within two interwoven realities: gendered and racial. These women experienced oppression as they navigated through the difficult terrains of the dominant culture, only to be further oppressed upon their return to their cultural community where the position of women was also rendered unequal. Chicana feminist theory was created in response to this oppressive positionality and aimed to facilitate political activism in the move toward equality.

Multiracial Feminist Thought

Another theory grounded in standpoint theory and feminism is multiracial feminism. Zinn and Dill (1996) explain multiracial feminist thought as emphasizing "race as a power system that interacts with other structured inequalities to shape genders" (p. 324). According to Burgess-Proctor (2006), it "proposes that these intersections occur simultaneously and, therefore, create a distinct *social location* for each individual" (p. 36). These social locations are standpoints that ultimately function to create co-cultures, where marginalized identities are lenses through which to address social injustices and inequalities.

LIVING CULTURE

Living With Homelessness   *Charles Vasquez*

When I was a child at the age of 6, I moved around a lot. I moved from family member to family member and from stranger to stranger. I never went to school consistently because it was better for the different people I lived with not to bother enrolling me. As a result, my schooling was interrupted many times over years and for different reasons.

When I was 7, I went on to live with my maternal grandmother; sometimes my mother would live with us. Because of my grandmother's alcoholism I was placed in foster care. I was there for a year. My mother fought to get me out and I was released to her custody provided she obtained stable housing. She did with the help of the Child Welfare Administration. We moved into an apartment in Harlem on 132nd Street between Lenox and Seventh Avenue. We lived there for about two years. Everything went well at first. I was in school and adjusting to a new life. It wasn't too long before taking me to school became more difficult for my mother when she began making friends, hanging out more, drinking, and being abusive. School was an on-again, off-again ordeal.

Then things changed even more quickly. There was a fire in our apartment. Neighbors said the fire was a result of a break-in. We moved in with my grandmother. We lived with grandma on and off, as we struggled through homelessness, because of grandma's and mom's alcoholism and mom's drug abuse. Going to school was a sort of a sanctuary. I could get two meals and a safe space. There came a time when I had the power to make choices in my life and move beyond my past.

As a teen, I dropped out of high school in the tenth grade. I was 17 at the time. It was partly because my mother had urged me to find a job. We needed the money. Plus, I couldn't afford staying in school. My mother couldn't afford buying school supplies and I didn't have money of my own. I washed my clothes by hand, sometimes without soap. Often my jeans wouldn't dry in time for school. I enjoyed going to school but was too embarrassed to go in wet clothes and no paper to write on. I decided to leave high school during the winter break. Later that summer, I found work in a health food store bagging groceries. I quickly moved up to the fish department, which translated into more money. I worked there for over a year. I soon discovered that having a job didn't help my situation at home. Mom and I just couldn't get along. I ended up on the street a lot but she always let me back in after a while.

At 18-years-old I was desperate to find a way out of my home and an opportunity to learn new skills. I turned to the army recruiting center. However, I was turned away. The staff sergeant told me to come back once I earned a general education diploma, also called a GED. The GED is a

LIVING CULTURE

five-subject exam taken by people who haven't earned a high school diploma. The subjects include math, reading, writing, science and social studies. Upon passing you get a certificate that is said to be equivalent to a high school diploma. It is known on the streets as the "good enough diploma." It was good enough to get a decent job that paid above minimum wage and, sometimes, benefits. I found a GED preparation course, which is always offered for free, took a few classes and a couple of practice exams. I didn't do well on the practice exams and decided to leave the course. Without a GED I was limited to working as a delivery boy or washing dishes.

One day, while on the street I saw an advertisement on the side of a city bus. It was an ad for a college claiming you could earn your GED while working toward an associate's degree. I enrolled. I was so excited. I took an entrance exam, and after I sat with an adviser to go over the results. I was disappointed to learn that I couldn't start classes until I fulfilled their math requirements. I stayed for about a week but I figured it would take me a few years to complete the requirements for the GED. Frustrated I left. Education didn't even cross my mind for another 6 years.

Enough was enough. I told myself that because I had endured suffering during most of my childhood and I could get by with nothing, that I could face the challenges of obtaining a higher education. I began by borrowing a GED book from the public library and studying for the GED exam. I started in April of 2003, and in May I took the exam. In July of the same year I obtained my GED certificate. In August I applied to community college.

Obtaining my GED and going to college didn't come without sacrifice. While studying for the GED exam, I stopped working or looking for a job. I applied for public assistance for temporary financial support. I received $200 a month and $186 in food stamps a month. I was able to get by and provided some financial help at home but that wasn't enough for my mother. For only reasons she knows about, she kicked me out for good in June of 2003. I went to the New York City men's shelter on Wards Island. Wards Island is an island off of Manhattan's Upper East Side and is owned by the City of New York. The men's homeless shelter houses about a thousand homeless men.

In the fall of 2003, I enrolled in the Borough of Manhattan Community College. However, I quickly discovered the shelter system didn't provide the most supportive environment for a student. While continuing my education presented challenges, trying to continue my education in the homeless system meant being deemed ineligible for services including permanent housing. Substance abuse treatment and counseling were the only ways to get on the waiting list for housing. I was told there weren't any alternatives.

The chaotic atmosphere in the shelter weighed on me. Men often overdosed on heroin in the bathroom, some died, still others recovered and

(Continued)

LIVING CULTURE

(Continued)

would be seen a few days later repeating the pattern. In the mornings I went to class and I spent the entire day away from the shelter. In the evenings I would rush back to make the ten o'clock curfew. At times I felt there was no way out. I spent 3 months in the public shelter system and another 9 months living at a private shelter at the landmark Church of Saint John the Divine on 111th Street on Amsterdam Avenue. The church of Saint John's was unsuccessful in helping me find permanent housing and I was sent back to the men's shelter at Wards Island for another 2 months.

I would not let circumstances stop me. I had spent a lifetime being jostled around with no choice in the matter. Now, as an adult, my past isn't going to affect me. I had a choice to make and, although it was hard at that moment, in time it would pay off. In January of 2004, I landed a well-paying job with the New York Academy of Medicine. Within a few months, I was able to save money and moved out of the shelter and into my first apartment. It felt good to finally have a place of my own. In May of 2006 I graduated from the Borough of Manhattan Community College with an associate's degree. I am glad I stuck it out. My life turned around for the better.

Consider:

1. Why was it difficult for the author to "move beyond" his past even though he viewed himself as having the "power to make choices"?

2. What recurring themes can you find in this narrative? Why do these matter?

3. What are the author's goals? What are his concerns? How are his goals and concerns similar to or different from your own? Why?

4. What enabled the author to persevere?

Muted Group Theory

Anthropologists Shirley and Edwin Ardener created muted group theory, which "suggests that people attached or assigned to subordinate groups may have a lot to say, but they tend to have relatively little power to say it" (Kramarae, 2005, p. 55). This power difference serves to mute or render silent certain groups because of their powerless state. According to Orbe (1998), these groups are inarticulate because they are unable to or are forced to use the dominant group's communicative structures although they do not represent an inclusive or diverse worldview. Similar to multiracial feminism, this theory includes "a range of other marginalizing differences as well including race, sexuality, age and class" (Kramarae, 2005, p. 55).

Language use can mute women's perspectives when, for example, managers, whether male or female, discuss nongendered activities like teamwork using metaphors of sports or construction reflecting historically male experiences. These metaphors are not problematic in and of themselves but cumulatively serve to minimize the importance of other types of experiences that supply equally valid representations such as cooking, raising children, or other historically female experiences. In doing so, they mute experiences that have been historically more important to women in favor of experiences that have been historically more important to men.

Communication scholars, namely Cheris Kramarae (1981), adopted muted group theory and proposed that "women perceive the world differently from men because of women's and men's different experience and activities rooted in the division of labor" (p. 3). Muted group theory is different from the aforementioned theories in that it specifically addresses the impact that systemic oppression has on the communication between the marginalized and the dominant. The communication processes used reflect how co-cultural group members negotiate their marginalized status within various social contexts.

Co-Cultural Group Theory

Using standpoint theory and muted group theory as a foundation, co-cultural group theory (CCGT) was developed to reveal what Orbe (1998) calls the "'basic truths' from the standpoint of persons whose societal existence is typically marginalized by dominant public structures" (p. 11). In order to better understand how co-cultures came into existence, Orbe suggests that there are five premises that situate co-cultural group theory.

The first premise is that we must recognize that people experience various levels of privilege, ranging from the most privileged to the least. The most privileged group in many Western cultures is typically men, European Americans, heterosexuals, the able-bodied, and middle and upper class. The second premise explains that because of their power position, dominant group members consciously or unconsciously create ways of communicating that place greater value on their communication style than those of the marginalized. As such, their experiences are perceived and treated as the norm. The third premise is that the communication structures of the dominant group prevent the marginalized from moving away from the margins and exclude their lived experiences from public communicative systems. This means that the dominant group invalidates the responses or communication styles of the co-cultural group members, which subsequently functions to further oppress them and keep them in the margins.

The fourth premise suggests that co-cultural group members "share a similar societal position" (Orbe, 1998, p. 13) of marginalization and underrepresentation. Even though two people are members of different co-cultural groups, they have similar experiences or viewpoints because of their shared marginalized status in society. The fifth and final premise is that co-cultural group members confront "oppressive dominant structures" by "strategically adopt[ing] certain communication behaviors when functioning within the confines of public communicative structures" (p. 13). In short, co-cultural group members respond to oppression by using a communication style that allows them to adapt to the dominant culture with the fewest negative consequences.

Orbe (1998) advances this understanding of relationship between marginalization and communication by identifying 25 different communicative practices of co-cultural group members that can be used to respond to their intergroup encounters with dominant group members. It is important to acknowledge that these practices and behaviors exist (see Orbe, 1998, pp. 14–15) because co-cultural group members respond to their societal oppression. Thus, these communication practices co-cultural members employ are a result. Therefore, it is important for people to hear these stories of marginalization that are historically ignored.

CO-CULTURAL GROUPS IN ACADEMIC SETTINGS

Researchers use multiple methods to uncover the experiences of co-cultural group members. Depending on various factors (e.g., number of participants, scale of the phenomenon), their voices can be unearthed in ways that allow you to see how complex your socially constructed identities are and how salient they are to your lived experiences. A person's co-cultural group membership becomes salient in a variety of interpersonal and social contexts or situations. A common theme between the studies discussed in the following sections is that many of these involve people who are learning to negotiate their identities within an academic setting. Although this is not the only context within which these experiences occur, the studies have been chosen because they may be relatable to you as a student and are exemplars of how these social identities (potentially) remain central to the self across the span of one's lifetime.

Rape Survivors as Co-Culture

One recently identified co-cultural group reflecting the primary tenets of co-cultural group theory is rape survivors. Burnett et al. (2009) recognized a disturbing trend on college campuses and in society that was sadly creating a co-cultural group. They argue that "the rape culture is in fact a co-culture wherein the voices of the female victims are muted" (p. 465). In their research, they identify four myths, or commonly held beliefs about rape that are untrue, believed to contribute to this rape culture and the attitudes toward both victims and perpetrators: (1) denial/minimization of victim injury; (2) organized sports perpetuating ideals of physical domination, while fraternities perpetuate a double standard regarding sexuality; (3) increased likelihood of alcohol consumption before sex; and (4) rape culture fostering silence (Burnett et al., 2009). Collectively, these myths contribute the establishment of a culture and cultural norms that perpetuate rape and fail to address the consequences they have for the survivor and society at large.

Interviews with both men and women about communication about date rape revealed some interesting results (Burnett et al., 2009). They found that there is ambiguity in what constitutes a date rape, which they argue works to mute "actual and potential date rape, but potentially marginalizes meaningful discourse on the topic and further entrenches rape culture on campus" (p. 472). Participants also could not clearly articulate what verbal and nonverbal behaviors communicate consent, which unfortunately sets the ground for boundaries to be crossed. A third finding was that students did communicate about the importance of "events and contexts prior to the potential occurrence of rape [which] suggest[s that] communication focuses on individual responsibility for one's safety" (Burnett et al., 2009, p. 472). They concluded that women who are raped or could possibly be raped are held to a greater level of responsibility for their safety than are male perpetrators. Thus, a double standard toward date rape exists. Consequently, females who are victims of date rape constitute a co-cultural group (Burnett et al., 2009). They are marginalized, oppressed, and subjugated because they are not a part of the dominant culture. As a result, they must manage their communication in response to the marginalized position.

International Students and New Immigrants as Co-Culture

Co-cultural group theory has been extended to include international identities of college students (Hopson & Orbe, 2007; Urban & Orbe, 2007). In addition to reflecting marginal standpoints such as race, ethnicity, and culture, these groups are further marginalized because of their status as outgroup members on an international level. They are in a foreign country and are placed in the precarious position of learning the inner workings of the dominant culture on a national and local (e.g., university) level while managing their co-cultural group membership. They most likely already have a strong cultural identity that becomes stronger when they are forced to develop double consciousness while navigating life in the host country. International students and new immigrants as well have co-cultural group status and experiences that inform them about marginality. The metaphor of the boiling frog is used to describe this marginalization from an international perspective discovered in an essay by a male student from Uruguay. He explains it as follows:

> They say that if you throw a frog in a pan with boiling water, it jumps out immediately; but if you slowly heat up the water with the frog inside, it does not notice it and becomes a soup. Once again I had to be taken out of the pond to realize the effect living in a new culture had had on me. Like the syndrome of the boiled frog, I had become numbed and I did not notice how I was changing. (as cited in Urban & Orbe, 2007, p. 133)

This student and others like him occupy a "positionality as cultural outsiders" (Urban & Orbe, 2007, p. 117), which influences their communication with others within the host culture. This shift in their communication becomes an integral part of their educational experience.

As co-cultural group members, international students were made aware of their minority status by dominant

Take a Side Trip:

If you would like to read more about related issues, visit Appendix D: Transnational Dominican Culture Through Phenomenological Analysis.

groups members and explained that, "[t] hey felt that it was expected of them to learn and adopt the new 'rules'" (Urban & Orbe, 2007, p. 124). They had difficulty understanding how to communicate with fellow students and professors, which involved trying to learn how to accurately encode and decode messages. They shared that "people of color, those with heavy non-native accents, and students whose culture significantly differed from the dominant U.S. culture seemed to struggle the most with their inability to 'blend in'" (pp. 124–125).

Matsunaga and Torigoe (2008) also argue that international status constitutes co-cultural group membership within some contexts. Their interviews with Koreans residing in Japan revealed specific efforts to manage one's identity management, which they suggest is somewhat similar to Du Bois's notion of a double consciousness. Rather than being torn between two cultural groups, Japan-residing Koreans experienced a neither/nor tension or orientation while attempting to assimilate to the dominant culture. They felt no connection to the larger dominant group or their ethnic group, hence this tension between identities. Matsunaga and Torigoe suggest that identity negotiation becomes central for co-cultural group members, as they must choose responses that are for the good of either the individual or the collective.

IMPLICATION OF CO-CULTURAL GROUP MEMBERSHIP ON INTERCULTURAL COMMUNICATION

Psychologists Eidelson and Eidelson identify five belief domains, echoed by Lyubansky and Eidelson (2005), that "focus on issues of direct relevance to a group member's perception of the in-group's circumstances and his or her willingness to take action on behalf of the group, even at the risk or cost of intergroup conflict" (p. 5). The five domains are (1) vulnerability, (2) injustice, (3) distrust, (4) superiority, and (5) helplessness (Lumby & Morrison, 2010) and each describes what co-cultural group members may believe as a result of being othered.

Lumby and Morrison (2010) state that vulnerability belief, the first domain, refers to a co-cultural group member's perception that the group is at risk of being a "collective target of pervasive threat and potential catastrophe" (p. 5). Because of the familiarity with systemic oppression, co-cultural group members are acclimated to the strong possibility that negative or dire outcomes will result from engaging with the mainstream society in their daily life (e.g., work, shopping, school, errands, etc.). There is an anticipation or expectation that they will experience "alienation and estrangement from the larger world" (p. 5). An example of this might be when Inga, a Yugoslavian exchange student, is shopping in a store and is ignored by the salespeople. She has a thick accent and speaks broken English, which seems to frustrate North Americans. Her past negative experiences (e.g., cultural memory) in other stores compels her to believe the current and future encounters will have similar outcomes of oppression.

The second domain, injustice belief, relates to the belief that the co-cultural group views themselves as victimized by other groups. This is "often based on individuals' belief that in-group members receive substandard outcomes due not to their own inadequacies but because some other, more powerful out-group has created a biased or rigged system" (Lumby & Morrison, 2010, p. 5). This is akin to a belief that as an inherently privileged group, members of the dominant group are a part of a larger system of oppression to which the co-cultural group and its members will be subjected. As a result, co-cultural group members with injustice beliefs are more likely to have a stronger allegiance to and identification with their group (Lumby & Morrision, 2010).

Distrust belief is the third domain and "focuses on the presumed hostility and malicious intent of other groups" (Lumby & Morrison, 2010, p. 5). What distinguishes this domain from the others is that the co-cultural group members have a "conviction that outsiders harbor malevolent designs toward the in-group" and are not to be trusted (p. 5). All of the domains can be experienced to varying degrees as an "accurate and functional assessment of the world of intergroup relations" (p. 5). In the case of the United States, the history of institutionalized slavery as well as the civil rights and feminist movements provide evidence of this. Both dominant and co-cultural groups have been "in competition for scarce resources" (p. 5), which undoubtedly breeds negative intergroup relations that are difficult to overcome. In more extreme cases, people who espouse this domain belief may also "border on paranoia, leading to hypervigilant social information processing and exaggerated perceptions of conspiracy" (p. 5).

The fourth domain is the superiority belief that "revolves around the conviction that the in-group [in this case the marginalized group] is morally superior, chosen, entitled, or destined for greatness—and the corresponding view of the out-group as contemptible, immoral, and inferior" (Lumby & Morrison, 2010, p. 5). This response to intergroup interactions can be perceived as a defense mechanism that developed as a result of past negative experiences in the cultural memory or to protect oneself from the outgroup. Lumby and Morrison (2010) further suggest that this perception of a superior status is a form of "selective recounting of a group's history" (p. 5) which may be viewed as a type of selective memory where the co-cultural group member fails to accurately remember the reality of an experience. This does not, however, imply that claims of oppression are to be easily dismissed. Rather, a person has reframed a narrative and, as Lumby and Morrison (2010) explain, "fails to provide supporting documentation for such accounts" (p. 5), which can become problematic regarding historical instances of oppression.

Such accounts can be counterproductive to larger discussions of those situations that occur where oppression is present. For example, Nadine, an older African American domestic, worked for the Thomases, a White family, most of her life. While sharing her life story with her grandchildren, she paints a picture of a blissful experience, to the surprise of her children. Nadine's children later share with the grandchildren the racism and discrimination their grandmother Nadine faced because of her gender, race, and class. The Thomases did employ her for many years, but there were several times where Nadine was treated poorly and she seemed to suppress these memories.

The final domain is the helplessness belief. This refers "to the individual's conviction that the in-group is unable to favorably influence or control events and outcomes through political or economic means" (Lumby & Morrison, 2010, pp. 5–6). When group members believe that they are ill equipped to change their circumstances, their way of thinking directly impedes any efforts to "organized political mobilization" (p. 6). The group weighs the costs and rewards of addressing systemic oppression and chooses to believe that such efforts are futile. The helplessness belief can be, as Lumby and Morrison (2010) suggest, "more demoralizing and debilitating than external impediments" (p. 6).

These domains provide a framework for understanding the responses co-cultural group members can have to systemic or societal oppression. Responses can vary in degree, preference, and appropriateness. They demonstrate how it is oftentimes difficult to ignore perceived and actual mistreatment from members of the dominant group. The experiences that typically illuminate these negative occurrences are oftentimes related to one's racial or ethnic identity; however, social science interest is growing and extending to include recently identified co-cultural groups that are also subjected to alienation and isolation.

REFLECT 9.4: Can you think of other groups that might be considered co-cultural groups that have not been discussed in the chapter? Make a claim about why they should be considered co-cultural groups.

FINAL THOUGHTS

As has been shown, your racial, ethnic, gender, physical capabilities, religious orientations, or sexual identities play a critical role in how you understand your self and the world you live in. Unfortunately, these standpoints are subjected to various forms of systemic oppression, which in turn create realities and experiences that are ignored, devalued, or unappreciated. These standpoints not only inform how you see and know your self, but they also directly impact how you communicate within your co-cultures and with members of the dominant group.

Whether the decision is to assimilate or accommodate in the face of systemic oppression (Cohen & Avanzino, 2010), co-cultural group members are subjected to situations where their otherness becomes central to their interactions with members of the dominant group. They are often forced to offer responses that cause them to either embrace or deny who they are, which is highly problematic. As discussed earlier in the case of people with disabilities, their physical and mental health is at risk because of the insensitivity of others. These co-cultural group members must choose how they will respond, which could have dire consequences. The same is said for gender, as evidenced by a history of women being oppressed in a patriarchal society. Communication strategies and behaviors are adapted in response to the oppression to which co-cultural group members are subjected. Regardless of the standpoint, several theories offer insightful lenses through which to understand marginalization and its effect on the lived experiences of the oppressed.

In terms of communication and relationships, co-cultural group membership has a significant impact on how you view yourself in general and how you choose to interact with others. The presence of the dominant culture, however, oftentimes serves as a barrier to understanding your identity because of the social hierarchy that dictates your perceived value. The studies discussing rape survivors, international students, and new immigrants use co-cultural group theory to demonstrate that societal oppression is pervasive and continues to serve as a barrier to success within a variety of social contexts. Not only do co-cultural group members struggle with learning how to appreciate their race, gender, ethnicity, sexual orientation, or religious orientation, but they also struggle in a society with rules, norms, and expectations to which they are expected to conform.

Although living in such a world is less than idyllic, it provides you with a lens through which to understand the consequences of marginalization. As Tim Wise (2008) notes, in order for the privileged to exist, there must be an underprivileged or underbenefitted. The experiences of the marginalized have long been ignored, and efforts to give voice to those co-cultural group members have been, and continue to be, laudable and necessary. Many people are under the misconception that the election of President Barack Obama marked the arrival of a post-racial America, and fail to recognize that although this is a landmark victory for this nation on several levels, systemic oppression remains a barrier to intercultural communication.

CONTINUE YOUR JOURNEY ONLINE

Visit: http://www.ncsl.org/issues-research/health/health-disparities-over view.aspx

Disparities in Health on the National Conference of State Legislatures (NCSL) website. Check out the links on this site to find out more about how co-cultural group membership affects access to health care. Explore what is being done through legislation and in other ways to end these disparities.

66 SAY WHAT?

Say What? provides excerpts from overheard real-life conversations in which people have communicated stereotypes. As you read these conversations, reflect on the following questions.

- Have you been in conversations like this before?
- Is there any one of these conversations that stick out to you more than the others?
- What do you think of this conversation?
- How did the stereotype help or hinder the conversation?
- Was there another way the stereotyper could have communicated to convey the same point?
- How do you feel when you hear this conversation or the specific stereotype?
- Do any of these conversations bother you more than others? Why or why not?
- Do any concepts, issues, or theories discussed in the chapter help explain why?

- **Say What?** I was traveling from Rome to Newark. At one point I noticed three young men of Middle Eastern origin with a strong Arabic accent. As I was observing them I noticed that their body language seemed mechanical; they went through every checkpoint distancing one another of about a 5-minute timing, and eventually met up and talked at random places. I noticed that the gate's computer screen said, right under the flashing "NEWARK NOW BOARDING," "NEXT FLIGHT CASABLANCA." At that point I went straight to board, realizing my anxiety was just a result of my imagination.

- **Say What?** The class was divided into small groups and given calculus problems to complete. There were about five of us in my group: four White students and an Asian student. I noticed that every time we had a question or problem the entire group looked to the Asian student for help. It didn't seem to matter that another student may have the same idea of how to go about things. Whatever the Asian student said, was what the group did. The Asian student did not appear to notice and if he did he did not bring the subject up.

- **Say What?** I was on the phone with my girlfriend and I brought up a Russian rock band I had seen featured on MTV. I mentioned that the girls in the group were very pretty. She immediately made a sound of disgust when I said this. "Dirty foreigners, I don't think Russians are pretty," she said. My eyebrows rose up a foot and I repeated what she said back to her in a condescending manner so she could hear how racist she sounded: "Dirty foreigners?"

- **Say What?** I began describing my problem to him. After two attempts he didn't understand, and I began speaking to him like he was a child, using sign language. "The fau-cet in-my-show-er [making sprinkling motions with my hands] is brooooo-ken. Can-you [pointing at him] fix-it?" I could tell that the super was embarrassed and a little mad at the same time. He then shook his head "yes" and shut the door behind him. I went back to my apartment expecting him to show up a few minutes later to fix the problem; however, it ended up to be a few days later.

REVIEW QUESTIONS

1. What does it mean to be marginalized or othered, according to the chapter? Why are the words *other* and *marginalize* appropriate to symbolically capture this experience?

2. Who has co-cultural group membership, according to the chapter?

3. What thoughts and emotions, based on the discussion in the chapter, led to W. E. B. Du Bois introducing the concept of double consciousness?

4. What does memory have to do with co-cultural group membership, according to the chapter?

5. Why does the chapter discuss four types of feminism? Is this level of depth appropriate given the chapter topic? Why or why not?

6. Compare and contrast muted group theory, standpoint theory, and co-cultural group theory, as discussed in the chapter?

7. What are the five belief domains discussed in the chapter as what co-cultural group members may believe as a result of their experience of being othered? Why would a co-cultural group member believe these to be true?

8. Why might the belief domains make communication between co-cultural group members and dominant group members difficult? Based on what you learned in the chapter, what strategies can you think of that might help in moments when communication is difficult between members of these groups?

9. The chapter discusses two co-cultural groups in academic settings. Did it surprise you to see these groups presented in this way? Using the concepts from the chapter, explain why or why not.

10. Based on the examples throughout the chapter, what tangible and intangible benefits do members of dominant groups possess?

KEY TERMS

Black feminist thought   197

Chicana feminist
   thought   197

co-cultural group (CCG)   188

co-cultural group theory
   (CCGT)   201

critical memory   194

dispelling stereotypes   190

distrust belief   204

double consciousness   191

feminism   196

helplessness belief   205

injustice belief   204

maintaining interpersonal
   barriers   190

marginalized   187

multiracial feminist
   thought   197

muted group theory   200

neither/nor tension   203

orientational others   185

othered   187

playing the game   195

re-membering   191

standpoint theory   196

superiority belief   204

vulnerability belief   204

REFERENCES

Andrews, V. L. (2003). Self-reflection and the reflected self: African American double consciousness and the social (psychological) mirror. *Journal of African American Studies, 7*, 59–79.

Berger, M., & Bettez, S. (2007). Multiracial feminism. In G. Ritzer (Ed.), *Blackwell encyclopedia of sociology.* Retrieved from http://www.blackwellreference .com/public/tocnode?query = berger + bettez&wi den = 0&result_number = 1&fields = bibliograph y&fields = content&from = search&id = g97814 05124331_yr2011_chunk_g978140512433119_ss1– 132&type = std

Burgess-Proctor, A. (2006). Intersections of race, class, gender, and crime: Future directions for feminist criminology. *Feminist Criminology, 1*, 27–47.

Burnett, A., Mattern, J. L., Herakova, L. L., Kahl D. H. Jr., Tobola, C., & Bornsen, S. E. (2009). Communicating/ muting date rape: A co-cultural theoretical analysis of communication factors related to rape culture on a college campus. *Journal of Applied Communication Research, 37*, 465–485.

Cohen, M., & Avanzino, S. (2010). We are people first: Framing organizational assimilation experiences of the physically disabled using co-cultural theory. *Communication Studies, 6*, 272–303.

Collins, P. H. (1989a). The social construction of Black feminist thought. *Signs: Journal of Women in Culture and Society, 14*, 745–773.

Collins, P. H. (1989b). A comparison of two works on Black family life. *Signs: Journal of Women in Culture and Society, 14*, 875–884.

Collins, P. H. (1990). *Black feminist thought: Knowledge, consciousness, and the politics of empowerment.* New York: Routledge.

Collins, P. H. (1996a). Sociological visions and revisions. *Contemporary Sociology, 25*, 328–331.

Collins, P. H. (1996b). What's in a name? Womanism, Black feminism, and beyond. *Black Scholar, 26*, 9–17.

Dillard, C. B. (2008). Re-membering culture: Bearing witness to the spirit of identity in research. *Race Ethnicity and Education, 11*, 87–93.

Du Bois, W. E. B. (1903/1989). *The souls of Black folk.* New York: Bantam Books.

Garcia, A. M. (1997). *Chicana feminist thought: The basic historical writings.* New York: Routledge.

Hartsock, N. C. M. (1983). The feminist standpoint: Developing the ground for a specifically feminist historical materialism. In S. Harding & M. Hintikka (Eds.), *Discovering reality: Feminist perspectives on epistemology, metaphysics, methodology, and philosophy of science* (pp. 283–310). Boston: D. Reidel.

hooks, b. (1990). *Yearning: Race, gender, and cultural politics.* Boston: South End Press.

Hopson, M. C., & Orbe, M. P. (2007). Playing the game: Recalling dialectical tensions for Black men in oppressive organizational structures. *The Howard Journal of Communication 18*, 69–86.

Houston, M. S. (1994). When Black women talk to White women: Why dialogues are difficult. In A. Gonzalez, M. Houston, & V. Chen (Eds.), *Our voices: Essays in culture, ethnicity, and communication* (pp. 133–139). Los Angeles: Roxbury.

Johnsrud, L. K., & Sadao, K. C. (1998). The common experience of "otherness": Ethnic and racial minority faculty. *The Review of Higher Education, 21*, 315–342.

Kramarae, C. (1981). *Women and men speaking: Frameworks for analysis.* Rowley, MA: Newbury House.

Kramarae, C. (2005). Muted group theory and communication: Asking dangerous questions. *Women and Language, 28*, 55–61.

Lumby, J., & Coleman, M. (2010). Leadership and diversity. *School Leadership and Management, 30*, 1–2.

Lumby, J., & Morrison, M. (2010). Leadership and diversity: theory and research. *School Leadership and Management, 30*, 3–17.

Lyubansky, M., & Eidelson, R. J. (2005). Revisiting Du Bois: The relationship between African American double consciousness and beliefs about racial and national group experiences. *Journal of Black Psychology, 31*, 3–26.

Matsunaga, M., & Torigoe, C. (2008). Looking at the Japan-residing Korean identities through the eyes of the "outsiders within": Application and extension of co-cultural theory. *Western Journal of Communication, 72*, 349–373.

McIntosh, P. (1988). *Working paper 189: White privilege and male privilege: A personal account of coming to see correspondences through work in women's studies*. Wellesley, MA: Wellesley College Center for Research on Women.

Orbe, M. P. (1996). Laying the foundation for co-cultural theory: An inductive approach to studying "non-dominant" communication strategies and the factors that influence them. *Communication Studies, 47,* 157–176.

Orbe, M. P. (1998). *Constructing co-cultural theory: An explication of culture, power, and communication.* Thousand Oaks, CA: Sage.

Orbe, M. P., & Harris, T. M. (2008). *Interracial communication: Theory to practice.* Thousand Oaks, CA: Sage.

Sadao, K. C. (2003). Living in two worlds: Success and the bicultural faculty of color. *The Review of Higher Education, 26,* 397–418.

Tatum, B. D. (2003). *"Why are all the Black kids sitting together in the cafeteria?": A psychologist explains the development of racial identity.* New York: Basic Books.

Thompson, B. (2002). Multiracial feminism: Recasting the chronology of second wave feminism. *Feminist Studies, 28,* 337–360.

Urban, E., & Orbe, M. P. (2007). The syndrome of the boiled frog: Exploring international students on U.S. campuses as co-cultural group members. *Journal of Intercultural Communication Research, 36,* 117–138.

Walker, A. (1988). *Living by the word: Selected writings 1973–1987.* San Diego: Harcourt Brace Jovanovich.

Wise, T. (September 13, 2008). This is your nation on White privilege (updated). *Red room writer profile.* Retrieved from http://www.redroom.com/blog/tim-wise/this-your-nation-white-privilege-updated?page = 4

Zinn, M. B., & Dill, B. D. (1996). Theorizing difference from multiracial feminism. *Feminist Studies, 22,* 321–331.

PART III

Navigating Inter/Cultural Communication in a Complex World

CHAPTER **10**

Advocacy

**Rachel Anderson
Droogsma**

Nebraska Wesleyan University

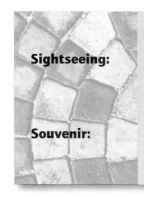

Journey Through Chapter 10

Sightseeing: On your journey, you will use the social constructionist perspective from a critical approach in order to visit with issues related to advocacy, including different types of advocacy from within and outside marginalized groups. The dark side of advocacy is addressed as well.

Souvenir: After your journey, you will take away a broader view of what advocacy entails, including a variety of types of advocacy. You will gain an appreciation for the difficulties inherent in any type of advocacy.

When Shin Fujiyama traveled to Honduras as a college sophomore in 2005, he visited a small village that had been destroyed by a hurricane in 1998 and had never been rebuilt (Students Helping Honduras, 2009). He was moved by the plight of the orphaned children living there, many of who lived in the streets (CNN, 2009, May 7a). A young girl in the village named Carmen asked Shin (who speaks fluent Spanish) if he could help the village build homes for her friends and family members. Inspired by the strength of the people and their great need, Shin pledged to return to help Carmen and the village. Upon arriving home to the University of Mary Washington in Fredericksburg, Virginia, Shin started a student group called Students Helping Honduras (SHH). SHH began raising money for the village by sponsoring bake sales and organizing fundraising walks on campus (CNN, 2009, May 7b). With the help of his sister Cosmo Fujiyama, Shin began visiting other college campuses to encourage more students to join them in their efforts. And they did. SHH is now a nonprofit organization with 25 student chapters (and growing) around the United States (Students Helping Honduras, 2009). The organization raised over $750,000 to support underserved people in Honduras, which has led to the construction of two elementary schools and the rebuilding of homes in

Photo 10.1   How do you feel when you help someone? Helping someone, whether through advocacy or merely holding the door open for someone with heavy packages, is often responded to with appreciation and joy. In the picture, grateful and joyous children surround smiling Shin Fujiyama in Honduras.

the village Shin visited as a sophomore. Shin, who graduated from college in 2007, continues to work as executive director of SHH and was honored as a CNN Hero for his work in Honduras (CNN, 2009, May 7b).

As a student, Shin witnessed the villagers' poverty and chose to believe he could make their lives better. Yet, students often feel helpless in the face of the injustices in the world. After learning about or witnessing the social inequalities that surround them, many students feel conflicting emotions. Sometimes guilt, sadness, anger, confusion, or even doubt surface when a person learns about or experiences the scope of the injustices that different cultural groups face. These common reactions to the realities of oppression are often perceived as barriers to reducing inequities. However, these emotions may also propel you to action. Like Shin Fujiyama, you can choose to believe that you can make the world a better place if you take action.

As you consider what you can do in the fight to end social inequities, consider being an advocate for marginalized groups discussed extensively in the previous chapter. Because their voices are not often heard in public platforms, marginalized group members face misunderstandings and oppression in society, including stereotypes, prejudice, and discrimination. According to Roy and Starosta (2001), "The goal of an intercultural communication researcher should not be limited to reporting about communication patterns in other cultures and how these compare to his or her own cultural patterns; instead s/he should be involved in an inquiry that seeks to liberate people from oppression" (p. 13).

This statement applies not only to researchers but to students of inter/cultural communication, as well. If you are like 66% of incoming college freshmen, you may already be inclined to take action to help people facing difficult circumstances (Jayson, 2006) and may simply be searching for a way to do so. On the other hand, advocacy is not for everyone, and not all marginalized groups desire advocacy. So, it is important to weigh your own motivation, the level of your commitment, and the needs of the group before you decide if you want to advocate.

This chapter, which reflects a critical, or power-based, inter/cultural communication perspective, helps you do this. It provides you with some of the ways you can advocate for people in marginalized groups, whether you are a member of the group you choose to advocate for or not. It also provides you with some forms your advocacy might take, and shares some of the difficulties of being an advocate. Throughout, the chapter offers real examples of some of the ways college students just like you are making a difference in marginalized people's lives.

ADVOCACY

For the purposes of this chapter on inter/cultural communication, advocacy can be defined as involving two components: communication and action. First, advocacy involves using communication to provide support to a marginalized group. Second, advocacy involves taking action to create change in society to benefit a marginalized group. Although communication in and of itself can be viewed as taking action, drawing distinctions between these two components helps illuminate the many forms your advocacy can take as well as how your advocacy might unfold. Whether you choose to advocate through everyday communication or to progress from communication to direct action, you will want to make sure your advocacy is ethical.

Advocacy through communication in support of a marginalized group can include educating others about the marginalized group, encouraging others to dialogue about their stereotypes of the group, or speaking in support of the group in private or public settings. If you choose to advocate through communication, your knowledge about the group should come from quality source material or research about the group and through direct communication with group members, and not secondhand knowledge you have acquired through the media or friends and family. If you do not possess quality information about the group, it would not be ethical to advocate on their behalf. Further, as you share your knowledge with others, your communication should encourage dialogue and mutual understanding rather than argument.

Advocacy through action, on the other hand, can include volunteering at a nonprofit agency that supports the group, joining an awareness campaign to change people's attitudes toward the group, or lobbying to create a change in policy that benefits the group. If you choose to advocate through action, the same ethical rules apply as for communication, but you must also consider whether or not you possess a platform from which to act on behalf of the group. This can mean that your standpoint gives the cultural group a different vantage point from which to relay their message or that you possess resources that may benefit the group. For example, you may be a member of a more powerful group, and your testimony on behalf of a marginalized group may hold more sway with members of other powerful cultural groups. Or, you may know how to use technology, such as blogs or websites, to share the group's message with a broader audience. You may also have the time to volunteer on behalf of an organization that supports the group's needs.

So how do you determine if you are the right person to advocate for a particular marginalized group? First, you must determine your own cultural standpoint, which shapes your opportunities to advocate. Feminist standpoint theory, which was discussed in Chapter 9, applies not only to women. The theory says that your social positioning shapes how you experience the world, the self, and what you know (Wood, 1994), and explains that inequities are built into society (Collins, 1990). In relation to advocacy, standpoint theory can help you determine: (1) your view of the social world, and how that view might impact your advocacy; and (2) which groups are marginalized and, therefore, may be in need of advocacy.

Start by determining which dominant cultural identities you share, if any. In the United States, for example, these might include being any of the following: White, male, middle to upper class, heterosexual, Christian, educated, or English speaking. Next, consider which, if any, of your identities place you outside of those dominant group identities, and therefore marginalize you. According to Naples (2003), whether you are conscious of it or not, "our social location shapes the way we proceed to gather information and draw conclusions from that information" (p. 191). So, it is important to ask yourself, how is your view of society limited? Understanding the perspectives of the marginalized group you wish to advocate for is vital to ensuring your advocacy is based on their needs and not your own assumptions about what the group needs. If you share dominant group characteristics, how will you work to reduce your blind spots and better understand the experiences of marginalized groups?

Finally, ask yourself if there is a group you have learned about or have contact with that faces constraints that you would like to help with. Does this group need advocacy? For example, are they marginalized and muted? Do you have a platform based on your standpoint to advocate for this group? If you are not sure you possess the resources necessary to advocate for the group or do not feel committed to the group's cause, advocacy is probably not the right path for you. However, if you have answered these questions affirmatively and think you can help the group achieve their goals, you are in a position to begin advocating for this group, whether you are a member of the group or not.

ADVOCACY FROM WITHIN OR OUTSIDE A MARGINALIZED GROUP

You might be wondering, "Which groups could I qualify to advocate for? Can I advocate for a group that I'm not a part of?" As long as you take steps to learn about the group's standpoints from quality, firsthand research sources, or dialogue with members of the cultural group you wish to advocate for, you can be an advocate whether you are a member of the group or not. Advocacy from within a marginalized group and advocacy from outside a marginalized group both present benefits and drawbacks.

Advocacy From Within a Marginalized Group

If you choose to advocate from within a marginalized group, known as insider advocacy, you may have greater authority when speaking on behalf of the group because, as a group member, you share the group's cultural experiences. Indeed, when people speak on behalf of their own cultural group, others tend to listen. Additionally, because many people want the best for their own cultural group, this may lead to a more accurate portrayal of the group's cause and concerns. For example, some scholars suggest that being a community "insider" may prevent abuses of power by researchers (Jandt & Tanno, 2001).

However, being a member of the marginalized group does not necessarily assure that group members' voices will be heard (Bishop, 2005). No advocate is without biases, and the role of advocate brings power that can be abused, even by ingroup members. For example, the advocate's personal experiences might not be representative of the entire group, so by speaking out the advocate might misrepresent the group's standpoints. Further complicating advocacy from within a marginalized group is the potential for negative judgment from people outside the group. Someone who calls the dominant group's attention to inequities may receive negative labels and may be scorned by people in power. Outgroup members may view cultural group insiders as biased in favor of their own group and, therefore, may deem an insider advocate less credible. Despite these potential challenges, if you are a group insider, your membership gives you insights into the marginalized group's experiences that outsiders simply do not have, and that is a tremendous advantage.

For those advocating from within their own racial group, a further issue can complicate their advocacy: the model minority stereotype. The label model minority is applied to members of marginalized groups who behave in ways that satisfy dominant group expectations. In other words, someone in a model minority group is perceived to be someone who acts consistently with the norms of the dominant culture and does not "cause problems" by pointing out issues of inequality or by drawing attention to stereotypes or discrimination. In return, a model minority is favored and is granted privileges by the dominant group. For example, Asian Americans in the United States are sometimes given the label model minority because of the academic excellence and quiet demeanor that is often stereotypically attributed to them. Perhaps as a result of group members' supposed model behavior, this group may face fewer negative stereotypes from the dominant group (White people) than people in other marginalized racial groups do. If someone from within a marginalized model minority group begins advocating on behalf of another nonmodel minority marginalized group, others' perceptions of this person's model status may be shattered and negative judgment and the removal of privileges may ensue. Ultimately, the potential for negative judgment exists for all within-group advocates. This does not mean, however, that people from inside marginalized groups should not become advocates. Instead, advocates must weigh the strength of their convictions and understand the potential consequences that might come with their advocacy.

One example of an effective advocate from within a marginalized group is J. McLane Layton, an adoptive mother who advocates for the rights of adopted children in the United States. Although adopted children and families might not seem like a marginalized cultural group at first glance, consider how few adopted kids' and adopted families' voices, concerns, and experiences are shared in broader society. Consider too the stereotypes that these families can face simply because they are not constructed biologically. McLane realized these injustices when she adopted her children from abroad and found that internationally adopted, and in some cases domestically adopted, children are not granted the same rights as biological children in the United States. For example, an internationally adopted child can never be president of the United States; they are considered foreign born for their entire lives even with full U.S. American citizenship and U.S. American parents. McLane became outraged by the many restrictions her children and family faced and realized the need for someone to speak for the community as a whole, so she founded Equality for Adopted Children (EACH, 2007) to share this group's experiences and needs with the public.

Advocacy from Outside a Marginalized Group

Those who engage in advocacy from outside the group, or outsider advocacy, face different potential benefits and obstacles. An outsider advocate may possess more privilege and have access to more resources. Thus, these advocates may be able to share the group's message in a more public way than members of the marginalized group can. Further, the dominant group may perceive outsiders' testimony on behalf of a marginalized group to be more convincing than testimony from someone inside the group advocating on the group's behalf.

Although dominant group members may be more inclined to listen to them, outsider advocates may not fully understand the experiences of the marginalized group for which they are advocating. It is easy for outside advocates to re-create inequities in their relationships with marginalized group members by making decisions for group members or failing to engage in dialogue with the group to ensure their needs are being met. For example, researchers Kamler and Threadgold (2003) discuss the difficulties of accurately representing the stories of a different cultural group (in this case Vietnamese women in Australia) due to their own identities as White, feminist women. In their article, Kamler and Threadgold note that every choice they made throughout the research process not only did not include the participants, but acted to shape the focus of the study according to what the researchers wanted, rather than what the women in the study wanted or needed. Their power, then, allowed them to distort the stories of these Vietnamese-Australian women despite their professed good intentions.

As a result of such potential abuses of power, outside advocates must constantly strive for equality in their relationships with the marginalized group. The best way to do this is for the advocate to listen critically to the group's concerns during constant and ongoing dialogue. Starosta (2003) notes that intercultural communication is better defined by mutual listening than reciprocal talking. According to Starosta (2003), when engaged in effective intercultural listening, the listener analyzes the speech of the other person first from the standpoint of the other's culture and then from the standpoint of his or her own culture. The listener recognizes the other's cultural influences and the listener's own stereotypes about the other culture that need to be set aside. Only by listening in this way can an advocate begin to understand marginalized group members' cultural standpoints.

One example of an outsider advocate is a straight ally. A straight ally is a heterosexual person who promotes lesbian, gay, bisexual, and transgender (LGBT) people's rights. Although they are outside the community, by dialoguing with and listening to their LGBT friends and acquaintances, they can be powerful advocates for equality for people of all sexual orientations. Another example of an outsider advocate are the members of the organization Out and Equal, who label themselves *workplace advocates* for members of the LGBT community (Out and Equal, 2010). The organization trains members of the LGBT community and its allies to create workplaces that are safe for members of the LGBT community.

Take a Side Trip:

If you would like to read more about related issues, visit Appendix A: Navajo Culture Explored Through Ethnography.

LIVING CULTURE

Creating an Organ Donation Health Campaign
Susan E. Morgan

Purdue University

I am always struck by how important it is to follow the principles and lessons learned from academic readings to the real world. When I am designing and planning campaigns that are designed to reach minority populations (generally African Americans), I am careful to learn about the ways in which the population I am trying to reach view a health issue differently from the rest of the population. A primary principle of persuasion is that you view your topic through the eyes of your audience and think about what would be persuasive to them, not what would be persuasive to you and people like you.

I help develop campaigns to promote registering to become a potential organ donor when people come to an office to get or renew their driver's licenses or identification cards in the state of Michigan. Rather than develop one single statewide campaign, we tailored a couple of different campaigns to the state's primary populations. For African Americans, we did this in three different ways. First, we identified concerns that were especially salient to the African American community regarding organ donation, such as the perception of unfairness in the organ allocation system and suspicion that the medical system may be corrupt. Essentially, there is a concern that if African Americans donate, their organs will most likely go to help wealthy, influential White people. In a study we did on African Americans' conversations with family members about their willingness to donate their organs after they die, we recorded the following exchange:

Person 1: Just the fact that the doctors won't give their full, like, all to try to save me if they knew that I was an organ donor. Probably wouldn't give their all to try to save me if I wasn't, if I wasn't one.

Person 2: Yeah.

Person 1: Going on who's your doctor.

Person 2: Yeah, and how much money you've got, too.

Person 1: You're right. They don't want to keep poor people alive.

Person 2: No, they don't.

Clearly, these attitudes toward organ donation were important to acknowledge so we could create an effective campaign.

(Continued)

LIVING CULTURE

(Continued)

Second, we created messages that specifically targeted these concerns. For example, we created posters and billboards that featured the stories of local African Americans in Detroit whose lives were saved through organ donation by other Michiganders. African Americans are disproportionately in need of transplants and actually receive organs at a greater rate than Whites and we wanted to get that message out to the community.

Third, we made sure that our channels of communication made sense for the population we were trying to reach. Instead of using only billboards and newspaper ads, we also used ads on busses (because although many people in the Detroit area do not drive, they still need to go to drivers license offices to get identification cards) and placed our PSAs on radio stations popular with African Americans. Another part of our campaign involved in-person visits to driver's license offices by volunteers; we made sure that these volunteers had all been touched by organ donation in some way and were nearly all African American. Because the messages from volunteers were delivered orally, this was particularly appropriate for the African American community; there are general cultural preferences for this channel of communication because of a long history of oral tradition within this community.

Our efforts to create a culture-centered campaign that communicated in a way that was culturally competent paid off extremely well. We were able to increase donor registrations by over 1,800%, a nearly unheard of outcome for any type of health campaign. All in all, our experiences have reaffirmed the importance of understanding the perspective of a cultural community and communicating in ways that are most appropriate for that community.

Consider:

1. What role did members of the community being served play in this health campaign?

2. How did those working on the campaign step outside of themselves and their assumptions? Why is this important?

3. Why would the author, not a member of the culture she advocated for, work with this culture?

4. Can you think of other health issues that would benefit from this type of outreach?

Group Insiders and Outsiders Working Together

Both within and outside of the group advocates are vital to improving the status of marginalized groups everywhere. Group causes that are promoted by people regardless of group membership are more likely to succeed. By forming a combined team, advocates from within the group bring their strengths to the cause, such as being closer to the group's cultural experiences, and advocates from outside of the group bring their strengths to the cause, such as their greater privilege and voice in society. Think about the civil rights movement and its example of how advocates can work together to achieve their goals. In 1961, for example, 13 young people—7 Black and 6 White—volunteered to ride busses together in the South to challenge racial segregation there; these Freedom Riders' actions sparked violence and further protests and eventually led to the Supreme Court overturning state segregation laws in transportation (Arsenault, 2006).

As the Freedom Riders example illustrates, working across cultural groups lays the groundwork for peace, both among the groups working together and within and across nations. Peacebuilding, which is a process of conflict resolution that attempts to remove the causes of violence among different groups, "requires a process of nonviolent, social change toward equality" (Fisher, 1993, p. 250). In this way, communication among different co-cultural groups striving for a common goal of advocating for marginalized people's rights is vital to achieving mutual understanding and peace. Indeed, the dialogue that results from insiders and outsiders working together may encourage positive change among group members, too, perhaps leading to the formation of a third culture. Third culture building becomes possible when two parties negotiate cultural differences and merge cultural traits to create a new culture (Starosta & Olorunnisola, as cited in Chen & Starosta, 1998). In other words, people from different groups take parts of one another's cultures to create a new culture that makes sense to both parties.

Starosta and Olorunnisola (as cited in Chen & Starosta, 1998) describe five phases of building a third culture, beginning with initial contact with someone different and ending with the creation of a new co-culture. First, people make judgments of the other group from a distance and process that information internally. Second, people gather information about the other group and start to learn the difference between the other's cultural identity and individual identity. Third, open dialogue occurs, leading both parties to have a greater awareness of the differences between their cultures; these differences, however, are viewed positively and with equality. At this point, because cultural differences have been recognized and explored, cultural and racial barriers are valued and no longer hinder mutual understanding. Fourth, the parties in the third culture test their new culture to make sure it works for them and adjust it as necessary. Finally, if the parties decide they really like the new culture, they can decide to adopt it. In sum, you can actually create a new co-culture by finding allies across cultural groups. Third cultures are a powerful example of how to break down barriers, create change that benefits marginalized groups, and promote peaceful intercultural relationships. That is an exciting prospect.

Another reason to work together is that cultural identities are not fixed. Instead, they are fluid. As such, a dominant group member may become marginalized. This change in social status may be the result of the loss of a job, because of an illness or natural disaster, or due to a change in the amount of power a person's co-culture holds over time, among other reasons. Similarly, a marginalized group member may become more dominant. In other words, if you care only about the issues that impact you and your cultural group(s), you may find yourself isolated and without assistance when you need it.

REFLECT 10.1: Have you ever been an advocate for a group in the past? Were you a member of the group or an outsider? What about your status as insider or outsider was helpful to you as an advocate, and what was a potential drawback?

TYPES OF ADVOCACY

If you have decided you are ready to make a difference and know whom you want to help, your advocacy can take many forms. A few forms of advocacy are highlighted here to help you get started, but regardless of which form advocacy takes, an advocate must be creative and flexible to meet the group's needs.

Individual Advocacy

There are some fairly simple things you can do on your own to make a positive difference in society for marginalized groups. Once you possess quality information about a marginalized group that is stereotyped or misunderstood by the general public, simply sharing your information with others through individual advocacy can create change. Consider advocacy through interpersonal communication, through research and learning, or through individual action or volunteering.

Advocacy Through Interpersonal Communication

At some point, you have probably heard or participated in stereotyping or expressing prejudice or discrimination toward people in a certain cultural group. When you hear such comments, it is tempting to not say anything and "keep the peace" with the person who said the comment, particularly if the person is a friend or relative. However, remaining silent only allows the oppression of people in marginalized groups to continue. Instead, pledge to speak up when you hear such comments. This is not done to create an argument or make the speaker feel bad, but instead to have a conversation about what the speaker's words really mean thereby drawing attention to and calling into question their underlying assumptions.

REFLECT 10.2: Have you ever confronted someone's negative comment about a cultural group? What did you say to get the conversation started? Did your approach work or not, and why? How might you do this differently in the future?

For example, after taking an intercultural communication course, Nick Thompson was having lunch with his boss when his boss made negative comments about Muslims, implying that all Muslims were terrorists. Nick said that prior to taking intercultural communication he might have ignored his boss' comments, partly out of fear of insulting his boss and partly out of a lack of accurate information about Muslims. Having learned some facts about Muslims in his intercultural communication course, however, Nick felt confident dealing with the prejudiced comments from his boss against Muslims. Instead of being confrontational, Nick started by asking his boss why he held the belief that Muslims were terrorists. When his boss identified media coverage, which he said "obviously" showed Muslims were terrorists, Nick asked him if he had ever had any negative experiences with Muslims personally. His boss said no, not directly. Nick then shared with his boss what he had learned about Muslims in his intercultural communication class. He told his boss that Islam is a religion of peace and that the media presents a skewed perspective of Muslims. Although Nick may not have changed his boss's mind that day, by starting a conversation with open-ended questions and respectfully challenging his remarks, Nick planted the seeds of change in his boss's mind that will hopefully lead his boss to reconsider his assumptions.

If you are not sure how you could discuss bigoted speech when you hear it, check out the website Teaching Tolerance, which is a project of the Southern Poverty Law Center. Bigoted speech is talk that expresses intolerance or prejudice. On the website, you can view a handbook called, Speak Up! (Teaching Tolerance, n.d.) that includes ideas about how to respond to bigoted comments based on your relationship with the speaker. Above all else, aim to dialogue with people about their thoughts and attitudes toward different cultural groups because open communication is the best way to advocate for marginalized groups. Of course, you can also show respect to cultural groups through your own words by avoiding biased speech. If someone finds something you said offensive and tells you so, try to remain open to what that person has to say. Although it is difficult to be critiqued, sometimes people are blind to their biases and need someone else to tell them when they offend. Being open-minded about someone else's critiques helps make advocating easier for that person.

Besides critiquing the words of ourselves and others, advocates should consider responding when they see someone being discriminated against, as well. As discussed in Chapter 1, discrimination occurs when someone is treated differently, and usually negatively, due to cultural identity. You may see someone being discriminated against at work or in a public place. When discrimination occurs in public places and by or to strangers, advocates may or may not feel safe intervening. If you do not feel safe intervening, report the incident to the appropriate authorities or to an advocate group. If you do feel safe intervening, however, you can choose to take action by making simple, direct statements to the perpetrator. Sam Johnson, for example, was holding his partner's hand while walking along a beach boardwalk when a group of men approached them and began to taunt them about being gay. A heterosexual couple walking ahead of Sam and his partner on the boardwalk quickly rushed to their side and told the group: "If we can hold hands and go for a walk here, so can they." The couple stood next to Sam and his partner, and the group of harassers rapidly dispersed.

Sadly, whether or not bystanders attempt to intervene, physical violence that is rooted in hate can occur. In December 2008, two brothers walked home from a New York City bar together arm-in-arm, as is the cultural norm in their home country of Ecuador (McFadden, 2008). A group of homophobic young men used this nonverbal behavior to classify the brothers as homosexual and beat one of the brothers nearly to death with a baseball bat thereby committing a hate crime. A hate crime is a crime in which a perpetrator attacks a victim due to the individual's perceived membership in a particular group. Although bystanders witnessed this event and called for help, no one tried to intervene directly. As this example shows, seeking help from those with training to provide it may sometimes be a better option than intervening directly because, in this example, bystander intervention may have led to the advocate's injury or death. So remember that your own safety, as well as your ability to help, should always be considered prior to communicating for advocacy. It is important to weigh your ability to make a positive difference prior to communicating your support of the group.

Advocacy Through Research and Learning

Many students use research about a marginalized group or groups to learn how they can best advocate for that group(s). Conducting research firsthand is a great starting point. When the researcher encourages dialogue with the researched, rather than a researcher assuming what the group in question needs, the research is stronger. Bishop (2005) encourages co-cultural group members to tell stories of their experiences, which the researcher and group members later analyze together. Foley and Valenzuela (2005) also advocate a conversational style of interviewing that they claim encourages participants in their studies to share more. Later, these participants assist researchers in understanding their experiences and are free to edit their words. In these ways, researchers demonstrate to participants their respect for them and their lives. For an advocate, dialogue should not just be viewed as an ideal to strive for, but the foundation upon which research is built. An open dialogue between researcher and researched ensures that the research is mutually guided and mutually beneficial. So, if you choose to research a marginalized group, include people from the group in your study and gain their active participation in the research.

Interacting with participants is the best way to learn about their cultural standpoints. Jessica Lee used her final research paper in intercultural communication to learn about the LGBT community. Her cousin had recently shared with her that she is a lesbian, and Jessica wanted to understand her better and chose research to do so. Jessica interviewed her cousin as well as two other members of the LGBT community in order to understand their cultural standpoints. After conducting her research, Jessica realized that much of her prior knowledge about LGBT people was based on stereotypical media portrayals of LGBT people. In class, Jessica shared her research, made a commitment to share her newfound knowledge with her friends, and pledged to speak up when she heard people use prejudiced language to describe LGBT people.

Your research might take you outside of your university campus, as well. For example, after growing up with both Jewish and Muslim family members, Mohamed Seck chose to study the Palestinian/Israeli conflict firsthand. He attended an Arabic immersion study abroad program in Jordan and then traveled to both Palestine and Israel to meet with Palestinians in refugee camps and speak to Israeli Jews to gain both sides of the story. Mohamed realized that the conflict went beyond religion and, at least for the Palestinian refugees he spoke with, had nothing to do with religion. From the perspective of regular, everyday people in Palestine, Mohamed found that: "Palestinians don't hate Jewish people. They just want to live a normal life." Mohamed plans to spend another year in Jordan and then hopes to use his research on conflicts in the Middle East to shape United States foreign policy.

Although not everyone will have the opportunity to travel to a different country as an advocate, you can choose research or paper topics that allow you to gain knowledge about a culture or cultural issue that is new to you. Moreover, learning does not end when you earn a college degree. Make learning about cultural issues and cultural groups a priority through-out your life, not just when you are in college. Educating yourself about the diverse cultures around you helps combat the one-sided views that the media and, often the general public, present about culturally different others. So, use your curiosity about different cultures to educate yourself and then consider sharing that information with others.

Advocacy Through Volunteering

You can also be an advocate by volunteering for causes you believe in. Check the nonprofit agencies that support marginalized groups in your community and see if they need your help. Students often do not realize that they can volunteer in homeless shelters, domestic abuse centers, refugee and immigrant support centers, and other agencies that serve marginalized populations. You might be surprised at how little time it takes to make a difference in nonprofit agencies that are often strapped for time and finances.

REFLECT 10.3: Have you ever volunteered your time for an organization or cause? What did you learn from this experience that you would not have known had you not volunteered?

After being motivated to serve his community by his football coach, Ben Martinez and other members of his football team began volunteering once a week at the local food pantry. His experience helping community members in need every week transformed Ben's view of the world. Before volunteering, Ben had not realized people in his community were hungry, but after seeing and interacting with hungry people, he realized that they were just like him and his teammates; they were simply going through a hard time. Ben made a commitment to continue serving the hungry and to educate others about their existence and need. Therefore, another benefit of volunteering is that it often allows for empathy with marginalized group members, providing the volunteer with greater perspective on members' standpoints. The volunteer can then use firsthand knowledge to advocate for the marginalized group, as Ben now does.

Small Group Advocacy

Margaret Mead (n.d.) said it best: "Never doubt that a small group of thoughtful, committed citizens can change the world. Indeed, it is the only thing that ever has." Depending on the marginalized group you choose to advocate for and the needs of that group, you may find that small group advocacy could be particularly effective in reaching the group's goals. A group of people, after all, can sometimes reach a larger and more diverse audience and have a broader impact than one person alone. So, you may consider forming a student group or other organized small group of like-minded people who, like you, are interested in advocating for the marginalized group to create social change.

If you are wondering what you can accomplish as a student with a few friends, look no further than Shin Fujiyama's story at the beginning of this chapter. Indeed, Students Helping Honduras's motto is "where students create change" (Students Helping Honduras, 2009). Even though Shin was a college student, he saw the need of the people in the Honduran

Photo 10.2 Can you imagine what it is like to be homeless? Living a life in which what you take for granted, like a home and food to eat, is a luxury is not pleasant to imagine. Minnesota State University, Mankato, students hold cardboard signs with facts about homelessness on campus to raise awareness about homelessness on the day of an art show in the same theme.

Copyright 2010 by Rachel Anderson Droogsma.

village, realized that he could advocate for them, and took action.

Service Learning

If you identify a marginalized population in need of help and are passionate about serving them, your passion may be contagious, just as Shin's was (and is). And you do not have to start your own nonprofit organization in order to make a difference. You can also participate, alone or with a group of friends, in service opportunities organized through a class, student group, college, or outside nonprofit organization. Many college campuses offer volunteer opportunities during spring break with organizations such as Habitat for Humanity, and others send students to areas of high need like New Orleans for rebuilding efforts following Hurricane Katrina.

Courses that incorporate service learning, the fusion of traditional coursework with community service in which students meet the needs of community members or organizations through their coursework, are also wonderful places to learn about marginalized populations and their needs. If you enroll in a course that allows you to participate in a service-learning project, view the project as an opportunity to understand your community's needs better and not just another assignment. Service projects allow students and community members to partner together to draw attention to the needs and inequities of people in the community. Students at Minnesota State University, Mankato, participated in a service project that allowed them to advocate for homeless women, children, and families in their community. At the request of a local homeless shelter, the students organized an art project that encouraged former and current shelter guests to create art to share their experiences of homelessness with the public. The shelter hoped that the art would help the public understand that homeless people exist in the community and need the public's support. Students in the class helped plan the art creation sessions with shelter guests as well as the public display of that art, entitled "Views of Homelessness," throughout the community. On the day of the display on campus, members of the class stood all over campus holding cardboard signs with facts about homelessness. Following the project, the class committed to educating their friends and family members about homelessness, and several signed up to volunteer at local organizations for the homeless. In these ways, students in a class can become passionate, informed advocates for homeless people in the community.

Social Movements

When a cause catches on, it can become a social movement. A social movement occurs when people band together around a common goal. Throughout history, people, often young people like yourself, have initiated social movements and generated social change. Although you may feel like you do not have much influence as a young person or as a student, nothing could be further from the truth. The passion and energy of young people can transform society. Once you begin advocating for a cause, if enough people become involved, you could start a social movement yourself.

For example, as a college student, Eboo Patel became aware of the misunderstandings between religions and the increased extremism in faiths around the world and, in response, founded the Interfaith Youth Core (Patel, 2008). The Interfaith Youth Core trains young people from all faiths to promote religious pluralism. The organization began with just a few of Patel's college friends and is now a nationwide and worldwide movement (Interfaith Youth Core, n.d.). By empowering young people of faith to talk to one another and serve their communities together, the movement hopes to fight religious extremism and bigotry against various faiths. Powered by Patel's beliefs that people of faith are tied together by similar common values and that young people are the ones who must fuel the interfaith movement, the Interfaith Youth Core is now a worldwide force for social change.

Another social movement that was inspired by the work of local advocates is the Clothesline Project, an international grassroots public art project that aims to end violence against women (Clothesline Project, n.d.). Through T-shirt art, survivors and the loved ones of murder victims tell their stories anonymously; the colors of the T-shirts represent the type of violence the survivors endured or if the person was murdered by an abuser. T-shirts are hung on clotheslines in public spaces in the community where the survivors live to break the silence surrounding violence against women. This activist public art project, which began with a small group of women in Massachusetts, now exists all over the world (Droogsma, 2009). It encourages survivors of abuse and the loved ones of those murdered by abusers to advocate for themselves and others like them by anonymously creating a T-shirt. Local displays of the Clothesline Project appear all over the country and world every year, particularly during October, Domestic Violence Awareness Month, and April, Sexual Assault Awareness Month.

Whatever your cause is and whomever you choose to advocate for, realize that you *can* make a difference if you choose to. Sometimes the impact of your actions may be seen locally and other times globally, but what matters it that people band together to create the change they want to see in society.

THE DARK SIDE OF ADVOCACY

Although the examples throughout this chapter highlight the tremendous accomplishments of individual advocates, advocacy groups, and social movements, advocacy for marginalized groups is not easy and is not always successful. When advocates decide to commit to a cause, they must realize the hardships they may face. The harsh realities of advocacy include the fact that social change takes time, if it comes at all, and may bring danger to the advocate. Advocates also sometimes impose their own desires on marginalized group members, thus recreating or reinforcing inequities with group members. Moreover, social change does not come easily; after all, dominant group members do not relinquish their power overnight, nor do they quickly recognize the inequities in society that create hardships for marginalized groups.

As a result of these issues, it is important to understand that advocates can face burnout if their efforts to share their passion with others fail, or if the social change they desire is long in coming. Passion, ultimately, is not enough to create change; other people must also believe in the advocate's cause and offer their time and energy to achieve the goal. Financial and other resources are also necessary to share the group's message and support its efforts. Without additional resources and support, even the most well-intentioned cause may fail. In addition, certain social, political, economic conditions can make advocacy particularly difficult. Further, when advocates become consumed with seeking additional support for the group's cause, they face the danger of becoming detached from the very group they seek to help. Remaining in constant contact with group members and engaging in genuine dialogue with them, as well as forming a support network of people committed to the cause, is vital to remain personally energized and connected to the group's needs.

Perhaps as a result of some of these difficulties even worthy causes and well-intentioned advocates can engage in unethical advocacy. Unethical advocacy occurs when the advocate acts independently on behalf of the group without their informed consent, when the support the advocate attempts to provide is misinformed or contributes to the group's silencing, or when the advocate's actions benefit the advocate rather than the group.

REFLECT 10.4: Has someone ever assumed they knew what was best for you even though you disagreed? How did it feel to have someone think they knew you and your needs better than you did?

A 2011 investigation by *60 Minutes* raised questions about Greg Mortenson, a famous advocate for marginalized people (Kroft et al., 2011). Mortenson, founder of the Central Asia Institute (CAI) and author of the bestselling book *Three Cups of Tea,* gained national and international publicity for CAI's work building schools in remote areas of Pakistan and Afghanistan. Although Mortenson has positively impacted the lives of many children in both countries, accusations that he pocketed some of the money donors gave to CAI to build schools so that he could pay for the promotion of his books, among other claims of unethical behavior, have called Mortenson's credibility as an advocate into question.

In order to avoid the dark side of advocacy, students and researchers of inter/cultural communication must listen to cultural group members' concerns and weigh their own motivations for advocacy before determining whether or not advocacy is appropriate. Great abuses of power occur when an advocate *decides for* the marginalized group members that they are oppressed or that they need advocacy for a certain issue. Indeed, "Many have rightly questioned the arrogance that may accompany efforts to emancipate 'others'" (Kincheloe & McLaren, 2005, p. 308). Speaking for the concerns of a cultural group can represent an abuse of power when it strips participants of their agency and leaves them othered.

For example, many U.S. Americans misunderstand Muslim women's wearing of hijab (also called a headscarf) and stereotype the women who choose to wear it as oppressed (Cooke, 2001), even though research with American Muslim women who wear hijab reveals that some Muslim women embrace hijab as an empowering choice (Gerami, 1996; Mule & Barthel, 1992). These hijab wearers reject the notion that Western or revealing clothing is freeing and that they must wear such clothing in order to be valued or considered beautiful (Droogsma, 2007). So, advocating for the banning of hijab, as has happened in France, in order to "free" Muslim women from this clothing choice would be potentially unethical because such advocacy may be based on misinformed assumptions instead of on the standpoints of group members.

Instead, advocates must seek out the perspectives of group members and listen carefully to their concerns before rushing to advocate for these groups. According to Sauceda (2003), "We have to diffuse our own defensiveness by learning to listen without judgment for understanding, not advocacy" (p. 390). This does not mean that you should not be an advocate; it means you should not determine ahead of time what the group wants, thinks, or needs and instead should keep an open mind. When advocates fail to listen openly to the concerns of marginalized group members, their biases continue to determine what the group "needs." Quality source material about group members or dialogue with group members, then,

Photo 10.3   Do you see cherished animals or delicious food? Cows are cherished in India and turtles, frogs, and dogs are pets in America. However, cows in America, frogs in France, turtles in Creole culture, and dogs in China are all considered tasty. When even something as basic as the value of another living creature varies from one culture to the next, you can imagine all of the potential subtleties involved when advocating for a cultural group of which you are not a member.

becomes the only way to determine if the group or individuals feel oppressed at all, and if the group wants an advocate to act on their behalf.

A final point worth restating is that advocacy can sometimes be dangerous. As mentioned earlier in the chapter, speaking up and acting out in support of a marginalized group can put an advocate's safety at risk. Further, leading a movement for social change makes an advocate vulnerable as others, particularly people likely to lose power if the social change occurs, direct their anger at the advocate. Throughout history, advocates have lost their lives in pursuit of causes they believed in. Such extreme backlash against an advocate is rare in the United States. Yet, advocates may face negative judgments or threats of some sort. Therefore, it is important to consider the consequences of your advocacy and to assess whether or not the price of your advocacy is a price you are willing to pay.

FINAL THOUGHTS

In the words of Martin Luther King Jr. (1963): "Injustice anywhere is a threat to justice everywhere." Consider advocating for oppressed groups, whether or not you are a part of one, because each person's empowerment is tied to one another. As part of the human community and as a citizen of the world, you hold the power to create change, if you choose, in people's attitudes toward different cultural groups, in policies that create and sustain inequities, in the realities of life for persons in marginalized groups, and in yourself. Ultimately, as ethical students of inter/cultural communication, remain open to opportunities for advocacy throughout this course and throughout your life. Each person's actions can help build a better community and world.

CONTINUE YOUR JOURNEY ONLINE

Visit: The websites of some of the organizations mentioned in this chapter:

Out and Equal, http://outandequal.org

EACH, www.equalityforadoptedchildren.org

Teaching Tolerance, www.tolerance.org/handbook/speak/speak

Students Helping Honduras (recently renamed the Central American Children's Institute), www.studentshelpinghonduras.org

Interfaith Youth Core, www.ifyc.org

The Clothesline Project, www.clotheslineproject.org

As you visit these websites, consider for which group(s) you would be most likely to advocate. Consider how your cultural group identity plays a role in that preference.

Note

The examples in this chapter are real students' stories. Student names have been used with permission. Nick Thompson, Sam Johnson, Jessica Lee, and Ben Martinez are pseudonyms.

66 SAY WHAT?

Say What? provides excerpts from overheard real-life conversations in which people have communicated stereotypes. As you read these conversations, reflect on the following questions.

- Have you been in conversations like this before?
- Is there any one of these conversations that stick out to you more than the others?
- What do you think of this conversation?
- How did the stereotype help or hinder the conversation?
- Was there another way the stereotyper could have communicated to convey the same point?
- How do you feel when you hear this conversation or the specific stereotype?
- Do any of these conversations bother you more than others? Why or why not?
- Do any concepts, issues, or theories discussed in the chapter help explain why?

- **Say What?** His arm was cut severely. I had never, ever seen so much blood. He was wheeled into a room where he was still bleeding profusely. I waited outside. To make matters worse, a male nurse came out of the room and made a very disturbing comment to me. He said, "Are you afraid of blood? Does blood gross you out because I know a lot of girls are? If you are, I would suggest you not go in the room because you might thump to the floor." After the nurse made that comment to me, I responded quietly, "No, I'm not, but thanks."

- **Say What?** My boyfriend Ronald and I were watching an episode of *Designer's Challenge* a Home and Garden network series. I stated that I would not pay a designer $5,000 to decorate a child's room since I could successfully decorate it myself. Ronald responded, "As Jews they could afford to spend that much money to hire a designer." I launched into a thorough defense of those of Jewish faith. After my historical discourse, I shifted the discussion to my personal feelings toward Ronald's use of derogatory stereotypes and reminded him that it was both offensive and unnecessary to belittle someone else because of their race, ethnicity, or in this case religious beliefs.

- **Say What?** We were joking back and forth, playing the game where we see who can make the other one laugh the most, my roommate Kris came up with the comment, "Most students must think I'm a lesbian because I'm always in my sweats and I never do my hair and makeup when I go to class." I proceeded to tell her what she already knew, that all lesbians do not wear sweats with no makeup and her comment was unfair.

- **Say What?** "Oh it figures it would be an Asian driving." He proceeded with, "Well it's a fact that all Asians are horrible drivers." The three of us began to talk about his comment. I said, "We all have Asian friends; how can you say that? I mean, anyone can be a crummy driver. I don't see how it has anything to do with a nationality."

REVIEW QUESTIONS

1. According to the chapter, who do advocates try to help? Why?

2. What are the benefits and problems the chapter associates with advocating from within a marginalized group? From outside?

3. Is the model minority privileged or marginalized? Explain your answer based on the chapter discussion.

4. Why does the chapter say that understanding your standpoint is important if you want to be an advocate?

5. When advocating through interpersonal communication, discussed in the chapter, how might the ingroup and outgroup membership of those involved play a role?

6. In what way does research and learning, like reading this chapter, help a person to become an advocate?

7. Where would a person go to get involved with service learning? What are the benefits, according to the chapter?

8. Based on the chapter discussion of the dark side of advocacy, revisit two of the examples from the chapter and consider how these could have gone badly.

9. What factors might influence whether advocacy is successful? Use examples from the chapter to explain your answers.

10. Based on the examples provided throughout the chapter, create a list of motivations people have for becoming advocates.

KEY TERMS

advocacy   215

bigoted speech   223

hate crime   223

individual advocacy   222

insider advocacy   216

intercultural listening   218

model minority   217

outsider advocacy   218

peacebuilding   221

service learning   226

small group advocacy   225

social movement   227

straight ally   218

third culture building   221

unethical advocacy   228

REFERENCES

Arsenault, R. (2006). *Freedom riders: 1961 and the struggle for racial justice.* New York: Oxford University Press.

Bishop, R. (2005). Freeing ourselves from neocolonial domination in research: A Kaupapa Maori approach to creating knowledge. In N. K. Denzin & Y. S. Lincoln (Eds.), *The Sage handbook of qualitative research* (pp. 109–138). Thousand Oaks, CA: Sage.

Chen, G., & Starosta, W. (1998). *Foundations of intercultural communication.* Boston: Allyn & Bacon.

Clothesline Project. (n.d.). *The Clothesline Project.* Retrieved from http://www.clotheslineproject .org

CNN. (2009, May 7a). Building sunshine village. *CNN Heroes.* Retrieved from http://www.cnn.com/video/#/video/living/2009/05/07/cnnheroes.fujiyama.extra2.cnn

CNN. (2009, May 7b). CNN heroes: Shin Fujiyama. *CNN Heroes.* Retrieved from http://www.cnn.com/video/#/video/living/2009/05/07/cnnheroes.shin.fujiyama.profile.cnn

Collins, P. H. (1990). *Black feminist thought: Knowledge, consciousness, and the politics of empowerment.* Boston: Unwin Hyman.

Cooke, M. (2001). *Women claim Islam.* New York: Routledge.

Droogsma, R. A. (2007). Redefining hijab: American Muslim women's standpoints on veiling. *Journal of Applied Communication Research, 35,* 294–319.

Droogsma, R. A. (2009). "I am the woman next door": The Clothesline Project as woman abuse survivors' societal critique. *Communication, Culture, & Critique, 2,* 480–502.

Equality for Adopted Children. (2007). Founder biography. Retrieved from http://www.equalityforadoptedchildren.org/about_each/founder_biography.htm

Fisher, R. J. (1993). The potential for peacebuilding: Forging a bridge from peacekeeping to peacemaking. *Peace and Change, 18,* 247–266.

Foley, D., & Valenzuela, A. (2005). Critical ethnography: The politics of collaboration. In N. K. Denzin & Y. S. Lincoln (Eds.), *The Sage handbook of qualitative research,* (pp. 217–234). Thousand Oaks, CA: Sage.

Gerami, S. (1996). *Women and fundamentalism.* New York: Garland.

Interfaith Youth Core. (n.d.). *What we do.* Retrieved from http://www.ifyc.org/about_core

Jandt, F. E., & Tanno, D. V. (2001). Decoding domination, encoding self-determination: Intercultural communication research processes. *Howard Journal of Communications, 12,* 119–135.

Jayson, S. (2006, Oct 23). Generation Y gets involved. *USA Today.* Retrieved from http://www.usatoday.com/news/nation/2006-10-23-gen-next-cover_x.htm

Kamler, B., & Threadgold, T. (2003). Translating difference: Questions of representation in cross-cultural research encounters. *Journal of intercultural studies, 24,* pp. 137–151.

Kincheloe, J. L., & McLaren, P. (2005). Rethinking critical theory and qualitative research. In N. K. Denzin & Y. S. Lincoln (Eds.), *The Sage handbook of*

qualitative research, (pp. 303–342). Thousand Oaks, CA: Sage.

King, M. L. K. (1963). *Quote from letter from Birmingham Jail.* Retrieved from http://www.quotationspage.com/quote/24974.html

Kroft, S. (Writer), Klug, R., & Flaum, A. T. (Directors). (2011, April 17). Greg Mortenson. In A. Court, K. Livelli, & M. Usman, *60 Minutes.* New York: CBS.

McFadden, R. D. (2008, December 8). Attack on Ecuadorean brothers investigated as a hate crime. *New York Times.* Retrieved from http://www.nytimes.com/2008/12/09/nyregion/09assault.html

Mead, M. (n.d.). *Quote from About.com Women's History.* Retrieved from http://womenshistory.about.com/cs/quotes/a/qu_margaretmead.htm

Mule, P., & Barthel, D. (1992). The return to the veil: Individual autonomy versus social esteem. *Sociological Forum, 7,* 323–332.

Naples, N. A. (2003). *Feminism and method: Ethnography, discourse analysis, and activist research.* New York: Routledge.

Out and Equal. (2010). *Allies at work: Creating a lesbian, gay, bisexual, and transgender inclusive work environment.* Retrieved from http://www.outandequal.org/Allies-At-Work

Patel, E. (2008). *Acts of faith: The story of an American Muslim, the struggle for the soul of a generation.* Boston: Beacon Press.

Roy, A., & Starosta, W. J. (2001). Hans-Georg Gadamer, language, and intercultural communication. *Language and Intercultural Communication, 1,* 6–20.

Sauceda, J. M. (2003). Effective strategies for mediating co-cultural conflict. In L. Samovar & R. Porter (Eds.), *Intercultural communication: A reader* (pp. 385–405). Belmont, CA: Wadsworth.

Starosta, W. J. (2003, July). *Intercultural listening: Collected reflections, collated refractions.* Paper presented to a joint session of the World Communication Association and the International Listening Association, Stockholm, Sweden.

Students Helping Honduras. (2009). *Our mission.* Retrieved from http://www.studentshelpinghonduras.org/about

Teaching Tolerance. (n.d.). *Speak up!* Retrieved from http://www.tolerance.org/publication/speak/speak

Wood, J. T. (1994). Saying it makes it so: The discursive construction of sexual harassment. In S. G. Bingham (Ed.), *Conceptualizing sexual harassment as discursive practice,* (pp. 17–44). Westport, CT: Praeger.

Media and Culture

Mark P. Orbe

Western Michigan University

*The "Reality" of
Media Effects*

Journey Through Chapter 11

Sightseeing: On your journey, you will visit basic concepts related to media and culture that reflect social scientific and social construction perspectives. After a discussion of types of media and various media theories, the chapter will offer you reality television and its representations and constructions of various cultures in order to further examine these theories. Media effects and media literacy are also discussed.

Souvenir: After your journey, you will be a better informed media consumer and media critic aware of various theories through which to view and understand the media to which you are exposed daily and its relation to culture.

The media is a powerful presence in people's lives. Within the field of communication, media is the term used to refer to the particular medium used to deliver a message to a large, anonymous, diverse audience (Pearce, 2009a). Media studies involve research on media effects, which refer to the influence that the media has on audiences, and media representations, which are portrayals of various cultural groups. At the core of social construction is the idea that there is no such thing as objective reality (Pearce, 1995). Instead, scholars who advocate for this foundation stress that all knowledge is historically and culturally specific (Allen, 2005). Media, as a powerful social system, plays an important role in creating a person's sense of reality (Gergen, 1999). Even those persons who closely monitor their media consumption are not immune to media effects. Media consumption

Photo 11.1   Did you ever feel like a celebrity? Due to international media representations, children unaccustomed to seeing non-Japanese foreigners or *gaijin* may treat them like celebrities. In this photo, a U.S. American is asked for his autograph by a group of children happy to meet him on a bus.

Copyright 2010 Anastacia Kurylo.

refers to what and how much media you are exposed to. The problem is that a lot of the messages that people get from the media are taken in unconsciously. People may think that they can be exposed to the media without being influenced by it, but this seems to be an impossible thing to do.

The first step in recognizing the role that the media plays in your life is to take inventory of your own media consumption. Think about a "normal" day. Given the hectic nature of many students' lives while in school, it may be helpful to list a normal day when attending and not attending college. First, list the number of hours you spend each day watching television. Within this figure, be sure to include time typically spent watching DVDs and time spent watching television shows or movies online. Next, add the number of hours spent listening to music, reading books, newspapers, and magazines, surfing the Internet, and so forth. Second, conduct a mental inventory of how different cultural groups, such as Middle Easterners, senior citizens, people with disabilities, or persons who identify as lesbian, gay, bisexual, or transgendered (LGBT), are portrayed in various media forms. Do you notice any patterns? This simple, two-step process is a good point of reflection in terms of understanding how the media influences our perceptions of others.

This chapter focuses on the role that media plays in terms of inter/cultural communication. First, you are introduced to a general overview of media concepts and terms. Second, a brief explanation of different media theories is offered. In order to provide insight into one specific type of media from multiple theoretical perspectives, the third section applies these concepts and theories to different examples of reality television in the United States (Orbe, 1998, 2008; Orbe & Hopson, 2002). Last, the chapter concludes by explaining what media literacy is, and how it is an important set of skills to negotiate media influences.

REFLECT 11.1: Based on your own inventory, were you surprised at how much you are exposed to different media forms? How has your use of media changed over time? What, if any, impact do you think these images have on how you feel about yourself and others?

MEDIA

Most people immediately think of television when they hear the word *media*; however, there are many different forms of mediums. Traditionally, media was comprised of a few different types of industries: printed media, recordings, radio, movies, and television. However, recent technological advances—including the increased use of computers—have created easy access to various mass media mediums. In this regard, lines between interpersonal and mass communication have been blurred (Pearce, 2009a). The following section provides brief descriptions of traditional media genres including printed media, recordings, movies, radio, and television. As you read each of these sections, remember what many inter/cultural communication scholars (e.g., Squires, 2009) believe: Media images are an important source of information for people especially in terms of cultural groups with whom they may not have frequent, meaningful interactions. In other words, over time, each of these media sources individually and collectively works to shape your perceptions of others, and directly or indirectly, your communication interactions.

Printed Media

Printed media is the term used to refer to books, newspapers, and magazines. This type of mass media is the oldest. Scholars have traced the history of print media back to over 4,500 years ago when various religious, legal, and personal narratives were published on clay tablets. Although the earliest books were limited to the elite members of society, technological advances like the printing press allowed the medium to enter popular culture with increasing influence (McLuhan, 1962).

Photo 11.2   Well intentioned or offensive? Sometimes behaviors motivated by the best intentions can be construed as offensive. For example, in this picture the Spanish men's Olympic basketball team poses, pre-Beijing Olympics, for an advertisement in a Spanish magazine.

Newspapers, like books, were an early form of mass communication. Dating back to the first century, newspapers moved from elite usage to mass consumption over time. Although many people are moving away from traditional consumption to reading news online, newspapers continue to be a central source of information. Magazines also have an impressive history. Within the United States, the first magazine can be traced to the 1740s. As the industrial revolution developed, so did the number of magazines. By 1900, more than 5,000 different magazines were being published in the United States. Today, a variety of magazines are available including those specifically aimed at women and men, sports fans, professionals, families, youth, and different cultural groups.

Recordings

In 1877, Thomas Edison invented a "talking machine" that allowed him to hear his rendition of "Mary Had a Little Lamb" repeated back to him. His invention set in motion the development of a powerful medium of mass communication. Early recordings have little similarity, in terms of quality, to the digital processes used today. However, the principal concept remains largely the same: Use technology to produce audio images for mass consumption. Most people immediately think about various types of music that have been made popular through recordings. However, other mass mediated messages—like many of Martin Luther King Jr.'s civil rights speeches in the 1960s—were also distributed to mass audiences through this medium.

Movies

The history of motion (moving) pictures can also be traced back to the 19th century inventions of Thomas Edison. Even before the talking motion-picture era exploded in the 1930s and 1940s, one film powerfully illustrated the impact that this form of mass media could have on the larger society. In 1915, one of the first full-length films of its kind, *Birth of a Nation,* was released to critical acclaim. However, in terms of race relations, the film was criticized for its promotion of African American racial stereotypes. The movie industry has long represented a billion dollar capital venture; however, it has also remained a prominent source of mass mediated images that arguably reinforce existing cultural stereotypes of underrepresented groups (Jackson, 2006; Squires, 2009).

Radio

In 1901, Guglielmo Marconi sent wireless sound across the Atlantic Ocean. This initial breakthrough was followed by successful voice transmission several years later and the creation of the first toll station, which charged advertisers for airtime, going on the air in 1922. From the outset, radio met important cultural needs. It provided a medium for political leaders, like President Franklin D. Roosevelt, to communicate about important issues directly to the U.S. American public. Radio also served as a key source for entertainment including electronic vaudeville, situation comedies, and soap operas. Today, radio continues to function as an influential source of information and entertainment in many cultures. With advanced technology (e.g., computers, satellites), the influence of radio has remained significant.

Take a Side Trip:

 If you would like to read more about related issues, visit Appendix B: Local Culture Explored Through Discourse Analysis.

Television

The story of television dates back to the 1920s and 1930s. During the earlier years, many television shows were adopted from radio; these included different quiz shows, soap operas, and situation comedies. Unlike radio, however, television did not start with experimental, noncommercial stations. Television began with established networks supported by advertising sponsors. Like other media forms, television initially was primarily used by a small (wealthy) segment of society. The middle of the 20th century (late 1940s to early 1950s) witnessed an explosion of viewers. In fact, the number of television sets in U.S. American homes went from 172,000 to 17 million in one 4-year period (1948–1952). With the invention of various new media technologies, U.S. American viewers now can have access to hundreds of television channels (Squires, 2009).

LIVING CULTURE

Shushing, Shelving, and Stamping   *Marie L. Radford*

Rutgers, The State University of New Jersey

If anyone doubted that the traditional stereotype of the librarian is alive and well, convincing evidence to confirm this is easily found. One example is an editorial by Parks from the April 11, 2010 Newark *Sunday Star-Ledger* about the impact on libraries of New Jersey Governor Chris Christie's proposed 74% budget reduction to NJ library funding. Parks's editorial supports the librarian's struggle for funding restoration, but even though he is touting the value of libraries in promoting literacy and open, democratic access to information, he opens his article by evoking stereotypical images. He writes: "In both stereotype and practice, New Jersey's librarians are a fairly unexcitable bunch, more prone to shushing than they are to hyperbole. So take this into consideration as you read this from Edison Public Library director Judith Mansbach. 'If this goes through, it's going to be devastating'" (Parks, 2010). The three-column article decries the proposed cuts and mentions a May 6 librarian rally in Trenton, the state capitol. Parks returns to the library stereotype by ending on this note: "Needless to say they could use your help. So if you value your local library—or literacy in general—please make your view known to your legislators. It'll be one time your librarian won't shush you for raising your voice" (Parks, 2010).

This example is one of countless newspaper articles, blogs, cartoons, television shows, commercials, novels, advertisements, motion pictures, and so forth in a broad range of mediated discourse that continue to call to mind the librarian stereotype. Librarians, usually female, are consistently portrayed as bespectacled, mousy, unassuming, sexually repressed introverts who primarily engage in three behaviors—shushing, stamping, and shelving books. The male librarian stereotype, although less prominent, is also unflattering to the profession. Usually portrayed as prissy with the ubiquitous horn-rimmed glasses and bow tie, he is distinctly feminine and, also, therefore accorded the low status of the female librarian.

In another example, during the presidential election of 2008, Republican candidate Sarah Palin was referred to in the news media and on the Internet as the "sexy librarian" type. This characterization fully evokes the idea of the stereotype complete with glasses, bunlike hairdo, and buttoned-up suit with modest high-collared blouse, especially seen before her makeover in the early part of her campaign for the nomination. If one searches in the Google.com Images search engine for "sexy librarian," pictures of Palin are retrieved (see for example http://ktuu.images.worldnow.com/images/7240504_BG5.jpg). Regardless of a person's political affiliation,

LIVING CULTURE

it is of interest to observe how the media portrayed a sitting governor and contender for the U.S. presidency as a member of a feminized profession that is easily objectified, seen as powerless, and open to ridicule. Many librarians were not pleased by this comparison because they objected to Palin's censorship attempt to remove controversial books from the Wasilla public library (Kranich, 2008).

This stereotype has persisted since the early 1900s, despite the information age that has transformed the profession as now being immersed in sophisticated digitized systems and sources. Library collections and archives have rapidly evolved from mainly print ones to rich hybrids featuring full text e-collections of journal articles, e-books, and other web-based resources. Information services are now offered to online users 24/7 via live chat, e-mail, instant messaging, and texting.

I published an article in *Library Quarterly* (Radford & Radford, 1997) that used Foucauldian and feminist thought to analyze the enduring librarian stereotype in the film *Party Girl.* The analysis raised a number of fundamental issues such as the following:

> Who is speaking through the stereotype of the female librarian, and to what ends? What interests does the stereotype serve (certainly not those of women)? How can the image of subservience and powerlessness that it affords to women be challenged and changed? It is not enough to cry out that the stereotype is "wrong," "inaccurate," or "unfair." Such responses are expected, common and futile. It is time to dig deeper, to describe the conditions from which the stereotype is made possible, and to analyze the systems of power/knowledge that go to the very heart of what it means to be male and female, powerful and marginalized, valued and devalued. (p. 263)

Some may dismiss stereotypical texts and images as harmless, cute, or humorous and chide librarians to get a sense of humor. As one who has studied the librarian stereotype in depth, I have come to view these media representations as far from harmless, with serious, anti-intellectual, and antifeminist messages.

References

Kranich, N. (2008, September 18). What's *Daddy's Roommate* doing in Wasilla? *The Nation.* Retrieved from http://www.thenation.com/article/whats-daddys-roommate-doing-wasilla

(Continued)

LIVING CULTURE

(Continued)

Parks, B. (2010, April 11). Budget imperils New Jersey's libraries. *The Sunday Star-Ledger.* Retrieved from http://blog.nj.com/njv_guest_blog/2010/04/budget_imperils_new_jerseys_li.html

Radford, M. L., & Radford, G. P. (1997). Power, knowledge, and fear: Feminism, Foucault and the stereotype of the female librarian. *The Library Quarterly, 67,* 250–266.

Consider:

1. Where have you found stereotypes of librarians? Who communicated these to you (e.g., media, friends, family, instructors)?

2. Why does the author view the librarian stereotype as a problem? In what ways, if at all, is the librarian stereotype consequential?

3. Do stereotypes of librarians matter? To whom? Why?

4. How does this narrative relate to stereotypes of other cultural groups?

All types of media function as a cultural socialization agent. However, of all the different types of media, scholars have spent the most time researching the impact that television has had on personal, cultural, and societal perceptions. This is largely due to the rapid growth of the television industry and its pervasiveness in everyday life. As a socialization agent, the mass mediated images that appear on television, via the news, soap operas, situation comedies, dramas, talk shows, sporting events, and so forth, can have a tremendous influence on how people view themselves and others. Because of this, the governments in some countries ban certain types of programming or only allow television shows that support specific agendas. As such, programs that are produced and aired are oftentimes subject to political, religious, cultural, and social agendas in countries throughout the world. This idea is explored in detail in the concluding sections of this chapter.

All of the different media forms previously discussed—books, magazines, newspapers, recordings, movies, radio, and television—continue to influence your perceptions of self and others. On one hand, people are spending more and more time interacting with new media technologies. Some might argue that this reduces the influence of other mediums. However, on the other hand, it is important to recognize that new media technologies are also enhancing the impact that media has on

Take a Side Trip:

If you would like to read more about related issues, visit Appendix E: South African Culture Explored Through Content Analysis.

people as a whole. For instance, think about what you can do with computers, enhanced recording devices like TiVo, and handheld personal devices. Having these new media technologies allows you to listen to your favorite radio program that airs hundreds of miles away, watch a television show that you missed, read your childhood hometown newspaper, enjoy a video from an independent new band, or see a movie that did not appear in a local theater.

> **REFLECT 11.2:** What are your favorite books, magazines, mp3s, movies, radio stations, and television shows? Do these feature particular cultural groups that you identify with?

MEDIA THEORIES

As human use of media has grown, scholars have become increasingly interested in understanding its impact. The study of media effects has been traced back to the late 19th century (Werder, 2009). However, the exponential growth of the media in the last 75 years has triggered an explosion of research and theorizing aimed to explain how media affect a person's everyday life. This section provides a brief chronology of different media theories. The relevance of these theories to inter/cultural communication is addressed in the following section.

Direct Effects Theory

The earliest media theories were based on the concern that media could be an all-powerful source of influence. Scholars assuming this approach believed that audiences were passive consumers of the media that had direct impacts on viewers. Consequently, this line of theorizing has been described as direct effects theory and was prevalent in the early 20th century (Werder, 2009). These theorists argued that the media images entered naive viewers' consciousness and had immediate consequences. Because of this, direct effects theory was also known as a magic bullet or hypodermic needle approach. Most contemporary communication researchers view these theories as oversimplistic and not giving enough credit to the general public. Yet, some seem to continue to embrace this approach when they argue that certain shows cause viewers to engage in problematic behaviors, such as violence, that is presumed to stem from watching violent television or playing violent video games.

Limited Effects Model

Over time, scholars tested the assumptions of a direct effects approach and found little scientific evidence to support their claims. These results lead scholars to advocate for a limited effects model—a theoretical perspective that argued that media has little influence on people. This model was supported by research that showed that media consumers selectively exposed themselves to media messages that were consistent to their existing belief, attitudes, and values (e.g., Lazarsfeld, Berelson, & Gaudet, 1948). Following the results of this research, theorists concluded that media only had minimal effects on a person's everyday life.

Uses and Gratifications Theory

Uses and gratifications theory is another theory that seeks understanding into how the media influences everyday life. This theoretical approach acknowledges audiences as active users of media who are motivated to use different types of media programming to fulfill different needs (Katz, Blumler, & Gurevich, 1973). According to this theory, media influences vary depending on the functions that the various forms play in the lives of consumers. Research found that viewers were purposeful in their media consumption and actively selected media to satisfy specific needs and wants (Pearce, 2009b).

Cumulative Effects Models

As scholars continued to study media influences, more complex theoretical foundations began to emerge. These new media frameworks acknowledged a balance of potential media effects *and* active media consumption, and are known as cumulative effects models. One such theory focuses on the agenda setting function that the media plays. Early on, scholars within this approach asserted that the media cannot tell people how to think, but it does tell people what to think about. In other words, the media guides people in establishing what is viewed as important. The more you view an issue in the media, the more you feel it is important. More recent work within this area has led scholars to describe ways in which the media also provides direction as to how people should think about the issues that they deem as important (McCombs, 2004).

Cultivation Theory

For many, media represents a window into the world, especially worlds that are not part of their immediate settings. This perspective prompted scholars to explore the relationship between reality and reality as portrayed on television. According to cultivation theory, media consumption works to create distorted perceptions of the world (Gerbner, Gross, Morgan, Signorielli, & Shanahan, 2002). The main idea of the theory is that heavy users—people who have substantial, ongoing exposure to television—begin to view the real world as it exists on television. Cultivation theory research established specific psychological processes that occur with heavy television users. This is the strongest media effects model to date since the magic bullet theory (Werder, 2009).

Critical Cultural Studies of Media

Critical cultural studies continue to extend the work of media scholars interested in exploring the power of the media. This theoretical approach understands the media as a tool of society's most powerful group to remain in power (Hall, 1997) and emerged as a response to previous theories that did not address power inequality. Through this theory, scholars examine how the media relate to matters of ideology, race, gender, social class, and other forms of human diversity. One of the main ideas of this theoretical framework is that the media play a key role in maintaining existing power inequalities such as those discussed in Chapter 8. This is done through subtle influences that typically go unnoticed by viewers.

Each of these media theories provide insight into how mass-mediated images influence a person's perceptions of self, others, and society as a whole. Most contemporary scholars reject earlier theorizing attempts (i.e., direct effects and limit effects models) as too simplistic in their beliefs that the media is all-powerful or totally harmless. The other theories briefly described here remain relevant to discussions of media influences on inter/cultural communication in the 21st century. Taken together, they are useful for understanding how mass-mediated representations have a cumulative effect in cultivating a societal agenda where cultural difference remains a salient issue that influences inter/cultural communication.

REFLECT 11.3: Are you the type of person that watches lots of reality television or do you despise all reality television? Or, are you like many people who have at least one reality television program that is your "guilty pleasure"—something that you only reluctantly admit to watching? Why?

FOCUS ON REALITY TELEVISION

For many traditionally aged college students, the world has never been without an array of reality television programs. As explained in this section, reality-based programming has a history that spans 60-plus years. However, in recent years, reality television has become the most popular form of entertainment (Schroeder, 2006). Given its mass appeal in the United States and abroad (Hill, 2005), it has moved from the margins of television culture to its core in a dominating fashion. From a television executive perspective, reality television represents an attractive form of programming. It has low production costs. It can easily be marketed for foreign distribution. It also can be produced without dependence on unionized actors and writers (Murray & Ouellette, 2004). These factors, as well as huge popularity among diverse audiences, have propelled reality television from "another fad that overstayed its welcome" (Smith & Wood, 2003, p. 3) to a staple in contemporary television culture.

Although this section focuses on reality TV in the United States, this type of programming has proven to be popular (and profitable) in many countries across the world. In fact, these cheap-to-produce shows have used proven formulae to attract large audiences in many different countries. Kraidy and Sender's (2011) collection of essays offer insight into various global perspectives of reality television. In particular, they demonstrate the rapid globalization of reality television programming and how different shows and formats have been adapted to local, state, and national cultural norms. This includes analyses of *Afghan Star*—Afghanistan's version of *American Idol*—and how Muslim audiences reacted to female contestants' onstage dress and dancing given cultural norms (see also Kraidy, 2010).

Despite its inter/cultural importance, lucrative nature, and mass appeal, reality television critics abound. To many, it remains an extreme form of "trash television" (Geiser-Getz, 1995) that is cheap, sensationalized programming. Given these criticisms, media scholars have failed to study it with any substantial progress (Murray & Ouellette, 2004). Other scholars argue that reality television encompasses a huge variety of high- and low-quality programming—all of which, as forms of popular culture, deserve scholarly attention (Orbe, 2008). Reality television will continue to dominate the television landscape as long as viewers continue to watch in record-breaking numbers. Even if you personally do not watch reality television, it is becoming increasingly hard to avoid (Reiss & Wiltz, 2004, p. 25). Many people admit that they view at least one reality television show regularly that they describe as "a guilty pleasure." As you read through the broad definition provided in the next section, think about your own experiences with reality television. Also, think about how your perceptions of these programs are influenced by the cultural groups to which you belong (Warren, Orbe, & Greer-Williams, 2003).

Defining Reality Television

What do you think of when you hear the phrase, *reality television?* If you are like many people, you immediately think of some of the most popular shows in recent times: *American Idol, Survivor,* or *Dancing With the Stars.* Others might be more aware of different cable shows such as *The Real World, Run's House,* or *America's Next Top Model.* However, what most people do not realize is that reality television includes an amazingly diverse array of shows.

According to Smith and Wood (2003), "As a genre, reality television involves placing 'ordinary' people before the camera and deriving some entertainment value from the perception of their activities being unscripted" (p. 2). Several critics have described the *unrealistic* nature of reality television, including how many shows appear increasingly scripted and manipulated through producers' editing (e.g., Orbe, 1998). However, the definition offered by Smith and Wood focuses on the fact that reality television is sold, and largely perceived, as unscripted. As such, the "reality" in reality television can be best understood as a social construction—one that uses the seemingly unscripted life experiences of everyday people to create a form of entertainment that the viewing public consumes.

Brief History of Reality Television

Based on the definition offered in the last paragraph, reality television covers a wide range of programming formats. One of the earliest reality television shows was *Candid Camera* (1948), known as "the granddaddy of the reality TV" (Rowan, 2000). This classic show has spawned a number of others that set up various pranks on unsuspecting targets (e.g., *Punk'd, Scare Tactics, Girls Behaving Badly*). Other types of reality television (discussed subsequently) appear to be straightforward—until a big hoax is revealed (e.g., *My Big Fat Obnoxious Fiance, Hell Date, Boy Meets Boy*). These types of shows have gained popularity as viewers get bored with regular reality television shows (Orbe, 2008).

Another early form of reality television involved competition-based game shows whereby contestants were faced with trivia questions. Over time, game shows became a staple of daytime television (e.g., *The Price is Right, Family Feud*) and also gained immense popularity in primetime slots as well (e.g., *Who Wants to be a Millionaire?, Deal or No Deal, Are You Smarter Than a 5th Grader?*). More recently, other competition shows pit people against one another as they seek a big monetary prize (e.g., *Big Brother, Survivor*), professional contracts (e.g., *Last Comic Standing, The Apprentice, America's Best Dance Crew*), or the chance to find love (e.g., *The Bachelor/Bachelorette, Joe Millionaire, Next*).

An early popular form of reality television programming in the United States began in the early 1980s with the introduction of *COPS* (Geiser-Getz, 1995). This show allowed viewers to follow police officers in major U.S. cities as they went about their day-to-day interactions with the general public. In addition to other similar shows (e.g., *Dog The Bounty Hunter*), *COPS* spawned a number of reality television programs focusing on solving crimes (*America's Most Wanted*) or existing unknowns (e.g., *Unsolved Mysteries*). With the public's interest in the criminal aspects of everyday life established, an extension of this type of reality television appeared: court shows. Initially these focused on various small court proceedings (e.g., *The People's Court*); however, more recently these have focused on particular types of court cases (e.g., *Divorce Court*) or the entertaining personalities of particular judges (e.g., *Judge Judy, Judge Mathis*).

For many people, MTV's *The Real World* remains the most commonly recognized form of reality television: the documentary soap opera (Andrejevic & Colby, 2006). This popular show launched a number of similar shows including MTV's *Laguna Beach: The Real Orange County* and BET's *College Hill,* as well as TLC's *Little People, Big World.* Other documentary-based shows revolve around following people as they engage in various personal or professional activities (e.g., *Sheer Genius, Doctor 90210*). More recently, other shows follow celebrities within their own daily lives (e.g., *The Anna Nicole Show, The Osbournes, Run's House, My Life on the D-List*) or as they compete for various prizes (*Celebrity Apprentice, Celebrity Fit Club*). The popularity of celebrity-based reality television has led VH1 to create an entire block of shows, known as "celebreality" (Orbe, 2008).

The final type of reality television programming features transformative improvements. This type of programming typically involves individuals, or a team of individuals, working with people to achieve dramatic makeovers in terms of personal appearance or style (e.g., *Queer Eye for the Straight Guy*), weight (*The Biggest Loser*), personal identity (e.g., *Made*), or family empowerment (e.g., *Supernanny*). Alternatively, the focus of different makeovers is living spaces (e.g., *Trading Spaces, Extreme Makeover: Home Edition, Curb Appeal*) or personal automobiles (e.g., *Pimp My Ride*).

Media Analysis of Reality Television

Each of the different media theories described earlier in the chapter can provide a lens to studying reality television. As expected, different theoretical lenses can result in different understandings of the role that reality-based programming has on

Photo 11.3 What counts as family to you? Historically, U.S. American media has often represented family as a nuclear family with heterosexual parents and two children—a boy and a girl. Today, reality television has helped to expand people's idea of what family means. These photos provide some examples of family.

inter/cultural communication. The final section of this chapter draws from different media theories to explore how reality television impacts how people perceive themselves and others through a cultural prism.

Currently, there is certainly no agreement as to the impact that reality television has on societal perceptions of different cultural groups. Some communication scholars might argue that the influence is minimal (limited effects model). These scholars would point to how viewers selectively expose themselves to certain shows that feature images of cultural groups that are consistent with their existing perceptions. For instance, they would note that many of the reality television shows (e.g., *Real Housewives of Atlanta, Let's Talk About Pep, Snoop Dogg's Fatherhood, College Hill*) with predominately African American casts are watched most faithfully by African American audiences whose existing perceptions of African American life are largely established. According to this approach, the images contained in the show—both positive and negative—have little effect on their audiences.

A related theoretical approach to studying reality television might argue that it fulfills different needs for different viewers (uses and gratifications theory). For example, most viewers watch reality television shows for entertainment purposes. Specific shows that provide an educational function (e.g., *TLC's Little People, Big World,* or *Intervention*) may be more influential in affecting perceptions of others (e.g., little people or drug addicts). However, communication scholars from this approach would argue that these shows do more to reinforce existing perceptions than create new ones. In this context, it is important to remember that viewers do not watch television as "blank slates"; instead they come with significant preexisting ideas about culture that are not easily changed.

Other media scholars might disagree. They would argue that reality television shows have a direct impact on how viewers develop their perceptions of self and others (direct effects theory). These scholars would join societal leaders who have criticized many reality television shows for their negatively stereotypical depictions of different cultural groups. Take the case of the MTV hit show, *Jersey Shore*. The show featured several young Italian Americans from the U.S. Northeast whose lives revolve around "GTL" (Gym, Tan, and Laundry), drinking, partying, and hooking up. In fact, the stars of the show proudly described themselves as *guidos* and *guidettes*—terms that they embrace but historically have been regarded as highly offensive slurs. Several national Italian American organizations were so concerned about the negative stereotypical images featured on the show that they called for a boycott from advertisers—several of which withdrew their support from the show. In the end, the controversy generated significant buzz for the show, and propelled it into one of the most watched shows on cable. According to this theoretical perspective, the result of the show, especially for viewers with little interaction with Italian Americans, was an advancement of negative images for this ethnic group.

Agenda-setting theorists would focus on how reality television images contribute to what viewers deem as most important or relevant in society. For instance, think about the central themes of most reality television programming. Producers could showcase stories that highlight inter/cultural understanding, intergroup harmony, and cultural similarity that could work to provide models for viewers who are motivated to engage in healthy, authentic intercultural relationships. However, most often reality television shows contain images that reflect intercultural misunderstanding (e.g., *Wife Swap, Charm School*), intergroup conflict (e.g., *Survivor, Real World/Road Rules: The Duel*), and cultural differences (e.g., *Trading Spouses, Big Brother*). The rationale for this is that drama, conflict, and competition make for "good" television. Viewers, it is presumed, are not interested in watching people who get along and work together with little to no conflict. Although some might argue that this is true, it does not negate the fact that these are the images that people see the most and come to regard as the most prevalent in society. Agenda-setting theorists would argue that by watching reality television, viewers come to believe that different racial groups can never get along, different religious groups will always have conflict, and women and men come from different planets.

The idea that media images generally, and those that appear on reality television shows specifically, help to create distorted perceptions of the world is consistent with cultivation theory. As such, some cultivation theorists would focus their attention on heavy users of reality television and explore how substantial exposure to this type of programming affects their sense of reality. Scholars might conclude that heavy users believe that the world is filled with more cultural conflict than actually exists. This perception is likely to be paired with rigid stereotypes of different cultural groups that have appeared across various reality television shows. For instance, the recent influx of programs featuring transgendered persons (e.g., *RuPaul's Drag Race, Transform Me, America's Next Top Model, The Real World*) might lead heavy users to blur the lines of sexuality in ways that distort the reality of persons who identify as gay, lesbian, bisexual, and/or transgendered.

Of all the media approaches previously discussed, critical cultural studies scholars would be most condemning of reality television shows. These scholars would argue that reality-based television is one of the newest forms of mass mediated exploitation—one in which everyday people are lured into a process by which their life experiences are manipulated to create stories designed to reap the biggest profits for media owners. According to this media lens, reality television shows are inexpensive to produce, yet generate large amounts of income through constant programming rotations and product placement or promotion. Think about it for a moment: Did you ever wonder why the *American Idol* judges all have Coca-Cola cups in front of them? Or how many Cover Girl products are included on *America's Next Top Model?* Or how many MTV shows feature specific musicians, different food and beverage products, and electronic devices (e.g., reality television cast members who are often heard declaring: "We just got a message on our Teen Mobile cell phones!")?

Critical cultural studies scholars would reveal how reality television shows promote certain products in a capitalist world. Viewers interested in the content of the shows are constantly exposed to commercial products. However, this media lens would also reveal the ways in which reality television sells certain ideologies like those related to beauty standards, personal safety, and the American dream. In this regard, reality-based programming works alongside other mass media images to subtly convince viewers to participate in a world where they are primarily consumers. Consider, for instance, how the promotion of culturally specific beauty standards promotes billions of dollars in spending. The same could be said for products related to public safety (desperately needed in the violent world that exists on television) and purchases made to secure the American dream (in spite of person's actual need for the item or their ability to afford them). In the end, existing societal inequalities within a culture continue to persist.

REFLECT 11.4: Think about how culture is represented on one particular reality television show that you have seen. Based on your perceptions of the show, which one of the media theories serves as the most valuable lens to understand how the show might impact its viewers?

NEGOTIATING MEDIA EFFECTS

As illustrated throughout this chapter, media functions as a powerful influence in people's lives. In particular, it represents a substantial social system that contributes to a person's sense of reality. Much has been written about negative media effects, including the ways in which media images promote negative cultural stereotypes (Squires, 2009; Warren et al., 2003). However, it is also important to recognize that reality TV can have both positive and negative effects when it comes to intercultural communication, including providing positive images of different cultural groups (Terreri, 2004), educating people about life issues (Palmer, 2004) and promoting stories of intercultural cooperation (Kiesewetter, 2004). For instance, Pullen (2007) suggests that reality programming on MTV (e.g., *The Real World, Road Rules, Singled Out, Undressed, Next,* etc.) has had a positive effect on how persons who are lesbian, gay, bisexual, transgendered, or queer are perceived by viewers. In particular, he argues that the consistent inclusion of LGBTQ persons on these shows works to normalize nonheterosexual experiences that ultimately leads to greater societal acceptability. Similar arguments can be made regarding other shows that provide substantial exposure to underrepresented groups like that which has been seen in TLC's *Little People, Big World,* A&E's *Intervention,* or the National Geographic Channel's *Taboo.*

Yet, most media critics, those who study and analyze media and its effects, have focused on how this unique form of media programming has fallen short of it potential. For the most part, it appears that most reality-based shows have continued the cultural stereotyping that exists across media forms (Darling, 2004; Orbe & Harris, 2008). The fact that shows are sold as reality leads some scholars (e.g., Orbe, 1998) to argue that the images are even more damaging than other types of programming that viewers regard as more fabricated. For example, this appears to be the case for heavy users of reality television who seemingly perceive African American women in largely stereotypical ways. This dynamic is evidenced in Boylorn's (2008) autoethnographic writing where, despite her academic credentials and professionalism, she describes how White students expected her to take on the characteristics of popular reality TV stars like "New York" (aka Tiffany Pollard) from VH1's *Flavor of Love.* What remains unclear is if her students were relying on mass-mediated fueled stereotypes or if her metastereotypes were actually more influential than she believes (Sigelman & Tuch, 1997; Torres & Charles, 2004). Metastereotypes are your perceptions of the stereotypes you think outgroup members have about your ingroups. In either case, however, reality TV images are seen as influential to everyday experiences of inter/cultural communication.

In the end, it is also important to recognize that the various forms of media can have both positive and negative effects in regards to intercultural communication. The key question is how can people maximize positive media effects while minimizing negative ones? One answer to this question is through the development of media literacy skills.

MEDIA LITERACY

One means to negotiate the power that the media has over you is to develop critical literacy skills (Fecho, 1998). In recent years, communication scholars have advocated that media consumers must develop media literacy. Media literacy, by definition, involves developing a critical understanding of how mass media operates, including learning to read messages behind the media's images.

According to Gerbner (2000), media literacy involves three specific skills. First, media consumers must be able to identify the techniques used to create the images that are perceived to be real. This involves understanding how reality television show producers use visual images, music, lighting, camera angles, and the editing process to influence media images. Second, media consumers must come to understand that the media are businesses geared toward earning profits. When interacting with reality television, ask yourself: Why are certain images of particular cultural groups featured more than others? How do they work to promote images that are profitable in today's society? Third, media consumers must learn to recognize how specific mass media images project particular ideologies (e.g., cultural superiority) and values (e.g., ethnocentrism). In terms of reality television, becoming media literate means that you critically acknowledge the values inherent in the images that are shown and recognize how specific techniques influence viewers in subtle and not-so-subtle ways (Gerbner, 2000).

Photo 11.4 What do you see when you critically examine this cartoon? The media uses stereotypes to provide a simplified view of cultural groups. This view is often inaccurate and self-perpetuating. Here men are stereotyped as tough but unreasonable; women are stereotyped as nurturing but nagging.

Throughout this section, the focus has been on how reality television works to shape your perception of self and others. Media literacy, however, applies to all forms of the media, not just the mass-mediated images that people see on television. Becoming media literate means that you develop a critical eye for how various media forms—recordings, radio, movies, newspapers, magazines, and new media technologies—function as a cultural socialization agent in terms of how people view the world around them. The increased awareness that comes with media literacy will never eliminate media effects, but it can help to diminish the negative impact that the media has on your everyday life. In terms of inter/cultural communication, becoming media literate enhances the potential for media consumption to lead to greater understanding of how other cultural group members are both different from and similar to ourselves. "Reality TV has evolved into a genre that many media experts believe presents even meaner, more competitive, and more hurtful versions of 'reality' to an ever-expanding audience" (Balkin, 2004, p. 10). Viewers who practice media literacy must understand how the images are produced to maximize profits and how "the meanings and values of reality TV [vary] across national, regional, gendered, classed, and religious contexts" (Sender, 2011, p. 1).

FINAL THOUGHTS

This chapter described the significant role that media plays in terms of how people are socialized to think about themselves, others, and the process of inter/cultural communication. It included a general overview of basic media concepts, terms, and theories. The focus of the chapter was the fairly recent explosion of reality television and how this particular type of programming potentially affects everyday interactions where culture exists as an important issue. Hopefully, this chapter raised your awareness of how the media impacts your own perceptions and motivates you to become more media literate as an informed consumer of the media. Although this chapter focused on reality TV in the United States, understanding the similarities and differences of reality television shows across cultures, and the ways in which cultural values, norms, and beliefs necessitate local adaptation will represent another important step in advanced understanding of inter/cultural communication across national boundaries as this media genre expands further.

CONTINUE YOUR JOURNEY ONLINE

Visit: http://gawker.com

Gawker. As the name of the site suggests, people come to Gawker to just watch. You are encouraged to do the same. Whether celebrity gossip or recent news stories are of interest to you, explore the site. Pick a single culture and look for example of how that culture is represented on the site. Draw some conclusions. Do the same for other cultural groups. Compare. Consider what messages the media sends about these various groups and their interactions amongst each other.

66 SAY WHAT?

Say What? provides excerpts from overheard real-life conversations in which people have communicated stereotypes. As you read these conversations, reflect on the following questions.

- Have you been in conversations like this before?
- Is there any one of these conversations that stick out to you more than the others?
- What do you think of this conversation?
- How did the stereotype help or hinder the conversation?
- Was there another way the stereotyper could have communicated to convey the same point?
- How do you feel when you hear this conversation or the specific stereotype?
- Do any of these conversations bother you more than others? Why or why not?
- Do any concepts, issues, or theories discussed in the chapter help explain why?

- **Say What?** My roommate and I were watching television when the show *COPS* came on. In this show, arrests of all different types of criminals are depicted. The first arrest that was shown was of a young African American male who was charged with the possession of drugs. Right after this arrest was shown, my roommate stated, "It figures." I asked her what she was referring to.

- **Say What?** "He could move around the stage like he was an actual fairy playing in the woods," remarked Jen. In an attempt to be funny, Patrick blurted out something along the lines of "I don't think he was acting; he was just flaming!" Jennifer and I gave a small chuckle after hearing this remark; however, Chris did not find it so funny. With a look that could kill, he quickly gazed over at Patrick and asked him what he meant by that statement. "Were you implying that all theater actors are homosexuals, or that all gay men are girly?" Chris asked in a stern voice.

- **Say What?** I call my roommate to buy me a copy of the paper. She walks in about 40 minutes later with her father, and she hands me the paper. Her father jokes that I owe him five dollars. I start complaining. I can't believe this class is going to cost me money. Her father laughs and says he's kidding, and my roommate snickers and says, "She's just being a Jew, so cheap!" The response after Rachel said the stereotype was her and her father laughing, and me smiling because I've heard this a million times before. I'm used to being made fun of for being a "cheap Jew."

- **Say What?** "Is it true that sorority girls are snobby and stupid and all they do is party? Because that's what I've heard and all the movies I've seen are like that." I laughed a little and explained to her that my sorority has the highest cumulative grade point average out of all the sororities on campus, most of the girls are making the dean's list, and one of the focal points of my sorority in general is the maintenance of quality grades of our members.

REVIEW QUESTIONS

1. How do media socially construct reality? Use at least one theory discussed in the chapter to explain your answer.

2. Compare and contrast the ways in which at least two of the five types of media described in the chapter are cultural socialization agents. Take into consideration the social contexts in which each might be used.

3. What is the hypodermic needle approach, as defined by the chapter? Do you agree with it?

4. Why are the media theories discussed in the chapter relevant for inter/cultural communication?

5. Which media theories discussed in the chapter view media as all-powerful influences on passive audiences?

6. Apply at least two media theories to a single example of a reality television program referenced in the chapter.

7. According to the chapter, what was an early form of reality television? Consider one of the more recent examples mentioned and discuss how reality television has changed. How do these changes reflect the culture? What impact might these changes have on the audience?

8. The chapter says, "Critical cultural studies scholars would be most condemning of reality television shows." Why?

9. How could a person become more media literate? Why is it important for inter/cultural communication?

10. Based on the chapter discussion, describe how specific types of shows contribute or take away from more productive inter/cultural understanding?

KEY TERMS

agenda setting function   244

critical cultural studies   244

cultivation theory   244

cultural socialization
   agent   242

cumulative effects
   model   244

direct effects theory   243

heavy user   244

hypodermic needle
   approach   243

limited effects model   243

magic bullet   243

media   235

media consumption   235

media critic   250

media effects   235

media literacy   250

media representation   235

metastereotype   250

printed media   237

reality television   246

uses and gratifications
   theory   244

REFERENCES

Allen, B. J. (2005). Social constructionism. In S. May & D. K. Mumby (Eds.), *Engaging organizational communication theory and research: Multiple perspectives* (pp. 35–53). Thousand Oaks, CA: Sage.

Andrejevic, M., & Colby, D. (2006). Racism and reality TV: The case of MTV's *Road Rules*. In D. S. Escoffery (Ed.), *How real is reality TV? Essays on representation and truth* (pp. 195–211). Jefferson, NC: McFarland & Company.

Balkin, K. (2004). Introduction. In K. Balkin's (Ed.), *Reality TV* (pp. 9–11). New York: Thomson/Gale.

Boylorn, R. (2008). As seen on TV: An autoethnographic reflection on race and reality television. *Critical Studies in Media Communication, 25,* 413–433.

Darling, C. (2004). Reality TV encourages racial stereotyping. In K. Balkin's (Ed.), *Reality TV* (pp. 40–43). New York: Thomson/Gale.

Fecho, B. (1998). Crossing boundaries of race in a critical literacy classroom. In D. E. Alvermann, K. A. Hinchman, D. W. Moore, S. F. Phelps, & D. R. Waff (Eds.), *Reconceptualizing the literacies in adolescent's lives* (pp. 75–102). Mahwah, NJ: Lawrence Erlbaum.

Geiser-Getz, G. C. (1995). COPS and the comic frame: Humor and meaning-making in reality-based television. *Electronic Journal of Communication/ La Revue Electronique de Communication,* 5(1).

Gerbner, G. (2000). *Becoming media literate.* Retrieved from http://www.context.org/ICLIB/IC38/Gerbner .htm.

Gerbner, G., Gross, L., Morgan, M., Signorielli, N., & Shanahan, J. (2002). Growing up with television: Cultivation process. In J. Bryant & D. Zillman (Eds.), *Media effects: Advances in theory and research* (pp. 43–67). Mahwah, NJ: Lawrence Erlbaum.

Gergen, K. J. (1999). *An invitation to social construction.* London: Sage.

Hall, S. (1997). *Representation: Cultural representations and signifying practices.* London: Sage.

Hill, A. (2005). *Reality TV: Audiences and popular factual television.* London: Routledge.

Jackson, R. L. (2006). *Scripting the Black masculine body: Identity, discourse, and racial politics in popular media.* Albany: State University of New York Press.

Katz, E., Blumler, J. G., & Gurevitch, M. (1973). Uses and gratifications research. *Public Opinion Quarterly, 37,* 509–523.

Kiesewetter, J. (2004). Some reality TV shows encourage cooperation. In K. Balkin's (Ed.), *Reality TV* (pp. 37–39). New York: Thomson/Gale.

Kraidy, M. M. (2010). *Reality television and Arab politics.* Cambridge, UK: Cambridge University Press.

Kraidy, M. M., & Sender, K. (2011). *The politics of reality television: Global perspectives.* New York: Routledge.

Lazarsfeld, P. F., Berelson, B., & Gaudet, H. (1948). *The people's choice: How the voter makes up his mind in a presidential campaign.* New York: Columbia University Press.

McCombs, M. (2004). *Setting the agenda.* Cambridge, UK: Polity Press.

McLuhan, M. (1962). *The Gutenberg galaxy.* Toronto: University of Toronto Press.

Murray, S., & Oulette, L. (Eds.). (2004). *Reality TV: Remaking television culture.* New York: New York University Press.

Orbe, M. P. (1998). Constructions of reality of MTV's *The Real World*: An analysis of the restrictive coding of Black masculinity. *Southern Communication Journal, 64,* 32–47.

Orbe, M. P. (2008). Representations of race in reality TV: Watch and discuss. *Critical Studies in Media Communication, 25,* 345–352.

Orbe, M. P., & Harris, T. M. (2008). *Interracial communication: Theory into practice.* Thousand Oaks, CA: Sage.

Orbe, M. P., & Hopson, M. C. (2002). Looking at the front door: Exploring images of the Black male on MTV's *The Real World.* In J. N. Martin, T. K. Nakayama & L. A. Flores (Eds.), *Readings in intercultural communication: Experiences & contexts* (pp. 219–226). Boston: McGraw-Hill.

Palmer, K. S. (2004). Reality TV helps young people learn about life. In K. Balkin's (Ed.), *Reality TV* (pp. 52–53). New York: Thomson/Gale.

Pearce, K. J. (2009a). Media and mass communication theories. In S. W. Littlejohn & K. A. Foss (Eds.),

Encyclopedia of communication theory (pp. 623–627). Thousand Oaks, CA: Sage.

Pearce, K. J. (2009b). Uses, gratifications, and dependency. In S. W. Littlejohn & K. A. Foss (Eds.), *Encyclopedia of communication theory* (pp. 978–980). Thousand Oaks, CA: Sage.

Pearce, W. B. (1995). A sailing guide for social constructivists. In W. Leeds-Hurwitz (Ed.), *Social approaches to communication* (pp. 88–113). New York: Guilford Press.

Pullen, C. (2007). *Documenting gay men: Identity and performance in reality television and documentary film.* Jefferson, NC: McFarland & Company.

Reiss, S., & Wiltz, J. (2004). Fascination with fame attracts reality TV viewers. In K. Balkin's (Ed.), *Reality TV* (pp. 25–27). New York: Thomson/Gale.

Rowan, B. (2000). Reality TV takes hold. Retrieved from http://www.infoplease.com/spot/realitytv1.html

Schroeder, E. R. (2006). "Sexual racism" and reality television: Privileging the White male prerogative on MTV's *The Real World.* In D. S. Escoffery (Ed.), *How real is reality TV: Essays on representation and truth* (pp. 180–195). Jefferson, NC: McFarland & Company.

Sender, K. (2011). Real worlds: Migrating genres, traveling participants, shifting theories. In M. M. Kraidy & K. Sender (Eds.), *The politics of reality television: Global perspectives* (pp. 1–11). New York: Routledge.

Sigelman, L., & Tuch, S. A. (1997). Metastereotypes: Blacks' perceptions of White's stereotypes of Blacks. *Public Opinion Quarterly, 61,* 87–101.

Smith, M. J., & Wood, A. F. (Eds.). (2003). *Survivor lessons: Essays on communication and reality television.* Jefferson, NC: McFarland & Company.

Squires, C. (2009). *African Americans and the media.* Malden, MA: Polity Press.

Terreri, J. (2004). Reality TV can offer a positive religious message. In K. Balkin's (Ed.), *Reality TV* (pp. 34–36). New York: Thomson/Gale.

Torres, K. C., & Charles, C. Z. (2004). Metastereotypes and the Black White divide: A qualitative view on an elite college campus. *DuBois Review, 1,* 115–149.

Warren, K. T., Orbe, M. P., & Greer-Williams, N. (2003). Perceiving conflict: Similarities and differences among Latino/as, African Americans, and European Americans. In D. I. Rios & A. N. Mohamed (Eds.), *Brown and Black communication: Latino and African American conflict and convergence in mass media* (pp. 13–26). Westport, CT: Praeger.

Werder, O. H. (2009). Media effects theories. In S. W. Littlejohn & K. A. Foss (Eds.), *Encyclopedia of communication theory* (pp. 632–635). Thousand Oaks, CA: Sage.

Technology and Culture

Tatyana Dumova
Point Park University

Journey Through Chapter 12

Sightseeing: On your journey, you will use the social constructionist and social scientific perspectives to visit Web 2.0 and explore how it is used to represent and construct culture by generating shared intercultural spaces, fostering global intercultural conversations, reducing barriers to intercultural communication, promoting educational opportunities, and stimulating cultural exchange. Relevant societal, legal, and ethical issues will also be addressed.

Souvenir: After your journey, you will have a thorough understanding of a range of issues relevant to technology and culture in a modern world.

As people move through the 21st century, what is the impact of technology on culture? Particularly, what is the impact of technology on communication within and between cultures? Technology is the practical application of human knowledge and the tools and techniques a society produces to meet people's needs. The technological imperative introduced in Chapter 1 suggests that technology is central to the understanding of the dynamic nature of inter/cultural communication. In today's society, technology is becoming omnipresent and is markedly transforming the way people interact. One difficulty in examining technology is that technological applications are numerous and take many forms. Another difficulty is that technology is constantly changing. As a result, it is impossible to discuss all the relevant issues. The current chapter focuses on communication technologies that have proliferated most recently and with which you may be most familiar and applies a functional approach emphasizing what technology does. The chapter concentrates on the role of communication technology in generating shared intercultural spaces, fostering global intercultural conversations, and reducing barriers to intercultural communication. Additionally, the chapter discusses issues related to promoting educational opportunities and stimulating cultural exchange and also examines culturally relevant societal, legal, and ethical issues associated with the latest advances in digital communication technologies.

GENERATING SHARED INTERCULTURAL SPACES THROUGH SOCIAL MEDIA

In the age of mobile Web, technology is increasingly viewed as a platform to connect, share, and build relationships among people of different cultures. The proliferation of social interaction technologies makes this shift possible. Social interaction technologies are Internet-based tools and techniques designed to initiate, maintain, share, and distribute interactive and collaborative activities and spaces online (Dumova & Fiordo, 2010). These tools involve a broad spectrum of second-generation web applications and services commonly known as Web 2.0, such as online social networks, blogs, wikis, podcasts, web feeds, social bookmarks, folksonomies, mashups, and virtual worlds. Analysts have observed the dynamic and interactive nature of Web 2.0 tools and applications and their profound impact on culture. One way technology affects culture is through facilitating shared intercultural spaces. Such technologically mediated environments support intercultural sharing and collaboration and enhance traditional forms of cultural participation. They include video and photo sharing networks, wiki-based collaborative websites, and real-time short-messaging services. Social media—including social networking sites, blogs, Twitter, and YouTube—are particularly productive at generating shared intercultural spaces.

Social media refer to a range of online applications, including social networks, blogs, and wikis through which people can create and distribute content and engage in social interactions. In recent years, social media have become a truly global phenomenon demonstrating explosive growth throughout the world, regardless of the economic, social, and cultural differences between regions. A few statistics illustrate this point. A study published by the Nielsen Company (2010) found an 82% increase in the time global consumers spend on online social networks. In December 2009, users spent on average more than 5.5 hours per month on popular networking sites such as Facebook and Twitter, as compared to 3 hours in December 2008 (Nielsen Company, 2010). The study involved users in the United States, the United Kingdom, Australia, Switzerland, Germany, France, Spain, Italy, Brazil, and Japan. United States–based Facebook was found the number-one global social networking destination with 206.9 million monthly visitors to the site (Nielsen Company, 2010). Another survey of Internet users in more than 50 countries conducted by a global media planning and marketing company, Universal McCann (2010), revealed that 1.5 billion active Internet users around the world visited social networks on a daily basis.

One notable dimension of social media is the growth of user-generated content involving widespread user participation in the production and distribution of online content. For example, this includes reader-contributed news, user-created video, blog posts, comments, user tags, product ratings, and the like. With the emergence of applications such as Blogger, Facebook, Wikipedia, YouTube, and Flickr, traditional distinctions between the production and consumption of content in Internet's cultural spaces have begun to blur (Lull, 2007). Bruns (2009) calls the phenomenon "produsage" referring to the combined roles of the participants as producers and users at the same time. Jenkins (2009) draws an even bigger picture by denoting this new mode of production of shared intercultural spaces as the birth of a new culture. However, Shirky (2010) points out the current lack of cultural institutions, norms, and self-regulation necessary for the use of new technologies. Although it is debatable

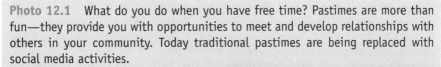

Photo 12.1   What do you do when you have free time? Pastimes are more than fun—they provide you with opportunities to meet and develop relationships with others in your community. Today traditional pastimes are being replaced with social media activities.

Copyright 2010 Bill Edwards and Michael Kurylo.

whether social media constitute a new culture, it is clear that emerging media, especially social networking sites, blogs, Twitter, and YouTube, create and facilitate shared intercultural spaces.

Social Networking Sites

In the last few years, social networking has moved to the forefront of Web 2.0 technologies and has become the primary platform for content creation and sharing. A social networking site allows members to post and update their personal online profiles, add friends to their network, exchange messages, and share photos and videos. In 2003, Mark Zuckerberg created a prototype of Facebook, a site originally intended for Harvard students only, in his college dormitory. By December 2011, this biggest and perhaps most well-known social networking service has reached 845 million users (Facebook, 2012). No doubt you have your own Facebook page. Facebook and MySpace took over the European social networking scene, as well as that of the United States, Canada, Australia, and the Arab world. As of January 2012, Facebook remains the top search term on the Internet (Universal McCann, 2012). In China, domestic social networking sites such as 51 and Xiaonei are most visited. VKontakte is the largest social network in Russia, while Orkut is most popular in India and Brazil. CyWorld dominates in South Korea, Mixi in Japan, and Friendster in the Philippines.

Besides a network of friends, users can also join a network started by a school, college, nonprofit organization, or business. In this way, Facebook provides people the opportunity to create virtual cultural communities where community members can check in to see how one another are doing, find out the latest news, and listen to each other vent about their problems or celebrate their successes. Oftentimes, because of the young age of early technology adaptors, Facebook involves generational cultural communities wherein parents or teachers posting a message might seem out of place.

REFLECT 12.1: What role do social networking sites such as Facebook and MySpace play in your everyday life? Do these aid with inter/cultural communication? How?

A common goal may serve as a focal point for creating an online purpose group. After you propose an idea or cause, your friends and other users can join you and form a dedicated social network, which can grow exponentially. Take the example of a viral communication campaign that took place on Facebook in January 2010 after a devastating earthquake happened in Haiti. In addition to a centralized Facebook global relief effort page with more than half a million visitors, thousands of smaller dedicated networks emerged. A grassroots relief group in Miami Beach, Florida, began from a single call for donations to 10 Facebook friends. Soon, the group enlisted over 1,200 people and brought $20 million worth of relief supplies to Haiti, according to the *Miami Herald* (Stone, 2010). In this and innumerable other ways, social networking sites generate shared intercultural spaces.

Blogs

Since the late 1990s, online users have utilized blogs or online journals as one of the most ubiquitous social media tools to connect with millions of other people worldwide. Rosana Hermann, a Brazilian blogger, who received wide international recognition for having the best blog written in Portuguese, has been blogging since 1999. In her own words, blogs have brought her "friends, travel, opportunities, work and awards" (as cited in Sinico, 2009a). She advises that a person must write with passion to succeed. Blog publishing and reading has become popular on a global scale, particularly in China, India, South Korea, Russia, and Brazil. In Germany, on the opposite side, blogging seems to have reached its peak, with only half of Internet users reading blogs, and even less writing them (Universal McCann, 2009). In the United States, blogging has begun to give way to the now more popular activity of social networking. Researchers from the Pew Internet and American Life Project indicate that since 2006, blogging has dropped 14% among teenagers and young adults but remained steady among the older adults. On average, 1 in 10 adults in the United States maintains a blog, and this trend has been fairly consistent since 2005 (Lenhart, Purcell, Smith, & Zickuhr, 2010).

REFLECT 12.2: Do you read blogs? Are they written by those within or outside your culture? How does reading these blogs aid in your inter/cultural understanding?

Like social networking sites, blogs generate shared intercultural spaces that can be used for social activism. A German blogger Markus Beckedahl, initiated an online petition to the Bundestag, the national parliament of Germany, to protest plans to impose Internet censorship. It was signed by 134,000 people and was taken into consideration by the lawmakers (Sinico, 2009b). In Russia, where the government traditionally keeps a tight lid on information, blogs became a premiere venue for breaking news. After several confrontations with the authorities, the Russian blogosphere was officially acknowledged when blogger Rustem Adagamov was invited as a reporter to a formal event at the Moscow Kremlin.

Apparently, blogging has emerged as a harbinger of a new globalized virtual culture. However, researchers still argue over whether or not and to what degree intercultural differences influence bloggers. One cross-cultural analysis of American, German, and Russian blog writers (Haferkamp, Lam-chi, & Krämer, 2011) found that Russian bloggers tend to be more reserved and often feel more insecure towards receiving comments than American and German bloggers.

Twitter

Since the use of emoticons (see Table 12.1) when e-mails began, people have searched for concise ways to communicate online. In this way, Twitter provides a different kind of shared intercultural space than social networking sites or blogs, which are more time consuming. Twitter was launched in 2006 as a service for sending and receiving short (under 140 characters) messages, or tweets, over the Web or a cellular network. It gained nearly instant popularity with the millennial audience. Within 3 years, one in five U.S. Americans between 18 and 24 years used Twitter or similar services (Lenhart & Fox, 2009). Twitter has received wide recognition in the world with 175 million messages posted daily and half a billion registered profiles (Bennett, 2012). Jaiku, based in Finland, is another microblogging service that is popular in Europe. The Plurk network is popular in Taiwan, the Philippines, and Indonesia.

Twitter became especially known during the January 2011 political protests in Egypt, when many Egyptians used Twitter updates as a source of up-to-date news. It may surprise you to know that more than half of all Twitter users come from outside the United States (O'Dell, 2010). Twitter's micromessaging platform has introduced the notion of a real-time

Table 12.1   Emoticons for Cultural Groups.

Do these symbols represent your culture? We create new language to help us communicate. Even with the expansion of the Internet, traditional identities like ethnicity are still maintained through, for example, these types of emoticons.

Emoticon	Meaning
(^_^)	Asian Smiley
@ : -)	East Indian Smiley
- : -)	Punk Rocker Smiley
(- :	Australian Smiley
`\=o-o=/'	Eyeglass Wearer Smiley

Source: Adapted from "The Canonical Smiley (and Other 1-Line Symbols) List" by James Marshall. Copyright 1994, 1995 by James Marshall.

web. Now global netizens stay constantly and instantaneously updated, while Twitter becomes the "pulse of the planet," wrote *Wired* magazine. On May 12, 2009, NASA astronaut Mike Massimino (2010) tweeted from outer space: "From orbit: Launch was awesome!!". In less than a year, Massimino has gained over 1 million followers on the Twitter network. Although Twitter's business model is still uncertain, the value of real-time micromessaging is apparent at least to the Library of Congress, one of the largest cultural depositories in the world, which archives Twitter content due to its immense impact on contemporary culture.

There is no limit to the creative adaptations of new technologies, and Twitter is no exception. An international online book club, One Book, One Twitter, for example, held a discussion of an award-winning fantasy novel *American Gods* by Neil Gaiman on Twitter, chapter by chapter. In his blog, Neil Gaiman (2010) wrote that he was "pleased and impressed with the depth and intelligence" that people were bringing to the conversation during Twitter-based discussions. Another Twitter-like platform, Tumblr, also incorporates social networking functions and makes special emphasis on the usability of the interface which allows users to share not only text but also photos, videos, music, links, and quotes from their favorite blogs. These services, and others yet to come, are valuable and important generators of shared intercultural spaces.

YouTube

YouTube originated in 2005 as an online video sharing website, but quickly became a gateway to cultural participation on a worldwide scale. It was successful in overcoming technical barriers for the diffusion of online video by providing a simple interface that encompassed a range of social networking features. With YouTube, you can become a director and producer of your own content. Users can upload, share, and view videos as well as receive comments. YouTube is a shared intercultural space with 3 billion views per day. YouTube is recognized not only as the leader in online video entertainment, but also as the premier destination for a free exchange of user-generated video content: More than 48 hours of video are uploaded to the site every minute (YouTube, 2012).

For example, Hawaiian-born musician Jake Shimabukuro explains, "One of the biggest things that happened for me was YouTube" (as cited in Harrington, 2010). Shimabukuro became widely recognized as "the Hendrix of the ukulele" after a 4-minute video clip of his performance of the Beatles song "While My Guitar Gently Weeps" in New York City's Central Park appeared on YouTube. The next year, his CD became a world music sensation. Shimabukuro, who was planning to be an elementary schoolteacher, became a world-touring ukulele artist entertaining international audiences. It should be noted that cultural exchange has long been in existence, for example, the ukulele itself is considered to be a variation of a small Iberian four-string guitar brought to Hawaii by European immigrants. However, the advent of the new Web 2.0 age has accelerated this process by creating shared intercultural spaces not limited by geographic or national boundaries. With the emergence of social interaction technologies, information, and culture disseminate in truly unprecedented ways.

Several attempts to theorize how new communication technologies create shared intercultural spaces are worthy of special note. Some theorists suggest that technology and modern society are "mutually embedded" (Barney, 2009, p. 35). These theorists ask the question: Does society make the Internet what it is or does Internet technology make society what it is? Other theorists (e.g., Lister, Dovey, Giddings, Grant, & Kelly, 2003) view new technologies, including the Internet, as socially constructed. The social construction of technology perspective maintains that technology is subordinate to the way it is used in society and specific sociocultural contexts in which everyone is a "culture producer" able to initiate, develop, and maintain diverse cultural experiences. Digital technologies greatly expand the availability of channels for cultural activity and create many new forms of cultural construction.

For others, the Internet is cultural technology (Lull, 2007) in a sense that it connects people with distant cultural resources; blurs the distinctions between technology and culture direct and mediated experience; and creates new opportunities for cultural activity. The push and pull of culture model (Lull, 2007) offers perhaps one of the most captivating conceptualizations of the dynamic relationship between culture and technology. According to this model, *push* signifies structure and tradition and refers to those aspects of culture that are inherited by people, for example, primary language, religion, collective memory, core values, and everyday customs. *Pull* represents the active role of the self as an agent of cultural construction and places emphasis on individual, user-driven tendencies. The technological advances brought about by the rise of Internet-based tools and applications affect both sides of culture: push culture and pull culture. Lull finds that with the adoption of new technologies the locus of cultural activity increasingly shifts from groups to individual persons who select resources, build social networks, and create individual identities.

FOSTERING GLOBAL INTERCULTURAL CONVERSATIONS

The proliferation of social media applications has brought about profound changes in the way people around the world interact with each other. Reflecting on the famous Marshall McLuhan's statement, "the medium is the message," contemporary communication experts claim that in social media, "the content is the conversation" (Technorati, 2009; see Technorati, 2011 for the latest *State of the Blogosphere* report). Putting this another way, Brian Solis, the author of the *Social Media Manifesto*, similarly argues that conversation—the art of listening, learning, and sharing—is key to cultivating relationships, whether online or in the real world. Solis (2008) concludes that "monologue has given way to dialog." This is a dialogue in which people are increasingly using the Internet to contribute to the conversation and to listen to and monitor the conversation, according to Susannah Fox, associate director of the Pew Research Center's Internet and American Life Project, an expert team that has followed the changing habits of U.S. Internet users for a decade (as cited in Straczynski, 2009).

Rephrasing the classical Lasswellian formula of communication, who says what in which channel to whom with what effect, Solis (2008) identifies a new model of communication in the interaction era which evolves from conversation: Who hears what, who says what to whom, in what channel, with what inter, and with what effect? His interpretation emphasizes the interactive nature of social media and their unprecedented potential for fostering two-way conversations among people. The question remains: How can these newly discovered powers of social media properly be engaged to empower people, make their voices heard, and establish global conversations? Consider for a moment any intercultural conversation you have had through social media whether as an exchange student, speaking with an outsourced customer service representative, seeking information or entertainment, or engaging in your own activism. The role of social media in fostering global intercultural conversations in these ways becomes especially evident in times of crisis.

During the recent wave of revolutionary unrest in the Middle East, a 26-year-old journalist Rachel Beth Anderson (About Rachel Beth Anderson, 2011; see also Sniderman, 2011) documented the tumultuous events for PBS *Frontline*, *Pittsburgh Tribune-Review*, and *Ahram Online*. In 2011

Anderson was able to share her photographs and weekly videos about the revolution in Libya and Libyan youth through the support of an international grassroots initiative, One Day on Earth (see www.onedayonearth.org/profile/LibyaTrueStory). In addition, she conducted multimedia workshops for 15 young citizen journalists in Libya in partnership with Small World News, a media company providing journalism training and affordable tools to journalists and citizens in crisis areas and conflict zones around the world. Anderson grew up in North Dakota and earned a bachelor's degree in broadcast journalism from the University of Nebraska – Lincoln in 2007. After participating in a Fulbright-funded journalism program in Egypt, she started reporting as an independent journalist and raised money to produce her first multimedia news stories from Libya (www.LibyaTrueStory.com) using Kickstarter.com.

As this example suggests, global problems require global discussions, and social interaction technologies provide a venue for them. For example, CNN and YouTube organized a joint interactive debate during the 2009 United Nations world Summit on Climate Change in Copenhagen, Denmark. The debate was simultaneously broadcast on the CNN network and webcast on YouTube. An underlying idea behind this enterprise was to give common people a voice during this gathering of world leaders. YouTube members submitted more than 4,000 text and video questions to a panel of experts. They uploaded nearly 1,000 videos on climate change effects during the Raise Your Voice contest on YouTube (CNN, 2009). The creators of the two highest rated videos, which explored environmental changes, were from Brazil and the Philippines and were invited to come to Denmark.

Meaningful, solution-seeking conversations in particular during the 2009 CNN/YouTube debate was very different from the politically motivated wrangling at the summit's negotiating table. A culminating moment occurred during a debate with the government and corporate leaders from different countries, when a 12-year-old boy from Kuala Lumpur, Malaysia, asked the panel of experts via CNN/You Tube what world they planned on leaving for his generation. This CNN/YouTube debate demonstrates how **legacy media** that include traditional forms of media such as television, radio, and print discussed in the previous chapter, together with social interaction technologies, can provide opportunities for people all over the world to hear the opinion of the growing generation expressed in creative ways.

The CNN/YouTube debate reveals the particular role that technological advances can play in fostering and promoting the power of collective reasoning through conversation. It displays the efficiency of crowdsourcing whether at a global or local level. Jeff Howe, a contributing editor to *Wired* magazine, coined the term **crowdsourcing** in 2006 to refer to the "wisdom of crowds" in solving problems. With roots in the open source software development movement, crowdsourcing uses the collective intelligence of groups—creativity, insight, knowledge—amplified by the use of social media. Harnessing group wisdom can be beneficial in diverse fields that range from science and research to business. However, in crowdsourcing, "outsourcing" a task to a group of people or community implies that it is done for a cause and without pay. For example, Yelp, a cross between social networking and a review site, uses customer ratings and reviews in a local search for businesses, products, or services. Founded in San Francisco, it literally thrived on an idea of social engagement. From the United States, Yelp extended first to Canada, then Europe. It created a community of writers, which produced over 17 million reviews attracting 50 million readers every month (Yelp, 2011). Lull's (2007) notion of cultural technology explains how these types of contemporary advances in global communication enabled by social media provide new platforms for cultural participation and engagement. Whether or not technology can bring about social change by holding public dialog on a global scale or crowdsourcing the solutions to important problems is yet to be determined.

LIVING CULTURE

Staying Connected   *Satomi Sugiyama*

Franklin College Switzerland

The impact of technologies on intercultural communication is undeniable. From transportation technologies to communication technologies, they have exerted and continue to exert significant influence on the way we interact with those from our culture and those from cultures different from our own. I have been observing and conducting interviews with college students of various cultural backgrounds regarding how they use communication technologies and how they make sense of them. These students study away from their home country and have developed new relationships with those who grew up in different parts of the world. At the same time, they also maintain preexisting relationships with family, friends, and others with whom they grew up. As a consequence, their "relationally close" friends and family members are not necessarily physically within close proximity. Under this circumstance, these students navigate among a geographically dispersed network of people.

A student from the Dominican Republic explained to me how he stayed in touch with his friends when he was back in his home country:

> I was catching up with them telling them about my (reverse culture) shock, and they were telling me about their (reverse culture) shock, and how everything has changed, and we just talked, yeah . . . cell phone was very interesting. One of them was in the Philippines, I got a call from Cairo, and Spain. . . . and I got goose bumps, because it's so exciting how people meet in this geographic place, and just in one day, everyone was in every different part of the world you can possibly imagine, with all different kinds of weather, all different kinds of cultures, and you can't help thinking about it, it just gives me goose bumps, it's amazing!

A student from Bahrain told me how she was able to mobilize young people across cultures online to promote peace for the Middle East without "meeting" each other. About core staff members of the organization she manages online, she said, "These five people, I've never met them before. Not once. . . . All we do is Skype, phones, and e-mail, and that's it."

A student from Jordan shared her experience of how her mother becomes very anxious when she does not answer her mobile phone. She said, "If my phone is off, she goes crazy. And if I don't answer, she's like, 'Why aren't you answering?' She's like, 'send me at least a message.' And sometimes I don't have credit so I don't reply so she goes crazy!" She explained how her mother then calls all of her friends until she is able to locate her.

(Continued)

LIVING CULTURE

(Continued)

Another student from Jordan said that her friends with whom she grew up are currently all over the world. Because she has been so close to them since first grade, "It's hard not to talk to them everyday cause I was used to always being with them. So we kind of have to stay in touch." She explained that Facebook is a primary medium for this.

I myself have been living away from my home country, taking advantage of some of the most recent technologies to navigate my geographically dispersed relationships. From Switzerland, I excitedly sent a Japanese text message to my mother in Japan saying "Hi, I can now send you messages from my mobile in Japanese characters!" Previously she was able to use Japanese characters but I could not so we were not able to interact using Japanese characters on our mobiles before. She immediately texted me back saying "how convenient!" We exchanged several Japanese text messages consecutively, which made us feel like I was with her back in Japan.

Last winter when I was in Japan sitting in a car with my friend, we called each other to make sure my Swiss phone worked in Japan. We laughed at the fact that the phone call would be considered an international phone call even though we were sitting right next to each other.

These anecdotes highlight issues concerning intercultural communication and technologies. On one hand, we are able to develop and sustain intercultural relationships regardless of our physical geographical location. On the other hand, our connectedness to familiar geographically dispersed others via these communication technologies blurs our sense of being in a new cultural environment in which there are unlimited opportunities to develop new relationships. With ever-developing communication technologies, our relationships become more complex in terms of those who are close in proximity and those who are close relationally, demanding reconsideration for how we define "us."

Consider:

1. In what way is the author using the word *connected?*

2. How are other technologies similar or different to cell phones for their use in intercultural communication?

3. How do technology and identity intersect?

4. How does technology make the world both smaller and bigger?

REDUCING BARRIERS TO INTERCULTURAL COMMUNICATION

The growth of the Internet and Web 2.0 applications makes it possible for people and organizations to communicate and collaborate across geographical borders as shown in Table 12.2, reducing barriers to intercultural communication. For example, the barriers of space, time, and language have traditionally reduced the possibility of success in cross-cultural endeavors. However, these are often irrelevant to communication that takes place over the Internet. Electronic collaboration in general and Wikipedia in particular provide examples of how technology reduces barriers to intercultural communication.

Electronic Collaboration

Electronic collaboration or e-collaboration refers to a complex range of social interactions including computer-supported collaborative work, information and resource sharing, and decision making facilitated by Internet-based technologies. Electronic collaboration enables ordinary people, organizations and businesses to reach outcomes that they would not be able to achieve on their own. Global e-collaboration is the process of cooperation between geographically dispersed teams in two or more countries working together toward a common goal and using digital technologies. There are two types of collaborative tools that promote e-collaboration: synchronous and asynchronous collaborative technologies. Synchronous collaborative technologies, such as instant messaging, online chat, audio-video conferencing and virtual worlds, enable real-time collaboration and allow team members to interact without any time delay in an instantaneous fashion. Asynchronous collaborative technologies do not involve real-time collaboration but, nonetheless, allow team members to interact over time. These started with e-mail, intranets, newsgroups, and listservs and evolved to online bulletin boards, group calendars, collaborative document management systems, collaborative websites, and web-based knowledge repositories (Araujo, 2009).

Synchronous and asynchronous technologies are invaluable for reducing barriers to intercultural communication. However, they are limited in their ability to do so, in part, because of cultural norms and values that impact how willing people are to use and adapt these technologies. In one study (Riopelle et al., 2003), the Hain Celestial company's sales and marketing team consisting of 20 members in the United States, France, Belgium, Argentina, and China was involved in global product marketing. Although originally team members employed audio and video conferencing as well as online document sharing to accomplish their tasks, after 6 months of collaborative work they rejected these virtual tools. In contrast, in the same study, e-mail exchange, instant messaging, and telephone calls became the primary methods of communication for seven members of the ASC NewBiz product development team (Riopelle et al., 2003). The authors of the study argue that culture played a critical role in the adoption or rejection of collaborative technologies.

The Celestial team, which worked with a client based in Paris, rejected virtual tools in part as a result of the general preference for face-to-face, unmediated interactions in French culture, where much meaning is derived from nonverbal cues. For French members, Internet connectivity was not the ideal way to share information. As further evidence of this, note that implementation of Internet technologies in France has been slower than in the United States, Japan, and in other European countries. On the contrary, the ASC NewBiz collaboration involved members

Table 12.2   Internet Usage by Country.

Where do the people with whom you communicate online live? Internet usage statistics like these are quickly made out of date as technological advancements make Internet access easier and more affordable.

Country	Internet Users (Millions)	Penetration (%)	User Growth 2000–2009 (%)
Australia	17	80.1	158.1
Bahrain	0.4	55.3	293.0 *
Belarus	3.1	32.2	1,626.10
Brazil	72	36.2	1,340.60
Canada	25.1	74.9	97.5
China	384	28.7	1,606.70
Cuba	1.4	12.7	2,316.70
Egypt	16.6	21.1	3,596.90
France	43.1	69.3	407.1
Germany	61.9	75.3	158.2
India	81	7	1,110.0 *
Iran	32.2	48.5	12,780.00
Italy	30	51.7	127.5
Japan	96	75.5	103.9
Mexico	27.6	24.8	917.5
Mongolia	0.33	10.9	1,000.00
Myanmar (Burma)	0.2	0.2	29,900.0 *
Norway	4.2	90.9	92.5
Russia	45.2	32.3	1,359.70
Saudi Arabia	7.8	27.1	2,250.0 *
Singapore	3.4	72.4	102.0 *
South Africa	5.3	10.8	120.8
South Korea	37.5	77.3	96.8
Spain	29.1	71.8	440
Sweden	8	89.2	99.7
Syria	3.5	16.4	4,900.0 *
Tunisia	3.5	33.4	3,400.00
Turkey	26.5	34.5	1,225.00
Turkmenistan	0.07	1.5	3,140.0 *
Ukraine	10.3	22.7	5,077.00
United Arab Emirates	3.5	74.10	132.0 *
United Kingdom	46.7	76.4	203.1
United States	234.3	76.3	145.8
Uzbekistan	2.5	8.9	23,166.0 *
Vietnam	22.8	25.7	9,013.0 *
Yemen	0.3	1.6	1,700.0 *

Source: Adapted from "Usage and Population Statistics" by Internet World Stats, 2009. Copyright 2011 Anastacia Kurylo.
* data for 2000–2007

Photo 12.2   Asynchronous technologically mediated communication has considerable room for miscommunication. Reading this conversation from bottom to top, try to identify where the miscommunication is. What general rule of e-mail would you create so that this type of miscommunication can be prevented?

From: Sam
Sent: Tuesday, October 11, 1:33 PM
To: Pat
Subject: RE: Can you prepare a few labels for me? Thank you.

Regular labels

From: Pat
Sent: Tuesday October 11, 1:32 PM
To: Sam
Subject: RE: Can you prepare a few labels for me? Thank you.

Let me know what kind of labels you need.

From: Sam
Sent: Tuesday October 11, 1:15 PM
To: Pat
Subject: Can you prepare a few labels for me? Thank you.

Copyright 2011 Michael Kurylo.

in the United States and Japan. For the ASC NewBiz team members, both asynchronous and synchronous collaborative technologies suited their tasks and extended opportunities to overcome the time zone gap, and even resolve language differences. Results of this study indicate that the relationship between technology and culture is not necessarily one-way with technology influencing culture. In addition, cultural traditions, values, beliefs, and practices may have an impact on the development of technology and the place it occupies in people's lives.

Wikipedia

Wikipedia, a free online encyclopedia, is probably one of the most remarkable examples of international, cross-cultural electronic collaboration. It represents a collaborative effort of thousands of voluntary contributors from around the world who share their knowledge with the global community. In 2009, Wikipedia's readership surpassed that of other well-known information, news, and reference sources including National Public Radio, *New York Times,*

CNN, BBC News, Merriam Webster, and Britannica. Today, 400 million users visit Wikipedia every month to obtain information (Wikimedia Foundation, 2010). Wikipedia employs a set of explicit policies designed to encourage free information exchange, knowledge sharing, and collaboration. Its guidelines for contributors aim to ensure a neutral point of view, verifiability of information, and quality control.

Started by Jimmy Wales and Larry Sanger in 2001, Wikipedia used the so-called wiki technology developed by Ward Cunningham in the mid-1990s. Wikis are collaborative websites that can be edited by anyone, including nontechnical people and nonexperts. The term comes from the Hawaiian *wiki-wiki,* which means "fast." In choosing a name for his invention, Cunningham referred to the ease of creating a wiki-based website. He could not predict the enormous popularity that wikis have gained only a few years later. Indeed, since 2001, Wikipedia has grown exponentially. As of February 2012, Wikipedia has encountered 21,271,964 entries written in 284 languages and represents an innumerable variety of cultural groups (meta.wikipedia.org, 2012).

REFLECT 12.3: How accurately is your local community represented on Wikipedia? What would you change about its entry?

Yet, there are some who remain convinced of the negative impact of the Internet and Web 2.0 on culture, innovation, creativity, and values. Despite the exceptional popularity of Wikipedia and the widespread adoption of social media, critics argue that participatory sites promote "the cult of the amateur" (Keen, 2007) and have an undermining effect on culture. "It's ignorance meets egoism meets bad taste meets mob rule," says a Wikipedia opponent (Keen, 2007). In his opinion, high-quality content on a large scale increasingly gives way to the anarchy of the self-broadcasting culture, which creates a cultural vacuum unconstrained by professional standards or cultural authority. Moreover, although research in neuroscience shows that the use of the Internet develops visual-spatial intelligence, this enhancement comes with a cost. The prevalence of visual sources of information results in reduced higher-order cognitive processes, including abstract and critical thinking (Greenfield, 2009). These critiques suggest that although technology breaks down barriers to intercultural communication, people benefit most from a balance in their production and consumption of visual and print information especially when they collaborate interculturally.

PROMOTING EDUCATIONAL OPPORTUNITIES AND STIMULATING CULTURAL EXCHANGE

The emergence of a new generation of digital technologies and tools has significant implications for the world of education, including a vast potential for connecting learners like yourself around the world, stimulating cultural exchange, and fostering global collaborative education. All of these opportunities are no longer bound by the confines of physical space or the limitations of a traditional school setting. Information sharing and the co-creation of knowledge have become the cornerstones of a new learning culture. In today's networked world, participatory learning is seen as a mode of learning in which new technologies enable learners of any age to work jointly to aggregate their ideas, views, and experiences and achieve individual and group learning goals. Participatory learners use computer technologies and Web 2.0 tools to interact and share their knowledge with others and ultimately contribute to the creation and dissemination of knowledge throughout the world.

Technology presents an array of opportunities to bridge distance and connect learners locally, nationally, and internationally. It is not uncommon today to hold class meetings with speakers and participants joining the discussion from various parts of the world via synchronous distance learning techniques provided by various video and audio conferencing systems and including web-based platforms like Adobe Connect and Blackboard Collaborate. Mobile communication devices such as smartphones, portable media players, as well as tablet computers and e-book readers make it possible to extend the physical space of a classroom into personal learning spaces where students can continue learning at their own pace, synchronously or asynchronously, receiving timely support when and where they need it.

During the last decade, Massachusetts Institute of Technology (MIT) has been engaged in OpenCourseWare, a large-scale global collaborative education initiative aimed to advance knowledge and digitally enabled education worldwide. OpenCourseWare makes possible web-based sharing of instructional materials such as course syllabi, assignments, and audio and video lectures of MIT faculty with learners across the globe. In 2010 the project involved 2,000 courses in 33 academic disciplines (OpenCourseWare, 2011). The OpenCourseWare website (ocw.mit.edu) is accessed by a broad international audience of students, educators, and self-learners, with more than half of all traffic coming from Southeast Asian countries, Western Europe, and Latin America. Many courses have been translated into foreign languages: Spanish, Portuguese, Persian, Vietnamese, Thai, Simplified Chinese, Traditional Chinese, French, German, and Ukrainian. Overall, 100 million people around the world have visited the site (OpenCourseWare, 2011). As this example shows, technology has made important contributions to promoting educational opportunities and stimulating cultural exchange.

REFLECT 12.4: Would you be comfortable knowing that your course paper will be graded overseas? Why or why not? In your opinion, what are the advantages and disadvantages of outsourcing?

SOCIETAL, LEGAL, AND ETHICAL ISSUES

The proliferation of digital devices such as digital cameras, audio and video recorders, and MP3 players poses important challenges to traditional modes of communication and has a range of essential social, legal, and ethical implications that warrant consideration. This section specifically discusses personal property, intellectual property, and cybercrime to explicate some of these issues. These topics are important especially when communicating outside of the familiar context of your own culture you may not be aware of the threats to and laws about personal privacy, intellectual property, and cybercrime.

Personal Property and Privacy

Corporate and individual identity thieves do not need to pick your pocket literally. Instead, they can do it virtually and from anywhere, without you even knowing who did it or that it happened at all. According to the Electronic Privacy Information Center (www.epic.org), profiling is the recording and classification of consumer behavior. **Consumer profiling** may occur through aggregating information from purchase data, both offline and online including through supermarket savings cards, credit card transactions, credit records, product warranty cards, white pages, surveys, sweepstakes and contest entries, property records, motor vehicle data, smartphone and feature phone records, the sale of magazine and catalog subscriptions, U.S. Census data, and health care records.

Privacy concerns came to the forefront of public attention when Facebook introduced a number of significant changes to its privacy policy. Although advances in digital technologies have blurred the line between private and public, people are starting to recognize the need to reconsider the state of privacy in the 21st century. When it comes to **Internet privacy**, the key questions for individuals, businesses, government agencies, nonprofit organizations, teachers, and students alike are what information about their identities, locations and relocations, personal relations, purchases, and medical histories is gathered, how it is stored, with whom it is shared, and how it can be protected from misuse.

While technological possibilities for tracking consumer behavior have grown, so too have resources protecting privacy online. You may find the Internet itself the best starting point to obtain relevant information on common online scams, and how to secure your computer and protect your personal data from identity theft. The Center for Democracy and Technology (www.cdt.org), PrivacyActivism.org, Electronic Frontier Foundation (www.eff.org), and Privacy Rights Clearinghouse (www.privacyrights.org) are nonprofit organizations that offer extensive information about privacy issues and the Internet. Since 2007, International Data Privacy Day has been observed on January 28 to celebrate "the dignity of the individual expressed through personal information" (dataprivacyday2010.org). When you communicate online, whether with friends on Facebook or checking out at your favorite online store, it is important to understand societal, legal, and ethical issues related to privacy for your own security as well as for others.

Intellectual Property and Copyright

The World Intellectual Property Organization (WIPO) defines **intellectual property** as "creations of the mind" which include inventions (patents), industrial designs, symbols, and trademarks used in commerce, as well as literary, musical, and artistic works. Intellectual property is traditionally divided into two categories, industrial property and copyright. **Copyright** refers to the protection of original works of authorship, such as poems, novels, plays, films, musical works, performances, radio and television programs, drawings, paintings, photographs, sculptures, architectural designs, and computer software (WIPO, 2004).

Plagiarism refers to using others' ideas and words as your own (intentionally or unintentionally) without clearly acknowledging the source of information. The term itself comes from a Latin word *plagium,* which means "kidnapping." **Internet plagiarism** has become a particular concern because of the increasing availability and accessibility of information. In the United States, expression of original ideas is considered intellectual property and is protected by law, and plagiarism is viewed as a serious breach of ethics. Those caught in plagiarism face serious disciplinary measures such as expulsion from a university or loss of a job or professional standing.

Copyright law also applies to peer-to-peer networking. **Peer-to-peer (P2P) networks** allow users to share files, programs, or computer desktops with anyone over the Internet. Sharing of software, music, movies, games, and other copyrighted works across peer-to-peer networks can lead you to inadvertently break copyright laws domestically or internationally. If you download or store copyrighted materials such as MP3 audio files or video on your computer without the permission of the copyright owner, you may be violating the copyright law.

Continued improvements in information and communication technologies and the ease of digitization and reproduction of copyrighted material have posed challenges to copyright in the digital environment. In the United States, the Digital Millennium Copyright Act (1998) was signed into law on October 28, 1998. The act served as an amendment to the older copyright laws of the United States. It protected Internet service providers from liability for copyright infringement by their users, created new rules for digital materials, updated old rules and procedures regarding archival preservation, and offered protection for international copyright holders in the United States. Additionally, because of the tensions between open collaboration and copyright infringement, new licenses for copyright protection have been established. A growing number of educational institutions around the world, including MIT's OpenCourseWare, use Creative Commons licenses. Creative Commons (CC) licenses provide authors with a flexible range of protections and freedoms consistent with the rules of copyright by changing their copyright terms from "all rights reserved" to "some rights reserved." According to its website creativecommons.org, Creative Commons is a nonprofit organization that aims to increase sharing and improve collaboration.

Fighting Cybercrime

Crime that is committed using a computer network or system and using the Internet Protocol (TCP/IP) can occur practically any time and any place. It can take many forms from illegal music downloads to e-book piracy to computer viruses, spam, hacking, phishing, data and identity theft, and cyberbullying. Cyberbullying has received particular attention in recent years because of suicide deaths related to incidences of cyberbullying that invoked issues related to sexual identity and body image, suggesting that intercultural issues related to cybercrime occur locally as well as globally.

For those that do occur globally, however, the Council of Europe's Convention on Cybercrime entered into force on July 1, 2004. It provides a foundation for international cooperation against cybercrime. The convention is the first international treaty on crimes committed via the Internet and other computer networks, dealing particularly with infringements of copyright, computer-related fraud, child pornography, and violations of network security (Council of Europe, 2004). Developed by member countries of the Council of Europe and several nonmember states including the United States, Canada, Japan, and South Africa, the convention established "a common criminal policy aimed at the protection of society against cybercrime by adopting appropriate legislation and fostering international cooperation," states the treaty. Among other international initiatives aimed at battling cybercrime is Safer Internet Day celebrated on February 9 in more than 50 countries. Joining world efforts in cyber safety, Facebook has formed an international advisory board—Facebook Safety Advisory Board—on issues related to online security and user safety throughout the Facebook network. The board is comprised of representatives of several leading North American and European Internet safety organizations.

In this age of technology, there are still important challenges and concerns relating to the success of innovative endeavors in the areas of information, news, business, education, and health, which, if unresolved, may have negative implications for intercultural communication.

Strong safeguards for privacy and Internet safety and a progressive intellectual property system are recognized as the essential conditions for the progress of culture in a digital age.

The Internet has demonstrated a potential for becoming the major channel for communication and interaction between people around the world. It is capable of bringing information and cultural resources to the most remote places on Earth. E-mail and text messages, blogs, and social networking sites open up new opportunities for exchanging ideas and information; they also can create new targets for censorship. Attempts to disrupt the free flow of online information, introduce online censorship, detain bloggers, and block social networking sites has occurred in Iran, China, Vietnam, Egypt, Tunisia, and Uzbekistan. U.S. Secretary of State Hilary Clinton (2010), who is considered one of the most renowned defenders of Internet freedoms in the world, established herself as "the Web's first global diplomat." In her speech on January 21, 2010, at the Newseum in Washington, DC, Clinton urged world governments to provide their people with open access to the key freedoms of the Internet age: freedom of expression, freedom of worship, freedom from fear of cyber attacks, and freedom to connect. While "the spread of information networks is forming a new nervous system for our planet," she said, "we need to synchronize our technological progress with our principles" (Clinton, 2010).

FINAL THOUGHTS

Recent technological developments such as the growth of social media applications and the widespread adoption of mobile communication devices create a range of previously unknown opportunities and challenges for fostering communication within and across cultures (Dumova, 2012). Internet-based social interaction technologies help generate shared intercultural spaces by giving rise to an explosion of user-generated content and creating technologically mediated intercultural spaces like YouTube, Wikipedia, and the Twitterverse. Social networking, blogging, and microblogging increasingly facilitate intercultural conversations and two-way communication between people of diverse cultural backgrounds. Technology helps eliminate the traditional barriers of space, time, and language and serves as a platform for intercultural participation, collaboration, and engagement. In addition, the evolution of the Internet toward embracing Web 2.0 applications offers new prospects for cultural exchange and learning across geographical and information divides. Despite certain skepticism about lowering the barriers to knowledge sharing and the products of collaborative knowledge making, these trends suggest the importance of technology-enabled interactions and collaboration in maintaining a continuous dialog between world cultures, advancing innovative means of social connectedness, and building a better world.

CONTINUE YOUR JOURNEY ONLINE

Visit: http://one.laptop.org

One Laptop Per Child website. This site demonstrates the potential for technology to transform intercultural spaces and places. As you look through the site, consider whether this is an example of globalization. If so, ponder the implications, both positive and negative, of this type of intercultural outreach through technology.

66 SAY WHAT?

Say What? provides excerpts from overheard real-life conversations in which people have communicated stereotypes. As you read these conversations, reflect on the following questions.

- Have you been in conversations like this before?
- Is there any one of these conversations that stick out to you more than the others?
- What do you think of this conversation?
- How did the stereotype help or hinder the conversation?
- Was there another way the stereotyper could have communicated to convey the same point?
- How do you feel when you hear this conversation or the specific stereotype?
- Do any of these conversations bother you more than others? Why or why not?
- Do any concepts, issues, or theories discussed in the chapter help explain why?

- **Say What?** "Women are horrible drivers because they eat while driving, they only use their rearview mirrors for applying makeup, and they always have to use their cell phones! You know that you do the same thing. Run out of the house for work, holding on to coffee, and putting on your lipstick, causing a mess out there on the street," he said to me. I respond giggling, "I am always doing something else while driving, but personally I do not think that I am a bad driver. Not only do I not think that I am not a bad driver, but I know many men that eat while driving and talk on their cell phones while driving also. I also know that my insurance is a lot cheaper than many of the guys around me. That says something in itself when it comes to men driving."

- **Say What?** All of a sudden she notices a headline on the website and reads it aloud. "Moss arrested, but will play in upcoming game." I replied, "Who is Randy Moss?" She says, "Some football player who was accused of a felony. They are so violent. They must have bad attitudes. Why do they all do that?" I yelled to her, "Hey, that's a stereotype."

- **Say What?** Toward the end of the night two people came in. One was a gentleman, dressed sharply, an older man, carrying an array of folders and a leather briefcase. He walked sternly to the desk, and two of the three people at the desk flocked to him. Next to him was a short woman, in her early 40s . . . a little on the heavy side, and seemed smallish next to the gentleman. She too was well dressed in a business suit, but seemed preoccupied since she was on the telephone. As we all smiled at him and proceeded to check him in, he smiled and said, "I'm not your guest, Ms. Samuels right here is, I am the driver of her car."

- **Say What?** "I called on the telephone to make a dermatologist appointment for my son. I asked whether the doctor whom I had used before would be willing to have an infant as a patient even though he was not a pediatric dermatologist. The receptionist, trying to be of help, responded, "Yeah. I guess. But you may be better off seeing, well, we have a female doctor. She may work out better." She assumed that the female doctor, by virtue of her being female, would naturally be better equipped to handle an infant. Despite her suggestion, I made the appointment for the male doctor I originally had inquired about."

REVIEW QUESTIONS

1. What are social interaction technologies? Why do they matter for intercultural communication, according to the chapter?

2. Name the examples of social media discussed in the chapter. What are the pros and cons of each in terms of their usefulness for facilitating intercultural communication?

3. Think of examples of how organizations can use crowdsourcing. Consider the social, economic, and ethical implications crowdsourcing may have.

4. How can cultural patterns like those discussed in Chapter 2 affect team collaboration that uses Web 2.0 technologies discussed in the current chapter?

5. Based on what you have learned in the chapter, where may global collaborative education initiatives be most helpful? In what communities? Industries? Cultures? Countries?

6. Visit Facebook's privacy page and become familiar with its privacy policy. If you were on the Facebook Safety Advisory Board, what changes to the current policies would you recommend to protect the personal privacy of Facebook members? Use chapter content to support your answer.

7. Are initiatives such as Safer Internet Day and Data Privacy Day helpful in raising awareness about the legal and ethical issues related to protecting online privacy? In your opinion, what else can be done to stop cybercrime?

8. What role might culture play in the legal and ethical issues involved with Internet use according to the discussion and examples in the chapter?

9. Consider the value of a global diplomat. Based on what you have read throughout the chapter, list five reasons why having one is beneficial.

10. How does theory help you understand the role of culture and technology in contemporary society? Use chapter content to support your answer.

KEY TERMS

asynchronous collaborative technology   267

blog   260

consumer profiling   272

copyright   272

Creative Commons (CC) License   273

crowdsourcing   264

cultural technology   263

cybercrime   273

Digital Millennium Copyright Act   273

e-collaboration   267

functional approach   257

global collaborative education   271

global e-collaboration   267

intellectual property   272

Internet plagiarism   272

Internet privacy   272

legacy media   264

micromessaging   261

participatory learning   270

REFERENCES

About Rachel Beth Anderson. (2011, April 2). *CBS News.* Retrieved from http://www.cbsnews.com/8301–504943_162–20057117–10391715.html

Araujo, A. L. (2009). Instrumental and social influences on adoption of collaborative technologies in global virtual teams. In J. Salmons & L. Wilson (Eds.), *Handbook of research on electronic collaboration and organizational synergy* (pp. 400–408). Hershey, PA: Information Science Reference.

Barney, D. (2009). *The network society.* Malden, MA: Polity Press.

Bennett, S. (2012, February 23). *Just how big is Twitter in 2012?* [Infographic]. Retrieved from http://www.mediabistro.com/alltwitter/twitter-statistics-2012_b18914

Bruns, A. (2009). *Blogs, Wikipedia, Second Life, and beyond: From production to produsage.* New York: Peter Lang.

Clinton, H. R. (2010). *Remarks on Internet freedom* (Transcript). Retrieved http://www.state.gov/secretary/rm/2010/01/135519.htm

CNN. (2009, December 16). *Experts clash at CNN/YouTube climate change debate.* Retrieved from http://edition.cnn.com/2009/TECH/science/12/15/youtube.climate.debate.cop15/

Council of Europe. (2004). *Convention on cybercrime* (CETS No. 185). Retrieved http://conventions.coe.int/Treaty/en/Reports/Html/185.htm

The Digital Millennium Copyright Act of 1998. Pub. L. No. 105–304, 112 Stat. 2860.

Dumova, T. (2012). Social interaction technologies and the future of blogging. In T. Dumova & R. Fiordo (Eds.), *Blogging in the global society: Cultural, political and geographical aspects* (pp. 249–274). Hershey, PA: Information Science Reference.

Dumova, T., & Fiordo, R. (2010). Preface. In T. Dumova & R. Fiordo (Eds.), *Handbook of research on social interaction technologies and collaboration software: Concepts and trends* (Vol. 1, pp. xl-xlvi). Hershey, PA: Information Science Reference.

Facebook. (2012). *Fact sheet.* Retrieved from http://newsroom.fb.com/content/default.aspx?NewsAreaId = 22

Gaiman, N. (2010, May 14). *One book, one Twitter, one wondering author, one wandering character.* Retrieved from http://journal.neilgaiman.com/2010/05/one-book-one-twitter-one-wondering.html

Greenfield, P. M. (2009). Technology and informal education: What is taught, what is learned. *Science, 323*(5910), 69–71.

Haferkamp, N., Lam-chi, A. D., & Krämer, N. C. (2011). Jumping the border in the blogosphere? A cross-cultural comparative study on the motives of American, Russian, and German bloggers for writing and commenting. *International Journal of Interactive Communication Systems and Technologies, 1*(2), 14–28.

Harrington, J. (2010, March 3). *Jake Shimabukuro, 'Hendrix of ukulele,' hits Bay Area for 3 shows.* Retrieved from http://www.mercurynews.com/top-stories/ci_14641432

Jenkins, H. (2009). *Confronting the challenges of participatory culture: Media education for the 21st century.* Cambridge, MA: MIT Press.

Keen, A. (2007). *The cult of the amateur: How today's Internet is killing our culture.* New York: Doubleday/Currency.

Lenhart, A., & Fox, S. (2009). *Twitter and status updating* (Pew Internet Project data memo). Retrieved from http://www.pewinternet.org/Reports/2009/Twitter-and-status-updating.aspx

Lenhart, A., Purcell, K., Smith, A., & Zickuhr, K. (2010, February 3). *Social media & mobile Internet use among teens and young adults*. Washington, DC: Pew Internet & American Life Project. Retrieved from http://pewinternet.org/Reports/2010/Social-Media-and-Young-Adults.aspx

Lister, M., Dovey, J., Giddings, S., Grant, I., & Kelly, K. (2003). *New media: A critical introduction*. New York: Routledge.

Lull, J. (2007). *Culture-on-demand: Communication in a crisis world*. Malden, MA: Blackwell Publishing.

meta.wikipedia.org. (2012). *List of Wikipedias*. Retrieved from http://meta.wikimedia.org/wiki/List_of_Wikipedias

Mike Massimino@Astro_Mike. (2010). Retrieved June 2, 2010, from http://twitter.com/Astro_Mike

Nielsen Company. (2010, January 22). *Led by Facebook, Twitter, global time spent on social media sites up 82% year over year*. Retrieved from http://blog.nielsen.com/nielsenwire/global/led-by-facebook-twitter-global-time-spent-on-social-media-sites-up-82-year-over-year/

O'Dell, J. (2010, April 8). *Majority of Twitter accounts are outside the U.S.* Retrieved http://mashable.com/2010/04/08/international-twitter/

OpenCourseWare. (2011). *Our history*. Retrieved from http://ocw.mit.edu/about/our-history/

Riopelle, K., Gluesing, J. C., Alcordo, T. C., Baba, M. L., Britt, D., McKether, Monplaisir, L., Ratner, H.,Wagner, K. H. (2003). Context, task, and the evolution of technology use in global virtual teams. In C. B. Gibson & S. G. Cohen (Eds.), *Virtual teams that work: Creating conditions for virtual team effectiveness* (pp. 239–264). San Francisco: Jossey-Bass.

Shirky, C. (2010). *Cognitive surplus: Creativity and generosity in a connected age*. New York: Penguin Press.

Sinico, S. (Ed.). (2009a, December 7). *Ten years of blogging in Brazil*. Retrieved from http://www.dw-world.de/dw/article/0,,4966083,00.html

Sinico, S. (Ed.) (2009b, December 18). *Internet pioneer Markus Beckedahl on the German blogosphere*. Retrieved from http://www.dw-world.de/dw/article/0,,4966022,00.html

Solis, B. (2008). *New communication theory and the new roles for the new world of marketing*. Retrieved from http://www.briansolis.com/2008/07/new-communication-theory-and-new-roles/

Sniderman, Z. (2011, March 30). *U.S. journalist in Libya finds audience via Kickstarter*. Retrieved from http://mashable.com/2011/03/30/libya-kickstarter-journalist/

Straczynski, S. (2009, October 19). *19% of U.S. Internet users tweet: New Pew research shows the speedy rise of status update services*. Retrieved from http://www.adweek.com/aw/content_display/news/digital/e3i209e6b1f462c1a585a0a82cde0ab20b4

Stone, R. (2010, May 20). Grass-roots Haitian-relief agency maps its own route to success. *The Miami Herald*. Retrieved from http://www.miamiherald.com/2010/05/20/1638243/grass-roots-haitian-relief-agency.html

Technorati. (2009). *State of the blogosphere 2009*. Retrieved from http://technorati.com/social-media/article/state-of-the-blogosphere-2009-introduction/page-3/

Technorati. (2011, November 4). *State of the blogosphere 2011*. Retrieved from http://technorati.com/social-media/feature/state-of-the-blogosphere-2011/

Universal McCann. (2009). *Wave 4 – Power to the people: Social media tracker*. Retrieved from http://www.universalmccann.com/wave/

Universal McCann. (2010). *Wave 5 – The socialization of brands: Social media tracker – 2010*. Retrieved from http://www.umww.com/global/knowledge/view?id = 128

Universal McCann. (2011). *Wave 6 – The business of social: Social media tracker 2012*. Retrieved from http://umww.at/global/knowledge/view?Id = 226

Wikimedia Foundation. (2010). *Wikimedia Foundation annual report 2009–2010*. San Francisco: Author. Retrieved from http://wikimediafoundation.org/wiki/Annual_Report

World Intellectual Property Organization (WIPO). (2004). WIPO intellectual property handbook: Policy, law and use (Publication No. 489). Geneva, Switzerland: Author.

Yelp. (2011). *About us*. Retrieved from http://www.yelp.com/about

YouTube. (2012). *Statistics*. Retrieved from http://www.youtube.com/t/press_statistics

PART IV

Looking to the Future of Inter/Cultural Communication: Research and Practice

CHAPTER **13**

Social Scientific
Approach to
Culture

**Jan Pieter van
Oudenhoven**
University of Groningen

Journey Through Chapter 13

Sightseeing: On your journey, you will visit with a social scientific approach used to conduct research to study how cultural groups are and can be represented. In doing so, you will learn about research methods, ethics, and limitations of conducting a study using a social scientific approach.

Souvenir: After your journey, you will take away an understanding of some basic differences between a social scientific and interpretivist approach based in a social scientific perspective. You will also learn concepts that would provide fundamental knowledge for you to be able to conduct your own social scientific study of inter/cultural communication if you wished to do so.

A popular Dutch TV series shows the experiences of children from different countries who change families for a couple of weeks. To brief her daughter for her stay in the Netherlands, a Surinamese mother teaches her Dutch culture: "Be aware, darling, in the Netherlands they always dine at a fixed time, mostly at 6 p.m. So, even if you're not hungry, you'll have to eat at six. And the Dutch go to bed at a fixed time, even if they are not sleepy." The daughter accepts the lessons on the Dutch norms without any problem, because she finds the country interesting. In the Netherlands there are highways that run one above the other, and such a thing she has never seen in real life.

This little story illustrates several aspects of the concept of culture: a subjective aspect referring to social phenomena such as habits, norms, values and opinions, and an objective aspect referring to material products such as books, agricultural instruments, and viaducts. This classification in social and material human products follows the widely used definition of culture by Herskovits (1958) as "the man-made part of environment" (p. 305). According to this definition, culture does not only encompass immaterial things such as school rules and wedding rituals, but also material things such as mosques and brothels. All of these comprise the way of life of a culture discussed in Chapter 1. In the current chapter, you will learn about the differences between a social scientific approach and interpretivist approach to research that is based on a social construction approach. Next, you will learn about objectivity and specific steps required in the research process when conducting a social scientific study. You will then learn about ethical considerations in and the limitations of social scientific research.

The Surinamese girl in the vignette at the start of this chapter was particularly thrilled by viaducts, a material product. It was easy to explain to her that in a densely populated country such as Holland, overpasses are necessary in order not to have a permanent traffic jam. Social science (or quantitative) researchers, however, are more fascinated by social products, the immaterial social aspects of life, for instance why the Dutch are precise with time as are those in other monochromic cultures such as in the United States. Social products like this are often more difficult to explain than material products and often require comparisons to be made clear.

For example, comparison between agricultural and industrialized societies helps to demonstrate the importance of monochromic time. In the colder climates of the more industrialized North American regions, being on time is important because factories and offices have fixed opening hours. In contrast, warmer climates—often the setting of agricultural societies like most South American countries—allow for more flexible dining and sleeping times. Even in relatively similar cultures, the same words, another type of social product, may evoke different reactions in intercultural encounters. For instance saying "Hello, how are you today" in the United States is a form of greeting and not so much an invitation to be informed about the well-being of the other. In the Netherlands it is common to view such a greeting as an invitation to tell how you feel and that might take some time.

The transmission of culture takes place by means of enculturation and socialization. Enculturation as discussed in Chapter 6 refers to a broad process of acquiring elements of a culture—both informally, for instance in the street or in bars, among friends, and formally, for instance at school. Much of what people learn happens in the street, often by imitating others. For instance, many children learn important social rules of life, such as fair play by playing marbles. Language acquisition is the most important universal example of informal enculturation. Socialization is a formal, focused, normative form of enculturation in which knowledge and values are imposed upon the individual. Studying the Koran, the Bible, or the Torah—all three meant as an introduction into the religious community—are examples of socialization, and so are going to college, or receiving military training.

Although concerned with understanding and appreciating differences between cultures, all members of a community do not share culture equally. There are individual differences in the extent to which members of a community adhere to a specific culture. This is called intracultural variability. Some cultural members identify highly with the norms, values, and ideas of a community, whereas others distance themselves from some beliefs. This depends on what Pelto (1968) called tightness versus looseness of a culture. In a tight culture, few varieties of behavior may be found across different situations, whereas in a loose culture many varieties of behavior may be found across different situations. For example, complex societies with a vast differentiation of professions, such as industrial societies, tend to have a more loose culture. Societies with little differentiation of professions, such as fishing societies, tend to possess a tighter culture. As is clear from the examples already mentioned, culture affects the behavior of individuals.

REFLECT 13.1: Iran and the United States have different cultures. Try, as much as you can on the basis of factual knowledge, to compare the two societies on the dimension of tightness versus looseness. What would be acceptable ways of informal communication between female and male students in the two countries?

However, culture is not static, but adapts itself to social, ecological, and economic circumstances. For example, individuals influence cultures. The relative racial tolerance in South Africa can be attributed to some extent to the former president Mandela who helped the culture make the shift from apartheid. Thus, culture influences behavior, but does not determine behavior. An example of environmental influences on culture would be the strict Jewish and Islamic prescriptions for preparing meals. These prescriptions are more functional in the Middle East where food gets more easily rotten than in colder regions. An economic example is the growth in wealth in the Western world since World War II, which combined with the invention of the birth control pill, has greatly facilitated the emancipation of women. Greater wealth has created more opportunities for women for prolonged education and for making a living on their own. The birth control pill has made it possible for women to choose the number of children, if any, they want and when.

Meta-Theory

What is the—conscious or unconscious—theory behind the social scientific researcher's behavior? The answer to this question refers to what, with a posh word, is called *meta-theory*. Learn more about meta-theory by visiting the meta-theory textboxes interspersed throughout the chapter.

TWO APPROACHES TO RESEARCH

Finding good and valid explanations and insights about cultural phenomena requires research. There are two different—complementary—approaches to study cultural and intercultural phenomena: the interpretivist approach and the social scientific approach. The researchers of the first approach, the interpretivist approach, try to interpret and understand cultural phenomena. An important task of these researchers is to interpret what people do and say in order to get a deep and holistic understanding of their culture. The second approach, the social scientific approach, is focused on drawing firm, reliable, valid, and objective conclusions about the cultural phenomena, about the relations between the phenomena, and the causes of them in order to predict and explain behavior. This approach is discussed at length in this chapter.

SOCIAL SCIENTIFIC APPROACH

Social scientific research stands for a systematic, empirical way of collecting, analysing, and interpreting data to answer questions, test hypotheses, and shed light on problems concerning social behavior. In order to make good and adequate comparisons, social scientific researchers want to be as sure as possible about their conclusions. This is because they want these to be valid universally. The term generalizable means that it must be possible to generalize these conclusions about social behavior to other comparable groups of people. Therefore, they apply and prefer well-tested instruments such as questionnaires or observation instruments to conduct their studies, prefer to study their objects from a certain distance, and may sometimes not even see the people they investigate. Social scientific researchers may remain outsiders and view this as ideal because they want to be as objective as possible. Additionally, they rely heavily on statistics to analyze their data and value that, through their quantitative methods, other researchers are able to check their conclusions.

Meta-Theory

Ontology

Ontology (or the science of being) deals with fundamental questions, such as "What can be said to exist?" All researchers have some basic theoretical assumptions about the object of their study. The **ontological assumption,** refers to the *nature of things.* The social scientific approach is an **empirical approach.** This means that researchers assume that the objects of their study, in this case elements of culture, exist and can be observed. If they can be observed, they can be studied. For example, cultural differences in the expressions of religions can be observed. Thoughts can also be studied because people can express their thoughts and opinions.

An example of a social scientific study is a 32-country survey on emotional display rules (Matsumoto et al., 2008). Over 5,300 respondents filled out a questionnaire in which they indicated what they should do if they felt each of seven emotions (anger, contempt, disgust, fear, happiness, sadness, and surprise) toward 21 different targets in private and public contexts. The authors found a universal trend to greater expression of emotions toward ingroup than to outgroups. In addition, they found that in individualistic cultures (e.g., Canada and the United States) there is a higher endorsement of expressing emotions than in collectivistic cultures (e.g., Hong Kong and Indonesia).

REFLECT 13.2: What percent of people would need to behave in a certain way for you to be willing to claim that most members of that group behaved in that way?

ETIC AND EMIC PERSPECTIVES

The two approaches to studying culture, social scientific and interpretivist, both seek to discover patterns in human behavior. You might say that the interpretivist approach's virtue is empathy, while the social scientific approach's virtue is objectivity. The distinction between the interpretivist and social scientific approaches resembles the distinction between emic and etic approaches respectively. Table 13.1 provides an overview of the differences between the emic and etic approaches. The emic approach attempts to understand the culture from within or inside the cultural system being studied and the etic approach attempts to understand the culture from outside the cultural system being studied. There are benefits to both. The emic and etic distinction is foundational to and provides insight into the research methods each approach chooses. In order to take an etic perspective, social scientific researchers prioritize objectivity when they conceptualize and conduct their studies.

OBJECTIVITY

By keeping a certain distance to the object of study, the social scientific researcher may more easily discover differences but also similarities between cultures. Take the phenomenon of marriage as an example, also mentioned in Chapter 8. All over the world there are still more arranged marriages than romantic marriages (Jankowiak & Fisher, 1992). An arranged marriage may be desirable if it can improve the economic position of the family, strengthen existing social networks, or seem to offer a guarantee for the groom that the bride is a virgin. These and other factors may enhance and maintain the stability of the relationship. In

Table 13.1 Differences Between Etic and Emic Approaches.

Which approach do you prefer? Researchers benefit from understanding their own preferences and biases in the research process.

Etic Approach	Emic Approach
Analytical	Interpretative
Primarily quantitative	Primarily qualitative
Primarily comparative across cultures	Attention to variation within cultures
Focus on isolated variables	Focus on networks of variables
Emphasis on universal aspects	Emphasis on unique aspects
Concepts and variables introduced externally through prediction	Concepts and variables developed from experience within the culture
Empirical: data are the source of knowledge	Constructivist: constructs are the source of knowledge
Culture seen as a determinant of behavior	Culture and behavior are seen as interdependent
Investigates behavior from outside the community studied	Investigates behavior from inside the community studied

contrast, romantic marriages in the Western world are characterized by strong emotions, sexual attraction, and love between the specific people getting married. For many Westerners it may seem hard to imagine marrying without being in love with their partner. Nevertheless, those in arranged marriages do not appear to be less happy (Goodwin, 1999). Whereas romantic marriages often start with a high degree of satisfaction, which tends to decrease over time, arranged couples start with a lower satisfaction, which tends to rise over the years.

Interestingly, there is one principle working in both types of relationships: the social psychological law that similarity leads to attraction. In arranged marriages, family members—mostly the parents—usually look for a partner who shares many aspects (attitudes, economic position, religion, ethnicity) with the person to be married. As a consequence of the similarity, the chance that they will feel attracted to each other will be high. In romantic marriages, individuals also seem to choose partners that are similar in many respects (attitudes, social status, religion, and degree of attractiveness), although there they themselves are responsible for the selection. In short, if you were to look from a distance at these two types of marriages that seem to be so different, you can see that they have many aspects in common. A social scientific approach allows a researcher to take a step back from any emotional and psychological investment in a topic and view the big picture objectively.

LIVING CULTURE

A Day   *Kurt Lemko*

San Francisco, California, United States

Tuesday, March 2

I don't think he's going to call me.

A day in the life of a gay man is not drastically dissimilar than that of a hetero. We think about, worry about, dream about, and stress about many of the same things.

I start the day 5 minutes late. I know I can hit the snooze button because my roommate, who gets up immediately after me, doesn't have to wake up early. His grandmother died the night before, and he is flying to Nashville later today for her funeral. I have no living grandparents and my only living parent, my father, will be 80 this year. When he passes away, my siblings and I will become the oldest generation of my immediate family. That's strange. I don't feel like the adult I perceived my parents to be when they were my age.

Still 5 minutes behind, I hope to catch a streetcar, which would shave 10 minutes off my commute. The streetcar I desire never comes, so I end up walking—very briskly. I pass a homeless guy sleeping in a public pay toilet trying to keep dry in the rain. It puts my tardiness in perspective.

It doesn't really matter that I'm a few minutes late because my supervisor has been out for a week. Her mother has a brain tumor. We learn that her mother's prognosis is not good, and she must undergo surgery and chemotherapy. My supervisor will be out the remainder of the week, maybe longer. It's a heavy morning.

LIVING CULTURE

On a happier note, today is payday! Unfortunately, it includes a furloughed holiday for which I didn't get paid, making this check 10 % lower than normal. I could have used the extra money. I just bought my first house 2 weeks ago, and the bills from contractors are hitting me hard. Even with automatic deposit, I still may bounce the rent check. I'm praying a large deposit gets credited to my account before my landlord deposits my check. I nervously monitor the status of my bank account online every few hours and hope for the best.

The carpenter calls and tells me there's a gas leak in my house. It's coming from the broken wall heater. I thought I smelled gas when I was there 2 days earlier. Thankfully, the wall heater is being replaced today. Disaster averted.

Tuesday night is yoga night, most definitely needed after a stressful day at work. I started yoga about 6 months ago after being diagnosed with degenerative disc disease. Yoga is critical for my physical well-being, but is also mentally and emotionally soothing.

What I really want to do tonight, however, is my chest routine. With the house purchase taking over my life, it's been 2 weeks since I last did chest. As Jack McFarland in *Will and Grace* said, "No pecs, no sex." Being a gay man, my desire to look good trumps my desire to feel good. Chest it is.

Even as a gay man living in the gay bubble of the Castro, my daily concerns are fairly typical . . . getting to work on time, the health of my father, growing older, paying my bills, making my rent, my physical well-being, staying in shape. Physical appearance and sex are a huge part of our lives, as it is with most men. The main difference for gays is that sex is easy to get. In the absence of girls, boys will be boys.

I end the evening at a bar known for its raunchy Tuesdays. There's a speakeasy password to enter, and it's busy when I arrive. They have a pants check, which apparently some guys have already taken advantage of. Almost immediately, I run into an old colleague from 10 years ago, then a friend, then another friend. Anonymity is not in the cards tonight.

Then I see him . . . the hottest guy in the bar. His tight, muscular body is incredible. Huge arms, strong shoulders, incredible abs. I can't help but stare at him. I watch other guys hit on him, but, one after another, he rejects them. I remove my shirt in hopes he'll notice me.

I don't consider myself good looking by any stretch of the imagination, but at 39, I'm in the best shape of my life. Consequently, I am attracting better looking guys these days, which is odd for a former 110-pound weakling. I see him checking me out. Might he be interested?

After my third drink, I approach him. I touch his back, and he turns around. We exchange names. He smiles and pulls me close. I can't believe it!

(Continued)

LIVING CULTURE

(Continued)

Of all the people here, he's interested in me! I caress his body and marvel at his perfect muscles.

I want everybody else to disappear so we can be alone, but we're joined by three other guys. I want to talk to him and get to know him, but there is only silence among the group. I want to look into his beautiful eyes, but instead I am on my knees. He must be special . . . I have never done this for anyone in a bar before.

It's the end of the night, and the bar is closing. They call "last call for alcohol." One by one, the guys in my group leave, except for him. "That was fun," he says. "I was watching you earlier but didn't know how to approach you. I'm glad you came over." We exchange names again, but I forget it. I want his number but don't want to assume he's still interested in me. Instead, I give him my phone number on a cocktail napkin. If he calls me, I'll know he's interested.

I long to see him again. I long to get to know him better. I long to hug him and kiss him and hold him close. I long to have a boyfriend. I long to have a partner with whom I can travel, fall in love, marry, and grow old. I long to be with him together, alone.

I don't think he's going to call me.

LIVING CULTURE

A Love   *Jack Bennett*

Astoria, New York, United States

I fell in love at the age of 17, unequivocal, heart-wrenching, body-shaking, mind-racing love; Romeo and Juliet didn't have shit on me. I fell in love with the most beautiful person I have ever met. Of course, not everything is that easy, we lived 333.44 miles away and I was unsure whether I was loved back. The summer after my senior year of high school was spent talking on the phone to the one person I wanted to be holding. We spent months apart, yet our bond grew impenetrable through phone calls alone, but I still didn't know if I was loved back. Were we friends? Lovers? Soul mates?

It wasn't until the fall of my freshman year in college that I knew. Thanks to the lighthouse on the beach, a brother's bed, and the painful goodbye, I was sure the rest of our days would be spent together. I was loved back. Four months later, under a sole lamppost in a parking lot with freezing

LIVING CULTURE

Wisconsin rain pouring down, I got down on one knee and proposed. An elated yet tearful, "Yes!" was the answer.

Our life together began a year later in New York City when I transferred schools. Of course New York held a large appeal to a midwestern boy like me, but I would have transferred to a community college in Tennessee if it meant I could be with the one I loved. College took a backseat to our relationship. We were best friends that spent every single free second together; late night walks to Magnolia Bakery, sunrises at Battery Park, odd movies in the Village, we were inseparable. Our love grew so strong our first year together, and we had our whole lives planned out: A wedding on 11/11/11, children by the name of Joaquin and Mason, it seemed our biggest problem was whether we would live in the East or West Village.

Like all epic love stories, mine fell apart. I fell in love with someone that needed freedom from an average life, a sense of adventure and danger that can only come from foreign travels, and desires that couldn't be filled by only one person. Much to my surprise, I decided over late-night drinks with a friend that I would spend one last night with the person I was meant to spend the rest of my life with.

Later that night when he came home:

Me: "You cut your hair."

Him: "I'm moving out."

Me: "No. You don't get to do this. It's over."

Goodbye to the late-night cupcakes followed by sunrises, goodbye to my closest and best friend, goodbye to my fiancé, and goodbye to the only form of true love I may ever feel.

Consider:

1. When you read these narratives do you see differences or similarities?

2. Why does the author of "A Day" say that the life of a gay man is not "drastically dissimilar"?

3. Social scientists generalize across a vast range of experiences in order to make claims about how people think, feel, and behave. What would you need to consider in order to conduct a study about same-sex relationships to enable you to generalize your results?

4. How might bias affect how you would study this culture?

RESEARCH METHOD

In order to conduct research from a social scientific perspective, the research process takes a typically linear form. Specifically, it involves data collection, analysis and interpretation, and the presentation and use of findings. Each of these are discussed separately.

Meta-Theory

Epistemology

The **epistemological assumption** refers to *how* researchers acquire scientific knowledge, or how the phenomena can be studied. It deals with the way researchers can get to know the things studied. This may happen directly by studying material objects, or indirectly by studying the social behavior of people. The social scientific approach has a strong preference for empirical methods. These are methods that are focused on objects of study that can be perceived, observed, and measured, so that a fellow researcher can check the conclusions by repeating the study thereby replicating the measurements. A good example of research according to the scientific approach is the observation study "How to Order a Beer" by Pika, Nicoladis, and Marentette (2009) which showed that Germans would start with the thumb to indicate the number of beers wanted, whereas English Canadians would start with their index finger. You can easily try to replicate this study among a group of fellow students.

Data Collection

One way to collect data is content analysis, which is a technique for analyzing the information and content in written documents such as books, letters, newspapers, or other media such as television programs, movies, YouTube, Facebook, advertisement, or conversations. Content analysis is widely used both by interpretivist and social scientific researchers. Social scientific researchers heavily rely on quantitative computer programs of analysis to detect patterns in the data. An example would be a comparative analysis of speeches by political leaders from different parties in different countries to find out which are the main values for a party and for a nation. In the United States it could be *hope* for Barack Obama, in South Africa *reconciliation* for Desmond Tutu. In the Netherlands it would be *respect* (See Appendix E for an illustration of a content analysis).

Another way of examining intercultural communication is systematic observation. In systematic observation, researchers explore the topic they are studying, such as differences between cultures, by viewing people's behavior and making precise records of these. People from nation to nation vary much in their behavior, because they are brought up differently. Some of these differences may affect intercultural communication. For example, in intercultural communication sometimes confusion may arise between conversation partners originating from different cultures. People have learned the cultural rules of how to engage in conversations with others. You may not be aware of these cultural habits, particularly not of the nonverbal rules. One of these rules regards differences in conversation distances. For instance, Japanese, both men and women, keep approximately the same distance as U.S. American men, but U.S. American women dare to approach each other almost one foot more than Japanese women do (Sussman & Rosenfeld, 1982). As a consequence, Japanese may feel uncomfortable by the close distance when having a conversation with U.S. American women. Interestingly, participants from Venezuela keep much less distance when they speak Spanish, but increase their conversation distance when speaking English. The Surinamese girl in the Netherlands will probably notice that the Dutch keep more distance to each other than she is accustomed to and might conclude that the Dutch are less warm to each other. Studies on conversational distance would use systematic observation as a research method.

Because the most obvious way of getting answers is to ask questions, not surprisingly, the most widely used instrument is the questionnaire. Almost everybody will have participated in some form of survey. A survey usually consists of a series of questions that are asked in written form, but an interviewer may also ask the questions orally. There are open questions, such as "What would be some reasons to pay taxes?" and closed questions such as "Choose one of the following reasons why a person should pay taxes: for education, for health care, for construction of roads." Although it may look easy to construct questionnaires, it is not. Questions should not be suggestive, should be easy to understand, and refer to one aspect of the issue studied per question. (See Appendix F for an illustration of survey research).

The most typical and superior way of collecting data within the social scientific approach is experimentation because it can inform about causality, the association between events that suggests one event results in the other event. Therefore a more elaborate description of experiments is given here. As laypersons do, researchers put people in social categories, and search for relations between social phenomena. These processes help people to create order in the mass of stimuli with which they are confronted. Although these are helpful in general they are far from always totally accurate. One common distortion is that people too often take a relationship between events in life as a causal relationship. People are keen on causality because it makes their lives more predictable or seemingly so. Social scientific researchers are interested in differences between social categories, in relations between variables, and in causality. In contrast to laypersons, they have more time and better methods to come to less distorted observations and conclusions, in particular with respect to causality. Therefore social scientists often use experiments because they most convincingly identify cause-and-effect relations.

Experiments enable the researcher to manipulate an environment, such as conversational distance, in order to observe the effect of this manipulation on the dependent variables (e.g., feelings of comfort). At the same time, all other factors that also might have an effect on the dependent variable (e.g., kind of music or attractiveness of conversation partner) are controlled for. Another characteristic of experiments is random assignment. This requires that all participants be assigned to the experimental conditions by chance only. Random assignment assures that personal characteristics of the participants are unrelated to the manipulated variable. One of the most famous experiments is Henri Tajfel's creation of minimal groups. What he found was that when he assigned members to minimal groups, groups based on trivial criteria such as the color of their pen, the members identified with their group, such as red pens versus blue pens, and showed ingroup favoritism. They judged their own group more favorably, and distributed higher material rewards to their own group than to the other groups. One can easily understand that ingroup favoritism will be even stronger among real groups such as cultural groups.

Psychology and communication journals report thousands of experiments a year. Many of them are creative and often successful manipulations of psychological states such as mood. Examples are bringing participants in a winning mood versus loosing mood by manipulating the outcome of a contest, inducing sexual rivalry by having two male participants fulfilling a task in the presence of a highly attractive female experimenter, creating competition or patriotism by showing pictures of national football or soccer teams in the background, letting participants believe that they are brilliant or dumb by giving them fake feedback about their scores on an intelligence test, and so forth.

Unfortunately, a problem with respect to intercultural research is that researchers cannot always easily induce the essential elements of culture. For example, it is not possible to assign at random participants to a Chinese condition or a Turkish condition. Manipulating realistic conditions of marriages by assigning participants to groups based on arranged marriages or romantic marriages would be even more difficult. Assigning participants at random to real types of marriages is beyond the power of a social scientific researcher. In order to overcome these problems social scientific researchers must rely on quasi-experiments. Quasi-experiments are experiments which cannot be entirely controlled by the researcher but occur naturally. The researcher will, for example, compare real representatives of Turkish and Chinese cultures. However, doing so runs the risk of letting other aspects (e.g., height, family background, intelligence) influence the data. To deal with that problem all kinds of sophisticated statistical procedures are used. Such quasi-experiments have at least one advantage over true experiments and that is that a person does not have to worry about the authenticity of the independent variable culture. (See Appendix G for an illustration of an experimental design).

Analysis and Interpretation

In order to answer questions about intercultural communication, social scientific researchers look at differences between groups (e.g., Are U.S. Americans more religious than Europeans?) and relations between variables (e.g., Is religiosity related to charity?). Statistics help to answer these questions. First there is descriptive statistics. For an example, see Figure 13.1. They describe people; they provide a summary of what characterizes individuals (e.g., their amount of money, their number of children if any, their weight, their IQ) or what they do (e.g., how often they go to the movies, what time they spend on eating, how much time they spend on gossiping).

Statistics also help researchers draw conclusions about the phenomena they study. This branch of statistics is called inferential statistics. For example, a group of 50 Scottish students with an average IQ of 125 has a whiskey consumption per person of five bottles per year, and a second group of 50 Scottish students with an average IQ of 120 takes in six bottles a person per year; how sure can the researcher be that the difference in IQ between the two groups is real and should not be attributed to chance? How can the researcher determine that there is a relationship between drinking whiskey and IQ? And if there is a relation, how does the researcher find out whether drinking whiskey affects IQ, or, the other way around, whether

Figure 13.1   Where Were Babies Born in 2009?

Is this just a bunch of numbers or meaningful information? Statistics enable us to compare groups and identify patterns. This pie chart illustrates the continents in which babies were born in 2009.

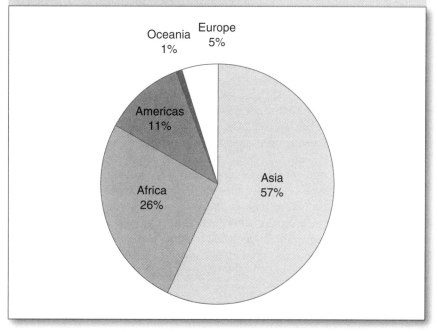

Source: Adapted from "Where Do Babies Come From?" *Newsweek,* October 19, 2009. Copyright 2010 Anastacia Kurylo.

a lower IQ brings people to drink more whiskey? These bits of information referring respectively to *differences between groups,* and to *relations between variables* are essential to understand the world.

Differences Between Groups

Human beings are interested in differences between people. Therefore they put other human beings into social categories such as males and females, young and old, poor and rich, Black and White, individualistic and collectivistic, Republicans and Democrats, and so forth. Particularly the distinction between male and female is so important that almost all languages constantly urge the speakers to tell whether the subject is a *he* or *she,* whether the subject is *bello* or *bella, beau or belle,* or whether a thing is *hers* or *his.* Categorizing other people is functional because knowing in what category an individual belongs provides a lot of information of how to deal with that individual. Social scientists too like to categorize people because they want to check if characteristics can be reliably attributed to specific social categories and they want to know to what degree social categories differ. For that purpose statistics is useful. First, the mean or average is an important measure. A mean is the sum of all scores in a set divided by the number of scores. The mean is only to be used or is only informative if the data show—approximately—a normal distribution which implies that most numbers are to be found in the middle of a symmetrical bell curve (see Figure 13.2). This would show where most cases fall and, therefore, the most typical case can be identified. In contrast, knowing the mean of a very skewed distribution does not reveal what the typical case is like. Most data in the natural world follow a normal distribution. Examples are weight and height, altitude of mountains, daily temperatures, and IQ. In a perfectly normal distribution, the mean also is the mode (the most frequent value) and the median (the score that divides the set of data in half).

Additional statistical tests can be conducted to determine the degree of dispersion, which refers to the extent to which data are spread out or the extent to which they deviate from the mean or average. It tells whether the distribution is too steep, suggesting a narrow range of the scores in the data, or too flat, suggesting a great variety of scores in the data. In Figure 13.3, a steep and a flat distribution are shown. The more the data are spread out, the more difficult it is to identify a typical case that commonly occurs in the data. Knowing the dispersion or variance helps the researcher to describe the data. Additionally, knowing the means and variance of two or more groups of data allows the researcher to compare whether differences between the groups are real or, as it is officially labeled, whether they are statistically significant. Statistical significance is achieved if a statistical test indicates that one can be 95% sure that the results have not happened by chance. There are many more sophisticated ways to analyze differences between groups, but many of them are based on the principles of analysis of variance.

Figure 13.2 Normal Distribution.

Does this mean anything to you? This is an example of a normal distribution, where mean, mode, and median collapse and provides valuable information about the data it represents.

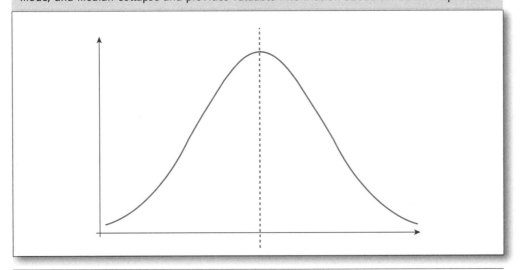

Figure 13.3   Steep Distribution and Flat Distribution.

Do either of these look normal to you? Steep distributions with a high standard deviation and flat distributions with a low standard deviation do not represent the tendencies in a population.

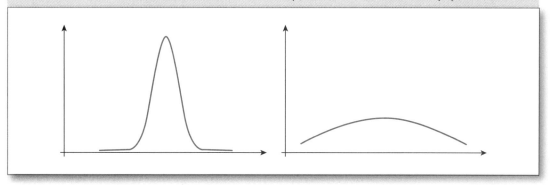

Copyright 2011 Jan Pieter van Oudenhoven.

Relationships Between Variables

In daily life, people experience many associations between characteristics or variables: Well-being increases with health; hours of study are associated with marks for exams; memberships in clubs are associated with invitations for social parties, and belief in God goes with belief in life after death. In science, there is a way of expressing the magnitude of a relationship, the correlation. A correlation is the degree of relatedness between two variables. An example of a moderately high correlation can be found between cultural similarity and attraction. Individuals feel attracted to cultural groups who are like themselves in many respects, particularly, with regard to attitudes, which is understandable because consensus is convenient. This principle is known within social psychology as the *similarity-attraction hypothesis*. This mechanism may explain why cultural majority groups in Western immigration countries prefer immigrants from (West) European descent. There also are negative correlations, in which the higher the score for one variable, the lower the score for the other variable, such as between consumption of alcohol and the percentage of Muslims in a society. The reason is that Islam does not allow its followers to drink alcohol.

There are hundreds of studies that show relations between dimensions of national cultures, as determined by Hofstede (1991), and psychological phenomena such as political beliefs, or consumption behavior. De Mooij and Hofstede (2010), for instance, report that in high power distance societies, where status is important, products such as jewelry, watches, and whiskey are frequently advertised to show a person's success. In high uncertainty avoidance cultures, advertisement of mineral water is common, because mineral water suggests certainty regarding the absence of pathogenic bacteria.

Correlations often are interesting in their own right, but you must be cautious in interpreting their meaning. A correlation means that there is an association, but it does not say which is the cause and which is the effect. Similarity of attitudes may lead to mutual liking, but liking may also lead people to agree more easily. Or there may not be any causal relationship at all. For example, individuals from the same clubs may have similar attitudes, and as a consequence of visiting the clubs, may be more likely to get to know each other and develop friendships.

Defining Elements of a Social Scientific Approach

Whatever the focus of research—finding causality, relationships or differences, or just description—instruments are used such as questionnaires, diaries, ratings, MRI scans, interviews, and implicit attitude tests. The instruments may vary widely, but they all must possess two qualities that are integral to a social scientific approach: validity and reliability. Validity is a must because researchers want to know that the instrument *truly and correctly* measures what it indicates; reliability is a must because researchers want an instrument to yield *consistent* measurements. An instrument is valid if it measures what it intends to measure. The most global but subjective form is face validity, which refers to whether the measure looks on the surface as if it is measuring what it should, or put simply: Does the measure make sense? The only valuable aspect of face validity is that it more easily invites people to participate. There is for instance a psychological test, the Rorschach inkblot test, showing vague configurations, which is used to determine deeper motivations of individuals. Many clients are reluctant to take the test because the way psychologists interpret the ink dots is not clear to them. In contrast, an instrument with face validity makes more immediate sense to a participant. The second, construct validity, tells whether the instrument measures the theoretical concept. For instance, does a high score on an honesty scale correlate with actual honest behavior as observed in another setting? Does it correlate with patterns of behavior with which it is expected to correlate? A third way to determine the validity of a measure is to check it against a certain criterion that is used as a standard. Can the measure, an academic motivation test for instance, predict academic achievement? If so, it has predictive validity.

REFLECT 13.3: In all languages, name-calling is common. Interestingly, the names differ from country to country (van Oudenhoven et al., 2008), though they tend to all refer to a lack of certain cultural values. For example, *loser* refers to lack of societal success. What are frequently used words used for name-calling in your culture, and to which values do they refer? Do you think each name sounds mild or severe to a person of another culture?

The second major quality of an instrument is its reliability, which is the extent to which the instrument provides consistent results when the characteristics of the object measured have not been changed. An instrument is reliable if it measures the same thing more than once and results in the same outcome. The most widely reported form of reliability is internal consistency, which indicates the extent to which the items of an instrument yield similar results. A researcher can also compare the scores on two parallel forms of the instrument to assess the reliability of the instrument. In this case, there are two exemplars of the same test consisting of approximately similar items. The test is reliable if a high correlation is found between the scores on the two tests. Another way to determine the reliability is the test-retest method. The instrument should at different moments yield similar results unless the characteristic it measures has been changed. Again the degree of correlation would be used to determine the degree of reliability. Validity and reliability are crucial in scientific measurement because they deal with content (validity) and certainty (reliability). Consider a comparison with the medical practice: People want physicians to come to the right diagnosis (validity) and to apply procedures that consistently yield the same results (reliability).

Presentation and Use of Findings and Claims

Social scientific researchers have relatively simple procedures in the way they disseminate their findings. In most cases, they present their preliminary findings at conferences where they get feedback from their colleagues. This positive and negative feedback helps them to improve their papers, which they subsequently submit to scholarly journals. There again they receive feedback, this time structured feedback by two or three reviewers, in order to revise their paper, provided their research was sufficiently well performed and reported. Next, from the moment it is accepted, they will be the legal authors of the paper. Usually they will then see the paper published within one year. From the moment of publication they share their knowledge with a broader audience, although most of them are professionals from the same or related fields. These publications enable other researchers who are interested to try to replicate the findings. If they do, the study has contributed to the domain of scientific interest. If the studies are potentially interesting for a broader audience, press releases are directed to the media, which may decide to pay attention to it. Reactions from the general public may further provide feedback to the researchers, which can encourage the researcher to continue with their studies or to improve them.

ETHICAL CONSIDERATIONS FOR SOCIAL SCIENTISTS

Ethics deal with issues beyond the quest of scientists to answer their theoretical questions or find solutions to societal problems. Research ethics refer to the moral rules or standards governing the conduct of the members of the scientific community. In the case of social sciences, moral rules are particularly important because participants can be damaged by the researchers or—sometimes—may benefit from being the object of study. For example, social scientific researchers may use experiments in which they manipulate behavior even in ways that may possibly harm the participant, varying from causing some feelings of insecurity to actual psychological or physical harm. Now, we have a look at the major ethical issues that have to be dealt with, and how their potentially disturbing effects on research can be minimized.

REFLECT 13.4: Suppose one of your instructors has, because of your participation in research, information about the IQ and emotional stability of you and your fellow students. Think of a set of rules that you would find necessary to guarantee a sufficient level of confidentiality.

Voluntary Participation

People should not be forced into participation in a study. Students, particularly freshmen students, form an important group in many studies. They are put under pressure to participate as part of their academic tasks. Similarly, employees of organizations or the military are often required by their superiors to fill out questionnaires. Many of them participate because they have to. However, they may experience it as a violation of their privacy, or it may make them unnecessarily nervous, or remind them of earlier unpleasant experiences. Therefore, they must be clearly allowed not to participate in the research, for instance by being offered an alternative task. This way voluntary participation will be guaranteed.

Protection From Harm

Obviously, participants may not be exposed to situations in which they can physically or psychologically be hurt. An exception may be if the potential benefits of the study for the individual are larger than the risks. Too often in experimental research participants are brought into certain moods, which may influence the person's psychological well-being beyond the experimental session. For instance, the participant may be brought into a depressed mood, or may temporarily be convinced of being much less intelligent or much smarter than the average participant in the experiment. The researcher has the obligation to explain the study to the participants after the experiment, but that may not always be sufficient to prevent lasting harmful effects of having been deceived.

Protection of Privacy

This issue of privacy refers to anonymity, which is particularly relevant for social scientific research, and confidentiality, which is even more relevant for interpretivist research. Anonymity means that apart from the investigator, nobody has access to the data and that the data that may identify the participants are secured and not made available to others. Nor must it be possible from the presentation of the results in a report to be traceable to whom the data refer, for instance by mentioning the profession of someone (e.g., judge) in combination with the city where that individual lives. For example, in some cities there may be only a few judges such that a person can easily find out which judge is being discussed in the study. Confidentiality means that information about whom the interviewee or person observed is should remain undisclosed unless otherwise agreed. Confidentiality is required if participants allow information about them to be made public. Because participants may not be aware of the harmful consequences that this may have for them, it is the duty of the researcher in such cases to warn the participant.

Providing Information to Participants

Researchers are obliged to give as much information about the study as possible to the participants before and after the study. Sometimes it is not possible to investigate if the researcher gives all the information beforehand. Instead, in such cases, deception is used. For instance, think of a study about the unconscious influences of cultural markers such as exotic surnames or accents on the selection of employees, or a study about the relationship between cultural background and productivity of work teams in which case participants who were aware of the aims of the study could bias its results. When deception is used, a debriefing should be provided. Debriefing is the practice of explaining fully the purpose of the study after the participants have completed the task. However, deception in research should be avoided as much as possible. Ideally, researchers should also inform the participants as much as is possible about the results of the study. This can be done, for instance, by sending a brief report or an e-mail message, by placing a summary of the study on a website, or by organizing a meeting in which the researchers present their conclusions. The last one is a particularly rewarding way of debriefing, because the participants are personally interested in the results, and they may give feedback to the researchers about the validity of the results.

Ethical Codes

Ethical principles and codes of conducts are found in many national associations for psychologists (Leach & Harbin, 1997). They are found among those in the United States, Europe, Chile, South Africa, Australia, and China. They are most outspoken, elaborate, and widely published or ventilated in the United States. Many U.S. textbooks on research methods include a chapter on ethical issues. This does not necessarily mean that U.S. researchers are the most ethical researchers, but it does show that they take it seriously. A problem might arise, though, when the rules are applied too rigidly or are too legalistic. For instance, immigrants in many nations may be put off by having to fill out an informed consent form. They may have had uncomfortable experiences with immigration officials and be reluctant to fill out forms if they do not have to. Less educated participants might be reluctant to fill out forms because they have trouble reading the texts.

Ethical codes for research are indispensable and they exist all over the world. Nations stress different aspects. The largest differences are found between China and the United States (Leach & Harbin, 1997). With respect to research, all nations emphasize the principles of protection of physical and psychological harm, and confidentiality of data. Apparently these are universal principles. All individuals around the globe understand that researchers have to act in accordance with these principles.

LIMITATIONS OF THE SOCIAL SCIENTIFIC APPROACH

In conducting social scientific research, three limitations should be taken into consideration. These include (1) researcher bias, (2) cultural context, and (3) confounding variables. These limitations mean that the results of social scientific studies are limited in their ability to explain and predict the phenomena they represent.

Researcher Bias

The potential for researcher bias, in an otherwise objective study, is a limitation of social scientific research. Once involved in research on social behavior, a researcher may forget that the way the studies are being done, the methods of investigation, the choice of topics, or the way the people are approached are not self-evident and have been the result of some selection process, of which the researcher may only partly be aware. For each of the chosen options there are always feasible alternative ways of answering the theoretical and practical questions of the study. Because, to some extent, researcher bias may never be known, results of a social scientific study are limited in their explanatory value.

Cultural Context

Another limitation is that the social scientific approach to culture is not culture free. For example, many psychological phenomena are susceptible to cultural influences. Methods, theories, and research topics are influenced by the culture to which a researcher belongs. Psychologies as a consequence are to some degree indigenous. They reflect to some extent the way of thinking that is dominant within a certain culture. That also applies to the dominant psychology, which has primarily developed in Western societies. Not surprisingly *the individual* is often a *too* crucial and a *too* dominant concept in Western psychology. Most clearly, this is the case in personality psychology that has individual differences as its topic. Even *social* psychology is defined as the investigation of "how the thoughts, feelings and behaviors of individuals are influenced by the actual, imagined or implied presence of others" (Allport, 1968, p. 3, as cited in Hogg & Vaughan, 2005). Cultural context and its often invisible impact on social scientific research present a limitation for this type of research.

Meta-Theory

Axiology

For a long time, general psychology has tried to formulate universal laws. However, these so-called universal laws were developed within a specific culture. This is because social scientists study the behavior of individuals in interaction with their cultural environment. Despite the desire to seek universal law, it is not possible to really understand human behavior if researchers do not take into account the way in which individual and culture influence each other. This appreciation represents an assumption of the social scientific approach important for understanding how axiology or value theory applies to social scientific research.

As members of a cultural community, scientists are susceptible to the mainstream way and content of thinking within their own culture. Karl Popper (1967) mentioned that scientific statements do not always correctly represent the real world. Statements are always based on a limited number of observations within a cultural context. Moreover, scientists are influenced by their cultural environment. In social scientific research, Western psychology has been dominant, which implies that many psychological *laws* are based on Western behavioral patterns. Time and again, established theories, developed in the West, appear not to apply outside the Western world.

The concept of attachment style provides an example of Western theories that fall short of universality. It refers to a variety of behavioral patterns for approaching people whose use is determined by a person's contact, in particular, with his or her mother as a child. This theory takes for granted that the child is part of a nuclear family consisting of mother, father, and children. In many cultures, however, a child forms part of an extended family with many people around who all can teach the child to acquire a sense of security. Another example of lack of universal consensus is the impossibility to develop an intelligence test that is culture free. How do you measure intelligence in an illiterate society? How do people react to a test situation if they are not accustomed to it? Moreover, what is considered to be intelligent varies from culture to culture. For example, Jerome Bruner (1973) has even defined intelligence as the capacity to get by in a particular culture.

Culture may creep into science in many ways. First is in the selection of topics. Gender studies, for example, will take place in cultures, where emancipation of women is desired and a realistic option. Racism does not get any attention in some societies whereas it may become a dominant topic in societies with racial tensions. Topics like intelligence and achievement look more culture free, but tend to be more often chosen in a society such as individualistic cultures, where individual differences in talent and motivation are stressed. Second, as the culture philosopher Thomas Kuhn (1962) pointed out, methodological rules and concepts are not culture free. Definitions of concepts such as intelligence, happiness, poverty, and unemployment differ from culture to culture and from period to period. Should researchers call housewives unemployed? Is poverty absolute or relative? Cultures may even differ more strongly with regard to the meaning they attach to certain events. Is killing infants to regulate the composition of the family child murder or family planning? Is beating of wives mistreatment or maintenance of order? Is widow burning a crime or a nuptial obligation? Is placing parents in a house for the elderly a hard-hearted act or an act of care? Are Palestinian suicide actions terror or patriotism?

Third, scientists experience the influence of the dominant interpretation within the culture of which they are part in the form of researcher bias. Nowadays researchers are more aware of the influence of culture on their interpretation of human behavior. As discussed in Chapter 1, intercultural imperatives have reinforced that social scientists need to be aware of their cultural biases and pay attention to checking whether their findings may be generalized to other cultures. The Netherlands offers an example of the influence of culture on social scientific thinking. In the last four decades the Netherlands has witnessed a considerable immigration from Muslim countries: More than a million added to a population of 16.7 million. This has challenged the relatively large consensus about issues regarding homosexuality, male-female relations, and the role of religion in this society. This confusion is also, not surprisingly, reflected by social scientific researchers in their various interpretations of the current national culture.

Confounding Variables

The social scientific approach searches for universal patterns (etics). When researchers compare patterns in existing cultures they may forget that other aspects co-vary. There is always some degree of confounding variables, such as language, wealth, climate, political situation, general level of education, and so forth, that are active at the same time in such a way as to make it difficult to deduce which is the explanatory variable. Social scientific researchers should be well aware of the possible effects of these other variables as a limitation of their research when comparing different cultures.

FINAL THOUGHTS

Within the field of intercultural communication, there are two research approaches: the interpretivist approach and the social scientific approach. Social scientific researchers love objectivity, are quantitatively oriented, rely on statistics, look for causal explanations of social and cultural behavior, and are interested in discovering universal patterns of behavior. By keeping a certain distance to the object of study, the researcher may more easily discover differences but also similarities between cultures. Knowing how cultures differ and also discovering similarities promotes understanding of other cultures and facilitates intercultural communication. The interpretivist approach offers the obvious alternative to social scientific research. However, when dealing with cultural phenomena it is better not to consider the interpretivist approach as merely an alternative, but as a complementary approach, which is extensively discussed in the next chapter.

CONTINUE YOUR JOURNEY ONLINE

Visit: http://www.davidmatsumoto.com/research.php and **http://www .jamescmccroskey.com/measures**

David Matsumoto's research products website and James McCroskey's research measures website. Explore these sites to discover how communication is translated into numbers through research instruments that measure behavior. Have fun answering the questions on these instruments and scoring your own behavior. As you do, take a moment to think critically about the ability of these to measure behavior.

REVIEW QUESTIONS

1. Based on the discussion in the chapter, explain what a social scientific approach is in your own words.

2. Why do emic and etic approaches, as discussed in the chapter, matter when conducting research?

3. Why is objectivity important for a social scientific approach according to this chapter?

4. What are the steps in the research process described in this chapter? Why is each step important?

5. What methods of data collection are associated with a social scientific approach in the chapter? Compare and contrast these.

6. Explain what a correlation is in your own words. Provide an example.

7. When would validity and reliability be ascertained in the process of conducting research, according to the different types discussed in the chapter?

8. Name three of the ethical issues discussed in the chapter. Explain why these are necessary considerations for a researcher. Why might these sometimes be difficult to handle when conducting intercultural research?

9. What are some limitations of a social scientific approach, especially for the study of inter/cultural communication?

10. Select one case study that takes a social scientific approach from the appendices. Analyze the case study based on the description of the social scientific research process discussed in this chapter. Incorporate issues of data collection, analysis and interpretation, and presentation or use of findings and claims.

KEY TERMS

anonymity   298

causality   291

confidentiality   298

confounding variable   301

construct validity   296

content analysis   290

correlation   295

debriefing   299

emic approach   285

empirical approach   284

epistemological
   assumption   290

etic approach   285

experiment   291

face validity   296

generalizable   284

internal consistency   296

intracultural variability   282

loose culture   282

minimal group   291

normal distribution   294

ontological assumption   284

predictive validity   296

quasi-experiment   292

random assignment   291

reliability   296

research ethics   297

social products   282

social scientific
   research   284

socialization   282

statistical significance   294

systematic observation   290

test-retest method   296

tight culture   282

validity   296

REFERENCES

Bruner, J. (1973). *Beyond the information given.* New York: Norton.

De Mooij, M., & Hofstede, G. (2010). The Hofstede model applications to global branding and advertising strategy and research. *International Journal of Advertising, 29,* 85–110.

Goodwin, R. (1999). *Personal relations across cultures.* London: Routledge.

Herskovits, M. J. (1958). *Cultural anthropology.* New York: Knopf.

Hofstede, G. (1991). *Cultures and organizations: Software of the mind.* London: McGraw-Hill.

Hogg, M. A., & Vaughan, G. M. (2005). *Social psychology.* Harlow, UK: Pearson Education Limited.

Jankowiak, W. R., & Fisher (1992). A cross-cultural perspective on romantic love. *Ethology, 31,* 149–155.

Kuhn, T. S. (1962). *The structure of scientific revolutions.* Chicago: University of Chicago Press.

Leach, M. M., & Harbin, J. J. (1997). Psychological ethics codes: A comparison of twenty-four countries. *International Journal of Psychology, 32,* 181–192.

Matsumoto, D., Yoo, S.H., Fontaine, J. (2008). Mapping expressive differences around the world: The relationship between emotional display rules and individualism versus collectivism. *Journal of Cross-Cultural Psychology, 39*(1), 55–74.

Pelto, P. J. (1968). The differences between "tight" and "loose" societies. *Transaction, 5,* 37–40.

Pika, S., Nicoladis, E., & Marentette, P. (2009). How to order a beer: Cultural differences in the use of conventional gestures for numbers. *Journal of Cross-Cultural Psychology, 40*(1), 70–80.

Popper, K. R. (1967). *The logic of scientific discovery.* New York: Harper & Row.

Sussman, N. M., & Rosenfeld, H. M. (1982). Influence of culture, language, and sex on conversational distance. *Journal of Personality and Social Psychology, 42,* 66–74.

van Oudenhoven, J. P., et al. (2008). Terms of abuse as expression and reinforcement of cultures. *International Journal of Intercultural Relations, 32,* 174–185.

CHAPTER **14**

Interpretivist Approach to Culture

David Boromisza-Habashi

University of Colorado Boulder

Journey Through Chapter 14

Sightseeing: On your journey, you will visit with a social construction approach to conducting research, known as the interpretivist approach, which explores how cultures are constructed products of communication processes. In doing so, you will learn about research methods, ethics, and limitations of conducting a study using an interpretivist approach.

Souvenir: After your journey, you will take away an understanding of some basic differences between a social scientific and interpretivist approach. You will also learn concepts that provide fundamental knowledge for you to conduct your own interpretivist study of inter/cultural communication if you wish to do so.

In 1972, the American anthropologist Charles Briggs arrived in Córdova, New Mexico. In this small village located about 30 miles north of Santa Fe, Briggs wanted to study the local wood-carving industry, language use, folklore, and ritual. As most anthropologists would do, Briggs set out to interview members of the community who kindly accepted his presence. However, he had a difficult time getting informants to answer his questions. For example, Aurelio Trujillo, one of Briggs's elderly key informants, frequently made scriptural allusions during interviews instead of directly answering questions. In his book Learning How to Ask *(1986), Briggs provides readers with the transcript of one of these extended allusions (p. 85).*

1	AT	Pero al cabo que Dios	But in the end God
2		los sabe premiar	knows how to reward them
3		lo mismo que premia al	just as He rewards a
4		((pecador)),	((sinner)),
5		porque dice	because He says
6		"perdonar al inocente,"	"pardon the innocent,"
7		dice,	He says,
8		"porque no sabe lo que	"because he knows not what he
9		hace."	does."
10		Y todos semos [sic] HIJOS,	And we are all CHILDREN,
11		todos semos BROTHERS,	we are all BROTHERS,
12		todos semos hermanos.	we are all brothers and sisters.
13	CB	Sí.	Yes.
14	AT	Y muchos no,	But not for many,
15		porque tiene un nickel	because she or he has a nickel
16		more que el otro;	more than the other;
17		es ORGULLO.	it's PRIDE.
18		Mire,	Look,
19		la VANIDAD	VANITY
20		se acaba,	comes to an end,
21		no tiene fin.	it is pointless.
22		EL DINERO se acaba,	MONEY comes to an end
23		no tiene fin.	it is pointless.
24		De modo que hay tres cosas	And so there are three things
25		que no tienen fin.	that are pointless.
26		Y la AMISTAD REINA EN LA VIDA.	And FRIENDSHIP REIGNS IN LIFE.

Puzzled and somewhat frustrated, Briggs decided to spend time in the field making sense of his informants' and respondents' reluctance to answer his questions with direct answers. During his 10 years of fieldwork in Córdova, he made a number of discoveries about what happened in the course of those initial interviews. First, according to Córdovan communicative norms, for a young person like Briggs (who was 19 at the time), questioning others was not considered an appropriate mode of learning about local ways. The young were expected to begin to learn by imitation, achieve a certain level of expertise, and only then ask questions. Second, Trujillo was acting in a way that was considered wholly appropriate for an elder in the community. He was performing pedagogical discourse in order to contribute to young Briggs's moral development. Young Córdovans were taught not to interrupt elders during these moments and only to signal their attention and occasionally ask for clarification. (On line 13, Briggs fortunately did exactly what he was supposed to do.) Third, scriptural allusions lent the highest possible degree of legitimacy to Trujillo's words according to local communicative norms. Finally, Briggs had to realize that when he thought his respondents were giving nonanswers to his questions they were actually doing important interpersonal work. Mr. Trujillo's use of English lexical items ("brothers" on line 11, "nickel more" on lines 15–16) and his reference to pride, vanity, and avarice (vices Mexicanos commonly associated with Anglo-Americans) signaled that he treated Briggs as an Anglo outsider, and as one in need of moral education. His final utterance on line 26 (And FRIENDSHIP REIGNS IN LIFE.) was, however, an indication that Trujillo did not regard Briggs's background as an obstacle to a developing friendship between the two of them which, in the end, lasted for decades.

Most people accept as a fact that those living outside the boundaries of the social environment they consider their own are likely to view the world and live their lives in a different way than they do. These differences sometimes lead to problems in how they communicate or act together with people they regard as cultural others. You do not have to think about large-scale conflicts or international warfare to understand how these differences organize relationships among members of social groups. When interacting with those outside your communities, you may sometimes get things right but you may often get things wrong too. For example, some of Briggs's behavior, though accidental, was right in the conversation with Mr. Trujillo. To explore the kind of research being conducted in the preceding excerpt, the current chapter highlights an interpretivist approach to the study of inter/cultural communication based in a social construction approach. You will learn the research method used by interpretivist researchers, the ethical issues these researchers confront, and the limitations of interpretivist studies.

REFLECT 14.1: If you studied your own culture through interpretivist methods, what do you think you would find out? Do you think you would be surprised by the results of your study?

Intercultural communication is a complicated affair because when people communicate in ways that seem inappropriate, they have to deal with the social consequences of their mistakes. The intercultural practitioner (Agar, 1994) requires local knowledge to be able to communicate well with the "natives." Agar goes as far as to argue that the main reason practitioners talk about culture is that they face problems when communicating with people from other parts of the world. According to Agar (1994), "Culture is something the [intercultural practitioner] creates, a story he or she tells, one that highlights and explains the differences—to both sides—that created the problem in the first place" (p. 227). From this perspective, people do not *have* cultures; a speech community's culture needs to be *made* (for example, see Figure 14.1 on page 313). When you, as an intercultural practitioner, are confronted with the unfamiliar ways of a community, you need to make sense of those ways from your own perspective. To do so, you can use a variety of interpretative methods. You can apply the interpretative techniques described in this chapter and you can read existing studies about the community's ways. The results of your sense-making will be the culture you will then attribute to the community and use to communicate with communal members. You can then test this culture you create against cultural members' reactions to your communicative conduct. You would critically evaluate and recreate your understanding of this culture if it does not seem to "work."

What *culture* as an interpretive concept suggests, among other things, is that you are committed to regarding the unfamiliar communication patterns of an unfamiliar speech community as on a par with yours—not as inferior, only different. Briggs adopted this approach when he assumed that his *Mexicano* respondents ascribed different meanings to his interview questions than he did. This use of the concept highlights culture as a realm of practice, as a system of locally meaningful social action and organization as discussed in Chapter 5.

Meta-Theory

What basic theoretical assumptions guide the interpretivist (qualitative) approach to culture and intercultural communication? Throughout the chapter you will have the opportunity to take a brief look at three categories of assumptions: ontology, epistemology, and axiology.

TWO APPROACHES TO RESEARCH

Interpretivist researchers go about capturing and explicating culture in different ways than social scientists. Social scientists set out to make accurate predictions about how people in various social groups will act in particular situations, and what their attitudes will be toward particular objects and issues. While interpretivist research generates claims with some predictive power, its chief aim is not prediction but the interpretation of the meaning of communicative practices from the perspective of those speakers who engage in those practices. Intercultural communication researchers working in this research tradition are interested in what happens when members of two speech communities come into contact. Speech communities "shar[e] rules for the conduct and interpretation of speech, and rules for the interpretation of at least one linguistic variety" (Hymes, 1972, p. 54). Although a social scientist would make claims like "Mexicano speakers will communicate in Way X in Situation Y," an interpretivist claim would look more like this: "Mexicano speakers tend to communicate in Way X in Situation Y because they believe *Z*." Inevitably, this kind of study will provide insight into how members of a speech community make sense of their everyday experiences and behavior.

INTERPRETIVIST APPROACH

An irony in adopting an interpretivist approach to intercultural communication is that this approach requires interaction with the speech communities whose communicative practices the researcher intends to study. Therefore, the interpretivist study of intercultural communication requires intercultural communication. As an interpretivist scholar, Briggs wanted to capture the cultural logic of language use among Mexicanos, but in order to do that he had to communicate with them relying on the Anglo-American speech patterns with which he was familiar. In doing so, Briggs had to deal with the social consequences of situations in which the two cultural systems for communication were at odds.

Intercultural communication scholars respond to this paradox in two ways. One way is that they use qualitative research methodologies that take into account that their chief research instruments are their own social selves and their own communication. The other way is that they learn to become aware of and reflect on the research process as a social encounter between members of two speech communities. Interpretivist approaches are referred to as interpretivist because they place emphasis on capturing how participants of intercultural communication episodes make sense of those episodes. There are two separate but intertwined domains of sense-making involved in the interpretivist research process: the researcher makes sense of how speakers make sense of communicative conduct.

EMIC AND ETIC PERSPECTIVES

The anthropologist Kenneth Pike (1967) created the distinction between *emic* and *etic* to bring scholars' attention to an essential feature of interpretivist research, namely that interpretive frameworks that originated on the outside (etic) and the inside (emic) of the cultural system being studied are distinct but mutually inform one another. Recall approaches discussed in Chapter 13. In the example from the beginning of this chapter, Briggs used the Anglo-American notion of the interview to begin to examine why his respondents were reluctant to answer his questions. Briggs, ultimately, had to treat the interview as an etic category because he could not take for granted that the Mexicanos would recognize this communicative genre. He was also forced to realize that his attempts to conduct interviews violated Mexicano norms for asking questions in order to learn from others. Gaining an understanding of this indigenous system of norms required an emic approach. In his discussion of this experience, Briggs (1986) used his interpretation of Mexicano norms for communication to demonstrate that the Anglo-American interview was just as much a culturally distinctive communicative genre as Córdovan scriptural allusions in pedagogical discourse to a Mexicano.

The interpretivist approach to culture and intercultural communication requires you to move back and forth between etic and emic ways of sense-making. You begin studying the communicative conduct of a speech community with externally conceived (etic) ideas and expectations about how communication works. You then try to make sense of local ways on communal members' terms (this is the emic move); and finally you are able to see your etic ideas in the light of this emic interpretation. Carbaugh and Hastings (1992) refer to the etic ideas interpretivist researchers start with as communication activity theories, the emic understanding of culturally specific communicative practices as situated theories, and the return to your original etic ideas and expectations as evaluation. They caution that this process is by no means linear but cyclical. You can think of using the etic and emic approaches as using a pair of eyes. With the use of both eyes you see more clearly than through one. An interpretivist researcher who incorporates both an emic and etic approach also sees more clearly what is being studied.

REFLECT 14.2: What are the formal or informal activity theories you rely on in your everyday life?

Scholars working in the interpretivist tradition are not interested in viewing themselves as objective natural scientists who strive to minimize their personal involvement in the populations they study by relying on research instruments (e.g., surveys, lab experiments) and complex statistical analytic procedures. Although interpretivist researchers do not deny the value of research instruments and statistics, they call into question the strategy of using these methods to socially distance the researcher from the target population. Instead of trying to minimize their social involvement in the data collection process in the name of objectivity, interpretivist researchers acknowledge their own involvement and interest in their target communities and study the meanings of their communicative practices from that acknowledged position. Imagine a middle-aged male researcher trying to observe communication among children playing on a playground, or a U.S. American scholar, male or female, trying to recruit Taliban insurgents for interviews. They realize the methodological necessity of accepting and carefully studying the nature of interpretivist research as a social encounter in order to achieve reflexivity.

REFLEXIVITY

Reflexivity is the practice of systematic reflection on research as socially situated interaction. To elaborate on the claim that interpretivist research is a reflexive activity, you can use a framework designed by Hymes (1972) for capturing elements of the social context of communicative action. Research is best viewed as a sociocultural activity taking place in particular physical *settings* with particular kinds of *participants* who work toward a variety of *ends* and *goals*. It also consists of a finite range of *acts*, relies on a range of communicative channels or *instruments*, follows a set of *norms*, has a certain *key* or emotional tone, and employs various types of communication or *genres*. In a manner of speaking, the interpretivist researcher exercising reflexivity turns the researcher's own social self into a research instrument. The researcher is professionally *and* personally involved in the data collection process.

Now, consider the example at the beginning of this chapter using Hymes's framework. Briggs needed to exercise reflexivity in order to figure out what went wrong in his interview with his informant. He had to take into account that the interview took place in Córdova (*setting*). In addition, he was a 19-year-old Anglo-American outsider and Mr. Trujillo was an elderly Mexicano (*participants*). Briggs wanted to conduct research and to write publications down the road (*ends*). Mr. Trujillo wanted to exercise his authority as an elder and teach Briggs about what was right and what was wrong (*ends*). Briggs thought he could rely on the communicative act of questioning, while Mr. Trujillo engaged in "scriptural allusions" (*acts*). You get the sense that the emotional tone of Briggs's questions was most likely matter-of-fact and direct, whereas Mr. Trujillo's pedagogical discourse must have sounded much more ceremonial (*key*). The norms they observed in their interaction differed as well. While Briggs held that everyone with the proper academic credentials should be allowed to ask questions and conduct interviews, Mr. Trujillo believed that young people should not ask questions if they wanted to learn about local ways; they should instead imitate those with experience (*norms*). What Briggs was expecting to do with Mr. Trujillo conformed to the communicative genre of interviewing, whereas Mr. Trujillo implemented the genre of pedagogical discourse (*genre*).

The two of them agreed on one thing only: Both used verbal interaction as communicative channel (*instrument*). The example of this research interview demonstrates the potential difficulty of intercultural communication for interpretivist researchers. Briggs's exercise of reflexivity about the interaction aided his ability to understand this difficulty.

RESEARCH METHOD

This section is designed to introduce to you what interpretivist (or qualitative) researchers interested in the cultural aspect of communication do. The research process consists of four overlapping phases: (1) data collection, (2) analysis, (3) interpretation, and (4) presentation or use of findings and claims. Keep in mind that in contrast to the linear presentation of these phases, interpretivist researchers often work on multiple phases at the same time. They may also decide to return to a previous phase in the light of a subsequent one. For example, it is sometimes the case that researchers decide to collect more data when they are not satisfied with their interpretation of how participants make sense of a particular communicative practice.

Photo 14.1   What is your first thought when you see these photos of classrooms? The interpretivist researcher must take a step back from familiar cultural knowledge and their bias to gain an emic perspective on a culture.

Copyright 2010 Bill Edwards.

Data Collection

From the interpretivist perspective, data collection is the principled, rigorous study of a culturally specific system of communication. Data collection must be principled and systematic in two ways. First, data collected in the process of fieldwork need to be documented in the form of field notes, transcripts, and collections of documents. Second, the researcher is required to reflect on the research process in the speech community as a social encounter (Hervik, 1994). This latter requirement of reflexivity is a fundamentally important feature of interpretivist work.

Two techniques that many interpretivist researchers use in the field are participant observation and interviewing. Participant observation requires the researcher to spend time among the people whose ways he or she wants to study, interact with them and, in the process of interaction, develop a sense of the local, cultural knowledge that informs their everyday conduct. Participant observation is more than participation because the researcher painstakingly observes communal members, and it is more than observation because the researcher never pretends to be just a fly on the wall. Participant observers write elaborate field notes in which they document their experiences in the field using a variety of strategies to capture as much of what they see as possible, carefully separating their own impressions from observations. Field notes are sometimes reconstructed from words or phrases that the researcher quickly jotted down in the field to serve as a reminder of important observations. Because such jottings are often scribbled during a quick bathroom break from a corporate meeting, or in the back of a police cruiser while the observed officers are driving over bumpy roads at high speed, making sense of them can take quite a bit of detective work.

Interpretivist researchers also interview communal members in order to collect members' accounts of their experiences and opinions. Interviews fall into five categories or genres (Lindlof & Taylor, 2002): (1) Ethnographic interviews take place in the field and are generally informal and spontaneous. (2) Informant interviews ask savvy key informants to speak about the world around them. (3) Respondent interviews ask any communal member with relevant experience to speak about a particular subject. (4) Narrative interviews involve the elicitation of participants' stories. Finally, (5) focus group interviews involve multiple informants being interviewed simultaneously and allow insight into how members of a speech community reach consensus or disagree about their views.

Meta-Theory

Epistemology

Epistemology, introduced in Chapter 13, is a body of beliefs about how and what you can learn about things that exist in the world. To find out about speech communities' ways of making sense of their everyday experience using language, the interpretivist researcher (or the inter/cultural practitioner) must engage in sense-making. These intertwined sense-making processes give interpretivist epistemology its special character. Following Lindlof and Taylor (2002) you can identify interpretivism's basic epistemological assumptions as follows:

1. Interpretivist research wants to break with the tradition of social science modeled on the natural sciences, in that it does not assume the existence of a single reality and it is not interested in objective accounts of that reality. Rather, it is interested in how particular cultural groups make sense of their experience and create multiple realities together for particular social purposes.

2. Interpretive research should strive to achieve a deep understanding of human actions, motives, and feelings. The researcher should keep in mind that knowledge can only be created from particular perspectives in interaction with those being studied.

3. Reports based on interpretivist research should represent how the target population engages in meaningful social action. Those representations should be used as evidence for their research claims.

Figure 14.1   Linguistic Map for Answers to "What Do You Call an Easy Course?"

Which word do you use? Interpretivist researchers can use multimethod research.

Understanding a speech community can begin with identifying differences in language use as identified in these maps, compiled with 9,500 respondents, and extending to an in-depth ethnography of the lived experience that both motivates and explains these cultural distinctions.

- gut (14.65%)
- crip course (4.98%)
- blow-off (36.57%)
- other (not shown) (43.79%)

gut

crip course

blow-off

Source: Adapted from "Dialect Survey Map and Results." Available at www4.uwm.edu/FLL/linguistics/dialect/maps.html. Copyright 2010 Bert Vaux.

Researchers carefully transcribe their interviews and sound or audio recordings they create in the field. Transcription is a particularly useful source of insight because, once completed, transcripts provide the opportunity for the researcher to delve into the fine details of communicative conduct. The researcher must make careful choices about what to transcribe and transcription symbols. Some researchers are satisfied with capturing all words spoken, others mark pauses, intonation, emphasis, and all *uhs* and *ums*. These types of choices render transcription an act of interpretation (Bird, 2005). As such, interpretivist researchers tend not to rely on public transcripts created by media, political, or business organizations as transparent representations of reality because they have reason to believe that these organizations represent talk in a way that bolsters their reputation and influence (Park & Bucholtz, 2009).

Nonetheless, researchers often analyze records of communicative conduct others have created. These records may include official transcripts and documents, news reports, or other researchers' transcripts, among others. The methodological issue in this case is that the researcher who treats these records as data needs to make an attempt to reconstruct the social position or perspective from which the records were created. What interests shaped a corporation's or a government's official account of its involvement in a catastrophic event? What motivated a news outlet to edit an interview in a particular way? What intellectual or political agenda guided the way another scholar recorded a particular event? This process of reconstruction involves the researcher exercising reflexivity on someone else's (e.g., the corporation's, the government's, etc.) behalf.

Interpretivist researchers tend to rely on four research traditions (ethnography, discourse analysis, rhetorical analysis, phenomenological analysis) when collecting and analyzing communication and interpreting the findings resulting from their research. The appendices to this volume give you a sense of these traditions that interpretivist researchers rely on to make sense of culturally specific communication practices.

Analysis and Interpretation

The discussion of analysis and interpretation are combined in this section because the interpretivist research process often moves back and forth between these two stages. Interpretivist methodological approaches to inter/cultural communication are interested in (1) how language use is meaningful to members of particular speech communities, and (2) what happens when members of different speech communities engage one another in communication, using different systems of communicative resources to achieve their goals. Interpretivists hold that the meaning of communicative conduct is not to be found in words, phrases, sounds, and gestures. Instead, the meaning of spoken or written communication is the result of sense-making, the process of attributing meaning to talk in interaction with others. For example, the word *khawaga* ("foreigner" or "gringo") in Egyptian colloquial Arabic can function as a playful put-down when Egyptians use it to address foreigners, as a term of endearment among Coptic Christians (i.e., members of the Egyptian Christian community), and as a vehicle of discrimination when Egyptian Muslims Orthodox use it to describe Coptic Christians.

Meta-Theory

Ontology

Introduced in Chapter 13, ontology addresses the nature of things in the world. Interpretivists accept that a defining feature of humans is their sense-making through language use. As a result, observable language use can be regarded as the site, and evidence, of human sense-making. Such sense-making, or meaning-giving, will contain universal features and culturally variable resources. For example, telling jokes about a person's own and others' fathers-in-law on Rossell Island in Papua New Guinea will draw on universal features of joke-telling and on the local, cultural logic of matrilineal kinship system (Levinson, 2005).

Analysis is the process of breaking up and categorizing a person's experience of communication in an unfamiliar speech community using emergent analytic categories. Analysis ensures that the analyst is distanced from preconceived culturally specific notions about how communication works and focuses on communication *as communal members understand it*. It is the process of putting together the analytic categories into a coherent whole, an interpretation of a speech community's ways of speaking.

For example, a researcher may take the transcript of a conversation where speakers from two different speech communities seem to have trouble understanding the other's intentions. The researcher could analyze the conversation by identifying particular lines where speakers display lack of understanding or confusion, and describing how, in each instance, participants end up being at cross purposes. Interpretation may entail explaining why, from the perspective of the communicative norms of each speaker, the other seemed to violate those norms. This is what Kenneth Liberman (1990) did when he tried to understand why Aboriginals of Australia's Western Desert had so much trouble communicating according to Anglo-Australian expectations in a courtroom setting. He noticed that Aboriginal defendants attempted to voice agreement with the Anglo judge at every turn of the conversation regardless of what the judge's question was. Based on his study of Aboriginal ways of speaking, Liberman was able to explain that Aboriginal defendants were observing a central communicative norm of their speech community: In a public meeting, in order to settle a matter of dispute a person should work toward communitywide consensus, not disagreement.

Defining Elements of Interpretivist Analysis

All interpretivist approaches share three unique defining elements: (1) rich points, (2) abduction, and (3) the multiple overdetermination of pattern (Agar, 1999, 2004). Rich points are moments in a person's experience in a speech community that feature intense surprise and confusion and a similarly intense sense of fascination. Interpretivists use these moments as invitations to study the cultural system they understand only partially, or not at all, and use these to

Photo 14.2 What belongings make you think of your family? Like souvenirs from other cultures, family treasures are not just objects but also remind us of what our families mean to us and represent for us. Regardless of culture, family often means strength, support, food, and education. Cultural artifacts like this quilt made with family photos can be studied to find out about cultural values.

Copyright 2011 Terrence F. Wilburg.

move beyond the limitation of their etic perspective. Rich points can occur in entirely mundane and unexpected moments of communication. A rich point Mike Agar (1994) experienced involved him standing at the door of his apartment in Austria at 7 a.m., trying to figure out why a man with an official badge was asking him to pay his electricity bill in cash. This moment prompted Agar, who was born and raised in the United States, to investigate the differences between the U. S. American and Austrian systems of banking and utility payment. Such reflection helped him understand the confusing communicative situation he had experienced as a rich point.

Abduction, one of three modes of reasoning along with deduction and induction, is the process of identifying underlying cultural assumptions about the local meaning of communicative conduct. Inter/cultural researchers or practitioners like yourself rarely have the luxury to patiently wait until they have accumulated enough observations to make strong claims about the meaning of seemingly strange communicative conduct and about underlying premises that make them meaningful. Instead, they formulate, test, and refine premises as they go along. In essence, abduction refers to a process in which you encounter strange behavior that you feel you must make sense of in the moment (observation or rich point), you try to understand the communicative conduct you have just witnessed from the community's perspective (conclusion), and you also try to guess what they must believe for their conduct to seem meaningful *to them* (premise). Abduction feeds into the process of induction.

Induction involves reasoning from observations toward conclusions based on established premises. Inductive reasoning asks the question: Does the cultural premise I have identified make communicative conduct meaningful from the community's perspective? Inductive reasoning in interpretivist research requires the researcher to observe particular acts of communication first and then reach a conclusion about their meaning on the basis of an underlying cultural premise. Induction, however, can only work together with abduction (Agar, 1999). In contrast, deduction involves reasoning from established premises toward their logical consequences. The use of hypotheses for the purpose of making predictions about behavior, the analytic procedure typical of social scientific research as discussed in Chapter 13, involves deductive reasoning. Deductive and inductive logic share a common feature, namely that in both types of reasoning the premises remain unchanged.

REFLECT 14.3: What relationship do you see between stereotyping and the process of abduction? Should this be of concern to interpretivist researchers? If you were an interpretivist researcher how might you handle this issue when approaching your study?

Interpretation can stop when the researcher achieves the multiple overdetermination of pattern, that is, when the researcher is able to confirm, on the basis of multiple data sources (e.g., interviews with multiple respondents, recordings, documents, etc.) and inductive reasoning that the cultural premise (i.e., norm, belief) used in the interpretation can be regarded as accurate. Interpretation is complete when rich points no longer occur. These interpretations constitute the research findings of the study. These findings sometimes provide researchers opportunities to critically evaluate the activity theories they brought to the research project.

Returning to Briggs provides an example of these three defining elements of an interpretivist approach. In Briggs's case, the rich point he experienced was that an older interviewee was not willing to provide direct answers to direct interview questions. Briggs had to gradually establish a set of premises or cultural beliefs and norms to make sense of this observation and to conduct productive research in Córdova. Upon entry into the community, he experienced a rich point that made no sense to him because he could not point to a cultural premise in the light of which the rich point could make sense. As a result, he had a hard time getting his research project off the ground. As time passed, however, he engaged in abduction through which he was able to formulate a premise that represented the community's point of view. As you have already seen in the introduction to this chapter, he observed that young members of the community were not expected to learn about communal ways by asking questions; rather, they were expected to imitate more experienced community members. Knowing this, his informants' resistance to questions began to make sense to Briggs and, as a result of the inductive testing of the premise, he could be sure that his interpretation of a Mexicano belief about appropriate ways of learning and asking questions was true. Equally important, he could finally conduct productive research and pursue the multiple overdetermination of pattern.

**LIVING
CULTURE**

Community Living   *Brad Crownover*

College of Mount Saint Vincent

A few years ago, I completed an ethnographic case study of a group of mostly Latino men residing in a care-giving facility for people living with HIV/AIDS. I considered this an excellent place to study the kinds of communication practices that perhaps establish a sense of community among a group of people. It never occurred to me that maybe I wouldn't find community. The limitation I created for myself as a researcher was in how I let the commonalities shared by those living together in this unique situation establish for me a kind of myth of community. Here was a group of men living, eating, celebrating, and mourning together in a location that was spatially and culturally isolated. The men shared a language and in some cases, even, a common nationality. Not to mention the men shared a common health crisis. Taken on the surface, these commonalities seemed to initially suggest that the site and the people I studied would be a good place to start if one wanted to find a sense of community.

Instead, what my study revealed were some deeply rooted cultural tensions around masculinity and what it means to be known as having HIV/AIDS. Direct and indirect negative communication involving these tensions overwhelmed the positive communication that arguably could have been evidenced at the research site. So while the commonalities of being male, having a shared language, and experiencing a health crisis brought the men together physically, ultimately, these commonalities only served to force a group of men into interaction who otherwise would have probably avoided direct contact. For example, living in this common place forced many men to have to deal with problems of being "seen" as someone who is gay, whether or not it was the case. For many of the men this was something they had actively avoided for most of their lives. Although it is not my intent to blanket all of Hispanic/Latino culture, the definition of what it means to be a man in this culture hasn't exactly extended to include being gay as a qualification.

Perhaps even more crippling than this, though, was the fear and stigma that some of the men attached to their HIV status and being known as having the disease. Most of the men I interviewed had not told their families and friends about their HIV-positive status. This was rooted in their very real fears of losing whatever support they were getting out of these relationships, a fear of further stigmatization and a fear of being seen as less than a man both because of the disease and because they could be perceived as having broken with cultural rules of what it means to be a

LIVING CULTURE

man. The majority of the men I interacted with were attempting to get away from a cultural experience, which more often than not, reinforced that they had little or no value in the broader Latino community, expressly as a result of their HIV-positive status.

As I began to draw conclusions from my study, I found that the commonalities the men experienced through culture also framed and impeded communication around the following: (1) sexuality; (2) masculinity; and (3) shame associated with being gay, being perceived as being gay, having HIV/AIDS, or being perceived as having HIV/AIDS. All of this is captured in the following exchange between three residents I recorded in my field notes:

One night, I was sitting and talking to a couple of residents in the dining room. As Silvio came into the room, two residents I was speaking to began teasing him by calling him "El Macho." Silvio didn't seem to mind this nickname. The four of us talked as a group for a short while and then the conversation took an abrupt turn. One of the residents, Alejandro, began to question how Silvio had contracted HIV. The conversation turned so quickly and intensified at such a quick pace that I was only able to capture the core of what was being said. What I was absolutely sure of, by the words that Alejandro was choosing and the way in which he was speaking to Silvio, was that he was accusing Silvio of looking down on "maricónes" (best translation in this circumstance = faggots) and that Silvio had no right to do so since he had contracted HIV by having sex with a man. The third resident remained silent, but looked on with what I would describe as a smirk.

After the initial turn in the conversation, the talk slowed down a bit and Alejandro kept driving his general point home to Silvio that he had no right to see himself as above gay men. The third resident occasionally would reinforce something that Alejandro said by making a similar comment. Silvio remained in the dining room, but moved around the room to get coffee and to take something out of the refrigerator. After a short while of this, Silvio left the room. In writing my fieldnotes immediately following the event, I couldn't recall anything that Silvio directly said to defend himself. Reflecting on this exchange, it seemed as if Silvio used movement to deflect what he was being said to him.

Once Silvio left the room, the other two residents began talking about Silvio and whether or not they thought he was gay. A short time later, Silvio returned only to leave again. Perhaps Silvio's return to the dining room was evidence of him attempting to stop others from gossiping about him.

(Continued)

LIVING CULTURE

(Continued)

I saw this situation involving Silvio and the two other residents as capturing what I had begun to see as a deeply complex and personal tension among residents to maintain an individual identity against direct and indirect pressure to accept a group identity. In this circumstance, Silvio seemed to be identified by some residents as reflective of what some of the men in the group were: men who have sex with men but who will not admit it.

To my sincere disappointment, communication in this care-giving facility for people living with HIV/AIDS functioned largely as a way to impede the construction of community among the men I studied. A sense of community could have been an invaluable care-giving tool.

Consider:

1. What do you think about the author's ideas related to there being the potential for a "myth of community?" How do you think this added to researcher bias, if at all?

2. What did the author mean when he wrote that "direct and indirect negative communication . . . overwhelmed positive communication"? What do you think of this idea?

3. What can we glean from the description of Silvio's nonverbal communication in the field note excerpt?

4. In what ways does the researcher demonstrate the validity on his study, discussed in brief here?

Presentation and Use of Findings and Claims

As a result of the analysis and interpretation of data, researchers have two ways to make use of their findings and claims. They can present them to the audiences of their choice, such as fellow researchers, students of culture and communication, or larger, popular audiences, and they can use them in interaction with members of the speech communities they study.

Van Maanen (1988) distinguishes four kinds of "tales" interpretivist researchers tell to report their findings and claims. Realist tales present the researcher as an all-seeing and all-knowing objective observer who reports on the details of the ways of cultural others. Objectivism in the realist tale does not mean that the researcher claims to be a completely objective observer in the field. No interpretivist researcher would claim that today.

Objectivism in the realist tale means that the researcher minimizes the discussion of the researcher's own involvement in the field and instead focuses on reporting observations. Confessional tales include explicit reflection on the difficulties, dilemmas and complexity inherent in the fieldwork process and show the researcher at work. Briggs's account of his frustrating initial interviews is an example of a confessional tale. Impressionist tales tend to purposely violate the conventions of realist tales and flirt with the conventions of literary genres like fiction and poetry. Impressionist tales contain plotlines, interesting characters, stylistic flair, intrigue, and drama. Finally, critical tales report the plight of those on the margins of society and critically evaluate social structures that create inequality and injustice. Researchers often blend these four forms of representation in their research reports.

Findings about culture and intercultural communication often have practical value in that they help cultural outsiders do a better job interacting with members of a given speech community. Some U. S. colleges and universities, for example, rely on intercultural communication research to design orientations for international and study abroad students. This practice-oriented view of culture leads to two important realizations. First, interpretivist research is closely modeled on the way people make sense of their experience on a daily basis. When communicating with people whom you view as cultural others you often run into surprises, try to come up with explanations for why they act the way they do, and look across various conversations to make sure that you have your explanation right. When interpretivists talk about rich points, abduction, and multiply overdetermined patterns, they are turning the basic facets of everyday experience into rigorous research methodology. Second, because of the strong relationship between interpretivist research methods and everyday sense-making strategies, interpretivist findings can be used to inform your interactions with cultural others. For example, Briggs's study of qualitative interviewing can function as a useful reminder to all intercultural practitioners that there can be innumerable reasons why members of another speech community are reluctant to directly answer your questions about local ways of life. Their reluctance may not necessarily be a sign of their dislike for you or their unwillingness to engage with you but rather the sign of incompatible cultural ideals about proper ways to communicate.

REFLECT 14.4: Based on your personality, preferences, and viewpoints, would you be more comfortable studying intercultural communication using a social scientific approach or interpretivist approach? Why?

ETHICAL CONSIDERATIONS FOR INTERPRETIVISTS

Social scientific and interpretivist scholarship share a concern with many of the same ethical issues (see Chapter 13 for the discussion of issues such as consent, debriefing, anonymity, confidentiality, and participant safety). In addition, ethical interpretivist research strives to achieve two ends: to engage with members of the community in an ethically principled manner, and to shape the social consequentiality of their research. There are a number of organizations tasked with making sure that interpretivist researchers engage with the communities they study in an ethical manner, such as professional associations and institutional review boards. These organizations tend to require that the researcher be open about the goals, methods, and outcomes of the research toward communal members, and protect respondents or informants by granting them anonymity and confidentiality.

However, it is not always the case that the researcher can be completely open about the methods used, and sometimes even needs the protection of communal members. In his account of doing fieldwork among street children in Port-au-Prince, Haiti, the anthropologist J. Christopher Kovats-Bernat (2002) tells how he sometimes needed to leave his shirt untucked to give the impression that he was carrying a concealed weapon, and how he relied on street children's local knowledge to ensure his own and his research assistant's personal safety. Kovats-Bernat writes:

> I applied a *localized ethic* . . . I took stock of the good advice and recommendations of the local population in deciding what conversations (and silences) were important, what information was too costly to life and limb to get to, the amount of exposure to violence considered acceptable, the questions that were dangerous to ask, and the patterns of behavior that were important to follow for the safety and security of myself and those around me. (p. 7, emphasis in original)

Most interpretivist scholars intend their research to make a difference in the world, but they often disagree about the ways in which interpretivist research on culture and communication can, or should, make a difference. You can get a good sense of this debate from an exchange that took place between critical media scholar John Fiske and ethnographers of communication Gerry Philipsen and Donal Carbaugh. These three scholars confronted the issue of the influence of ethnographic research in the world on the pages of the U.S. American scholarly communication journal *Quarterly Journal of Speech* (Carbaugh, 1991; Fiske, 1990, 1991; Philipsen, 1991). Fiske proposed that the objective of the cultural researcher should be to point out examples of injustice and inequality in modern industrialized societies. Carbaugh and Philipsen responded by arguing that a researcher approaching a target speech community with the intent to identify injustice was making an assumption that might lead to misinterpretations as discussed in Chapter 10. What if communal members do not make sense of their own life experience as an example of injustice? The main objective of cultural research, they suggested, was to explicate the meanings communal members ascribe to their own communication practices. The critical approach Fiske represents sets out to bring about social change. Carbaugh and Philipsen call upon interpretivist researchers to represent complex social worlds on the terms of those who populate them, and to contribute to existing knowledge about how social worlds work. This disagreement points to two ethically informed modes of thinking about the role of research in the world.

researchers have a variety of technologies and methodologies at their disposal, all experiences in the field are inevitably filtered through the researcher's senses, prior experience, expectations, ambitions, and theoretical preferences. This means that interpretivist researchers cannot simply ask or hire others to administer a survey questionnaire, which requires their extensive training.

Resources

Fieldwork and analysis consume large amounts of time and money. Interpretivist researchers working in distant lands often cannot afford or have the time to return to the field to conduct additional fieldwork or member checks. Without unlimited resources, researchers make decisions about which resources are needed and how these may best be used to ensure the quality of the study. As such, choices are made that may also limit the study.

Access

Some communities are easier to gain access to than others that may be more difficult to penetrate. Conducting fieldwork among affluent, influential, or otherwise privileged groups of people (e.g., in corporations) can be difficult, and sometimes impossible. Similarly, stigmatized communities (such as gangs) may provide limited or no access. This may affect how thoroughly and how well communities can be represented in the research results.

FINAL THOUGHTS

At the end of this chapter a question that may be on your mind is this: Can I ever become a successful inter/cultural practitioner if I don't receive extensive training in qualitative methods? The answer is yes because you can benefit from appreciating the differences between the inter/cultural researcher and practitioner.

A difference between an interpretivist researcher and an inter/cultural practitioner like you is tacit and explicit knowledge of communicative practices (Tracy, 2002). Tacit knowledge is the knowledge you already possess that allows you to communicate. Explicit knowledge helps you reflect on how you have achieved interactional ends using communicative resources. Explicit knowledge also enables you to teach communicative practices and strategies to others. For example, you may already be able to grasp intuitively an unfamiliar speech community's ways of speaking. With the help of concepts used in inter/cultural communication research you may now be able to articulate how you have achieved that knowledge in interaction with communal members.

An additional difference is that interpretivist research has accumulated a sizeable body of knowledge about sense-making techniques. As an inter/cultural practitioner, you can borrow from the researcher's toolkit and use those tools to your advantage. The next time you ask questions from members of an unfamiliar speech community and you are struggling to get direct answers, think about Briggs and Mr. Trujillo.

CONTINUE YOUR JOURNEY ONLINE

Visit: http://www.military.org

Military.org. This site provides an online community so that "30 million Americans with military affinity stay connected and informed." As you explore the vast resources at this site, make observations about what this cultural community is like. Think about how you would conduct a study of this community using an interpretivist approach. What would be some difficulties that might arise in conducting an interpretivist study of this community?

REVIEW QUESTIONS

1. Based on the discussion of interpretivist research at the start of the chapter, why is it valuable to study speech communities in order to understand inter/cultural communication?

2. According to the chapter, how is data collection "principled and systematic" in interpretivist research?

3. When was the last time you experienced a rich point? What happened? How do rich points relate to interpretivist study of inter/cultural communication?

4. Name five ways discussed in the chapter in which an interpretivist research project's validity can be spoiled. Why is each important to be aware of when studying inter/cultural communication?

5. Compare and contrast issues of ontology and epistemology discussed in the textboxes in this chapter and in Chapter 13.

6. Name three of the ethical issues discussed in the chapter. Explain why these are necessary considerations for a researcher. Why might these sometimes be difficult to handle when conducting inter/cultural research?

7. What are some limitations of an interpretivist approach, especially for the study of inter/cultural communication?

8. Why does the chapter stress the importance of understanding that the researcher is an instrument in interpretivist research?

9. Select one case study that takes an interpretivist approach from the appendices. Analyze the case study based on the description of the interpretivist research process discussed in this chapter. Incorporate issues of data collection, analysis and interpretation, and presentation or use of findings and claims.

10. Studying one's own culture using interpretivist methods can be more difficult than studying a culture in which the researcher is not a member. Based on what you have learned about interpretivist methods in the chapter, do you think this is so? Why?

KEY TERMS

abduction   316

communication
    activity theory   309

confessional tale   321

critical tales   321

deduction   317

ethnographic interview   312

explicit knowledge   325

field notes   312

focus group interview   312

impressionist tale   321

induction   317

informant interview   312

interpretivist research   308

member check   323

multiple overdetermination
    of pattern   317

narrative interview   312

participant observation   312

realist tale   320

reflexivity   310

respondent
    interview   312

rich point   315

sense-making   314

tacit knowledge   325

transcribe   314

triangulation   324

REFERENCES

Agar, M. (1994). The intercultural frame. *International Journal of Intercultural Relations, 18,* 221–237.

Agar, M. (1999). How to ask for a study in Qualitatish. *Qualitative Health Research, 9,* 684–697.

Agar, M. (2004). Know when to hold 'em, know when to fold 'em: Qualitative thinking outside the university. *Qualitative Health Research, 14,* 100–112.

Bird, C. M. (2005). How I stopped dreading and learned to love transcription. *Qualitative Inquiry, 11,* 226–248.

Briggs, C. L. (1986). *Learning how to ask: A sociolinguistic appraisal of the role of the interview in social science research.* Cambridge, UK: Cambridge University Press.

Carbaugh, D. (1991). Communication and cultural interpretation. *Quarterly Journal of Speech, 77,* 336–342.

Carbaugh, D., & Hastings, S. O. (1992). A role for communication in ethnography and cultural analysis. *Communication Theory, 2,* 156–165.

Chen, V., & Pearce, W. B. (1995). Even if a thing of beauty, can a case study be a joy forever? In W. Leeds-Hurwitz (Ed.), *Social approaches to communication* (pp. 135–154). New York: Guilford Press.

Fiske, J. (1990). Review of *Talking American: Cultural discourses on Donahue,* by Donal Carbaugh. *Quarterly Journal of Speech, 76,* 450–451.

Fiske, J. (1991). Writing ethnographies: Contribution to a dialogue. *Quarterly Journal of Speech, 77,* 330–335.

Geertz, C. (1983). *Local knowledge: Further essays in interpretive anthropology.* New York: Basic Books.

Hervik, P. (1994). Shared reasoning in the field: Reflexivity beyond the author. In K. Hastrup & P. Hervik (Eds.), *Social experience and anthropological knowledge* (pp. 78–100). Boston: Routledge.

Hymes, D. (1972). Models of the interaction of language and social life. In J. J. Gumperz & D. Hymes (Eds.), *Directions in sociolinguistics: The ethnography of communication* (pp. 35–71). New York: Holt, Rinehart and Winston.

Kovats-Bernat, J. C. (2002). Negotiating dangerous fields: Pragmatic strategies for fieldwork amid violence and terror. *American Anthropologist, 104,* 1–15.

Levinson, S. C. (2005). Living with Manny's dangerous idea. *Discourse Studies, 7,* 431–453.

Liberman, K. (1990). Intercultural communication in Central Australia. In D. Carbaugh (ed.), *Cultural communication and intercultural contact* (pp. 177–183). Hillsdale, NJ: Lawrence Erlbaum.

Lindlof, T. R., & Taylor, B. C. (2002). *Qualitative communication research methods.* Thousand Oaks, CA: Sage.

Park, J. S.-Y., & Bucholtz, M. (2009). Introduction. Public transcripts: Entextualization and linguistic representation in institutional contexts. *Text & Talk, 29,* 485–502.

Philipsen, G. (1991). Two issues in the evaluation of ethnographic studies of communicative practices. *Quarterly Journal of Speech, 77,* 327–329.

Pike, K. L. (1967). *Language in relation to a unified theory of the structure of human behavior.* The Hague, Paris: Mouton & Co.

Taylor, B. C., & Trujillo, N. (2001). Qualitative research methods. In F. Jablin & L. Putnam (Eds.), *The new handbook of organizational communication* (pp. 161–194). Newbury Park, CA: Sage.

Tracy, K. (2002). *Everyday talk: Building and reflecting identities.* New York: Guilford Press.

Van Maanen, J. (1988). *Tales of the field: On writing ethnography.* Chicago: University of Chicago Press.

Challenges and Opportunities in Inter/Cultural Communication

Anastacia Kurylo

Marymount Manhattan College

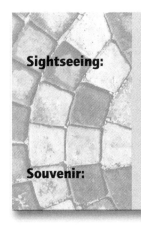

Journey Through Chapter 15

Sightseeing: On your journey, you will visit with some challenges and opportunities presented by inter/cultural communication regardless of whether you view culture as representation or construction. Relevant concepts and theories associated with these challenges and opportunities will be discussed, including relational empathy, which is offered as a response to these challenges.

Souvenir: After your journey, you will take away greater insight into and motivation for inter/cultural communication and your role within it as an agent for change.

The future of inter/cultural communication looks surprisingly similar to the past. Although new technologies have developed to facilitate, or hinder, inter/cultural communication, inter/cultural communication practitioners will continue to face many of the same challenges. It is important to understand these challenges in order to appreciate and navigate inter/cultural communication no matter what method of communication is used. This chapter emphasizes concepts relevant to challenges faced by inter/cultural communication practitioners. A discussion of relational empathy complements the chapter's discussion of these issues. In addition, the future of inter/cultural communication continues to provide many of the same opportunities as in the past. The chapter discusses these as well. The chapter concludes with a discussion of the important role you play in the future of inter/cultural communication.

REFLECT 15.1: What do you think the future of inter/cultural communication will look like? How will it change? How will it stay the same? Why?

CHALLENGES

The challenges to inter/cultural communication that this section discusses are too often easily overlooked and, yet, integral to any inter/cultural practitioner. Among these challenges are reductionism, the assumption of differences, functions of prejudice, and the communication of privilege. Although each of these presents a challenge, having awareness of each will help you navigate your inter/cultural interactions.

Reductionism

Inter/cultural communication practitioners often seek information to familiarize themselves with a culture. Although various options are available to find information about a culture, the Internet may be the most accessible way to find information because it allows for easier production of and access to an enormous of amount information on nearly any topic. The information that a person walks away with after such a search, however, may represent only a small portion of all the various issues related to that topic. Searching the Internet is a metaphor for how people search for information about a culture in general. Such searches present a challenge for inter/cultural practitioners because they promote reductionism. In reductionism, people reduce complex and vast amounts of information about a culture to smaller chunks of information in a way that is presumed to reflect the essence of that culture.

For example, if you perform an Internet search about a culture, you are likely to get millions of pages of hits referencing websites discussing that culture. For example, searching for "Dominican Republic" produced 298 million hits. How many of these would you search through? Likely, you would limit yourself to the first few pages of hits so that you can get the basic idea of the information available on the most popular sites about this country. This process is necessarily selective. As a result of this selectivity, the information you take away from that search may reflect only the most unique, interesting, obvious, or often repeated information about the culture rather than a representative sample of the information available and relevant to your interest in the culture. Although the results of your search might seem to give you the essence of relevant information, they would not necessarily represent the most relevant or useful information about the culture.

Sorting through the vast amount of information on cultural groups, the variety of sources of information, and determining their credibility can be overwhelming. Information processing theory explains that people have a limited cognitive capacity to process information and, so, they process information in selective ways (e.g., Fiske & Taylor, 1984). In addition to limited cognitive resources, a person's ability to process information is limited by time, energy, and access. All of these make it difficult to weed through information, think critically about it, and measure it against preconceptions. As a result of these limitations, people only access a small amount of all the possible information available at any given time about a culture.

Reducing information in this way, however, is *not* inherently problematic. To the contrary, as information processing theory articulates, reducing information is a necessary process, albeit a biased one. It is a result of the bias used to select information that reductionism can occur.

Because people have limited cognitive capacity, resources, time, energy, and access, a search for information about a culture is not typically an exhaustive search. Instead, people often stop looking for information once they find enough to verify what they already think they know about a topic rather than moving forward to critically analyze information and seek out additional information. In doing so, people reaffirm their original conclusions and produce hypothesis confirming information (Hamilton, Sherman, & Ruvolo, 2000). When hypothesis confirmation is based on a person's stereotypes about a cultural group, reductionism is particularly problematic because it not only provides a selective and essentialized view of the culture, but it may reinforce inaccurate preconceptions about the culture as well.

Despite much psychology research during the 1930s, scholars did not find conclusive evidence that stereotypes are accurate (e.g., Katz & Braly, 1933; LaPiere, 1936). Instead, the findings of these studies more often suggest that stereotypes provide an inaccurate, and therefore false, basis for decision making (e.g., Hinton, 2000; Judd & Park, 1993). As a result, most scholars abandoned the quest to determine stereotype accuracy and resigned themselves to the conclusion that people use stereotypes because they *think* stereotypes are accurate, not because they *are* accurate. This is not to say that all stereotypes are inaccurate; but in general most people would have no basis for claiming stereotypes are accurate given that even scientists are unable to do so.

Reductionism presents a challenge for inter/cultural practitioners who wish to find out information about a culture because it hampers a person's ability to understand, appreciate, and experience the complexity of cultural groups. When reductionism is based in stereotype, the result can be particularly detrimental for the inter/cultural practitioner. This is because it would sacrifice a more complicated view of a culture in favor of an essentialized and inaccurate representation of that culture. Awareness of the limits of information processing and the problem of reductionism can help inter/cultural practitioners to overcome this challenge.

Assumption of Differences

Another challenge for inter/cultural practitioners is their assumption of differences. A focus on cultural differences has dominated inter/cultural communication research for a long time. In general, inter/cultural communication researchers have also prioritized intergroup differences over intergroup similarities. A focus on differences seems reasonable. After all, if people assume that all cultures are the same, they may overlook the variability between cultures that can cause miscommunication or conflict. For example, being aware of and appreciating differences can be particularly helpful to alleviate culture shock or the anxiety a person may feel when they have entered a new cultural environment, as discussed in Chapter 6. Barna (1998) even argues that assuming similarities is a stumbling block in inter/cultural communication and that people need to understand and appreciate each other and their differences in order to "exchange ideas and information, find ways to live and work together, or just make the kind of impression we want to make" (p. 174).

However, the assumption that differences between cultures matter above all else has become an obsession that has hampered Barna's larger goal of treating "each encounter as an individual case, searching for whatever perceptions and communication means are held in common and proceed[ing] from there" (p. 174). Although appreciating differences is a practical way to approach inter/cultural communication, it can also provide a challenge for inter/cultural practitioners. Imagine how overwhelming it would be to have a conversation with someone from a different culture, which can arguably mean every conversation, if you assumed that the other person was different from you. If you assume differences matter in each intercultural interaction, merely approaching someone to talk could be an unbearably stressful situation. Instead, being provisional throughout inter/cultural interactions is an important way to respond to this challenge. Inter/cultural practitioners may benefit from being flexible and open in conversation while having an awareness of the possibility that differences (or similarities) may (or may not) matter.

Functions of Prejudice

When people talk about inter/cultural communication, the topic of prejudice is often discussed. It may not be surprising to you, then, to learn that prejudice is a challenge faced by inter/cultural practitioners. However, in addition to prejudice itself, what is *not* often discussed is the benefit people gain or "functions" served from holding and communicating prejudice. In an effort to understand the practical reasons that might account for why people are prejudiced, Brislin (2000) based on Katz (1960) articulates four functions of prejudice.

1. The utilitarian function of prejudice suggests that people use prejudice to gain intrinsic rewards (e.g., greater self-esteem) or extrinsic rewards (e.g., profit).

2. The knowledge function of prejudice suggests that prejudice aids in information processing because stereotypes help filter information.

3. The ego defensive function of prejudice suggests that people use prejudice to protect their sense of who they are by being aggressive toward outgroup members.

4. The value expressive function of prejudice suggests that people use prejudice to view their ingroups as ethically and morally superior to other groups.

Considering these four benefits that people gain from being prejudiced, it is not surprising that there is prejudice in the world. Inter/cultural practitioners, just like anyone else, benefit from being prejudiced. Therefore, inter/cultural practitioners face the challenge of needing to look beyond the benefits they gain from having prejudices against outgroup members and their preferences for ingroup members (see Figure 15.1).

One way to do so is to see the benefits of diversity. For example, large corporations like American Express, Ernst & Young, and Avon have taken initiative in this area by hiring diversity and inclusion specialists as part of their human resource management teams. In doing so, these corporations demonstrate that they appreciate the benefits of a diverse work force. By valuing heterogeneity, these corporations allow a broader range of ideas to emerge that can give their company a competitive edge in the marketplace. Rather than allowing prejudice to guide inter/cultural communication, inter/cultural communication practitioners can choose to view members of other cultures as valuable contributors to their conversations, personal and professional lives, and society more broadly.

Figure 15.1   Depiction of the Inherent Difficulty in Shifting Between Ingroups and Outgroups. What is depicted in this cartoon? Ingroup favoritism and outgroup prejudice. The process of ingrouping and outgrouping looks cute when performed by stick figures but less so when it involves people. This process is not likely to change in the future.

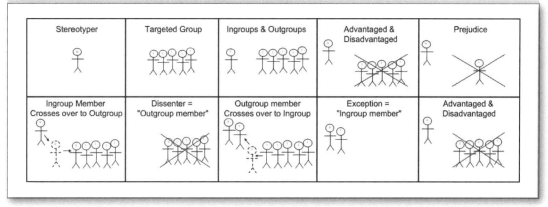

Copyright 2011 Anastacia Kurylo.

REFLECT 15.2: What way do you use stereotypes, prejudice, and discrimination in your life? How might you change this in the future, if at all?

Communicating Privilege

As discussed in Chapter 8, people regularly communicate privilege without realizing it. In doing so, they inadvertently reproduce and reinforce the power that dominant groups have over marginalized group members. Asking, "So do you have a boyfriend?" to a female with whom you are trying to make friends even though you do not know her sexual orientation treats heterosexuality as the norm. Similarly, the doctor in the narrative titled, "New Jersey" in Chapter 7 communicates that his patient is a foreigner, without knowing this to be the case, by asking, "So, what brought you to this country?" A challenge for even the most well-intentioned and open-minded inter/cultural practitioners is that they can perpetuate privilege without realizing they are doing so.

Consider the following excerpt from Mary Jane Collier, an inter/cultural communication scholar, about her experience with privilege:

At hotels where we stay for our academic conferences, I have not once been asked whether I could fetch some extra towels or quickly clean a particular room, whereas several of my female colleagues of color do get asked such questions. (as cited in Collier, Hegde, Lee, Nakayama, & Yep, 2002, p. 258)

Although mistaken identity can occur when people wear clothes that resemble the uniforms worn by employees, the mistaken identity in Collier's story is more problematic because unlike clothing, skin color can not be easily altered. The way privilege is communicated, whether the privileged group represents class, sexual orientation, gender, race, and so forth, is a challenge for inter/cultural communication because it is subtle, taken-for-granted, and easily overlooked. The subtle way in which privilege creeps into behavior can be more insidious, powerful, and hurtful than overt behavior, which is more easily identified and dismissed. Inter/cultural practitioners who are mindful of the way their behavior may unintentionally reproduce privilege may more easily navigate inter/cultural interaction.

Reductionism, the assumption of differences, functions of prejudice, and the communication of privilege are challenges that inter/cultural practitioners can overcome. An exemplar of this is the story of Keshia Thomas, an 18-year-old Black woman from Ann Arbor in Michigan. In 1996, she used her body to protect a man wearing a jacket with a confederate flag at a Klu Klux Klan rally. He was being beaten with sticks by a crowd of anti–Klu Klux Klan demonstrators (Worklan, 1996). In doing so, Thomas overcame each of these challenges and created a third culture, a concept introduced in Chapter 10, in which race, even in what seemed to be an inherently racial context, was not relevant.

CONFRONTING CHALLENGES THROUGH RELATIONAL EMPATHY

With so many difficult challenges to deal with, it would be easy for the inter/cultural communicator to become discouraged or disheartened. Fortunately, there are many ways to overcome the obstacles that people face in communicating in inter/cultural situations. Although it requires effort, you can minimize the temptation of reductionism, overcome the assumption of difference, reduce prejudice, and become more aware of how you communicate privilege. If you can meet these challenges effectively, it will enable you to take advantage of the many opportunities offered by inter/cultural communication. Before those opportunities are presented, consider some of the principles that need to govern communicative behavior in inter/cultural situations.

Benjamin Broome, an intercultural communication scholar who has many years of experience working with a variety of conflicts around the world, proposed a concept called relational empathy, which enables people to engage perceived cultural differences by creating shared meaning between communicators (Broome, 2009). You are probably familiar with the traditional concept of empathy, which asks you to put yourself in the place of the other person when taking action or responding to messages. Although the decentering and perspective taking involved in empathy are critical aspects of any form of communication or relationship with others, it is difficult to enact them in intercultural situations. In fact, by treating culturally different others as you would like to be treated by them you may easily fall prey to the very reductionism, prejudice, and hidden communication of privilege that you are trying to avoid. That is because your own experience is not usually an accurate gauge in culturally unfamiliar situations. What might be good for you could be disrespectful or even damaging for the other.

Relational empathy goes beyond the traditional edict to "place yourself in the place of the other," emphasizing instead the creation of a third culture in the intercultural encounter. This third culture is a set of understandings and norms for communicating that may not have existed before in either of the cultural orientations brought to the encounter by the participants. Rather than each person relying on their own understandings about the perspective of the other, they can engage in dialogue that allows them to create a mutually shared set of meanings from which they can draw as they communicate with one another. By focusing on the creation of a third culture, people can avoid most of the pitfalls presented by the challenges discussed in the previous section. Consider more closely the following set of five principles that guide relational empathy.

Understanding Is a Dynamic Process

A person can have no direct knowledge of another's inner world, and can never be totally accurate in interpreting what another person is thinking or feeling. Through relational empathy, people participate in creating the understandings that come to exist between them during the conversation they have with another person. Learning about another person or about another culture is not so much a search for "truth" as it is a process, one that is ongoing, with new knowledge emerging during the intercultural encounter itself. In this way, the learning process is always in flux and new knowledge must be integrated with current knowledge. Keeping yourself constantly open to new learning is a challenging but rewarding process. Intercultural encounters are full of surprises, and while more energy is required than during encounters with familiar friends, the potential for growth is high.

Embracing Differences Promotes Learning

Although cultural differences can sometimes seem insurmountable, they are often good opportunities for learning—about yourself, about the other, and about new and interesting aspects of culture. However, such learning does not happen on it own, and relational empathy is particularly important when there are significant differences between the subjective worlds of the participants. Relational empathy reduces your tendency to judge others by your own feelings, choices, and preferences. It allows you to communicate on a deeper level and apprehend the other person more completely. For example, discussion about race can foster inter/ cultural understanding provided communicators are willing to steer through, rather than around, the potential conflict that may arise from doing so. By producing shared meaning, discussants can both come to understand better the issues surrounding race and the experience of race by each other.

Cognition and Affect Are Inseparable and Complementary

Emotions are almost always a major part of intercultural conflicts, and they often make it quite difficult to engage in meaningful discussion about the issues that divide the parties. People are often told to keep emotions out of the conflict and that these will derail the possibility of productive conflict management. Common advice is to approach the situation "rationally" rather than "emotionally." Relational empathy suggests that cognition and affect are inseparable and complementary, not divided and at odds with one another. In fact, emotions must be acknowledged and expressed, in productive ways, when a person is involved in intercultural conflict. Despite the misconception that emotions have no place in conflict, they can actually contribute to the discussion, if handled appropriately. They demonstrate a person's commitment to the issues and willingness to trust the other, and they draw attention to issues that might otherwise not surface or remain intentionally hidden. In addition, you must not forget positive emotions, such as feelings of compassion and sensitivity to the situation of the other person. These emotions can be beneficial in establishing a relationship with the other that is strong enough to withstand the difficult discussions that are necessary to deal with divisive issues. Of course, cultures differ in when, how, and with whom feelings are expressed, so managing emotions is tricky business in the intercultural context. But through relational empathy, interactants can discover *together* an appropriate way to handle emotions and feelings, creating their own set of norms for dealing with the volatility of emotional aspects of conflict.

Meanings Are Situated in Context

When you encounter cultural differences, keep in mind that your own behavior and the actions of the other are embedded in the context surrounding the encounter. They cannot be divorced from the setting and the circumstances in which you find yourself. It is easy (and natural) to interpret your own actions (particularly when you make mistakes or engage in inappropriate or harmful behaviors) as resulting from external conditions, while the negative actions of the other person are often interpreted as intentional and due to that individual's personality or character. Relational empathy helps people perceive conflicts as context dependent, and it challenges people to work hard to understand the constraints and entitlements that influence the goals and behaviors of all participants. This may not make it any easier to accept the frustration and confusion people are experiencing, but by situating their interpretations in both the immediate and larger context, people can more realistically work through the differences that would otherwise divide them.

Synthesis Requires Dialogue

In Western societies, a great deal of emphasis is placed on compromise. These societies tend to believe that to successfully resolve differences, both sides must give up some of what they want and reach a middle position. As you may have experienced, such compromise often results in an overall feeling of dissatisfaction, and often the agreement does not hold up because both sides feel they have lost something important. Relational empathy suggests that the most desirable outcome in a conflict is one in which both sides are able to synthesize their goals and achieve these without severely compromising important goals. Surprisingly, there are often creative ways to do so, but the key is dialogue. This means sharing perspectives, listening respectively to each other, and keeping an open mind. Through dialogue, participants can expand their own horizons so that they come to encompass the other's goals and desired outcomes. This can be a tedious process, and it requires a lot of patience, but in the end it can be worth the extra effort. Although compromise is often a quicker and simpler conflict management style, it is deceptively so. Dialogue based on relational empathy requires considerable time and effort, and there is no guarantee it will yield the desired outcome, but it is the best way to reach an outcome that can genuinely satisfy all parties to a conflict.

These basic principles of relational empathy make it possible for inter/cultural conflict to be productive and beneficial to those involved, reducing prejudice and discrimination, and making it less likely that you will fall prey to reductionism and overemphasis on differences. As you have read, relational empathy requires more than merely putting yourself in another person's shoes. It is a dynamic process that necessitates taking steps to synthesize conflicting perspectives. Although this process is important for everyday interactions, it is critical in the intercultural encounter.

Broome (2005) provides an example of relational empathy put into practice in his description of dialogue groups that were formed across the dividing line in Cyprus. Coming together after years of conflict and separation, Greek-Cypriots and Turkish-Cypriots from all walks of life met together over a 9-month period for an intense series of dialogue sessions. They started out with little understanding of each other and very different positions about the conflict. Over time, by practicing the principles of relational empathy, they were able to reach a collective vision for the future of Cyprus. This vision incorporated elements of each group's goals, but it also created new goals that had not existed within either community. More important, the group was able to establish a unique culture among the members, characterized by respect, listening, openness to differences, and a commitment to stay together and continue working on the issues until they could produce a satisfying product that genuinely represented everyone's interests and needs. Both their collective vision statement and their group culture represented a synthesis of horizons in the purest sense. Afterwards they put their vision into action, creating dozens of new groups and hundreds of projects that brought people together across the dividing line of the conflict.

Photo 15.1   What has your culture adapted from other cultures? Because cultures are so distinct and interesting, people welcome culture into our lives in numerous and varied ways. Away from his home in Japan, a man sips a Margarita, a Mexican drink, while celebrating the New Year in a New York City loft.

Copyright 2010 Michael Kurylo.

Practicing relational empathy in intercultural encounters not only helps people meet the challenges of intercultural communication, but it positions them to take advantage of the opportunities offered by conversations

---

Note

This section, Confronting Challenges Through Relational Empathy, was contributed by Benjamin Broome, author of the relational empathy concept. It draws from material published in Broome, B. J. (2009). Building relational empathy through an interactive design process. In Dennis D. J. Sandole, Sean Byrne, Ingrid Staroste-Sandole, & Jessica Senihi (Eds), *Handbook of conflict analysis and resolution* (pp. 184–200). New York: Routledge.

and relationships with culturally different others. In this way, inter/cultural communication is not merely a set of obstacles to overcome or problem to be solved. It is a setting for learning and personal growth, and perhaps the only way that you can shape your future world so that it is a place where people can lead productive and satisfying lives.

LIVING CULTURE

Toward Internarrativity: Reflections of a Humble Interculturalist   *William J. Starosta*

Howard University

This year marks for me 42 years of wandering down unmarked paths, then deer trails, then carriage paths, then highways in research in intercultural communication. I started my study toward the world's first PhD degree called Intercultural Communication at Indiana University as an essentialist rhetorician, and as an internationalist. In 1970, culture equaled nation, and those of a nation communicated alike. Those of a nation were ungendered, high or low context, they used monochronic or polychronic time, they practiced identical proxemics, they uniformly looked to the future or to the past. Then, an undergraduate year of study in India and 30 years of teaching at a historically Black university shattered most of what I "knew."

I started to (un)learn through direct experience, both from an undergraduate year as a student and fieldworker amidst India's diversity, armed only with some Hindi and the advice "accept, accept, accept," and from friendships I formed with students and colleagues at Howard University that provided me deeper insight into the way mainstream researchers are viewed through Afrocentric eyes. I doubted my belief in culture. Culture was not a thing, it was an ongoing (re)creation, a site of contestation and intersectionalities clashing with bright, acrimonious sparks.

The closer I stood to culture, the more I saw the feminist's crystalline reflections, deflections, refractions, and diffusions of identity: The nearer I came, the more I saw myself gazing at a reflective surface that revealed me and my assumptions as much as it did any intrinsic quality of the culture being studied. It was at an invited plenary address in Sweden with the World Communication Association and the International Listening Association that I reached a critical realization: I no longer viewed culture as a thing "out there." I could no longer apprehend "it" by seeing it from one fixed position. This thing called culture could be known only through *intercultural listening,* a process of reciprocal attending to the cultural nuances of the other. Upon returning home I saw all matters of gendering

LIVING CULTURE

and racing and culturing with new eyes. I was in a place of becoming and dispute, a place replete with hierarchies and domination and hegemony, and was co-moving with students who, with me, were seeking a secure definition. Every meeting became an adventure, and every conversation a co-creation. I therefore formulated five conceptual tools to locate a place "beyond culture":

1. Dialectics

The cultural is a range of places on a scale, not a fixed location; it grows from a series of opposed choices (at this moment am I foreign or local, Black or mainstream?) that are accessed only through the triangulations of a particular intercultural exchange. We will know from our essentialisms roughly where to search for culture, but we know only at an actual moment what we will find.

2. Asian Insights

In a Daoist spirit, one may leave behind a unitary belief in essentialisms that equate with nation, and instead move in places of competing but complementary forces. The activation of one's most familiar cultural possibilities is met by the resistance and corrections of alternate cultural possibilities. While the solo researcher may be able to plot cultural starting points, all final cultural destinations will be mutually negotiated. Forces of privilege and power will try to define the conversation, and to keep it within comfortable and controllable bounds, but will fail. Every truth that tries to stand alone will be viewed dialectically against the counterstandards of equal truths.

3. Merging Horizons

Hans Georg Gadamer looked for a place of merged horizons, a place of interlinguisticality, a place governed by philosophic hermeneutics. In his view, each person carries a set of prejudices that incline her to see the world in a familiar way. This equates roughly with "culture." But the responsible researcher does not stay forever defined by these initial prejudices. She sees over the horizon, beyond the individual range of sight. In Edward T. Hall's parlance, she goes "beyond culture." Cultural prejudices earlier followed blindly now become options and starting points.

(Continued)

LIVING CULTURE

(Continued)

4. Multiple Authenticities

My work in intercultural communication repeatedly came back to the "authentic." Is it authentic for a White scholar to research a Black rhetor? Is it authentic for a patriarchic theory of acculturation to be applied to women? Is it authentic to credit an experience that had been gained by means of book knowledge, not daily living? My answer to the problem of authenticity was to work toward "double-emic" perspectives and criticism. Each participant to an exchange brings pertinent cultural, generational, and gendered experience. Though individuals have formed a community identity by means of different paths, they may yet come to share an emic understanding. The interpretation of intercultural and interethnic events requires a critic or facilitator to develop both (or all) of the cultural group's emic perspectives and use these to generate possible points of nonparallel interpretations of the event at hand. The intercultural critic may then try to explain those places where the various cultural group members will be inclined to view the matter at hand differently. This critic would have little to say about "right" or "wrong," just about matching or nonmatching understandings of the issue at hand.

5. Internarrativity

Finally, the interculturalist of the future will develop tools for internarrativity. In the Fisherian tradition, humans narrate. They build stories that are true to internal logic, true to the individual's experience, true to the collective experience of the narrator and others, and good, or moral, in some larger sense. The transplanetary interculturalist will hone tools to locate coherence within cultural narratives and compatibilities among rival narratives. She will find ways around difference, even while philosophically recognizing socialized difference as the starting point of culture. She will listen for the emergence of unnoticed differences of linguisticality and cultural prejudice, and ease the route toward new and productive interunderstandings.

Consider:

1. What view of culture does the author have now? How has this changed over time?

2. How do travel and immersion within cultural groups affect the author's view of culture?

LIVING CULTURE

3. Why is the issue of authenticity problematic? How does the author handle this?

4. In your own words, what view of the future does the author have? How does this relate to your view of the future?

OPPORTUNITIES

Relational empathy provides a way to respond to the challenges of inter/cultural communication. Inter/cultural communication practitioners benefit from looking beyond challenges, however, to understand inter/cultural communication as providing opportunities as well. Merging and emerging cultures, redefinition, and dialectical tensions are three opportunities that inter/cultural communication provides. Each of these is discussed in this section.

Merging and Emerging Cultures

One opportunity that inter/cultural communication provides is the infinite possibility of new cultural identities that comes from the intermingling, merging, subdividing, and emergence of cultures. Interethnic and interracial marriages produce multiethnic and multiracial children. New cultural groups emerge in response to political, social, and economic factors such as the emergence of the Tea Party in the United States in recent years. Nations subdivide and create independent states. In order to adapt to these cultural shifts, inter/cultural practitioners may need to change how they view culture. Culture can no longer easily be viewed as reflecting strict geographical or ideological borders. Instead, culture is less definable, more dynamic, and interminably open to change. Although this amorphous view of culture can be uncomfortable for some, Hegde entices scholars to welcome a state of flux.

> Categories leak, assumptions run dry, and we need to get our field a little dirty in terms of deconstructing the neat categories—the sanitized divisions between categories and areas. . . . My suggestion is that we get intellectually "impure." (as cited in Collier et al., 2002, p. 239)

Inter/cultural communication practitioners can benefit from this messier view as well. Neat cultural boxes no longer line up in predictable ways. Yet, in this messiness, there is opportunity.

For example, groups that have been historically marginalized like the majority populations in Egypt and Libya have become dominant groups. Even cultures that emerge with little fanfare like the Occupy Wall Street movement can shift their cultural identity within weeks to become the prominent topic in news coverage. The ways in which cultures merge and emerge provide opportunities for inter/cultural practitioners open to these shifts. Even those who are ethnocentric (discussed in Chapter 3), chauvinistic with an extreme, nearly militant, version of ethnocentrism, or xenophobic with a fear of those who are different or foreign may find themselves needing to respond or adjust to these shifts.

In response to these shifts some people may espouse cultural relativism. Cultural relativism takes a "to each their own" approach and views all cultural groups as distinct and accepts that each has a right to believe and behave in its own culturally appropriate way. However, cultural relativism may not be a practical response because merging cultures, in particular, necessarily integrate their beliefs and behaviors in unpredictable ways that challenge a relativistic view. Similarly, the polar opposite of relativism, cultural universalism, may not be a useful response either. Cultural universalism prioritizes similarities in beliefs and behaviors across cultures arguing that "we're all basically the same." At the extreme, those who espouse cultural universalism may pejoratively ask, "Why does that culture have to do things *so* differently?" The merging of cultures challenges those who take a universalistic approach to confront and engage differences rather than disregard or discount differences. In contrast to relativism and universalism, cultural pluralism may provide a better response to the merging and emerging of cultures. Cultural pluralism envisions an ideal in which dominant cultures and co-cultures coexist and coparticipate in the culture-at-large. The merging and emerging of cultures provides an opportunity for inter/cultural practitioners to espouse a cultural pluralistic approach as a practical response to the increased messiness of cultural boundaries.

Take a Side Trip:

If you would like to read more about related issues, visit Appendix D: Transnational Dominican Culture Through Phenomenological Analysis.

Photo 15.2 What approach works best when cultures merge? This photo represents a cultural relativistic approach to culture. The happy couple use their clothing to represent their respective cultural heritage.

Copyright 2010 Michael Kurylo.

Redefinition

Another opportunity that inter/cultural communication provides for inter/cultural practitioners is redefinition. Redefinition involves the development of new language and the emergence of new meaning for already existent language. The Sapir-Whorf hypothesis helps explain why the meaning of language is not fixed but is always potentially changing. For example, according to the Defense of Marriage Act passed in 1996, the U.S. government defines marriage as occurring between a man and a woman. Yet, the Marriage Equality Act passed in June 2011 makes same-sex marriage legal in New York State. The coexistence of this seeming contradiction is evidence of the fluidity of language and its meaning.

The Sapir-Whorf hypothesis in its theorizing about language explains how redefinition occurs through linguistic relativity and linguistic determinism shown in Figure 15.2. Respectively, the two components of this theory argue that language changes over time in response to the needs of a culture and also that language produces change in a culture. Linguistic relativity describes the way in which language evolves to reflect changes in the culture in which it is created. For example, consider the word *truthiness* discussed in Chapter 1. The word was coined as a response to a culture's need to concisely describe or represent this thing within the culture. As a culture changes and new experiences within the culture warrant attention and discussion, new language develops.

Linguistic determinism describes the way in which language shapes culture. For example, prior to the creation of the term *date rape* or the term *sexual harassment,* unwanted sexual advances of these kinds were often not taken seriously in the United States, resulted in little if any punishment, and were blamed on the victim, predominantly female, by focusing on her actions rather than the perpetrators. Once the terms were created and came into common usage they began to shape the way cultural group members thought about these acts resulting in more serious attention given to accusations, the incorporation of formal complaint and disciplinary procedures, and a shift in focus to the perpetrator.

REFLECT 15.3: What new words do you remember being introduced? Do you think these words were created as a response to changes within the culture itself? Why or why not?

Change within a culture, even with something as seemingly simple as a word, takes time. Still today in U.S. American culture, as discussed in Chapter 9, when the topic of a specific date rape is raised, questions about clothing, intoxication, and intimacy are asked problematically focusing on the victim's actions in the rape. Asking, "What was she wearing?" or "Was she drunk?" focus the blame on the victim. Although change within a culture often happens slowly, redefinition provides the opportunity for that change to take place. Although it may seem that there is little any single person can do to take advantage of the opportunity offered by redefinitions, consider that the examples discussed here initially required only a handful of advocates to persevere in order for the redefinition to gain momentum. In this way, redefinition provides an opportunity for inter/cultural practitioners.

Dialectical Tensions

Dialectical tensions provide another opportunity for inter/cultural communication practitioners. Numerous dialectical tensions are involved in inter/cultural communication. The narrative in this chapter addresses some of these tensions. Additionally, Chapter 1 discusses the representation and construction of culture as a tension that can be understood through structuration theory. In Chapter 7, individual identity and cultural identity provide yet another tension. Chapters 12 and 13 identify emic and etic tensions in inter/cultural communication research.

Dialectical tensions are counter to the assumption that the goal of inter/cultural communication is to find a best way to communicate. Instead, appreciating the dialectical tensions involved in inter/cultural communication means that you accept that there is no solution to the "problem" of inter/cultural communication. Instead, there are only tensions that are momentarily resolved as values, identities, cultures, and viewpoints shift over time. Dialectics allow people to be pushed and pulled, thereby, energizing them to be mindful and to act. They require dialogue, debate, activity, and engagement with ideas and perspectives that people might not otherwise embrace. In this way dialectical tensions provide opportunity for inter/cultural practitioners.

Figure 15.2 Sapir-Whorf Hypothesis.

Can the chicken and the egg argument be applied here? Language is a powerful tool of a culture and is also a valuable way in which cultures are themselves produced.

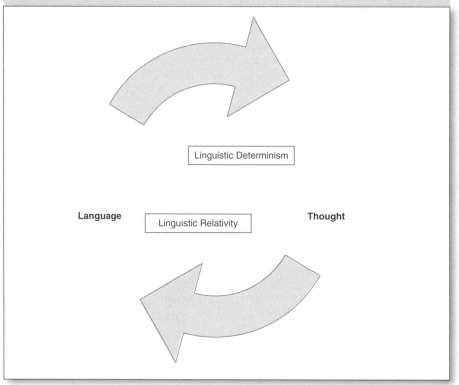

Linguistic Determinism

Language   Linguistic Relativity   Thought

Copyright 2011 Anastacia Kurylo

REFLECT 15.4: Of the topics discussed in this chapter that will be relevant to the future of inter/cultural communication, which do you think will be the most relevant to your life as you graduate, seek and find employment, and pursue romantic relationships and your own ideas of family?

FINAL THOUGHTS

Inter/cultural communication theories and concepts presented throughout the text have provided insights that enable scholars and practitioners alike to explore the challenges and opportunities inherent in inter/cultural communication. Social scientific and social construction approaches provide the foundation for these theories and concepts. As articulated in Chapter 1, structuration theory describes how these two approaches work together. Inter/cultural practitioners benefit from understanding how they have the agency to construct culture and how current representations of culture that are often taken for granted limit them. Because of the limits representations place on agency, change may be slow, but there is movement.

Inter/cultural communication can involve a variety of important high stakes issues including but not limited to health care, outsourcing, environmental issues, the military, social services, equal rights, and immigration among others. Through reading this text you have the framework to navigate inter/cultural communication and understand related high stakes issues like these that are consequential for people's lives. Although you may have initially assumed you already knew a lot about inter/cultural communication when you began reading this text, you may realize now that you have completed the text that your education related to inter/cultural communication has just begun. Regardless of whether you take additional classes in college, engage in training workshops and programs sponsored by your employer, or undertake your own research, you have much to gain from learning more about inter/cultural communication. Although you may now have a greater appreciation of how important inter/cultural communication is to you, you may still not realize just how important you are to inter/cultural communication. The way in which you do the following is consequential.

- View differences and similarities between cultural groups.
- Become interculturally competent.
- Construct identity—yours and others—in cultural moments.
- Use language to inter/culturally communicate and engage in conflict.
- Identify and interact with your ingroups and outgroups.
- View yourself in relation to co-cultural groups.
- View and respond to privilege.
- Advocate for others.
- Critically examine the media and its role in how you come to understand culture.
- Incorporate Web 2.0 technology into your inter/cultural exchanges.
- Approach your research and study of cultures.

It is not an overstatement to say that how you navigate the challenges and opportunities discussed in this chapter will determine the future for inter/cultural communication. What happens tomorrow begins with what you do today.

CONTINUE YOUR JOURNEY ONLINE

Visit: United Nations website. Explore this site to become familiar with the United Nations, its goals, available resources, and relevant current events. Look for the challenges and opportunities for inter/cultural communication practitioners that are expressed through this website.

http://www.un.org/en/

Read more about Benjamin Broome's work in Cyprus by downloading his book (2005), *Building Bridges Across the Green Line,* available at an affiliated United Nations website.

http://www.undp-act.org/data/articles/building_bridges_english.pdf

" SAY WHAT?

Say What? provides excerpts from overheard real-life conversations in which people have communicated stereotypes. As you read these conversations, reflect on the following questions.

- Have you been in conversations like this before?
- Is there any one of these conversations that stick out to you more than the others?
- What do you think of this conversation?
- How did the stereotype help or hinder the conversation?
- Was there another way the stereotyper could have communicated to convey the same point?
- How do you feel when you hear this conversation or the specific stereotype?
- Do any of these conversations bother you more than others? Why or why not?
- Do any concepts, issues, or theories discussed in the chapter help explain why?

- **Say What?** All three of us at the table noticed two Asian girls entering the diner. My friend said that they were in the same honors English class in high school. She then went on to say the stereotype that "all Asian people are smart," and how she felt somewhat stupid in the class. After my friend told her story, my other friend and I had a response of being speechless. There were just too many things implied in one simple story that were better off left alone.

- **Say What?** I was using a calculator to facilitate the addition of a long list of numbers. When the final number was given the response was, "I knew that; Can't you tell I'm Asian? We are good at mathematics!" I didn't know if this person was merely making a joke, or he felt like I had possibly discriminated against him in some way. It was obvious that I did not know how to respond. So he did the work for me. His next remark was with a smile, "I am just kidding." As I realized he was relaxed and in good spirits I relaxed as well, shrugged it off and cracked a smile.

- **Say What?** I was watching a group of parents who were celebrating one boy's birthday at the police museum's children's play area. The boys immediately took to their surroundings and acted out their police fantasies. Of the twenty kids playing cops and robbers, the one continually selected to play the robber was the only black kid.

- **Say What?** Tim asked Mike how his night was and if he had made any tips. Mike replied "I bartended for a Bar Mitzvah, what do you think?" implying that of course he didn't make any money because he was working a Jewish party. Initially, Mike, Dave, who was Jewish, and I laughed. Tim realizing that Dave would not take kindly to that comment stayed silent and gave Mike a sneer. However, Dave immediately confronted Mike saying, "What's that supposed to mean?"

REVIEW QUESTIONS

1. What stumbling block to intercultural communication should be viewed differently, according to the chapter? Why?

2. What is reductionism? Why might it be a problem for intercultural communication, according to the chapter?

3. What is hypothesis confirming information? Based on the chapter discussion, how can this be avoided?

4. How does the chapter say that prejudice is involved in the future of intercultural communication?

5. According to the chapter, why is provisionalism important for inter/cultural communication? How would a person engage in provisionalism?

6. What are the basic principles of relational empathy according to Broome (2009) discussed in the chapter? How are these relevant to inter/cultural communication?

7. What dialectical tensions are mentioned in the chapter? Why are these productive rather than destructive for inter/cultural communication?

8. What does it mean that language creates culture and that culture creates language? How might the examples of sexual harassment and date rape discussed in the chapter each be an example of both of these concepts?

9. Name two challenges and two opportunities discussed in the chapter that are most relevant and meaningful for your life. Demonstrate that you understand why these are challenges in your answer.

10. According to the chapter, how will you contribute to the future of inter/cultural communication?

KEY TERMS

chauvinistic   341

cultural pluralism   342

cultural relativism   341

cultural universalism   342

ego defensive function
of prejudice   332

hypothesis confirming
information   331

information processing
theory   330

knowledge function of
prejudice   332

linguistic determinism   343

linguistic relativity   342

provisional   332

redefinition   342

reductionism   330

relational empathy   337

Sapir-Whorf hypothesis   342

utilitarian function
of prejudice   332

value expressive
function of prejudice   332

xenophobic   341

REFERENCES

Barna, L. (1998). Stumbling blocks in intercultural communication. In M. Bennett (Ed.) *Basic concepts of intercultural communication*. Yarmouth, MN: Intercultural Press.

Brislin, R. W. (2000). *Understanding culture's influence on behavior* (2nd ed.). Fort Worth, TX: Harcourt.

Broome, B. J. (2005). *Building bridges across the green line: A guide to intercultural communication in Cyprus*. New York: United Nations Development Programme (UNDP).

Broome, B. J. (2009). Building relational empathy through an interactive design process. In D. D. J. Sandole, S. Byrne, I. Staroste-Sandole, J. Senihi (Eds), *Handbook of conflict analysis and resolution* (pp. 184–200). New York: Routledge.

Collier, M. J., Hegde, R. S., Lee, W., Nakayama, T. K. & Yep, G. A. (2002). Dialogue on the edges: Ferment in communication and culture. In M. J. Collier (Ed.). *Transforming communication about culture, International and Intercultural Communication Annual* (Vol. 24, pp. 219–280). Thousand Oaks, CA: Sage.

Crandall, C. S., Eshleman, A., & O'Brien, L. (2002). Social norms and the expression and suppression of prejudice: The struggle for internalization. *Journal of Personality and Social Psychology, 82,* 359–378.

Fiske, S. T., & Taylor, S. E. (1984). *Social cognition* (1st ed.). Reading, MA: Addison-Wesley.

Hamilton, D. L., Sherman, S. J., & Ruvolo, C. M. (1990). Stereotype-based expectancies: Effects on information processing and social behavior. *Journal of Social Issues, 46,* 35–60.

Hinton, P. R. (2000). *Stereotypes, culture, and cognition: Psychology focus*. Philadelphia: Psychology Press.

Judd, C. M., & Park, B. (1993). Definition and assessment of accuracy in social stereotypes. *Psychological Review, 100,* 109–128.

Katz, D. (1960). The functional approach to the study of attitudes. *Public Opinion Quarterly, 24,* 163–204.

Katz, D., & Braly, K. W. (1933). Racial stereotypes of one hundred college students. *Journal of Abnormal Social Psychology, 28,* 280–290.

LaPiere, R. T. (1936). Type-rationalizations of group antipathy. *Social Forces, 15,* 232–237.

Worklan, P. (1996, June 26) Black teen blocks assault at Klan rally. *Chicago Tribune*. Retrieved from http://articles.chicagotribune.com/1996-06-25/news/9606250300_1_klan-rally-confederate-flag-unidentified-man.

PART V

Appendices: Studies of Inter/Cultural Communication

Appendix A

NAVAJO CULTURE EXPLORED THROUGH ETHNOGRAPHY

Charles A. Braithwaite

University of Nebraska–Lincoln

Overview

Based in social construction, Braithwaite's interpretivist study uses ethnographic fieldwork to explore how Navajo culture is enacted in Diné College curriculum and classrooms. As you read about this study, consider how your own culture has been communicated to you throughout your culture's educational communication practices.

WHY DID I STUDY THIS CULTURE?[1]

I recognized very early on in my teaching career that the college classroom is not immune from the influence of culture. For example, when I require my public speaking students to choose speech topics that are "original" and "creative," I am imposing the Euro-American preference for individualism and the belief that we are all unique. Just as I weave my cultural assumptions into my classes, so do other teachers who come from different cultural perspectives. To examine this cultural phenomenon, I chose to study college teachers at Diné College, a bilingual/bicultural college on the Navajo Nation[2]. Diné College is unique in explicitly integrating Navajo culture throughout its educational communication practices.

WHY DID I USE THIS METHOD?

There are at least two reasons why ethnographic research, which describes and explicates culturally specific communication practices in the classroom, is important for both researchers and educators concerned with communication education. First, ethnographic studies of classroom interaction provide an opportunity for instructors to present cross-cultural comparisons for their students. For example, both Philips (1983) and Dumont (1972) detail the rules for silence among some American Indian communities and discuss how this communicative conduct affects classroom behavior. A second and related reason for examining ethnographic studies of communication practices in education is for instructors to begin to explore their own taken-for-granted assumptions about the nature of their pedagogy. According to Philipsen (1992),

> The ethnographer of speaking is a naturalist, who watches, listens, and records communicative conduct in its natural setting. The ethnographer describes what is to be found in a given speech community as well as what regular patterns can be observed there. (p. 7)

Additionally, it is especially important to use ethnography of speaking field methods in studying Native peoples, who have a long history of stressing the oral tradition, because the spoken word carries such a powerful force in the lives of these people (Philips, 1983; Pratt, 1994). As will be described, instructors at Diné College openly discuss how their own culture should be incorporated into the classroom. This provides Anglo teachers, such as myself, an opportunity to reflect on how their assumptions about education are shaped by their culture.

WHO DID I STUDY?

Diné College is located on the Navajo Nation, which is North America's largest Indian nation. The Navajo number is over 210,750 and the Nation covers an area approximately the size of West Virginia. Diné College is composed of a main campus in Tsaile, Arizona (Navajo Nation), as well as six additional locations in other parts of Arizona and New Mexico. Starting with around 500 students in 1969, the Diné College system has grown to over 1,500 full-time equivalent students, with almost 600 full-time students at the Tsaile campus alone. The Diné College system has an impressive retention rate of students: 88% (McCombs, 1995). The Diné College system (originally called Navajo Community College or NCC) was established in 1968 as the first tribally controlled community college in the United States (Denny, 1996). What makes this system at Diné College unique is the overt attempt to impose Navajo culture into all aspects of their educational communication practices. In summarizing the history of Diné College, Denny (1996) states that

> Diné College is a Navajo Bilingual/Bicultural Education institution. Navajo language and culture is the core of the college curriculum. NCC's main mission is to integrate Navajo and Western Culture. Students would then be able to adjust within the western society and still retain their culture by knowing who they are and where they come from. (p. 1)

In the introduction to each general catalog, Diné College states:

> The educational philosophy of Diné College is Sa'ah Naagháí Bik'eh Hózhóón, the Diné traditional living system, which places human life in harmony with the natural world and the universe. The philosophy provides principles both for protection from the imperfections in life and for the development of well-being. (Navajo Community College, 1995a, p. 6)

Method

How Did I Conduct This Study?

Ethnographic study involves establishing contact and developing relationships with participants, conducting participant/observation in context, and systematic collection and analysis of data. Because I believe no researcher should examine a community without giving back something in return, I became active in Diné College and its community. First, by attending recruitment fairs for Navajo students for 4 years; then in other ways, including advising Navajo students who were considering transferring to 4-year institutions. In return, I was given permission by the dean of instruction and the department heads to sit in on classes and participate in activities at Diné College.

Eight months of participant/observation began by arranging to live in the dormitory at Diné College with other students. When at the college, I ate in the cafeteria, and used the library and computer center in order to spend as much time as possible in context. I also sat in on various administration, committee, and planning meetings. I participated in many off-campus activities as well. Systematic data collection involved observing over 100 hours of classroom interaction. These included courses I attended such as Navajo Oral History, Navajo History, Navajo Astronomy, and Speech Communication which were taught almost exclusively in English and had instructors recommended as examples of "good" teaching.

In each class I was introduced by the instructor and most often functioned as an observer rather than a participant in class discussion. One of the basic tenets of the ethnography of communication is the assumption that communicative practices are distinctive to a context, they are systematic within that context, and they are traceable though observation (Hymes, 1962; 1972). Therefore, I collected as much data as possible concerning communicative practices in the classroom. The 300 pages of field notes from the classrooms I observed consisted of descriptions of class content and, more importantly, specific verbal and nonverbal speech events by the faculty which were related to Sa'ah Naagháí Bik'eh Hózhóón. Additional sources of data included documents published by Diné College, course textbooks, and semistructured interviews (Merton & Kendall, 1946) with students and faculty. I stopped collecting data when I identified recurring patterns of interaction (Braithwaite, 1995; Katz, 1983) and stopped seeing something "new."

All documents and descriptions provided by Diné College emphasize how Sa'ah Naagháí Bik'eh Hózhóón is the core of all education throughout the system. In fact, course syllabi for all courses are *required* to include a statement acknowledging the centrality of this particular cultural perspective. One of the most common statements on course syllabi reads: "Course goals as related to SNBH: This course will integrate Diné holistic teachings in accordance with the pedagogical paradigm: Nitsáhákees, Nahat'á, Naayée'ehgo Na'nitin (protection-way teachings) and Hózhoojík'ehgo na'nitin (blessing way teachings)" (Navajo Community College, 1995b, p. 6).

Given the college's overt goal of incorporating SNBH[3] throughout the curriculum, I wanted to discover how this educational philosophy was actually incorporated in practice into the day-to-day behavior in the college classroom. The objective of my study was to describe and explicate Navajo educational communication practices as they were enacted at a Diné college.

WHAT DID I FIND OUT?

Ethnographic fieldwork at Diné College suggests that Sa'ah Naagháí Bik'eh Hózhóón is enacted in the curriculum and the classroom by incorporating the following four aspects of Navajo philosophy into lectures, activities, and assignments: (1) focusing on the Navajo sense of place; (2) focusing on the duality in life; (3) focusing on Diné identity; and (4) using the rhetorical form of enactment.

A Sense of Place

The creation of the four worlds, the significance of living between the four sacred mountains, and importance of the four directions have been central in trying to understand Navajo life. So it is not surprising that instructors at Diné College focus on the Navajo sense of place in enacting Sa'ah Naagháí Bik'eh Hózhóón in the curriculum and the classroom. How does the sense of place emerge in the Diné College classroom? In all of the classes I visited, there were considerable discussions of places, place names, and the significance of certain locations. All Diné College students are taught how the college was built to conform to traditional Navajo philosophy of place. According to Aronilth (1992), who is a medicine man and teacher of a required course on Navajo philosophy at Diné College, "The N.C.C. campus has an entrance to the east where our prayers, songs, learnings and knowledge begin. The circular drive represents the road of life, both inside a hogan [which is the traditional Navajo dwelling] around the fireplace and outside on the road of life" (p. 13). He goes on to describe how the placement of each building is significant, and stresses that the students need to understand the meaning of this placement if they are to understand their education at Diné College.

All classroom discussions surrounding Navajo traditional beliefs are associated with discussions of the four sacred mountains, the four directions, the four seasons, the four parts of the day, and the four worlds through which the Navajo emerged. All of these drawings and stories begin with orienting the students toward the four directions, and each event and character in the stories is tied to a particular direction. For example, students are taught that First Man was created in the East, First Woman was created in the West; Talking God is associated with the East, Changing Woman is associated with the West; turquoise is associated with the South, jet black is associated with the North. Always these directions are tied to the four sacred mountains: Blanca Peak to the East, San Francisco Peak to the West, Mt. Hesperus to the North, and Mt. Taylor to the South, between which is located the Navajo Nation. This teaching of the importance of place is intended to help students understand aspects of Navajo culture and some students stated that these were not clear to them until they came to Diné College. For example, after a discussion of the relationship between the East and certain kinds of knowledge, one student said he had not understood the significance of facing the East in the morning until this was explained to him.

Duality in Life

In the required reading for all students and faculty at Diné College, *Foundation of Navajo Culture,* Aronilth (1992) highlights the prescription to "learn to understand that education identifies itself as a male and female concept, but of equal value" (p. 171). Just as many Navajo traditional beliefs emerge from a sense of place, so too are they discussed as having a dual nature of male and female. Nowhere is this more evident than in the stories of the four worlds through which Navajos emerged to reach the world we live in today. Students were taught that all persons have a male side and a female side, with the left being the warriors—or male—and the right being the gentle—or female. Talking God is presented sometimes as a male god, and sometimes as a female god (Calling God). Stories of White Shell Boy are presented along with stories of Abalone Shell Girl. The natural elements are presented as air and sunlight being male, while water and earth are female. Even the term Sa'ah Naagháí Bik'eh Hózhóón contains this duality, with sa'ah naagháí equated with the male component, and bik'eh hózhóón being the female (Farella, 1984).

In public speaking classes, the instructor communicated to the students the importance of making the best and most effective uses of their male and female sides. Males are encouraged to "tone down" their speaking voices, and females are encouraged to "speak up" in order to compete with the males. In one case, the public speaking instructor had some of the Navajo women go out into the parking lot, stand about 25 yards away, face into the wind, and introduce themselves aloud by saying their clan affiliations. The instructor kept asking the women to speak louder until they could be heard easily.

Diné Identity

There are approximately 30 Navajo clans (Navajo Curriculum Center, 1993), which emerged from the four original clans created by Changing Woman (one of the original Holy People of the Navajo): Near the Water Clan (To'ahani), Tower House Clan (Kinyaa'aanii), Bitter Water Clan (Todich'iinii), and Mud Clan (Hastlishnii). The traditional Navajo way of relating to one another is based on identifying oneself with the mother's clan, the father's clan, the maternal grandfather's clan, and the paternal grandfather's clan. How this impacts the classroom is in the emphasis on presenting one's clan affiliations upon being introduced.

Introductions

Diné value introductions. This is articulated most explicitly in Aronilth's (1992) instructions given to all Diné College students:

For a Diné, it is the teaching and belief of our forefathers, that an introduction is a large part of what makes us unique.

1. Because our name is the foundation of who we are, while the spirit of our clan is the roots of our life. Our name and clan have to go together.

2. A proper introduction has a lot to do with the way we feel, think, talk, and categorize our words.

3. Expressing our clan is based upon our capacity to love and on receiving love, which is how we understand how effective and good we are.

4. Our clan system plays a very important part in our behavior and attitude.

5. By introducing yourself properly, you will feel more at ease and you will feel more of a home atmosphere.

6. How you say your words and how you use your words will be clearer and more categorized.

7. You may discover that you have relatives that were previously unknown, then there is a good understanding.

8. If you do not introduce yourself properly, you will have a nervous feeling, you may not feel comfortable, or at home among other people.

9. Your body will tighten up and you will get out of control speaking.

For all these reasons, as Diné, we need to understand the proper method of our introduction. (pp. 26–27)

In Diné introduction, individuals each must give their name and the clan they represent. At the beginning of each semester, students will introduce themselves by their clans as a Diné, a different tribe or even a different race. Other individuals, who are not Navajo, may give their name and the race they represent. Each Navajo instructor at Diné began the semester by way of this type of introduction. Every time a student or Navajo guest speaker would start a presentation, they first went through this introduction. Although I was acutely aware of this prescription while being an observer, I failed to remember the significance of clan introductions when I returned to my role as professor. When I taught a summer course for Navajo transfer students, I invited several graduates of Diné College to talk to my students about how they succeeded when they went to a 4-year university. When my first guest speaker came to class, I started to ask questions immediately after I introduced him. The speaker politely told me he would answer my questions after he had "properly" introduced himself to the class.

Enactment

As can be seen from the previous discussions of place, duality, and identity, the subject of being a Navajo is central to the communication practices at Diné College. Therefore, it should not be surprising that faculty make extensive use of their personal experiences to support the teaching of Sa'ah Naagháí Bik'eh Hózhóón. Each Navajo faculty member I observed drew upon their own life as a Navajo, and the lives of their Navajo relatives, to corroborate SNBH themes in their lectures and discussions. I recognized this type of testimonial to be an example of the rhetorical form of *enactment*. According to Campbell and Jamieson (1977), enactment is a form in which "the speaker incarnates the argument, is the proof of the truth of what is said" (p. 9). This goes beyond merely establishing credibility as a speaker on a particular topic. In using enactment, the speaker becomes a method of validation of the point being made.

This rhetorical form of enactment was made most evident when instructors demonstrated the usefulness of oral histories in understanding Navajo life. One instructor told how his grandfather participated in the Long Walk as a child. The stories his grandfather told to his grandmother, who then passed these stories on to the instructor, were vividly presented to the students as an illustration of the richness found in oral history. After the instructor told a particularly riveting account of how his 6-year-old grandfather was captured at Canyon De Chelly by Kit Carson, the instructor stopped and asked, "How did I do my research? I know my Navajo History!" In another case, the instructor described a trip he had made to New York City. He told of not being able to get a sense of direction as he walked among the large buildings, and how that led to him feeling lost for the first time in his life. This was presented as an illustration of how a sense of direction is "built in us (Navajo)," but that sense is lost upon leaving the land between the four sacred mountains.

Data

Sample of Field Notes

January 24, Location: Navajo Community College, classroom bldg. #1, 2nd floor. Time: 1–5pm (mix of sun and snow that day—everyone bundled up) Participants this day: Dean, H., O. J., N., S., 20 students

- Met with Dean and H.
- Dean approved my proposal to spend time in the classroom.
- Turned me over to H. (after saying that H. verbally approved)
- H. lectured on Diné—importance of learning identity for students.
- H. took me in a class without warning (them or me!).
- Students seemed completely at ease with strangers being there (didn't seem to really look at us).
- Teacher came over to explain what they were doing (using dominoes to count in Navajo).
- (H. told me how they do a whole game of Bingo in the intro course to teach numbers!).
- H. introduced me to O. J.
- (Everyone seemed so excited that I was doing this articulation stuff).
- Spent 1 1/2 hours with H. and O. J. talking about the Navajo Language program.
- Visits by N. and S.
- OJ asked for advice on finishing a BA (in ED?). Promised I would get College of Education stuff to him.

WHY DOES THIS MATTER?

Although the purpose of most community college education is to help students regarding employment or moving on to higher education, a central goal of Diné College is to "strengthen personal foundations for responsible learning and living consistent with Sa'ah Naagháí Bik'eh Hózhóón" and to "promote Navajo language and culture" (Navajo Community College, 1995a, p. 6). This means that Navajo instructors will use themes and techniques like those described above to help students understand who they are as a people and what that means to each individual Navajo. For example, one discussion contrasted the Western assertion that Native peoples came from across the Bering Strait with the Navajo view that Native peoples came from an underworld. As part of this discussion, the instructor asked, "What is the truth? The objective of talking about this is for you to find out who you are. Where do you belong; what can you use to live your life?" Later, in a discussion about how Anglos off the reservation will call Navajos names like Geronimo and Cochise, the instructor cautioned, "If you don't know your history, you will have a personality conflict." Comments such as these illustrate how much of the education at Diné College is concerned with the student *as a Navajo,* in addition to providing a solid educational base in English, math, science, and so forth.

Why is there so much of a focus on Navajo cultural identity in the instruction at Diné College? Pratt (1994) states that "with the loss of language and the loss of tribally competent role models, people of Indian decent are struggling to find an identity" (p. 13). Mercer (1990) argues that "identity only becomes an issue when it is in crisis, when something assumed to be fixed, coherent and stable is displaced by experience of doubt and uncertainty" (p. 43). Mercer claims that issues of identity can be problematic when environments exist which call that identity into question. This is certainly the case for the Navajo, given the problems facing them today: poverty, alcoholism, declining federal revenue, diminishing natural resources, and the number of Navajos choosing to move off the reservation. Faculty and students at Diné College are highly aware of the challenges facing them as a people, as evidenced by the number of lecture, paper, and speech topics I heard which focused on understanding and improving the Navajo people.

A focus on the Navajo as a unique people, which is endemic to the instructional practices at Diné College, helps explain the distinctive concern for a sense of place and on the duality in life. By focusing attention on the role of the sacred mountains, rivers, and other sacred places on the Navajo Nation, the students are taught to view their land as part of who they are as a people. Aronilth (1992) states that "this type of learning can give us a positive Navajo image and identity. It will give us a good foundation to be strong and have courage as a person" (p. 18). The heightened awareness of the duality of the male and female in all persons also helps to communicate what it takes to be a successful Navajo. By accepting and embracing the dual nature of persons, Navajo students are taught that this is the path toward being "whole."

The Navajo instructors' technique of referring to communal places, times, and directions as a source of strength for the students provides an interesting contrast to the focus on learning in the Anglo college classroom, where so much of what is important in life is discussed as coming from the "self" and the interpersonal dyadic "relationship." In contexts where an Anglo instructor may tell students to "get in touch with themselves" in order to understand the nature of their behavior, a Navajo instructor may tell students to "learn from our elders" to understand how people should behave.

NOTES

1. A longer version of this essay was published as Braithwaite, C. A. (1997). Sa'ah Naagháí Bik'eh Hózhóón: An ethnography of Navajo educational communication practices. *Communication Education, 46,* 219–233.

2. The author wishes to thank the faculty, students, staff, and administration of Diné College for their assistance and support.

3. Using the acronym SNBH to stand for Sa'ah Naagháí Bik'eh Hózhóón is common in the documents and speech found at Diné College. However, some Navajo instructors object to the use of this abbreviation, which they say was developed to accommodate those that are not fluent in Navajo, primarily Anglos.

QUESTIONS TO CONSIDER

Culture

1. Imagine you were going to interact with a member of this culture. Based on this study, might you do anything differently in a conversation with someone from this culture than you would with someone from your own culture? Why or why not?

2. How is the culture discussed in the study similar to and different to your own?

3. How does what you learned about this culture relate to what you understand about your own culture?

4. What theories, concepts, or issues discussed in this text are relevant to this study?

5. What new theories, concepts, or issues have you learned from this study?

6. Is culture discussed here as a representation that affects communication or as a construction created by communication?

Research Method

1. What would you have done differently if you were to conduct a similar study? Why?

2. If you were going to conduct research on a cultural group, would you use this method? Why or why not?

3. What are the limitations of the research conducted that are identified by the author? Can you think of other limitations the author has not discussed?

4. What are some pros and cons of using this method?

5. How did the researcher construct the identity of cultural group members? What did the researcher do or say that communicated this?

6. What questions do you have about this method?

REFERENCES

Aronilth, W. (1992). *Foundation of Navajo culture.* Tsaile, Navajo Nation: Diné College.

Braithwaite, C. A., & Braithwaite, D. O. (1991). Instructional communication strategies for adapting to a multicultural basic course. *Basic Course Annual III,* 3, 145–160.

Braithwaite, D. O. (1995). Ritualized embarrassment at "coed" wedding and baby showers. *Communication Reports, 8,* 145–157.

Campbell, K. K., & Jamieson, K. (1977). Form and genre in rhetorical criticism: An introduction. In K. K. Campbell & K. Jamieson (Eds.). *Form and genre: Shaping rhetorical action* (pp. 9–32). Falls Church, VA: Speech Communication Association.

Denny, A. (1996). The History of NCC Campus-Tsaile Arizona [on-line]. Retrieved from http://crystal. ncc.cc.nm.us/webzine/ncchistory.html

Dumont, R. V. (1972). Learning English and how to be silent: Studies in Souix and Cherokee classrooms. In C. B. Cazden, V. P. John, & D. Hymes (Eds.), *Functions of language in the classroom.* (pp. 32–65). New York: Teachers College Press.

Farella, J. R. (1984). *The Main Stalk: A synthesis of Navajo philosophy.* Tucson: University of Arizona Press.

Hymes, D. (1962). The ethnography of speaking. In. T. Gladwin & W. Sturtevant (Eds.), *Anthropology and human behavior* (pp. 13–53). Washington, DC: Anthropological Society of Washington.

Hymes, D. (1972). Models of the interaction of language and social life. In J. Gumperz & D. Hymes (Eds.), *Directions in sociolinguistics: The ethnography of communication* (pp. 35–71). New York: Holt, Rinehart and Winston.

Katz, J. (1983). A theory of qualitative methodology: The social system of analytic fieldwork. In R. M. Emerson, (Ed.), *Contemporary field research: A collection of readings* (pp. 127–148). Boston: Little, Brown and Company.

McCombs, E. (1995). *Navajo Community College institutional report,* 1992–95. Tsaile, Navajo Nation: Diné College Press.

Mercer, K. (1990). Welcome to the jungle: Identity and diversity in postmodern politics. In J. Rutherford (Ed.), *Identity: Community, culture, difference* (pp. 43–71). London: Lawrence & Wishart.

Merton, R., & Kendall, P. (1946). The focused interview. *American Journal of Sociology, 51,* 541–557.

Navajo Community College (1995a). *Navajo Community College 1995–96 general catalog.* Tsaile, Navajo Nation: Diné College Press.

Navajo Community College (1995b). *Navajo history & Indian studies program course syllabi, 1995–96.* Tsaile, Navajo Nation: Diné College Press.

Navajo Curriculum Center (1993). *A history of Navajo clans.* Chinle, AZ: Rough Rock Demonstration School.

Philips, S. (1983). *The invisible culture: Communication in classroom and community on the Warm Springs Indian Reservation.* New York: Longman.

Philipsen, G. (1992). *Speaking culturally.* Albany: State University of New York Press.

Pratt, S. (1994, November). *Conducting research among American Indians: A 90's perspective.* Paper presented at the Speech Communication Association Annual Convention, New Orleans, LA.

Appendix B

LOCAL CULTURE EXPLORED THROUGH DISCOURSE ANALYSIS

Kathleen C. Haspel

Fairleigh Dickinson University

Overview

Based in social construction, Haspel's study uses discourse analysis to explore how local culture is enacted in call-in talk shows. As you read about this study, consider how your own culture is portable because it transcends the limitations of space and place.

WHY DID I STUDY THIS CULTURE?

As a native of Staten Island, a borough of New York City, I have always felt as if my hometown had a distinctive local culture, despite being part of a multicultural city. This is reflected in the very way that Staten Islanders (and other members of the "outer" boroughs, Brooklyn, Queens, and the Bronx) refer to Manhattan, as "the city." Non–New Yorkers have often asked me why I refer to a city I am situated in this way. The answer to this question is what drives my research into local constructions of culture, namely how culture and cultural identity are built and put on display in our talk and text or discourse. Local culture is essentially what you do and say in your interactions with others that makes you you—not just as an individual, but as a member of some distinctive group of people. In other words, local culture is defined and displayed through members' distinctive communication practices situated in a particular place.

Our cultural identities—and by extension, our membership in local cultures—are tied to place. This is evident in the ways in which we identify ourselves. On the first day of class in any given course, when I ask students to introduce themselves, they invariably do so in terms of where they are from, which may be "Ashley from Long Beach Island," or "Ashley from South Jersey." When people call into talk shows on radio and television, too, they are identified in terms of where they are from. A host may say, "Kathleen from Madison, New Jersey, you're on the air," or simply, "Madison, New Jersey," giving precedence to place over personal reference. Sometimes we state or *avow* our local cultural identities (I often say "I'm originally from New York" because I now live in New Jersey). But more often than not, they are brought to our attention by others who *ascribe* an identity to us the moment we open our mouths, based on what we say (as in the names we give to bubbly soft drinks, whether *pop* or *soda*) and how we say it, and the situation we say it in. For example, in a supermarket out West (my way of referring to the western United States from the East Coast) I asked for soda, to which a clerk responded, "you must be from the East." As with other things that are familiar yet important to us, we may take elements of our local culture for granted, only noticing them when we are removed from them. But because local culture is defined by our talk, it never really leaves us. As a common refrain goes (one I heard many times when I moved away from New York), "You can take the girl out of New York [or your hometown], but you cannot take New York [or your hometown] out of the girl." I am fascinated by this phenomenon: that culture is transportable yet tied to place.

And so, early in my education in the field of communication, and again more recently, I set out to look for the webs of significance or building blocks to the city that is said to be culture (Geertz, 1983). My site of exploration of local culture, ironically, has been discourse that is removed from a particular place, namely talk that is "on the air" (broadcast on radio and TV). To me, the threads of culture are spun from language use and woven through discourse. I use a range of methods to closely examine these threads, how they are woven together, and what they are used to do, collectively called *discourse analysis*. The units of analysis for discourse analysts are the contents of text and talk—which can be as small as an exhalation (a *sigh*) or nonverbal utterance (*uh*), or as large as a story (e.g., an eyewitness account of 9/11 told on a talk show) or even a collection of stories (as in the "Discourse of 9/11")—studied in context.

WHY DID I USE THIS METHOD?

I use discourse analysis because it is like a box of tools that can be used for a variety of specialized jobs, yet is geared toward making the inner workings of talk and text understandable to anyone. Discourse analysis is used and understood by people in other disciplines than communication who study language use, including linguists, teachers of English as a second language, sociologists, anthropologists, and social psychologists (Schiffrin, Tannen, & Hamilton, 2003). Having studied English and linguistics as an undergraduate and master's student before embarking on a lifelong study of communication, I was attracted to discourse analysis because of the attention it draws to language and how it is used across contexts. Unlike some forms of linguistic analysis, discourse analysis looks at language beyond the level of the sentence and moves into the realm of social practice, so that talk is considered action. That is, we "do" things with talk, like show who we are and "where we are coming from." I like the flexibility discourse analysis gives me to work with data sets (samples of talk and text) of various sizes. It can be used to study entire bodies of knowledge, called *discourses;* large collections of conversational practices, called *corpuses;* small sets of particular forms of talk or text, called *instances* or *excerpts;* or case studies. If culture could be defined by an entire population or a single person's communication, through everything they say or a single utterance, then discourse analysis seemed to be the most appropriate method for my mission, looking for constructions of local culture in talk.

Method

How Did I Conduct This Study?

In addition to recording these talk shows, I sat in on the programs to observe how they were produced in the studio, in an effort to broaden my understanding of the context in which the talk I was studying was produced. I took field notes on the ways in which callers were identified by screeners (who typed their information into a terminal visible to the host) in terms of their location and topic, and the means by which they were selected to be "put on air" or rejected. These field notes included documentation of every person who called each program, where each was calling from, and what each person was calling about, which later helped me create logs of the tape recordings of each program. Each call/caller was given a number in my log so that I could track the sequence of calls in a program.

I created codes to mark calls in which callers avowed a certain identity in the context of the talk (e.g., "I'm a New York City school teacher"), which I came to call *credentialing,* and those in which callers told of their personal experience with the topic of discussion, that is, their local knowledge of it, which I call *personal experience narratives.* I selected a sample of calls (about 10%) from each program for transcription and closer analysis of the discourse. I used a method of transcription developed by conversation analysts and used widely in studies of discourse (Schegloff, 2007), which uses symbols to capture what is said in interaction, how it is said, and how it is organized (in lines and turns at talk that are numbered). This detailed method of transcription aids in understanding discourse in the context of its use, that is, in the talk.

To seek out signs of cultural significance, I examined participants' references to persons (including pronouns), places, and activities, as well as indexical expressions, which are terms that *index* or point out details of context, such as location, direction, and proximity (Levinson, 1983). I highlighted these references in the transcripts, then organized them into categories (e.g., place names, use of here/there), making sure to mark the transcript and line numbers where they appeared so that I could quote and cite to support my claims so that readers of my work can see for themselves how and where units of discourse were produced in the discourse.

In my first attempts to explore local culture (as a graduate student learning interpretivist methods), I set out to study what I called *commuter culture* in social (and not so social) interaction on New York City ferries and subways, using ethnographic methods. Although I enjoyed playing participant observer on my daily trips between Staten Island and Manhattan, I found it difficult to separate my self as researcher from my self as cultural member/commuter. Afraid I would somehow miss something, I began to tape record what commuters said in their interactions while writing field notes about the situations in which they interacted. I was fascinated with the talk I recorded, as if I captured a piece of the site of study and carried it home with me. Listening to talk on public transportation in my own home allowed me to recapture my sense of being there, *in situ* (the situation where the talk or data was collected), yet focus my analysis on the talk itself. Discourse analysis allowed me to take the position of observer from multiple vantage points—giving me critical distance from the communication I was studying while at the same time drawing close attention to its inner workings—like being able to zoom from global view to street view on an electronic map.

Although discourse analysts do not, as a rule, make and test hypotheses, like all researchers we are driven by research questions. However, these are usually derived *inductively,* from the talk itself, rather than from preexisting theory. As an avid radio listener who had worked at college and community radio stations, I had a sense of what I was looking for, but remained opened to discovery. First, I wondered whether locally produced talk would look, sound, or act differently than talk produced on national broadcasts. Second, I was looking for indications of a unified local culture among the callers in their ways of speaking. Third, I wanted to know if callers to talk shows contributed local knowledge to the news talk produced on these programs, or whether their discourse merely constituted a culture of complaint and conflict as critics have claimed.

WHO DID I STUDY?

I chose to study call-in talk shows (initially on radio, later on TV), because of the focus on talk and accessibility to a broad range of subjects (participants) they provide. I selected programs that produced news talk (on public affairs) as opposed to advice talk (on personal problems), and those that consisted primarily of dialogue between callers and hosts or guests of programs, rather than those dominated by hosts' monologues. For my initial study, I studied talk produced during the same week of programming on one nationally syndicated commercial talk show and one tri-state (New York, New Jersey, and Connecticut) public radio station.

WHAT DID I FIND OUT?

I found that location matters to people speaking as cultural members—in a number of ways. This is evident in the various ways they identify themselves, refer to others, refer to the places where they live and work, describe what they do, and indicate their proximity to the places they are talking about and the people with whom they are talking (on the air). In short, through their talk, people not only connect with others, they map out the ways in which they are tied to others and tied to place, effectively situating themselves as members of local cultures.

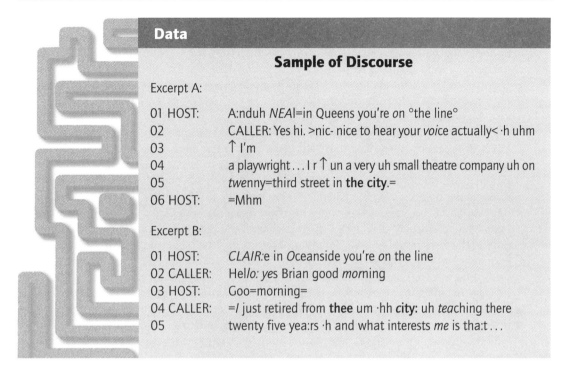

Data

Sample of Discourse

Excerpt A:

```
01 HOST:     A:nduh NEAI=in Queens you're on °the line°
02           CALLER: Yes hi. >nic- nice to hear your voice actually< ·h uhm
03           ↑ I'm
04           a playwright . . . I r ↑ un a very uh small theatre company uh on
05           twenny=third street in the city.=
06 HOST:     =Mhm
```

Excerpt B:

```
01 HOST:     CLAIR:e in Oceanside you're on the line
02 CALLER:   Hello: yes Brian good morning
03 HOST:     Goo=morning=
04 CALLER:   =I just retired from thee um ·hh city: uh teaching there
05           twenty five yea:rs ·h and what interests me is tha:t . . .
```

Orientation and Design of Talk

First, although callers are identified by hosts who introduce them in terms of where they are calling from, the place names are initially supplied by callers (who give them to screeners), and at times are adjusted once the caller is on the air, showing how speakers orient and design their talk for the audience they think is listening. For example, in a discussion of racial conflict and hate crime incidents in ethnic enclaves of the boroughs of New York City, callers identified themselves as being from neighborhoods in Brooklyn and Queens locally known for such crimes (e.g., "I'm from Howard Beach" and "I'm from Bensonhurst"). This shows that when callers identify themselves in terms of place, they may also indicate their race, class, or position on an issue, or call up public memories of local news stories without explanation, which is evidently useful when delicate topics are discussed (Haspel & Tracy, 2007). Place names do more than tell us who a speaker takes her audience to be and what she assumes they know (Schegloff, 1972). They identify people in relation to others, marking alignments between people as members of a local culture, or cultural boundaries between members of one local culture and another (e.g., Haspel & Tracy, 2007).

Membership Categorization Devices

Second, references to places, persons, and activities can be inference rich, or what might be more commonly referred to as *loaded* terms. That is, callers' references to place may be so dependent on the local context of talk, location, and situation that it is left to audience members to draw inferences from the talk to figure out what they mean. Returning to the earlier example of "the city," callers from the New York City area to both regional and national talk shows use this term to refer to (1) the island of Manhattan, if they were located beyond it; (2) the place, building, or occupation within which they work; (3) any number of municipal institutions (e.g., Board of Education, New York Police Department) which they called to criticize; and (4) the population of New York City in general (as in "the city voted overwhelmingly democratic"). In using this reference, callers are telling us something about who they take their audience to be: members of a group who have sufficient local knowledge to understand what they are talking about without further explanation. Discourse analysts call these kinds of labels or references that rely heavily on a commonsense knowledge shared by speakers and listeners *membership categorization devices* or *MCDs* (Silverman, 1998).

One function of MCDs used in public discourse (as in talk shows and public meetings) is to single out members of the audience for criticism, or to show one's alignment (siding) with one faction of the audience as opposed to another (Haspel & Tracy, 2007). In one extreme case, while discussing New York City politics with the host, a caller used racist discourse to refer to the former and first Black mayor of New York City, David Dinkins, as "the washroom attendant," adding, "you know who I'm talking about?" with a snicker. The caller was not only using a familiar reference he had apparently heard the host and others use on the program; he was "fishing" for the host to acknowledge his attempt at a tacitly racist inside joke, one based on shared but not stated knowledge (Pomerantz, 1980). The caller's seemingly simple reference not only demeaned David Dinkins by casting him in a subservient occupation once held by African Americans rather than acknowledging him as mayor, but condescended to people in the audience who may have aligned themselves with Mayor Dinkins, as other African Americans, Democrats, or New Yorkers. In such cases, speakers use MCDs to *ascribe* cultural identities to others that mark their difference and distance from them, which implicitly assigns a cultural identity to the speaker as well—or allows us to infer one, without stating it (Antaki, 1998).

In summary, references to persons, places, topics, and experiences can be shown, through discourse analysis, to operate as so much more than content. Discourse markers, specifically pronouns, indexical expressions, and MCDs, help us to interpret talk and text in a cultural context that is rooted in place even when the discourse is produced in a place far removed from the local culture such as "on the air" (Haspel, 2007).

WHY DOES THIS MATTER?

Using methods of discourse analysis to study the talk of New Yorkers and others on the air allowed me to see and hear that culture is located in communication, no matter where it takes place. This is important in the context of our increasingly interconnected world and converging media that some fear are threatening the very existence of distinct local cultures. Yet the analysis of public, mediated discourse, like that produced on broadcast talk shows, demonstrates that people mark their cultural membership and boundaries in their ways of communicating. As our means of interacting with others—familiar and strange—grow more immediate, intimate, and mobile with advancements in communication technology, the local construction of culture in discourse may grow even more evident to us. That people make efforts to demonstrate where they are speaking from, locally and culturally, even when they are addressing their talk "to the world" is potentially quite significant. The ways in which callers to talk shows construct their identities, and connect to or distance themselves from others may not seem relevant in an age of social networking. However, if we consider broadcast talk a mediated forum of discussion similar to online chat or social networking sites, we can see how communication practices in all of these forums are related.

With your newfound attention to discourse and appreciation of methods for studying it, you may now be able to see and understand the webs of cultural significance you construct every day in your communication with others. One place we can detect threads of cultural significance woven through talk to show how we are connected to one another is in the ways we orient to others in our talk and text. By *orient to others,* I mean the ways in which we show others "where we are coming from," which is an idiomatic expression in American English for our position in a discussion, our perspective on some issue, or our world view, all of which stem from our experiences situated in a certain place—where we live, work, grew up, went to school–and in networks of relationships we built there. We might call that place home, that starting place from which we navigate and network. These are terms we know and regularly use regarding social networking on the Internet, but they have their origins in social interaction.

If we extend this analogy a bit further, just as the address at the top of the page tracks our journey when we navigate the World Wide Web, so does our discourse. As noted earlier and as reflected in your own experiences, when we open our mouths we show others where we come from—geographically, relationally, and ideologically—but also show them where we have been. Orientation to others may extend to communication accommodation, so that we Easterners may find ourselves pronouncing that *r* after vowels or calling soda *pop* like those we consider to be Westerners do when we address them, even though we still sound different from them. We can speak as our unique selves and address others at the same time, because as cultural members we learn how to code switch. Discourse analysis of subtle shifts in indexical expressions and pronouns and inference-rich references to place allow us to see code switching in action, up close, in context. Learning how to analyze and understand discourse on a local level effectively equips us with our own global tracking device, in talk and text. Consider now how your place in the world, where you are coming from, is marked and tracked in the talk and text you produce and exchange every day, and why, in an age of global electronic communication, it should matter.

QUESTIONS TO CONSIDER

Culture

1. Imagine you were going to interact with a member of this culture. Based on this study, might you do anything differently in a conversation with someone from this culture than you would with someone from your own culture? Why or why not?

2. How is the culture discussed in the study similar to and different to your own?

3. How does what you learned about this culture relate to what you understand about your own culture?

4. What theories, concepts, or issues discussed in this text are relevant to this study?

5. What new theories, concepts, or issues have you learned from this study?

6. Is culture discussed here as a representation that affects communication or as a construction created by communication?

Research Method

1. What would you have done differently if you were to conduct a similar study? Why?

2. If you were going to conduct research on a cultural group, would you use this method? Why or why not?

3. What are the limitations of the research conducted that are identified by the author? Can you think of other limitations the author has not discussed?

4. What are some pros and cons of using this method?

5. How did the researcher construct the identity of cultural group members? What did the researcher do or say that communicated this?

6. What questions do you have about this method?

REFERENCES

Antaki, C. (1998). Identity ascriptions in their time and place: "Fagin" and "The Terminally Dim." In C. Antaki & S. Widdicombe (Eds.), *Identities in talk* (pp. 71–86). London: Sage.

Geertz, C. (1983). Common sense as a cultural system. In *Local knowledge: Further essays in interpretive anthropology* (pp. 73–93). New York: Basic Books.

Haspel, K. C. & Tracy, K. (2007). Marking and shifting lines in the sand: Discursive moves of ordinary democracy. In K. Tracy, B. Gronbeck, & J. P. McDaniel (Eds.), *The prettier doll: Rhetoric, discourse and ordinary democracy* (pp. 142–175). Tuscaloosa: University of Alabama Press.

Haspel, K. C. (2007). Order from chaos: The sensemaking structure and therapeutic function of mediated eyewitness accounts of the September 11th attacks. *American Communication Journal, 9,* [Electronic publication]. http://www.acjournal.org/holdings/vol9/spring/articles/sensemaking.html

Levinson, S. C. (1983). Deixis. In *Pragmatics* (pp. 54–96). Cambridge, UK: Cambridge University Press.

Pomerantz, A. (1980). Telling my side: "Limited Access" as a "Fishing" device. *Sociological Inquiry, 50,* 186–198.

Schegloff, E. (1972). Notes on a conversational practice: Formulating place. In P. P. Gigioli (Ed.), *Language and social context* (pp. 95–135). New York: Penguin Books.

Schegloff, E. A. (2007). *Sequence organization in interaction: A primer in conversation analysis* (Vol. I). New York: Cambridge University Press.

Schiffrin, D., Tannen, D., & Hamilton, H. E. (Eds.) (2003). *The handbook of discourse analysis*. Malden, MA: Blackwell.

Silverman, D. (1998). Membership categorization analysis. In *Harvey Sacks: Social science & conversation analysis* (pp. 74–97). New York: Oxford University Press.

Appendix C

DAGAABA CULTURE OF GHANA EXPLORED
THROUGH RHETORICAL ANALYSIS

Anthony Y. Naaeke

Marymount Manhattan College

Overview

Based in social construction, Naaeke's interpretivist study uses rhetorical analysis to explore narratives within Dagaaba culture. As you read about this study, consider what lessons about your own culture are embedded in the familiar myths you have read or heard in your life.

WHY DID I STUDY THIS CULTURE?

This essay engages in a rhetorical analysis of some aspects of the culture of the Dagaaba of Ghana. Since the 1950s, the United Nations Educational, Scientific and Cultural Organization (UNESCO) has called for the documentation, preservation, and dissemination of cultural traditions worldwide making it essential to seize any opportunity to participate in this worthwhile program. Particularly in sub-Saharan Africa, cultures are undergoing change as a result of contact with Western and Eastern societies in the wake of globalization. The values of the Dagaaba can enlighten other cultures and dispel stereotypes. I also chose to write about the Dagaaba because I am a member of this culture and have written about this culture in other contexts. Because Dagaaba view themselves as part of a process that begins at birth and ends not simply with physical death, but in a spiritual world hereafter, I focus on Dagaaba worldview regarding procreation, sense of right and wrong, and destiny. In my study, I conduct a narrative analysis of Dagaaba stories because these aspects of Dagaaba culture expressed in these stories summarize the life cycle of a person within the Dagaaba society and this is essential for understanding Dagaaba and their worldview. As a Dagao, I have listened to these stories while growing up in Ghana. The stories are well known, common, but beginning not to be actively told because of formal education whose curriculum does not encourage the study of local language but focuses on teaching English language. For this reason it is important to record and study these stories for posterity.

WHY DID I USE THIS METHOD?

The essay explores Dagaaba culture by using a cultural or narrative analysis approach to rhetorical criticism because the Dagaaba are a story-telling people. The narrative approach to rhetorical criticism enables the critic to examine and discover how stories "discourage or facilitate particular outcomes" and how stories "function as tools for empowerment or to build community within a group" (Foss, 1996, p. 400). Foss states further that analysis of narratives is important for what it can "reveal about an individual's or culture's identity, what things mean to them" (p. 401). Malidoma P. Some (1998), a Dagara (variant of Dagaaba) shama and scholar asserts:

> Stories open a world wherein relating to others and the world is automatic, and they boost imagination toward a place of better self-knowledge. Without stories, a society will find it difficult to hold itself together. It is as if stories bond people together and allow each individual to better comprehend what their place is in the world, and how their place holds everything else together. Indigenous teachings are derived from stories that they see as eternal blueprints for human wisdom. (p. 250)

For the Dagaaba, the rhetorical function of mythical narratives is similar to what Foss (1996) has observed. Hence, from both Western and Dagaaba perspectives, I am confident that Dagaaba narratives play a significant rhetorical function.

WHO DID I STUDY?

The Dagaaba reside in the Upper West Region of Ghana. The region shares geographical borders with la Cote d'Ivoire (Ivory Coast) in the West, Burkina Faso in the North and the Upper East and Northern regions to the East and South of Ghana respectively. The Upper West region of Ghana occupies about 18,500 square kilometers, which represents approximately 7.8% of Ghana's total landmass of 258,538 square kilometers. The region is home to about 450,000 people, that is, about 4% of Ghana's total population. The language spoken is called *Dagaare* or *Dagara*. Geographically, the land occupied by the Dagaaba is flat with low trees. The year is divided into two distinct seasons—dry and wet—the latter lasting from late April through October. Temperatures range between 20 and 35 degrees Celsius (68–95 degrees Fahrenheit). The people are mainly subsistence farmers who derive their livelihood from cultivating the land and rearing animals (for more on Dagaaba culture see Naaeke, 2010). For entertainment, Dagaaba tell stories, especially when the moonlight shines brightly at night. According to Angsotinge (1986), Dagaaba find stories entertaining and pleasurable "not so much because of the intrinsic content-elements of the tale but because of the socio-psychological functions that become manifest in the perception of the narrative" (p. 2). In addition to the entertainment value, the didactic value of Dagaaba narratives is that they "inculcate virtues in the younger generation," (p. 60) especially those stories that condemn vice and antisocial behavior such as "failure to show hospitality, thievery, murder, gossip, greed, and witchcraft" (p. 60).

Method

How Did I Conduct This Study?

Rhetorical analysis, or criticism, entails a conscious reflection on the symbols that we encounter every day, such as movies, stories, words, and posters, and why they affect or influence our perception and actions. One way of doing rhetorical analysis is narrative criticism, introduced by Walter R. Fisher (1984). This approach to rhetorical criticism recognizes narration as a way of persuasion that is different from the methods of persuasion introduced by Aristotle that place emphasis on appealing to the reason of an audience. It also conveys the fact that narratives "are meaningful for everyone, across culture, time, and place" (Burgchardt, 2000, p. 289). Narrative criticism shows another way of analyzing discourse that does not privilege logic and yet conveys sensible and comprehensible messages. Some of these include stories, parables, riddles, myths, and folklore. As Foss (1996) explains, narratives or stories have a "capacity to reveal how we organize experience" (p. 399).

As Shuter (2000) argues, rhetorical critics must be aware that analytical frameworks "are reflections of the cultures that produced them" and that "Aristotle's rhetorical framework is not culturally compatible with non-Western rhetorics" (p. 13). Luciates, Condit, and Caudill (1999) articulate the virtue of incorporating peripheral cultures in the rhetorical corpus as follows:

> The incorporation of marginalized voices into the contemporary study of rhetoric has significantly challenged the historical biases represented in the canon of great works privileged by the rhetorical tradition, including both technical and philosophical treatises, as well as those texts identified as exemplars of rhetoric-in-action. (p. 535)

The addition of such voices has also challenged the methods employed in the study and enactment of rhetoric. Therefore, the narrative paradigm gives a voice to societies, such as the Dagaaba in the study of rhetorical theory and criticism.

In this narrative rhetorical analysis, I analyze three stories told within Dagaaba culture by posing and answering three main questions that are central to mythological narratives, namely, (1) Where do we come from? (2) What is our conception of right and wrong? and (3) Where are we going? Narratives vary in detail and style depending on the narrator, the historical context at the time of the narration, and the location (village) from which the narrator comes. The narratives I analyze were recorded by Jack Goody (1972), an English ethnographer, Gervase T. Angsotinge (1986), and Paschal Kyoore. Angsotinge and Kyoore are Dagaaba scholars and folklorists.

WHAT DID I FIND OUT?

Let us now take a closer look at some Dagaaba narratives regarding procreation, social values of right and wrong, and conception of life after death from a rhetorical point of view.

The *Bagre*

The following narrative opens our eyes to routine domestic chores of women among the Dagaaba.

The boy's mother, when darkness fell, asked the father, "What shall we do to get another child in addition so there'll be two"?

The boy's father said to her, "The day after tomorrow I will go to my elder's place, to the spider who will help us to climb up to God's place and get a child."

Day had broken and the boy's mother went to the woods to fetch firewood. She searched till she came to a well-wooded bank. When she got there she saw a creature; a boa constrictor and his mate were playing there. At this the woman broke out laughing.

The boa constrictor called the woman to come near and he asked her why she was laughing. And she answered, "It's nothing, except the playing gave me pleasure. That's why I laughed."

The boa constrictor said to her, "Do you know this pleasure?" And she replied, "No I don't" and he told her to sit there. She sat quietly. The boa constrictor slept with his mate. They did their work and woman saw and asked him to sleep with her too. He slept with the woman and she got up. When she had done so, she told him his play had pleased her when she had said this the snake told her if she played that game, she'd give birth to many children.

Then the woman got up and ran off to her own house. She reached there and told the man that she'd seen something, a certain game. And the man asked, "What game was that?" She replied, "Wait till I show you." She went to lie down and called the man. He came there and lay down too, and then the woman showed him what to do. And the man enjoyed it too and laughed softly, saying it was true the game was pleasing. (Excerpt from *Black Bagre*, 1934–2020)

Procreation

All cultures seek answers to questions about their origins and the Dagaaba are no exception. To answer the question about how humans learned how to procreate, Dagaaba tell a story recorded by Jack Goody in his book, *The Myth of the Bagre* (1972). The *bagre* myth is a traditional myth that seeks in part to explain Dagaaba origins, including the origin of life and death in Dagaaba cosmology. Among the Dagaaba, it is part of the responsibilities of women to go to the woods to fetch firewood for domestic use. While searching for wood, women sometimes see snakes. When Dagaaba see a snake their immediate reaction is to try to kill it. So, it is interesting to note that in the bagre story the woman does not try to kill the snakes but is rather looking at them and finding pleasure in what they are doing. Consistent with Dagaaba culture that values learning by observation and participation (Suom-Dery, 2000, p. 213), the woman in the bagre myth learns about procreation from the snake. Three lessons for Dagaaba people are embedded in the *Myth of the Bagre*.

One lesson taught from this story is that contrary to the subordinate role and place that women play in Dagaaba society, the woman in this story is both the discoverer of how to procreate and initiator of sexual activity. She resists the social construction of her role and place in the society by proactively seeking knowledge about procreation and then becoming the teacher of her husband. This constitutes a reversal of roles in a society where men dominate women as head of the family, initiator of sexual activity, and custodians of cultural heritage. By becoming an active agent of self-emancipation from the cultural norm of "subjection of women to men" (Naaeke, 2010, p. 104), the woman may also be said to be resisting the society's construction of barrenness. For the Dagaaba, the worth of a woman is in child bearing. A barren woman is scorned upon. Barrenness is often a legitimate reason for a man to marry a second wife (Naaeke, 2005, p. 8). Hence, it may appear that this woman resists this social construct by finding a way to provide for her own fecundity.

A second lesson taught from this story regards the woman speaking to a snake. In Dagaaba folklore and mythology, as in stories from other cultures (e.g., George Orwell's *Animal Farm*) it is not unusual for animals, birds, or objects to speak. Just as the woman in the biblical narrative of Genesis engaged in dialogue with a snake leading to the discovery of the knowledge of good and evil, the woman in this Dagaaba narrative may be said to be a hero in the sense that she is willing to take a risk in a society where she is expected to be docile and submissive. She ventures into the woods (separation) where she encounters a stranger and after a brief conversation, she is willing to take a chance at learning something new. She is willing to dare, to take a risk (initiation). The venture yields good results in the sense that she learns to copulate and have children, and returns to share the knowledge with her man (return) (Naaeke, 2005, p. 8). In this way, she completes the journey of a hero as described by Joseph Campbell (1973). A hero ventures forth from the world of common day into a region of supernatural wonder (separation); fabulous forces are there encountered and a decisive victory is won (initiation); the hero comes back from this mysterious adventure with the power to bestow boons on his fellow man (return; Campbell, 1973, p. 30; Naaeke, 2005, p. 8). Hence, the woman in the story can be said to be a hero.

A third lesson taught, from the standpoint of binary oppositions introduced by Levi-Strauss (1978), is that the story reveals some cultural elements of Dagaaba cosmology where cosmic spirits are sometimes shown as personified objects of the universe that are conceived not just as natural phenomena but as personal beings with spiritual interiority. One of the cosmic spirits is *wie* (bush). In this story, the woman goes from home (domestic environment) to wie (a place other than domestic; bush; wild environment). By going to wie, it may be said that the woman is actually going to the cosmic spirit where an encounter with the spiritual world is possible (Suom-Dery, 2000, p. 56). As religious people, Dagaaba believe in the power of spiritual beings that are part and parcel of their cosmology. These beings inhabit the bush (wie) as opposed to the home. Medicine men, diviners, and other spiritual agents among the Dagaaba receive knowledge and power from these spirits. Therefore, wie is a place of encounter between human beings and the spiritual world—a place of transformation and rebirth. However, the binary opposition occurs because according to Dagaaba cosmology, animals are lower in rank to human beings. The immediate superiors to human beings who teach or reveal things to human beings are the *kontome* (beings of the wild). Kontome are said to be the brain behind the discovery of many aspects of Dagaaba culture—art, music, magic, hunting, medicine, and so on. It is, therefore, surprising that the snake and not kontome is responsible for teaching human beings how to copulate and procreate.

In summary, the story introduces several elements of Dagaaba culture. These are the role of woman as knowledge seeker and hero even in a society that does not typically value women in these ways, and the value of even the lowest creature to provide knowledge. These may seem unreasonable or even contradictory to an outsider. Yet there is intrinsic narrative rationality for the Dagaaba when they listen to the story. The woman becomes the active agent in the liberation of her subservient role in a patriarchal society. In some respects, she is like the biblical Eve who gains knowledge of good and evil by having a conversation with a snake and eating the fruit that she and Adam were forbidden by God to eat. In contemporary Western societies, she could easily be identified with champions of women liberation. Additionally, it is important to note that, like Hannah in the Bible (1 Samuel Chapters 1 & 2), the woman goes to the spiritual world to lament her condition and in return, receives the favor of a fecundity and knowledge of procreation. Hearing the story and properly understanding its meaning can help Dagaaba women to learn that it is possible to empower themselves by venturing into the *spiritual world* to seek knowledge, transformation and rebirth from a society that constructs her as subservient to men and worthless if barren.

The Lion, the Wolf, and the Goat

Below is an abridged version of a narrative that illustrates Dagaaba response or reaction to the question of good and evil.

A long time ago, there lived the lion, the wolf and the goat. They all lived as friends. One day the wolf went hunting but he found no prey. He was returning home, still feeling hungry, when he met the goat. The goat had also gone hunting. He was lucky to find plenty of grass by the river side. He ate as much as he wanted. He then went and drank from the river. On his way home, the goat found some honey in the tree. He climbed the tree and filled his pot with the honey. He then descended and started to go home. As he was going home, he met the wolf who was also returning home from a fruitless search for food. The wolf saw that the goat was full and was even carrying something in his pot. The wolf planned to eat the goat and initiated a conversation with the goat during which the wolf became upset and began to chase the goat.

The two of them ran until the goat dashed into a thick grove. The wolf followed in hot pursuit. As soon as they entered the grove they came upon the lion and his wife.

When the lion's wife saw the wolf and the goat she started to groan in pain and asked the lion to get him some medicine. The lion turned around and asked the wolf and the goat, "Which of you can procure medicine to cure my wife?" The wolf immediately pointed at the goat and said, "Mr. Lion, have you not heard that the ancestors of the goat are renowned medicine men? You should ask him. I am sure he will know what kind of medicine your wife will need." The goat said, "Truly, my ancestors are famous medicine men. I am carrying some ingredients in my pot here to go home and prepare some medicine. I went hunting for some herbs this morning. I found all of them except one important ingredient which I urgently need for the preparation of the medicine." "What is that particular ingredient that you need to prepare the medicine?" demanded the lion. "I need the brains of one animal. However, that animal is bigger and stronger than me," replied the goat.

The wolf pleaded with the goat to tell lion the name of the animal he needs to make the medicine for the lioness. The goat said, "I need the brains of a wolf to prepare the medicine." At this, the lion pounced on the wolf and tore up a limb. He gave it to the goat. The goat dipped it into the pot of honey and passed it to the lioness. When the lioness had eaten all of the wolf, the lion himself was feeling hungry and wished he could eat the goat. So, he too started to complain of a headache. He asked the goat to procure some medicine for him too. The goat quickly came up with a plan and escaped from the lion. (Angsotinge, 1986, pp. 218–223)

Social Values of Right and Wrong

A second concern of mythical narratives regards the question of social norms on right and wrong. Like many cultures, Dagaaba battles with the question of why bad things happen to good people and, conversely, why good things happen to bad people. The answer to these questions is given in narratives, such as the myth of "The Lion, the Wolf, and the Goat." The immediate lesson to learn from this narrative is that it is better to do what is right than what is wrong and that evil will never win over good. However, there are deeper lessons that the narrative teaches. For example, from the point of view of binary oppositions, there is opposition between bush and home, domestic animal (goat) and wild animal (wolf or lion), small and big, weak and strong, wise and foolish. For the Dagaaba, the strong is supposed to protect the weak, but in this narrative, the strong (wolf) wants to trample upon the weak (goat). By some ingenuity of the weak, the stronger party loses in the end. Additionally, the lion is supposed to act as a mediator between the goat and the wolf, but he woefully fails in this task. The small but intelligent goat outsmarts the powerful lion and manages to escape from its threats. All in all, Dagaaba want to teach through this narrative that it is always good to maintain proper relationships with others and with nature and to do what is good and not evil. Moreover, when others do not behave appropriately, ingenuity may help the less fortunate.

Although the preceding narrative seems to suggest that Dagaaba narratives have a clear-cut lesson on right and wrong, that doesn't seem to be the whole truth. According to Paschal Kyoore (personal communication, February 1, 2010), "The main character of Dagara tales, *Deberlere* or *Bader* (Spider), almost always triumphs in his tricks and malice against 'good' characters in the tales. He tricks the little as well as the big animals, and listeners relish his intelligence and wit." As a resolution to this apparent contradiction in Dagaaba narratives, Kyoore observes that though *Deberlere,* the protagonist of many Dagaaba narratives, is a trickster, his character is meant to teach the youth that "intelligence and wit are handy for the little one who is vulnerable to the size and strength of those that are bigger, but at the same time it is not acceptable to take advantage of our friends" as *Deberlere* always does. In one particular story, *Deperlere* is not depicted as the hero or victor as he is usually in Dagaaba stories. Here, he is made to suffer for his bad behavior thereby serving as a lesson to Dagaaba youth that those who are small, weak, or underprivileged will not automatically be vindicated on account of their situation or ingenuity and that bad behavior will not be rewarded no matter who engages in it.

Life After Death

A third concern of mythical narratives is eschatological. Eschatological myths attempt to answer the question: Where are we going? or What is the end? "For the Dagaaba, the end of life is a mystery and unlike other cultures that have eschatological myths (see Biblical Book of Revelation), Dagaaba have no such myths" (Kuukure, 1985, p. 110). Dagaaba perceive death as a passage to a different way of life. Dagaaba understand death as going home to the land of the ancestors (Kuukure, 1985). Their beliefs about death and the hereafter are celebrated in rituals rather than narratives (Kuukure, 1985; Some, 1998). A central feature of a Dagaaba funeral ritual is the *paala* (pyre).

To briefly analyze the paala as a cultural snapshot of Dagaaba consolatory rhetoric, the paala is a place where the deceased is displayed for public viewing and mourning. It is made of wood tied together with fiber to make a giant chair with a canopy of cloths for shade. Around the paala are material displays of food, animals, and clothing meant to indicate the achievements of the deceased. Money is often strewn around the corpse. The money symbolizes the contribution of the donor toward the safe spiritual journey of the deceased to the land of the ancestors. Dagaaba believe that the deceased will need money to pay a ferry toll in order to cross a bridge connecting the land of the living to that of the ancestors.

The paala faces east if the deceased is male indicating that in life he usually woke up early in the morning, before or as the sun is rising, to go to work on the farm. If the deceased is female, the paala faces west to indicate that as a hardworking woman she was usually busy at work until the sun sets. The deceased is dressed and seated in a dignified position to show him or her honor and respect. For a deceased man, a bow is laid across his folded legs and a quiver hangs from his shoulder to indicate that in life he was a hunter and guardian of his household. On a deceased woman's lap is placed her shrine basket (*tiib-pele*) and in her hand an unscraped calabash. These objects symbolize her hardworking and hospitable character, often shown by offering a calabash of water to visitors and holding seeds for sowing in the fields (Kuukure, 1985, p. 115). The value of this ritual for the Dagaaba is that as the community grieves and beholds this ritual farewell to the deceased, they are summoned and challenged to uphold the values of the community just as the deceased did.

WHY DOES THIS MATTER?

By studying and analyzing these narratives, the fundamental rhetorical functions of myths or narrative for the Dagaaba, as for other cultures, becomes clear. As Hart (1997) and Foss (1996) observe, myths provide a heightened sense of authority, continuity, coherence, community, choice, and agreement (Hart, 1997, pp. 243–244). Narratives enable the critic to examine and discover how stories "discourage or facilitate particular outcomes" (Foss, 1996, p. 400) or "function as tools for empowerment or to build community within a group" (p. 401). In the narratives and ritual I discussed, Dagaaba find a sense of continuity and communion with their past and present. The narratives help Dagaaba children know that they share commonality in worldview and a sense of right and wrong. Additionally, these narratives help people who are not Dagaaba to know something about Dagaaba culture.

In recounting and analyzing these Dagaaba narratives, I realize that themes that the narratives address are common across cultures. Western and non-Western cultures alike pose similar questions and have narratives that answer similar questions. For example, U.S. American society responds to the question of procreation in the poem, "The butterfly and the bee," by William Lisle Bowles. Judeo-Christian traditions respond to the question of good and evil by teaching the Ten Commandments. With regard to death and the hereafter, the Judeo-Christian tradition answers with teachings about heaven and hell. Although the stories that each culture constructs to answer these questions may differ, there are similarities in the meaning of the message.

QUESTIONS TO CONSIDER

Culture

1. Imagine you were going to interact with a member of this culture. Based on this study, might you do anything differently in a conversation with someone from this culture than you would with someone from your own culture? Why or why not?

2. How is the culture discussed in the study similar to and different to your own?

3. How does what you learned about this culture relate to what you understand about your own culture?

4. What theories, concepts, or issues discussed in this text are relevant to this study?

5. What new theories, concepts, or issues have you learned from this study?

6. Is culture discussed here as a representation that affects communication or as a construction created by communication?

Research Method

1. What would you have done differently if you were to conduct a similar study? Why?

2. If you were going to conduct research on a cultural group, would you use this method? Why or why not?

3. What are the limitations of the research conducted that are identified by the author? Can you think of other limitations the author has not discussed?

4. What are some pros and cons of using this method?

5. How did the researcher construct the identity of cultural group members? What did the researcher do or say that communicated this?

6. What questions do you have about this method?

REFERENCES

Angsotinge, G. T. (1986). *Wisdom of the ancestors: An analysis of the oral narratives of the Dagaaba of northern Ghana.* PhD dissertation.

Burgchardt, C. R. (2000). *Readings in rhetorical criticism* (2nd ed.). State College, PA: Strata Publishing.

Campbell, J. (1973). *The hero with a thousand faces.* Princeton, NJ: Princeton University Press.

Fisher, W. R. (1984/2000). Narration as a human communication paradigm: The case of public moral agreement. In C. R. Burgchardt (Ed.), *Readings in rhetorical criticism* (2nd ed., pp. 290-312). State College, PA: Strata Publishing.

Foss, S. K. (1996). *Rhetorical criticism: Exploration & practice.* Prospect Heights, IL: Waveland Press.

Goody, J. (1972). *The myth of the bagre.* Oxford, UK: Clarendon Press.

Hart, R. P. (1997). *Modern rhetorical criticism.* Needham Height, MA: Allyn & Bacon.

Kuukure, E. (1985). *The destiny of man: Dagaare beliefs in dialogue with Christian eschatology.* New York: Peter Lang.

Levi-Strauss, C. (1978). *Myth and meaning.* New York: Shocken Books.

Luciates, J. L., Condit, C. M., & Caudill, S. (1999). *Contemporary rhetorical theory: A reader.* New York: Guilford Press.

Martin, J. N., Nakayama, T. K., & Flores, L. A. (2002). *Readings in intercultural communication: experiences and contexts.* New York: McGraw-Hill.

Naaeke, A. Y. (2005). The cultural relevance of myth: A reader-response analysis of the bagre myth with reference to the role and place of women in the Dagaaba society. *Journal of Dagaare Studies, 5,* 1–10.

Naaeke, A. Y. (2010). *Critical essays on Dagaaba rhetoric.* New York: Peter Lang.

Shuter, R. (2000). The cultures of rhetoric. In A. Gonzalez, D. V. Tanno (Eds.), *Rhetoric in intercultural contexts* (pp. 11-17). Thousand Oaks, CA: Sage.

Some, P. M. (1998). *The healing wisdom of Africa: Finding life purpose through nature, ritual, and community.* New York: Penguin Putnam.

Suom-Dery, E. (2000). *Family as subject of moral education in the African context: Incarnating Christian ethics among the Dagara of north-western Ghana.* Hamburg: Kovac.

Appendix D

TRANSNATIONAL DOMINICAN CULTURE EXPLORED THROUGH PHENOMENOLOGICAL ANALYSIS

Wilfredo Alvarez

Northeastern Illinois University

Mark P. Orbe

Ewa L. Urban

Nayibe A. Tavares

Western Michigan University

Overview

Based in social construction, Alvarez, Orbe, Urban, and Tavares provide a critical study using phenomenological analysis to explore how transnational Dominican culture is constructed through language and nonverbal behavior. As you read about this study, reflect upon how you interact with international students and, more broadly, those who embody a transnational culture.

WHY DID WE STUDY THIS CULTURE?

Transnational culture exists when individuals create a cultural home that resembles—yet is geographically apart from—their homeland. Recent enrollment of international students on U.S. campuses reached a record high number of 623,805 individuals (Institute for International Education, 2008). Colleges and universities greatly benefit from international students' presence and their cultural, academic, and financial contributions. However, many colleges and universities struggle with providing fitting support to this diverse group of individuals (Galloway & Jenkins, 2005). International students' adjustment to college is much more difficult than it is for their U.S. American peers due to a variety of additional challenges caused by cultural, social, linguistic, and educational differences (Fritz, Chin, & DeMarinis, 2008; Sumer, Poyrazli, & Grahame, 2008). Adjustment difficulties are more prevalent among international students of color, those with stronger foreign accents or communication difficulties,

379

or those whose cultures differ significantly from the culture of the majority of the host country (Hanassab, 2006). However, according to Dawson (2009), Latin American students, especially Dominicans, possess a strong sense of community that facilitates a sense of belonging, provides a supportive network, and helps alleviate stress related to negative—particularly discriminatory—experiences. Moreover, we chose to study transnational Dominican culture because we were all interested in how this particular group negotiated their roles as international students.

WHY DID WE USE THIS METHOD?

As researchers, we wanted to gather narratives from Dominican students in an unrestricted manner. Therefore, phenomenology appeared to be a logical choice. We drew heavily from the work of Merleau-Ponty (1962), Husserl (1962), Lanigan (1979), and Nelson (1989) in creating the methodological framework for our study. These scholars have used phenomenology as a qualitative methodology to ask essential questions like "what it is like to have a certain experience?" (van Manen, 1990, p. 45). In other words, phenomenology allowed us to gather descriptions of Dominican students' lived experiences, and then work to understand the central components of these experiences from their perspectives. The scholars that we list above have done considerable work that has provided a model for a straightforward, yet rigorous, way to conduct research.

Specifically, we decided to use focus groups in this research project. According to Patton (1983), the purpose of focus groups is to gather information through a process where individuals can consider their own views in the context of others. In other words, how people describe their experiences are shared as others in the group report similar and different experiences. Past research has indicated that this methodological approach is valuable, especially when examining the complex lives of individuals from diverse backgrounds (Orbe, 2000). Consequently, focus group discussion appeared as a logical choice for our study.

WHO DID WE STUDY?

We studied international students from the Dominican Republic (DR). Within the United States, the enrollment of international students from the Dominican Republic grew by 20% from the academic year 2006–07 to 2007–08 (Institute for International Education, 2008). This trend is reflected at the campus described in this study, where recent partnerships between the institutions and the DR government resulted in a dramatic increase in the number of Dominican students. For instance, at the university where data was collected, the number of DR students grew from 1 student in 2007 to a 101 students in 2008 (Office of Student Academic and Institutional Research, 2009). As of 2010, approximately 130 Dominican students are attending classes. They constitute the third largest international student group at the university, and have the highest grade point average among international students. Our study explored the communicative experiences of Dominican students; in particular we focused on how they communicate to create Dominican culture in a midsized U.S. midwestern city.

Method

How Did We Conduct This Study?

We conducted this study using volunteers who agreed to participate in focus group discussions. Participants were 10 female and 16 male Dominican international students who had received a government-sponsored scholarship to study in the United States. In order to learn about their experiences, we conducted five focus groups, each lasting between 60 to 90 minutes. In these sessions, we used a topical protocol to learn about how participants described their cross-cultural adaptation process; communication with other international students; communication with U.S. American faculty, staff, and students; and the impact of the international student experience on self-identity. All focus groups were conducted in English, but four of the five focus groups were cofacilitated by a native Spanish speaker from the Dominican Republic. This allowed participants to ask for clarification when questions were not clear and use Spanish when answering questions in English was difficult. All of the focus groups conducted were tape recorded, and transcribed verbatim. For instance, when participants used Spanish, a native Spanish speaker on our research team provided an English translation. This allowed both linguistic voices to be included in our data. The result of this process was 140 pages of text.

Phenomenology involves a three-stage process: (1) gathering descriptions of lived experiences (description), (2) reviewing these descriptions in order to reveal essential themes (reduction of data, or *capta*—the term that phenomenologists use), and (3) discovering how the essential themes collectively reflect the phenomenon (interpretation) (Nelson, 1989). Having gathered the descriptions through focus groups, we began the process of reduction while transcribing each tape and organizing the text into preliminary themes. This process involved reading the text several times and reflecting upon what phrases or statements appeared as especially revealing about the experience (van Manen, 1990). During this time, several key themes emerged. Finally, during interpretation, another level of reflection (Merleau-Ponty, 1962), we sought an overarching picture that interconnects the essential themes. The identification, interpretation, and articulation of major themes benefitted greatly from the diversity of our research team—which included both Dominicans and non-Dominicans, as well as those who had various experiences with being an international student (or not).

Data

M: Let me just jump on something that you said. We want to get an idea of how studying in the U.S. has changed you. If we were going to ask you, how has this experience changed you? You may have one answer... but if we could ask your father, or others at home, what would they say? I kinda want everyone to answer—wow, look at all of the hands going up! Why don't we start here and go around. Wow (to Ewa) look at all of them grabbing paper to write things down!

WMU-M: Well, first... no matter how good your English is, or how long you've been coming here—I've been coming here since I was 6 years old. It doesn't matter. You have a different culture. When I came to the university for the first time, every time I came here I was hanging around my family and friends. But when you get to the point when you are around people that you don't know, it's different. There's one thing that's different... I don't know if you guys feel like this or not but... we have a different way of greeting people. If we greet a girl you are going to give her a kiss on the cheek. Here it is not like that. So a lot of us have problems like that.

WHAT DID WE FIND OUT?

The focus group discussions that we facilitated revealed several salient cultural elements that illustrated how the international students re-created Dominican culture on campus. Creating a transnational culture primarily occurred through elements of culture such as language, nonverbal behaviors such as paralanguage (i.e., speech rate, pitch, volume), greetings, time, and touch, collectivistic value orientation, as well as issues related to food. Of these, nonverbal behaviors and language appeared as especially significant.

Language

Language can act as a vehicle for cultural group exclusion and inclusion in various social contexts. Perceptions of language abilities were the most significant issue in the transcripts. In our study, language appeared to be a great source of difficulty and anxiety for the Dominican international students. Most of the Dominican students believed that their English was limited; this seemed to lead to Dominican students' feelings of exclusion from the larger cultural context. For example, several of the students expressed that routine interactions such as communicating with their instructors produced anxiety because they did not know how the instructors would react to their perceived deficiency in terms of linguistic abilities. This issue is revealed in one of the students' statements:

What I thought would be the most difficult part was the language . . . when I came here I knew some words, but I didn't know about being in classes. I know that I can watch television, listen to some music, but I didn't know how it was going to be when we were in class with a professor.

In contrast, the Dominican students expressed their preference to interact with ingroup members and primarily speak their native language. These communicative practices created a context of inclusion for them by, in essence, re-creating their culture on campus. As one student stated, "All Dominicans talk to each other because it's more like helpful and you feel more comfortable." In this sense, language acted as a "membership card" that allowed the students to feel included and reinforced their cultural identity, something that the larger context was not achieving. On several occasions, one or more of the Dominican student coresearchers expressed why staying in their group and speaking their language was so important to them. For instance, one shared that "I have my Dominican or Hispanic friends. Because I can speak my own language." The forcefulness of this statement implies that speaking in one's own language is an important way that individuals enact culture and sustain cultural identity when crossing cultural borders. These accounts illustrate how, in an intercultural context, language acts to preserve cultural identity, form and maintain relationships, and allow group cohesion.

Nonverbal Behaviors

Nonverbal behaviors and outgroup members' perceptions of those behaviors during social interaction represented another major issue that participants raised during the focus group discussions. Through nonverbal performances based on paralanguage (i.e., speech rate, pitch, and volume), greetings, use of space, and touch, coresearchers enacted and re-created their culture on campus. Time emerged as a distinct theme and is discussed in a separate section. Nonverbal behaviors, overall, came across as a strong mode of cultural enactment across the focus group discussions. Out of these nonverbal behaviors, one particular aspect of paralanguage—volume—appeared as especially salient. These paralinguistic behaviors, enacted by the Dominican students on campus, are captured by this comment from a male student: "No, you [we] have a loud reputation. So, that's why . . . sometimes I didn't notice that I was talking loud. It's just for me . . . , it's normal. I don't notice. Maybe it's not our fault . . . it's just cultural." Similar accounts can be read across the focus group transcripts. For instance, another student added: "Dominicans are really loud people. We pass by and greet one another passionately."

The Dominican students shared that they felt that other people misinterpreted their nonverbal behaviors when interacting with other Dominicans. This illustrates how cultural norms can function as powerful mediators in how we interpret other people's communication and interact with them. The following statement by a male student illustrates this point: "Sometimes people misunderstand . . . like we are so loud, or if we are with the girls we have to be hugging them. It's just friendship, it's nothing beyond that . . . People sometimes misunderstand that." Another student aptly articulated Dominican culture nonverbal enactment through the use of space and touch, and how this was perceived by outgroup members: "In the American culture, there's more bubbles, there's more space . . . we don't have that so much. We don't have that much space. We are really touchy, really huggy, we are really concentrated [when interacting with others]."

These behaviors were also perceived differently by outgroup members when these violated cultural norms of cross-gender interaction in public. In fact, some Dominican male students had been accused of sexual harassing behaviors, which forced one student to change his behavior: "Believe me I don't want to go and kiss another American girl now without previously knowing her."

Cultural Value Orientations

Cultural value orientation is a significant element of culture that Dominican students enacted through their communicative practices on campus. For instance, there were several cases when students expressed their need to make their family proud, and to collaborate with other classmates and colleagues because this was important to them. The Dominican students did not understand why many of their U.S. American counterparts did not seem to share their feelings about collaboration. These stories illustrate how Dominicans enacted their collectivistic value orientation in a rigidly individualistic cultural context such as the United States. A response from a male student, asked why he worked so hard to get good grades, illustrates the collectivistic cultural value orientation: "But I always go back and find my motivation there. I can easily say I don't want to do this anymore and quit. But it is not about me, it's also about my family." This collectivistic cultural value orientation was expressed throughout the focus group discussions.

The Dominican students' collectivistic value orientation was also exemplified through their sense of community. In fact, participants referred to the Dominican community on campus as "the family"—a constant source of support. Participants described how the support helped them adjust to U.S. culture, but also excel in their academic studies. For instance, one student talked about how Dominicans constantly studied together: "We every time do that. Like, you will get, like better results if you work together. And we do that a lot." Other students emphatically expressed that the primary factor helping them succeed as international students was "dedication and the motivation of your peers." Furthermore, one student pointed out that "we're [Dominicans] the international group with the highest GPA in the university, because we work together!" Another student quickly added, "Yeah, that's why! We work together!"

Time

Time orientation also emerged as a significant culture-related issue for Dominican participants. During the focus group discussions, participants often brought up that time norms were a major issue because U.S. norms were vastly different from the ones in their country. The following comment from one of the students illustrates this point: "A big thing is punctuality here. It is something that we [Dominicans] really have to learn. We Dominicans, we say if we have a party the party starts at 9 p.m.—everybody will get there at 12 a.m., or maybe 1 a.m." This observation exemplifies Dominican norms about punctuality and how much they differ from time orientations in the United States. Accordingly, through their reactions and behaviors toward time norms, participants continually enacted their native culture in their new cultural system.

The transcripts from the focus group discussions also revealed the Dominican students' realizations of how being immersed in U.S. American culture was changing their perceptions and behaviors related to time orientation. A female student expressed this the following way: "With punctuality, being on time . . . I think I'm used to the American style now of being on time and it's really annoying when people are late back at home." Another student offered the following advice to other students to manage the time norms back in their country: "If you want them early, you say 'I want you guys here at 1 and you know you're gonna start like at 2 or something.'" These comments demonstrate how the Dominican students' interactions within U.S. culture gave them useful insights into their own cultural norms and how they could alter any previous taken-for-granted behaviors. Additionally, the following comment displays a female student's newly discovered sense of exasperation with her native country's time orientation: "You know public transportation here is very good. In my country it's not like that. It's true. Public transportation in my country is never on time." In general, these narratives illustrate how these international students reacted to and negotiated the cultural differences associated with time in their host culture.

Food

Although we did not anticipate it, food was probably the most frequently raised cultural issue that the participants brought up throughout the focus group discussions. Food is a significant cultural element in any culture and these students' passionate accounts about food demonstrate how, through a constant pursuit of and talk about their native food, they recreated their culture. A male student's account captures this point: "American food isn't that good. I would say that most Americans like Dominican food [agreement from others]." Other students made observations about how Americans cook their food versus how Dominicans cook in the Dominican Republic: "I think it's not American food in general. It's that it's not made from scratch, like our food. If we're gonna cook, um, mashed potatoes, we buy actual potatoes and then . . ." Another student expressed: "Yes, I don't know, one of the things that I struggled when I came was with the food at the beginning."

The challenge of not having access to their native food on a regular basis provided another way that the participants recreated culture and signified the cultural meaning of food. A female student vividly captures the participants' struggles with food in their new cultural environment: "For me it was very difficult the first time I was here . . . And the first week, in the cafeteria, I was like pizza every time? At home, we only had pizza for special celebrations . . . And here every day. It's kind of weird for me."

Interestingly, food also functioned to facilitate the participants' adaptation to their new environment. Being away from their native foods made it real that they were not in their culture anymore so eating their food or other foods that resembled their own made them feel closer to home. For instance, one student responded that one of the reasons why he enjoyed spending time with his Chinese friends was because "I eat Chinese food, and I like that because they make rice [important ingredient in Dominicans' diet]." In this sense, food is not only something that humans consume for nutrition purposes but also a fundamental cultural "ingredient" that frames our cultural identity and our sense of "groupness" and community.

WHY DOES THIS MATTER?

We initially decided to study international students from the Dominican Republic for two primary reasons: (1) each of us had a personal or professional interest in the topic, and (2) this particular group of students was underrepresented in terms of existing research. The use of phenomenology allowed us to reveal how talking, behaving, socializing, working, and even eating were ways in which transnational Dominicans enacted important aspects of their cultural identities when away from their homeland.

In short, our study reveals that Dominican international students in the United States re-create Dominican culture on campus as a means of cultural adaptation. In particular, our analysis explains how this was achieved through the cultural elements of language, nonverbal behaviors (e.g., speech rate, dialect, volume, and touch), greetings, collectivism, time orientation, and food. As demonstrated through earlier sections, re-creating Dominican culture on campus allowed students to maintain or strengthen their cultural identity, work collectively with others to formulate a sense of cultural familiarity, and benefit from a sense of co-cultural community. From the perspective of study participants, having a substantial number of Dominican students was a crucial factor in their ability to adjust to U.S. American campus life. In this regard, their cultural adaptation did not follow the traditional model of assimilation but instead reflected the creation of an ethnic enclave on campus—a concentration of a particular cultural group who remains self-sufficiently separated from the larger population (Waldinger, 1993).

This research study represents a phenomenological examination of how Dominican students in the United States utilize the creation of co-cultural community as a means of cultural adaptation. Through this particular methodological approach, we were able to provide insight into a cultural group that historically has been largely ignored by communication scholars.

QUESTIONS TO CONSIDER

Culture

1. Imagine you were going to interact with a member of this culture. Based on this study, might you do anything differently in a conversation with someone from this culture than you would with someone from your own culture? Why or why not?

2. How is the culture discussed in the study similar to and different to your own?

3. How does what you learned about this culture relate to what you understand about your own culture?

4. What theories, concepts, or issues discussed in this text are relevant to this study?

5. What new theories, concepts, or issues have you learned from this study?

6. Is culture discussed here as a representation that affects communication or as a construction created by communication?

Research Method

1. What would you have done differently if you were to conduct a similar study? Why?

2. If you were going to conduct research on a cultural group, would you use this method? Why or why not?

3. What are the limitations of the research conducted that are identified by the authors? Can you think of other limitations the authors have not discussed?

4. What are some pros and cons of using this method?

5. How did the researchers construct the identity of cultural group members? What did the researchers do or say that communicated this?

6. What questions do you have about this method?

REFERENCES

Dawson, B. A. (2009). Discrimination, stress, and acculturation among Dominican immigrant women. *Hispanic Journal of Behavioral Sciences, 31,* 96–111.

Fritz, M. V., Chin, D., & DeMarinis, V. (2008). Stressors, anxiety, acculturation and adjustment among international and North American students. *International Journal of Intercultural Relations, 32,* 244–259.

Galloway, F. J., & Jenkins, J. R. (2005). The adjustment problems faced by international students in the United States: A comparison of international students and administrative perceptions at two private, religiously affiliated universities. *NASPA Journal, 42,* 175–187.

Hanassab, S. (2006). Diversity, international students, and perceived discrimination: Implications for educators and counselor. *Journal of Studies in International Education, 10,* 157–172.

Husserl, E. (1962). *Ideas: General introduction to pure phenomenology.* London: Collier Macmillan.

Institute for International Education. (2008). *Open doors 2008: International students in the United States.* Washington DC: Institute of International Education. Retrieved from http://opendoors.iienetwork.org/?p = 131590

Lanigan, R. L. (1979). The phenomenology of human communication. *Philosophy Today, 23*(i), 3–15.

Merleau-Ponty, M. (1948/1962). *The invisible and the visible* (C. Smith, Trans., F. Williams, Trans. Rev.). Boston: Routledge Kegan Paul.

Nelson, J. L. (1989). Phenomenology as feminist methodology: Explicating interviews. In K. Carter & C. Spitzack (Eds.), *Doing research on women's communication: Perspectives on theory and method* (pp. 221–241). Norwood, NJ: Ablex.

Office of Student Academic and Institutional Research (2009). *International student enrollment by country: Fall 2007 and fall 2008.* Kalamazoo: Western Michigan University. Retrieved from http://www.wmich.edu/ir/factbook/2008/enrollment/mapint.pdf

Orbe, M. P. (2000). Centralizing diverse racial/ethnic voices in scholarly research: The value of phenomenological inquiry. *International Journal of Intercultural Relations, 24,* 603–621.

Patton, M. Q. (1983). *Qualitative evaluation methods.* London: Sage.

Sumer, S. Poyrazli, S., & Grahame, K. (2008). Predictors of depression and anxiety among international students. *Journal of Counseling and Development, 86,* 429–437.

van Manen, M. (1990). *Researching lived experience: Human science for action sensitive pedagogy.* Ontario, Canada: State University of New York Press.

Waldinger, R. (1993). The ethnic enclave debate revisited. *International Journal of Urban and Regional Research, 17,* 428–436.

Appendix E

SOUTH AFRICAN CULTURE EXPLORED
THROUGH CONTENT ANALYSIS

Adrian Furnham

University College London

> ### Overview
>
> Furnham's social scientific study uses content analysis to explore how traditional gender roles are portrayed through television advertisements in South Africa. As you read about this study, consider what messages the media sends within your culture about men and women, as well as other cultural groups.

WHY DID I STUDY THIS CULTURE?

I grew up in South Africa, a country famed for many things including its beauty and sporting prowess, but also its cruel, oppressive, political policies. South Africa is the biggest, richest, and most populous country in the region of Southern Africa. When I was growing up (I was in high school 1965–1969) it was the high point of apartheid—the political policy of "separate development." There was much censorship and strict segregation not only of the races but of the sexes. So hotels had a bar for White men only, and a ladies bar where both sexes of the same race could mix. The government of the time was nervous about the spreading of liberal ideas with respect to racial equality and had strict censorship concerning imported films, theater, and books. Indeed it resisted any television until 1975.

Along with obvious issues like interracial contact, South Africa is of interest because of the role of women in society. Rissik (1994) notes:

> Although the status of women in each group in South Africa is different, there is one common factor: women in any group are less equal to men. As in almost all countries men have dominated the scene, making necessary for women not only to strive to reach the top in their fields, but to struggle against male domination as well. (p. 75)

She later writes:

> Most South African men are totally unwilling to do domestic chores, household shopping and the like. Some of this is because they have wives who do not work and hence they feel it is the "wife's job." But more often the resistance goes deeper as men feel it is "women's work" and therefore beneath them to get involved in it. It's a perception that is changing—but very, very slowly. . . . Among many South Africans and particularly men, there is a deep-rooted belief that women only work "if they have to." It often comes as quite a shock to them when they learn that many women, just like the men, work for personal fulfilment; to support or help support their families; to make their own decisions, and be in control of their own lives. (pp. 82–83)

It seems, therefore, that South Africa remains a rather traditional society when it comes to sex differences seeming to be almost 20 years behind various Western countries. I have done studies in many countries including Italy, New Zealand, and Zimbabwe and where I now live (Great Britain). It was time to investigate issues in the land of my birth.

My interest was in how things had changed 7 years after the end of apartheid in 1994 and at the beginning of the millennium. Were males and females, of all races and backgrounds, still tied to their traditional roles of breadwinner and homemaker? I decided to do a content analysis of television advertisements 25 years after television had come to South Africa. The study of television advertisements and what it tells us about a society has attracted a great deal of research (Eisend, 2009; McArthur & Resko, 1975).

WHY DID I USE THIS METHOD?

There are various methods to examine television advertisements, but the one I chose was content analysis, which is a method many different scientists use to systematically examine material for specific themes. It offers a method to explore data quantitatively and test hypotheses. It is a consistent, reliable way of classification looking for meaning and patterns in the content of material. Content analysis is sometimes called an unobtrusive measure where those researched are unaware that they are being studied. Content analysis is usually, but not exclusively, the analysis of public and archival material like public records, books, the mass media, or even private records like diaries. Content analysis can be variously defined. Smith (2000) calls content analysis the impartial and consistent application of explicitly defined procedures of analysis to all selected material. Essentially it is a tool for objectively and systematically identifying and categorizing the specific characteristics of behavior or messages. It can be used to test hypothesis like who says what to whom, how, and with what effect. It analyses the content of specific material usually forming categories and counting the incidence of those categories in the material. Content analysis remains at the heart of many research programs as it is generally acknowledged that the beginning of good science is reliable classification and taxonomization.

Content analysis tends to do two things: (1) to specify content characteristics or categories to be measured and (2) specify and apply the rules used for identifying and recording these categories. Essentially this means defining recording units that may be words or terms, themes, characters, paragraphs, or items. It is the sensitivity, comprehensiveness, and distinctness of the content categories that is crucial to the success of this methodology (Nachmias & Nachmias, 1981). Most researchers have three options with respect to coding systems: (1) use a preexisting coding system, (2) adapt in a minor (or major) way a preexisting system, or (3) devise a completely new coding system. Regardless, all the material has to be coded twice by different judges, raters, or coders working independently so that we can be sure that they view the data in the same way.

Method

How Did I Conduct This Study?

Along with a talented student, I conducted an analysis of 118 South African television advertisements in 2000 (Furnham & Spencer-Bowdage, 2002). The South African advertisements were recorded from the South African Broadcasting Corporation, during a 2-week period in April 2000 recorded during evening peak time (7 p.m.–11 p.m.). Repeated advertisements were discounted along with those few (around 5%) whose central characters were animals or children, and where there was no obvious central character. In all, 77 were found to be suitable for analysis and 116 characters were analyzed. A wide range of products were advertised, particularly food and beverages, household goods, cars, financial services, and clothes.

The content analysis carried out in this study was based on a coding scheme originally devised by McArthur and Resko (1975) so that comparisons with previous studies can be made (see Furnham & Mak, 1999). Nearly all 50 studies in this area have used a variation on this original category scheme developed 35 years ago (Furnham & Farragher, 2000). We adapted it slightly to better suit the data and the aims of the research. Any adult portrayed in a central role, either visually, vocally, or both, was suitable as a central figure. Where there appeared to be two or more central characters and a voice-over, then all were analyzed. For each used advertisement, the one or two most central characters were coded. Twelve attributes relevant to the study were measured. Advertisements were watched twice all the way through. They were then watched as many times as necessary to complete the analysis.

The second author (a female in her early 20s) completed the first round of coding; next a male in his 50s familiar with this task coded 10% of the South African advertisement and 10% of the British advertisements. It was thought desirable to have one coder of each sex as well as for them to be different in age. The second coder was first trained in the meaning of each of the categories. Following Krippendorf (1980), a reliability level was calculated and this was .95, which is in the acceptable range as specified by Krippendorf's canonical form correlation. The majority of categories scored between 93% and 100% reliability. Discussion resolved differences between coders in the coding of all the advertisements.

Knowledge of content analysis, how to do it properly and what it can reveal, is a great advantage for any researcher in the social sciences. I chose this method for three reasons. First, all of the other studies in this area (the depiction of gender in television) used this method. Second, this would mean I could compare my findings with other studies. Third, it was by far the most appropriate method to study this particular issue. Of course, a person could study gender roles in a society by many other methods (e.g., interviews, questionnaires) but to study how people are portrayed in the media, it seems content analysis is the most relevant and sensitive method.

WHO DID I STUDY?

From the Soweto rising (1976) till the end of apartheid (1994) there was considerable tension and bloodshed in South Africa. International boycotts had a profound effect on the economy and the country sank further and further into chaos. However, with end of apartheid and the election of Nelson Mandela, a new "rainbow" nation was born and there was considerable optimism in South Africa. It has been called the Rainbow Nation because it is made up of a multicolored tapestry of different ethnic groups including four major African groups (Xhosa, Zulu, Ndebele, and Sotho), and the coloreds or mixed-race people, Indians, and the Whites (mainly of European origin). Overall the Africans now make up around 90% of the population. No country, however, can escape its past. South Africa has experienced strong censorship and resisted changes in society. Television has been subject to considerable governmental regulation and control. South Africa is still a conservative country with a mixture of puritan laws and regard for traditional culture in part because of the domination on Calvinist Afrikaners but also because many of the large Black groups (Xhosa and Zulu) are themselves very conservative. This is manifest to a large extent in the traditional role of males and females.

WHAT DID I FIND OUT?

Portrayal of Traditional Sex Roles

Our study showed that males and females were portrayed in traditional ways on television. Men were more likely to do the talking. They were more likely to be in the expert or authority role while women were more likely to be (appreciative) product users. Men were shown as independent and women as dependent. Men also seemed more rational, giving factual, logical arguments. Women were portrayed as buying products for social approval or for self-enhancement: clothes, beauty or body products, and the like. Men were seen to buy things that were more practical and useful. In this sense, traditional sex roles are portrayed.

Would you notice this if you sat through a few hours of South African television and watched all the advertisements? The answer to this question is probably no in that the television advertisements are made professionally and attempting to sell modern products and services, some of which are international in distribution. In fact, they may seem strikingly familiar wherever you come from. The second reason why the advertisements would not be surprising is that these gender-role stereotypes are still found around the world. Universally it seems men are portrayed as logical, expert, and professional while women are portrayed as emotional, dependent shoppers. However this is a matter of degree. South African advertisements may be more conservative and gender-role stereotypic than you might find in Europe or North America.

Advertisements That Mirror South African Society

Do the findings of this study mirror the society from which they come? The answer to this question is more complex but Eisend (2009) claims to have answered it. That is, advertisements do mirror the society. Over the past 15 years in South Africa since the end of apartheid, more women have entered the labor market but primarily as unskilled workers. Further, despite many attempts to empower previously disadvantaged groups, there is high unemployment. Most noticeable of all is the conservative nature of the sex roles in South African society that this study highlights. This is perhaps seen most dramatically in the newly elected South African president Jacob Zuma who has four wives and 20 children and described himself as a traditional Zulu. South Africa is still traditional in terms of its gender-role expectations and socialization and these advertisements reflect gender roles in that society.

It would be naive to believe that a person could get a good understanding of the sex roles in South Africa by only conducting the content analysis discussed here. However, people do remark on how television does say something about a culture when they watch either "foreign channels" or local television in a foreign country. Drawing conclusions from this study, or indeed other similar studies, however, has limitations. First, culture changes over time and this means studies have to be regularly updated. The study reported was done 10 years ago. Second, there is always the question of the representativeness of the particular advertisements analyzed. We know that different products are advertised on different channels, at different times of day, and in different seasons. One sample of television advertisements can, therefore, be unrepresentative of the total number appearing. Third, there is a relationship between many variables (i.e., age, education, social class) and television watching. In a developing country such as South Africa most homes still do not possess television sets and programs and advertisements are aimed at the more affluent. In this sense, what they show is not representative of the total population. Fourth, the medium may affect the content. It would be interesting, relevant, and important to do the same content analysis of radio programs as well as the print media (newspapers, magazines) to see if the same results would occur. Fifth, all content analysis is a function of the content categories and it could be that interesting, subtle, and important categories were not included in this analysis.

WHY DOES THIS MATTER?

There are lots of published papers on gender stereotypes that examine the ability, competence, and personality generally associated with specific gender stereotypes. This work focuses on two topics: the *nature* of stereotypes (i.e., how people in a particular culture perceive men and women) and the *actual existence* of sex differences. It suggests that although there are observable and measurable differences in the behaviors of men and women, those differences are smaller and fewer than prevailing notions about stereotyping suggests. It has also been acknowledged that gender stereotypes are heavily influenced by culture. Best and Williams (1994), for instance, found greater stereotyping in poorer countries with a lower literacy rate. They found, in their study of 14 countries, that economic and educational advancement tends to be accompanied by a reduction in the tendency to view men as stronger and more active than women. Content analytic studies such as those reported here offer an opportunity to test specific hypotheses about the origin and maintenance of gender-role stereotypes in any culture. These studies have examined differences in stereotyping between men and women, between the past and the present, and between two or more countries.

Advertisements are of particular interest to psychologists because of their unique and rich nature. Manstead and McCulloch (1981) note:

> On the one hand, the images they contain are drawn from society at large and can therefore be viewed as reflecting prevailing cultural values. Due to the nature of advertisements they are highly condensed and designed to be easily comprehensible to aid their effectiveness. (p. 171)

They argue that due to these constraints, some degree of stereotyping is inevitable and that the need to represent typical people in typical situations leads to the production of compromises or composites of stereotypes of gender roles. Because the actors and situations featured in advertisements must be readily and quickly identifiable by their audience, they have to be consistent with prevailing cultural values (Manstead & McCulloch, 1981, p. 171). However, it should be acknowledged that many researchers have concluded that currently many advertisements are neither simple nor stable but open to more than one possible interpretation.

McArthur and Resko's (1975) pioneering paper was one of the first to address the issue of sex-role stereotyping in television advertisements, using a clear and comprehensive category proforma. It paved the way for numerous further studies that extended the research to many other countries, and in many cases were able to show similar findings demonstrating significant gender differences in the portrayal of central characters (Furnham & Mak, 1999). They found their results clearly indicated "that the men and women presented to the viewing audience in television commercials differ in several noteworthy respects" (McArthur & Resko, 1975, p. 217).

Furnham and Mak's review (1999) of many studies in different cultures demonstrates that female figures in television commercials were less likely than males to possess expertise; whereas, the male model was typically an authority or expert on the product being advertised, the female model was almost always a product user or consumer. Both in their credentials and in their behavior, the women in these advertisements were portrayed as less knowledgeable than men. Proportionately fewer women than men were depicted in an occupational setting. In fact, only 11% of the central figures depicted in such a setting were women. This figure is substantially lower than women's actual representation in occupational settings inasmuch as they comprise 37% of the labor force in the United States. Thus, comparing stereotyped depictions and actual behavior shows a meaningful discrepancy between the two.

Many authors have since replicated McArthur and Resko's findings, and some 26 years later, research continues to explore the stereotypes found in television commercials. Researchers are looking not only at expanding their work into different categories and countries, but also longitudinally, that is, looking at the changes that have taken place over the years. With colleagues I have conducted two large reviews on the now nearly 50 studies in this area that have done content analyses in America and Australia as well as Serbia and Zimbabwe. We (Furnham & Mak, 1999) reviewed and compared fourteen studies conducted on five continents over a period of 25 years (see also Furnham & Paltzer, 2010, for an updated review). Of the various studies, three used data from the United States, two from Great Britain, and one each from Australia, Denmark, France, Hong Kong, Indonesia, Italy, Kenya, Mexico, and Portugal.

The discrepancy between depictions of males and females and its consistency over time is meaningful. In 9 out of 11 studies it was found that males were more likely to be the voice-over of an advertisement, while females were often portrayed visually. The majority of studies also found that in respect to credibility, males were more likely than females to act as the authority of a product. Age also showed consistency among the studies, with females being shown as younger than males. Reward type showed consistency (9 of 14 studies), with men in general being shown as associated with pleasurable rewards, while females advertise more products that yield social or self-enhancement. Advertisements that sell home and body products were consistently shown to be female dominated. The background used in a commercial only showed consistency in that females were often shown against a children's background. A commercial's end comment also demonstrated a pattern whereby males more frequently make the end comment in an advertisement than females. There was much less consistency neither in the role of the central figure (notably autonomous vs. dependent) nor in the location of advertisement (home vs. work).

Finally, because studies have been done in the same country over a long period (up to 30 years) it is possible to see trends. Therefore it is possible to test the hypothesis that over time fewer characters are shown in traditional sex roles. Thus, in a medical context, the doctor is a male and the nurse a female; or the homemaker a female and the "professional" a male. However, the results have shown that changes in the way people are portrayed have occurred more in developing than developed countries. Despite some change, what is most clear and valuable to know based on this type of research is that there remains a great deal of gender stereotyping in advertising particularly as it relates to occupational roles and status. This is a hot issue for those interested in gender politics. One central question occurs in all this work: Do the media reflect the society in which they are located, or do the media shape that society? However, an answer has been provided to the old chestnut "mirror or mould" argument by Eisend (2009). In over 60 studies done in many countries, it may be concluded that television and advertisements in particular mirror society.

Although I have lived in England for 35 years, I go back to South Africa regularly to see my mother who still lives there. It is, I suppose like all countries, very different from the country I left 35 years ago. But the fundamentals of culture do not change that much, and nor does South African television which seems staid, differential to authority, and under strict government control. Does my modest content analytic study of South African television advertisements offer a window on the gender roles in that society in which I was raised? Yes, I believe it does, but this needs to be replicated and updated and, more important, supplemented by other studies using different methods.

QUESTIONS TO CONSIDER

Culture

1. Imagine you were going to interact with a member of this culture. Based on this study, might you do anything differently in a conversation with someone from this culture than you would with someone from your own culture? Why or why not?

2. How is the culture discussed in the study similar to and different to your own?

3. How does what you learned about this culture relate to what you understand about your own culture?

4. What theories, concepts, or issues discussed in this text are relevant to this study?

5. What new theories, concepts, or issues have you learned from this study?

6. Is culture discussed here as a representation that affects communication or as a construction created by communication?

Research Method

1. What would you have done differently if you were to conduct a similar study? Why?

2. If you were going to conduct research on a cultural group, would you use this method? Why or why not?

3. What are the limitations of the research conducted that are identified by the author? Can you think of other limitations the author has not discussed?

4. What are some pros and cons of using this method?

5. How did the researcher construct the identity of cultural group members? What did the researcher do or say that communicated this?

6. What questions do you have about this method?

REFERENCES

Best, D., & Williams, J. (1994). Masculinity/femininity in the self and ideal self descriptions of university students in fourteen countries. In A. Bouvy, F. Van de Vijver, P. Boski, & P. Schmitz (Eds.), *Journeys in cross cultural psychology* (pp. 297–306) Lisse, The Netherlands: Swets and Zeitlinger.

Eisend, M. (2009). A meta-analysis of gender roles in advertising. *Journal of the Academy of Marketing Science, 17,* 1–20.

Furnham, A., & Farragher, E. (2000). A cross-cultural analysis of sex-role stereotyping in television advertisements: a comparison between Great Britain and New Zealand. *Journal of Broadcasting & Electronic Media, 44,* 415–436.

Furnham, A., & Mak, T. (1999). Sex-role stereotyping in television commercials: A review and comparison of fourteen studies done on five continents over 25 Years. *Sex Roles, 41,* 413–437.

Furnham, A., & Paltzer, S. (2010). The portrayal of men and women in television advertisements: An updated review of 30 studies published since 2000. *Scandinavian Journal of Psychology, 51,* 216–236.

Furnham, A., & Spencer-Bowdage, S. (2002). Sex role stereotyping in television advertisements: A content analysis of advertisements from South Africa and Great Britain. *Communications, 27,* 457–483.

Krippendorf, K. (1980). *Content analysis: An introduction to its methodology.* London: Sage.

Manstead, A., & McCulloch, C. (1981). Sex-role stereotyping in British television advertisements. *British Journal of Social Psychology, 20,* 171–180.

McArthur, L. Z., & Resko, B. G. (1975). The portrayal of men and women in American television commercials. *Journal of Social Psychology, 97,* 209–220.

Nachmias, C. & Nachmias, D. (1981). *Research methods in the social sciences.* New York: Arnold.

Rissik, D. (1994). *Culture shock South Africa!* Singapore: Times Books.

Smith, C. (2000). Content analysis and narrative analysis. In H. Reis & C. Judd (Eds.), *Handbook of research methods in social and personality psychology* (pp. 313–335). Cambridge, UK: CUP.

Appendix F

KOREAN CULTURE EXPLORED THROUGH SURVEY RESEARCH

Seung Hee Yoo

David Matsumoto

San Francisco State University

Overview

Yoo and Matsumoto's social scientific study uses survey research to examine display rules used by South Koreans. As you read about this study, consider what the display rules are in your culture and whether these might be lost in translation when interacting with someone from another culture.

WHY DID WE STUDY THIS CULTURE?

The number of cross-cultural psychological studies conducted on Koreans, while steadily increasing, is still relatively low. Instead, many times, results obtained from the Japanese are generalized to Korea and other East Asian countries. Even though geographically close to one another, South Korea and Japan vary from one another on several important aspects. For example, South Korea and Japan differ on Hofstede's (2001) cultural dimensions (see Table F.1). They also vastly differ in ecological and social factors such as affluence, land size, type of government, and religion to name a few, which have all shown to be related to important cultural values and psychological processes. These differences between Japan and South Korea indicate that the results from studies on the Japanese may not generalize to South Koreans. This suggests the need for more research on South Koreans on a variety of topics on which studies of Japanese have been treated as representative and generalizable to Koreans.

On a more personal note, both of us have an interest in South Korea because of our experiences in Korea. One of us, Seung Hee Yoo, is Korean and the other, David Matsumoto, spent many years in Korea. This is why in the present paper we chose to focus on the display rules of South Koreans. Display rules, defined in Chapter 2, are norms about expressing emotions in various social contexts (Ekman, 1972).

Table F.1 Hofstede's Cultural Dimensions for South Korea and Japan.

	Rankings (out of 50 countries)	
Hofstede's Cultural Dimensions	**South Korea**	**Japan**
Individualism-collectivism	43	22/23
Power distance	27/28	33
Uncertainty avoidance	16/17	7
Masculinity	41	1

Source: Adapted from Hofstede, G.H. (2001).

We were specifically interested in examining whether Korean's display rules of expressing anger are affected by the status of the interactant. Anger is the emotion most consistently linked with hierarchy, power, and status (Tiedens, Ellsworth, & Mesquita, 2000; Timmers, Fischer, & Manstead, 1998). Because South Koreans score high on power distance, hierarchy, and status differentiation, we hypothesized that South Koreans' display rules about expressing anger would differ depending on the interactants' status.

WHY DID WE USE THIS METHOD?

We used surveys to assess display rules in our present study. This was because we believed that surveys would be the most direct way of measuring these norms. Adults all have norms about displaying emotions to others and therefore would be able to report on them. We believed that by asking participants what they believe they *should* do in various contexts, as opposed to what they *would* do, we would be able to considerably reduce socially desirable responding biases and accurately measure display rules shared by members of the culture (Matsumoto et al., 2008). Using a survey is of course not without limitations. One limitation is that surveys can only assess conscious display rules, but not unconscious ones. Another limitation is that there may be discrepancies between self-report and actual behavior. In other words, the display rules assessed by surveys may not always be used in actual interactions.

WHO DID WE STUDY?

Participants were 196 Korean university students from various universities in Seoul, South Korea (Males = 112, Females = 84), all born and raised in South Korea. Their mean age was 21.56 years (Standard deviation [SD] = 2.39). All participants signed a consent form and then completed a set of questionnaires as part of a multinational study on cultural display rules (Matsumoto et al., 2008) either during class or at home. The questionnaire of interest to this study is the modified Display Rules Assessment Inventory (DRAI; Matsumoto, Yoo, Hirayama, & Petrova, 2005).

Method

How Did We Conduct This Study?

The DRAI is a questionnaire that assesses display rules, or norms about how to express emotions in various social contexts (Matsumoto, et al., 2005; Matsumoto et al., 2008). According to Ekman (1972), emotional expressions can be modified by display rules in several different ways. Individuals can simply express their emotions as much as they feel it (express). They can also amplify (express more than their feelings), deamplify (express less than their feelings), mask (not show their feelings by showing a different emotion), qualify (show their feelings with another emotion), or neutralize (not express any emotions) their emotions. Individuals will modify their emotions in one of these ways depending on what is appropriate for the social situation.

The targets of emotions assessed in the DRAI are 21 interactants from four groups—family, friends, classmates, and professors—in two different settings of interaction-private and public (for more details see Matsumoto et al., 2008 or go to www.davidmatsumoto.com). In the present study, we examined Koreans' display rules about expressing anger in public to interactants of varying status, male and female professors in their 50s (higher status), male and female same class year classmates (same status), and male and female students of a lower class year (lower status). These interactants were chosen because previous research has shown that these interactants were perceived by Korean university students as being higher, the same, or lower in power compared to them (Holtgraves & Yang, 1992).

One example of the questions asked of the participants is "What do you believe you should do if you are interacting with a classmate of the same class year who is male at the university cafeteria in plain view within earshot of others, and you feel anger toward him?" Definitions of terms such as *classmate* (e.g., classmate refers to acquaintances in school) and *anger* were provided to participants.

The English version of the DRAI was first translated to Korean and then the Korean version was backtranslated to English by two different bilingual speakers and discrepancies between the two translations were discussed and resolved (Brislin, 1970). This was to ensure that the meaning of terms in the Korean DRAI were semantically equivalent to the ones in the English DRAI (i.e., to establish linguistic equivalence). The order of the interactants referenced in the survey was arranged in eight different ways to eliminate possible order effects.

WHAT DID WE FIND OUT?

In order to examine whether South Koreans' display rules to express anger to an interactant depended on the status of the interactant, we compared participants' Express scores across the six interactant types. Express scores are the number of times participants reported that they would express their anger as much as they feel it. We also examined if sex of the interactants and the participant were factors that influenced the results.

Display Rules Based on Status

Participants reported display rules to express anger the most to the same year classmates, and then to lower class year students, and the least to professors. They also reported display rules to express anger more to interactants of the same sex. Female participants reported display rules to express anger more to women interactants than to men interactants, and vice versa for male participants. There was also an interaction between interactant, sex of interactant, and sex of the participant. Female participants reported display rules to express anger more to female same year classmates than to male same year classmates. Male participants reported display rules to express anger more to male same year and lower classmates than to female same year and lower classmates, respectively.

These results indicate that Koreans have different display rules about expressing their anger depending on the status of the person. Participants reported having the display rules to express anger the least with professors. This is not surprising because professors would represent to the participants, who were all university students, interactants who were of a higher status than them and who have direct power over them. This would be particularly true in a high power distant and hierarchical country like Korea where respecting adults is an important norm learned in childhood. Expressing anger—an emotion that is associated with greater power, status, and dominance (Hess, Blairy, & Kleck, 2000; Knudson, 1996; Tiedens et al., 2000)—to professors therefore would not be appropriate. Not only would it be disrespectful, it would also serve no purpose as expressing anger would not be a successful way to establish power.

An interesting pattern of results was obtained regarding interactants of same and lower status. To understand these results, it is important to know that in Korea there is a clear hierarchy among students based on age and class year. A student who is of a higher class year is called *sunbae* and a student of a lower class year is called *hoobae*. When students start their freshman year in college, they are taken care of by their sunbaes, who give them various advice about school, take them out to meals, and do whatever else to make them feel welcome. They are viewed as role models to hoobaes. This informal mentor type relationship extends beyond the 4 years in college and oftentimes lasts throughout life. It is expected that hoobaes treat their sunbaes with respect. The hoobaes use the honorific form of language to their sunbaes (unless they become very close) and generally have to do as the sunbaes tell them (especially while in college).

In our study, display rules to express anger toward same year classmates were reported more frequently than display rules to express to students of lower class year. This may be because participants interacting with same year classmates who anger them may have the need to establish, maintain, or regain power and control in the group (Timmers, Fischer, & Manstead, 1998). Otherwise, they run the risk of looking weak. Expressing anger to establish power would not be as necessary to do to lower class year students, because they already have power over them because of the sunbae and hoobae relationship.

Another possible explanation for the results is that people have display rules to express anger to targets with whom they feel most comfortable and close. It is likely that participants were the closest to same class year classmates and same sex interactants compared to professors, lower class year classmates, and opposite sex interactants. People tend to self-disclose and reveal their vulnerabilities to someone with whom they are close (Collins & Miller, 1994). They may have felt the most comfortable and safe to express the anger that they felt to these interactants.

WHY DOES THIS MATTER?

One important aspect of intercultural communication is understanding emotional expressions, which may sometimes be difficult because there are cross cultural differences in how people display their emotions (Matsumoto, 2001). Gaining knowledge of display rules could be one way in which understanding of emotional expressions can be made easier. This in turn would make intercultural communication less ambiguous and uncertain (Gudykunst & Nishida, 2001), especially in interactions that differ in status.

Even though the existence and maintenance of hierarchies are universal aspects of human life because of their importance for social order and efficiency in groups (Matsumoto, 2007; Tiedens et al., 2000), they would be especially important and relevant in Korea, where cultural values of power distance, hierarchy, and status differentiation are high (Hofstede, 2001; Matsumoto, 2007; Schwartz, 2004). Koreans accept and emphasize power and status differences between people and have norms that guide them to change their behavior depending on the status of the interactant. Furthermore, Koreans like those from other East Asian countries are raised on Confucian values, which include values related to relational hierarchy in society such as loyalty to superiors, ordering relationship by status, and filial piety (Zhang, Lin, Nonaka, & Beom, 2005).

The present study found that the status of the interactant is related to Koreans' display rules about expressing anger. They have the display rules to express anger the least to someone of a higher status than them, and most to someone of the same status. Future studies on display rules should also use multiple methods, including measurements of facial expressions in social interactions. For example, future studies might examine whether Koreans' actual emotional expressions of anger are shown in ways that are consistent with their norms about display rules. Another interesting future research would be examining how this power dynamic changes if they are interacting with someone of a different ethnicity.

We believe that understanding display rules of different cultures would be very helpful in the intercultural communication process. It would allow people to understand and interpret the meaning behind the emotional expressions of their interactants from a different culture. Being aware of cultural norms has been shown to be associated with positive intercultural adaptation and adjustment (Ward, 2001). Knowledge of cultural norms, especially about expressive behavior and interactional styles, can help to reduce the uncertainty and ambiguity of intercultural interactions, thus, lowering stress and anxiety. Hopefully, understanding these differences can help to improve cross-cultural understanding and cooperation.

QUESTIONS TO CONSIDER

Culture

1. Imagine you were going to interact with a member of this culture. Based on this study, might you do anything differently in a conversation with someone from this culture than you would with someone from your own culture? Why or why not?

2. How is the culture discussed in the study similar to and different to your own?

3. How does what you learned about this culture relate to what you understand about your own culture?

4. What theories, concepts, or issues discussed in this text are relevant to this study?

5. What new theories, concepts, or issues have you learned from this study?

6. Is culture discussed here as a representation that affects communication or as a construction created by communication?

Research Method

1. What would you have done differently if you were to conduct a similar study? Why?

2. If you were going to conduct research on a cultural group, would you use this method? Why or why not?

3. What are the limitations of the research conducted that are identified by the authors? Can you think of other limitations the authors have not discussed?

4. What are some pros and cons of using this method?

5. How did the researchers construct the identity of cultural group members? What did the researchers do or say that communicated this?

6. What questions do you have about this method?

REFERENCES

Brislin, R. (1970). Back translation for cross-cultural research. *Journal of Cross-Cultural Psychology, 1,* 185–216.

Collins, N. L., & Miller, L. C. (1994). Self-disclosure and liking: A meta-analytic review. *Psychological Bulletin, 116,* 457–475.

Ekman, P. (1972). Universal and cultural differences in facial expression of emotion. In J. R. Cole (Ed.), *Nebraska Symposium on Motivation, 1971* (pp. 207–283). Lincoln: Nebraska University Press.

Gudykunst, W. B., & Nishida, T. (2001). Anxiety, uncertainty, and perceived effectiveness of communication across relationships and cultures. *International Journal of Intercultural Relations, 25,* 55–71.

Hess, U., Blairy, S., & Kleck, R. E. (2000). The influence of facial emotion displays, gender, and ethnicity on judgments of dominance and affiliation. *Journal of Nonverbal Behavior, 24,* 265–285.

Hofstede, G. H. (2001). *Culture's consequences: Comparing values, behaviors, institutions, and organizations across nations.* Thousand Oaks, CA: Sage.

Holtgraves, T., & Yang, J. N. (1992). Interpersonal underpinnings of request strategies: General principles and differences due to culture and gender. *Journal of Personality and Social Psychology, 62,* 246–256.

Knudson, B. (1996). Facial expressions of emotion influence interpersonal trait inferences. *Journal of Nonverbal Behavior, 20,* 165–182.

Matsumoto, D. (2001). Culture and emotion. In D. Matsumoto (Ed.), *Handbook of culture and psychology* (pp. 171–194). New York: Oxford University Press.

Matsumoto, D. (2007). Individual and cultural differences in status differentiation: The Status Differentiation Scale. *Journal of Cross-Cultural Psychology, 38,* 413–431.

Matsumoto, D., Yoo, S. H., Hirayama, S., & Petrova, G. (2005). Development and initial validation of a measure of display rules: The Display Rule Assessment Inventory (DRAI). *Emotion, 5,* 23–40.

Matsumoto, D., Yoo, S. H., Fontaine, J., Anguas-Wong, A. M., Ariola, M., Ataca, B., Bond, M. H. et al. (2008). Mapping expressive differences around the world: The relationship between emotional display rules and individualism v. collectivism. *Journal of Cross-Cultural Psychology, 39,* 55–74.

Schwartz, S. H. (2004). Mapping and interpreting cultural differences around the world. In H. Vinken, J. Soeters & P. Ester (Eds.), *Comparing cultures, dimensions of culture in a comparative perspective* (pp. 43–73). Leiden, The Netherlands: Brill.

Tiedens, L. Z., Ellsworth, P. C., & Mesquita, B. (2000). Sentimental stereotypes: Emotional expectations for high- and low-status group members. *Personality and Social Psychology Bulletin, 26,* 560–575.

Timmers, M., Fischer, A. H., & Manstead, A. S. R. (1998). Gender differences in motives for regulating emotions. *Personality and Social Psychology Bulletin, 24,* 974–985.

Ward, C. (2001). The A, B, Cs of acculturation. In D. Matsumoto (Ed.), *Handbook of culture and psychology* (pp. 411–445). New York: Oxford University Press.

Zhang, Y. B., Lin, M-C., Nonaka, A., & Beom, K. (2005). Harmony, hierarchy and conservatism: A cross-cultural comparison of Confucian values in China, Korea, Japan, and Taiwan. *Communication Research Reports, 22,* 107–115.

Appendix G

JAPANESE CULTURE EXPLORED THROUGH EXPERIMENTAL DESIGN

Yohtaro Takano

University of Tokyo

Overview

Takano's social scientific case study uses experimental design to explore conformity behavior among Japanese. As you read about this study, consider what assumptions you have about other cultures that might be disproved if you were to come into casual contact with or conduct a study of members of that cultural group.

WHY DID I STUDY THIS CULTURE?

An ethnic joke put it: A luxury liner was sinking. To urge passengers to dive into the sea, the captain said to an American passenger, "If you dive, you'll be a hero." He said to a Japanese passenger, "All others are diving." As seen in this joke, Japanese people are believed to always follow others. The representative image of Japanese is now collectivism (or groupism), which refers to a tendency to put priority on a group's interests at the sacrifice of an individual's.

The common view that Japanese are collectivistic is a central dogma of Japanology. It has been innumerably repeated that Japanese people always act as others in their group do, have no independent self, willingly sacrifice themselves for their business corporation, and so on. This common view provided a basis for self-construal theory (Markus & Kitayama, 1991), which has been dominating psychological cross-cultural studies in recent years.

Why did I study Japanese culture? I am Japanese. So, it would have been surprising if I had not been interested in Japanese culture in comparison with other cultures, especially considering that I experienced American culture for 5 years when I stayed in the United States some decades ago. Before going to the United States, I had read a number of books in Japanology (e.g., Benedict, 1946; Nakane, 1967), which served to establish the common view that the Japanese were collectivists. In everyday contacts with Americans (which will hereafter refer to the people in the United States), however, I did not find any essential difference between Americans and Japanese concerning collectivism (and its antonym, individualism), although Americans were usually regarded as the most individualistic people in the world.

In the history of psychology, however, it has been repeatedly found that our intuition may be grossly misleading. So I tried to find empirical studies that directly compared Japanese and Americans on individualism and collectivism. Fortunately, cross-national studies on individualism and collectivism were flourishing in psychology in the 1980s and 90s. I was able to locate 17 such studies, most of which had been conducted by those researchers who believed in the common view. Surprisingly, all but one of those studies were inconsistent with the common view, which was so widely held (see Takano & Osaka, 1997, 1999). Also surprisingly, most of the researchers who conducted those studies did not explicitly comment on the fact that their own data did not support the common view.

The only study that supported the common view was a famous study by Hofstede (1980), which stimulated subsequent cross-national comparisons on individualism and collectivism. However, a close examination of this study revealed that he had misinterpreted his data: More specifically, his "individualism factor" extracted from his factor analysis actually had nothing to do with individualism (see Takano & Osaka, 1999). Even supporters of the common view agreed with us in that Hofstede's factor interpretation was invalid (Heine, Lehman, Peng, & Greenholtz, 2002). Thus, it turned out that virtually no formal empirical study supported the common view, which had been formed largely on the basis of arbitrarily chosen casual observations such as personal experiences, anecdotes, proverbs, and so on (see Mouer & Sugimoto, 1986).

Among the reviewed 17 studies were four conformity experiments that examined Japanese participants to be compared to American counterparts in an experimental paradigm devised by Asch (1956). If the common view were correct, "collectivistic Japanese" should conform to their group more often than "individualistic Americans." Contrary to this expectation, however, those four studies found essentially no difference in conformity between Japanese and Americans.

But this summary needs one qualification: One of the above four studies (Williams & Sogon, 1984) reported two experiments. In the first experiment, the researchers recruited Japanese college students from various parts of their college campus to form experimental groups just like the original study by Asch (1956), and found that the level of their conformity was comparable to that of American college students. In the second experiment, however, each group was composed solely of members of the same college club, and the conformity level was extraordinarily high, much higher than that of American students.

Heine and colleagues (2002) focused on this latter finding, and argued that the conformity level was extraordinarily high because all the participants belonged to the same ingroup. In Japanology, it is often claimed that Japanese behave in collectivistic ways only in their own ingroup (e.g., Nakane, 1967, 1970). Heine and fellow researchers (2002) reasoned that Japanese participants did not conform to the experimental group more often than American counterparts in the other conformity experiments because the group was composed not of ingroup members but of outgroup members.

We had anticipated this interpretation and suggested a possibility that the ingroup versus outgroup distinction was confounded with another variable, vertical discipline, which is a kind of social force that makes people submissive to their superiors in some types of social setting (Takano & Osaka, 1997, 1999). In the second experiment of Williams and Sogon (1984) where the extraordinarily high conformity level was observed, participants were recruited intentionally from formal sports clubs (baseball and Japanese fencing) that demanded strict vertical discipline from its members because the primary goal of these clubs was to train their members and win intercollegiate games. Therefore, it is possible that the sports club participants showed the extraordinarily high conformity rate not because the experimental group was composed of members of an ingroup (i.e., a college club) but because their particular ingroup (i.e., a formal sports club) demanded unusually strict vertical discipline. Lummis (1981), who had once been a marine, noted that the behavioral patterns usually ascribed to "Japanese collectivism" would all apply to American marines. Nobody would consider the behavioral patterns seen in the Marine Corps as representative of those of the whole American nation. Similarly, it may be unwarranted to generalize the behavioral pattern of Japanese college students in formal sports clubs to "Japanese culture."

If the extraordinarily high conformity level observed in the second experiment of Williams and Sogon (1984) was due to the unusually strict vertical discipline rather than ingroup membership, the conformity level would be much lower in those ingroups that do not impose strict vertical discipline on their members. We conducted a conformity experiment in Japan to test this prediction (Takano & Sogon, 2008).

WHY DID I USE THIS METHOD?

The research method that we employed was experimentation. Conformity has been explored mainly through the famous experimental paradigm devised by Asch (1956). We had to compare our prospective data to those already obtained in the Asch-type conformity experiments conducted in the United States. So, we had no choice other than conducting an experiment.

More generally, however, experimentation has desirable properties for cross-cultural research especially in the following two respects: First, it examines actual behavior. Most cross-cultural studies are conducted by means of questionnaires. A questionnaire study is relatively easy to conduct. Because cross-cultural studies are hard to conduct as compared with intracultural studies, this property of questionnaires is a great advantage for cross-cultural research. However, a questionnaire study has a serious drawback as well. To easily obtain information about respondents, a questionnaire study relies on self-report (e.g., "How do I respond when my mother opposes my decision?"). But it is well known that self-report sometimes deviates from actual behavior to a considerable extent.

The second important merit of experimentation is that it can examine behavior in the same situation across different cultures. Suppose, for example, that American soldiers obeyed an order from their superior officer, whereas German college students refused to obey an order from their professor. Should we conclude that Americans are more obedient than Germans? Obviously not. Rebellious soldiers could be jailed or even executed, whereas rebellious students could not. To compare different cultural groups appropriately, it is necessary to observe their behavior in the same situation. In responding to a questionnaire, people in different cultural groups may imagine different situations because typical situations may be different between different cultures. In an experiment, we are able to prepare an identical situation for different cultural groups (although we have to be cautious about a possibility that a physically identical situation may have psychologically different meanings for different cultural groups).

WHO DID I STUDY?

To separate the target variable (i.e., ingroup membership) from the confounding variable (i.e., strict vertical discipline), we recruited participants from Japanese college clubs that were not formal sports clubs (e.g., tea ceremony, brass band, and so on). Although a variety of clubs were included in the experiment, every experimental group was composed solely of members of the same club. Since Heine et al. (2002) claimed that the college clubs in the second experiment of Williams and Sogon (1984) were ingroups, it will be justified to consider that the college clubs in our experiment were also ingroups. We had another reason for regarding these clubs as ingroups: The participants had been belonging to the same club for 28 months on the average.

Method

How Did I Conduct This Study?

I followed the experimental procedures in Asch (1956) as faithfully as possible so that the conformity level of Japanese participants in my experiment could be properly compared to that of American participants in Asch-type conformity experiments. In Asch's experiment, participants were shown one standard line and three comparison lines. Their task was to judge which comparison line had the same length as the standard line. Participants performed this task in a small group of five to nine. In each group, only one participant was a real testee; the others were all confederates who cooperated with the experimenter. Participants provided answers orally one by one in a fixed order across all trials; the real testee always answered second to the last.

In two thirds of trials, the confederates unanimously provided predetermined wrong answers. The line-length task was very easy because the three comparison lines had obviously different lengths; the proportion of correct answers was almost 100% when a separate group of participants performed this task individually (see Asch, 1956). If the real testee made the same answer as the confederates' unanimous wrong answer, accordingly, it could be reasonably concluded that he conformed to the group (incidentally, all the participants in Asch's experiment were male).

The mean proportion of trials wherein the real testees conformed to their groups was 37% in Asch's (1956) original experiment. This conformity rate was shockingly high because it betrayed the popular image of "independent Americans." However, the average conformity rate was 25% in eight subsequent studies that applied the same procedures to Americans (Bond & Smith, 1996). When participants were Japanese, the average conformity rate was 23% in the above four studies, except for 51% percent in Williams and Sogon's (1984) second experiment.

We employed these nonsports clubs because we knew that vertical discipline was very loose in these clubs. To confirm this, however, we asked participants to fill in a questionnaire, where they intuitively assessed the degree of vertical discipline in their own club.

WHAT DID I FIND OUT?

First, let's see if the precondition for our experiment was satisfied: Was vertical discipline less strict in our nonsports clubs than in Williams and Sogon's (1984) formal sports clubs? Although it was impossible to ask Williams and Sogon's (1984) participants to rate severity of vertical discipline in their own formal sports clubs by slipping back in time to the early 1980s, I instead asked the second author of Williams and Sogon (1984) to deliver the questionnaire to current members of the very same sports clubs of the very same university that provided participants for their second experiment. In the questionnaire, severity of vertical discipline was assessed on a 9-point rating scale (0 = very loose; 8 = very severe). As expected, the participants in our conformity experiment reported that vertical discipline was loose in their nonsports clubs (mean rating was 2.0), whereas the current members of the formal sports clubs reported that it was on the severe side (mean rating was 5.3). The second author of Williams and Sogon (1984) told me that vertical discipline in formal sports clubs had loosened considerably at his university as well as many other universities in Japan since their study had been conducted nearly 25 years earlier. The vertical discipline in those formal sports clubs might have been much severer when they conducted their second experiment. At any rate, the precondition for our experiment was satisfied.

Now return to our primary concern: Was the conformity rate high or low in the ingroups where vertical discipline was less strict? In our experiment, the mean conformity rate was 25.2% (Takano & Sogon, 2008). This is much lower than 51% reported in Williams and Sogon's (1984) second experiment; and essentially identical to the aforementioned average conformity rate, 25%, across eight studies conducted in the United States after Asch (Bond & Smith, 1996).

Japanese Do Not Conform More Often Than Americans

These findings strongly suggest that Williams and Sogon's (1984) extraordinarily high conformity rate, 51%, should not be attributed to the ingroup membership claimed by Heine and colleagues (2002), but should be attributed to the unusually strict vertical discipline in the formal sports clubs that provided participants for their second experiment. In the U.S. studies, participants tend to show somewhat higher conformity rates in ingroups than the above 25% observed in outgroups (Bond & Smith, 1996). It is thus implausible that the conformity rate is higher for Japanese than for Americans in their respective ingroups. Therefore, it can be concluded again that Japanese do not conform more often than Americans.

WHY DOES THIS MATTER?

Our conformity experiment thus further confirmed that empirical evidence was inconsistent with the common view that Japanese are more collectivistic than Americans. In a sense, this is not surprising because the basis of the common view was not scientific empirical studies but casual observations (Mouer & Sugimoto, 1986). It is well known that intuitive judgments based on casual observations are susceptible to a variety of cognitive biases (e.g., Gilovich, 1991; Kahneman, Slovic, & Tversky, 1982). For example, people tend to look for confirmatory instances that would support their preconception (e.g., Baron, 1988; Evans & Over, 1996; Wason, 1960). It is highly probable that many anecdotes invoked to endorse the common view were selected by this kind of biased search process because it is possible to find out a comparable number of opposite anecdotes showing that Japanese behave in individualistic ways and Americans behave in collectivistic ways, if we look for them selectively (Mouer & Sugimoto, 1986; Takano, 2008). Scientific studies are much less susceptible to such a biased search process. Because scientific studies do not support "Japanese collectivism," this common view is better conceived of as a stereotype than a reality.

Cultural stereotypes portray different cultures as heterogeneous (i.e., essentially different) groups of people. The common view often leads us to feel as if Japanese and Americans are totally different kinds of creatures: Every Japanese always acts in obviously collectivistic ways, whereas every American always acts in obviously individualistic ways. These images tend to put down roots in our minds without our awareness. Heterogeneity is stressed especially at times of intergroup conflict because perception of heterogeneity makes it easier to take aggressive behavior against the "heterogeneous" people.

An American veteran who had once trained new soldiers for the Vietnam War told a television reporter that he had instructed his soldiers that Vietnamese were subhumans; for example, their narrow eyes could not see objects clearly. According to his explanation, the reason for this instruction was that if they thought that enemies were also humans, they could not kill the enemies (Yamamoto, Higashino, Miyamoto, & Sakai, 2008).

Norwegian criminalist, Nils Christie, who studied concentration camps set up by the Nazis in Norway during World War II, made a similar comment. He investigated why some Norwegian guards killed detained Yugoslavians while others did not, and found that those who did not kill Yugoslavian inmates had personal conversations with them and were in some cases shown photographs of their families. For Norwegian guards, it was hard to kill Yugoslavian inmates who were recognized as humans just like themselves (Yamazaki, Minagi, Komura, & Yamada, 2009).

In the case of the common view, Americans stressed "Japanese collectivism" and Japanese stressed "American individualism" during World War II (Dower, 1986). "Japanese collectivism" (specifically, "Japanese collectivistic economy") was again stressed amidst "Japan bashing" at the time of the 1980s trade conflict between the United States and Japan.

A cultural stereotype makes a different culture look heterogeneous, and thus could cause or intensify a conflict with that culture. In the current world where intercultural contacts are rapidly increasing, it is important to confirm whether a portrait of a culture is valid or not on the basis of cautious empirical investigation as to what is the reality.

QUESTIONS TO CONSIDER

Culture

1. Imagine you were going to interact with a member of this culture. Based on this case study, might you do anything differently in a conversation with someone from this culture than you would with someone from your own culture? Why or why not?

2. How is the culture discussed in the case study similar to and different to your own?

3. How does what you learned about this culture relate to what you understand about your own culture?

4. What theories, concepts, or issues discussed in this text are relevant to this case study?

5. What new theories, concepts, or issues have you learned from this case study?

6. Is culture discussed here as a representation that affects communication or as a construction created by communication?

Research Method

1. What would you have done differently if you were to conduct a similar study? Why?

2. If you were going to conduct research on a cultural group, would you use this method? Why or why not?

3. What are the limitations of the research conducted that are identified by the author? Can you think of other limitations the author has not discussed?

4. What are some pros and cons of using this method?

5. How did the researcher construct the identity of cultural group members? What did the researcher do or say that communicated this?

6. What questions do you have about this method?

REFERENCES

Asch, S. E. (1956). Studies of independence and conformity: I. A minority of one against a unanimous majority. *Psychological Monographs, 70*(9), Whole No. 416.

Baron, J. (1988). *Thinking and deciding.* Cambridge, UK: Cambridge University Press.

Benedict, R. (1946). *The chrysanthemum and the sword: Patterns of Japanese culture.* Boston: Houghton Mifflin.

Bond R., & Smith, P. B. (1996). Culture and conformity: A meta-analysis of studies using Asch's (1952b, 1956) line judgment task. *Psychological Bulletin, 119,* 111–137.

Dower, J. W. (1986). *War without mercy: Race and power in the Pacific war.* New York: Pantheon Books.

Evans, J. St. B. T., & Over, D. E. (1996). *Rationality and reasoning.* London: Psychology Press.

Gilovich, T. (1991). *How we know what isn't so: The fallibility of human reasoning in everyday life.* New York: The Free Press.

Heine, S. J., Lehman, D. R., Peng, K., & Greenholtz, J. (2002). What's wrong with cross-cultural comparisons of subjective Likert scales: The reference-group effect. *Journal of Personality and Social Psychology, 82,* 903–918.

Hofstede, G. (1980). *Culture's consequences.* Beverly Hills, CA: Sage.

Kahneman, D., Slovic, P., & Tversky, A. (Eds.). (1982). *Judgment under uncertainty: Heuristics and biases.* Cambridge, UK: Cambridge University Press.

Lummis, C. D. (1981). *Uchi naru gaikoku: "Kiku to katana" saikou* [An internal foreign country: "The chrysanthemum and the sword" reconsidered]. Tokyo: Jiji-Tusuushin-Sha.

Markus, H. R., & Kitayama, S. (1991). Culture and the self: Implications for cognition, emotion, and motivation. *Psychological Review, 98,* 224–253.

Mouer, R. E., & Sugimoto, Y. (1986). *Images of Japanese society: A study in the social construction of reality.* London: Routledge & Kegan Paul.

Nakane, C. (1967). *Tate shakai no ningen kankei: Tan-itsu shakai no riron* [Human relations in the vertical society: A theory of the unilateral society]. Tokyo: Koudansha.

Nakane, C. (1970). *Japanese society.* Berkeley: University of California Press.

Takano, Y. (2008). *"Shuudan-shugi" toiu sakkaku: Nihon-jin-ron no omoi-chigai to sono yurai* [Collectivism as an illusion: A misconception in Japanology and its origin]. Tokyo: Shinyo-sha.

Takano, Y., & Osaka, E. (1997). "Nihon-jin no shuudanshugi" to "amerika-jin no kojinshugi": Tsuusetsu no saikentou ["Japanese collectivism" and "American individualism": Reexamining the dominant view]. *Japanese Journal of Psychology, 68,* 312–327.

Takano, Y., & Osaka, E. (1999). An unsupported common view: Comparing Japan and the U.S. on individualism/collectivism. *Asian Journal of Social Psychology, 2,* 311–341.

Takano, Y., & Sogon, S. (2008). Are Japanese more collectivistic than Americans? Examining conformity in ingroups and the reference-group effect. *Journal of Cross-Cultural Psychology, 39,* 237–250.

Wason, P. C. (1960). On the failure to eliminate hypotheses in a conceptual task. *Quarterly Journal of Experimental Psychology, 12,* 129–140.

Williams, T. P., & Sogon, S. (1984). Group composition and conforming behavior in Japanese students. *Japanese Psychological Research, 26,* 231–234.

Yamamoto, N., Higashino, M. (Producers), Miyamoto, Y., & Sakai, Y. (Directors). (2008). *Heishi tachi no akumu* [Nightmares of soldiers]. [Motion picture]. Japan: NHK.

Yamazaki, S., Minagi, H. (Producers), Komura, K., & Yamada, R. (Directors). (2009). *Hanzai-gakusha Nirusu Kurisuti: Shuujin ni yasashii kuni karano houkoku* [A criminalist, Nils Christie: A report from a country gentle to prisoners]. [Motion picture]. Japan: NHK.

Glossary

abduction   Process of identifying underlying cultural assumptions about the local meaning of communicative conduct.

accent   Way of pronouncing words that is indicative of a specific speech community.

accommodative dilemma   When a person or people have to communicatively manage miscategorizations of overt or covert abuse toward them.

accommodative move   Behavioral attempt to accommodate that may be welcomed and can engender a genuine cooperative response in many cultures.

accountable   Something that demands an explanation.

acculturation   Process of learning and adapting one's identity to others who are not in one's own cultural groups.

advocacy   Using communication to provide support to a marginalized group; involves taking action to create change in society to benefit a marginalized group.

affective dimension   One of the dimensions of intercultural communication competence (ICC) which refers to emotional abilities.

affective resourcefulness   One component of the identity negotiation model, which refers to a person's ability to relate to self and others in various intercultural situations.

agenda setting function   Refers to how the media guides people in establishing what is viewed as important: The more a topic is discussed in the media, the more important it seems.

anonymity   Means that, apart from the investigator, nobody has access to data that may identify the participants of a study because these are secured and not made available to others. Additionally, the presentation of the data and results in any report about the study can not be traceable to specific participants.

anxiety/uncertainty management model (AUM)   Suggests that when people meet those from a different culture they cannot necessarily assume that they will behave in the same way as someone from their own culture, and, therefore, this uncertainty will cause anxiety. The extent to which a person is able to manage this anxiety influences the level of effective communication.

ascription   Process by which others attribute identities to individuals.

asynchronous collaborative technology   Technology that do not allow for communication in real time and instead require a delay between sending and receiving messages. These technologies began with e-mail, intranets, newsgroups, and listservs and evolved to online bulletin boards, group calendars, collaborative document management systems, collaborative websites, and web-based knowledge repositories.

avowal   Process by which individuals portray themselves.

behavioral dimension   One of the dimensions of intercultural communication competence (ICC) which refers to the applied skills that people have through their ability to communicate.

behavioral resourcefulness   One component of the identity negotiation model, which refers to a person's ability to be flexible and behave in a way that is appropriate to the situation.

being-in-the-world   Concept drawing attention to the particularities of a person's senses about things, beliefs about people or classes of people, and emotions.

bigoted speech   Talk that expresses intolerance or prejudice.

Black feminist thought   Theoretical framework for understanding a double oppression; serves as a form of social activism on behalf of African American women ignored by the feminist movement.

blog   Typically composed of journal-type entries that appear in reverse chronological order and can be updated from any stationary or mobile device with Internet access.

breach   Violation of taken-for-granted practice(s).

categorization threat   Act of being falsely foisted with an outgroup label. The term *threat* is intended to reflect the potential dire consequences of the label.

causality   Association between events that suggests one event results in the other event.

chauvinistic   Extreme, nearly militant, version of ethnocentrism.

Chicana feminist thought   Perspective that allowed women to respond to the patriarchal system of machismo, recognized as an oppressive force; similar to feminist thought, but with particular emphasis on the unique experiences of Latin women.

co-created contract   Means by which all parties co-create their set of expectations for each other and their relationship.

co-cultural group (CCG)   Marginalized group whose members make valuable contributions to society and their respective communities but are disenfranchised by the dominant group.

co-cultural group theory (CCGT)   Another name for co-cultural communication theory. Theorizes about the creation of co-cultural groups and provides five premises to understand this process.

code switching   Occurs when a person who speaks two or more languages shifts between these in a conversation.

cognitive complexity   Refers to one's ability to form unique categories in his or her mind. A more cognitively complex person is able to form categories that are distinct and to rely less on generalization.

cognitive concept of culture   Provides a collective mental map used to perceive the world; a filtered way of sensing, believing, and feeling.

cognitive dimension   One of the dimensions of intercultural communication competence (ICC) which refers to the mental abilities that pertain to communication competence.

cognitive resourcefulness   One component of the identity negotiation model, which refers to both the knowledge a person has, as well as the individual's ability to use that knowledge to deal with unfamiliar and new situations.

collective harmony   State of being demonstrated when the needs of the group are more significant than the needs of the individual.

collectivist culture   One end of the continuum of Hofstede's collectivism-individualism intercultural dimension where the self is not as important as the social groups to which the individual belongs, and self-credit is viewed as inappropriate.

colonialism   Involves the placement of settlements of a cultural population on distant lands.

communal layer   Sense of identity that members of a group share; emerges out of networks and groups.

communication   Use of symbolic code to send messages and create meaning.

communication accommodation theory Provides a framework which explores the reasons for, and consequences arising from, speakers converging toward and diverging away from each other in their communication behavior.

communication activity theory   Provides a framework for culturally specific communicative practices as situated theories; an emic understanding of communicative practices.

communication competence   Effective and appropriate communication. A communication exchange is effective when the speaker accomplishes his or her goal in that particular exchange and appropriate when the speaker accomplishes this goal in a manner that is both expected and accepted in that given social context.

communication practice   Expressive action performed in specific contexts; how people actually do communication in their specific social scenes.

communication theory of culture   Refers to the social construction of culture produced through communication practices.

communication theory of identity (CTI) Examines how communication shapes and reflects identity and foregrounds the communicative nature of self-identity and the social identities people enact when they interact with others. CTI asserts that identity is a dynamic phenomenon that cannot be separated from communication.

community   Organization of diverse people and practices.

conferred dominance   Process of most people in a culture, consciously or unconsciously, giving one group power over another.

confessional tale   Story a researcher uses to present findings that show the research process at work; includes explicit reflection on the difficulties, dilemmas, and complexity inherent in the fieldwork process.

confidentiality   Refers to the practice in research whereby information about the interviewee or person observed should remain undisclosed unless otherwise agreed. Confidentiality is also required if participants allow information about them to be made public. If participants may not be aware of the harmful consequences that may have for them, it is the duty of the researcher in such cases to warn them.

conflict marker   Communication practice employed during conflict or when talking about conflict that indicates serious interactional trouble.

confounding variable   Variable that is active at the same time as another variable in such a way as to make it difficult to deduce which is the explanatory variable.

Confucian dynamism   Explains a cultural preference for employers or employees to be dependable, respectful, and desirous to ensure that harmonious relationship's exists.

conscious competence Level of intercultural communication competence in which a communicator deliberately adapts competent behavior and is alert to the nuances of the communication context.

conscious incompetence   Level of intercultural communication competence in which the communicator is aware that he or she is not communicating as effectively as expected or not exhibiting the appropriate behaviors in an intercultural context, but does not know the particulars of what contributes to the incompetence.

consent   Creates and maintains acceptance and agreement to ideas thereby making these ideas unquestionable and commonsensical.

construct validity   Signifies whether the research instrument measures the theoretical concept being studied.

consumer profiling Aggregating of information on consumer behavior from purchase data, both offline and online including through supermarket savings cards, credit card transactions, credit records, product warranty cards, white pages, surveys, sweepstakes and contest entries, property records, motor vehicle data, cell and mobile phone records, the sale of magazine and catalog subscriptions, U.S. Census data, and health care records.

contact culture Cultural group in which members need less personal space and touch frequently during interaction.

content analysis Technique for analyzing the information and content in written documents; widely used both by interpretivist and social scientific researchers.

conversational style Aspects of directness and intonation in speech which are ways of producing particular speech codes.

copyright Protection of original works of authorship, such as poems, novels, plays, films, musical works, performances, radio and television programs, drawings, paintings, photographs, sculptures, architectural designs, and computer software.

correlation Degree of relatedness between two variables.

Creative Commons (CC) license Provides protection and freedom regarding that which is copyrighted; created by the Creative Commons nonprofit organization that aims to increase sharing and improve collaboration.

critical approach Explores how power, such as that which is associated with wealth, whiteness, heterosexuality, or maleness, is constructed through the use of symbols and the impact of this power on people's lives.

critical cultural studies Examine how the media relate to matters of ideology, race, gender, social class, and other forms of human diversity.

critical memory Process of remembering a critical event related to one's standpoint.

critical tale Story the researcher uses to present findings that report the plight of those on the margins of society and critically evaluate social structures that create inequality and injustice.

cross-cultural communication Refers to how different cultures vary in their communication behavior.

crowdsourcing Large groups of people working together collaboratively to solve problems whether at a global or local level.

cultivation theory Theorizes that media consumption works to create distorted perceptions of the world in that people—through repeated, heavy exposure to television—begin to view the real world as it exists on television.

cultural communication Focuses on the way in which communication enables people to create their cultural identities; is often invisible when interacting with people who share the same cultural identity.

cultural construction Group identity created through the consistent and repetitive communication of symbols in communication practices.

cultural contracts theory (CCT) Presents a model to explain how avowals and ascriptions can result in various conditions under which identity conflicts must be managed; CCT maintains that as people negotiate identities they are also agreeing to figuratively "sign" one or more cultural contracts.

cultural discourse Expressive system including communication practices, acts, events, and styles that involves symbols as well as symbolic forms, norms, and their associated meanings.

cultural enactment Occurs when a person engages in a cultural communication practice, such as speaking a certain language.

cultural expressive system Lifeblood of culture composed of three types of communication practices that are prominently active in social scenes: (1) specific acts, (2) events, and (3) styles of social interaction.

cultural identity   Reflection of how people's social and cultural groups influence their thoughts and behaviors.

cultural imperialism   Refers to the process of domination through the proliferation and global spread of cultural products.

cultural migration   Flow of people, social networks, and cultural values from one cultural context, such as a nation-state, to another.

cultural moment   Specific point in communication when culture, usually taken for granted, can be easily identified.

cultural more   Component of a culture that can be learned, such as its norms, values, and customs.

cultural participation   Extent to which people use particular speech codes and other communicative modes in order to display membership in socially recognizable communities.

cultural perspective   Focuses on conversation. Views culture not as something that people carry around, live in, or "are" in some obvious sense; rather, views culture as a symbolic and material category for patterned ways of communicating.

cultural pluralism   Envisions an ideal in which dominant cultures and co-cultures coexist and coparticipate in the larger culture.

cultural relativism   Takes a "to each their own attitude" and views all cultural groups as distinct and unique in their own culturally appropriate ways.

cultural representation   Uses symbols to reflect various aspects of a shared group identity.

cultural socialization agent   Refers to how mass mediated images can have a tremendous influence on how individuals see themselves and others.

cultural technology   Technology that connects people with distant cultural resources, blurs the distinctions between technology and social life as well as direct and mediated experience, and creates new opportunities for cultural activity.

cultural universalism   Values similarities in beliefs and behaviors across cultures.

culture   Any group of people that share a way of life.

culture-bearer   One who learns in a specialized way, acts in particular ways, believes particular things, and feels certain ways about the world; everyone plays this role.

culture shock   Anxiety a person may feel when entering a new cultural environment.

culture-specific speech acts   Social actions which are particular to a speech community.

cumulative effects model   Acknowledges and incorporates a balance of potential media effects and active media consumption.

cybercrime   Crime committed using a computer network or system and using the Transmission Control Protocol/Internet Protocol (TCP/IP); can occur practically anytime and any place and can take many forms from illegal music downloads to e-book piracy to computer viruses, spam, hacking, phishing, data and identity theft, and cyber bullying.

debriefing   Practice of explaining fully the purpose of the study after the participants have completed the task.

deduction   Reasoning from established premises toward their logical consequences; for example, the use of hypotheses in order to make predications about behavior.

demographic   Makeup of a culture's population such as size, gender, age, location, and so forth.

demographic imperative   Suggests that people are motivated to be culturally aware in response to changes in the makeup of a culture's population.

dialectical tension   Stress resulting from the interaction of opposing forces (e.g., ideas, arguments) pulling on one another.

dialogic   Refers to how cultural enactments interact with, can be compared to, and exist with other cultural enactments.

dialogic approach   Focuses on conversation and the use of symbols in everyday talk to construct meaning.

Digital Millennium Copyright Act   Amendment to the older copyright laws of the United States. It protected Internet service providers from liability for copyright infringement by their users, created new rules for digital materials, updated old rules and procedures regarding archival preservation, and offered protection for international copyright holders in the United States.

direct effects theory   Argues that media images enter naive viewers' consciousness and have immediate consequences; also known as the magic bullet or hypodermic needle approach.

discrimination   Extension of prejudice into behavior in a way that causes different, negative, and consequential treatment of a member of the stereotyped group.

dispelling stereotypes   Communication practice a co-cultural group member uses to problematize stereotypes.

display rule   Defines the appropriate type of emotional expression in any given situation.

distinctive concept of culture   Distinguishes the habits of one human group from another human group.

distrust belief   Refers to a co-cultural group member's belief that outsiders such as dominant group members are not to be trusted as evidenced by historical instances of prejudice, discrimination, and oppression such as slavery.

diversity   Presence of a variety of cultural groups.

dominant group   Group composed of people in society with greater power, privileges, and social status.

double consciousness   Refers to the life of a marginalized person expected to live simultaneously in two worlds: a Black world and a White world; the internal tensions and struggles experienced by many African Americans as a result of living simultaneously in these two different worlds with vastly juxtaposed landscapes.

e-collaboration   Electronic collaboration; complex range of social interactions involving computer-supported collaborative work.

economic imperative   Suggests that people are motivated to be more culturally aware in order to benefit from and be responsive to political, social, economic, and environmental events around the world that shape global economies.

effective communication   Communication in which there are minimal misunderstandings.

ego defensive function of prejudice   Uses prejudice to protect one's sense of self.

emic approach   Attempts to understand the culture from within or inside the cultural system being studied.

empathy   Ability to understand someone else's perspective by imagining one's self in the other person's situation.

empirical approach   Researchers' assumption that the objects of their study exist and can be observed.

enacted layer   Consists of the ways in which people decide, both consciously and unconsciously, to project their identities to others in interaction through their communicative practices.

enculturation   Manner in which individuals first learn who they are through their interactions with people in their native cultural groups, such as family members, friends, and people in their communities.

epistemological assumption (epistemology) Assumptions about how things can be studied; a basic theoretical assumption.

ethical imperative   Suggests that people are motivated to be more culturally aware in order to be moral, just, and fair.

ethnocentrism   Viewing the world from the perspective of one's own culture and evaluating other people and cultures using one's own cultural values as the ideal.

ethnographic interview   Process that takes place in the field by a researcher and is generally informal and spontaneous.

ethnolinguistic identity theory   Suggests that the higher one's ingroup vitality, the more members are willing to invest in their ingroup emotionally, psychologically, and with respect to collective action to foster their own group's interests.

ethnonym   Label people adopt for their ingroup.

ethnophaulism   Racial or ethnic slur.

etic approach   Attempts to understand the culture from outside the cultural system being studied.

evaluative concept of culture   Having access to and appreciation of the best that a society has to offer as in the expression "to be cultured." To lack culture, in this evaluative sense, is to be ignorant, vulgar, or unappreciative of the "finer" aspects of life.

exclusiveness   Refers to how a cultural group may not welcome intrusion from outside groups.

experiment   Research in which the researcher manipulates an independent variable in an environment (e.g., conversation distance) in order to observe the effect of this manipulation on the dependent variables (e.g., feelings of comfort). At the same time all other variables (e.g., attractiveness of conversation partner) that might also have an effect on the dependent variable are controlled for.

explicit knowledge   Reflection on how communicative resources are used to achieve interactional ends.

external component   Obvious component of culture such as its art, food, and religion(s).

face   A person's positively valued social identity.

face negotiation theory   Suggests that collectivist cultural members focus on group well-being over self, while individualists emphasize the self over and above the group. Specifically, rather than cause problems that would result in a loss of face, collectivists tend to use compromise, avoiding, and compliance conflict management styles.

face-threat   Action that harms a person's face.

face validity   Refers to whether, on the surface, the research instrument looks as if it is measuring what it should; the most global but subjective form of validity.

face-work   Refers to identity management of face, how people make themselves look good in the presence of others, protect or regain face when it has been threatened, and make sure others are viewed positively as well.

feminine culture   Culture that focuses on nurturance, values relationships, involves equality between males and females, and downplays individual accomplishments.

feminism   Active approach to addressing the oppression women experience in a patriarchal society.

field notes   Method researchers use to document their experiences in the field using a variety of strategies to document as much of what they see as possible, carefully separating their own impressions from observations.

first-world   Term originally used to designate the dominant economic powers of the West (e.g., the United States), characterized by a capitalist system of production.

focus group interview Process that involves multiple informants being interviewed simultaneously and allows insight into how members of a speech community reach consensus or disagree about their views.

form of address Way of calling or referring to a person or people.

fourth-world Cultural groups of indigenous people who suffer even more economic marginalization and social oppression than groups ruled or controlled by foreign powers.

fragmentation Occurs when aspects of social identities do not feel integrated with each other contributing to feelings of distance and alienation.

functional approach Focuses on what technology "does."

generalizable Describes conclusions reached by researchers that are universally valid; statements about social behavior extended beyond the specific people studied and applied to other comparable groups of people.

generalization Statement about the characteristics and behaviors that describe a percentage of the members of a culture group.

generalized other Process whereby people develop an idea of who they are by looking at themselves through the lens of how they think others perceive them.

generic concept of culture Views culture as a way of distinguishing the human animal from other animals by highlighting uniquely human accomplishments (e.g., language ability, artistic expression, musical abilities); views humans as above and unlike all other species.

giving-face Intentional support of another person's identity; often used to counter face-threats.

global collaborative education Initiative aimed to advance knowledge and digitally enabled education worldwide.

global e-collaboration Process of cooperation between geographically dispersed teams in two or more countries working together toward a common goal using digital technologies.

global village A world in which various communication technologies bring people together from different regions of the globe.

globalization Process whereby people's lives and local communities are increasingly influenced by economic, technological, and cultural forces that operate worldwide.

group vitality Refers to three separate, but interrelated, dimensions of status, demographics, and institutional support that provide social advantages for cultural groups in terms of pride in the group's history, sheer numbers of its members, and the visibility of its culture and communicative codes.

group-related power Power present in relationships between different groups in a culture.

hate crime Crime in which a perpetrator attacks a victim due to the perception that the victim is a member of a particular group.

heavy user (of television) Person who has substantial, ongoing exposure to television.

hegemony Refers to the process whereby ideas that support the interests and beliefs of the powerful become fixed, unquestionable, and commonsensical.

helplessness belief Refers to a co-cultural group member's belief that he or she is ill-equipped to change his or her own circumstances and that such efforts are futile because of the systematic oppression that works against them.

heterogeneous culture Culture in which there exists great diversity in the cultural identities of its group members.

high context culture Culture in which cultural group members use language and behavior that assumes that others know much of what they know.

high culture   Culture associated with the upper class and the value placed on the so-called finer aspects of life such as arts and education.

high sensation seeker   Person who is drawn to novel and exciting experiences and who is often motivated to seek intercultural contact because of the element of novelty involved in interacting with someone of a different culture.

history   Stories people tell themselves to make sense of who they are.

homogenous culture   Culture without cultural diversity and instead comprised of populations with similar demographic characteristics.

honorific   Title or other term that references status.

hypodermic needle approach   Another name for the direct effects theory.

hypothesis confirming information   Refers to the tendency of a person to stop looking for answers once an answer that verifies what is already thought is found.

identity   Basic and predominantly fixed features of a person's personality acquired in childhood.

identity denial   When people are denied the right to identify with the group in which they view themselves as belonging, for example through the question: Where do you really come from?

identity gap   Unreconciled contradiction in identity that may result in fragmented identity if not resolved.

identity management theory (IMT)   Asserts that in addition to cultural identities, relational identities are people's most significant identities. In order to be competent communicators, individuals must be able to manage and negotiate relational identities competently.

identity negotiation   People's efforts to reconcile or negotiate tensions with regard to their identities.

identity tourism   Process whereby individuals take on the identities of other cultures, races, ethnicities, genders, social classes, sexualities, and (dis)abilities for recreational purposes.

ideology   Refers to the collective beliefs, attitudes, perceptions, and values that are known to and guide the actions of cultural members.

immigration   Process of moving from one nation-state to another to settle more or less permanently.

imperialism   Refers to how dominant cultures exercise their powerful influence on other cultures around the globe through the dissemination of attitudes, ideas, practices, and products.

impressionist tale   Story the researcher uses to present findings that tends to purposely violate the conventions of realist tales and flirts with the conventions of literary genres like fiction and poetry.

indexicality   Describes how one term, phrase, or other aspect of what is communicated references something that is not communicated explicitly

individual advocacy   Occurs when a person shares quality information about a marginalized group that would otherwise be stereotyped or misunderstood by the general public; includes advocacy through interpersonal communication, through research and learning, or through individual action or volunteering.

individual layer   Intrapersonal identity that a person possesses, consisting of self-concept and self-image.

individualistic culture   One end of the continuum of Hofstede's collectivism-individualism intercultural dimension wherein self-reliance and individual achievement are positively valued.

individuating information   Unique characteristics of a person such as personality or temperament.

induction Reasoning from observations toward conclusions based on established premises; requires the researcher to observe particular acts of communication first and then reach a conclusion about their meaning on the basis of an underlying cultural premise.

informant interview Process in which a researcher asks savvy key informants, regardless of their cultural group membership, to speak about the world around them.

information processing theory Explains that people have a limited cognitive capacity to process information and, therefore, they process information in selective ways.

infrahumanization effect Tendency for people to attribute and express human qualities to members of their ingroup and less human and more animalistic properties to members of their outgroup.

ingroup Social category or group with which one strongly identifies.

injustice belief Co-cultural group member's belief that members of the dominant group will act through a larger system of oppression to which the co-cultural group and its members will be subjected, such as a biased judicial system.

insider advocacy Involves an advocate who is a member of the marginalized group for whom advocacy is undertaken. This person may have more authority from which to advocate by virtue of being personally familiar with the group and also more potential for bias than advocates who do not belong to the group.

institutional support Refers to the extent to which a group and its culture are reflected in the main structures of society, such as in the media, politics, the law, and so forth.

integrated model of intercultural communication competence (IMICC) Interconnects five variables that contribute to intercultural communication competence.

intellectual property Creations of individual ideas which include inventions (patents), industrial designs, symbols and trademarks used in commerce, as well as literary, musical, and artistic works.

interactional dilemma Conversational choice which, by serving one aim, directly competes with an equally desirable ideal.

interaction involvement Conversational exchange requiring mindfulness and active listening.

inter/cultural communication Reflects how each conversation involves cultural as well as intercultural communication

intercultural communication Communication between and among those from different cultures.

intercultural communication competence (ICC) Uses effective and appropriate communication in a context where cultural variables significantly influence the outcome of the interaction.

intercultural imperative Suggests that people are motivated toward greater awareness about intercultural communication; six imperatives represent societal level reasons for why people benefit from broader cultural awareness.

intercultural listening Analyzes the speech of the other person first from the standpoint of the other's culture and then from the standpoint of one's own culture.

intercultural transition Process of moving between cultural contexts ranging from relatively short periods of time to long durations and permanent resettlement.

intergroup boundary Boundary that is symbolically equivalent to a geographical border, yet is reflected in psychological and communicative dimensions.

intergroup communication (IGC) Views intercultural communication as an intergroup exchange in which the social and historical relations between cultures is critical to the communication activity; views social identity as being a focal part of any interaction which can often hamper effective communication.

intergroup communication perspective   Studies the effects of talking to someone from another culture based solely on a person's being a member of that group rather than talking to the person based on individuating information.

intergroup contact   Conversations with, and observations of, another culture through its media, literature, and knowledge of its history.

intergroup interaction   Talking to someone from another culture based solely on the individual's being a member of that group.

intergroup status hierarchy   Refers to how a society views the cultural groups that comprise a society and their relative positions within that society.

inter-individual interaction   Talking to someone from another culture based on individuating information.

internal components   Subtle and sometimes unspoken dimensions of a culture (e.g., rules about appropriate proxemic behavior).

internal consistency   Used to ascertain reliability; the extent to which the items of a research instrument yield similar results.

Internet plagiarism   Using others' ideas and words as one's own (intentionally or unintentionally) without clearly acknowledging the online source of that information.

Internet privacy   Protection of information about identities, locations and relocations, personal relations, purchases, and medical histories; the desire for security in how this information is gathered, stored, shared, and how it can be protected from misuse.

interpenetration   Occurs when identities cohere.

interpersonal ideology   Rules for interaction.

interpretivist approach   Guides researchers toward understanding how symbols are used and interpreted in given contexts to create meaning by those who use them.

interpretivist research   Generates claims with some predictive power; its chief aim is not prediction but the interpretation of the meaning of communicative practices from the perspective of those speakers who engage in those practices.

intersectionality   Refers to how race, social class, gender, sexuality, ability, and nationality simultaneously operate within a single person.

intracultural variability   Idea that some cultural members identify highly with the norms, values, and ideas of a community, whereas others distance themselves from some beliefs.

I-Other dialectic   Logic that asserts, "how I see myself is heavily influenced by how I see others and how they see me."

knowledge function of prejudice   Uses prejudice to help process the enormous amount of information with which people come into contact.

language selection   Language a person chooses to speak at a particular moment.

language suicide   Occurs when communication codes of members of low vitality groups fade away and become extinct.

legacy media   Traditional forms of media such as television, radio, and print.

lens   Perspective people take on the world guided by the norms and values of the culture with which they identify.

limited effects model   Presents a theoretical perspective arguing that media has little influence on individuals.

linguistic determinism   Describes the way in which language shapes culture.

linguistic intergroup bias   Refers to the way linguistic subtleties can be interpreted by listening to the language people use to describe or report on the actions of ingroups and outgroups. If an ingroup is behaving in a socially positive manner, then the act is described in global traits terms. If an outgroup member committed this same act, they would be described only in specific behavioral terms. This allows perceptions of ingroup members overall to be favorable while for outgroup members it doesn't generalize beyond the single act.

linguistic landscape   Powerful means of establishing and legitimizing a sense of ingroup pride and vitality through ethnic or cultural enclaves.

linguistic relativity   Describes the way in which language evolves to reflect changes in the culture in which it is created.

linguistic shibboleth   Word or term that when communicated can identify someone as being a member of a distinctive group.

long-term orientation   One of Hofstede's value dimensions. Countries which demonstrate a short-term orientation tend to prefer fast results, focus on social and status obligations, and enjoy stability whereas cultures with a long-term orientation look further into the future in order to understand the benefits and consequences of their actions.

looking glass self   Asserts that people learn who they are by the image that is projected unto them by others.

loose culture   Culture in which many behaviors are allowed across different situations.

lose face   Results when a person's face is challenged by a face-threat.

low context culture   Culture in which cultural group members provide a lot of detail in their conversations and they do not make assumptions about their speech partner's knowledge.

low culture   Culture associated with the lower class, with those who are less educated, and with popular culture.

macroscopic power   Way power is set up in a given culture or society at a particular time in history; the circulation of power on a larger social scale and it includes government and politics, social policy and the law, religious institutions, educational systems, health care institutions, family and kinship systems, mass media, and other social institutions.

magic bullet   Another name for the direct effects theory.

maintaining interpersonal barriers   Communication practice used by a co-cultural group member to create psychological distance using their nonverbal behavior (e.g., space, eye contact, physical distance) or topical avoidance (e.g., topical shifts) to minimize or reduce communication with a dominant group member who is engaging in behavior deemed offensive or inappropriate.

majority identity   Identity representative of a dominant group in society.

marginalized   Describes individuals or groups that do not fall into the mainstream and who are forced to the fringes of society where they are essentially ignored and deemed a part of the underclass.

markedness   Way in which people add to what they are saying in order to demonstrate that something is atypical (e.g., using the phrase *male nurse*).

masculine culture   One end of the continuum of Hofstede's masculinity-femininity intercultural dimension wherein strength and external wealth are viewed as important aspects of life.

media   Refers to the particular medium used to deliver a message to a large, anonymous, diverse audience.

media consumption   Amount and content of media to which a person is exposed.

media critic   Person who studies and analyzes media and its effects.

media effects   Influence that the media has on audiences.

media imperialism   Domination or control through media products.

media literacy   Involves developing a critical understanding of how mass media operates, including learning to read messages behind the media's images.

media representation   Portrayal of various cultural groups in the media.

member check   Process whereby interpretivists seek out opportunities to ask community members to read or listen to their account of the communal ways and comment on whether or not they consider it an accurate representation of their everyday experiences.

membering   Uses culture to identify a person's membership with those in some cultures and not with others.

membership categorization device   Way of referencing people which puts them into assumed categories.

metastereotype   Perception of the stereotype a person thinks outgroup members have about that individual's ingroups.

micromessaging   Generic name for sending short (under 140 characters) messages.

microscopic power   Way power occurs in individual and social transactions—in conversations with others, interpersonal relationships, or inter/cultural encounters.

mindful communicator   Involves continually creating new categories in a person's mind to accommodate new information being received. Instead of operating on "auto-pilot," or mindlessly, a mindful communicator is deliberate in his or her communication behavior.

mindfulness   Involves creating mental categories to accommodate new information in the communication exchange; being active, tuned-in, and involved in an interaction.

minimal group   Group membership based on trivial criteria; although the membership is based on seemingly unimportant criteria, once associated with a group (e.g., those with black pens and those with blue pens) the members show ingroup favoritism.

minority identity   Identity that is representative of those without power, privilege, or social status and who are, therefore, not representative of dominant groups in society.

model minority   Marginalized groups who behave in ways that satisfy dominant group expectations; groups whose members do not "cause problems" by pointing out issues of inequality or by drawing people's attention to stereotypes or discrimination against his or her cultural group. In return the group and its members are favored and granted privileges by the dominant group.

monochronic   Describes cultures that view time as following a linear trajectory in which specific times are allocated to specific tasks or events.

multicultural worldview   Open-minded view that welcomes a variety of cultural perspectives.

multiple overdetermination of pattern   Occurs when researchers are able to confirm, on the basis of multiple data sources (e.g., interviews with multiple respondents, recordings, documents, etc.) and inductive reasoning, that the cultural premise used in the interpretation can be regarded accurate.

multiracial feminist thought   Views race as interacting with other systems of power, such as gender, to perpetuate inequalities.

muted group theory   Makes the argument that people live in a hierarchically structured society where some people experience privileges more so than others. As a result of this power difference, certain groups are muted or rendered silent by their powerless state.

narrative Extended speech act practice with cultural variability.

narrative interview Process in which a researcher elicits participants' stories.

neither/nor tension Tension felt between identities when an individual does not feel connected to the larger, dominant group nor to his or her self-identified group.

noncontact culture Cultural group in which members maintain more space and touch less frequently during interaction.

nonverbal communication Uses behavior, other than language, to send and receive messages and create symbolic meaning.

normal distribution Occurs when most numbers in a data set are to be found in the middle of a symmetrical bell curve. This distribution shows where most cases fall and, therefore, identifies the most common case in the study. Ideally, the researcher's hypothesis would have predicted this typical case.

novelty Situation that is both unpredictable and challenging.

ontological assumption Ontology; that which is assumed about the nature of things; a basic theoretical assumption.

oppression Social forces that limit, restrict, block, and foreclose an individual's—or a group's—pursuit of a good life.

orienting to culture Process in which a conversational participant explicitly labels his or her own, or others', practices as cultural.

orientational others Those individuals whose opinions and perceptions are valued and trusted.

other-face Refers to concern with ensuring the other person in a conversation does not lose face.

othered Occurs if someone is not mainstream or does not conform to what society deems normal and is, therefore, treated differently because of that person's cultural identity.

otherness Refers to specific locations in a particular social group where individuals are deemed to have deviated from the cultural standard or center.

outgroup Social category or group with which a person does not identify.

outsider advocacy Involves an advocate who is not a member of the marginalized group for whom advocacy is undertaken. While they may have greater credibility with dominant group members, they may also not fully understand the experiences of the marginalized group for whom they are advocating. An outside advocate must also constantly strive for equality in his or her relationship with the marginalized group.

paradox of privilege Explains the situation in which society gives a person advantages because the person belongs to the dominant cultural group but that person does not personally feel privileged.

participant observation Requires the researcher to spend time among the people whose ways he or she wants to study, interact with them and, in the process of interaction, develop a sense of the local, cultural knowledge that informs their everyday conduct.

participatory learning Mode of learning in which new technologies enable learners of any age to work jointly to aggregate their ideas, views, and experiences to achieve individual and group learning goals.

part-whole nature of an expressive system Identifies that expressive acts do not stand alone but are parts of larger social sequences.

peacebuilding Process of conflict resolution that attempts to remove the causes of violence among different groups.

peace imperative Suggests that people are motivated for more cultural awareness in order to create or maintain intercultural stability.

peer-to-peer (P2P) network   System of sharing files, programs, or computer desktops with anyone over the Internet.

permeability of intergroup boundaries   Refers to whether the characteristics of a group are so unique as to be inaccessible (and impermeable) to outgroups.

person referencing   Different terms for referencing and addressing people, including forms of address, honorifics, and membership categorization devices.

plagiarism   Occurs when one person uses another's ideas and words (intentionally or unintentionally) without clearly acknowledging the source of information.

playing the game   Learning how to navigate through organizational structures.

polarization   Treating differences between cultures as if they reflect two extreme opposite poles of behavior.

polychronic   Describes cultures that view time as multidimensional; many tasks may be dealt with at once.

power   Ability to control circumstances (like access to financial, social, and cultural resources) and to get things done (like fulfilling personal goals and dreams and helping others achieve theirs); all individual and social relationships operate within relations of power.

power distance   One of Hofstede's value dimensions representing the extent to which a culture accepts inequality for people within the society and assents to centralized power and status differentials.

practices of people in place   Something people do with each other, as a system of practices, as a way of organizing themselves together, and as a way of accounting for that organization.

predictive validity   Indicates the validity of a research instrument to make accurate predictions by checking it against a certain criterion that is used as a standard.

prejudice   Hostile attitude toward a member of a cultural group because the person is a member of that group and is assumed to have qualities stereotypically associated with that group.

printed media   Refers to books, newspapers, and magazines.

privilege   Frequently invisible and normalized process whereby a person is granted more value—and given better treatment—solely based on this person's membership in a group.

progressivity   Progression or advancement toward completing certain conversational actions.

provisional   Being flexible and open in conversation while having an awareness of the possibility that differences (or similarities) may (or may not) matter.

proxemics   Use of personal space.

push and pull of culture model   Provides a framework in which "push" signifies structure and tradition and refers to those aspects of culture that are inherited by people (e.g., primary language, religion, collective memory, core values, and everyday customs); "pull" signifies the active role of the self as an agent of cultural construction and places emphasis on individual, user-driven tendencies. The technological advances brought about by the rise of Internet-based tools and applications affect both sides of culture: push culture and pull culture.

pyramid model of intercultural competence   Shows the development of intercultural competence as a process, from the person level of one's attitudes, to the interpersonal level of interacting with other people.

quasi-completed contract   Type of cultural contract that is most well aligned with accommodation. It may involve a part of one's identity being accepted while another is rejected or not appreciated.

quasi-experiment   Experiment in which the independent variable cannot be controlled by the researcher but occurs naturally.

random assignment   Requires that all participants be assigned to the experimental conditions by chance only.

ready-to-sign contract   Type of cultural contract that is readily available as if a person has the contract in his or her pocket when he or she encounters different values, norms, or beliefs. The expectation is that conflict is best resolved by the other party "signing" or agreeing to the ready to sign contract. This contract is potentially the most problematic unless both parties agree to a homogenous way of doing things.

realist tale   Story the researcher uses to present findings in a way that represents the researcher as an all-seeing and all-knowing objective observer who reports on the details of the ways of those from other cultural groups.

reality television   Television programming sold, and largely perceived, as unscripted; the "reality" in reality television can be best understood as a social construction—one that uses the seemingly unscripted life experiences of everyday people to create a form of entertainment that is consumed by the viewing public.

redefinition   Involves the development of new language and the emergence of new meaning for already existent language.

reductionism   Reduction of complex information to smaller chunks which risks overlooking more complicated ideas.

reflexivity   Necessity of careful reflection on the research process that acknowledges the social interaction between researcher and communal members.

relational empathy   Enables people to engage perceived cultural differences through the creation of shared meaning and, in doing so, produce a third culture.

relational identity   Identity which emphasizes the *we* not *I* or *you*; Involves privately shared systems of understanding between those in the relationship.

relational layer   Consists of how identity is produced and negotiated throughout communication in relationships.

reliability   Extent to which the research instrument provides consistent results when the characteristics of the object measured have not been changed; an instrument is valid if it measures what it intends to measure.

re-membering   Recalling from past experience and interpreting this in new ways through the present.

repressive   Restricting or restraining people through the control of resources such as money, knowledge, and various social institutions.

research ethics   Moral rules or standards governing the conduct of the members of the scientific community.

respondent interview   Process in which a researcher asks any communal member with relevant experience to speak about a particular subject.

retroactive speech halo effect   Notion that fast speech rates and standard accents are construed as positive attributes of speakers across many cultures. Hence the effect is manifest in that if one believes a speaker is of high status, the speaker would be heard to sound more standard accented and faster in speech rate than if no status information was available or if the person was known to be of low status.

rich point   Moment in a researcher's experience within a speech community that features intense surprise and confusion and a similarly intense sense of fascination.

roster-like approach   Lists all of the aspects of a person's identity and considers these (more superficial) characteristics of an individual.

Sapir-Whorf hypothesis   Presents a theory that involves linguistic relativity and linguistic determinism; argues that language changes over time both in response to the needs of a culture and in such a way as to produce change in a culture.

save face   Actions a person takes to avoid losing face.

second-world   Economic powers, such as the Soviet Union and its satellites, featuring a socialist system of production.

self   Stable, core set of identities within a person that comprise that person's system for thinking and behaving.

self-awareness imperative   Suggests that people are motivated for cultural awareness in order to be self-reflexive and understand their thoughts and behaviors.

self-consciousness   General awareness of one's self in society.

self-efficacy   Individual's belief in the capacity or ability to alter his or her circumstances.

self-esteem   Refers to how an individual values him- or herself. Social and environmental cues facilitate self-appraisals.

self-identity   Self constructed through shared meanings of understanding with others. This dynamic negotiated communicative process contrasts with identity as a fixed and stable feature of self.

sense-making   Process of attributing meaning to talk in interaction with others.

service learning   Fusion of traditional coursework with community service in which students meet the needs of community members or organizations through their coursework.

short-term orientation   Value dimension that tends to prefer fast results, and focuses on social and status obligations.

small group advocacy   Advocates for the needs of a marginalized group.

social construction approach   Stresses the way in which cultures are created through symbols. A social construction approach espouses the view that there is no reality of a culture outside of those who communicate about that culture.

social construction of technology perspective   Views technology as subordinate to the way it is used in society and specific sociocultural contexts in which everyone is a "culture producer" able to initiate, develop, and maintain diverse cultural experiences.

social identity theory   Asserts that when an ingroup identity is made or becomes salient, people often wish to emphasize characteristics of their group which they hold dear. The theory suggests that by expressing that group's distinctive characteristics, group members can thereby assume unqualified pride in their membership in this group. Moreover, the theory suggests that by such expressed public identification with the group, this translates into a greater sense of personal worth. This view of their ingroup is bolstered by a more negative view of their outgroup.

social interaction technology   Internet-based tools and techniques designed to initiate, maintain, share, and distribute interactive and collaborative activities and spaces online.

social media   Range of online applications, including social networks, blogs, and wikis through which people can create and distribute content and engage in social interactions.

social movement   Occurs when people band together around a common goal such that momentum is built towards reaching that goal.

social networking site   Internet site that allows members to post and update their personal online profiles, add friends to their network, exchange messages, and share photos and videos.

social products Immaterial social aspects of life.

social scene Place people can identify and recognize as significant in their lives such as a church service, a sporting event, a family dinner, a court room, and so forth.

social scientific approach (to culture) Stresses the way in which cultures are represented symbolically and helps to distinguish differences and similarities among cultures.

social scientific research Stands for a systematic, empirical way of collecting, analysing, and interpreting data to answer questions, test hypotheses, and shed light on problems concerning social behavior.

socialization Formal, focused, normative form of enculturation in which knowledge and values are imposed upon the individual.

speech act Utterances (e.g., questions) characterized by their social function.

speech code Patterned way of speaking which is shared and intelligible among community members.

speech community Community sharing rules for conduct and the interpretation of speech codes.

stance Displays what is assumed to be a speaker's opinion, belief, or attitude.

standpoint theory Acknowledges that people have certain vantage points from which they each view the world.

statistical significance Extent to which statistical tests indicate that the researcher can be 95% sure that the results have not happened by chance.

status Refers to the influence and power a group has economically, historically, socially, and linguistically within a culture.

stereotyping Expectation that all cultural group members will have the same characteristics.

straight ally Heterosexual person who promotes lesbian, gay, bisexual, and transgender (LGBT) people's rights.

stranger Someone who is geographically near such that two people can engage in communication but culturally distant such that he or she comes from a culture that is distinctly different from the other person.

structural privilege Refers to how whiteness is associated with unearned advantages, opportunities, and access to a social system with advantages.

structuration theory Articulates how social constructions are imposed upon by cultural representations.

subjective group vitality Refers to how people view their own and others groups' vitalities.

superiority belief Refers to a co-cultural group member's sense of superiority over the dominant group.

symbol Expresses meaning using language and behavior; comprised of verbal or nonverbal codes, distinct behavior units such as a wave or the word *hello*, that represent meaning.

symbolic forms Communication acts within larger sequences of actions.

symbolic interactionism Explicates how people make sense of the world in their everyday interactions. This theory explains how people learn their cultural norms and values, as well as create their sense of self, through these interactions. Theoretical tenets of symbolic interactionism assert that people do not construct their understanding of themselves and the world in isolation; rather people understand themselves and others through intersubjective interaction.

symbolic intercultural space The moment when a communication exchange has been affected by cultural differences.

synchronous collaborative technology Technology such as instant messaging, online chat, audio-video conferencing, and virtual worlds that enables real-time collaboration and allows team members to interact without any time delay in an instantaneous fashion.

systematic observation Way researchers explore the topic they are studying, such as differences between cultures, by viewing people's behavior and making precise records of these.

tacit knowledge Knowledge a person already possesses that allows this person to communicate.

taken-for-granted knowledge Something that one typically does not have to think about; it is just assumed.

technological imperative Suggests that people are motivated for more intercultural awareness in order to be connected to the global village.

technology Practical application of human knowledge and the tools and techniques produced by a society to meet people's needs.

tensional force Communication practice that ignites tension between a creative impulse and common practice.

test-retest method Used to ascertain reliability; the extent to which a research instrument should at different moments yield similar results unless the characteristic it measures has been changed.

theoretical approach Provides researchers with preexisting ideas about what is important to look for and how to do so.

thick intersectionality Highlights lived experiences and the biography of the person.

third culture building Occurs when two parties negotiate cultural differences and merge cultural traits to create a new culture.

third-world Cultures constituted by the experience of being ruled or controlled by others; views of these cultures are often saturated with images of poverty, disease, and war.

tight culture Culture in which few forms of behavior are permitted across different situations.

transcribe Process by which researchers capture, to the extent desired or necessary, all words spoken, pauses, intonation, emphasis, and all *uhs* and *ums* as well as other relevant nonverbal behavior in order to produce a documented artifact of an interaction (i.e., a transcript).

transcript Verbatim typed-out version of exactly what each person said.

triangulation Taking multiple perspectives on the same observation in order to ensure that the interpretation of that observation is accurate. This can be done by conducting member checks, consulting multiple researchers observing the same example of communicative conduct, or using multiple sources of data.

turn-taking Quick back-and-forth that occurs within conversation in which each person literally takes a turn talking.

tweet Short (under 140 characters) message sent and received through Twitter which was launched in 2006; a specific form of micromessaging sent through Twitter.

uncertainty avoidance One of Hofstede's value dimensions representing the extent to which a culture prefers order and structure and shuns ambiguity, free thinking, and alternative lifestyles.

unconscious competence Level of intercultural communication competence where the communicator is so conversant in communicating with people of other cultures that he or she communicates competently without putting conscious effort.

unconscious incompetence Level of intercultural communication competence where the communicator is communicating without being effective or appropriate and is unaware that he or she is doing so.

unearned advantage   Entitlements available to certain groups in a culture that everyone should have, such as feeling that one's life is valuable or experiencing safety in public spaces.

unethical advocacy   Occurs when the advocate is acting independent of the group to take action on behalf of the group; also occurs when the support an advocate attempts to provide to a group is misinformed or contributes to the group's silencing.

user-generated content   Reader-contributed news, user-created video, blog posts, comments, user tags, product ratings, and the like.

uses and gratifications theory   Suggests that media influences vary depending on the functions that the various forms play in the lives of consumers; acknowledges audiences as active users of media who are motivated to use different types of media programming to fulfill different needs.

utilitarian function of prejudice   Uses prejudice to gain intrinsic (e.g., greater self-esteem) or extrinsic rewards (e.g., profit).

validity   Signifies whether the research instrument truly and correctly measures what it intends.

value expressive function of prejudice   Uses prejudice to increase self-confidence and view one's own groups more positively thereby protecting individual and group identity.

verbal communication   Uses language to send and receive messages and create symbolic meaning.

vernacular language   Native or indigenous language that is not of a standardized variety.

vulnerability belief Refers to a co-cultural group member's perception that his or her group is at risk for negative or dire outcomes as group members engage with mainstream society in daily life.

way of life   Aspects of a culture that make up the life of its members including language, norms and values, and so forth.

Web 2.0   Tools that involve a broad spectrum of second-generation web applications and services such as online social networks, blogs, wikis, podcasts, RSS feeds, social bookmarks, folksonomies, mashups, and virtual worlds.

whiteness   Cultural identity that acquires meaning through its relationship to other groups; a major force in the social world that conceals its power through its invisibility.

wiki   Collaborative website that can be edited by anyone, including nontechnical people and nonexperts.

willingness to communicate (WTC)   Importance of a variety of both psychological and contextual variables that influence a person's desire to communicate with someone from another culture.

xenophobic   Fear of those who are different or foreign.

Index

About the Editor

Anastacia Kurylo (PhD, Rutgers University) is Assistant Professor of Communication Arts at Marymount Manhattan College in New York City. She teaches courses in interpersonal communication, advanced interpersonal communication theory, gender and communication, organizational communication, communication theory, public speaking, intercultural communication, and stereotypes and communication. In her 15 years of teaching, she has taught at numerous colleges including Borough of Manhattan Community College, Marymount Manhattan College, Molloy College, New York University, Pace University, Rutgers University, and St. John's University. Her research interests include the examination of stereotypes communicated in interpersonal, intercultural, and organizational contexts and the implications of these for stereotype maintenance. She also studies pedagogy and mentorship as well as emotion and culture. She has published five teaching activities, four book chapters, a recent interdisciplinary article on stereotypes published in *Qualitative Research in Psychology,* and her blog TheCommunicatedStereotype.com. She is currently writing *The Communicated Stereotype: From Media to Everyday Talk* to be published in 2013. She is a former president of the New Jersey Communication Association and serves as a reviewer or editorial board member for several journals and associations. She enjoys spending time with her family, creating mosaics, eating in cafes, and working on research with her students.

About the Contributors

Wilfredo Alvarez (PhD, University of Colorado at Boulder) is Assistant Professor in the Department of Communication, Media and Theatre at Northeastern Illinois University in Chicago. His research and teaching interests include interpersonal/organizational communication and social identity, specifically issues related to communication and race, social class, and immigration. Some of his past research examined the everyday communication experiences of Latina/o immigrant custodial workers within U.S. higher education organizations. Originally from Santo Domingo, Dominican Republic, he has had invaluable cultural experiences living in New York, Florida, Colorado, and Illinois.

Lily A. Arasaratnam (PhD, Rutgers University) is Director of Master of Arts (Christian Studies) at Alphacrucis College in Sydney, Australia. Prior to her current position she was an assistant professor at the Department of Speech Communication at Oregon State University, followed by Macquarie University in Sydney. Her social scientific research relates sensation seeking to intercultural communication, with emphasis on intercultural communication competence. She serves as a reviewer for several major communication journals and her research on intercultural communication models has been published in both national and international journals. She is bilingual and has lived in four countries and nine cities so far.

Jack Bennett is currently earning his undergraduate degree in communication arts and psychology. He has worked as a research assistant on work related to stereotypes and culture. Originally from Minnesota, he now lives in New York working as a store manager for a retail company.

David Boromisza-Habashi (PhD, University of Massachusetts, Amherst) is Assistant Professor in the Department of Communication at the University of Colorado Boulder. His ethnographic research focuses on the sociocultural basis of observable language use. As an ethnographer of communication, he is pursuing two directions in his research: He studies the cultural foundations of speaking in public and the interactional basis of qualitative sense-making in a group context. Originally from Budapest, Hungary, he has gained valuable intercultural experiences living and working in Hungary, Egypt, and the United States where he and his wife, Nora, are raising their two daughters, Anna and Mira, as trilingual citizens.

Charles A. Braithwaite (PhD, University of Washington) is Fellow in the Center for Great Plains Studies, a Graduate Fellow in the Department of Anthropology, and Senior Lecturer in the Department of Communication Studies at the University of Nebraska, Lincoln. He teaches courses such as intercultural communication, ethnographic research methods, conflict management, interviewing, and nonverbal communication. He has a special interest in American Indian and First Nations higher education, and had conducted extensive research on the

Navajo Nation, and with the U-Mo'n-Ho'n (Omaha), the Ho-Chunk (Winnebago), and the Ponca tribes of Nebraska. He has served as editor of *Great Plains Quarterly* since 2000.

Donal Carbaugh (PhD, University of Washington) is Professor of Communication, Director of the Graduate Program, Chair of the International Studies Council, and Samuel F. Conti Faculty Fellow at the University of Massachusetts, Amherst. His book, *Cultures in Conversation* (2005) was designated the Outstanding Book of the Year by the International and Intercultural Communication Division of the National Communication Association. His most recent edited book with Patrice Buzzanell is *Distinctive Qualities in Communication Research* (2009). He has enjoyed lecturing at the United Nations (in New York and Geneva), at various universities, embassies, and other places across the United States, Europe, and Asia.

Brian Cogan (PhD, New York University) is Associate Professor of the Department of Communications at Molloy College in Long Island, New York. His specific areas of research interest are punk rock, comic books, and the intersection of politics and popular culture. He is the author, coauthor and coeditor of numerous books, articles, and anthologies on popular culture, music, and the media. He is also on the editorial board of the *Journal of Popular Culture* and on the editorial board of ABC-CLIO's popular culture project. A native New Yorker, he has been a drummer/vocalist in the pop-punk band, In-Crowd, since 1987.

Brad Crownover (PhD, Rutgers University) is Assistant Professor of Communication at the College of Mount Saint Vincent in Riverdale, New York. He teaches in the areas of strategic/promotional communication, human communication, theatre/acting, organizational communication, and intercultural communication. His research and writing focuses on relationships and how they are developed among organizations, products, and their publics; between people of different and similar cultures; and the relationship an actor creates with his or her character, other characters, artifacts, space, and an audience.

Satarupa Dasgupta (PhD, Temple University) is Assistant Professor and Faculty Fellow at the College of Nursing, New York University. Her research interests include sexual health behavior among high-risk populations, community health advocacy, risk reduction communication, identity studies, press freedom measurement, and South Asian popular culture. She has published several book chapters and peer-reviewed journal articles, and serves as a reviewer for two journals.

Rachel Anderson Droogsma (PhD, Howard University) is Assistant Professor of Communication Studies at Nebraska Wesleyan University in Lincoln, Nebraska. Her research, which has been published in the *Journal of Applied Communication Research* and *Communication, Culture, and Critique,* explores the ways women in marginalized groups resist oppression through communication. She pursues activist research and engages her students in service learning projects that benefit people in need in her community.

Tatyana Dumova (PhD, Bowling Green State University) is Associate Professor of Multimedia in the School of Communication at Point Park University in Pittsburgh, Pennsylvania. Her research focuses on the social implications of information and communication technologies and the role of technology in teaching and learning. She has presented and published her research nationally and internationally. Most recently, she has lead edited the two-volume *Handbook of Research on Social Interaction Technologies and Collaboration Software: Concepts* *and Trends* (2010) and *Blogging in the Global Society: Cultural, Political and Geographical Aspects* (2012). Dumova is also the editor of the *International Journal of Interactive Communication Systems and Technologies.*

Bill Edwards (PhD, Southern Illinois University at Carbondale) is Professor of Communication at Columbus State University, Columbus, Georgia. He began teaching intercultural communication in the 1970s. He has traveled to over 30 countries, mostly developing economies, to better understand the problems of intercultural communication. For recreation, he enjoys the game Go (a game originating in China over 2,000 years ago), kayaking, and handball.

Anita Foeman (PhD, Temple University) is Professor in the Department of Communication Studies at West Chester University in Pennsylvania. Her research investigates communication patterns of multiracial people and families. Her most recent work in this area explores how interracial couples make decisions about their children's education. Since 2006 she has been studying the relationship between DNA ancestral data, family narratives, and the social construction of race.

Adrian Furnham (DPhil, DSc, DLitt, Oxford University) is Professor of Psychology at University College London and a Fellow of the British Psychological Society. He has written over 700 scientific papers and 60 books, and is on the editorial board of a number of international journals, as well as the past elected president of the International Society for the Study of Individual Differences. Since 2007, he has been nominated by *HR Magazine* as one of the 20 Most Influential People in HR. He rides a bicycle to work early in the morning, does not have a mobile phone, and hopes never to retire.

Howard Giles (PhD, DSc, University of Bristol) is Professor of Communication at the University of California, Santa Barbara. His research is in the general area of intergroup communication, language attitudes, and accommodation, with a particular cross-cultural interest in intergenerational encounters as well as police-civilian interactions. He is now working on *The Handbook of Intergroup Communication* (2012). Founding editor of the *Journal of Language and Social Psychology* and the *Journal of Asian Pacific Communication,* and past editor of *Human Communication Research,* he has been past president of the International Communication Association and the International Association of Language & Social Psychology.

Jane Giles (BSc, University of Bristol) is part of Van Buren Consulting, where she is a Timeslips Certified Consultant for Sage Timeslips. She graduated with honors in psychology and a postgraduate certificate in education. After 4 years teaching high school sciences, she became an analyst/programmer with the UK leader in pension management software, one of whose clients was the Queen of England. She is a proud recipient of a Parent-Teacher-Student Association (PTSA) honorary service award for computerizing production of a junior high yearbook, never having seen one before moving to California. One of her hobbies has been publishing empirical research and theory on different aspects of intergroup communication, including bilingualism.

Cerise L. Glenn (PhD, Howard University) is Assistant Professor in the Department of Communication Studies at the University of North Carolina at Greensboro. She examines how various aspects of social identity, especially race/ethnicity, gender, and socioeconomic status, intersect in various contexts. Her research and teaching interests center on social constructions of difference (diversity), particularly identity negotiation and representations of underrepresented groups in organizational, intercultural/international, and mass-mediated contexts.

Tina M. Harris (PhD, University of Kentucky, Lexington) is Professor in the Department of Communication Studies at the University of Georgia. She is the 2011 Religious Communication Association Scholar of the Year for her research on religious communication and a 2010 Josiah T. Meigs Distinguished Teaching Professor and a 2006 recipient of the Georgia Board of Regents' Scholarship of Teaching and Learning Award for her teaching and scholarship on race and pedagogy. Her research expertise is on interracial communication, interracial dating, race relations, racial representations and the media, and the intersection of race, health, religious/Christian frameworks, and communication. She is a nationally renowned interracial communication scholar and has coauthored the leading textbook *Interracial Communication: Theory to Practice* (2008) with communication scholar Mark P. Orbe.

Kathleen C. Haspel (PhD, Rutgers University) is Associate Professor of Communication Studies at Fairleigh Dickinson University in Madison, New Jersey. Her research examines narrative and discursive practices in public and institutional contexts, such as call-in radio and television news programs, public meetings, and emergency service calls. Her recent work examines narratives of crisis, race, and place. Her work has been published in the *Journal of Communication,* the *American Communication Journal,* the *International Encyclopedia of Communication,* and other edited volumes. She has served as chair of the Language and Social Interaction division of the National Communication Association.

Ronald L. Jackson II (PhD, Howard University) is Professor and Head of Media & Cinema Studies and African American Studies at the University of Illinois. He is also Professor in the Institute of Communications Research. In his teaching and research, he explores how and why people negotiate and define themselves as they do. His research examines how theories of identity relate to intercultural and gender communication. Communication. He is editor of *Critical Studies in Media Communication* and of the recently released book *Global Masculinities and Manhood* (with Murali Balaji).

Kurt Lemko (MA, San Diego State University) works for the City and County of San Francisco as an Operations Analyst. He aims to get back into his field of urban geography doing neighborhood revitalization work. His hobbies include traveling, gardening, lifting weights at the gym, bicycling, and hiking. He enjoys the San Francisco nightlife on weekends, but mostly he loves hanging out with his friends.

David Linton (PhD, New York University) is Professor of Communication Arts at Marymount Manhattan College in New York. He has been on the faculty for more than 20 years. His research interests and publications are wide ranging, including such topics as the media environment of Elizabethan England, the reading behavior of the Virgin Mary, the history of the Luddite movement, and the formation of literary and media canons. He is writing a book about the social construction and images of menstruation and teaches an interdisciplinary course on this subject in addition to a course in communications theory, media, and public speaking.

David Matsumoto (PhD, University of California at Berkeley) is Professor of Psychology and Director of the Culture and Emotion Research Laboratory at San Francisco State

University. He has studied culture, emotion, social interaction, and communication for over 25 years. His books include well-known titles such as *Culture and Psychology* (2013) and the *Cambridge Dictionary of Psychology* (2009). He is the recipient of many awards and honors in the field of psychology, including being named a G. Stanley Hall lecturer by the American Psychological Association. He is the series editor for Cambridge University Press' series on *Culture and Psychology,* and he is also editor-in-chief for the *Journal of Cross-Cultural Psychology.*

Susan E. Morgan (PhD, University of Arizona) is Professor in the Department of Communication at Purdue University, West Lafayette, Indiana. Her research interests involve the design and evaluation of persuasive messages targeting health behavior change in multicultural populations. Her research has been supported by over $9 million in grants. Her latest research involves conducting and evaluating multimedia campaigns to promote organ donation in worksite and community settings. She serves on the editorial board of 5 journals and is an active reviewer for 15 journals. She has published over 50 articles and the book, *From Numbers to Words: Reporting Statistical Results for the Social Sciences* (2002).

Anthony Y. Naaeke (PhD, Duquesne University) is Assistant Professor of Communication Arts at Marymount Manhattan College in New York. His research focuses on persuasion in cultural and religious discourse as well as the rhetoric of intercultural and development communication. He is the author of *Kaleidoscope Catechesis: Missionary Catechesis in Africa, Particularly in the Diocese of Wa in Ghana,* (2006) and *Critical Essays in Dagaaba Rhetoric* (2010).

Mark P. Orbe (PhD, Ohio University) is Professor of Communication and Diversity in the School of Communication at Western Michigan University where he also holds a joint appointment in the Center for Gender and Women's Studies. His teaching and research interests focus on the inextricable relationship between culture, power, and communication.

Jan Pieter van Oudenhoven (PhD, University of Leiden) is Professor of Psychology at the University of Groningen in the Netherlands. Since 1976 he has been a social and cross-cultural psychologist at the University of Groningen. He has published on topics such as international cooperation, national cultures, and individual factors of adaptation of migrants, acculturation, and cross-cultural differences in moral principles. He is on the editorial board of three journals, is president-elect of the International Academy of Intercultural Research, and has over 200 publications on social and cross-cultural topics. He started his career in Latin America as a UNESCO associate expert in educational programs for farmers.

Marie L. Radford (PhD, Rutgers University) is Chair of the Department of Library and Information Science and Associate Professor at Rutgers, The State University of New Jersey, School of Communication & Information in New Brunswick, New Jersey. Previously, she was acting dean of Pratt Institute's School of Information and Library Science in Brooklyn, New York. Her research interests are interpersonal communication in face-to-face and virtual environments, nonverbal communication, cultural studies, and media stereotypes of female librarians. She has published and presented in numerous national and international scholarly venues. Her latest books are *Leading the Reference Renaissance* (2012) and *Conducting the Reference Interview* (2009).

Jessica S. Robles (PhD, University of Colorado at Boulder) is Lecturer in Communication at the University of New Hampshire. Her research involves discourse analytic approaches to interaction in interpersonal, institutional, cultural, and intercultural contexts particularly around morality and conflict. She has authored and coauthored numerous publications and presentations on discursive practices in situations related to health, political, and family communication. She is an active member of language and social interaction divisions at National Communication Association (NCA), International Communication Association (ICA), and regional conferences.

William J. Starosta (PhD, Indiana University) is Professor of Communication and Culture at Howard University, Washington, DC. He has taught for 38 years at the postgraduate level. His research interests include intercultural communication, South and East Asian communication, rhetoric and culture, identity, centrisms, intercultural listening, third culture building, interethnic rhetoric, internarrativity, and interpretive methods. He has authored or edited five books, was recognized as an Eastern Communication Association Research Fellow, served on 14 international editorial boards, and founded *The Howard Journal of Communications*. His writing appears in the journals of six disciplines.

Satomi Sugiyama (PhD, Rutgers University) is Associate Professor of Communication and Media Studies at Franklin College Switzerland. She has been conducting research on the way young people perceive and use mobile communication technologies in various cultural contexts. She has presented and published her work in numerous international venues. These include a coauthored article on mobile phones as fashion statements with James Katz in the journal *New Media and Society* as well as several collections of essays.

Yohtaro Takano (PhD, Cornell University) is Professor at the Department of Psychology, Graduate School of Humanities and Sociology, University of Tokyo. His interests cover a wide range of research areas from form recognition to culture. For example, he theoretically explained and empirically demonstrated the foreign language side effect (i.e., a temporary decline of intellectual ability accompanying foreign language usage). In English, he has published journal articles on mental rotation, mirror reversal, linguistic relativity, and individualism/collectivism in addition to the foreign language side effect. In Japanese, he has published books, book chapters, and journal articles in other areas as well.

Nayibe A. Tavares is an undergraduate student in the College of Arts & Sciences at Western Michigan University. Born and raised in the Dominican Republic, she is a French major and pre-law minor with plans for attending law school following graduation. In support of her work on this project, she received a 2009 College of Arts & Sciences Undergraduate Research and Creative Arts Award.

Ewa L. Urban (MA, Western Michigan University; MA, University of Silesia, Poland) is an Associate Director for Assessment and Technology and a PhD candidate in higher education leadership at Western Michigan University. Her current research interests focus on intercultural communication, international students' career transitions, outcomes, and internationalization of higher education.

Charles Vasquez Jr. (AA, Borough of Manhattan Community College) is attending Hunter College majoring in computer science. Raised in New York City, he has interned as a programmer at Emblem Health, and worked in the community as a HIV/AIDS peer educator, an assistant researcher for the New York Academy of Medicine and as a field interviewer for Beth Israel

Hospital Continuum Health Partners. He has a green thumb, loves to kayak, and lives in the Bronx with his wife Avy, daughters Anevy Esperanza and Elyna Annora, and parrot Candelita.

Bernadette Watson (PhD, The University of Queensland) is Senior Lecturer in the School of Psychology at The University of Queensland, Australia. Her research focuses on effective communication in intergroup contexts. Much of her research has been investigating communication behaviors between health professionals and patients and good patient health outcomes. This includes research on the influence of identity and intergroup processes both on patient-health professional communication and on communication in multidisciplinary health teams. She is a board member of the International Association of Language and Social Psychology. She has written a number of book chapters covering communication issues and is author on a number of peer-reviewed articles on health communication.

Kesha Morant Williams (PhD, Howard University) is Assistant Professor of Interpersonal and Organizational Communication in the Department of Communication Studies Arts &Sciences at Penn State Berks. Her research interest includes interpersonal relationships, health communication, and popular media examined through a cultural lens. She is also interested in African American communication, prosocial and antisocial behaviors, decision making, and entertainment-education.

Gust A. Yep (PhD, University of Southern California) is Professor of Communication Studies and a member of the Graduate Core Faculty of Sexuality Studies at San Francisco State University. His research focuses on communication at the intersections of culture, race, class, gender, sexuality, and nation. In addition to three books, he has published more than 60 articles in various disciplinary and interdisciplinary journals and anthologies. A recipient of numerous teaching, mentoring, research, and community service awards, he is a former editor of the National Communication Association (NCA) Non-Serial Publications Program. He serves on several journal editorial boards.

Seung Hee Yoo (PhD, Yale University) is Assistant Professor of Psychology at San Francisco State University. She received her BA in psychology from Yonsei University in Seoul, Korea, and her research interests include interpersonal functions of emotion, cultural display rules, and intercultural interactions.

⑤SAGE research**methods**

The essential online tool for researchers from the world's leading methods publisher

Find exactly what you are looking for, from basic explanations to advanced discussion

More content and new features added this year!

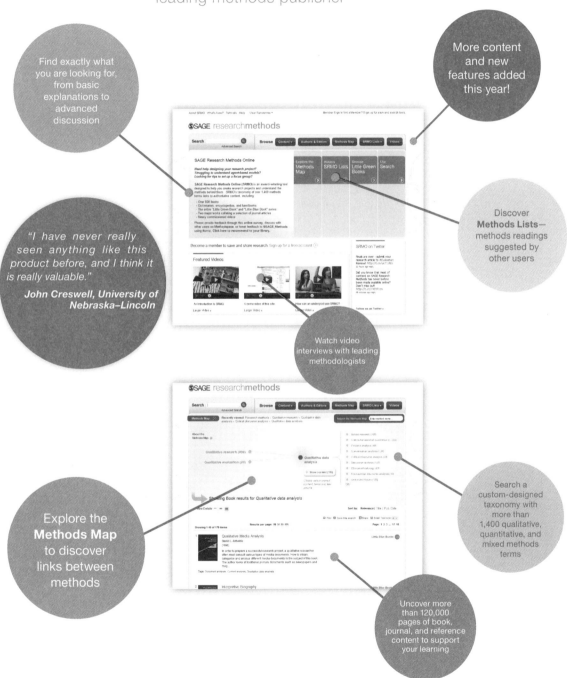

"I have never really seen anything like this product before, and I think it is really valuable."

John Creswell, University of Nebraska–Lincoln

Discover **Methods Lists**— methods readings suggested by other users

Watch video interviews with leading methodologists

Explore the **Methods Map** to discover links between methods

Search a custom-designed taxonomy with more than 1,400 qualitative, quantitative, and mixed methods terms

Uncover more than 120,000 pages of book, journal, and reference content to support your learning

Find out more at
www.sageresearchmethods.com